Who's Who in Christianity

Who's Who in Christianity is an invaluable reference guide to the leading men and women who have influenced the course of Christian history, including the founding fathers, saints, popes, monarchs, philanthropists, theologians, missionaries and heretics.

The book encompasses both Eastern and Western churches and the lives and opinions of personalities who have shaped the past twenty Christian centuries, from Jesus of Galilee to Pope John Paul II, and from Paul of Tarsus to Mother Teresa.

Who's Who in Christianity provides:

- an accessible and user-friendly A–Z layout
- detailed bibliographical information on each prominent figure
- a glossary of technical terms
- a chronology of the chief historical events
- an invaluable guide for scholars, teachers, clergy, students and general readers

Lavinia Cohn-Sherbok is co-author of *A Dictionary of Judaism and Christianity* (1991) and *Jewish and Christian Mysticism* (1995).

D0465642

WHO'S WHO SERIES

Available from Routledge worldwide:

Who's Who in Military History
John Keegan and Andrew Wheatcroft

Who's Who in Nazi Germany
Robert S. Wistrich

Who's Who in Contemporary World Politics
Alan Palmer

Who's Who in Russia since 1900
Martin McCauley

Who's Who in Dickens
Donald Hawes

Available in USA from Oxford University Press:

Who's Who in the Old Testament
Joan Comay

Who's Who in the New Testament
Ronald Brownrigg

Who's Who in Classical Mythology
Michael Grant and John Hazel

Who's Who in Non-Classical Mythology
Egerton Sykes, new edition revised by Alan Kendall

Who's Who in Shakespeare
Peter Quennell and Hamish Johnson

Who's Who in World War Two
Edited by John Keegan

Who's Who in Jewish History
Joan Comay, new edition revised by Lavinia Cohn-Sherbok

Who's Who in Christianity

Lavinia Cohn-Sherbok

London and New York

First published 1998
by Routledge
11 New Fetter Lane, London EC4P 4EE

Simultaneously published in the USA and Canada
by Routledge
29 West 35th Street, New York, NY 10001

Reprinted 1998

© 1998 Lavinia Cohn-Sherbok

Typeset in Sabon by
RefineCatch Limited, Bungay, Suffolk
Printed and bound in Great Britain by
TJ International Ltd, Padstow, Cornwall

British Library Cataloguing in Publication Data
A catalogue record for this book is available from the British Library

Library of Congress Cataloging in Publication Data
A catalog record for this book is available from the Library of Congress

ISBN 0–415–13582–6 (hbk)
ISBN 0–415–13583–4 (pbk)

In memory of my father, Graham Heath (1899–1969)
ἀνὴρ ἀγαθὸς καὶ δίκαιος

Contents

Preface

Who's Who in Christianity is intended as an accessible introduction to the lives and ideas of twelve hundred of the most prominent people in the history of the Christian Church. Inevitably, with such a limitation on numbers, selection has not always been easy. Some individuals, such as Jesus himself, Paul, Thomas Aquinas, Martin Luther and Pope John XXIII, could under no circumstances be overlooked. Others were chosen as representatives of particular schools of opinion or historical movements. The primary criterion for inclusion was whether the particular individual has had a continuing effect on the life of the Christian Church. Thus there is a tendency to prefer denomination founders over historians, missionaries over the more obscure theologians, order founders over devotional writers. Included are an array of apostles, saints, philosophers, ecclesiastical leaders, mystics and prominent secular figures who have had a significant impact on Church history.

Ultimately it is hoped that all the people chosen are 'reference worthy' and a serious attempt has been made to take a global perspective. The Eastern as well as the Western Church is represented; leaders from the Third as well as the Developed World have their place and, within the constraints of historical objectivity, distinguished women have not been forgotten. Each entry gives a short biographical sketch. This is followed by a brief explanation of the significance of the individual's contribution. The subsequent history of his or her work is also described. Each entry should be seen as a small piece of a vast jigsaw, the whole portraying the vibrant, ongoing life of the Christian Church. It must be admitted that not every contribution has been constructive. Through its long history, the Church has taken many odd turns and there have been disastrous moments. None the less even the most dedicated critic of Christianity will find a great deal to admire as well as much to deplore.

Each entry concludes with a very short bibliography which is intended to lead the student into a deeper knowledge of the subject. Besides these suggestions, there are many useful encyclopaedias and general works of reference. A list of these can be found at the end of the book.

Notes on the use of Who's Who in Christianity

Alphabetisation

Entries are listed alphabetically ignoring spaces, hyphens and apostrophes. Headings which contain identical names, but different numbers (e.g. Pius I, Pius II) are listed with the lower number first.

Names

In order to facilitate ease of reference, the names used are those by which the person is commonly known in the English-speaking world. Thus it is Francis (not Francesco) of Assisi, but Leonardo (not Leonard) da Vinci. Inevitably inconsistencies will be noted. People are normally listed under their surnames. However, the use of surnames was not universal until the modern era and thus many early entries are placed in the alphabetical order of their Christian name. To give examples, Martin Luther is listed under Luther, but St Martin of Tours is under Martin. Popes and monarchs are put in alphabetical order of their official titles, so John XXIII not Roncalli.

Dates

The following abbreviations are used: b. = born, d. = died, *c.* = circa (about) and ? = uncertain. References to historical periods or events may occur without dates in the texts of entries; readers are referred to the chronology on p. xiii.

Cross-references

Names in small capitals indicate that there is a separate entry for that person.

Bibliographies

The list of references placed after each entry is in no way intended to be exhaustive. It is offered merely as a suggestion as to where the curious reader may find more extensive information. Where possible the recommendations are works in English and it is indicated where no English translations are available. In addition there is a list of useful encyclopaedias and general works of reference on the history of the Christian Church on p. 361.

Glossary

The glossary contains explanations of any technical words which appear in the text. It also attempts to give one-sentence summaries of the various theological positions found among Christians.

Category lists

The Category lists at the end of the book give the student a summary of all the entries in a particular category, such as denomination founders, missionaries or saints. A complete list (with dates) of all the Popes is also included. Those Popes who have individual entries are identified in bold.

Brief chronology

AD

29/30/33	Crucifixion of JESUS. PETER emerges as leader of the early Church.
c. 50	Council of Jerusalem. PAUL, PETER and JAMES agree that Gentile Christians should not have to keep Jewish law.
60–100	MARK, MATTHEW and LUKE's Gospels written.
64	Christians blamed for the great fire of Rome in the reign of the Emperor Nero.
70	Destruction of Jerusalem by the Romans.
81–96	Persecution of Christians during the reign of the Emperor Domitian.
84	Christians excommunicated from the Jewish synagogue.
144	MARCION excommunicated for rejecting the Hebrew Scriptures.
250	Persecution of Christians during the reign of the Emperor Decius.
303	Persecution of Christians during the reign of the Emperor Diocletian.
c. 305	ANTONY OF EGYPT organises his rule for hermits.
325	Council of Nicaea condemns ideas of ARIUS.
330	Emperor CONSTANTINE inaugurates Byzantium as Constantinople, the 'New Rome'.
337	Emperor CONSTANTINE baptised a Christian on his deathbed.
381	First Council of Constantinople. Constantinople assigned most senior see after Rome.
382	The Canon of the Old Testament and the New Testament is established.
410	Rome is sacked by the Goths led by Alaric.
416	The Council of Carthage condemns the doctrines of PELAGIUS.
431	Council of Ephesus condemns the doctrines of NESTORIUS and describes the Virgin MARY as *Theotokos* (God-bearer).
451	Council of Chalcedon affirms that JESUS CHRIST is one person in two natures. The conclusions of the Council are rejected by the 'Oriental' Orthodox Churches of Egypt and Syria.
482–519	Temporary schism between East and West arising from ZENO's Henoticon.
496	Clovis, King of the Franks, accepts Christianity.
532	The Church of St Sophia is rebuilt by the Emperor JUSTINIAN.
c. 540	St BENEDICT draws up his monastic Rule.
553	The Second Council of Constantinople affirms that Christ is perfect in both Godhead and humanity and is made known to us in two natures which concur in one person.
c. 563	St COLUMBA establishes his headquarters in Iona.
597	AUGUSTINE OF CANTERBURY sent by Pope GREGORY THE GREAT to England.
622	The year 0 of the Islamic calendar.
638	Arabs conquer the city of Jerusalem.

664	Synod of Whitby. Roman usage triumphs over the Celtic in the British Church.
681	Third Council of Constantinople confirms that JESUS CHRIST has both a human and a divine will.
726	Outbreak of the Iconoclastic Controversy.
732	Muslim advance from the Iberian peninsula into France halted.
787	Second Council of Nicaea upholds the veneration of icons.
800	CHARLEMAGNE crowned Holy Roman Emperor by Pope LEO III.
815–43	Re-emergence of the Iconoclastic Controversy ends with the restoration of icons.
863–7	Communion broken between Patriarch PHOTIUS of Constantinople and Pope NICHOLAS I of Rome.
909	The monastery at Cluny is founded.
988	Prince VLADIMIR of Kiev is converted to Christianity.
996–1021	Persecution of the Coptic Church by the Muslims.
1054	Anathemas are exchanged between Rome and the Patriarch Michael CERULARIUS.
1059	Papal elections are placed in the hands of the Cardinal Bishops.
1084	Carthusian Order founded by St BRUNO.
1095	Pope URBAN II preaches the First Crusade against the Muslim Turks.
1146	Preaching of Second Crusade by St BERNARD OF CLAIRVAUX.
1187	The Muslim Emperor Saladin captures Jerusalem.
1189–92	Third Crusade.
1204	Latin troops sack the city of Constantinople in the Fourth Crusade.
1209	FRANCIS OF ASSISI sets up his order of friars.
1215	Fourth Lateran Council orders annual confession and other pastoral reforms.
1216	St DOMINIC establishes his order of friars.
1232	Pope GREGORY IX establishes the Papal Inquisition.
1244	Jerusalem finally conquered by the Muslims.
1302	Pope BONIFACE VIII proclaims the universal jurisdiction of the Pope.
1305	The French Pope CLEMENT V moves the papal headquarters to Avignon.
1337–51	In the Hesychast controversy, the teachings of GREGORY PALAMAS are upheld.
1348–9	The Black Death rages throughout Europe.
1378–82	John WYCLIFFE preaches against clerical corruption and papal authority.
1378	The start of the Great Schism with the election of two Popes.
1414–18	The Council of Constance affirms the primacy of general councils over the Papacy and condemns John HUS.
1429	The Great Schism ends under Pope MARTIN V.
1431–49	The Council of Basle reaffirms the authority of the Papacy.
1453	The City of Constantinople falls to the Muslim Ottoman Turks.
1479	Under King FERDINAND and Queen ISABELLA the Inquisition is established in Spain.
1492	The Muslims are expelled from Spain.
1493/4	Pope ALEXANDER VI partitions the New World between Spain and Portugal.
1506	The foundation stone of St PETER's Church in Rome is laid.
1517	Martin LUTHER posts ninety-five theses against the sale of Indulgences on the door of Wittenberg Church.

1534	The Act of Supremacy establishes King HENRY VIII as supreme head of the English Church.
1536	John CALVIN establishes his authority in Geneva.
1540	Pope PAUL III approves the foundation of the Jesuit Order, founded by IGNATIUS LOYOLA.
1545–64	In three Sessions, the Council of Trent redefines the content and agenda of Roman Catholicism.
1553–8	Queen MARY I tries to re-establish Catholicism in England.
1555	The Peace of Augsburg establishes the principle *'cuius regio, eius religio'*, in which the region follows the religion of the prince.
1559	Under Queen ELIZABETH I, the moderately Protestant Church of England is established independent of papal control.
1577	The definitive statement of Lutheranism, the Formula of Concord, is issued.
1593	King HENRY IV of France converts to Catholicism, thus ending the French Wars of Religion.
1598	The Edict of Nantes guarantees toleration for French Protestants.
1611	The King JAMES Authorised Version of the English Bible is published.
1618	The Synod of Dort condemns the doctrines associated with ARMINIUS.
1620	The *Mayflower* sails to America to found a colony which guarantees religious freedom.
1633	The Sisters of Charity are founded by St VINCENT DE PAUL.
1648	The Peace of Westphalia ends the Thirty Years War.
1653	The papal bull *Cum Occasione* condemns the five Jansenist propositions.
1666	Schism of the Old Believers in Russia.
1682	The Gallican Articles are issued in France.
1685	LOUIS XIV revokes the Edict of Nantes.
1701	Society for the Propagation of the Gospel in Foreign Parts is founded in London.
1721	PETER THE GREAT takes control of the Russian Church and abolishes the Moscow Patriarchate.
1726	The beginning of the 'Great Awakening' in North America.
1738	Conversion of John WESLEY.
1773	Pope CLEMENT XIV suppresses the Jesuit Order.
1781	Emperor JOSEPH II issues the Patent of Toleration.
1783	The British acknowledge the independence of the American colonies.
1789	Meeting of the French Estates General heralds the start of the French Revolution.
1799	SCHLEIERMACHER appeals to feeling as the grounds of religious belief.
1800	Start of the 'Second Great Awakening' in the United States of America.
1807	The slave trade is made illegal in Great Britain. First Protestant missionary arrives in China.
1815	Treaty of Vienna restores the map of Europe after the collapse of the empire of Napoleon.
1817	Robert MOFFAT arrives as a missionary in South Africa.
1821	Greeks revolt against Muslim Turkish rule.
1829	Parliament passes the Act of Roman Catholic Emancipation in Britain.
1833	Start of the Oxford Movement in England.
1839	Pope GREGORY XVI condemns slavery in a papal bull.
1841	The Niger Expedition is sponsored by the African Civilisation Society.

1847	Brigham YOUNG establishes the Mormon centre at Salt Lake City.
1854	Pope PIUS IX establishes the Immaculate Conception of the Blessed Virgin MARY as an article of faith.
1858	BERNADETTE has visions at Lourdes.
1859	Charles DARWIN's *Origin of Species* is published.
1867	The first Lambeth Conference of Bishops of the Anglican Church takes place.
1868/70	The First Vatican Council passes the decree of papal infallibility.
1875	The World Alliance of Reformed and Presbyterian Churches is founded in Geneva.
1891	Pope LEO XIII issues the encyclical *Rerum Novarum* on social problems.
1895	Beginning of the World Student Christian Federation (SCM).
1906/7	Separation of Church and State in France.
1907	Papal encyclical 'Pascendi' condemns Modernism.
1910	Edinburgh Missionary Conference leads to the establishment of the International Missionary Council.
1914–8	First World War.
1918	Re-establishment of the Russian Patriarchate. Decree on the separation of Church and State in Russia issued by the new Soviet government.
1919	Karl BARTH publishes his *Commentary on the Epistle to the Romans*.
1927	Faith and Order Movement founded in Lausanne.
1934	Creation of the Confessing Church of Germany in defiance of the Nazi government.
1939–45	Second World War.
1948	Foundation of the World Council of Churches.
1950	Pope PIUS XII declares the Virgin Mary's bodily assumption into Heaven to be an article of the Catholic faith.
1960	John F. Kennedy is the first Roman Catholic to be elected President of the United States.
1961	The Russian Orthodox Church joins the World Council of Churches, but the Roman Catholics continue to stand aloof.
1962–5	The Second Vatican Council embarks on 'opening' the Roman Catholic Church to the modern world.
1966	The Cultural Revolution closes all Christian Churches in China.
1968	The Encyclical *Humanae Vitae* reiterates the Roman Catholic Church's opposition to artificial methods of contraception.
1979	Pope JOHN PAUL II condemns the 'excesses' of liberation theology.
1989/90	The Eastern European bloc countries shake off their Communist regimes. Churches are re-established.

A

Abelard, Peter (1079–1142) Theologian. Abelard was born at Pallet, near Nantes in France. He attracted large audiences to his theological lectures at the Cathedral Schools of Paris. After his love affair with Héloïse, the niece of Fulbert, Canon of Notre Dame, he was forced to retire, initially to the monastery of St Denis. His book *Theologia Summi Boni* (*c.* 1120) was condemned at the Council of Soissons in 1121, but by 1136 he was teaching again in Paris. In 1140 some of his doctrines were condemned at the Council of Sens, St BERNARD OF CLAIRVAUX leading the movement against him. Abelard immediately appealed to Innocent II, but the Pope confirmed the Council's decision. Subsequently Abelard withdrew, and he died at the Priory of St Marcel, Chalon-sur-Saône. Abelard's other works include his defence *Theologia Christiana* (*c.* 1124), his own history *Historia Calamitatum*, his ethical treatise *Scito Te Ipsum* and his dialectical anthology *Sic et Non*. He is remembered for his tragic personal life and for his doctrine of the atonement, which he expounded in his commentary on the Epistle to the Romans. He argued that JESUS's death effected atonement not because it was a ransom paid to the devil or the repayment of a debt due to God, but because it inspired love in the sinner. Thus its value was exemplary rather than propitiatory.

B. Radice (ed.), *The Letters of Abelard and Heloise* (1974); D.E. Luscombe, *The School of Peter Abelard* (1969).

Aberhart, William (1878–1943) Politician, Preacher and Broadcaster. Aberhart was born in Ontario, Canada. Initially he earned his living as a schoolteacher and, in his spare time, he taught a Bible class at the Westbourne Baptist Church. This was very successful and led to the founding of the Prophetic Bible Institute and a regular radio ministry. In the 1930s his programmes inspired a religious revival throughout Alberta and Western Saskatchewan. During the years of the Great Depression, he formed the Social Credit party which won a landslide victory in the Alberta provincial election of 1935. Aberhart became Premier and headed the evangelical and politically Conservative administration until his death in 1943. Apart from his political activities, Aberhart is significant in that he was one of the first evangelists to realise the potential of radio as a missionary tool. He was succeeded as Premier of Alberta by his student Ernest Manning.

J.W. Grant (ed.), *The Churches and the Canadian Experience* (1963); C.B. Macpherson, *Democracy in Alberta: Social Credit and the Party System* (1962).

Acacius (d. 489) Patriarch. Acacius was Patriarch of Constantinople from 471 to 489. During this period, a temporary schism arose between the Church of Rome and the Churches of the East. Sponsored by the Eastern Emperor ZENO, Acacius and Peter Mongos, the Patriarch of Alexandria, devised the Henoticon formula. Orthodoxy continued to be defined by the decisions of Nicaea and Chalcedon and NESTORIUS and EUTYCHES continued to be condemned. At the same time, concessions were made to the moderate Monophysites. However, the formula was rejected both by the Pope and by the extreme Egyptian Monophysites. Acacius himself was condemned by Felix III. The 'Acacian Schism', as it was known, continued after Acacius's death and the Churches were only reconciled in 518 when the names of Acacius and his five successors were removed from the Diptychs (the list of names for whom special prayers were said).

W.H.C. Frend, *The Rise of the Monophysite Movement* (1972); J. Meyendorff, *Imperial Unity and Christian Divisions* (1989).

Acarie, Barbe Jeanne [Mary of the Incarnation] (1566–1618)   Order Founder.

From an early age, she wished to join a religious order, but instead married Pierre Acarie, Vicomte de Villemore, obeying her parents' wishes. In 1603 she succeeded in establishing the Carmelite Order in Paris and she was also influential in establishing the Ursulines and helping Pierre de BÉRULLE. When she was widowed in 1613, she joined the Carmel at Amiens, taking the name Mary of the Incarnation. She spent the last years of her life at the house in Pontoise. She was a noted mystic, but left no writings.

L.C. Sheppard, *Barbe Acarie* (1953).

Adamnan (c. 624–704)   Saint and Devotional Writer.

Adamnan was a native of Ireland. In 679 he was elected Abbot of Iona. He was the author of *De Locis Sanctis* and a life of St COLUMBA. He is mainly remembered for his attempts to persuade the Celtic Church to conform with the customs of Rome. In particular he succeeded in persuading the monks of Ireland to follow the Roman method for dating Easter, but the monks of Iona did not accept the authority of Rome in these matters until after Adamnan's death.

D.A. Bullough, 'Columba, Adamnan and the achievement of Iona', *Scottish Historical Review*, xliii (1964) and xliv (1965).

Aelfric (c. 955–c. 1020)   Theologian.

Aelfric joined the Benedictine community at Winchester; later he moved to Cerne Abbas and in 1005 he was elected the first Abbot of Eynsham. He was the author of an English homily on the liturgical year and another on doctrine. He also produced a collection of lives of the saints, a life of St ETHELWOLD and an English translation of BEDE's *De Temporibus*. Aelfric's teachings were revived by the Protestant Reformers who argued that he denied both the doctrine of transubstantiation and that of the Immaculate Conception of the Blessed Virgin MARY. He is primarily remembered as a leader of the tenth- and eleventh-century Benedictine revival.

P.A.M. Clemoes, 'The chronology of Aelfric's works', in P.A.M. Clemoes (ed.), *The Anglo-Saxons* (1959); J.C. Pope (ed.), *Homilies of Aelfric* (1967–8) [with introduction and notes].

Agatha (before fourth century)   Legendary Saint.

Agatha is venerated as a virgin martyr. She is listed in the ancient martyrologies and in the Canon of the Roman Mass. Almost nothing is known of her life, although it is said that she was handed over to a prostitute and her breasts were cut off. In Christian art, she is generally shown clasping a knife in one hand and a plate on which her breasts are laid in the other. She was very popular, particularly in the fifth century, and is the patron saint of the city of Catania (where she died), of bell-founders, jewellers and wet-nurses. She is also often invoked when fires break out.

V.L. Kennedy, *The Saints of the Canon of the Mass* (1938).

Agnes (before fourth century)   Legendary Saint.

Agnes is venerated as a virgin martyr and as the patron saint of chastity. She is listed in the ancient martyrologies and in the Canon of the Roman Mass. Almost nothing is known of the facts of her life. She is thought to have been put to death at the age of twelve or thirteen and her cult has existed since the fourth century. In iconography she is generally portrayed with a lamb (presumably because the word for lamb in Latin is 'agnus').

V.L. Kennedy, *The Saints of the Canon of the Mass* (1938).

Agricola, Johann (*c.* 1494–1566)   Theologian. Agricola was a native of Eisleben, Germany, and was a pupil of Martin LUTHER at the University of Wittenberg. After a brief ministry in Frankfurt and Eisleben, he returned to Wittenberg, but failed to be appointed to a chair, which was given instead to Philip MELANCHTHON. He was labelled an antinomian by Luther since he taught that the doctrine of justification by faith implied that Christians were no longer bound by the moral law. Against this Luther taught that the moral law was necessary as a means of leading the sinner to repentance. Agricola moved to Berlin where he was appointed General Superintendent and Court Preacher by the Elector of Brandenberg. In 1544 he helped to draw up the Interim of Augsburg which was commissioned by the Emperor CHARLES V to provide a provisional religious settlement between the Catholic and Protestant subjects of the Empire. In addition to his revival of antinomian teaching, Agricola is also remembered as the first compiler of collections of German proverbs.

A. McGrath, *Reformation Theology: An Introduction* (1988); LW. Spitz, *The Religious Renaissance of the German Humanists* (1963).

Aidan (d. 651)   Saint and Missionary. OSWALD, King of Northumbria, had asked the monks of Iona to send a missionary to convert his subjects to Christianity. After the failure of the first mission, the task was given to Aidan and he was consecrated Bishop of Lindisfarne in 635. Using the island as his headquarters, he founded a monastery and a school and embarked on a series of missionary visits. Largely through his efforts, the Celtic form of Christianity was established throughout the Kingdom of Northumbria. The work was continued after his death by his successor Oswin and his students Eata, Cedd, CHAD and WILFRID. Some authorities argue that he was more significant than AUGUSTINE OF CANTERBURY in bringing the Christian religion to England.

Bede, *Historia Ecclesiastica* [many editions]; A.C. Frier, *Aidan, the Apostle of the North* (1884); J.B. Lightfoot, *Leaders in the Northern Church* (1913).

Alacoque, Marguérite-Marie (1647–90)   Saint, Mystic and Cult Founder. Alacoque entered the Convent of the Visitation at Paray-le-Monial, France, in 1671. She lived a life of strict austerity in the convent and in time became Novice Mistress and Assistant Superior. Between 1673 and 1675 she reported several visions in which she saw the heart of Jesus burning with love for humanity. She believed that she was commanded to establish regular devotions to the Sacred Heart, which included a regular Mass on the first Friday of the month and an annual feast of the Sacred Heart to be celebrated on the Friday immediately after the conclusion of the Corpus Christi season. Initially her visions were discounted and ridiculed by her superiors, but gradually the cult of the Sacred Heart of Jesus spread throughout the Roman Catholic world. It was formally recognised by the Church in 1765 and its founder was beatified in 1864 and canonised in 1920.

M.-M. Alacoque, *Autobiography*, edited and translated by V. Kerns (1961).

Alban (second/third century)   Saint and Martyr. According to BEDE, Alban was a pagan living in the Romano-British city of Verulamium. He was converted to the Christian faith by a priest whom he was sheltering. When his house was searched, Alban disguised himself in the priest's cloak and was arrested and executed in his place. Alban is remembered as the first British martyr, though there is scholarly disagreement as to whether his martyrdom belongs to the early third-century Severan persecutions or to those of Diocletian in the fourth century. Verulamium is now called St Albans in the saint's honour. The cult of St Alban dates to 429 and St Albans Cathedral is built over his shrine.

Bede, *Historia Ecclesiastica* [many editions]; W. Levison, 'St Alban and St Albans', *Antiquity*, xv (1941).

Albertus Magnus (*c.* 1200–*c.* 1280) Saint, Bishop, Philosopher and Theologian. Albertus was born in Lauingen in Germany. Before entering the Dominican order, he studied at the University of Padua and subsequently he taught at Hildesheim, Freiberg, Ratisbon and Strasbourg. In about 1241 he moved to Paris where he held a chair in theology and where THOMAS AQUINAS was among his pupils. In 1248 he was transferred to Cologne where he started a new Dominican centre and between 1253 and 1256 he was Provincial of the German province. After a visit to Rome, where at the request of the Pope he had held a disputation on the oneness of the intellect, he was consecrated Bishop of Ratisbon in 1260. At the end of his life he moved between various German Dominican houses and he eventually died in Cologne. Albertus's works include the *Tractatus de Natura Boni*, a *Summa Theologica*, a commentary on the *Ethics* of Aristotle and various biblical commentaries. He is an important figure in the history of Christian thought in that he saw the relevance of Aristotelian ideas for Christian theology and he defended the distinction between the truths derived from revelation and those deduced by human reason. Although his work was eclipsed by that of his student Aquinas, he was recognised as an authority by contemporaries such as Roger BACON

and Ulrich of Strasbourg. Many legends concerning his miraculous powers grew up in the late Middle Ages. He was named a Doctor of the Church in 1931.

F.J. Catania, 'Bibliography of St Albert the Great', *The Modern Schoolman*, xxxvii (1959); J.A. Weisheipl (ed.), *Albertus Magnus and the Sciences* (1980).

Albright, Jacob (1759–1808) Sect Founder. Albright was born in Pennsylvania and grew up as a Lutheran. As a young man he served as a soldier and later he became a successful brickmaker. In 1791, after the deaths of several of his children, he became a member of the Methodist Episcopal Church and began a new career as a preacher. When his efforts were rejected by the Methodist leadership, he created his own organisation with himself as its first Bishop. At first the new body was known as the 'so-called Albright people', but it later became the Evangelical Association. Arminian in doctrine, the Church was organised on Methodist lines. In 1922 it became the Evangelical Church and, after amalgamation with the United Brethren in Christ in 1946, the Evangelical United Brethren Church.

R.W. Albright, *A History of the Evangelical Church* (1942).

Alcuin (*c.* 735–804) Educator. Alcuin was born in York. He was educated at the cathedral school where his teacher had been a pupil of BEDE. In 781 he joined the household of CHARLEMAGNE where he organised the palace library. On his appointment as Abbot of Tours in 796, he set up an important school which numbered among its students RABANUS MAURUS. One result of his educational work was the development of the Carolingian minuscule style of handwriting which was easy to read and which was an important factor in the preservation of ancient texts from further scribal corruptions. He was the author of several educational manuals, commentaries on the

Bible, polemical texts, a sacramentary and a series of letters which give a vivid picture of his life and times. He is generally regarded as one of the initiators of the Carolingian renaissance.

W. Levison, *England and the Continent in the Eighth Century* (1946); L. Wallach, *Alcuin and Charlemagne* (1959).

Alexander II (d. 1073) Pope. Anselm (his baptismal name) was born in Baggio, Italy and he was a pupil of LANFRANC at the monastery school in Bec. He was consecrated Bishop of Lucca in 1057 and was elected Pope in 1061. However, the Holy Roman Emperor HENRY IV did not support his candidacy and had an alternative churchman, Cadalus of Parma, elected as Antipope, Honorius II. The schism lasted until Honorius died in 1072, although Alexander II (as he was called) was generally recognised as the true successor to St PETER. In his youth, Alexander had been a supporter of the reforming Patarines. As Pope, he tried to put these ideals into practice. He held four synods in Rome. He enforced clerical celibacy, renewed the decrees against simony (the sale of ecclesiastical preferments) and even went so far as to depose the Archbishop of Milan for selling offices. He was also not afraid to confront the secular authorities – at the end of his life he excommunicated the Emperor's advisors. He also condemned the persecution of the Jews in Spain and southern France and he encouraged the Christian kings against the Muslims in Spain. He insisted that new Archbishops should present themselves in person at Rome to receive the pallium, the symbol of their office, and thus he increased the influence of the Papacy. In English history, he is remembered for his support of William of Normandy's invasion of England in 1066.

H.K. Mann, *The Lives of the Popes in the Early Middle Ages*, Vol. 6. (1925); R. Somerville, *Papacy, Councils and Canon Law in the 11th–12th Centuries* (1990).

Alexander III (d. 1181) Pope. Alexander III was born Orlando Bandinelli in Siena, Italy. In his adult life, he was a successful teacher of Canon Law at the University of Bologna and he was elected Pope in 1159, in succession to HADRIAN IV. His candidacy was not supported by the Emperor FREDERICK BARBAROSSA, who set up three antipopes in succession, Victor IV, Pascal III and Callistus III. In 1177 the Emperor was defeated by the Lombard League at Legnano, and in consequence, he acknowledged Alexander's right to the Papacy. In 1179 Alexander called the Third Lateran Council. Among several measures, the Council established that the right to elect a Pope was restricted to the College of Cardinals which must have a two-thirds majority in favour of the winning candidate. Alexander was also the author of various theological treatises and he was a keen patron of scholarship. In English history he is remembered as the Pope who supported Archbishop Thomas BECKET and who imposed penance on King HENRY II.

F. Barlow, *Thomas Becket* (1986); R. Somerville, *Papacy, Councils and Canon Law in the 11th–12th Centuries* (1990).

Alexander VI (1431–1503) Pope. Alexander, a nephew of Pope Callistus III, was born Rodrigo Borgia in Spain. At the age of twenty-five he became a Cardinal and was appointed Chancellor of the Roman Church in 1457. His scandalous private life earned a rebuke from Pope PIUS II, but he was influential during the pontificates of Paul II and SIXTUS IV. Although he was known to be the father of Cesare and Lucrezia Borgia, he was elected Pope in 1492. It was during his reign that the New World was divided between Spain and Portugal. His patronage of the arts, the excommunication and subsequent execution of the reformer Girolamo SAVONAROLA and the general opportunism and corruption of his court were the significant features of his Pontificate. The activities of Popes such as Alexander gave the sixteenth-century Protestant Reformers grounds for criticising the Roman Catholic Church.

P. de Roo (ed.), *Materials for a History of Pope Alexander VI*, 5 vols (1924); G. Parker, *At the Court of the Borgia* (1963); H. Vander Linden, 'Alexander VI and the demarkation of the maritime and colonial domains of Spain and Portugal, 1493–1494', *American Historical Review*, xxii (1917).

Alexander VII (1599–1667) Pope. Alexander was born Fabio Chigi in Siena, Italy. After serving as Inquisitor of Malta and papal nuncio in Cologne, he was created a Cardinal in 1652 and was elected Pope in 1655. He is chiefly remembered for his opposition to Jansenism and Laxism and for his support of the Jesuit Order. In 1656, he condemned the *Augustinus* of Cornelius JANSEN and in 1665 and 1666 he condemned forty-five Laxist propositions.

L. Pastor, *The History of the Popes from the Close of the Middle Ages*, Vol. 31 (1940).

Alexander VIII (1610–91) Pope. Alexander VIII was born Pietro Ottoboni in Venice. He was educated at the University of Padua and, after acting as Auditor of the Rota Sacra Romana (the papal tribune), he was appointed a Cardinal in 1652 and consecrated Bishop of Brescia in 1654. He became Grand Inquisitor of Rome during the Pontificate of Innocent XI, and was elected Pope in 1689. He is remembered mainly for his condemnation in 1690 of both the Four Gallican Propositions of 1682 and the Thirty-One Propositions of Cornelius JANSEN. He also censured the doctrine of philosophic sin in that it maintained a distinction between divine and natural law.

M. Dubruel, 'Le Pape Alexandre VIII et les affaires de France', *Revue d'Histoire Ecclésiastique*, xv (1914) [no English translation available]; L. Pastor, *The History of the Popes from the Close of the Middle Ages*, Vol. 32 (1940).

Alexander of Hales (*c.* 1186–1245) Theologian. Alexander was born at Halesowen in England and was educated at the Universities of Oxford and Paris. In his own lectures he caused a sensation by using the 'Sentences' of PETER LOMBARD rather than texts from the Bible as his starting-point. In 1231 he became Archdeacon of Coventry, but he returned to Paris a few years later and joined the Franciscan Order. He continued to teach and BONAVENTURA was among his pupils. His writings include an unfinished *Summa Theologica* and a commentary on the 'Sentences'. He was the founder of the Franciscan school of theology.

I. Herscher, 'A bibliography of Alexander of Hales', *Franciscan Studies*, xxvi (1945).

Alexander, Cecil Frances (?1818–95) Poet and Educator. Alexander was a native of Dublin, Ireland and was the wife of William Alexander, who became Archbishop of Armagh. She dedicated her life to helping her husband in his pastoral work. She was the author of many children's hymns including 'All things bright and beautiful', 'Once in Royal David's city', sung at Christmas, and the Good Friday hymn 'There is a green hill far away'.

V. Wallace, *Mrs Alexander: A Life of the Hymn Writer* (1995).

Allen, Richard (1760–1831) Denomination Founder. Allen was born a slave and grew up in Delaware in the United States of America. He was converted to Methodism and succeeded in converting his owner and thereby gaining his freedom. Almost entirely self-educated, he was accepted as a Methodist preacher in 1784 and served as an assistant to Bishop ASBURY in his preaching missions. Many African-Americans were attracted to his ministry and in 1787 he formed the Free African Society. In 1794 this became the African Methodist Episcopal Church and it was dedicated by Bishop Asbury. Allen was ordained to the new denomination in 1799 and he became its first Bishop in 1816. Through his determination and industry, the Church had achieved a national standing by the time of his death.

H.D. Gregg, *History of the African Methodist Episcopal Church* (1980); E. Lincoln, *The Black Church in the African-American Experience* (1990); G.A. Singleton (ed.), *The Life, Experience and Gospel Labors of the Rt Rev. Richard Allen* (1960).

Alphege (954–1012) Saint, Martyr and Archbishop. Alphege joined a monastic community at Deerhurst in Wessex, England, but spent some time as a hermit. He was consecrated Bishop of Winchester in 984, succeeding ETHELWOLD, and was used by King Ethelred the Unready on a diplomatic mission against the invading Danes in 994. As a result of Alphege's intervention, the Danish leader, Anlaf, became a Christian. In 1005 Alphege was enthroned Archbishop of Canterbury, following AELFRIC. Meanwhile the Danes were overrunning the south of England and in 1011 Alphege was imprisoned at Greenwich. He refused to be ransomed and was eventually killed during the course of a drunken revel when the Danish feasters threw ox bones at him. According to Archbishop ANSELM, just as JOHN THE BAPTIST was a martyr for truth, so Alphege was a martyr for justice. His cult was long celebrated in Canterbury until it was overshadowed by that of Thomas BECKET.

Eadmer, *The Life of St Anselm*, edited by R.W. Southern (1962); R.W. Southern, *St Anselm and his Biographer* (1963).

Alphonsus Liguori (1696–1787) Saint, Order Founder and Devotional Writer. Alphonsus was born near Naples and initially practised as a lawyer. At the age of twenty-four, however, he joined a preaching order. In 1726 he was ordained priest and in 1730 he moved to Scala to be near his friend the Bishop of Castellmare. In 1732 he founded the Redemptorists (the

Congregation of the Most Holy Redeemer). The task of the new order was to perform mission work among the poor. After the Bishop's death, Alphonsus became Superior-General and in 1749 the rule of the order was formally approved by Pope BENEDICT XIV. In 1750 a corresponding house was set up for women. In 1762 Alphonsus was consecrated Bishop of Sant'Agata dei Goti, but he resigned in 1775 to dedicate himself to the affairs of the order. His devotional works include the *Annotations* (1748), *Theologia Moralis* (2 volumes, 1753 and 1755), the *Great Means of Prayer* (1759) and the *Way of Salvation* (1767). These works were very popular and were in sharp contrast with the sombre theology of the Jansenists. Alphonsus was declared a Doctor of the Church in 1871. His order continues its work to the present time.

A.C. Berthe, *Life of Alphonsus Liguori*, translated by H. Castle, 2 vols (1905).

Ambrose (*c.* 339–97) Saint and Bishop. Ambrose was born in Trier, Gaul and at first he practised as a lawyer. In about 370, he was appointed governor of the province of Milan and when Bishop AUXENTIUS died, he was invited to be his successor. At this stage Ambrose was not even baptised. After much hesitation he accepted the invitation and was baptised, ordained and consecrated. Unlike Auxentius who was an Arian, Ambrose was strictly orthodox and he became famous as a preacher. St AUGUSTINE, in particular, greatly admired him. He was fearless in his dealings with the secular authorities, imposing penance on the Emperor THEODOSIUS I after a massacre in Thessalonica and declaring that the Emperor was within the Church and not over it. Among his surviving works are *De Sacramentis*, which is the earliest witness to the prayer of consecration in the Roman Mass, *De Officiis Ministrorum*, on Christian ethics, and various letters, hymns and sermons. Some scholars also believe him to have been the author of the Athanasian Creed. Ambrose is counted among the four traditional Doctors of the Latin Church, the others being AUGUSTINE, GREGORY THE GREAT and JEROME.

N. McLynn, *Ambrose of Milan* (1995); D. Williams, *Ambrose of Milan* (1995).

Ames, William (1576–1633) Theologian. A student of William PERKINS at the University of Cambridge, Ames became known as an extreme Calvinist. After living in Colchester, where he was prevented from holding a parish by the Bishop of London, he settled in the Netherlands. There he was an observer at the Synod of Dort and was involved in the condemnation of Arminian theology. In 1622 he was appointed Professor of Theology at Franeker where he was regarded as one of the best theologians in Europe. His works include *De Conscientia eius Jure et Casibus* (1632), which was an important contribution to Calvinist moral theology, and *Medulla Theologiae*, a systematic exposition of Protestant principles.

William Ames, *Latin Works*, edited by M. Nethenus 5 vols (1658); K.L. Sprungen, *The Learned Doctor William Ames* (1972).

Anastasia (*c*. early fourth century) Saint and Martyr. Anastasia was probably martyred in Sirmium, and her relics were removed to Constantinople. A much later tradition makes her of noble Roman origin and a spiritual disciple of St John CHRYSOSTOM. Despite the paucity of information about her, Anastasia has been venerated in Rome since the fifth century and she is specifically remembered in the Prayer of Consecration in the Roman Mass.

V.L. Kennedy, *The Saints of the Canon of the Mass* (1938).

Andrew (first century) Saint and Apostle. Andrew was the brother of Simon PETER and he earned his living as a fisherman. In the Gospels, he is mentioned in connection with his call to discipleship, in the incident of the feeding of the five thousand, in the episode of the Greeks who wanted to see JESUS and as a listener to Jesus's prophecies about the End. According to EUSEBIUS OF CAESAREA's fourth-century history of the Church, Andrew was later a missionary in Scythia. An even later tradition has it that he was martyred at Patras in Archaia and he is supposed to have been crucified on a diagonal cross. He became the patron saint of Scotland because St Rule, in response to a dream, was supposed to have carried his relics from the place of martyrdom to a new burial spot in Fife.

F. Dvornik, *The Idea of Apostolicity and the Legend of the Apostle Andrew* (1958); P.M. Peterson, *Andrew, Brother of Simon Peter* (1958).

Andrewes, Launcelot (1555–1626) Bishop and Devotional Writer. Andrewes was born near London and was educated at the University of Cambridge. He was known as a remarkable preacher and he rose quickly in the Church. In 1601 he became Dean of Westminster, in 1605 Bishop of Chichester, in 1609 Bishop of Ely and in 1619 Bishop of Winchester. He took a full part in the affairs of state, participating in the Hampton Court Conference in 1604, sitting on the Essex divorce suit commission and on the official investigation of the Archbishop of Canterbury's accidental shooting of a gamekeeper. He also accompanied King JAMES I to Scotland in his attempt to make episcopacy acceptable to the Scots. He was one of the translators of the Authorised Version of the Bible, being responsible for most of the Pentateuch and the historical books of the Old Testament. Among his friends were Richard HOOKER and George HERBERT and, later, he was greatly revered by Archbishop William LAUD. His fame, however, rests on his reputation for sanctity and for his inspiring sermons. His *Ninety-Six*

Sermons and his *Preces Privatae* remain classics of Anglican spirituality.

P. Welsby, *Launcelot Andrewes* (1958); N. Lossky, *Launcelot Andrewes the Preacher* (1971).

Angela Merici (1474–1540) Saint and Order Founder. Angela was born in Desenzano, Italy. In her youth she joined a Franciscan Tertiary Order and devoted herself to a life of nursing and education. During a pilgrimage to the Holy Land in 1524, she suddenly and temporarily went blind. On her return to Italy, she founded a new women's religious order in Brescia. The order was named the Ursulines, after St URSULA. Angela wrote the Rule and was appointed Superior in 1537. The order was intended as a society of unmarried women, living in their own homes and dedicated to teaching. Over the course of time, community life and even enclosure have been introduced. None the less the Ursulines remain one of the most important teaching orders in the Roman Catholic Church.

P. Caraman, *St Angela* (1963); Sr Mary Monica, *Angela Merici and her Teaching Idea* (1927).

Angela of Foligno (*c.* 1248–1309) Mystic. Angela was born in Foligno, Italy, to a prominent family. After her husband and children died, she joined a Franciscan Tertiary Order and led a life of extreme austerity. She was the recipient of many visions which were recorded by her confessor, Brother Arnold. These were later circulated and published as the *Liber Visionum et Instructionum*. This has become a classic of Franciscan spirituality. Angela identified twenty steps of penitence through which she had passed before entering her mystical state – the climax of which was the vision of herself in God.

Angela of Foligno, *Liber Visionum et Instructionum*, translated by M.G. Steegman (1909).

Angelico, Fra (1387–1455) Artist. Fra Angelico was born in Fiesole, Italy, and at the age of twenty-six he joined the Dominican Order. During the time of the Great Schism he was forced to move first to Foligno and then to Cortona. On his return, he painted the frescos in the Convent of St Marco in Florence and was responsible for the decoration of two chapels in the Vatican. His painting is notable for its luminous colour and his wonderful sense of composition. Besides his frescos, his well-known works include the *Coronation of the Virgin*, the *Last Judgement* and the *Deposition from the Cross*. He is thought to have been offered the Archbishopric of Florence, but to have refused it in order to dedicate himself to art.

J. Pope-Hennessy, *Fra Angelico* (1974).

Anselm (*c.* 1033–1109) Archbishop, Saint and Theologian. Anselm was born in Aosta, Italy, but was educated at the monastery school at Bec, where he was taught by LANFRANC. He joined the order and became Prior of the community in 1063. In 1078 he was elected Abbot of Bec and then, in 1093, he succeeded Lanfranc as Archbishop of Canterbury. In attempting to impose the reforms of Pope GREGORY VII on the Church in England, he became embroiled in various controversies with King William II. In 1098 he was forced into exile and journeyed to Rome to consult the Pope about his difficulties. While he was in Rome, he attended both the Council of Bari and the Vatican Council of 1099. On his return to England, he became involved in fresh conflict with the new King, Henry I, and he refused to consecrate the King's Bishops. Again he went into exile until 1107 when a compromise was reached. Back in England he held a council to enforce the celibacy of the clergy; he also established a new see at Ely and consistently maintained the primacy of the See of Canterbury over that of York. Despite his significance in the history of Church–State relations in

England, Anselm is primarily remembered as a theologian. He was the author of various works of philosophical theology including the *Proslogion* in which he formulated his famous ontological proof for the existence of God. His *Cur Deus Homo* is an important contribution to the theology of the atonement. In it he argued that JESUS's death was an essential propitiation to the perfect justice and majesty of God. It was not, as had been argued by ORIGEN and GREGORY OF NYSSA, the payment of a ransom to the devil. Anselm always maintained that he did not seek to understand in order to believe, but that unless he believed he would not understand. His maxim, *fides quaerens intellectum* ('faith seeking understanding'), has become much used as a description of the Christian theological enterprise. It is not certain whether Anselm was ever formally canonised, but he has been venerated as a saint since the late Middle Ages. He was named a Doctor of the Church in 1720.

R.W. Southern, *Anselm* (1990); Eadmer, *Vita Anselmi*, edited and translated by R.W. Southern (1962).

Anselm of Laon (d. 1117)   Theologian and Educator. Although there is little evidence, it has been suggested that Anselm of Laon was a pupil of St ANSELM at the monastery school of Bec. His later life was spent in the Cathedral School of Laon where he attracted many pupils and where he was known as the 'Doctor Scholasticus'. Among his students were Peter ABELARD and GILBERT DE LA PORRÉE. After his death, his lectures on the Books of the Bible were expanded and systematised. He was not an innovative theologian, but his method of imparting and elucidating biblical texts was revolutionary. He used to set up opposing views and then proceed to reconcile them. This procedure was used with great effect by many later authorities, including Abelard himself in his *Sic et Non*.

B. Smalley, *The Study of the Bible in the Middle Ages* (1952).

Anskar (*c.* 801–65)   Saint and Missionary. Anskar was born in Picardy, France and was educated at the monastery at Corbie. At the invitation of King Harold, he moved to Denmark where he established a mission school at Hedeby. He was soon expelled by the pagan Danes and was forced to return to the Frankish court. Then, at the request of the Swedish king, he established the Bishopric of Birka and built the first Christian church on Swedish soil. In about 832 he became Archbishop of Hamburg and was elected first Abbot of Bremen. Later he returned to Denmark and succeeded in converting the King of Jutland, Erik. Throughout his life he was tireless in his efforts – preaching, founding schools and dispensing charity. He hoped to die as a martyr, but in this he was disappointed and he is buried at Bremen. After his death both Denmark and Sweden reverted to paganism, but the seed was sown and Christianity was established firmly in Scandinavia in the tenth century.

G.Waitz (ed), *Anskar, the Apostle of the North*, translated by C.H. Robinson (1921).

Antoninus (1389–1459)   Saint, Archbishop, Theologian and Economist. Antoninus was a native of Florence, and he joined the Dominican Order at Cortona at the age of sixteen. There he was a contemporary of Fra ANGELICO. He rose rapidly in the Church, becoming Prior of Cortona in 1418, of Fiesole in 1421, of Naples in 1428 and of Rome in 1430. He was appointed Auditor-General of the Papal Tribune in 1431; he was Vicar-General of the Dominican Order between 1432 and 1445 and was Archbishop of Florence from 1446. During this period he established the Convent of San Marco in Florence (frescos in which are painted by Fra Angelico). He was highly influential in secular affairs and was the author of a *Summa Theologica* and several other ethical works. Today he is particularly remembered as one of the first theologians to argue that it was not illegitimate to lend money on interest – thus paving the way for modern capitalism.

W.T. Gaughan, *Social Theories of St Antoninus from his Summa Theologica* (1951); B. Jarrett, *St Antonino and Mediaeval Economics* (1914).

Antony of Egypt (*c*. 260–356)   Saint and Mystic. Antony was born in Como, Italy. At an early age, he retired into the desert to dedicate his life to God. There he is said to have wrestled with demons disguised as wild beasts. According to his biographer St ATHANASIUS, from *c*. 306 he began to gather disciples whom he organised into a community of hermits bound by a communal Rule. He came out of seclusion in 355 when he spoke out against the teachings of ARIUS. He was an immensely popular saint in the Middle Ages. The Order of Hospitallers of St Antony was founded at the beginning of the twelfth century as a mendicant order and it spread throughout Western Europe. The temptations of St Antony are a popular subject for artists and he is regarded as having a particular interest in pigs and bells.

D. Chitty, *The Desert a City* (1966/1975); Athanasius, *The Life of St Antony*, edited and translated by R.C. Gregg (1980).

Antony of Padua (1195–1231)   Saint. Antony was born in Lisbon, Portugal. He joined the Augustinian Order at the age of fifteen, but later he transferred to the Franciscans with the intention of becoming a missionary. He sailed for Morocco, but because of poor health was forced to return. Then he was sent to the Hermitage of San Paolo, near Forlí in Italy, but he was soon appointed the first Lector in Theology of the Franciscan Order. He taught at Bologna, Montpellier and Toulouse, but his fame as an orator was so

great that he ultimately retired to Padua to concentrate on preaching. His sermons attracted huge crowds. He died at the age of thirty-six and his relics have always been venerated in Padua. He is known as the saint who specialises in the finding of lost articles. The origin of this is obscure, but may relate to an incident when a novice borrowed his Psalter without asking. He was compelled to return the book after being confronted by an appalling monster! Antony is also thought of as the patron of the poor; in many countries the Church maintains a charitable fund known as 'St Antony's bread'. Many miracles are ascribed to him and he remains one of the most popular saints. He was canonised almost immediately after his death and he was named a Doctor of the Church in 1946.

V. Gambosa, *St Antony*, translated by H. Partridge (1991); E. Gilliat-Smith, *St Antony of Padua According to his Contemporaries* (1926).

Aphraates (fourth century)   Church Father. Very little is known of the life of Aphraates. In his writings he emphasised the value of the ascetic life. He taught that God created the Universe and gave the Law to Moses; that JESUS is the Son of God and that at baptism the believer receives the Holy Spirit. His twenty-three tractates (known as the Homilies), written between 337 and 345, are the earliest evidence of the Syrian Church and, as such, are very valuable to the Church historian.

E.J. Duncan, *Baptism in the Demonstrations of Aphraates* (1945); J. Neusner, *Aprahat and Judaism* (1971).

Apollinarius (fourth century)   Heretic. Apollinarius was born in Beirut, Syria. He was an upholder of orthodoxy against the teachings of ARIUS, was a friend of ATHANASIUS and was consecrated Bishop of Laodicea in *c*. 360. However, teachings similar to his were condemned at the Council of Alexandria in 362 and his own doctrines were specifically repudiated at the Western Council of Rome in 377 and at the Eastern Councils of Alexandria in 378, Antioch in 379 and Constantinople in 381. Apollinarius himself left the Church in c. 375. His followers were outlawed in later decrees issued by the Emperor THEODOSIUS I. Few of his writings have survived, but he seems to have taught that JESUS had a human body, a human soul and a divine spirit. Thus, although he was truly God, he was not fully human. This was unacceptable to the orthodox because if Jesus was less than a full human being, he could neither be a perfect example to humanity nor have fully redeemed human nature.

H. Chadwick (ed.), *St Basil the Great and Apollinarius of Laodicea* (1956); C. Raven, *Apollinarianism* (1923); F. Young, *From Nicaea to Chalcedon* (1983).

Apollos (first century)   Missionary. According to the Acts of the Apostles, Apollos was a Jew, a native of Alexandria. He came as a preacher to Ephesus, but he knew only the baptism of JOHN THE BAPTIST, not that of JESUS. His theology was corrected by PRISCILLA and Aquila and he subsequently became a missionary in Corinth. According to the First Epistle to the Corinthians, he was a party leader within the Church. PAUL was compelled to point out that there should be no parties in Christianity: 'I planted, Apollos watered, but God gave the growth' (I Corinthians 3:6). Martin LUTHER conjectured that Apollos was the author of the Epistle to the Hebrews, but there is little evidence for this suggestion.

The Acts of the Apostles, Chapter 18.

Aquaviva, Claudius (1543–1615)   Educator. Aquaviva was born into an Italian aristocratic family and was educated at the University of Perugia. He entered the Jesuit order at the age of twenty-four and

in 1581 was elected Superior-General. The fifth General in the Society's history, he faced many problems including possible schism within the order. The Society was also threatened with an examination by the Inquisition and an attempt by Pope Sixtus V to change its constitution. Aquaviva must be regarded as the most important early consolidator of the order. He successfully negotiated the difficulties and strengthened the Society's position. In particular he is remembered for his encouragement of mission and for his sponsorship of the 'Ratio Studiorum'. This was a scheme of studies based on Classics, Philosophy and Theology and it formed the basis of the curriculum of Jesuit schools until the end of the eighteenth century.

J.H.C. Aveling, *The Jesuits* (1981); J.W. Donohue, *Jesuit Education* (1963).

Aristides (second century)   Philosopher and Theologian. Aristides is mentioned in the writings of JEROME and EUSEBIUS OF CAESAREA, but until the late nineteenth century nothing was known of his work. In 1878 an Armenian translation of his *Apology* was published and this was followed by a more complete Syriac version in 1889. The *Apology* discussed the existence and eternity of God and argues that Christians have a fuller understanding of God and a higher moral code than Greeks, Jews or barbarians. Aristides is also believed to be the author of a surviving ancient sermon on Luke 23:43.

J.R. Harris (ed.), 'Apology of Aristides', in J.A. Robinson (ed.), *Texts and Studies*, Vol. I (1891).

Arius (c. 250–c. 336)   Heretic. Little certain is known of the early life of Arius. He emerged as a successful preacher in Alexandria, North Africa, teaching the subordination of the person of Christ to the person of the Father. In c. 320 he was excommunicated by a synod in Alexandria and he travelled to the East to enlist the support of the Emperor

CONSTANTINE. After receiving a report from HOSIUS, Constantine summoned an Ecumenical Council at Nicaea in 325. Only fragments of Arius's own writings have survived, but his position is fully described by the orthodox ATHANASIUS. Arius insisted that the Son was not co-equal and co-eternal with the Father. Instead He was created by God as an instrument through which the world was created. Therefore there was a time when the Father was and the Son was not. After this theory was rejected by the Council, Arius was sent into exile, but as a result of his friendship with EUSEBIUS OF NICOMEDIA, he was allowed to return to Alexandria. The beliefs which bear his name were highly influential throughout the fourth century, but were unequivocally rejected by the orthodox because they denied the full divinity of JESUS.

R.C. Gregg and D.E. Groh, *Early Arianism. A View of Salvation* (1981); R.D. Williams, *Arius* (1987).

Arminius, Jacob   (1560–1609)   Theologian. Arminius was born in Oudewater, Holland. He was a student of Theodore BEZA in Geneva, but after an extensive education, he returned to Holland in 1587. He was ordained and served a congregation in Amsterdam. During this period he became increasingly unhappy about the Calvinist doctrine of predestination and he came into sharp conflict with many of his colleagues. In 1603 he was appointed to a chair in theology at the University of Leyden, but he had to vindicate himself against charges of Pelagianism and Socinianism. In this he was successful and he spent the remaining years of his life in Leyden working for the revision of the official doctrines of the Dutch Church. Among his many sympathisers was the theologian Hugo GROTIUS. The theology which goes by the general name of Arminianism is grounded in the conviction that human beings were created

with free will and that JESUS CHRIST died not merely for the elect, but for all humanity. These doctrines have been highly influential on the development of later Protestant theology, and the Calvinist and the Arminian positions have been in frequent conflict.

C. Bangs, *Arminius: A Study in the Dutch Reformation* (1971); A.W. Harrison, *Arminianism* (1937).

Arnauld, Antoine   (1612–94)   Theologian. The brother of Mère Angélique, the formidable Abbess and reformer of the Convent of Port-Royal, Arnauld was born in Paris. He was educated at the Sorbonne and was under the spiritual direction of the Abbé de Saint-Cyran. He was ordained in 1641 and became a prominent spokesman for Jansenism. He was the author of *De la Fréquente Communion* and the *Apologie de M. Jansenius*; both books caused considerable controversy and in 1656 he was censured by the Sorbonne for his teachings against the Jesuit methods of hearing confessions. His doctorate was restored in 1669 and he began an important treatise against the Calvinists, *La Perpétuité de la Foi Catholique Touchant l'Eucharistie*. In 1679 he moved to Brussels to avoid further religious controversy; there he continued to write until his death. Arnauld is remembered as the most successful proponent of Jansenism of his time.

N.J. Abercrombie, *The Origins of Jansenism* (1936).

Arnold of Brescia   (*c*. 1100–55)   Heretic. Little is known of Arnold's early life. He is thought to have been born in Brescia and to have been a student of Peter ABELARD at the University of Paris. He then joined the Canons Regular. He achieved notoriety by arguing that auricular confession was unnecessary, that the sinfulness of the priest could invalidate the Sacrament and that Christians should not exercise worldly power or amass material possessions. As a result of the efforts of St BERNARD OF CLAIRVAUX, these teachings were condemned, together with those of Abelard, in 1140 at the Council of Sens. Subsequently, Arnold argued that the Pope should abandon all temporal power and, as a result, he was excommunicated by Pope EUGENIUS III in 1148. In 1152 he was handed over by the Emperor FREDERICK BARBAROSSA to the Prefect of Rome. He was executed and his ashes were thrown into the River Tiber. After his death a movement grew up, known as the Arnoldists, which stressed the desirability of Christians abandoning worldly wealth. Arnold was one of several mediaeval thinkers who suffered for their attempts to bring the Church back to the New Testament ideal of poverty.

G.W. Greenaway, *Arnold of Brescia* (1931).

Arnold, Matthew   (1822–88) Poet. The son of the schoolmaster Thomas ARNOLD, Matthew Arnold was educated at his father's school and at Oxford University. For much of his adult life he was an Inspector of Schools but in 1857 he was elected Oxford Professor of Poetry for a period of ten years. Some of his poems have become classics of English literature, including 'Sohrab and Rustum', 'The Scholar-Gypsy' and 'Rugby Chapel'. He was also an eminent essayist and is remembered for his condemnation of the English upper classes as barbarians and the English middle classes as philistines. His poem 'Dover Beach' described the retreat of the 'Sea of Faith' in late Victorian England. A hundred years later this phrase was adopted by the followers of Don CUPITT to describe their non-supernaturalist interpretation of Christianity.

A.L. Rowse, *Matthew Arnold, Poet and Prophet* (1976); L. Trilling, *Matthew Arnold* (1949).

Arnold, Thomas (1795–1842) Educator. Arnold was educated at the University of Oxford and, after ordination, he became a Fellow of Oriel College. At the age of thirty-three, he was appointed Headmaster of Rugby School. He was very involved in the ecclesiastical issues of his time, but he is primarily remembered as the major reformer of the English public schools. At Rugby he emphasised moral and religious ideals, then athletic prowess and only thirdly the development of the intellect. He consistently extolled the ideal of the English gentleman and ensured that the older boys took responsibility for their juniors. His weekly sermons in the school chapel were said to have made an enormous impression on his schoolboy hearers and his educational principles rapidly spread to other schools.

A.P. Stanley (ed.), *The Life and Correspondence of Thomas Arnold*, 2 vols (1844); M. McCrum, *Thomas Arnold* (1989).

Asbury, Francis (1745–1816) Missionary. Asbury was born in Birmingham, England and joined the Methodist movement as a very young man. Between 1766 and 1771 he served as a travelling minister. Then, in response to an appeal from John WESLEY, he went as a missionary to the American colonies. In 1784, he and Thomas COKE were appointed Superintendents of the American Methodist Church and, despite the lack of episcopal ordination, they assumed the title of Bishop. Asbury was a tireless traveller and by the year of his death, Methodism was well established in America.

E.T. Clark (ed.), *The Journal and Letters of Francis Asbury*, 3 vols (1958); L.C. Rudolph, *Francis Asbury* (1966).

Aske, Robert (d. 1537) Rebel. Aske was born in Yorkshire and trained as a lawyer in London. In response to King HENRY VIII's suppression of the monasteries, in 1536 he led the rebellion in the north known as the Pilgrimage of Grace. Historians disagree as to how far religious belief, rather than economic hardship, was the inspiration for the revolt. Thirty thousand men assembled; they were promised concessions, safe conduct and free pardons. However, after a further outbreak occurred in 1537, Aske was hanged in chains together with two hundred fellow rebels as a 'fearful spectacle' to others. The failure of the Pilgrimage of Grace was an important landmark in the establishment of the Reformation in England.

G.R. Elton. 'Politics and the Pilgrimage of Grace', in Barbara C. Malament (ed.), *After the Reformation: Essays in Honour of J.H. Hexter* (1980).

Athanasius (*c.* 296–373) Saint, Bishop and Theologian. Athanasius attended the Council of Nicaea as the secretary of the Bishop of Alexandria. He was consecrated as Bishop of Alexandria in 328, but he was driven into exile in 336 because of his opposition to the doctrines of ARIUS. He was the author of a series of theological works including the well-known *De Incarnatione*, and he presided over the Council of Alexandria in 362 which reconciled many semi-Arians to orthodoxy. He also resisted other heresies. Although he was a personal friend of APOLLINARIUS, he did not hesitate to condemn his teachings which denied the full humanity of JESUS CHRIST. He also opposed the doctrines of the disciples of MACEDONIUS who denied the full divinity of the Holy Spirit. A supporter of monasticism, he wrote a biography of St ANTONY OF EGYPT. None the less, he is chiefly remembered for his implacable opposition to Arianism. He did not live to see the final triumph of his views at the Council of Constantinople in 381 when Apollinarianism was condemned and the Nicene doctrine of the Person of Christ upheld.

T.D. Barnes, *Athanasius and Constantius* (1993); A. Pettersen, *Athanasius* (1992); R.D. Williams, *Arius* (1987).

Athanasius the Athonite (*c.* 920–1003) Saint and Order Founder. Athanasius was born in Trebizond. In 961 he established the first monastery on Mount Athos, a peninsula which juts out into the Aegean Sea. By the time of his death there were no fewer than fifty-eight communities on the mountain, of which he was Abbot-General. Today Mount Athos is regarded as a holy place in the Eastern Orthodox Church. There are twenty monasteries on the site; all women and female animals are forbidden entrance and the communities are the custodians of many important ancient manuscripts.

R.M. Dawkins, *The Monks of Athos* (1936).

Athenagoras (second century) Philosopher. Athenagoras was the author of one of the earliest apologies for Christianity. Dedicated to the Emperor Marcus Aurelius and to his son Commodus, it defended the Christians against the charges of atheism, cannibalism and incest. Written from a Platonic standpoint, Athenagoras stresses the admirable conduct of Christians and demands equal rights of citizenship for them. He is also thought by some scholars to be the author of a work on the resurrection of the dead. His writings are significant in that they are among the first to uphold the doctrine of the Trinity.

The Apology of Athenagoras, edited and translated by W.R. Schoedel (1972); L.W. Barnard, *Athenagoras: A Study in Second Century Christian Apologetic* (1972).

Athenagoras (1886–1972) Patriarch and Ecumenist. Athenagoras was born in Vasilikon in Greece. As Archbishop of the Americas in the 1930s, he ended a schism within the United States Greek Church. In 1948 he became Ecumenical Patriarch (Patriarch of Constantinople). During his reign, he organised the Pan-orthodox Conferences of the National Orthodox Churches and did much to bring about better cooperation. He also revoked the orders of excommunication which had been in force between Rome and Constantinople since 1054. After a meeting with Pope PAUL VI in Jerusalem in 1964 greater understanding was achieved between the Churches of the East and West. Athenagoras was thus a highly significant figure in the ecumenical movement of the 1950s and 1960s.

C.G. Patelos (ed.), *The Orthodox Church in the Ecumenical Movement* (1978).

Augustine of Canterbury (d. 604/5) Saint, Missionary and Archbishop. Augustine was Prior of St Andrew's Monastery in Rome. He was sent by Pope GREGORY THE GREAT to bring the English people back to Christianity. In 597 he landed in Kent where Queen BERTHA, a princess from Paris, was already a believer. In 601 her husband King ETHELBERT was baptised and the See of Canterbury was established. Augustine himself was consecrated first Archbishop in Arles, France. He founded a monastery in Canterbury, built the first cathedral and founded a new see in Rochester and another in London. However, he failed to reach agreement with the existing Celtic churches who were unprepared to submit to the discipline of Rome. The surviving letters of Gregory and Augustine are interesting in their reaction to the paganism of the time. The missionaries were advised to take over the non-idolatrous rites and adapt them for use in the Christian festivals. Augustine himself is primarily (but erroneously) remembered as the first bringer of Christianity to England.

M. Deanesly, *Augustine of Canterbury* (1964).

Augustine of Hippo (354–430) Saint, Bishop and Theologian. Augustine was born in Tagaste, North Africa, to a Christian mother (MONICA) and a pagan father. Educated at the University of Carthage, as a young man he abandoned his faith, took a mistress and fathered a son. In *c.* 374 he became a Manichaean, but after coming under the influence of

Bishop AMBROSE in Milan, he was baptised in 387. On his return to North Africa, he was ordained and in 395 he was consecrated Bishop of Hippo. Augustine described his life before he became a Christian in his *Confessions* and this has become a classic of Christian spirituality. (His prayer 'O God make me chaste – but don't do it just yet' is known even outside Church circles.) However, Augustine is primarily remembered as a theologian. He defended Christian doctrine against the Manichaeans who believed in a fundamental conflict between darkness and light. In contrast, Augustine taught that God's creation was all good and that evil was merely the absence of good. Against the Donatists, he insisted that the unworthiness of God's ministers in no way affected the validity of the Sacraments, since JESUS CHRIST was the true minister. Against PELAGIUS and his followers, he defined original sin as the inherited guilt of the first man, Adam, and he taught that human beings could only be obedient to God through divine grace. His best-known work, the *Civitas Dei* (*City of God*), was written as a reply to pagans who were arguing that the fall of Rome to the Goths in 410 was the result of the abolition of idolatrous worship. The book became a theology of history, describing the fortunes of the two cities created by worldly and heavenly love. Augustine's writings have been immensely influential and he is a major figure in the history of Christian thought. In particular his teachings were much used by the Protestant Reformers against the Aristotelianism of THOMAS AQUINAS and the Schoolmen. Within the Roman Catholic world, the theologies of Augustine and Aquinas have been held together in a state of creative tension.

St Augustine, *Confessions*, edited and translated by H. Chadwick (1991); *The City of God*, edited and translated by G.E. McCracken, 7 Vols (1957–72); H. Chadwick, *Augustine* (1986); P. Brown, *Augustine of Hippo* (1967).

Aulen, Gustaf (1879–1977)   Theologian, Ecumenist and Bishop. Aulen was born in southern Sweden and educated at the University of Uppsala. After teaching systematic theology at Lund University, he was consecrated Bishop of Strängnäs in 1933. As a Bishop, he worked against Naziism in neutral Sweden and he was prominent in the ecumenical movement. He was a leader of the Motivsforschung school of theology, which emphasised the truth as opposed to the form of a doctrine. His best-known work was a treatise on the atonement.

Gustav Aulen, *The Faith of the Christian Church* (1961); Gustav Aulen, *Christus Victor*, edited and translated by A.G. Herbert (1931).

Auxentius (d. 373/4)   Bishop and Heretic. A native of Cappadocia, Auxentius was ordained in *c.* 343 and consecrated Bishop of Milan in 355. His Arian views were condemned at the Council of Ariminum in 359, the Council of Paris in 360 and the Synod of Rome in 372. Nevertheless he remained Bishop of Milan mainly because he had the support of the Emperor Valentinian I. He left no writings, but we know of him through references in the works of ATHANASIUS (who fulminated against him), HILARY OF POITIERS and BASIL. He was the most prominent supporter of Arianism of his time and his death paved the way for the final victory of orthodoxy.

R.P.C. Hanson, *The Search for the Christian Doctrine of God* (1991); D.N. Mclynn, *Ambrose of Milan* (1995).

Avancini, Nikola (1611–86)   Devotional writer. Avancini was born in Bretz near Trent and joined the Jesuit Order in 1627. He had a highly successful career, was Rector of several colleges and was appointed Provincial of the Austrian Province in 1676 and Assistant-Principal of the German Province in 1682. He was a prolific writer, but is now chiefly remembered for his *Vita et Doctrina Jesu Christi ex Quattuor Evangelistis Collecta*

('The life and doctrine of Jesus Christ collected from the four evangelists'). This is an anthology of daily meditations. It has become a spiritual classic and is still widely used today.

Nikola Avancini, *Vita et Doctrina Jesu Christi*, edited and translated by K.D. Mackenzie (1937).

Avvakum (*c.* 1621–82)   Saint and Martyr. The son of a village priest, Avvakum became known to the Russian imperial family and he served as Archpriest of Our Lady of Kazan in Moscow. However, he came into conflict with Patriarch NIKON in the matter of liturgical reforms and quickly became regarded as the champion of the Old Believers, the group which remained faithful to the old traditions. He was exiled in Siberia in 1653, returned to Moscow in 1664 and was exiled again. In 1666 he was excommunicated and, while his followers were cruelly persecuted, he was imprisoned. He continued to campaign against the reforms and in 1682 Czar Theodore sentenced him to be burnt at the stake. Avvakum is regarded as a saint by the surviving Old Believers and his autobiography is a classic of Russian literature.

Avvakum, *The Life of Archpriest Avvakum* (1963).

Aylward, Gladys (1902–70)   Missionary. Aylward initially worked as a parlourmaid in London. Because of her inadequate education, she was refused for training by several missionary societies. Undaunted, she saved her tiny wages to pay her own fare to China. In Yangcheng she opened a centre with another woman missionary in 1933. Then, in 1940, when the Japanese invaded China, she led a hundred children to safety in a perilous journey over the mountains. Later she opened an orphanage in Formosa. Aylward was the subject of a bestselling biography and several Hollywood films.

A. Burgess, *The Small Woman* (1957).

Azariah, Vednayakam Samuel (1874–1945) Missionary and Bishop. Azariah was born in Vellalanvillai near Madras, India. His father was a convert to Christianity from Hinduism. From an early age Azariah became involved in missions, forming the Indian Missionary Society of Tinnevelly in 1903 and the National Missionary Society in 1905. He was ordained in 1909 and in 1912 he was consecrated Missionary Bishop of Domakel. He was tireless in his efforts for Church union in India and he was Chairman of the Indian National Christian Council between 1929 and 1945 and the host of the World Missionary Conference when it was held at Madras in 1938. He is remembered as the first Indian Bishop of the Anglican Church and his influence was crucial at a time when indigenous churchmen were increasingly replacing foreign missionaries.

J.Z. Hodge, *Bishop Azariah of Domakel* (1946); A. Mathew, *Christian Missions, Education and Nationalism* (1988).

B

Bach, Johann Sebastian (1685–1750)
Musician. Bach served as court musician
in Weimar and Anhalt-Köthen. In 1723
he was appointed Cantor at the Thomas
School in Leipzig. His output was enormous, but he is chiefly remembered by
Christians for his oratorios: the *St Matthew Passion*; the *St John Passion*; and
the *Christmas Oratorio*, and for his *Mass
in B minor*. He was himself a Lutheran,
but his music is enjoyed by and speaks to
members of all denominations and none.

K. Geiringer and I. Geiringer, *Johann Sebastian
Bach* (1966).

Bacon, Francis (1561–1626) Politician
and Philosopher. Bacon was the son of
Queen ELIZABETH I's Lord Keeper. He
was educated at the University of Cambridge and was first elected a Member of
Parliament in 1584. He became Solicitor-
General in 1608, Attorney-General in
1613 and Lord Keeper in 1617. In 1618 he
was appointed Lord Chancellor, but he
was accused of corruption in 1620 and
retired in disgrace. He is chiefly remembered for his writings and his essays are
read to this day. He was an orthodox
member of the Church of England and
his writings reflect his preoccupations.
His essays on death and atheism are of
particular interest to Christians, the former beginning with the arresting sentence, 'Men fear death as children fear to
go into the dark'.

A. Quinton, *Francis Bacon* (1980).

Bacon, Roger (*c.* 1214–*c.* 1292) Philosopher and Scientist. An Englishman,
Bacon received much of his education in
Paris. He joined the Franciscan Order in
c. 1257 and was part of the household of
Cardinal de Foulques, who was to become Pope Clement IV. Clement encouraged his writings and Bacon wrote the
Opus Maius, the *Compendium Studii Philosophae* and the *Compendium Studii
Theologiae*. He is thought to have been
under suspicion in his order for promulgating dangerous doctrines, but the facts
of this are not known. Bacon was one of
the first to give lectures on the works of
Aristotle and, unusually for his time, he
emphasised the necessity of empirical
experience for the increase of scientific
knowledge. He was known as the 'Doctor Mirabilis' and his reputation was
submerged by later legends of his magical powers and extraordinary inventions.

S.C. Easton, *Roger Bacon and his Search for a Universal Science* (1952).

Baius, Michel (1513–89) Theologian.
A native of Flanders, Baius was educated
at the University of Louvain. After studying the theology of St AUGUSTINE OF
HIPPO, he developed his own radical position which included the denial of the
doctrines of papal infallibility and the
immaculate conception. He also reinter-
preted the doctrine of original sin. His
ideas were denounced in the Sorbonne
and several of his teachings were specifically condemned by Pope PIUS V in 1567.
In 1579 a further condemnation was issued by Pope GREGORY XIII in the bull
Provisionis Nostrae, to which Baius
submitted. He claimed that his theology
was misunderstood by the Church establishment, but he was anxious to remain

within the Roman Catholic fold. He is a significant figure in the history of Christian thought in that his ideas are generally seen as an anticipation of those of Cornelius JANSEN and his followers.

N.J. Abercrombie, *The Origins of Jansenism* (1936).

Baker, Sir Henry Williams (1821–77) Poet and Anthologist. Baker was the son of a British admiral and was educated at the University of Cambridge. After ordination, he served as a parish priest in the village of Monkland. He was the author of many well-known hymns, many of which are still sung today. These include 'The king of love my shepherd is' and 'Lord thy word abideth'. He was also largely responsible for the compilation of the best-known Anglican hymn book, *Hymns Ancient and Modern* (1861). Since the mid-nineteenth century, hymn singing has become one of the most popular characteristics of worship in the Church of England.

W.K.L. Clarke, *A Hundred Years of Hymns Ancient and Modern* (1960); F.J. Gillman, *The Evolution of the English Hymn* (1927).

Bale, John (1495–1563) Bishop, Polemicist and Historian. As a boy, Bale entered a Carmelite monastery and he was educated there and at the University of Cambridge. In his thirties, however, he left the order and became a determined Protestant. He was protected by Thomas CROMWELL, but was forced into exile between 1540 and 1547. With the accession of the Protestant King EDWARD VI he returned to England and in 1552 was consecrated to the Irish bishopric of Ossory. He spent Queen MARY's reign in the Netherlands and retired to Canterbury in 1559. He is chiefly remembered for his plays and for his *Illustrium Majoris Britanniae Scriptorum*, an important, if inaccurate, catalogue of British writers.

W.T. Davies, 'A bibliography of John Bale', *Oxford*

Bibliographical Society Proceedings, v (1940); L.P. Fairfield, *Bishop John Bale* (1976).

Ball, John (d. 1381) Rebel and Popular Economist. Ball was an English priest who served congregations in York and Colchester. In 1366 he was forbidden to preach after he had been teaching a popular version of the doctrines of John WYCLIFFE and by 1381 he was in prison. During the course of the Peasants' Revolt, led by Wat Tyler, the rebels released him from gaol in Maidstone. He was present when the rebels murdered Archbishop SIMON OF SUDBURY and he preached a fiery sermon based on the rhyme, 'When Adam delved and Eve span, Who was then the gentleman?' With the young king's promise of amnesty, the rebellion collapsed. Its leaders were executed and Ball, captured in Coventry, was sentenced to be hanged, drawn and quartered.

R.B. Dobson (ed.), *The Peasants' Revolt of 1381*, 2nd edn (1983).

Bancroft, Richard (1544–1610) Archbishop and Theologian. Bancroft was educated at the University of Cambridge. He rose rapidly in the Church, becoming Canon of Westminster in 1587, Bishop of London in 1597 and Archbishop of Canterbury in 1604. He is remembered for his determined opposition to both Puritanism and Presbyterianism: the failure of the Hampton Court Conference of 1604 was largely the result of his unwillingness to compromise. He was also responsible for the re-establishment of episcopacy in Scotland.

Tracts ascribed to Richard Bancroft, A. Peel (ed.) (1953); S.B. Babbage, *Puritanism and Richard Bancroft* (1962).

Barabbas (first century) Rebel or Robber. According to St MARK's Gospel (Chapter 15), it was the custom of the Roman Governor of Judaea to release one prisoner at the time of the Jewish festivals. The crowd chose Barabbas rather than JESUS. Nothing more is known of him except that possibly his first name was also Jesus. The special privilege of releasing a prisoner is not mentioned in any other source and is of doubtful historicity.

H.A. Rigg, 'Barabbas', *Journal of Biblical Literature*, lxiv (1945).

Barbara (? fourth century) Legendary Saint. Little certain is known of the life of St Barbara. According to legend she was shut up in a tower by her father to be protected from men. So great was her beauty that princes came from far and wide to woo her. While her father was away she was converted to Christianity and wanted to live as a hermit. Her father was furious. She was handed over to the secular authorities and died a martyr's death. Her father also died, having been struck by lightning. No firm date can be given for these events and Nicomedia, Heliopolis, Tuscany and Rome have all, at different times, laid claim to be the site of her martyrdom. She was a very popular saint in the Middle Ages and even today is invoked by those in danger of lightning.

D.H. Farmer (ed.), *The Oxford Dictionary of Saints*, 3rd edn (1992).

Barclay, John (1734–98) Denomination Founder. Barclay was born in Perthshire, Scotland and was educated at St Andrew's University. As a preacher, he served congregations in Errol and Fettercairn. In 1766 he was censured for his *Rejoice Evermore* or *Christ is All in All*. He defended himself in Edinburgh, but had to travel to England to receive ordination. In 1773 he set up the Berean Assembly in Edinburgh, so called after the noble congregation of Beroeia (Acts 17:10). He also visited London and Berean communities were established there and in Bristol. His teaching differed from that of Scottish Calvinism in that he believed that the hallmark of Christianity

lies in the assurance of salvation and that faith is merely the intellectual acceptance of the truths revealed in the Bible. Barclay worked tirelessly for his followers until his death and the Church grew in all major Scottish towns. By the mid-nineteenth century, however, the impetus was lost and most Bereans had merged with the Congregationalists.

J. Campbell, *The Berean Church – Especially in Edinburgh* (1937).

Barclay, Robert (1648–90) Theologian. A Scotsman, Barclay was educated in Paris. He joined the Society of Friends (Quakers) in 1667. He was the author of several works of Quaker theology, including *A Catechism and Confession of Faith*, the *Anarchy of the Ranters* and *An Apology for the True Christian Religion, being as Explanation and Vindication of the People Called Quakers*. He was imprisoned on several occasions for his convictions, but in 1677 he became a favourite of the Duke of York, who was to become King JAMES II. As a result of his influence, the colony of East New Jersey in America was handed over to the Friends as a refuge from persecution. Barclay himself was appointed Governor, although he never crossed the Atlantic Ocean. He is chiefly remembered for his pacifist ideals, which have remained an important hallmark of the Society.

E. Russell, *The History of Quakerism* (1943); D.E. Trueblood, *Robert Barclay* (1943).

Bardesanes (154–222) Heretic. Bardesanes was born in Edessa, the centre of Syriac-speaking Christianity, and he was a philosopher with an interest in astrology. His *Book of the Law of the Lands* is fragmentarily preserved in the work of EUSEBIUS OF CAESAREA and other early historians. He was also an important hymn-writer although only a single quotation survives in EPHRAEM SYRUS's writings. He seems to have taught a form of dualism and that JESUS's physical body was not of flesh. As a result he was excommunicated and had to flee Edessa. His doctrines survived and it has been conjectured that the apocryphal *Acts of Thomas* was produced in a circle influenced by his thinking.

H.J.W. Drijvers, *Bardaisan of Edessa* (1966).

Barlaam   Legendary Saint. Barlaam was an Indian hermit who supposedly converted JOASAPH, the son of a pagan king, to Christianity. Together Joasaph and Barlaam retired to the wilderness to lead lives of austerity and sanctity. This was a popular story in the Middle Ages; it may well be based on Buddhist sources, since it is similar to the life of the Buddha.

D.M. Lang (ed. and transl.), *Barlaam and Joasaph* (1966); R.L. Wolff, 'Barlaam and Joasaph', *Harvard Theological Review*, xxxii (1939).

Barnabas (first century)   Saint and Apostle. Barnabas was not one of the original twelve. According to Acts, 'Joseph, who was surnamed by the apostles Barnabas (which means "Son of Encouragement"), a Levite, a native of Cyprus, sold a field which belonged to him and brought the money and laid it at the apostles' feet' (Acts 4:36–7). He introduced PAUL, after his conversion, to the Church in Jerusalem and he was sent by the apostles to examine the new disciples of Antioch. He accompanied Paul on his first missionary journey and he was present at the Council of Jerusalem. On the second missionary journey, however, he quarrelled with Paul and sailed for Cyprus without him. He is mentioned in the First Epistle to the Corinthians, the Epistle to the Galatians and the Epistle to the Colossians. According to one legend, he died as a martyr in Salamis in *c.* 61. Alternatively he is thought to have founded the Church in Milan, Italy, and to have been its first Bishop. The apocryphal *Epistle of Barnabas* is almost certainly not his work.

The Acts of the Apostles, Chapters 4–15.

Barnardo, Thomas (1845–1905)   Educator and Philanthropist. A native of Dublin, Ireland, Barnardo joined the Plymouth Brethren in 1862 and came to London in 1866 to qualify as a physician. He was appalled by the number of destitute children he found on the city streets and he set up his first Home for Boys in 1870. The organisation grew rapidly. By 1876, he had attracted sufficient notice and funds to build a model village for homeless girls. From 1882 he began to send children to the British colonies abroad. This aspect of his work has attracted considerable criticism in recent years, but he genuinely believed that there were better employment prospects there. By the time of his death, nearly sixty thousand children had been admitted to his institutions. The work continues today, although increasingly the organisation recognises that adoption and fostering are better alternatives for parentless children.

J. Hitchman, *They Carried the Sword* (1966); N. Wymer, *Father of Nobody's Children* (1954).

Barnes, Ernest William (1874–1953) Bishop and Theologian. Educated at the University of Cambridge, Barnes taught mathematics at the university before being ordained in 1902. He became a Canon of Westminster in 1918 and Bishop of Birmingham in 1924. He is primarily remembered for his radical views, calling into question the literal historical truth of the virgin birth and the bodily resurrection of JESUS. In addition he was a determined and courageous pacifist who unequivocally condemned the use of nuclear weapons.

Ernest William Barnes, *Scientific Theory and Religion* (1933).

Barsumas of Nisibis (*c.* 415/20–*c.* 491/2) Bishop and Heretic. Barsumas was a follower of the semi-Nestorian IBAS of Edessa. Supported by the Persian King, he became Bishop of Nisibis where he founded an important school of theology. He attempted to establish the independence of his see from the Churches of the Roman Empire, and Nestorianism became the official doctrine. Clerical marriage was permitted and he himself married a nun. Ultimately he was assassinated by a group of Persian monks. Six of his letters have survived.

P. Gero, *Barsumas of Nisibis and Persian Christianity* (1981).

Barth, Karl (1886–1968) Theologian. Barth was born in Basle and was educated in the nineteenth-century liberal theological tradition. After the carnage of the First World War, he produced his ground-breaking *Commentary to the Epistle to the Romans*. Liberal theology, as taught by SCHLEIERMACHER and his followers, stressed the fatherhood of God and the brotherhood of man. Influenced by writers such as DOSTOIEVSKY and KIERKEGAARD, Barth's 'Crisis Theology' insisted on the absolute transcendence of God and the total inadequacy of unaided human reason. He taught that God revealed Himself only through His Word, that is in JESUS CHRIST. Human beings are dependent solely on divine grace for salvation since their own efforts count for nothing. His views spoke to his contemporaries, struggling to make sense of the tragedy of war. Liberal ideas had plainly failed and Barth was the most influential theologian of his day. He taught at the Universities of Göttingen, Münster and Bonn and was largely responsible for the Barmen Declaration of 1934, which refused to allow the Confessing Church of Germany to be an instrument of Nazi policy. Expelled from Germany, he returned to Switzerland where he taught until his retirement in 1962. A highly prolific writer, he is remembered for his multi-volumed *Church Dogmatics*, dealing with the Word of God, the doctrine of God, creation and reconciliation. The final section on redemption was never completed. During his lifetime, many regarded him as a prophet and, although his views are now less fashionable, no account of twentieth-century theology can ignore his monumental contribution.

R.J. Erler and R. Marquand (eds), *A Karl Barth Reader*, translated by G.W. Bromiley (1986); J. Bowden, *Karl Barth* (1971); G. Harsinger, *How to Read Karl Barth* (1970).

Bartholomew (first century) Apostle. Bartholomew is listed as one of the original twelve disciples in the Gospels, but he does not appear in any other context. Since the ninth century there have been attempts to identify him with Nathanael, 'the Israelite . . . in whom there is no guile' (John 1:47), but there is no evidence to connect the two. According to EUSEBIUS OF CAESAREA, he took the Gospel to India. Another legend has him preaching in Armenia where he was martyred by being flayed alive.

B.M. Metzger and M.D. Coogan (eds), *The Oxford Companion to the Bible* (1993).

Barton, Elizabeth (*c.* 1506–34) Rebel. Barton was born in Aldington, a country village in Kent. She claimed to have seen the Virgin MARY in visions and she became a nun in a community in nearby Canterbury. Subsequently she felt inspired to denounce King HENRY VIII's divorce of Catherine of Aragon. After an examination by Archbishop CRANMER, which may have involved torture, she admitted that her visions were faked and she was executed.

A. Neame, *The Holy Maid of Kent* (1971).

Basil (*c.* 330–79) Saint, Bishop and Theologian. Basil was the elder brother of St GREGORY OF NYSSA and a native of Caesarea in Cappadocia. After an extensive education (he studied in Athens with GREGORY OF NAZIANZUS) he was baptised and became a hermit. In 364, at the request of Eusebius, he returned to the world to combat the Arian heresy. His first books were attacks on the Arian bishop EUNOMIUS. Then in 370 he succeeded Eusebius as Bishop of Caesarea where he remained for the rest of his life. Although he corresponded with APOLLINARIUS, he was a determined warrior for orthodoxy. He confronted and outfaced the Arian Emperor Valens and he unswervingly opposed the Pneumatomachi who denied the divinity of the Holy Spirit. However, Basil is primarily remembered for his support of monasticism and for his caring and efficient administration of the clergy and poor of his diocese. He introduced the idea of community into the ascetic life and his pastoral supervision of charity was much imitated. Besides the books against Eunomius, he wrote an important collection of letters and a treatise on the Holy Spirit. One of the Three Cappadocian Fathers (the other two being Gregory of Nyssa and Gregory of Nazianzus), he is generally known as St Basil the Great.

P. Rousseau, *Basil of Caesarea* (1994); P.J. Fedwick, (ed.), *Basil of Caesarea* (1981).

Basilides (second century)　　Heretic. Basilides was a teacher in Alexandria, North Africa; we know of his doctrines through the writings of IRENAEUS and HIPPOLYTUS. He was a Gnostic who taught that the Gospel of Light descended from demi-gods through to JESUS and then to a chosen few who would return above. Only those who accepted this doctrine would attain salvation. He formed his own organisation in Alexandria; he and his followers practised magical rituals and the sect seems to have survived until at least the end of the second century. Basilides is a significant figure in that he illustrates the type of Gnostic speculation that was rife in the second-century Church.

Irenaeus, *Adversos Haereticos*, English translation (1977); W. Frend, *Saints and Sinners in the Early Church* (1985).

Bauer, Walter (1877–1960)　　Theologian. Bauer taught for many years at the University of Göttingen. He is remembered for his *Orthodoxy and Heresy in Earliest Christianity* (1934) in which he argued that the early Christian heresies were once widely held forms of the Christian religion. Orthodoxy was the product of the centralising of the Church establishment which overcame the less co-ordinated versions of the Christian message. Bauer was also responsible for a definitive New Testament lexicon.

Walter Bauer, *Orthodoxy and Heresy in Earliest Christianity*, R.A. Kraft and G. Krodell (eds) English translation (1972).

Baur, Ferdinand Christian (1792–1860) Theologian. Baur was born near Württemberg in Germany. For many years he taught at the University of Tübingen and he is regarded as the leader of the Tübingen school of Biblical criticism. Among his many books were *Symbolik und Mythologie*, *Paulus, der Apostel Jesu Christi* and *Kritische Untersuchungen über die Kanonischen Evangelien*. His views were radical for their time; he maintained that of the epistles, only those to the Romans, Galatians and Corinthians were of genuine Pauline authorship. He insisted on a late date for the Gospels, placing that of JOHN in the latter half of the second century. He also believed that there had been a deep-seated conflict between the early Jewish Church and the Hellenised Christianity of PAUL. Baur himself was influenced by the philosophical methods of HEGEL and the theology of SCHLEIERMACHER. Other members of the Tübingen school included Eduard Zeller, Albert Schwegler and Albrecht RITSCHL at the start of his career.

H. Harris, *The Tübingen School* (1975); P.C. Hodson, *The Formation of Historical Theology: A Study of Ferdinand Christian Baur* (1966).

Baxter, Richard (1615–91)　　Poet and Devotional Writer. Baxter was a native of Shropshire. In 1638 he was ordained to the Church of England ministry and he served congregations in Bridgnorth and Kidderminster. He fought on the Parliamentary side in the English Civil War, although he remained a moderate in his views. In 1660 he supported the Restoration of the monarchy, but his views on episcopacy led him to refuse the Bishopric of Hereford. At the Savoy Conference of 1661, he produced an alternative liturgy to the Book of Common Prayer, but he gained almost no concessions from the Bishops. Because of his Presbyterian leanings, he held no further benefices and he endured a certain amount of harassment until the accession of William and Mary in 1688. Baxter is remembered for his devotional writings. His classic, *The Saints' Everlasting Rest*, reveals his sincere piety and he was the author of hymns such as 'Ye holy angels bright' and 'He wants not friends who know thy love', which are still sung today.

Richard Baxter, *The Saints' Everlasting Rest*, edited by M. Monckton (1928); W.M. Lamont, *Richard Baxter and the Millennium* (1979); G.F. Nuttall, *Richard Baxter* (1965).

Bayly, Lewis (1563–1631) Bishop and Devotional Writer. Bayly was educated at the University of Oxford, England. He became chaplain to the Prince of Wales, then chaplain to King JAMES I and finally Bishop of Bangor. He is remembered for his devotional handbook, *The Practice of Piety*. Its original date of publication is unknown, but it was in its third edition by 1613 and its fifty-ninth by 1735. It was used as an aid to prayer in many Puritan households and was translated into many languages, including North American Indian dialects. John BUNYAN, the author of the *Pilgrim's Progress*, regarded it as a major influence on his life.

J.E. Bailey, ' Bishop Lewis Bayly and his *Practice of Piety*', *Manchester Quarterly*, ii (1883); Lewis Bayly, *The Practice of Piety*, edited by G. Webster (1842).

Becket, Thomas (*c.* 1118–70) Saint, Martyr and Archbishop. Becket was born in London and educated at Merton Abbey and Paris. After legal training he was ordained Deacon. He came to the notice of King HENRY II when he was in the household of Archbishop THEOBALD. In 1155 he was appointed Chancellor of England, in which position he was a loyal and successful servant of the King. Expecting the same commitment from him, Henry secured his election as Archbishop of Canterbury. Instead, Becket resigned as Chancellor, adopted an austere way of life and dedicated himself to the Church. He opposed the King in his claims for the secular courts and insisted on the churchman's right to appeal to Rome. In 1164 he was forced to flee to France and, although he was permitted to return to England in 1170, he promptly excommunicated several Bishops who had connived with the King. In fury, Henry demanded to be rid of 'this turbulent priest'. Four knights took him at his word. They rode to Canterbury and murdered the Archbishop in his own cathedral. The whole Christian world was aghast. The King was forced to do public penance and Becket was canonised in 1173. Canterbury became a major centre of pilgrimage and Chaucer's *Canterbury Tales*, describing one such journey, has become a classic of English literature.

F. Barlow, *Thomas Becket* (1986); B. Smalley, *The Becket Conflict and the Schools* (1973).

Becon, Thomas (*c.* 1512–67) Theologian. Becon was born in Norfolk. He was educated at the University of Cambridge and was a pupil of Hugh LATIMER. After ordination he served congregations in Kent and London and in 1547 he became a chaplain at the court of King EDWARD VI. A committed Protestant, he supported the Reformation and was imprisoned in the Tower of London during the reign of the Roman Catholic Queen MARY. He managed to escape and fled to Germany. At the accession of Queen ELIZABETH I in 1559, he returned to England and became a Canon of Canterbury Cathedral. His writings enjoyed great popularity in the sixteenth century. He is best remembered today for his 'Homily against adultery' in the *Book of Homilies*.

D.S. Bailey, *Thomas Becon and the Reformation of the Church of England* (1952).

Bede (*c.* 673–735) Saint and Historian. Bede was a native of County Durham, and at an early age he became a monk at the Benedictine community at Jarrow. At this period, Northumbria was a centre of learning and although Bede is thought never to have travelled abroad, he could read Latin, Greek and Hebrew. He was also well versed in Classical literature and he was familiar with the work of many of the Church Fathers. He is best known for his *Historia Ecclesiastica Gentis Anglorum*. For this monumental history he used copies of documents sent from foreign libraries and he also made careful use of oral traditions. For this he is often described as the 'Father of English History'. In addition he wrote a life of St CUTHBERT, a history of the community at Jarrow, historical chronicles, biblical expositions and a scientific treatise, *De Natura Rerum*. After his death he was given the title 'Venerable' and in 1899 he was declared a Doctor of the Church.

P.H. Blair, *The World of Bede* (1970); J.M. Wallace-Hadrill, *Bede's Ecclesiastical History of the English People* (1988); B. Ward, *The Venerable Bede* (1990).

Bell, George Kennedy Allen (1881–1958) Bishop, Ecumenist and Polemicist. The son of a clergyman, Bell was ordained in 1907 and became chaplain to Archbishop Davidson in 1914. In 1924 he became Dean of Canterbury and in 1929 Bishop of Chichester. From its inception, he was involved in the ecumenical movement, drafting the final message of the Stockholm Conference in 1929 and becoming

President of the Life and Work Movement in 1932. He was elected an honorary President of the World Council of Churches in 1954. However, Bell is primarily remembered for his confrontation with Nazi anti-semitism and his involvement with NIEMÖLLER, BONHOEFFER and the Confessing Church of Germany. During the Second World War, he courageously condemned the saturation bombing of German cities, thereby incurring the wrath of the Prime Minister, Winston Churchill. This may well have prevented his selection as Archbishop of Canterbury after the death of TEMPLE in 1944. Nevertheless he was unquestionably one of the outstanding churchmen of his era.

George Bell, *Christian Unity: the Anglican Position* (1948); R.C.D. Jasper, *George Bell, Bishop of Chichester* (1967).

Bellarmine, Robert (1542–1621) Archbishop, Saint and Theologian. Bellarmine was a native of Tuscany, Italy. Having joined the Jesuit Order in 1560, he taught theology at the University of Louvain from 1570 and he became a professor at the Collegium Romanum in 1576. In 1597 he was chosen to be personal theologian to the Pope; he became a Cardinal in 1599 and he was Archbishop of Capua between 1602 and 1605. He is remembered for his vigorous defence of Roman Catholicism against the Protestants, his most famous work being *Disputationes de Controversiis Christianae Fidei adversus huius Temporis Haereticos*. His views were moderate. He took an informed and friendly interest in the work of GALILEO and he argued for less direct papal interference in secular matters. Because of this, his true worth was not immediately recognised by the Church establishment and he was not canonised until 1930. The following year he was named a Doctor of the Church.

J. Brodrick, *Robert Bellarmine, Saint and Scholar* (1961).

Belloc, Joseph Hilaire Pierre (1870–1953) Historian and Critic. Belloc was born near Versailles, of Anglo-French parents. He was educated at Cardinal NEWMAN's Oratory School in Birmingham and at the University of Oxford. For a short period he was a Member of the British Parliament, but after 1910 he concentrated on journalism and his other writing. He consistently upheld the liberal Roman Catholic view and his essays, histories, biographies and travelogues were widely read during the middle years of the twentieth century. In particular, generations of children were brought up on his *Cautionary Verses*, which, in a light-hearted manner, encouraged them into civilised behaviour.

Hilaire Belloc, *Europe and the Faith* (1912); Hilaire Belloc, *Essays of a Catholic Layman in England* (1931); A.N. Wilson, *Hilaire Belloc* (1984).

Benedict (*c.* 480–*c.* 550) Saint and Order Founder. The brother of St SCHOLASTICA, Benedict was born in Nursia, Italy, and was educated in Rome. He became a hermit at Subiaco where he was joined by a group of disciples. In *c.* 525 he moved to Monte Cassino and it was there that he composed his famous Rule. This is the basis of all later Benedictine monasticism. It insists on stability of life, obedience and enthusiasm; the monks' lives are dedicated to the recitation of the Divine Office, study and manual labour; all worldly goods are held in common and the Abbot has full authority over the community. Benedict's form of monasticism spread throughout the Christian world and the Rule remains one of the most influential spiritual guides ever written.

J. McCann (ed. and transl.), *The Rule of St Benedict* (1952); J. Chapman, *St Benedict and the Sixth Century* (1929); E.R. Elder (ed.), *Benedictus: Studies in Honor of St Benedict of Nursia* (1981).

Benedict XII (d. 1342) Pope. Benedict was born Jacques Fournier. As a very young man he entered the Cistercian Order and was educated in Paris, France. Despite humble beginnings, he rose rapidly in the Church. In 1311 he was elected Abbot of Fontfroide; in 1317 he was consecrated Bishop of Pamiers; in 1326 he became Bishop of Mirepoix; he was made a Cardinal in 1327 and in 1334 he was elected the third in the succession of Avignon Popes. Benedict is remembered for his dedication to Church order. His firmness with the clergy and his reform of religious orders anticipated measures taken at the Council of Trent two hundred years later. Although he wished to restore the Papacy to Rome, he was prevented by King Philip VI of France and instead he drew up plans for the construction of a papal palace at Avignon. During his reign, the belief that the sinless souls of the faithful attain the beatific vision as soon as they die became official Catholic doctrine.

G. Mollat, *The Avignon Popes* (1963).

Benedict XIII (d. 1423) Antipope. Benedict XIII was born Pedro de Luna. An expert in Canon Law, he was made a Cardinal in 1375. After the death of Antipope CLEMENT VII in 1394, he was elected in his place on the understanding that he would resign in order to put an end to the papal schism which had begun in 1387 with Clement's election over URBAN VI. However, once elected, he maintained his position with utmost determination. He was deposed at the Council of Pisa in 1409 and again at the Council of Constance in 1417. Even after his allies had deserted him, and until the day of his death, he insisted that he was the one true Pope. This fiasco did much to discredit the institution of the Papacy in the century before the Protestant Reformation.

A. Glasfurd, *The Antipope (Peter de Luna 1342–1423): A Study in Obstinacy* (1965).

Benedict XIV (1675–1758) Pope. Benedict XIV was born Prospero Lorenzo

Lambertini. He trained as a lawyer, specialising in Canon Law, and became Bishop of Ancona in 1727, Cardinal in 1728, Archbishop of Bologna in 1731 and Pope in 1740. As Pope, he pursued conciliatory policies with his fellow European rulers; he made the position of the Jansenists easier in France and he did much to encourage art and learning in Rome. Among his many cultural activities, he established four academies dedicated to historical studies and he began the task of cataloguing all the Vatican manuscripts. A man of outstanding intellect, he was the author of several books, including a treatise on the Mass and an important volume on the beatification and canonisation of saints.

E. Morelli, *Tre Profili* (1955) [no English translation available].

Bengel, Johannes Albrecht (1687–1752) Theologian. Educated at Tübingen, Bengel was ordained a Lutheran minister in 1707. After teaching at a seminary in Denkendorf, he became superintendent of Herbrechtingen and later Alpirsbach. He was the author of several apocalyptic works, but he is chiefly remembered for his *Gnomon Novi Testamenti*, a New Testament commentary, much of which was translated by John WESLEY and which is still used by evangelical scholars today. Previously in 1734, he had published a critical edition of the New Testament. Although it has long been superseded, it is generally regarded as the start of modern scientific critical work in biblical studies.

J.D. Douglas (ed.), *The New International Dictionary of the Christian Church*, revised edition (1978).

Berdyaev, Nicolas (1874–1948) Philosopher and Theologian. Berdyaev was born in Kiev in the Ukraine. As a young man he supported the Marxist cause, but after the revolution, he was expelled from his position as Professor of Philosophy at the University of Moscow. By 1924 he had settled in France. There he wrote several books in which he attempted to reconcile Orthodox Christianity with the ideas of modern philosophy. Particularly influenced by the work of KANT, NIETZSCHE and DOSTOIEVSKY, he has been described as a 'Christian existentialist'. He is best known for his *Freedom and the Spirit* and *The Destiny of Man*.

Nicolas Berdyaev, *Dream and Reality* (1950) [Autobiography]; D.A. Lowne (ed. and transl.), *Christian Existentialism: A Berdyaev Anthology* (1965).

Berengar (c. 1010–88) Theologian. Berengar was a native of Tours, France. The details of his life are not known, but he was a pupil of FULBERT and by 1040 he was Archdeacon of Angers, where he remained until 1060. In 1070 he appears as Master of the Schools of Tours and at the end of his life he retired to a hermitage. Berengar is remembered for his teaching on the Eucharist. In the eleventh century, the official doctrine of the Church was that of PASCHASIUS RADBERTUS, namely that the presence of Christ in the Mass was not merely a spiritual presence, but involved the miraculous transformation of the elements into the body and blood of JESUS. By contrast, Berengar believed that the Christian does not literally eat and drink Christ's body and blood; instead, by sharing in the Eucharist, the faithful can participate in a spiritual communion with Jesus in his full glorified humanity. He endured much harassment for these views; treatises (such as that of LANFRANC) were written against him, but he never seems to have been excommunicated. Although his teaching had little influence in his own time, it forced his critics to examine the traditional doctrines and led the way to the rigorous scholastic argument of the next century.

A.J. Macdonald, *Berengar and the Reform of Sacramental Doctrine* (1930); R.W. Southern, 'Lanfranc of Bec and Berengar of Tours', in R.W. Hunt, W.A.

Pantin and R.W. Southern (eds), *Studies in Mediaeval History* (1948).

Berggrav, Eivind (1884–1959) Bishop and Polemicist. Berggrav was the son of a Norwegian Lutheran Bishop. After a varied clerical career, he became Bishop of Tromso in 1928 and of Oslo in 1937. Although a prolific writer and successful editor, he is chiefly remembered for his courageous stand against the Nazis in the Second World War. While Norway was occupied, he refused to co-operate with the puppet government and resigned his bishopric in 1941. At the same time he insisted that he retained the spiritual calling to which he had been ordained. He was imprisoned in a log cabin outside Oslo and lived under heavy guard until the end of the war.

Eivind Berggrav, *With God in Darkness* (1943); A. Johnston, *Eivind Berggrav*, English translation (1960).

Bergson, Henri (1859–1941) Philosopher. Bergson was born in Paris, to Jewish parents. Between 1900 and 1924 he held a chair at the Collège de France; he was elected to the Académie Française in 1914 and he was awarded the Nobel Prize in 1928. Among his most important writings were *Essai sur les Données Immédiates de la Conscience, Matière et Mémoire, L'Evolution Créatrice* and *Les Deux Sources de la Morale et de la Religion*. In his writings, Bergson emphasised the role of personal intuition in human activity and insisted that humanity should be open to the 'élan vital' as the source of free will and creativity. His work was particularly influential among the Modernists of the French Roman Catholic Church, who also rejected the intellectualism of traditional scholastic theology.

P.A. Gunter, *Henri Bergson: A Bibliography* (1974); J. Maritain, *Bergsonian Philosophy and Thomism* (1955); A.E. Pilkington, *Bergson and his Influence* (1976).

Berkeley, George (1685–1753) Bishop and Philosopher. A native of Ireland, Berkeley was educated at Trinity College, Dublin. He was appointed Dean of Derry in 1724 and, after a period as a travelling missionary in America, he was consecrated Bishop of Cloyne in 1734. He is primarily remembered for his philosophical writings, which included *A New Theory of Vision, Principles of Human Knowledge* and *Alciphron*. He made the distinction between the reality of material objects which exist in so far as they are perceived by spiritual beings (including God) and the reality of spirits which do exist in their own right. His ideas were much discussed by his contemporaries and he is an unusual figure in that he combined rigorous philosophical speculation with a genuine enthusiasm for spreading the Christian gospel.

T.E. Jessop, *A Bibliography of George Berkeley*, 2nd edition (1973); G. Warnock, *Berkeley* (1969); K.P. Winkler, *Berkeley: An Interpretation* (1989).

Bernadette (1844–79) Saint and Mystic. Bernadette Subirous was the daughter of a miller and grew up in the French village of Lourdes. Between 11 February and 16 July 1858, she claimed to have had eighteen visions of the Virgin MARY, who went by the title of the 'Immaculate Conception'. She joined the Order of the Sisters of Charity in 1866 and she died at the age of thirty-five. Miraculous healings took place at the Lourdes spring from the late 1850s and it was recognised as an official place of pilgrimage in 1862. Even today the faithful flock to the village seeking physical and mental cures and many well-documented healings have occurred. Bernadette was canonised in 1933.

R. Laurentin, B. Billet and P. Galland, *Lourdes: Histoire Authentique des Apparitions*, 6 vols (1961–4); R. Laurentin, *Bernadette of Lourdes*, translated by J. Drury (1979).

Bernard of Chartres (d. *c.* 1130) Theologian. Bernard was the elder brother of

THIERRY OF CHARTRES and was born in Brittany. Little is known of his life except that he was Chancellor of the School of Chartres from 1119 until at least 1124 and that GILBERT DE LA PORRÉE was among his pupils. None of his writings have survived, but JOHN OF SALISBURY describes him as an influential teacher, one who oversaw the morals as well as the intellects of his students, and as 'the most thorough-going Platonist of our age'. Partly as a result of his leadership, the School of Chartres was known for its Platonist traditions.

E. Gilson, 'Le Platonisme de Bernard de Chartres', *Revue Néoscolastique de Philosophie*', xxv (1923) [no English translation available].

Bernard of Clairvaux (1090–1153) Saint, Theologian, Mystic and Order Founder. Bernard was born near Dijon in France. As a young man he joined the Cistercian Order and was soon invited to found a new community at Clairvaux. This was to become one of the most important monastic houses in Europe. In 1128 he was responsible for the rule for the new Order of Knights Templar, which was to be accepted at the Synod of Troyes. The original purpose of the Templars was to provide aid to pilgrims making their way to the Holy Land, but over the years the order became hugely rich and powerful. Bernard was influential in the election of Pope Innocent II and in 1145, one of his students, Bernardo Pignatelli, was elected Pope EUGENIUS III, enhancing Bernard's reputation still further. He was tireless in his defence of Catholic doctrine and he secured the condemnation of the doctrines of ABELARD and ARNOLD OF BRESCIA at the Council of Sens of 1140. He was also entrusted with the preaching of the Second Crusade. His personality was as important as his activities. His ascetic temperament and deep religiosity impressed his contemporaries, but even in his lifetime, his unbending principles were the source of controversy. Under his leadership the Cistercian Order flourished. He was devoted to the Virgin MARY as the mother of God and did much to encourage her cult in the West. He was also the author of a number of mystical hymns; some, such as 'O sacred head sore wounded', are still sung today. His mystical treatise *De Diligendo Deo* has been described as 'one of the most outstanding of all mediaeval books of devotion'. Bernard was canonised soon after his death in 1174 and was named a Doctor of the Church in 1830.

E. Gilson, *The Mystical Theology of St Bernard* (1990); T. Merton, *The Last of the Fathers* (1954); A.V. Murray, *Abelard and St Bernard* (1967).

Bernard of Cluny (twelfth century) Poet and Polemicist. Little is known of his life except that he was a monk at the influential Benedictine house at Cluny. He is remembered as the author of a magnificent satirical poem entitled *De Contemptu Mundi*. In it he mocked the monastic corruption of his time and contrasted the short-lived pleasures of this life with the joys of the world to come. Several well-known hymns, such as 'Jerusalem the golden' and 'Brief life is here our portion', are based on verses from the poem.

Bernard of Cluny, *De Contemptu Mundi*, edited and translated by H.C. Hoskier (1929); G.J. Englehardt, 'The *De Contemptu Mundi* of Bernardus Morvalensis', *Mediaeval Studies*, xxii (1960), xxvi (1964) and xxix (1967).

Bernardino (1380–1444) Saint and Cult Founder. Bernardino was born in Massa di Carrera, Italy. As a young man he joined the Franciscan Observantine Order and was elected Vicar-General in 1438. In addition to doing much to reform the order, he was one of the most famous preachers of his time. He travelled on foot all over Italy and attracted huge crowds. As a result of his reputation, numbers in the order greatly increased and he set up new schools of theology in Perugia and Monteripido. He is particularly remembered for his encouragement of the cult of the Holy Name of JESUS. He was canonised only six years after his death.

J.R.H. Moorman, *A History of the Franciscan Order from its Origins to the Year 1517* (1968); I. Origo, *The World of San Bernardino* (1963).

Bertha (late sixth/early seventh century) Queen. Bertha was a Christian princess from Paris, who was married to the pagan King ETHELBERT of Kent some time before 597. A condition of her marriage was that she was permitted to practise her own religion with the aid of her chaplain LIUDHART. Although AUGUSTINE OF CANTERBURY converted Ethelbert and so established Christianity in the south of England, there is no evidence that she took any part in the mission.

M. Deanesly, *Augustine of Canterbury* (1964).

Bérulle, Pierre de (1575–1629) Theologian, Order Founder and Cardinal. De Bérulle was born in Sérilly, France. He was educated at the Sorbonne and was ordained to the priesthood in 1599. In 1611 he founded the French oratory. This was inspired by the Oratory of St PHILIP NERI, but differed in that it was a centralised organisation governed by a Superior-General. Its primary function was to train priests and to increase the respect of the laity for the priestly office. To this end, a group of secular priests lived together in community, but without vows. As a spiritual director, de Bérulle had considerable influence in the French court. Hoping for the conversion of England back to Catholicism, he was involved in the marriage negotiations between King CHARLES I of England and the French princess Henrietta Maria. His spiritual teachings were spread through his books, the best known of which were his *Discours de l'Etat et de la Grandeur de Jésus*, which was much used by Jacques BOSSUET. He was made a Car-

dinal two years before his death in recognition of his influence.

E.A. Livingstone, *The Oxford Dictionary of the Christian Church* (1997).

Besant, Annie (1847–1933) Educator and Sect Founder. Besant was born in London, and was educated at the University of London. Her marriage to a clergyman of the Church of England ended in divorce and she moved from Anglicanism to atheism, through spiritualism to Theosophy. She succeeded Mme BLAVATSKY as president of the Theosophical Society and proclaimed her adopted son, Jidder Krishnamurti, the new Messiah. He was said to be a reincarnation of the Supreme World Teacher. After 1889 she spent most of her life in India where she founded various educational institutions. As a result of her efforts, Theosophy became very fashionable in the West in the early years of the twentieth century, even among professing Christians. However, it received a severe blow when Krishnamurti repudiated the role assigned to him. Besant herself was the author of several works including *Esoteric Christianity, The Basis of Morality* and *India: Bond or Free?*

M. Gomes, *The Dawning of the Theosophical Movement* (1987); A. Taylor, *Annie Besant: A Biography* (1992).

Beuno (d. c. 640) Saint and Missionary. Little certain is known of the life of Beuno although he is the subject of a variety of legends. In particular he is said to have been the uncle of St WINIFRED and on one occasion to have brought her back to life. He was Abbot of the monastery at Clynnog, Wales and he is reputed to have conducted successful missions in both North Wales and Herefordshire.

A.W. Wade Evans (transl. and ed.), 'Beuno Sant', *Archaeologia Cambrensis*, lxxxv (1930).

Beza, Theodore (1519–1605) Theologian. Beza was born in Vézelay,

Burgundy. His family had intended him for the priesthood, but at the age of twenty-nine he formally embraced Protestantism. At the invitation of John CALVIN, he became Professor of Greek at the University of Geneva in 1558. In 1561 he played a leading part in the Colloquy of Poissy, which had been summoned by CATHERINE DE MEDICI to discuss the religious differences between Catholics and Protestants. When Calvin died in 1564, Beza assumed the leadership of the Swiss Calvinists. He is primarily remembered as a theologian and classicist. In 1564 he produced a major critical edition of the Greek New Testament for which he consulted all the available sources and variants. His *Confessio Christianae Fidei*, written in 1560, was a straightforward exploration of Calvinist theology and he was the author of a eulogistic biography of Calvin. He was also responsible for a history of the Reformed Churches of France. His works appeared in French and English as well as Latin and his influence was widespread. His biblical scholarship informed the translators of the English Authorised Version of the Bible (published in 1611) and his rigid doctrines of biblical literalism, double predestination and his defence of Church discipline did much to consolidate the thinking of the Reformed Churches in the seventeenth century.

H.M. Baird, *Theodore Beza: The Counsellor of the French Reformation* (1899); J.S. Bray, *Theodore Beza's Doctrine of Predestination* (1975); R.M. Kingdom, *Geneva and the Consolidation of the French Protestant Movement* (1967).

Biel, Gabriel (*c.* 1420–95) Philosopher and Economist. Biel was born in Speyer, Germany. He joined the Brethren of the Common Life and from 1485 he held the Chair of Theology at the new University of Tübingen. His nominalist philosophy was influenced by the views of WILLIAM OF OCKHAM and was expressed in works such as his *Epitome* and an exposition on the Canon of the Mass. However, he is

chiefly remembered for his economic theories. He argued that the just price of an article depended on economic rather than theological considerations – a view which laid the foundations for modern capitalism.

Gabriel Biel, *Treatise on the Power and Utility of Moneys*, translated by R.B. Burke (1930); H.A. Oberman, *The Harvest of Mediaeval Theology: Gabriel Biel and Late Mediaeval Nominalism* (1963).

Blake, William (1757–1827) Artist and Poet. Blake was trained in London as an engraver. He was the author of a series of volumes of poetry, all of which were illustrated by himself. These included the *Songs of Innocence*, the *Marriage of Heaven and Hell*, the *Songs of Experience*, *Milton* and *Jerusalem*. He also produced individual plates such as 'Elohim creating Adam' and a series of illustrations for the *Book of Job*. His work was not popular in his lifetime, but interest has increased since the end of the nineteenth century. Blake himself held unconventional religious views. He preached a gospel of extreme individualism and he was bitterly opposed to the moralism and rationalism of his own age, declaring, 'I must create a system or be enslav'd by another man's'. In England he is chiefly remembered for his poem 'Jerusalem' which is taken from *Milton*. With its notion of rebuilding Jerusalem 'in England's green and pleasant land', it has become an unofficial national anthem.

William Blake, *Poems*, edited by W.H. Stevenson (1989); P. Ackroyd, *Blake* (1995); J.G. Davies, *The Theology of William Blake* (1948); R. Lister, *William Blake: An Introduction to the Man and his Works* (1968).

Blasius (? fourth century) Legendary Saint. Little certain is known of St Blasius. He is thought to have been a bishop in Armenia who was martyred in the fourth century. In particular he is remembered for having saved a child who was choking on a fishbone and is therefore invoked by those who have illnesses or obstructions in their throats. He was supposedly martyred by being flayed with wool-combs before execution, so he is also the patron saint of wool-combers. He is one of the fourteen Auxiliary Saints, the holy helpers venerated for their help to human beings in particular difficulties.

G. Garitte, 'La Passion de S. Irénarque de Sébastée et la Passion de S. Blaise', *Analecta Bollandiana*, lxxiii (1955) [no English translation available].

Blavatsky, Helena Petrovna (1831–91) Cult Founder. Blavatsky was born in the Ukraine. She married young, but soon separated from her husband. With Henry Olcott she founded the Theosophical Society in New York in 1875, having spent many years in Tibet and India. She claimed that she had been taught by Tibetan Grand Masters who had revealed to her the secret knowledge that lies behind all religions. Her main work in which she expounded her doctrines was *Isis Unveiled*, published in 1877. Theosophy was popular among the middle classes in both the United States and Great Britain in the early twentieth century, and even committed church-goers joined the Society. Blavatsky was significant in the history of Christianity in that she led many Westerners to an awareness of the Eastern religious traditions. The Society did not set itself up as an alternative religion; its avowed aims were to form a nucleus of universal brotherhood, to encourage the study of comparative religion and to investigate the hidden laws of nature and the latent powers of human beings.

S. Cranston, *H. P. B. The Extraordinary Life and Influence of Helena Blavatsky* (1994); M. Gomes, *The Dawning of the Theosophical Movement* (1987).

Blemmydes, Nicephorus (*c.* 1197–1272) Theologian. After the sacking of Constantinople in the Fourth Crusade, Nicaea became a major centre of Greek Christianity. Blemmydes, a physician turned priest, was an outstanding figure in the city, founding a school, establishing a monastery and teaching philosophy. In his theological writings he attempted to reunite the Western and Eastern Churches and he is also remembered for his political ideas on Church and State.

P. Canart, 'Nicéphore Blemmyde et le Mémoire adressé aux envoyés de Grégoire IX', *Orientalia Christiana Periodica*, xxv (1959) [no English translation available].

Blondel, Maurice (1861–1949) Philosopher. Blondel was born in Dijon, France and, for the greater part of his career taught philosophy at the University of Aix-en-Provence. His books include *L'Action: Essai d'une Critique de la Vie et d'une Science de la Pratique* (his doctoral thesis), *Histoire et Dogme, Le Procès de l'Intelligence, Le Problème de la Philosophie Catholique* and *La Pensée*. He insisted that it is not only through the human intellect that the truth is found, but through the whole of experience. It follows then that faith cannot be equated with accepting received dogma intellectually, but is found by perceiving God beyond the natural order. This pragmatic emphasis was highly influential within the French Catholic Modernist movement, although Blondel himself rejected LOISY's views on dogma and history. He remained a devout Roman Catholic all his life and was regarded as one of the foremost religious thinkers of his time.

J.J. McNeill, *The Blondelian Synthesis* (1966).

Bloxam, John Rouse (1807–91) Liturgist. Bloxam was educated at Oxford University, England. At the age of twenty-six he was ordained to the Anglican ministry and, after a period of teaching at Oxford, he became the vicar of a country parish in 1862. At Oxford he had come under the influence of John Henry NEWMAN, under whom he had served a curacy at Littlemore Church. He did not follow Newman into the Roman Church, but he did introduce various traditional ceremonials into the regular services. As a result of his efforts, ornaments such as wooden alms dishes and altar candlesticks became commonplace in English parish churches. Bloxam has been described as the originator of the ceremonial revival within the Church of England. Many of the innovations aroused great hostility when they were first introduced because they were seen to smack of popish practice. None the less today very few Anglican churches lack traditional ornaments.

R.D. Middleton, *Newman and Bloxam: An Oxford Friendship* (1947).

Boehme, Jakob (1575–1624) Mystic. Boehme was born in Altseidenberg in Germany and earned his living as a shoemaker. During the course of his life he had various mystical experiences which he described in his books. Other works, published after his death, include a treatise on baptism and the eucharist, an allegorical reading of the Book of Genesis, and a discussion of the essence of God. He believed that God is the *ungrund*, the 'abyss', from which both good and wrath flow. The Christian life involves a mystical imitation of JESUS's death and resurrection and he insisted that each human being must make a choice between living on the lower natural plane, or on the higher spiritual one. Boehme was very critical of the Protestantism of his day and, on one occasion, he was forced to leave his village of Gorlitz in Silesia and take refuge with friends in Dresden. His work is not straightforward, but is complicated and hard to understand. It was none the less influential on William LAW and the Cambridge Platonists as well as on the later German Romantic movement.

J.J. Stoudt, *Sunrise to Eternity: A Study in Jakob Boehm's Life and Thought*, revised edition (1968).

Boehm, Martin (1725–1812) Bishop and Denomination Founder. Boehm was born in Pennsylvania, to a Mennonite family. In 1756 he became an itinerant preacher among the villages of Virginia and Pennsylvania, but he was later expelled by the Mennonite Church because he was prepared to embrace new ways and speak to his listeners in English. In 1768 he met Philip OTTERBEIN and they began working in partnership. This culminated in the foundation of the new Church of the United Brethren in Christ in 1800. This was Arminian and perfectionist in its theology, and Boehm and Otterbein were the Church's first Bishops. Since then the United Brethren have gone through various forms of organisation. There was a new constitution in 1889; the Church merged to become the Evangelical United Brethren in 1946 and since 1968 it has been part of the United Methodist Church.

R.T. Handy, *A History of the Churches of the United States and Canada* (1976).

Boesak, Allan (b. 1946) Theologian and Polemicist. Boesak was educated at the University of the Western Cape in South Africa and in the Netherlands. After ordination in 1968, he returned to South Africa where he served a congregation and acted as a university chaplain. He was deeply involved in the anti-apartheid movement and he emerged as a prominent black liberation theologian. In 1983 he founded the United Democratic Front and he was elected President of the World Alliance of Reformed Churches in 1985. That year he was detained in prison for over a month in connection with his political activities. Among his books were *Farewell to Innocence*, *Black Theology*, *Black Power* and *Black and Reformed: Apartheid, Liberation and the Calvinist Tradition*. He espoused a nonviolent approach to liberation and was very much influenced by the thought of Martin Luther KING. Sadly a scandal brought his career within the Church to a premature end.

A. Boesak, *Black Theology, Black Power* (1978).

Boethius, Anicius Manlius Torquatus Severinus (*c.* 480–*c.* 524) Philosopher, Politician and Saint. Boethius was the son of a Roman Consul and was educated in Athens and Alexandria. He was himself elected to the Consulship in 510, but was accused of treason, imprisoned and finally executed. Today he is remembered for his *De Consolatione Philosophae*, written in prison. This describes how the study of philosophy can lead the soul to God. There are no specifically Christian references in the work, so Boethius's religious affiliation used to be a matter of scholarly dispute. However, he is now generally agreed to have been the author of one treatise on the Trinity and of others refuting heresy. Because of his orthodoxy, he is now regarded in the Church as a martyr and he was canonised as St Severinus.

M. Gibson (ed.), *Boethius: His Life, Thought and Influence* (1981); H. Chadwick, *Boethius* (1981).

Boff, Leonardo (b. 1938) Theologian. Boff is a native of Brazil. After studying with Karl RAHNER at the University of Munich, he was ordained and became Professor of Theology in Petropolis, Brazil where he was also an advisor to the Brazilian Conference of Bishops. A prominent liberation theologian and champion of the poor, he is the author of *Jesus Christ, Liberator* and *Ecclesiogenesis: The Base Communities Reinvent the Church*. After the publication of his *Church, Charisma and Power* in 1981, he was summoned to Rome to explain himself and a year's silence was imposed on him. During this period he produced *Trinity and Society*. Boff teaches that JESUS is a liberator not merely from spiritual evil, but also from the material oppression of the rich and powerful; this is based on Boff's own ex-

perience of work among the dispossessed poor of South America. His conflict with the Roman Catholic establishment arises from his rejection of the hierarchical authoritarianism which he perceives as endemic within the Church.

Leonardo Boff, *Introducing Liberation Theology*, translated by Paul Burns (1987).

Bonaventura (*c.* 1221–74) Bishop, Mystic, Theologian and Saint. Bonaventura was born Giovanni di Fidanza near Viterbo, Italy. As a young man, he joined the Friars Minor and studied at the University of Paris under ALEXANDER OF HALES. During this period, he produced a commentary on the 'Sentences' of PETER LOMBARD and a treatise on the poverty of JESUS CHRIST. In 1257 he was elected Minister-General of the Friars Minor and he became Cardinal Bishop of Albano in 1273. A notably saintly man, Bonaventura was described as the 'prince of mystics' by Pope LEO XIII. He taught that all human reasoning and knowledge was vanity compared with the enlightenment given by God to his faithful servants. His most famous book, the *Itinerarium Mentis in Deum*, is regarded as a spiritual classic and he also wrote the authorised life of St FRANCIS.

Z. Hays, *The Hidden Centre* (1981); C.H. Tavard, *Transience and Permanence: The Nature of Theology according to St Bonaventura* (1954).

Bonhoeffer, Dietrich (1906–45) Theologian. Bonhoeffer was educated at the Universities of Tübingen and Berlin, in Germany. He was particularly influenced by the thought of HARNACK and BARTH. After ordination, he continued to teach at the University of Berlin. He was a moving spirit behind the Barmen Declaration, which refused to allow the Confessing Church of Germany to become an instrument of Nazi party policy. He became head of the Confessing Church seminary at Finkenwalde in 1935, but he was dismissed from his post at the university and the seminary was closed down by the Nazis in 1937. In 1943 he was arrested and he was hanged in Flossenberg prison just before the end of the Second World War. His most celebrated work, *Widerstand und Ergebung*, was a collection of his letters and papers written in prison. It did not contain a fully worked out theology, but gave a glimpse of what he called a 'religionless Christianity'. He argued that it was necessary for 'man come of age' to speak in a secular way about God and he interpreted the person of JESUS as 'the man-for-others'. His other books include *Sanctorum Communio*, *Akt und Sein*, *Die Nachfolge* and the posthumous *Ethik*. Bonhoeffer is widely regarded as a modern saint and martyr. Through his death, as well as through his writings, he has become perhaps the best-known of all twentieth-century Protestant theologians.

Dietrich Bonhoeffer, *Letters and Papers from Prison*, edited by E. Bethge (1967); J.W. de Gruchy, *Dietrich Bonhoeffer, Witness to Jesus Christ* (1988); C. Marsh, *Reclaiming Bonhoeffer* (1994).

Boniface (680–754) Archbishop, Saint and Missionary. Boniface's original name was Wynfrith and he was born in Devonshire, England. As a young man, he became a monk and, after acting as an emissary for the King of Wessex, he initially chose to spread the gospel in Frisia. In 719, with the backing of the Pope, he made a journey to Hesse and Thuringia where he met with great success. After a second visit to Rome, he returned to Germany and established new bishoprics and monasteries there. He was consecrated a Bishop in 722 and Archbishop in 732. In 741 he began a thorough-going reform of the Frankish Church; he presided over several councils and corrected many abuses. At the end of his life he decided to return to Frisia and there he was murdered by a band of pagans. It has been said that no Englishman has had a deeper influence on the history of Europe than St Boniface.

J.C. Sladden, *Boniface of Devon, Apostle of Germany* (1980).

Boniface VIII (c. 1234–1303) Pope. Boniface was born Benedict Gaetani in Angani, Italy. He was appointed Notary Apostolic to the Curia in 1276; he became a Cardinal in 1291 and he was elected Pope in 1294. His reign was dominated by the need for peace in Europe after the wars of the thirteenth century and by the problem of the Turkish occupation of the Holy Land. Boniface did little to solve either problem. He became locked in conflict with Philip the Fair of France by refusing to allow the King to impose extraordinary taxation on his clergy. During the course of the struggle, Boniface issued the bull *Unam Sanctam* which declared that there was but one Holy, Catholic and Apostolic Church and that there was no salvation outside that Church. Furthermore, the Pope had been granted the authority of spiritual power and for a secular power to oppose that power was tantamount to opposing God. In 1303, Boniface took steps to excommunicate Philip, but he was taken prisoner by a band of French mercenaries before the bull could be delivered. Although he was soon rescued from their clutches, he died soon afterwards. The reign of Boniface VIII illustrates the growth of national feeling in the late thirteenth century and the inevitable diminution of the Pope's secular powers in consequence.

T.S.R. Boase, *Boniface VIII* (1933); C.T. Wood (ed.), *Philip the Fair and Boniface VIII: State versus Papacy* (1967).

Bonino, José Miguez (b. 1924) Theologian. Bonino is a native of Argentina. A Methodist, he has taught at the Union Theological Seminary of Buenos Aires and has served as President of the World Council of Churches. A leading liberation theologian, he is none the less sensitive to the dangers of tying Third World theologies uncritically to Marxist ideology. Among his most important books are *Revolutionary Theology Comes of Age*, *Christians and Marxists: The Mutual Challenge to Revolution* and *Towards a Christian Political Ethic*.

José Miguez Bonino, *Towards a Christian Political Ethic* (1983); E. Dussel, *A History of the Church in Latin America*, translated by Alan P. Neely (1981).

Bonosus (d. *c.* 400) Bishop and Sect Founder. Bonosus was Bishop of Naissus. He seems to have taught that the Virgin MARY had other children after JESUS, thus denying her perpetual virginity. He was deposed after examination at the Council of Capua of 391. However, a sect of his followers, known as the Bonosiani, survived until the seventh century.

F.L. Cross (ed.), *The Oxford Dictionary of the Christian Church*, 2nd edition (1974).

Booth, Billington (1857–1940) Order Founder and Philanthropist. Booth was the second son of William and Catherine BOOTH. In 1883, he became joint Commander of the Salvation Army in Australia and in 1887 he moved to the United States of America. However, he found the Army too centralised and authoritarian and in 1896 he left to found the Volunteers of America. This is an evangelical welfare organisation; Protestant, though non-denominational in orientation, it operates numerous philanthropic institutions in the United States.

R. Sandall, *The History of the Salvation Army*, 3 vols (1947–55).

Booth, William (1829–1912) Order Founder and Philanthropist. Booth was born in Nottingham. As a young man he served as a preacher for the Methodist New Connection Church, but he left in 1861. With his wife, Catherine, he started a mission in the East End of London in 1865, which was the starting point of the Salvation Army. This rapidly became an international organisation. Booth was its first General and it was organised on militaristic lines with uniforms, brass bands, military ranks and the requirement of 'unquestioning obedience'. It presents an evangelical form of Christianity, and conversions are encouraged at mass meetings. Its philanthropic activities are remarkable. It maintains hostels, hospitals, schools, night shelters, soup kitchens and missing person bureaux. Booth and his children carried the organisation from Britain to the United States, Australia, Europe and India. His book, *In Darkest England – And the Way Out*, published in 1890, did much to publicise the deplorable social conditions in which the poor lived. When he died in 1912, there were sixteen thousand serving officers in the Army. Since 1931, the General has been elected by a High Council, but the organisation's commitment to the improvement of society has continued unabated.

William Booth, *In Darkest England – And the Way Out*, 6th edition (1970); R. Collier, *The General Next to God* (1965); R. Sandall *The History of the Salvation Army*, 3 vols (1947–55).

Borromeo, Charles (1538–84) Archbishop and Saint. Borromeo was born in Arona, Italy, of a noble family and was educated in Milan and Paris. From his early youth he was destined for the Church and he was appointed Cardinal Archbishop of Milan by his uncle Pope PIUS IV at the age of twenty-two. He played an important part in the final session of the Council of Trent and is thought to have been responsible for the drawing up of the new Catechism of 1566. This was an exposition of the Creed and the Ten Commandments and was intended for the use of priests. In his own archdiocese, in the face of considerable opposition, he instituted many far-reaching reforms. Living very simply himself, he founded seminaries, reformed monasteries, disciplined errant clergy, organised philanthropic institutions and Sunday Schools and encouraged the activities of the Jesuits. He is regarded as an important leader of the Counter-Reformation and continues to be seen as a model Bishop.

M. Yeo, *A Prince of Pastors* (1938); J. Headley and J. Tomaro (eds), *San Carlo Borromeo* (1988).

Bosco, Giovanni Melchior (1815–88) Saint, Educator and Order Founder. Bosco was born into a poor family in Becchi, Italy. He was ordained priest at the age of twenty-six and exercised his ministry in Turin. Anxious to do something for the poor boys he saw in the city, he founded night schools and work shops. In 1859, he drew up the Rule for a new order, the Salesians, the society of St FRANCIS OF SALES. Today the order has spread to many parts of the world and, together with its sister organisation, the Daughters of our Lady Help of Christians, is now the third largest order in the Roman Catholic Church. It maintains orphanages, schools, savings banks, asylums and agricultural colonies. The foundation of Bosco's system was reason and kindness; he used to say, 'Try to gain love before inspiring fear' and Salesian foundations are still guided by these principles.

E.J. Docherty, *Lambs in Wolfskins* (1953); L.C. Sheppard, *Life of Don Bosco* (1957).

Bossuet, Jacques Bénigné (1627–1704) Bishop and Theologian. Bossuet was born in Dijon, France, and was educated in Paris. At a very early age, he was picked out as an outstanding speaker, and after ordination he served as Archdeacon to the Cathedral Chapter at Metz for seven years, before moving to Paris. In 1670 he was appointed tutor to the French Dauphin and in 1681 he was consecrated Bishop of Meaux. Bossuet is now mainly remembered for his extraordinary preaching gifts and for his support of moderate Gallicanism. In 1682 he drew up the Four Gallican Articles which affirmed the powers of the General Council over the Pope and denied that

the Pope had power over the king in temporal and civil matters. He provided an important statement on the divine right of kings in his *Politique tirée de l'Écriture Sainte*. His philosophy of history was expounded in his *Discours sur l'Histoire Universelle* and he argued that divine providence was the key to historical causation. Towards the end of his life, he became more entrenched in his positions. He supported the Revocation of the Edict of Nantes in 1685, thus ending the privileges of Protestants and he was largely responsible for the condemnation of François FÉNELON's mystical spirituality. He engaged in a long correspondence with the philosopher Gottfried LEIBNIZ on the question of Christian unity and his *Méditations sur l'Evangile* and his *Élévations sur les Mystères* are generally considered to be spiritual classics.

W.J. Sparrow Simpson, *A Study of Bossuet* (1937).

Bourignon, Antoinette (1616–80) Mystic and Sect Founder. Bourignon was born in Lille in the Spanish Netherlands and grew up as a Roman Catholic. From her early youth she had visions in which God chose her to be the 'woman clothed with the sun' described in the Book of Revelation. She attempted to form an ascetic order, but this was not a success. Subsequently she attacked the established Churches and preached an extreme form of Quietism, maintaining that salvation was to be found in the illumination of the soul by the inner light of God. She attracted a group of followers and her ideas spread to Scotland where a sect known as the Bourignonians survived until the middle of the eighteenth century.

A.R. MacEwan, *Antoinette Bourignon, Quietist* (1910).

Bourne, Hugh (1772–1852) Denomination Founder. Bourne was born in Stoke-on-Trent, England, and, as a young man was a member of John WESLEY's

Methodist Church. He served as a local preacher, and, following the American model, he organised several mass camp meetings. These were not sanctioned by the official Methodist organisation and Bourne was expelled from the Church. In 1820, together with William CLOWES, he organised the first conference for a new group which was dedicated to the restoration of the original simplicity of Methodism. This came to be known as the Primitive Methodist Connexion and by 1852, the year of Bourne's death, it had over one hundred thousand members. It spread to Canada and the United States, but it did not describe itself as a Church until 1901. In 1932, the Primitive Methodists rejoined the Wesleyans and the United Methodists to form the Methodist Church.

A. Wilkes and J. Lovett, *Mow Cop and the Camp Meeting Movement* (1947); J.T. Williamson, *Hugh Bourne* (1952).

Bradwardine, Thomas (*c.* 1290–1349) Archbishop and Theologian. Bradwardine was born in Chichester, and was educated at the University of Oxford. He had a distinguished career within the Church, being Chancellor of St Paul's Cathedral, London, and Confessor to King Edward III; he was consecrated Archbishop of Canterbury in 1349. As well as being a distinguished mathematician, Bradwardine is remembered for his theological writings, particularly his *De Causa Dei Contra Pelagium*. Against the Pelagian heresy, he maintained that God's grace was necessary for salvation and that ultimately the cause of all human action is to be found in the will of God. This deterministic position anticipated the predestinarianism of John WYCLIFFE and the sixteenth-century Reformers.

G. Leff, *Bradwardine and the Pelagians* (1957).

Brainerd, David (1718–47) Missionary. Brainerd was born in Connecticut in the American colonies and he had a conversion experience at the age of eleven. Educated at Yale, he was expelled, according to his friend Jonathan EDWARDS, as a result of his 'intemperate and indiscreet zeal'. Subsequently he was taken on as a missionary by the Scottish Society for the Propagation of Christian Knowledge. During his short life, he was tireless in his efforts to convert the native American inhabitants of Pennsylvania to Christianity and he enjoyed some success. He is remembered for his journal which, published posthumously, has proved an inspiration to many later missionaries.

D. Brainerd, *Journal*, 1st edn (1749).

Bray, Thomas (1656–1730) Educator and Missionary. Bray was born in Shropshire, England, and was educated at the University of Oxford. After serving in a country parish, he was invited to become Commissioner for the American colony of Maryland. While waiting to sail, he worked on a scheme to organise parish libraries both at home and in America. This was highly successful and within his lifetime more than eighty parish libraries were established. He also founded the Society for the Promotion of Christian Knowledge (SPCK) and the Society for the Propagation of the Christian Gospel (SPG). The educational and missionary work of both societies continue to this day and many schools, teachers' training colleges and missions are maintained under their auspices.

W.K. Lowther Clarke, *A History of the SPCK* (1959); H.P. Thompson, *Into All Lands* (1951); H.P. Thompson, *Thomas Bray* (1954).

Bray, Vicar of (seventeenth century) Legendary Parson. The vicar of Bray is the hero of a well-known English folk song. It describes how the good vicar kept his benefice through all the religious twists and turns of the seventeenth century – the chorus reading, 'For whatsoever king may reign,/I'll STILL be the vicar of Bray, Sir!' It has proved impossible to identify this worthy cleric with any certainty.

Brent, Charles Henry (1862–1929) Bishop and Ecumenist. Brent was born in Ontario, and was educated at Trinity College in Toronto. After ordination in the Protestant Episcopal Church, he served in the United States; in 1901 he became Bishop of the Philippines and in 1918 he was consecrated Bishop of Western New York. Brent is remembered as an important figure in the early days of the ecumenical movement. As a result of his efforts, the American Episcopal Church was persuaded to convene the first World Conference on Faith and Order. This met in 1927 in Lausanne under his chairmanship. The main objective of the subsequent Faith and Order movement has been to bring about the reunion of the Christian Churches. In 1948 it merged with the Life and Work movement to form the World Council of Churches.

D.P. Gaines, *The World Council of Churches: A Study of its Background and History* (1966); F.W. Kates, *Charles Henry Brent* (1948).

Brewster, William (1567–1644) Polemicist and Church Leader. Brewster was born in Scrooby in England and was educated at the University of Cambridge. He served as British ambassador to Holland, but, by 1589, he had become part of a congregation which eventually separated itself from the Church of England. As a result of persecution, the whole community moved to Holland where Brewster set himself up as a publisher of Protestant literature. He was one of the pioneers who sailed on the *Mayflower* to establish the Plymouth colony in America. There he was the only Church officer. He led the congregation in prayer, but because he had never been ordained, he did not administer the Sacraments.

C.M. Andrews, *The Colonial Period in American History*, 4 vols (1934–8).

Bride (sixth century) Saint. Little certain is known of St Bride (Brigid of Ireland). She is thought to have been baptised by St PATRICK, to have become a nun and to have been elected Abbess of Kildare. There are many legends about her. She is said to have been able to multiply portions of food so that everyone was satisfied. On one occasion she is supposed to have appeared as the Virgin MARY to her Bishop in a dream. It was even rumoured that she herself was consecrated as a Bishop, although this seems somewhat improbable. She is an immensely popular saint in Ireland and Wales and is known as the patron of blacksmiths, healers and poets.

F. O'Brian, *St Brigid: Her Legend, History and Cult* (1938).

Bridget (1303–73) Saint, Mystic and Order Founder. Bridget was the daughter of a governor of Upland in Sweden. She married at a very early age, had eight children and was appointed lady-in-waiting to the Queen of Sweden. In about 1340 she began to have visions and, after the death of her husband, she retired from public life. In 1346 she founded the Brigittine order at Vadstena. This was organised in a double community, one of men and the other of women, who lived in separate parts of the monastery, but who shared a chapel. They were to live an austere life, but there was to be no limitation on the number of books they purchased. The order survives today in Germany, the Netherlands, England and Spain although the plan of double communities was abandoned in the sixteenth century. Bridget died in Italy. She was involved in the negotiations which brought Pope GREGORY XI back from Avignon to Rome. Her visions were held in great reverence throughout the Middle Ages. She is the patron saint of Sweden.

H. Redpath, *God's Ambassadress: St Bridget of Sweden* (1947).

Brooks, Phillips (1835–93) Bishop and Poet. Brooks was born in Boston, in the United States of America, and he was educated at Harvard University. After ordination in the American Episcopal Church, he served congregations first in Philadelphia and later back in Boston. He was consecrated Bishop of Boston in 1891. He was a famous preacher and was the author of *Lectures on Preaching*, which had originally been delivered to the students of Yale Divinity School. He was so well known that on a visit to England, he was invited to preach before Queen Victoria. He is chiefly remembered, however, for his much loved hymn, 'O little town of Bethlehem', which is sung regularly at Christmas throughout the English-speaking world.

R.W. Albright, *Focus on Infinity: A Life of Phillips Brooks* (1961).

Brown, John (1800–59) Rebel. Brown was a native of Connecticut. From 1854, he became convinced that he was divinely appointed to lead the campaign against slavery in the Union. Although he was probably mentally un-balanced, he organised a guerrilla cam-paign against the slave owners of Kansas and in 1856, he led an attack which re-sulted in five men being hacked to death in their homes. In 1859 he tried to set up a new free state as a slave refuge and centre for his operations. To this end, with twenty-one followers, he attacked the weapon store at Harper's Ferry, Virginia. The attack was easily repulsed by the United States army and Brown was arrested. Subsequently he was tried and hanged for treason. He is remem-bered as the hero of the marching song, 'John Brown's body lies a-mouldering in the grave/But his soul goes marching on'.

S.B. Oates, *To Purge his Land with Blood: A Biog-raphy of John Brown* (1970); J. Rossbach, *Ambiva-lent Conspirators: John Brown, the Secret Six and the Theory of Slave Violence* (1982).

Browne, Robert (*c.* 1553–1633) Theo-logian. Browne was born in Rutland, and was educated at the University of Cam-bridge. From 1579 he was preaching without the Bishops' permission, arguing that Bishops have no authority of them-selves. He was forbidden to preach by the Royal Council in 1580 and began organ-ising separatist Churches. He continued to insist that the congregation is the only true instrument of Church government. As a result of these activities, he was im-prisoned, and, on his release, he settled in Holland where he wrote his *Treatise of Reformation* and his *Book Which Sheweth the Life and Manners of all True Christians*. By 1585 he had returned to England where he conformed suf-ficiently to be ordained by Archbishop WHITGIFT. There is evidence that he continued to encourage separatist con-gregations, but for the rest of his life he served a parish in Northamptonshire. He died in prison, having assaulted a police constable. Browne has been described as the 'Father of English Congregationalism' and his followers were scornfully described as 'Brownists'.

C. Burrage, *The True Story of Robert Browne* (1906).

Browne, Sir Thomas (1605–82) Phil-osopher and Scientist. Browne studied medicine at the Universities of Oxford, Montpellier, Padua and Leyden. From 1637 he lived in Norwich where he prac-tised as a doctor. He is remembered as the author of the *Religio Medici* in which he attempted to work out his religious beliefs and reconcile them with his scientific knowledge. He also wrote *Pseudodoxia Epidemica* in which he distinguished between ancient myths and scientific truths and *Hydrotaphia or Urn Burial*, a study of the burial customs of many countries.

G.L. Keynes (ed.), *A Bibliography of Sir Thomas Browne*, 2nd edn (1968); C.A. Patrides (ed.), *Approaches to Sir Thomas Browne* (1982).

Brunner, Heinrich Emil (1889–1966) Theologian. Brunner was born in Winterthur, Switzerland. After serving as a pastor at Obstalden, he taught first at the University of Zürich and then at the Christian University of Tokyo. His work was particularly influenced by the philosophy of Søren KIERKEGAARD and the ideas of the Jewish theologian Martin Buber. Like Karl BARTH, he opposed the liberalism of Friedrich SCHLEIERMACHER and his followers, but he and Barth came into sharp disagreement over the question of natural theology. Barth insisted on an uncompromising doctrine of the total transcendent hiddenness of God, while Brunner believed that natural theology provided a starting point of contact between humanity and the gospel and that it was possible to speak of God in terms of analogy.

Emil Brunner, *Christianity and Civilization*, Gifford Lectures (1947/8, 1948/9); C.W. Kegley (ed.), *The Theology of Emil Brunner* (1962).

Bruno (1032–1101) Saint and Order Founder. Bruno was educated in Cologne and Rheims where he became Master of the Cathedral School in *c.* 1057. The future Pope URBAN II was among his pupils. He was appointed Chancellor of the diocese of Rheims, but he subsequently dedicated himself to the religious life. At first he sought the spiritual direction of ROBERT OF MOLESNE, who later founded the famous community of Citeaux, but in 1084, with a group of friends, he founded his own monastery near Grenoble. This was to become the first house of the Carthusian Order. In 1094, in obedience to the Pope, he moved to Italy where he founded another monastery at La Torre, having refused a bishopric. The Carthusians are a strict contemplative Order; the monks live separately from one another in silence and they dedicate their lives to prayer, work and the recitation of the daily office. The order has produced many famous mystics and is also known for the manufacture of Chartreuse, a liqueur.

E.M. Thompson, *The Carthusian Order in England* (1930).

Bucer, Martin (1491–1551) Theologian. Bucer was born in Sélestat in Alsace. At the age of fifteen, he joined the Dominican Order, but was released from his vows in 1521, after being converted by the views of Martin LUTHER. He was one of the first of the Reformers to marry; he settled in Strasbourg, was excommunicated by the Roman Catholic Church and became a leader of the Reformed community. He was involved in the drawing up of the constitutions of several new Churches and, between 1538 and 1541, John CALVIN was among his students. At the Conferences of Leipzig in 1539, Hagenau and Worms in 1540 and Regensburg in 1541, he was a leading Protestant negotiator against the Catholics. However, because he resisted the Interim Settlement of 1548, he was exiled to England where he became Regius Professor of Divinity at the University of Cambridge. He made suggestions for Archbishop CRANMER's 1549 revision of the Anglican Prayer Book and he dedicated his own book, *The Kingdom of Christ*, to the young King EDWARD VI. Bucer is primarily remembered for his influence on Protestant liturgy, particularly in the Scottish, English and Genevan versions.

H. Eells, *Martin Bucer* (1951); W.P. Stephens, *The Holy Spirit in the Theology of Martin Bucer* (1970); C. Hopf, *Martin Bucer and the English Reformation* (1946).

Buchman, Frank Nathan Daniel (1878–1961) Sect Founder. Buchman was born in Pennsylvania and as a young man he was ordained as a Lutheran pastor, but after an unhappy experience in the ministry, he resigned in 1908. Then, at a conference in Keswick, England, he experienced a religious conversion which led him to take up missionary work. In 1921 he founded the First Century Church Movement; this was followed by the Oxford Group in 1929 and Moral Rearmament in 1938. From 1929, he travelled widely bringing his message of moral and spiritual regeneration to Canada, the United States, Europe and the Near East. His movement had no regular meeting groups or hierarchy. People were brought in through personal contact or 'house parties' and great stress was laid on the 'Four Absolute Standards' – absolute purity, absolute unselfishness, absolute honesty and absolute love. Buchman's ideas were immensely influential on the professional classes of the United States and the British Commonwealth and 'Frank', as he was always called, made several important converts including, for a time, the theologian Emil BRUNNER.

Frank Buchman, *Remaking the World* (1947); T.E.N. Driberg, *The Mystery of Moral Rearmament* (1946); J.P. Thornton-Duesbury, *The Oxford Group* (1947).

Bulgakov, Sergius (1871–1944) Theologian and Ecumenist. Bulgakov was the son of a Russian Orthodox priest and was educated at a seminary in Orel and at the University of Moscow. After teaching at the Polytechnic Institute at Kiev and at Moscow, he was elected to the Duma. In 1918 he was ordained and in 1922 he was expelled from Russia by the Communist government. After a stay in Prague, he settled in Paris where he was a founder member of the Orthodox Theological Institute. He taught that the universe was created out of nothing as an emanation of the divine nature and that divine wisdom, or Sophia, is the agent of mediation between God and the universe. He was the author of many books including (in their English translations) *Agnus Dei, the God-Manhood, The Orthodox Church, The Comforter* and *The Wisdom of God.* Bulgakov is primarily remembered for his commitment to the ecumenical movement and for his teaching on Sophia.

J. Pain and N. Zernov (eds), *A Bulgakov Anthology* (1976); L. Zander, *God and the World: The World Conception of Father S. Bulgakov* (1948); D. Ford, *The Modern Theologian* (1997).

Bullinger, Johann Heinrich (1504–75) Theologian. Bullinger was born in Bremgarten, Switzerland, the son of the parish priest. He was educated at the University of Cologne where he studied the writings of the early Protestant Reformers. In 1531 he settled in Zürich where he succeeded Ulrich ZWINGLI as Chief Pastor. There he presided over the cantonal synod and did much for educational reform and Church administration. However, he is chiefly remembered for his writings. He was the author of a history of the Reformation and several important refutations of Anabaptist theology. He also was largely responsible for the two Helvetic Confessions of 1536 and 1566. The first was primarily an attempt to reconcile the views of Zwingli with those of Martin LUTHER. Although it was accepted by the Swiss Zwinglian Churches, it was rejected by the Lutherans. The second was a statement of moderate Calvinist theology and was received warmly throughout the Reformed world. Bullinger himself believed that the Christian was in a covenant relationship with God and although he accepted CALVIN's theories of predestination, he rejected the discipline of the theocratic state. Instead he supported Thomas ERASTUS for the rights of the State in ecclesiastical matters. He was particularly interested in the affairs of the English Church, offering hospitality to Protestant exiles in the reign of Queen MARY and refuting Pope PIUS V's bull of excommunication against Queen ELIZABETH I.

G.W. Bromiley (ed.), *Zwingli and Bullinger* (1953); D. Keep, *Henry Bullinger and the Elizabethan Church* (1970).

Bultmann, Rudolf (1884–1976) Theologian. Bultmann was educated at the Universities of Marburg, Tübingen and Berlin. Subsequently he returned to

Marburg where he taught the New Testament for thirty years. He was a pioneer in the form-critical method of analysing the text, and in his book *Die Geschichte der Synoptischen Tradition*, he adopted a position of extreme scepticism. Influenced by the philosophy of Martin HEIDEGGER, in his *Jesus*, he interpreted JESUS's call to discipleship as an existential moment of decision. In his commentary on the Gospel of St JOHN, he argued that the writer was greatly influenced by the Gnosticism of the first century, and in his essay 'Neues Testament und Mythologie', he insisted that the Gospel needed to be 'demythologised' of all its extraneous superstition and mythological elements. Bultmann is generally regarded as one of the most important New Testament scholars of the twentieth century and he has been influential on theologians since the Second World War.

Rudolf Bultmann, *New Testament Theology* (1952–5); C. Braaten and R.A. Harrisville (eds), *Kerygma and History: A Symposium on the Theology of Rudolf Bultmann* (1962); D. Fergusson, *Bultmann* (1992).

Bunting, Jabez (1779–1858) Denomination Leader. Bunting was born in Manchester, and was ordained to the Methodist ministry in 1799. He quickly became powerful within the movement; he was four times President of the Methodist Conference; he was President of the first Wesleyan Theological College at Hoxton and he was secretary of the Wesleyan Missionary Society for eighteen years. Although his tendency to centralise power was distrusted by many older members of the society, his genius for organisation was undisputed. It was largely through his efforts that Methodism became the influential Church that it is today.

W.R. Ward (ed.), *Early Victorian Methodism* (1976) [Jabez Bunting's correspondence]; R.E. Davies, *Methodism* (1963).

Bunyan, John (1628–88) Devotional Writer and Poet. Bunyan was born near Bedford, in humble circumstances. He fought in the English Civil War on the Parliamentarian side and in 1653 he joined an independent Church. He tried to pursue a career as a preacher, but after the restoration of King Charles II, he was frequently imprisoned for his efforts. He is remembered for his three great works, *The Pilgrim's Progress*, which was written while he was in prison, *The Holy War* and *Grace Abounding*. *The Pilgrim's Progress*, in particular, is a spiritual classic and remains a best seller to this day. It describes the Christian life in terms of a pilgrimage from the City of Destruction to the Celestial City. On his journey, the pilgrim, Christian, meets a host of splendid characters such as Obstinate, Pliable, Mr Worldly Wiseman, Apollyan and Giant Despair. After many tribulations, he finally succeeds in crossing the River of Death and is greeted by the Shining Ones on the other side. Bunyan was also the author of the much sung pilgrim hymn, 'Who would true valour see'.

F.M. Harrison, *A Bibliography of the Works of John Bunyan* (1932); M. Furlong, *Puritan's Progress: A Study of John Bunyan* (1975); C. Hill, *A Turbulent, Seditious and Factious People: John Bunyan and his Church* (1988).

Burchard (965–1025) Bishop and Lawyer. Burchard was consecrated Bishop of Worms in 1000 and did much to reform the diocese. He is remembered for his *Decretum*, an important collection of Canon Law which remained in force until the time of Pope GREGORY VII.

C. Munier 'Burchard, *Decretum* of', *New Catholic Encyclopaedia*, Vol. 2 (1967).

Burchard, John (d. 1506) Bishop and Liturgist. Burchard was born near Strasbourg, but moved to Rome in c. 1481. He was appointed Master of Ceremonies in 1483 and in 1503 he was consecrated Bishop of Orte and Civita Castellana and was elected to the College of Cardinals. Burchard is remembered for his *Ordo Servandus per Sacerdotem in Celebratione Missae* which is a collection of rubrics for the celebration of Mass. It was printed in later editions of the Roman Missal and formed the basis of PIUS V's *Ritus Celebrandi*. His diary is an important source for the history of the Papacy in this period.

J.W. Legg, *Tracts on the Mass* (1904).

Bushnell, Horace (1802–76) Theologian. Bushnell was born in Connecticut and was educated at Yale University. He initially trained as a lawyer, but instead chose to be ordained into the Congregational ministry and for many years he served as pastor. He was the author of many books including *Christian Nurture*, *Nature and the Supernatural* and *Forgiveness and Law*. He is remembered for his espousal of liberal theology in the Congregational Church, arguing, for example, that miracles should be seen as part of the laws of nature.

B.M. Cross, *Horace Bushnell* (1958).

Butler, Alban (1710–73) Historian and Devotional Writer. Butler was orphaned as a child and was educated at the Catholic Seminary at Douai. After ordination, he acted as chaplain to the Duke of Norfolk's household and travelled abroad a great deal. He is remembered for his monumental *Lives of the Fathers, Martyrs and Other Principal Saints* which covers the lives of sixteen hundred saints. Although it was designed as a devotional volume, there is much in it of historical value.

Alban Butler, *Lives of the Saints*, edited by D. Attwater, revised edition, 4 vols (1956).

Butler, Joseph (1692–1752) Bishop and Theologian. Butler was born in Wantage in England and was brought up as a Presbyterian. He became a member of the Church of England and was educated

at the University of Oxford. After ordination in 1718, he served congregations in County Durham and, after attracting the notice of Queen Caroline, he became Bishop of Bristol in 1738, Dean of St Paul's in 1740 and Bishop of Durham in 1750. He is chiefly remembered as a theologian. A firm advocate of natural theology and ethics, in his *Fifteen Sermons* he taught that virtue consisted in living in harmony with one's true nature; this he defined as being made up of self-love, conscience and benevolence. In his most famous work, the *Analogy of Religion*, he combated the Deism of his day by maintaining that the mysteries of natural and revealed religion are analogous to the mysteries that can be observed in nature and that this argues for God being the author of both. The *Analogy* was influential on such diverse thinkers as David HUME and John Henry NEWMAN and it remains a classic of British theology.

A.E. Baker, *Bishop Butler* (1923); P.A. Carlsson, *Butler's Ethics* (1964); I. Ramsey, *Joseph Butler* (1969).

Butler, Josephine (1828–1906) Philanthropist. Butler was born Josephine Grey in Dilston, England. She married the Revd George Butler at the age of twenty-four. Early in her marriage she began to set up refuges for reformed prostitutes. She came to the notice of the general public for her tireles advocacy of the repeal of the Contagious Diseases Acts, which was finally achieved in the 1880s. She also campaigned for the raising of the age of sexual consent. After a notorious case in which her associate, W.T. Stead, succeeded in procuring a very young girl, the necessary Act was passed through Parliament. She was a person of enormous courage and energy and was strengthened by her devoted prayer life which was modelled on that of St CATHERINE OF SIENA. In recent years she has become a feminist heroine.

Josephine Butler, *Personal Reminiscences of a Great Crusade* (1896); M.G. Fawcett, *Josephine Butler: Her Work and Principles* (1927); G. Petrie, *A Singular Iniquity: The Campaigns of Josephine Butler* (1971).

Byrd, William (*c.*1543–1623) Composer. Byrd was probably a native of Lincolnshire. Although a practising Roman Catholic, he became organist of Lincoln Cathedral in 1563 and moved to the Chapel Royal in 1570. He has been described as the 'father of the English anthem' and he is particularly remembered for his church music. Among his anthems which are still sung today are 'Christ rising again', 'Sing joyfully', 'Bow thine ear' and 'Sing merrily'.

H.K. Andrews, *The Technique of Byrd's Vocal Polyphony* (1966); E.H. Fellowes, *William Byrd* (1936); P. Le Huray, *Music and the Reformation in England 1547–1660* (1967).

C

Cabrini, Frances-Xavier (1850–1917) Saint, Missionary and Order Founder. Cabrini was born in S. Angelo Lodigiano, Italy and she initially trained to be a teacher. She volunteered to be a missionary in China, but was rejected for training on the grounds of health. Undaunted, in 1880 she founded her own women's missionary society, the Missionary Sisters of the Sacred Heart, and herself worked in New York among the newly arrived immigrants. Her order spread throughout America, Europe and Asia and has supported numerous schools and hospitals. Cabrini was canonised in 1946 and she is regarded as the patron saint of refugees and emigrants.

P. di Donato, *Immigrant Saint: The Life of Mother Cabrini* (1960).

Cajetan (1480–1547) Saint and Order Founder. Cajetan was born of a noble family in Vicenza, Italy. After ordination in 1516, he joined the Oratory of Divine Love. Then in 1524, together with Pietro Caraffa, who was to become Pope PAUL IV, he founded the Theatine Order. This was intended to be a community of secular priests who were engaged in pastoral work while being vowed to a life of poverty and austerity. The order spread throughout Europe and played an important part in the Counter-Reformation.

P.H. Hallett, *Catholic Reformer* (1959).

Cajetan, Thomas de Vio (1469–1534) Bishop and Theologian. Cajetan was born in Gaeta, Italy. Against the wishes of his noble parents, he joined the Dominican Order at the age of fifteen. A distinguished commentator on the writings of St THOMAS AQUINAS, he taught metaphysics at various Italian universities. In 1508 he became General of the Dominican Order; he was made a Cardinal in 1517 and he was consecrated Bishop of Gaeta in 1519. He was deeply involved in the ecclesiastical affairs of his time and his achievements include the defence of papal power at the 1511 Council of Pisa, the sending of the first Dominican missionary to the Americas and the election of CHARLES V as Holy Roman Emperor in 1519. However, he is chiefly remembered as the opponent of the Reformer Martin LUTHER. In 1518 they met for three days in Augsburg, but Cajetan was unable to persuade Luther to recant his opinions.

Catholic University of America, *Catholic Encyclopaedia* (1967).

Calvin, John (1509–64) Theologian and Denomination Founder. Calvin was born in Noyon, Picardy and was trained as a lawyer. By 1533 he was an avowed Protestant and was compelled to leave Paris where he was pursuing literary studies. He spent the next three years travelling through France, Italy and Switzerland. His first book, published in 1532, was a commentary on Seneca's *De Clementia*; then in 1534 he produced his first religious work, *Psychopannychia*, and this was followed in 1536 by his *Christianae Religionis Institutio*, which was a short summary of the Christian faith, expounded from a Protestant viewpoint. In response, he was invited by Guillaume

Farel to stay in Geneva and establish Protestantism there. Both Farel and Calvin were soon expelled from the city and between 1538 and 1541, Calvin lived in Strasbourg where he was a pupil of Martin BUCER and the pastor of the French refugee congregation. Then in 1541, the government of Geneva changed and Calvin returned. His aim was to found a theocracy, a holy city, and, although he held no official position, he largely fulfilled his objective. He established a system of education; he drew up a list of laws for both Church and State and he revised the liturgy. Geneva became a magnet for Protestant refugees from all over Europe; they imbibed Calvin's principles and returned to their own countries to spread the word. A prolific writer, Calvin conducted a voluminous correspondence and also wrote commentaries on almost all the books of the Bible. He was a frequent preacher and notes taken at his sermons have survived. In addition he revised the *Institutes* and the final 1559 version is a systematic exposition of his theology. It has been translated into many languages and gone through many editions. Calvin himself insisted that his theology was entirely based on the Bible. The doctrines associated with him include the total depravity of humanity, unconditional election, limited atonement and irresistible grace. The system, which is frequently contrasted with that of ARMINIUS, is relentless in its logic. If God is all-powerful and all-knowing, then God knows from all time who is to be numbered among the elect. This has nothing to do with good works or the cultivation of virtue. It is entirely the result of the boundless grace of God. Atonement was effected by the death of JESUS, but since only the elect are predestined to salvation, Jesus did not die for everyone, only for the chosen. John Calvin must be seen as one of the central figures of the Protestant Reformation. His influence on the thought of Christendom cannot be exaggerated.

John Calvin, *The Institutes of the Christian Religion*, edited and translated by J.T. Mcneill, 2 vols (1961); D.A. Erichson, *Bibliographia Calviniana*, reprinted (1960); A. McGrath, *A Life of John Calvin* (1990); T. Torrance, *The Hermeneutics of John Calvin* (1988); R.S. Wallace, *Calvin, Geneva and the Reformation* (1988).

Camillus (1550–1614)   Saint and Order Founder. Camillus was born near Naples and as a young man he was employed both as a soldier and as a labourer. In 1575 he was converted from his dissolute way of life and he tried to join first the Capuchin and then the Recollect Franciscan Orders. Because of a disease in his legs, he was compelled to leave the communities and for a time he worked in a hospital under the guidance of St PHILIP NERI. Ordained in 1584, he founded the Order of the Ministers of the Sick, or the Camillians who were dedicated to the service of the sick. His ideas on nursing were far in advance of his time and his care of the dying anticipated the practices of the modern hospice movement. Camillus is the patron saint of those who are ill and of those who look after them.

A.C. Oldmeadow, *The First Red Cross: Camillus de Cellis 1550–1614* (1923).

Campbell, Alexander (1788–1866)   Sect Founder. Campbell was the son of a Presbyterian minister and was educated at the University of Glasgow in Scotland. In 1809 he emigrated to Pennsylvania and there he was ordained into the Baptist ministry. However, in 1827 he left the Baptist Church and he founded the Disciples of Christ, who were also known as the Campbellites. Campbell's teaching emphasised baptism and the confession of JESUS CHRIST as saviour as the only necessary requirements of Christianity. He rejected both speculative theology and religious emotionalism and he was convinced that a union effected between the Churches based solely on the teachings of the New Testament would lead to an era of blessing. He was the author of numerous books and was the founder of Bethany College, West Virginia, which was created for the education of clergy.

J. Kellems, *Alexander Campbell and the Disciples* (1930).

Campion, Edmund (1540–81) Saint, Missionary and Martyr. Campion was born in London, and was educated at the University of Oxford. In 1569 he was ordained a deacon in the Church of England, but after a visit to Ireland, he renounced Anglicanism. He then enrolled in the seminary in Douai and in 1572 he was received into the Roman Catholic Church. He joined the Jesuit Order in 1573 and in 1580 he became part of a mission to reconvert England to Catholicism. He was a powerful speaker and achieved some success, but in 1581 he was arrested. Charged with conspiracy against Queen ELIZABETH I, he was tortured and executed. He is regarded as a saint and martyr in the Roman Church.

E. Waugh, *Edmund Campion* (1935).

Carey, William (1761–1834) Missionary. Carey was born in Northamptonshire. He was brought up in the Church of England, but joined the Baptist Church at the age of twenty-two. As a young man he supported himself as a cobbler while also teaching in a school and spreading the gospel. In 1792 he preached a famous sermon on the text, 'Expect great things from God; attempt great things for God', and four months later he founded the Baptist Missionary Society. The following year he sailed for India. He settled in Malda, in the province of Bengal, where he managed an indigo factory, while embarking on a programme of mission. Everywhere he went he established schools and medical centres. He also translated the Bible into Bengali. Subsequently he was appointed Professor of Sanskrit and Bengali at Fort William College in Calcutta. There he devoted himself to the translation of the

books of the Bible into the various Indian dialects and he produced grammars and dictionaries in Sanskrit, Marathi, Punjabi and Telugu. He also founded the Agricultural and Horticultural Society of India; he founded many new churches and he successfully campaigned for the abolition of suttee (widow burning). Carey has been described as the father of modern missionaries.

William Carey, *Enquiry into the Obligations of Christians to use means for the Conversion of Heathens*, edited by E.A. Payne (1961); S.P. Carey, *William Carey* (1923); E.D. Potts, *British Baptist Missionaries in India 1793–1837* (1967).

Carlile, Wilson (1847–1942) Philanthropist and Organisation Founder. Carlile began his career as a business man, but after enrolling in the London College of Divinity, he was ordained in 1880. In 1882 he founded the Church Army, which was designed to be an Anglican version of William BOOTH's Salvation Army. Carlile supervised prison missions, youth centres, canteens and hostels for the homeless, unmarried mothers, drug addicts, the elderly and discharged prisoners. Under his guidance as Chief Secretary, the Church Army became a highly successful organisation of lay-workers, all devoting themselves to philanthropic causes. The work of the Army continues today.

K. Heasman, *Army of the Church* (1968); E. Rowan, *Wilson Carlile and the Church Army*, 5th edn (1956).

Carlyle, Thomas (1795–1881) Historian and Popular Philosopher. Carlyle was educated at the University of Edinburgh in Scotland. He was the author of several well-received works of history – *The French Revolution, Oliver Cromwell* and *Frederick the Great*. He strongly opposed the materialism of his age and he also produced several quasi-religious works – *Sartor Resartus, On Heroes and Hero Worship* and *Past and Present*. These were highly influential and Carlyle was regarded as a sage in his lifetime. He taught a gospel of action and heroism; although he rejected organised Christianity, he firmly maintained that the 'religious principle lies unseen at the heart of all good men'.

F. Kaplan, *Thomas Carlyle: A Biography* (1983); J. Symons, *Thomas Carlyle: The Life and Ideals of a Prophet* (1952).

Carroll, John (1735–1815)   Archbishop and Missionary. Carroll was born in Maryland in the American colonies, but was educated in France. Having joined the Jesuit Order, he was ordained in 1769. In 1774 he returned to America where he practised as a missionary and actively supported the movement for independence. He was an associate of Benjamin Franklin, and through Franklin's influence he became Superior of Missions in 1784. Then in 1790 he was consecrated the first Roman Catholic Bishop in the United States. He insisted on the equal rights of Catholics with Protestants and was tireless in his attempts to consolidate the Roman Church in the new nation. He was appointed Archbishop of Baltimore in 1808, with four diocesan Bishops under his care. Carroll is remembered as an important figure in the history of the Roman Catholic Church in the United States.

A. Melville, *John Carroll of Baltimore* (1955).

Cartwright, Thomas (1535–1603)   Theologian and Polemicist. Cartwright was educated at the University of Cambridge. As a committed Protestant, he was forced to flee from England during the reign of Queen MARY. He returned with the accession of Queen ELIZABETH I and in 1569 he was appointed Lady Margaret Professor of Divinity at Cambridge. However, the following year he was deprived of his chair when he publicly declared that the Elizabethan constitution of the Church of England was less satisfactory than that of the apostolic Church. He travelled abroad and for a time stayed in Geneva where he made the acquaintance of Theodore BEZA. Returning to England, he advocated Presbyterianism in his *Second Admonition to Parliament*, although, later, he dissociated himself from the followers of Robert BROWNE. Arrested in 1590, he was tried by the Court of High Commission, but was released in 1592. On the accession of King JAMES I, he tried to influence the new king against the 'Romish' ceremonies of the Church of England by organising the Millenarian Petition of 1603. In response, the King summoned the Hampton Court Conference. In the event, Cartwright died before the Conference opened and little was conceded to the Puritan position. Cartwright is remembered as one of the most eminent and learned of the Elizabethan Protestant divines.

P. Collinson, *The Elizabethan Puritan Movement* (1967); A.F.S. Pearson, *Thomas Cartwright and Elizabethan Puritanism* (1925).

Cassian, John (*c.* 360–435)   Saint, Theologian and Devotional Writer. As a young man, Cassian joined a monastery in Bethlehem but he left to study the ascetic way of life in Egypt. In *c.* 402 he was ordained deacon in Constantinople and then visited Rome where he was invited to write a refutation of the opinions of NESTORIUS. Eventually he founded a monastery in Marseilles. His best-known work was his 'Institutes', in which he laid down rules for life in a religious community. This was the foundation for many later Rules, including that of St BENEDICT. He believed that the aim of the religious life was the contemplation of God; to this end it was necessary to study the Bible, withdraw from earthly striving, to practise love and humility and to avoid all occasions of temptation. Cassian is recognised as a saint in the Eastern, but not the Western Church.

O. Chadwick, *John Cassian: A Study in Primitive Monasticism*, 2nd edn (1968).

Catherine of Alexandria (? fourth century)   Legendary Saint and Martyr. She is said to have made a protest against the persecution of Christians and in consequence was herself broken on the wheel. The legend only became current in the tenth century, but she was none the less a popular saint in the Middle Ages. Whirling fireworks are still known as Catherine wheels in her honour and she is regarded as one of the Auxiliary Saints.

J. Capgrave, *The Life of St Katharine of Alexandria*, reprinted (1987); J.A. Robinson, 'The Passion of St Catherine and the Romance of Barlaam and Joasaph', *Journal of Theological Studies*, xxv (1924).

Catherine de' Medici (1519–89)   Monarch and Politician. Catherine was from a noble Florentine family and was related to Pope CLEMENT VII. She was married to King Henry II of France and became Regent on her husband's death. France at that time was embroiled in controversy between the Roman Catholics and the Protestant Huguenots. In 1561 Catherine called the Colloquy of Poissy in an attempt to find a political solution and initially she tried to work towards the toleration of Protestants. This policy had been abandoned by 1568 and in 1572 she was responsible for the notorious massacre of St BARTHOLOMEW's Day when the Huguenot Admiral Cligny was murdered together with several thousand Protestants. Catherine was a patron of literature and the arts, but she does not seem to have been interested in theological differences unless they served political ends.

J.E. Neale, *The Age of Catherine de Medici* (1943); N.M. Sutherland, *Catherine de Medici and the Ancien Regime* (1966).

Catherine of Genoa (1447–1510)   Saint, Mystic and Devotional Writer. Catherine was born Caterinetta Fieschi in Liguria, Italy, of a noble family. She was married at a very early age, but when she was twenty-seven she was released from her marriage vows. Her husband became a Franciscan Tertiary, but Catherine remained independent and dedicated herself to nursing the sick in St Laurence Hospital, Genoa. She led an intensely austere and spiritual life and produced two devotional classics, the *Dialogues on the Soul and the Body* and the *Treatise on Purgatory*. She was the subject of an important study on mysticism written by Baron VON HÜGEL.

Catherine of Genoa, *Dialogues* and *Treatise*, translated by C. Balfour and H.D. Irvine (1946); F. von Hügel, *The Mystical Elements of Religion as Studied in St Catherine of Genoa and her Friends*, 2 vols (1908).

Catherine of Siena (*c.* 1345–80)   Saint, Mystic and Devotional Writer. Catherine was born Caterina Benincasa in Siena, Italy. From her early youth she was subject to visions and, at the age of sixteen, she joined the Dominican Tertiaries. Through her spirituality and devotion to the Precious Blood of Jesus, she attracted many followers. Then, in 1376, she became involved in the politics of the Church when she entreated Pope GREGORY XI, who was based in Avignon, to return to Rome. Two years later she supported the cause of Pope URBAN VI in the Great Schism. Many of her letters have survived and she was the author of the devotional work *Dialogo*. She was canonised eighty years after her death and, since 1939, together with St FRANCIS OF ASSISI, she has been the patron saint of Italy.

Catherine of Siena, *Dialogo della Divina Providenza*, translated by Suzanne Noffke (1980); Raymond of Capua, *Legenda Major*, translated by G. Lamb (1960); G. Kaftal, *St Catherine in Tuscan Painting* (1949).

Cavasilas, Nikolaos (*c.* 1320–71)   Theologian and Mystic. Cavasilas was born in Thessalonica and, as a young man, was involved in politics, but little is known of his later life. He is remembered for his two treatises, *Life in Christ* and *The Exposition of the Divine Liturgy*. These volumes are generally regarded as classics of Eastern sacramental theology.

Nikolaos Cavasilas, *Life in Christ*, translated by C.J. de Catanzaro (1974); Nikolaos Cavasilas, *Interpretation of the Divine Liturgy*, translated by J.M. Hussey and P.A. McNulty (1960).

Cecilia (? second century) Legendary Saint and Martyr. Little certain is known of the life of St Cecilia. Some authorities believe that she died as a virgin martyr in Sicily in the late second century, but others put her death in Rome in the third century. She is the patron saint of music and is commonly portrayed playing the organ, but the musical connection was only established in the sixteenth century. One version of her story is known to English readers through the narrative of the Second Nun's tale in Geoffrey Chaucer's *Canterbury Tales*. Her body is said to have been found completely intact in the Church of St Cecilia in Rome when the church was undergoing repair in 1599.

D.H. Farmer (ed.), *The Oxford Dictionary of Saints*, 3rd edn (1992).

Celestine V (*c.* 1215–96) Saint, Pope and Order Founder. Celestine's baptismal name was Peter. At a young age he joined the Benedictine Order, but left to become a hermit on Mount Morrone in the Abruzzi, Italy. Many were attracted to his ascetic way of life and his rule led to the foundation of the powerful Celestine Order. Because of his sanctity, and in an attempt to reform the Papacy, he was elected Pope in 1294. By this stage he was an old man and his Pontificate was not a success. He was a complete innocent when it came to papal politics and he quickly came under the dominance of King Charles II of Naples. All was confusion and he abdicated of his own free will in the December of 1294. He was subsequently imprisoned by his intensely worldly successor BONIFACE VIII, and he died while in captivity. He was canonised by Pope CLEMENT V, partly as a public condemnation of Boniface's policies.

J.N.D. Kelly (ed.), *The Oxford Dictionary of Popes* (1986).

Celestius (fifth century) Heretical Theologian. Celestius practised as a lawyer in Rome, but he subsequently decided to dedicate his life to the spreading of the doctrines of PELAGIUS. He denied the doctrine of original sin, arguing that it was nothing to do with the first man, Adam, because sin could not be inherited. The logical consequence of this doctrine was that the Sacrament of baptism does not wash away the guilt of original sin (because there is no such thing) and that it merely enrols the infant into the Kingdom of God. In 412, Celestius was condemned at the Council of Carthage and in 415 at the Council of Diospolis. Celestius's writings are preserved (and refuted) in the work of St AUGUSTINE.

G. Bonner, *Augustine and Modern Research on Pelagianism* (1972); P. Brown, *Religion and Society in the Age of St Augustine* (1972).

Cerinthus (end of first century) Early Heretic. Cerinthus was a Gnostic who taught that God was far too exalted to have created the universe. Instead it came into being through the activities of angels or an inferior deity. He maintained that JESUS had been an ordinary human being who had become possessed by a supernatural power at his baptism. This left him just before his crucifixion. There is a legend recorded by EUSEBIUS OF CAESAREA that the Apostle JOHN fled from a bath-house when he heard that Cerinthus had entered it, thinking that his arrival would cause the roof to fall in! IRENAEUS argued that the Fourth Gospel was written as a refutation of the views of Cerinthus.

Eusebius, *Historia Ecclesiae*, translated by G.A. Williamson (1965); Irenaeus, 'Adversos haereticos', in F.R.M. Hitchcock (ed.), *Early Christian Classics*, 2 vols (1916).

Cerularius, Michael (d. 1059) Patriarch. Cerularius became a monk after the suicide of his brother and he was consecrated Patriarch of Constantinople in 1043. He disapproved of the practices of the Roman Church and, as Patriarch, he tried to force the Latin churches in Constantinople to adopt the Greek rite. When they insisted on their traditional modes of worship, he closed them down. The Roman Church promptly excommunicated Cerularius in 1053 and, in retaliation, the Patriarch pronounced anathemas on the Pope's representatives. In fact the differences between Rome and Constantinople went back for many centuries and rested on doctrines such as the origin of the Holy Spirit and the supremacy of the Pope. None the less the formal schism between East and West is conveniently dated from the time of Patriarch Michael and Pope LEO IX.

N.M. Zernov, *Eastern Christendom* (1961).

Chad (d. 672) Saint and Bishop. Chad was born in the Kingdom of Northumbria in Britain and, like his brother Cedd, had been a pupil of St AIDAN. In 664 he succeeded his brother as Abbot of Lastingham in Yorkshire. After a dubious consecration as Bishop of York, he was deposed by THEODORE OF TARSUS, but was chosen to be the first Bishop of Lichfield in 669. This was the first bishopric in the Saxon kingdom of Mercia and Chad established a successful episcopal organisation. According to BEDE's History, he was venerated as a saint soon after his death.

R. Vleeskruyer, *The Life of St Chad* (1954).

Challoner, Richard (1691–1781) Devotional Writer and Bishop. Challoner was born on the Isle of Lewis in Scotland of Presbyterian parents. After the death of his father, he was converted to Roman Catholicism and was educated at the Seminary at Douai. In 1730 he returned to the British Isles to join the London Mission, but he went back to Douai in 1738. In 1741 he was consecrated a Bishop. Challoner is remembered for his translations of the Bible and for his anthologies of prayers – *The Garden of the Soul* and *Meditations for Every Day of the Year*. These volumes have proved enduringly popular among English-speaking Roman Catholics.

E. Duffy (ed.), *Challoner and his Church* (1981).

Chalmers, James (1841–1901) Missionary. Chalmers was born in Ardishaig, Scotland. He experienced an evangelical conversion at the age of eighteen and was sponsored for training by the London Missionary Society. He began his missionary career in the Cook Islands, Polynesia, in 1867 and in 1877 he moved to the still unmissionised New Guinea. There he did much to open up the country and he helped the establishment of British rule. Chalmers is mainly remembered for his enlightened approach; he resisted any attempt to Westernise the customs of the New Guineans and encouraged them to become Christians in the context of their own culture – for this he was much respected and loved. In 1901, when exploring new territories, he was murdered by cannibals.

R. Lovett, *James Chalmers, his Autobiography and Letters* (1902).

Channing, William Ellery (1780–1842) Theologian. Channing was born in Newport, Rhode Island, and was educated at Harvard University. In 1803 he was appointed pastor of the Federal Street Congregational Church of Boston and in 1809, in a famous sermon, he preached the major doctrines of Unitarianism. He denied the doctrine of the Trinity, the divinity of Christ, the total depravity of human beings and any sub-stitutionary theory of atonement. He was committed to both pacifism and the abolition of slavery, but he is primarily remembered as the most important American Unitarian theologian. He himself never wished to belong to a distinct sect and always maintained that he 'desired to escape the narrow walls of a particular church'. None the less he was the moving spirit behind the 1820 Berry Street Conference for liberal-minded ministers, which led to the setting up of the American Unitarian Association.

R.L. Patterson, *The Philosophy of William Ellery Channing* (1952).

Chao, Tzu-Chen (1880–1979) Theologian. Chao was the Dean of the School of Religion at Yenching, China. In 1920, together with other leading Chinese thinkers, he formed the Apologetics group in Peking. The stated aim of the group was to spread Christianity as part of the regeneration of Chinese society. He was the author of several books including (in their English titles) *Chinese Philosophy*, *The Life of St Paul* and *The Interpretation of Christianity*. Much of his work has, however, never been translated. Chao believed that his country could only be restored through the creation of a new spirit in humanity and that this new spirit could only be found in JESUS CHRIST. His was a significant voice in China in the 1920s and 1930s and in 1948 he was a Co-President in the newly founded World Council of Churches.

Tzu-Chen Chao, 'The basis of social reconstruction', *Chinese Recorder*, liii (1922); Wing-Hung Lamb, *Chinese Theology in Construction* (1983).

Charlemagne (*c*. 742–814) Monarch. Charlemagne (Charles the Great) was the son of PEPIN III, King of the Franks. When Pepin died in 768, the kingdom was divided between Charlemagne and his brother Carloman. Carloman died in

771, leaving his lands to Charlemagne, and between 771 and 801, Charlemagne conquered Lombardy, Bavaria, Avar, Pannonia, Northern Spain and Barcelona. He established a strong central government and a clearly defined legal system. He was also a great patron of learning and did much to encourage the reform of the Church. ALCUIN was his advisor in religious and educational matters. Under his guidance a palace school and library were established and many scholars were attracted to the court, creating what has been described as a 'Carolingian renaissance'. On Christmas Day 800, Charlemagne was crowned Holy Roman Emperor by Pope LEO III. This act was an attempt to revive the old Roman Empire of the West in a new Christian form and it was set against the old Roman Empire of the East which still survived, governed from Constantinople. Although the new empire never attained its projected glory, it continued to exist in various forms until 1806.

P.D. King (ed.), *Charlemagne: Translated Sources* (1987); F.L. Ganshop, *The Carolingian and the Frankish Monarchy*, translated by J. Sondheimer (1971); L. Wallach, *Alcuin and Charlemagne* (1968).

Charles I (1600–49) Monarch. Charles I was the second son of JAMES I, King of England and Scotland. His elder brother died young and Charles inherited the throne in 1625. He had his own theological views; he consistently promoted High Church Arminian clergy in preference to followers of John CALVIN and, in 1633, William LAUD became Archbishop of Canterbury. Laud's policies were extremely unpopular. Charles himself was a firm believer in the divine right of kings and was very much influenced by his Roman Catholic wife, the French princess Henrietta Maria. Many of the King's subjects were infuriated by the tolerance shown to Catholics, coupled with the harsh measures meted out to the extreme disciples of the continental

Reformers. The Scots were appalled by his insistence that they follow the English Prayer Book and that their Church be controlled by English Bishops. The result in 1638 was that the Scots declared their Presbyterianism in the National Covenant. Ultimately, opposition to Charles's policies, political as well as religious, led to civil war, in which the rebels were victorious and the Church of England disestablished. Charles himself was executed by rebel army leaders in 1649, the only English King to meet this fate. For all his indecision and lack of political astuteness, Charles was a virtuous man who led an exemplary family life. Many considered his death to have been a martyrdom and he has remained a focus for extreme royalism and high Anglicanism ever since.

C. Petrie (ed.), *The Letters, Speeches and Proclamations of Charles I* (1935); C. Carlton, *Charles I, the Personal Monarch* (1984); A. Hughes, *The Causes of the English Civil War* (1991); C. Russell, *The Causes of the English Civil War* (1990).

Charles V (1500–58) Monarch. Charles was the son of Philip of Burgundy and Joanna of Spain (the daughter of FERDINAND and ISABELLA). He was thus the hereditary ruler of Burgundy, Spain, the Netherlands, the Spanish-American colonies and parts of Italy. Then in 1519 he was elected Holy Roman Emperor. During his reign he was compelled to confront the growth of Protestantism. In 1517 Martin LUTHER had nailed to the door of Wittenberg Church his ninety-five objections to the sale of indulgences. When he was not to be dissuaded from his position, he was placed under the ban of the Empire, but he was protected by the powerful Elector of Saxony. During the following years various compromises were debated, but in 1555, at the Diet of Augsburg, Charles was forced to concede the principle 'Cuius regio, eius religio' (whose kingdom, his religion), thus destroying for ever the unity of Western Christendom. He abdicated from power

the following year, leaving his son PHILIP II to succeed him.

M.-J. Rodriguez-Salgado, *The Changing Face of Empire: Charles V, Philip II and the Hapsburg Authority* (1988).

Chateaubriand, Vicomte François René de (1768–1848) Devotional Writer. Chateaubriand was born in St Malo, France, of aristocratic parents. Initially he supported the French Revolution, but during the Terror he fled to England, only returning to France in 1800. After the deaths of his mother and sister, he had experienced a deep religious conversion and Chateaubriand is chiefly remembered for his religious classic, *Génie du Christianisme, ou Beautés de la Religion Chrétienne*, published in 1802. This is a significant work in that it marks the passing of a rational defence of religion, based on natural theology, in favour of an emotional and aesthetic justification. In the *Génie*, Chateaubriand argued that Christianity is the most poetic religion known to humanity and is thus the main inspiration for the art and civilisation of Europe.

J. Evans, *Life of the Vicomte de Chateaubriand* (1939); V. Giraud, *Le Christianisme de Chateaubriand*, 2 vols (1925–8) [no English translation].

Chelcicky, Peter (c. 1390–1460) Theologian. Chelcicky was influenced by the theology of John WYCLIFFE and he started preaching in Prague, Bohemia in about 1420. He rejected the materialism of the Church and believed that society should be modelled on the basis of the doctrine of the body of Christ. He was the author of several books and his followers were known as the Chelcic Brethren. This group, together with the disciples of Archbishop Rokycana, became the core of the Bohemian brethren, later to be called the Unitas Fratrum or Moravians.

P. Brock, *The Political and Social Doctrines of the*

Unity of Czech Brethren in the 15th and Early 16th Centuries (1957); M. Spinka, 'Peter Chelcicky, the spiritual father of the unitas fratrum', *Church History*, xii (1943).

Chesterton, Gilbert Keith (1874–1936)

Poet, Novelist and Religious Writer. Chesterton was a highly popular writer in the early years of the twentieth century. He was brought up in the Church of England, but towards the end of his life he converted to Roman Catholicism. His best-known avowedly religious works were *Heretics* published in 1905, *Orthodoxy* published in 1908 and the hymn 'O God of earth and altar'. However, he was also the author of many short stories, including those about a Roman Catholic priest named Father Brown. Father Brown was a dim, inconspicuous character, who solved mysteries through his acute understanding of human nature. Through his unswerving integrity and lovable ordinariness, Father Brown has succeeded, perhaps better than anyone, in dispelling anti-Catholic prejudice in the Protestant English-speaking world.

G.K. Chesterton, *Autobiography* (1937); W.H. Auden (ed.), *G.K.Chesterton: A Selection from his Nonfictional Prose* (1970); C. Hollis, *The Mind of Chesterton* (1970).

Christopher (? third century)

Legendary Saint. Little certain is known of St Christopher. Supposedly he was a giant who earned his living by carrying people across a river. When a child asked to be ferried across, he was found to be so extraordinarily heavy that the giant was quite bowed down. On arriving on the other side, the child explained that he was JESUS CHRIST and that Christopher had carried the sins of the world on his shoulders. Later Christopher is thought to have been martyred. The legend has been a highly popular subject for wall paintings and Christopher is known as the patron saint of travellers.

C. Johnson, *St Christopher: The Patron Saint of Travellers* (1932).

Chrysostom, John (c. 347–407)

Saint and Patriarch. Chrysostom was born and educated in Antioch. After a time as a hermit, he gained fame as a preacher (the name Chrysostom means 'golden mouthed'). Between 386 and 398 he delivered a series of homilies on Scripture which were directed to the people of Antioch. In 398, against his own wishes, he became Patriarch of Constantinople, where he devoted his energies to reforming the city. Inevitably he aroused considerable hostility; he made powerful enemies and he was condemned at the Synod of Oak for teaching the doctrines of ORIGEN and speaking against the Empress. In spite of the support of Pope INNOCENT I and of his flock in Constantinople, he was sent into exile the following year and subsequently died of ill-treatment. He was the outstanding preacher of his time, but today he is remembered for giving his name to the liturgy which is in general use in the Eastern Orthodox Church. (The Prayer of St Chrysostom which is used in the Church of England is drawn from the Orthodox liturgy.) This dates from later than the time of Chrysostom and may have its origins in his liturgical reforms.

John Chrysostom, 'Homilies', *Library of the Fathers*, 16 vols (1839–53); P.J. Thompson (ed.), *The Orthodox Liturgy* (1939); J.N.D. Kelly, *Golden Mouth: The Story of John Chrysostom, Ascetic, Preacher, Bishop* (1995).

Clare (c. 1193–1253)

Saint and Order Founder. Clare was born in the town of Assisi, Italy. In 1212 she joined St FRANCIS at Portiuncula and dedicated herself to the religious life. After a time in a Benedictine Order, she formed her own community at Assisi, following Francis's Rule. Her nuns were known as the Poor Clares and they were famous for their poverty and austerity. The order spread throughout Europe, although differences arose as to the level of poverty which had to be observed. Clare herself was a person of great sanctity; on two occasions she is said to have saved Assisi from foreign armies, simply by appearing on the city walls with the Sacrament. She was canonised only two years after her death. The order which bears her name is still regarded as one of the most strict in the Western Church.

Clare of Assisi, *Works*, edited and translated by R.J. Armstrong (1988); N. de Roebeck, *St Clare of Assisi* (1980).

Claver, Peter (1580–1654)   Saint, Philanthropist and Missionary. Claver was born in Vedu, Spain. He was educated at the University of Barcelona and he joined the Jesuit Order in 1600. Sent by the Jesuits to Colombia, which was at that period a clearing house for the slave trade, he dedicated himself to the service of the Africans who arrived in appalling conditions in Cartagena. He provided basic medical care, preached to them and baptised them. He was canonised in 1888 and is much revered by Afro-Americans in both the United States of America and Latin America.

A. Lunn, *A Saint in the Slave Trade* (1935).

Clement V (1264–1314)   Pope. Clement was born Bertrand de Got, of an aristocratic French family. He was consecrated Bishop of Comminges in 1295, Archbishop of Bordeaux in 1299 and was elected Pope in 1305. His election was largely due to the influence of PHILIP THE FAIR of France; Philip had been humiliated by Pope BONIFACE VIII and was determined that it would not happen again. In obedience to his royal master, Clement annulled Boniface's bulls of excommunication and he agreed to dissolve the Knights Templar Order. He also established the papal court away from Rome in Avignon. There the Papacy remained for the next seventy years. Clement himself is remembered as a patron of scholarship; he founded the universities of Orléans and Perugia and interested himself in the problems of Canon Law.

G. Mollat, *The Avignon Popes* (1963); H.G. Richardson, 'Clement V and the See of Canterbury', *English Historical Review*, lvi (1941).

Clement VII (1478–1534)   Pope. Clement VII was born Giulio de' Medici and he was a cousin of Pope LEO X. He was appointed Archbishop of Florence and made a Cardinal in 1513 and he was highly influential during his cousin's Pontificate. In 1523 he himself was elected Pope. He was faced with the problem of Martin LUTHER's teachings spreading through Germany and King HENRY VIII of England's desire for a divorce from his wife Catherine of Aragon. Under these difficult circumstances he vacillated between supporting the policies of Francis I of France and those of the Holy Roman Emperor CHARLES V. In 1527 he was actually taken by the Emperor's troops and held in captivity. Clement VII is primarily remembered for his cultural activities; he was the patron of Cellini, MICHELANGELO and RAPHAEL.

H.M. Vaughan, *The Medici Popes, Leo X and Clement VII* (1908).

Clement VII (d. 1394)   Antipope. Clement was born Robert of Geneva. He was consecrated Archbishop of Cambrai in 1368 and was elected Pope by the French Cardinals in 1378. While URBAN VI had been elected in Rome and had the support of the Holy Roman Empire, England, Hungary, much of Italy and Scandinavia, Clement VII had his headquarters in Avignon and was supported by France, Naples, Savoy, Scotland, Spain and Sicily. The Great Western Schism, as this regrettable episode was known, lasted until 1417.

J.H. Smith, *The Great Schism 1378* (1970).

Clement XIV (1705–74)   Pope. Clement XIV was born Giovanni Ganganelli and he was a member of the Franciscan Order. He became a Cardinal in 1759 and, in 1769, after a long, acrimonious conclave, he was elected Pope. Clement is remembered as the Pope who suppressed the Jesuit Order. It has been conjectured that his election was the result of a secret agreement. In any event in 1773, in obedience to the wishes of his French and Spanish allies, who had gone so far as to threaten schism over the issue, Clement issued the brief 'Dominus ac Redemptor' and the order was suppressed. However, Catherine II of Russia and Frederick II of Prussia ignored the instruction and the order continued to work in their domains. Despite bowing to the pressure of the Catholic princes, Clement continued to face the erosion of papal power in an age of anti-clericalism and increased secularism.

J.C.H. Aveling, *The Jesuits* (1981); M.P. Harney, *The Jesuits in History* (1941).

Clement of Alexandria (*c.* 150–215) Saint and Theologian. Clement is thought to have been born in Athens. In 190 he became head of the Catechetical School in Alexandria, but was forced to flee from persecution in 202. His surviving works include the *Protrepticos*, the *Paidagogos* and the *Stromateis*. These describe the process of conversion, discipline and instruction in the Christian life. He also wrote a commentary on the scriptures and a homily on the stewardship of worldly wealth. Clement is primarily remembered for his teachings against Gnosticism, the belief that salvation is to be found in esoteric knowledge. Clement insisted that the only way to achieve immortality, righteousness and freedom is through the contemplation of JESUS CHRIST as the Logos of God. He believed that Christ was the only teacher and that faith was the only path that led to true enlightenment. Clement's writings are particularly interesting in that they attempt to understand the Christian faith in the light of the philosophy of the time. This has proved to be the way forward for most Christian philosophers of religion.

H. Chadwick, *Early Christian Thought and the Classical Tradition* (1984); S.R.C. Lilla, *Clement of Alexandria* (1971); E.F. Osborn, *The Philosophy of Clement of Alexandria* (1957).

Clement of Rome (late first century) Saint and Bishop. Clement was Bishop of Rome at the end of the first century. He was the author of an epistle to the Corinthians, in which he outlined his ideas on Church government and order. This was regarded as canonical by the Church in Corinth until nearly the end of the second century. In addition, many other apocryphal writings were circulated in his name, including another epistle to the Corinthians, the *Clementine Homilies*, the *Clementine Recognitions*, an apocalypse and two epitomes. In these works, Clement was portrayed as an intermediary between the original apostles and the late first-century Church. According to legend, Clement later became a missionary to the Crimea. He was martyred by being attached to an anchor and thrown into the sea.

J.B. Lightfoot, *Apostolic Fathers*, 2 vols (1890); A.C. Headlam, 'The Clementine literature', *Journal of Theological Studies*, iii (1901/2); B. Bowe, *A Church in Crisis* (1988).

Clitherow, Margaret (*c.* 1556–86) Saint. Clitherow was born Margaret Middleton and was a native of York. Although she was brought up as a Protestant, in 1574 she converted to Roman Catholicism. She refused to attend the parish church, she organised a school for young children and she illegally harboured priests. Although her husband John remained a Protestant, he chose to ignore her activities. Eventually she was arrested and, because she refused to plead either guilty or not guilty to the charge, she was crushed to death, in accordance with the laws of the time. She was canonised in 1970 as one of the Forty Martyrs of England and Wales.

M.T. Monro, *Blessed Margaret Clitherow* (1947).

Clovis (d. 511) Monarch. Clovis was the son of Childeric I and he himself became King of the Salian Franks in 481. His wife, St Clotilde, was a Christian, but Clovis became a member of the Church only after he was convinced that JESUS CHRIST had intervened in battle on his behalf in 496. Clovis greatly expanded his kingdom and, after defeating the Visigoths in 507, the Eastern Emperor conferred on him the title of Proconsul. With the support of the Emperor, and with his new Christian allies, he was able to establish a system of law within his dominions. He made Paris the capital of France and is generally regarded as the founder of the modern French nation.

J.M. Wallace-Hadrille, *The Long-Haired Kings and Other Studies in Frankish History* (1962).

Clowes, William (1780–1851) Sect Founder. Clowes was a native of Staffordshire. He was born into a drinking family, but was converted to Methodism and sobriety in 1805. However, because of his commitment to American-style camp meetings, he was expelled from the movement. His friends continued to support him as a preacher and, together with Hugh BOURNE, he founded the Primitive Methodist Connexion. He was an eloquent speaker and he devoted the rest of his life to spreading the Gospel in the Midlands and north of England.

J.T. Wilkinson, *William Clowes 1780–1851* (1951).

Coke, Thomas (1747–1814) Missionary. Coke was born in Brecon, Wales, and was educated at the University of Oxford. After ordination in the Church of England, he served as a curate in Somerset. From 1777, he worked with John WESLEY; he was appointed Methodist Superintendent for America with Francis ASBURY; he chaired the Christmas Conference of 1784 which laid down a constitution for the American Methodist Episcopal Church, and he was constantly travelling between America and England.

He also presided over the Methodist Connexion in Ireland; he organised missions to the West Indies, to Gibraltar, to Sierra Leone and to the Cape of Good Hope and he was a tireless campaigner against slavery. Coke was a man of enormous energy and he had considerable administrative ability. In the history of the Methodist movement, he is frequently described as Wesley's 'right-hand man'.

J. Vickers, *Thomas Coke* (1969); E.S. Bucke (ed.), *The History of American Methodism*, Vol. 1 (1964).

Colenso, John William (1814–83) Bishop and Theologian. Colenso was a native of Cornwall, and was educated at the University of Cambridge. After serving as a parish priest in Norfolk, he was consecrated Anglican Bishop of Natal, South Africa, in 1853. Colenso is primarily remembered for his liberal theological views. He made it clear that he did not believe in everlasting punishment, he taught that baptism is merely a symbol of the fact that human beings are already redeemed through the death of JESUS and he cast doubt on the Mosaic authorship and absolute historicity of the Pentateuch. The Archbishop of Cape Town was so appalled by these views that in 1863 he deposed him from his see. Undaunted, Colenso appealed to the Privy Council in London, who upheld his appeal. None the less the Archbishop solemnly consecrated a new Bishop of Natal in 1869 thus starting a schism in the Anglican Church of Natal that lasted until 1911. Colenso himself devoted the rest of his life to helping the people of Africa. He showed respect for African customs in his willingness to baptise polygamists and he consistently fought for just treatment. Many of his supporters in Britain were unhappy with these activities, but he was held in much respect in his diocese until the time of his death.

P.B. Hinchliff, *John William Colenso* (1964).

Coleridge, Samuel Taylor (1772–1834) Poet and Philosopher. Coleridge was the son of a country vicar and grew up in Devon. Although he never took his degree, he was educated at Cambridge University. In 1798, with William Wordsworth, he published his first selection of poems in a volume entitled *Lyrical Ballads*; this included the famous 'Ancient Mariner'. He was the author of several other books of verse as well as lectures on Shakespeare, *Lay Sermons, Aids to Reflection* and a monograph on the constitution of Church and State. As a young man, he had contemplated a career in the Unitarian ministry; later, inspired by the writings of the Jewish philosopher Baruch Spinoza and the German mystic, Jakob BOEHME, he turned to neo-Platonism and Pantheism. Then, after 1810, he turned back to the Church. He was interested in German biblical criticism and he believed that Christianity must be seen primarily as an ethical system. Coleridge is chiefly remembered as one of the greatest of the English poets; in the history of the Church, he must be seen as an important forerunner of the nineteenth-century Broad Church movement.

J.D. Boulger, *Coleridge as Religious Thinker* (1961); T. Mcfarland, *Coleridge and the Pantheist Tradition* (1969); C.R. Sanders, *Coleridge and the Broad Church Movement* (1942).

Colet, John (*c.* 1466–1519) Theologian. Colet was the son of a Lord Mayor of London and was educated at the University of Oxford. He gave a famous series of lectures on St PAUL's epistles in which he advocated a return to the simplicity and discipline of the early Church. In 1504 he became Dean of St Paul's Cathedral and he made use of his position to preach against the abuses and corruptions of his fellow clergy. He was a friend of Sir Thomas MORE and ERASMUS and, although suspected of heresy, was completely loyal to the Roman Catholic Church. On his father's death,

he used much of his inherited fortune to found St Paul's School. Colet is remembered as one of the greatest of the Renaissance humanist clergy.

E.W. Hunt, *Dean Colet and his Theology* (1956).

Coligny, Gaspard de (1519–72) Politician. Coligny was a member of the powerful Châtillon family and he spent his life in public service, ultimately becoming Admiral of France. During the late 1550s he was converted to Protestantism and, during the French Wars of Religion, he was regarded as the leading member of the Huguenot party. He was a favourite of the young King Charles, and CATHERINE DE' MEDICI became jealous of his influence. She ordered his murder, which prompted the massacre of St Bartholomew's Day during the course of which several thousand Protestants were slaughtered.

A.W. Whitehead, *Gaspard de Coligny: Admiral of France* (1904); S.L. England, *The Massacre of St Bartholomew* (1938).

Columba (*c.* 521–97) Saint and Missionary. Columba was born at Gartan in Ireland of a noble family. At an early age he became a monk and he founded monasteries at Derry, Durrow and possibly Kells. In 563 he moved to Iona, off the coast of Scotland where, with twelve companions, he established a famous religious house. He converted King Brude of the Picts to Christianity, but the extent of his missionary activities in Scotland has probably been exaggerated.

Adamnan of Iona, *Life of St Columba*, translated by R. Sharpe (1995); W.D. Simpson, *The Historical St Columba*, 2nd edn (1963).

Columbanus (*c.* 543–615) Saint, Theologian and Educator. Columbanus was born in Leinster, Ireland. A notable scholar, he could read both Hebrew and Greek. Towards the end of his life he founded a school in Luxorum, Burgundy. However, he was expelled from France after denouncing the vices of the Burgundian king. Subsequently he founded a monastery in Bobbio, North Italy. Columbanus's correspondence with Popes Boniface IV and GREGORY THE GREAT survive; his letters show him to have been an able debater who was both orthodox and learned.

F. MacManus, *St Columban* (1962).

Comenius, Johannes Amos (1592–1670) Bishop and Educator. Comenius was born in East Moravia and was educated at Prerov, Nassau and Heidelberg. He was ordained priest of the Bohemian Unitas Fratrum, of which Church he later became a Bishop. When all non-Catholic clergy were prevented from exercising their ministries in Bohemia, he moved to Poland where he became Rector of the Leszno Gymnasium. He was the author of *Janua Linguarum Reserata* and *Didactica Magna* and he was recognised as one of the foremost educationalists of his day. He spent the year 1641/2 in England where he outlined his plan for a 'Pansophic' college. Later he attempted to carry out a similar project in Sweden, Hungary and the Netherlands. He is primarily remembered for his *De Rerum Humanarum Emendatione Consultatio*. Only the first two volumes were published during his lifetime, but his belief that universal education was the key to founding a universal Church was highly influential in the nineteenth century.

Johannes Comenius, *Selections in Commemorations of the Third Centenary of Opera Didactica Omnia* (1957); J.E. Sadler, *J.A. Comenius and the Concept of Universal Education* (1966); M. Spinka, *John Amos Comenius, That Incomparable Moravian* (1943).

Cone, James Hal (b. 1938) Theologian. Cone was born in Arkansas in the United States of America and was educated at Garrett Theological Seminary and at North Western University. Subsequently he has taught at Union Theological Seminary in New York. Cone is a prominent expounder of black theology. Black theology in the United States has arisen out of the experience of slavery, oppression and exploitation. Cone is concerned with the interface between God's Word as revealed in Scripture on the one hand and the black experience on the other. As he himself puts it, 'Black theology seeks to analyse the satanic nature of Whiteness and by doing so to prepare Non-Whites for revolutionary action'.

James Cone, *A Black Theology of Liberation* (1970); G.S. Wilmore and James H. Cone, *Black Theology: A Documentary History 1966–1979* (1981).

Constantine (*c.* 274–337) Emperor. Constantine was the son of the Emperor Constantius Chlorus and HELENA. In 306 he was proclaimed Emperor of the West on the death of his father. This was confirmed after the Battle of Milvian Bridge in 312. According to legend, he had a dream before the battle in which the Christian God promised him victory. In 313, in the Edict of Milan, he decreed full toleration for the Christian Church. In 324 he also conquered the Eastern Empire. In 325, he summoned the Council of Nicaea. Despite the agreement reached, theological dissension persisted throughout Constantine's reign. In 330 Constantine founded the city of Constantinople as the capital of the Eastern Empire. He himself was baptised before he died and he was buried in a basilica in the new city. The authenticity of his conversion is much debated, but in any event, he was greatly involved in Church affairs and he established the precedent that the secular monarch should be the arbiter in ecclesiastical dispute.

T.D. Barnes, *The New Empire of Diocletian and Constantine* (1982); R. MacMillan, *Constantine* (1970).

Conzelmann, Hans (1915–89) Theologian. Conzelmann was a student of Rudolf BULTMANN at the University of

Marburg. He himself taught at the Universities of Zürich and Göttingen. A New Testament specialist, Conzelmann's best-known works are on the Third Gospel and the Acts of the Apostles. He was less sceptical than Bultmann about the historical value of the New Testament narratives and he was a participator in what has come to be called 'the new quest for the historical Jesus'.

Hans Conzelmann, *The Theology of St Luke* (1960); Hans Conzelmann, *The Acts of the Apostles* (1987).

Cosmas Melodus (eighth century) Saint, Bishop and Poet. Cosmas was the adopted brother of JOHN OF DAMASCUS. As a young man he joined a group of anchorites living near Jerusalem and in 743 he was consecrated Bishop of Meluma. Cosmas is remembered as a liturgical poet. Many of his odes have been incorporated into the liturgy of the Orthodox Church. He also may have been the author of a commentary on the poems of St GREGORY OF NAZIANZUS.

H.J.W. Tillyard, 'A canon on the recovery of the cross', *Byzantinische Zeitschrift*, xxviii (1928).

Coverdale, Miles (1488–1568) Bishop and Educator. Coverdale was born in York and he was educated at the University of Cambridge. He joined the Augustinian Order of Friars in 1514, but left in 1528, having been converted to Protestantism. After preaching Lutheran doctrines, he was forced to leave England. In Europe, he helped William TYNDALE in his translation of the Pentateuch and in 1535 his translation of the whole Bible was published. This was the first complete English Bible to be printed. It was based on Tyndale's work supplemented by Martin LUTHER's and Ulrich ZWINGLI's versions and the Latin Vulgate. Coverdale himself does not seem to have known Hebrew. Under the patronage of Thomas CROMWELL, he revised Matthew's Bible (first edited by John

ROGERS) which was published as the Great Bible. He was forced into exile again in 1540, but he returned to England during the reign of King EDWARD VI when he was consecrated Bishop of Exeter. Then, during the reign of Queen MARY, he lived in Geneva, where he may have been one of the committee which produced the Calvinistic Geneva Bible. He returned to England with the accession of Queen ELIZABETH I and he was one of the Bishops who took part in the consecration of Matthew PARKER as Archbishop of Canterbury. Coverdale is primarily remembered for the Bible translation which bears his name.

F.F. Bruce, *The English Bible*, 2nd edn (1970); J.F. Mozley, *Coverdale and his Bibles* (1953).

Cowper, William (1731–1800) Poet. Cowper was the son of a Church of England clergyman and grew up in Great Berkhamstead. He was trained as a lawyer. Throughout his adult life he was subject to fits of mania, alternating with periods of acute depression when he was convinced he was predestined to eternal punishment. He was the author of many poems, but in the Church he is remembered for such hymns as 'O for a closer walk with God' and 'God moves in a mysterious way'.

N. Nicholson, *William Cowper* (1951).

Cox, Richard (*c.* 1500–81) Theologian and Bishop. Cox was educated at the University of Cambridge. A convinced Protestant, he was closely involved in the compilation of the 1549 and 1552 Prayer Books. He was appointed Dean of Westminster in 1549, but was deprived in the reign of Queen MARY and went into exile. In Frankfurt, he emerged as the leader of the party that wished to retain the 1552 liturgy, while another faction, led by John KNOX, worked for still more radical reform. The two groups were known as the Coxians and Knoxians. On the accession of Queen ELIZABETH I in

1559, he returned to England where he was consecrated Bishop of Ely. He was involved in the translation of the Bishops' Bible of 1568, but eventually he resigned his see in protest at the use of candles and crucifix in the Queen's private chapel.

C.H. Garrett, *The Marian Exiles* (1938); M.M. Knoppen, *Tudor Puritanism* (1966).

Cranmer, Thomas (1489–1556) Liturgist, Archbishop and Martyr. Cranmer was born in Nottinghamshire and was educated at the University of Cambridge. He was useful to King HENRY VIII in the matter of his divorce from Queen Catherine of Aragon and, in consequence, was appointed Archbishop of Canterbury. Later he annulled the King's marriages to Anne Boleyn and to Anne of Cleves. He was a convinced Protestant; he encouraged the translation of the Bible into English and was responsible for the Ten Articles. During the reign of King EDWARD VI he was highly influential. On his initiative, continental theologians such as PETER MARTYR and Martin BUCER were invited to England, and he was largely responsible for the Prayer Books of 1549 and 1552. However, on the accession of the Roman Catholic Queen MARY, the daughter of King Henry and Queen Catherine, he was put on trial for treason and heresy. Initially he recanted his Protestantism, but in 1556 he reasserted his beliefs. He died with extraordinary courage, being burnt at the stake at Oxford. According to eyewitnesses, he plunged his right hand into the flames first because it was his right hand that had betrayed his true convictions by signing the document of recantation. Cranmer is remembered both for his martyrdom and for his wonderful prose style, which is preserved in the English Book of Common Prayer.

P. Avis and D. Selwyn (eds), *Thomas Cranmer: Churchman and Scholar* (1993); P. Brooks, *Cranmer in Context* (1989); D. Loades, *Thomas*

Cranmer and the English Reformation (1991); D. MacCulloch, *Thomas Cranmer: A Life* (1996).

Cromwell, Oliver (1599–1658) Politician. Cromwell was born in Huntingdon and was educated at the University of Cambridge. He was elected to Parliament in 1628 and 1640. In the Long Parliament he emerged as the leader of the Puritan party. In the English Civil War, he was responsible for organising the Parliamentary army and, when the King's forces were finally defeated, he was among those who signed the death warrant of King CHARLES I. Subsequently his army subdued both the Irish and the Scots and in 1653 he dismissed Parliament. From then on he effectively ruled alone, as Lord Protector, until his death in 1658. During this period, he made various attempts to reorganise the Church and reform the clergy. Despite his personal sincerity and his brilliant administrative powers, Cromwell's lack of success can be gauged by the people's eagerness to restore the pragmatic, High-Church King Charles II to the throne in 1660.

B. Coward, *Oliver Cromwell* (1991); C. Hill, *God's Englishman: Oliver Cromwell and the Puritan Revolution* (1970).

Cromwell, Thomas (*c.* 1485–1540) Politician. Cromwell was born in humble circumstances and spent some of his early life abroad as a soldier in the French army. Under the patronage of Cardinal WOLSEY, he was elected to the House of Commons in 1523 and after Wolsey's fall in 1529, he joined the household of King HENRY VIII. As the King's Vicar-General, he organised the dissolution of the monasteries; he brokered an unsuccessful Protestant marriage for the King (with Anne of Cleves); he encouraged the translation of the Bible into English and he defined the duties of the clergy. However, in 1540 he fell out of favour with the King. He was arrested, found guilty of treason and executed. His own religious convictions are not clear, but Cromwell must be regarded as an important contributor to the Protestant Reformation in England.

A.G. Dickens, *Thomas Cromwell and the English Reformation* (1959); G. Elton, *Thomas Cromwell* (1991).

Crowther, Samuel Ajayi (*c.* 1806–91) Missionary and Bishop. Crowther was born in Oshoyun, Yorubaland. At the age of fifteen, he was captured as a slave, but was freed by the British navy and taken to Sierra Leone. There he was baptised and trained to be a missionary. He served very successfully on the 1841 Niger expedition and, as a result, was sent to London for further training and ordination. After returning to Africa, he continued to work on the Niger mission and in 1864 he was consecrated Anglican Bishop of West Africa. White missionaries, however, were unwilling to work under a black Bishop and his leadership was under constant attack. Eventually, in 1889, worn down by criticism, he resigned. A white Bishop was appointed as his successor and the Niger Delta Pastorate seceded from the control of the Church of England. The episode of Crowther's episcopacy did not show the Anglican Church in its best light. Although official policy in the Church Missionary Society was to encourage self-government and the indigenisation of foreign Churches, this was all too often undermined by European prejudice.

J.F.A. Ajayi, *Christian Missions in Nigeria 1841–1891* (1968); J. Page, *Samuel Crowther: The Slave Boy of the Niger* (1932).

Cruden, Alexander (1701–70) Educator. Cruden was born in Aberdeen. A strict Presbyterian, he was extremely dedicated to the study of the Bible. In 1737 he published his famous Concordance to the Old and New Testaments which has remained a standard work ever since. Cruden's life was marked by considerable eccentricity.

After the publication of the Concordance, he set himself up as a regulator of public morals, calling himself 'Alexander the Corrector'. He was particularly exercised about swearing and breaking the Sabbath. In 1755, while wooing the daughter of the Lord Mayor of London, he even petitioned Parliament for the title to be bestowed officially. Unfortunately he was unsuccessful on both counts. None the less the Concordance remains a very useful reference volume.

E. Olivier, *The Eccentric Life of Alexander Cruden* (1934).

Cupitt, Don (b. 1934) Theologian. Cupitt was educated at the University of Cambridge and for most of his career served as Dean of Emmanuel College. He is the author of many books including *Taking Leave of God* (1980), *The Long-Legged Fly* (1987) and *The Time Being* (1992). He is associated with a non-realist vision of Christianity, arguing that human beings create their own meanings and values and that the Christian faith is not meant to be understood literally; it merely provides a framework through which its adherents come to terms with their own experiences. His ideas are discussed and promulgated in the 'Sea of Faith' group which meets regularly to discuss the consequences of interpreting religion in non-realist categories.

Don Cupitt, *Taking Leave of God* (1980); B. Hebblethwaite, *The Ocean of Truth* (1988).

Cuthbert (d. 687) Saint and Bishop. Inspired by a vision of St AIDAN, Cuthbert entered a monastery at Melrose in 651. Later he moved to Ripon for a while, but in 661 he returned and was elected Prior. Then in 664 he became Prior of Lindisfarne. There, against considerable opposition, he introduced certain Roman customs and he tightened discipline. During the twelve years he was at Lindisfarne he made several missionary journeys round Northumbria. Then in 676, he retired to a more solitary life on one of the Farne Islands. He refused the See of Hexham in 684, but in 685 he was consecrated Bishop of Lindisfarne. Cuthbert is remembered as the prominent figure of the Celtic Church of the late seventh century. His tomb is in Durham Cathedral.

C.F. Battiscombe (ed.), *The Relics of St Cuthbert* (1956); H. Colgrave, *St Cuthbert* (1947).

Cyprian (*c.* 200–58) Saint and Bishop. Cyprian was born in Carthage, North Africa. He was converted to Christianity in 246 and was consecrated Bishop of Carthage in 248. He quickly came into conflict with clergy in his diocese over the question of how those who had lapsed during a recent period of persecution should be received back into the Church. Subsequently he disagreed with Bishop Stephen of Rome over the nature of baptism. In his *De Catholicae Ecclesiae Unitate*, Cyprian argued that Sacraments were only valid within the Catholic Church and that therefore all those who had been baptised by schismatics or heretics must be rebaptised. These views were confirmed by two councils of African Bishops in 255–6, although Rome continued to insist that rebaptism was unnecessary since all baptisms were valid. During the Valerian persecutions in 257 Cyprian was banished from Carthage and he was later beheaded. He is remembered for his identification of the Christian ministry with the priestly and sacrificial functions outlined in the Old Testament and he was the author of the famous dictum, 'Habere non potest Deum patrem qui ecclesiam non habet matrem' (he cannot have God as his father, who does not have the Church as his mother).

G.S.M. Walker, *The Churchmanship of St Cyprian* (1968); P. Hinchliff, *Cyprian of Carthage* (1974).

Cyril (826–69) Saint and Missionary. Cyril was the brother of METHODIUS and was born in Thessalonica. After serving as librarian in the Church of St Sophia, Constantinople, he led a mission to the Khazars. Subsequently he travelled with his brother to Moravia where he organised the Slav Church. He is said to have invented the Glagolitic alphabet and to have conducted services in Slavonic. He is thus seen as the founder of Slavonic literature. He died in a monastery in Rome, but he is still revered in the Balkan states as the 'apostle of the Slavs'. With his brother, he was declared a 'Patron of Europe' in 1980.

F. Dvornik, *Byzantine Missions among the Slavs* (1970).

Cyril of Alexandria (d. 444) Saint, Patriarch and Theologian. Cyril was the nephew of Patriarch Theophilus and he succeeded his uncle as Patriarch of Alexandria in 412. He is primarily remembered as an indefatigable warrior for orthodoxy. He combated the teachings of NESTORIUS by sending him twelve condemnations. In 431, at the Council of Ephesus, he orchestrated the deposition of Nestorius from the Patriarchate of Constantinople. This decision was supported by the Emperor and Nestorius was exiled in Antioch. However, the Antiochene delegates, in their turn, attempted to depose Cyril and a compromise was reached only after further imperial intervention. Many of Cyril's theological works survive, including two anti-Arian treatises, a reply to the writings of JULIAN THE APOSTATE, several sermons and biblical exegeses and certain anti-Nestorian works including *That Christ is One*. He was a determined defender of the hypostatic union of the divine and the human in the person of JESUS CHRIST. Although he has been accused of Apollinarianism and Monophysitism because he occasionally uses the Greek term *phusis* to mean person as well as nature, his teachings must be seen as anticipating the final Chalcedon definition of the Trinity.

R.V. Sellers, *Two Ancient Christologies* (1940); J. McGuckin, *Cyril of Alexandria* (1993).

Cyril of Jerusalem (*c.*310–86) Saint, Bishop and Devotional Writer. Cyril was consecrated Bishop of Jerusalem in *c.* 350, but was banished by ACACIUS, the Arian Bishop of Caesarea, in 357. He was cleared of heresy by the Synod of Seleucia, but he was sent into exile again in 367. On his return in 378, GREGORY OF NYSSA reported that Cyril was both orthodox in his opinions and a rightful Bishop, who had unceasingly opposed the teachings of the heretic ARIUS. Cyril is primarily remembered for his twenty-four catecheses (instructions given to candidates before baptism). They give a full picture of the doctrines and liturgies of the Jerusalem Church of the fourth century.

W. Telfer, *Cyril of Jerusalem and Nemesius of Emesa* (1955).

D

Daly, Mary (b. 1928) Theologian. Daly was educated at the University of Fribourg, Switzerland, and has taught theology at Boston College in the United States of America. Her earliest book on the church, *The Church and the Second Sex*, was written 'in anger and hope', in response to the activities of the Second Vatican Council. Subsequently she disowned it as the work of a 'reformist foresister'. *Beyond God the Father* was written in 1973 and argued for the death of God the Father, beyond Christidolatry and for Sisterhood as antichurch. By the time she produced *Gyn-Ecology* in 1978, she had accepted that the notion of God cannot be separated from masculine imagery and she has since embarked on a post-Christian journey towards self-acceptance. Daly has proved an influential figure in the secular, as well as the Christian, women's movement and her uncompromising condemnation of the innate sexism of the Christian religion has not passed unnoticed.

Mary Daly, *Beyond God the Father: Towards a Philosophy of Women's Liberation* (1973); Mary Daly, *Gyn-Ecology: The Metaethics of Radical Feminism* (1978).

Damien, Father (1840–89) Missionary and Philanthropist. Father Damien was born Joseph de Veuster in Tremelo, Belgium. At the age of nineteen he joined the Fathers of the Sacred Heart of Jesus and Mary. He worked as a missionary first in the Sandwich Isles and then in Hawaii. In 1873 he moved to the island of Molokai which had been isolated as a leper colony. Single-handedly he cared for both the spiritual and physical needs of the lepers. By 1885 he himself had caught the disease, but he continued with his self-imposed task until he was on the point of death. His dedication was not always appreciated by the secular and religious authorities, but it aroused considerable interest in the outside world. His work has proved an inspiration to many and he is the subject of many biographies, including one by Robert Louis Stevenson.

Father Damien, *Letters*, edited by Father Pamphile (1889); R.L. Stevenson, *Father Damien* (1910).

Danjo, Ebina (1856–1937) Theologian. A member of the Samurai caste of Japan, Danjo was converted from Confucian philosophy to Christianity. He was taught by the missionary Captain L.C. James who gathered together a small group of Christian young men who became known as the Kumamoto Band. Later he became a preacher at Annaka. He taught that all humanity share to some degree the nature of God and through discovering their Godlike nature, human beings share in the experience of JESUS CHRIST. Danjo is generally considered to be the first original Christian Japanese theologian.

F. Notehelfer, 'Ebina Danjo: A Christian Samurai of the Meiji period', *Papers on Japan* (1963); I. Scheiner, *Christian Converts and Social Protest in Meiji Japan* (1970).

Dante Alighieri (1265–1321) Poet. Dante was a native of Florence, but as a result of his opposition to Pope BONIFACE VIII, he was exiled from the city and moved first to Verona and then to Ravenna. His masterpiece is the

Divina Commedia. This is an allegory of the soul's descent through sin and purgation and its subsequent ascent through the heights. The poet portrays himself as lost in the dark wood of sin. The Latin poet, Virgil, who represents philosophy, guides him through Hell and Purgatory and then Beatrice, his dead love, now representing theology and revelation, leads him to Paradise and the Beatific Vision. The *Divina Commedia* is one of the classics of Western Christianity and ranks with BUNYAN's *Pilgrim's Progress* and MILTON's *Paradise Lost* as a source of perennial inspiration.

Dante Alighieri, *The Divine Comedy*, edited by D.L. Sayers (1955); T. Bergin, *Dante* (1965); C. Grayson (ed.), *The World of Dante* (1980); G. Nuttall, *The Faith of Dante* (1969).

Darby, John Nelson (1800–82) Denomination Founder. Darby was born in Ireland and was educated at Trinity College, Dublin. After training as a lawyer, he was ordained as a Church of Ireland clergyman. However, in 1827, disenchanted with the complacency and apathy of the established Church, he wrote a tract entitled *On the Nature and Unity of the Church of Christ* and resigned his curacy. He joined a group of Plymouth Brethren in Dublin and quickly became their leader. In 1845 he quarrelled with the Brethren leader Benjamin Newton on questions of Church order and the interpretation of prophecy. In 1848 Newton was charged with heresy and the Brethren split into the Open and the Exclusive groups, Darby being the leader of the latter. He dedicated the rest of his life to preaching and made many visits abroad to Europe, to North America and to New Zealand. Under his care, the Exclusives became increasingly centralised and legalistic. Since his death they have had several further divisions among themselves.

F.R. Coad, *A History of the Brethren Movement* (1968); A. Reese, *The Approaching Advent of Christ: An Examination of the Teaching of J.N.*

Darby and his Followers (1937); H.H. Rowdon, *The Origins of the Brethren* (1967).

Darwin, Charles Robert (1809–82) Scientist. Darwin was educated at the University of Cambridge. In 1859 he published his *Origin of Species by Means of Natural Selection*. In this he argued that the earth's species were not created in their present form, but had evolved very slowly through the ages as the result of natural selection. Subsequently in 1871 he published *The Descent of Man*. The *Origin of Species*, coupled with LYELL's geological discoveries of the same period, caused a sensation in the Victorian Church. Not only did the theory contradict the biblical account of creation as found in the Book of Genesis, but it also implied that the world was not guided by a benevolent deity, but rather by an impersonal force ensuring the survival of the fittest. In addition, human beings could no longer be thought to be the result of a special, spiritual creation, but instead must be seen as part of the natural world. Christians have had different reactions to the insights of Darwinism. Many have assimilated the theory of evolution into their world view and understand the Genesis account as a spiritual myth; others, however, have denied the findings of the biologists and geologists and have stoutly continued to teach and believe in 'creation science'. Darwin himself was agnostic in his religious beliefs.

Charles Darwin, *The Origin of Species* (1859) [many editions]; N. Barlow (ed.), *Charles Darwin and the Voyage of the Beagle* (1945); G. Himmelfarb, *Darwin and the Darwinian Revolution* (1959); W. Irvine, *Apes, Angels and the Victorians* (1956); J.R. Moore, *The Post Darwinian Controversies* (1979).

David (sixth century) Saint. Little certain is known of the life of St David. According to legend, he was descended from a noble family, he became a priest and he founded twelve monasteries, all following highly ascetic rules. He seems to have attended the Synod of Brevi and is traditionally believed to have been chosen there to be Primate of the Welsh Church. He made a legendary visit to Jerusalem where he is said to have been consecrated Archbishop of Wales by the Patriarch. He is also thought to have been responsible for the transfer of the Bishop's seat from Caerleon to Menevia (now called St David's). Despite the lack of definite information, David is a highly popular figure and has been the patron saint of Wales since the twelfth century.

J.W. James (ed.), *Rhygyfarch's Life of St David* (1967); E.G. Bowen, *The Settlements of the Celtic Saints in Wales* (1956); S.M. Harris, *St David in the Liturgy* (1940).

Dearmer, Percy (1867–1936)   Poet and Liturgist. Dearmer was educated at the University of Oxford. After ordination, he served as a parish priest in London; following this he was appointed Professor of Ecclesiastical Art at the University of London and finally he became a Canon of Westminster Abbey. He was the author of a much used liturgical manual, *The Parson's Handbook*, published in 1899. However, he is chiefly remembered as a hymn-writer and for his great hymn collections, *The English Hymnal*, *Songs of Praise* and the *Oxford Book of Carols*. These are still used in the Anglican Church.

Percy Dearmer, *The Parson's Handbook*, edited by C.E. Pocknee, 13th edn (1965); N. Dearmer, *The Life of Percy Dearmer* (1940).

De Foucauld, Charles Eugène (1858–1916)   Order Founder and Missionary. De Foucauld was born in Strasbourg. After an adventurous period as a soldier and explorer, he joined a Trappist monastery in 1890. Seeking even greater austerity, he left to become a servant of the Poor Clares in the Holy Land. He was ordained priest in 1901 and then he settled in Algeria, first at Beni-Abbès and then in the remote Hoggar mountains.

There he lived the life of a hermit, dedicating himself to prayer and charity. In 1916, for obscure reasons, he was assassinated. Although he attracted no disciples in his lifetime, in 1923 his papers were published. This led to the setting up of various orders based on his Rule. These include the Little Brothers of Jesus and the Little Sisters of the Sacred Heart (both founded in 1933), the Little Sisters of Jesus (1939), the Little Brothers of the Gospel (1958) and the Little Sisters of the Gospel (1965). In all these orders, the members share in the life of the poor, earning their living by manual labour and maintaining a deep spirituality.

Charles de Foucauld, *Meditations of a Hermit* (1930); E. Hamilton, *The Desert my Dwelling: A Study of Charles de Foucauld* (1968); R. Voillaume, *Seeds of the Desert* (1955).

De Maistre, Joseph Marie (1753–1821)   Politician and Theologian. De Maistre was born in Chambéry, France. His experience of the French Revolution led him to an extreme conservative position. Between 1802 and 1816, he served as Savoy's ambassador to Russia. However, he is remembered for his highly authoritarian doctrine of the Papacy which he formulated in his book *Du Pape*, published in 1819. He argued that since it is God who bestows papal authority, the Pope is infallible in all spiritual matters. This view was highly influential on later ultramontane opinion and culminated in the formal declaration of papal infallibility at the First Vatican Council of 1869/70.

A. Caponigri, *Some Aspects of the Philosophy of Joseph de Maistres* (1945).

Demetrius (d. *c.* 231)   Saint and Bishop. Demetrius is remembered as the Bishop of Alexandria who appointed ORIGEN to the Catechitical School. He reprimanded him for preaching while still a layman in 216 and in 228 he banished him after he had been irregularly ordained by the Bishops of Caesarea and Jerusalem.

Demetrius is particularly venerated within the Coptic Church.

Eusebius, *Historia Ecclesiastica*, Vol. 6, translated by G.A. Williamson (1965).

Denis [Dionysius] (third century)   Saint. Little certain is known of St Denis. He is believed to have been one of seven Bishops who were sent from Rome to convert Gaul. According to tradition, he was martyred on Montmartre. Later in the seventh century his remains were transferred four miles north of Paris where a famous Benedictine monastery was built dedicated to the saint. Denis is chiefly remembered as the patron saint of Paris.

S. McK. Crosby, *The Abbey of St Denis* (1942).

De Nobili, Robert (1577–1656)   Missionary. De Nobili was born in Montepulciano, Italy. He joined the Jesuit Order in 1596 and in 1605 he arrived in India. Unlike the missionaries of the time, he adapted himself to Indian culture. He learned Sanskrit and he lived in the Brahmin quarter of Madura. He even allowed his first disciple to keep the Brahmin insignia. The local Church authorities were appalled, but de Nobili appealed to Pope Gregory XV who supported his stance. During his lifetime he baptised several thousand new converts. His vision in divorcing the essence of Christianity from its European setting proved an inspiration to later Christian missionaries.

V. Cronin, *A Pearl to India: The Life of Roberto de Nobili* (1959).

De Rancé, Armand-Jean le Bouthillier (1626–1700)   Order Founder. De Rancé was born into a noble French family and was the godson of Cardinal RICHELIEU. When young he was presented with several benefices, but in 1663 he renounced his worldly life and joined a Cistercian Order. After serving his novitiate, he assumed the position of Abbot at La

Trappe. He set himself to reform the monastery and in his *Traité de la Sainteté et des Devoirs de la Vie Monastique*, published in 1683, he argued that monastic life should be both austere and penitential. For the rest of his life he engaged in controversy, particularly with the Benedictine Jean Mabillon, who insisted that study was essential for the religious life. De Rancé is remembered as the founder of the Trappist Rule, which is one of the strictest in the Church. Trappist monks live in silence in a common dormitory. They eat no eggs, meat or fish and are dedicated to following the liturgical offices and to manual work.

A.J. Krailsheimer, *Armand-Jean de Rancé, Abbot of La Trappe* (1974); T. Merton, *Elected Silence* (1949).

Descartes, René (1596–1650)   Philosopher. Descartes was born in La Haye, France, and was educated at the Jesuit College of La Flèche. After a short military and legal career, he settled in Holland until a year before his death when he moved to Sweden at the invitation of Queen Christina. In his philosophy, Descartes tried to establish principles of absolute certainty using the methods of mathematics. He began with the famous dictum 'Cogito ergo sum' ('I think, therefore I am'). Working from the knowledge of his own self-consciousness, he argued for the existence of God and for his goodness. Descartes is a highly important figure in the history of philosophy. His methods foreshadowed the rationalism of Spinoza and LEIBNIZ as well as the empiricism of LOCKE, BERKELEY and HUME.

René Descartes, *Discourse on Method* (1637) [many translations and editions]; René Descartes, *Principles of Philosophy* (1644) [many translations and editions]; A. Kenny, *Descartes: A Study of his Philosophy* (1968).

Dibelius, Martin (1883–1947)   Theologian and Ecumenist. Dibelius was born in Dresden. From 1915 he taught at

Heidelberg University where he succeeded Johannes WEISS to the Chair of New Testament exegesis and criticism. He was an important proponent of the form-critical method of studying the text and in his *Die Formgeschichte des Evangeliums*, published in 1919, he argued that the Gospel writers were compilers of Church traditions and not independent authors. He was more conservative in his views than many of his contemporaries, such as Rudolf BULTMANN, and he believed that the preaching of the early Church was the medium through which the words of JESUS had been preserved. He was also a committed ecumenist and served as a leader of the Faith and Order Commission, endeavouring to provide a theological basis for the reunion of the Churches.

Martin Dibelius, *From Tradition to Gospel* (1934); H. Palmer, *The Logic of Gospel Criticism* (1968).

Dionysius Exiguus (d. sixth century) Historian. Dionysius was a Scythian monk who lived in Rome. He is remembered for his historical collection of papal letters dating from the fourth until the end of the fifth century. The collection provided a series of answers to problems arising out of Canon Law. In addition Dionysius continued CYRIL OF ALEXANDRIA's tables for the calculation of the date of Easter. Unlike Cyril, he used the supposed date of the Incarnation of JESUS CHRIST as the base year, rather than the date of the Emperor Diocletian's accession. Thus his work was the foundation of the BC/AD system.

C.W. Jones, 'The Victorian and Dionysiac Paschal tablets in the West', *Speculum*, ix (1934).

Dionysius of Alexandria (d. *c.* 264) Bishop and Theologian. Dionysius was a pupil of ORIGEN and became head of the Catechitical School of Alexandria. In 247 he was consecrated Bishop of Alexandria. During the Decian persecution, he had to flee to the Libyan desert and he

was also banished during the Valerian persecutions. Although only fragments of his writings survive, he is remembered for his determined opposition to the doctrines of SABELLIUS. His letter to Pope Dionysius on the godhead was prompted by the controversy. Dionysius has been accused of anticipating the teachings of the heretic ARIUS, but ATHANASIUS maintained that he was orthodox in his opinions.

W.A. Bienert, *Dionysius von Alexandrien* (1978) [no English translation available]; G.W. Clarke (ed.), *Dionysis of Alexandria: The Letters and Fragments* (forthcoming).

Dionysius, Pseudo- (fifth/sixth century) Mystic. Pseudo-Dionysius is the name given to an unknown mystical author. His writings include the *Celestial Hierarchy*, the *Divine Names*, *Mystical Theology* and ten surviving letters. The works are influenced by neo-Platonist philosophy and chart the ascent of the soul through a process of unknowing to its ultimate goal of union with God. The journey goes through the three stages of purgation, illumination and unification. This has been the pattern of many later mystical treatises and can be found in the works of HUGH OF ST VICTOR, ALBERTUS MAGNUS, THOMAS AQUINAS, DANTE and MILTON.

A. Louth, *Pseudo-Dionysius* (1982).

Dioscorus (d. 454) Patriarch. Dioscorus was the successor of CYRIL OF ALEXANDRIA to the Patriarchate of Alexandria. He presided over the Council of Ephesus which declared the teachings of EUTYCHES, the Monophysite opponent of Nestorianism, to be orthodox. However, the 451 Council of Chalcedon condemned Eutyches, and Dioscorus was deposed and banished to Pamphlagonia. The Coptic Church rejected the theological conclusions of Chalcedon and venerates Dioscorus to this day.

R.V. Sellers, *The Council of Chalcedon* (1953).

Dodd, Charles Harold (1884–1973) Theologian. Dodd was educated at the University of Oxford. Subsequently he taught New Testament studies first at Oxford, then at Manchester and finally at Cambridge. He was the author of several important books including the *Parables of the Kingdom*, *The Apostolic Preaching and its Development* and works on the Epistle to the Romans and the Johannine literature. He believed that JESUS taught a 'realised eschatology' (that the Kingdom of God was in the here and now), that the original teachings of the Apostles could be isolated (the 'kerygma') and that St PAUL's teaching on the Wrath of God implied that an impersonal process of retribution was built into the structure of the universe. These ideas were highly influential and Dodd is remembered as the most important British New Testament scholar of his generation.

W.D. Davies and D. Daube (eds), *The Background of the New Testament and its Eschatology: Essays in honour of C.H. Dodd* (1956); P.E. Hughes (ed.), *Creative Minds in Contemporary Theology* (1966).

Döllinger, Johann Joseph Ignaz von (1799–1890) Historian and Sect Founder. Döllinger was born in Bavaria. He was ordained to the Roman Catholic priesthood in 1822 and he taught Church history at the Universities of Aschaffenburg and Munich. A friend of NEWMAN, Gladstone and LAMENNAIS, his early ultramontane opinions were gradually eroded. He was the author of many books, including *Reformation* (3 volumes) and *Christientum und Kirche*. He disapproved of the papal decree of the Immaculate Conception of the Blessed Virgin MARY and he attacked the notion of papal infallibility in newspaper articles. These were later published as *The Pope and the Council*. He was excommunicated from the Roman Catholic Church for his refusal to accept the decree of the First Vatican Council and subsequently he was one of the founders of the Old Catholic Church. He also took part in discussions with members of the Church of England and the Orthodox Church and must be seen as an early ecumenist. In the end, however, he rejected some of the innovations of the Old Catholics and he seems to have died isolated from any branch of the Church.

Lord Acton, 'Döllinger's historical work', *English Historical Review*, v (1890); E.W. Kemp, 'The Church of England and the Old Catholic Churches', in E.G.W. Bill (ed.), *Anglican Initiatives in Christian Unity* (1967).

Dominic (1170–1221) Saint and Order Founder. Dominic was born in Calaruega, Spain, and was educated at the University of Palencia. In 1199 he was appointed a Canon of Osma and in 1203 he served as Bishop's chaplain on a royal embassy to the south of France. There he first began to preach against the Albigensian heresy. Then, in 1206, Dominic opened his first convent for young women in Prouille. He participated in Pope INNOCENT III's crusade against the Albigensians and in 1215 he proposed a new order of preaching friars at the Fourth Lateran Council. This was refused, but the new order was licensed by Pope HONORIUS III in 1216. The order was to live by voluntary alms; it would follow the Augustinian Rule and it would be dedicated to preaching and study. Known as the Black Friars, the Dominicans spread rapidly throughout Europe; they were leaders in the sending of missionaries to the New World; they established several universities and they took an important part in the Inquisition. Dominic himself spent the rest of his life organising the new order in Italy, France and Spain. He was canonised only thirteen years after his death.

F.C. Lehner (ed.), *St Dominic, Biographical Documents* (1964); W.A. Hinnebusch, *The History of the Dominican Order* (1966); M.H. Vicaire, *St Dominic and his Times*, 2 vols (1964).

Donatus (fourth century) Bishop and Heretic. The Donatist schism takes its name from Bishop Donatus, the successor of Bishop Majorinus, who was consecrated to replace Caecilian. The Donatists insisted that Caecilian's consecration had been invalid because one of his consecrators, Felix of Apthungi, had handed over the Scriptures when their possession had been forbidden in the Great Persecution of Diocletian. The dispute split the African Church. Theologically, the Donatists maintained that Sacraments were invalid if they were conferred by unworthy ministers. In contrast, St AUGUSTINE insisted that the Sacrament was unaffected by the merits or vices of the minister because the true minister was JESUS CHRIST. The Donatists maintained that they were the one true Church and, to the fury of the orthodox, they rebaptised all new converts from the Catholic Church. Although Donatism was condemned at the Synod of Arles of 314 and by the Emperor in 316, 347 and 411, the group persisted until the African Church was destroyed by the Arabs in the sixth or seventh century.

W.H.C. Frend, *The Donatist Church* (1952); G.G. Willis, *St Augustine and the Donatist Controversy* (1950).

Donne, John (*c.* 1573–1631)   Poet. Although Donne was born into a Roman Catholic family (he was a great-great-nephew of Sir Thomas MORE), he became an Anglican and was educated at the Universities of Oxford and Cambridge and at Lincoln's Inn. He served in the household of Lord Egerton, then Lord Chancellor of England, but was dismissed in disgrace after secretly marrying Egerton's niece. In 1615 he was ordained and in 1621 he was appointed Dean of St Paul's Cathedral, London. Although he was one of the most famous preachers of his day, he is now remembered as a poet. He was the author of both secular and religious verse and he is one of a group known as the metaphysical poets. His poems are marked by

extraordinary imagery and his religious verse shows a preoccupation with sin, death and judgement. T.S. ELIOT led a revival of interest in his work in this century.

John Donne, *Complete Poetry and Selected Prose*, edited by J. Hayward (1929); R.C. Bald, *John Donne: A Life* (1970).

Dorothea (? fourth century)   Legendary Saint. Dorothea is thought to have been martyred in the fourth century. It is said that on her way to execution, a young lawyer mocked her and demanded that she send him a gift of fruit and flowers from the Garden of Paradise. After her death an angel appeared and presented him with three heavenly roses and three heavenly apples. The legend has inspired many artists and writers throughout the centuries.

D.H. Farmer (ed.), *The Oxford Dictionary of Saints*, 3rd edn (1992).

Dorotheus of Gaza (sixth century)   Saint and Order Founder. Dorotheus founded a monastery near Gaza in the Holy Land. He was the author of a series of instructions on the monastic life which advocated humility and asceticism. They were based on the work of earlier writers and were highly influential. Armand-Jean DE RANCÉ, for example, made use of them in his Rule for the Trappist order.

Dorotheus, *Oeuvres Spirituelles*, edited by L. Regnault and J. de Préville, French translation (1963); E. Wheeler (ed. and trans), *Dorotheus of Gaza: Discourses and Sayings* (1977).

Dositheus (1641–1707)   Patriarch and Theologian. Dositheus was born in the Peloponnese and, as an orphan, was placed in a monastery at the age of eight. He was educated in Athens and in 1657 he entered the service of the Patriarch of Jerusalem. In 1661 he was appointed Archdeacon of Jerusalem; he was consecrated Archbishop of Caesarea in 1666 and he became Patriarch of Jerusalem in 1669. He is remembered for his dedicated opposition to Western theology. He presided over the Synod of Jerusalem in 1672 which produced a series of decrees designed to remove all Protestant influence from the Greek Church. He tried to limit the access of the Western religious orders to the Holy Places of Palestine and in 1680 he set up a printing press at Jassy to print books of traditional Greek theology. He set himself to reform the monasteries and the administration of the Greek Church and he sought to extend its influence into the Russian Orthodox Church. A man of tremendous erudition, he was the author of the *History of the Patriarchs of Jerusalem*, published after his death.

F.L. Cross (ed.), *The Oxford Dictionary of the Christian Church*, 2nd edn (1974).

Dostoievsky, Fyodor (1821–81) Novelist. Dostoievsky was born in Moscow. As a young man he became involved in the activities of a left-wing group and was sentenced to death by the authorities. At the very last moment, he was reprieved and was sent instead into exile in Siberia for ten years. He is remembered for his novels (in their English translations), *The House of the Dead*, *Notes from Underground*, *Crime and Punishment*, *The Idiot*, *The Possessed* and *The Brothers Karamazov*. In his books, Dostoievsky understands salvation as a free gift from God, but God himself cannot be found by human reason or determination. In this, together with the Danish philosopher Søren KIERKEGAARD, he is seen as a prophet both of the dialectical theology espoused by Karl BARTH and of modern existentialism.

Fyodor Dostoievsky, *Complete Letters*, edited and translated by D.A. Lowe and R. Meyer (1987); K. Mochulsky, *Dostoievsky: His Life and Work*, translated by M.A. Minchan (1967); V.V. Rosanov, *Dostoievsky and the Legend of the Grand Inquisitor*, translated by S.E. Roberts (1972); A. Vgrinsky, *Dostoievsky and the Human Condition after a Century* (1986).

Duns Scotus, Johannes (*c.* 1265–1308) Philosopher. Duns Scotus was born in Scotland and as a young man joined the Franciscan Order. During the course of his life, he lectured in philosophy at the Universities of Cambridge, Oxford, Paris and Cologne. He is remembered for his commentary on the 'Sentences' of PETER LOMBARD, a *Tractatus de Primo Principio* and various other works on logic. Unlike THOMAS AQUINAS, he believed that faith could not be compelled by logical proofs, but was a matter of will. He was the first to defend the doctrine of the Immaculate Conception and he maintained that faith, and not reason, was the cause of believing many of the Church's teachings. Thus he acknowledged a distinction between the sphere of philosophy and that of belief. His system has been the basis of all subsequent Franciscan theology.

E. Bettoni, *Duns Scotus* (1961); J.K. Ryan and B.M. Bonansea (eds), *John Duns Scotus 1265–1965* (1965).

Dunstan (*c.* 909–88) Saint and Archbishop. A nephew of Athelm, Archbishop of Canterbury, Dunstan was born in Somerset. After he was ordained as a priest, he became a hermit and then in 939 he was installed as Abbot of Glastonbury. There he reformed the monastery and successfully established the Rule of St BENEDICT in England. In 957 he became Bishop of Worcester, was consecrated Bishop of London, and in 960 he was installed as Archbishop of Canterbury. Working with King Edgar, Dunstan brought about many improvements within the English Church, mainly through the reform of the monastic houses. In particular, he probably inspired the Regularis Concordia, the code of monastic observance drawn up in *c.* 970 by St ETHELWOLD. He established new foundations at Peterborough, Ely and Thorney and he organised a system of tithes which ensured their financial security. In later centuries, Dunstan's archiepiscopate was regarded as a golden age within the English Church.

W. Stubbs (ed.), *Memorials of St Dunstan, Archbishop of Canterbury* (1874); E.S. Duckett, *Saint Dunstan of Canterbury* (1955).

Du Plessis-Mornay, Philippe (1549–1623) Politician. Du Plessis-Mornay was born of a noble family in Normandy, and was educated in Paris. As a Protestant, he fled from France after the St Bartholomew's Day massacre in 1572. During this period he lived for a time in London, where he published one treatise on the Church and another on the Christian religion. He became a leader of the Huguenot party and acted as a diplomatic agent for the Protestant Henry of Navarre. In 1589, he was appointed Governor of Saumur, where he built a new Protestant university. When Henry of Navarre succeeded to the throne of France as King HENRY IV, he converted to Roman Catholicism. Du Plessis-Mornay did not follow his example; he continued to work for the toleration of Protestants, and the Edict of Nantes was signed in 1598. The same year his treatise on the Eucharist was published. This was challenged by the Roman Catholic Bishop of Evreux in a public debate before the King, and du Plessis-Mornay was humiliatingly defeated. Subsequently he published his *Mysterium Iniquitatis sive Historia Papatus*. His later career illustrates the gradual eclipse of the Protestant party in France after 1600. In 1621 he was compelled to retire from Saumur. The terms of the Edict of Nantes were frequently infringed throughout the seventeenth century and it was finally revoked in 1685.

R. Patry, *Philippe du Plessis-Mornay: un Huguenot Homme d'Etat* (1933) [no English translation available]; W.J. Stankiewicz, *Politics and Religion in Seventeenth-Century France* (1960).

Durandus (c. 1275–1334) Bishop and Philosopher. Durandus of Saint-Pourcain was a member of the Dominican Order

and taught at the University of Paris. After a time as Lector at the papal court in Avignon, he became Bishop of Limoux in 1317, Bishop of Le Puy-en-Velay in 1318 and Bishop of Meaux in 1326. His teachings can be found in his commentary on the 'Sentences' of PETER LOMBARD, in his *De Paupertate Christi et Apostolorum*, in his *De Origine Potestatum et Jurisdictionum* and in his *De Visione Dei*. Durandus was a nominalist. He believed that universals can only be derived from instances and that understanding is a psychological, not a metaphysical, phenomenon. Despite the greater prestige of THOMAS AQUINAS, Durandus' ideas were much studied in the Middle Ages.

P. Fournier, 'Durand de Saint-Pourcain, Theologien', *Histoire Littéraire de la France*, xxxvii (1938) [no English translation available]; J. Koch, *Durandus de S. Porciano* (1927) [no English translation available].

Dürer, Albrecht (1471–1528) Artist. Dürer was born in Nuremburg, Germany where his father was a goldsmith. After extensive travel, he settled in Nuremberg and in the latter part of his life he worked for the Emperor Maximilian I. Dürer is remembered for his wood-cuts and engravings, some of which were used to illustrate the Bible. In particular his series of scenes from the *Apocalypse* (1497/8), *The Fall of Man* (1504) and *Melancholia* (1514) are widely known. Dürer remained a Roman Catholic, but he was a friend of Desiderius ERASMUS and Philip MELANCHTHON and after his death was much praised by Martin LUTHER.

Albrecht Dürer, *Works*, edited by C. Dodgson, G. Pauli and S.M. Peartree, 12 vols (1898–1911); C. White, *Dürer* (1971).

Durkheim, Emile (1858–1917) Philosopher. Durkheim was born in Epinal, Lorraine, of a Jewish family and was educated as a sociologist in Paris. Subsequently he taught at the Universities of

Bordeaux and Paris. In the history of Christianity, he is primarily remembered for his classic *The Elementary Forms of the Religious Life* published in 1912. In this he argued that religious ritual symbolises the social bonds within a group and he taught that divine authority is in fact a sublimation of the demands of society. Durkheim was one of several important twentieth-century figures who understood religion in terms of another discipline, rather than as revealing truths about a metaphysical world.

H. Alpert, *Emile Durkheim and his Sociology* (1939).

E

Eadmer (*c.* 1060–*c.* 1128) Historian. Eadmer was a member of the Benedictine monastery of Christchurch, Canterbury. He became ANSELM's secretary when Anselm was Archbishop of Canterbury and later wrote his biography. His writings give an interesting picture of the ecclesiastical disputes of the eleventh and twelfth centuries. He also wrote biographies of St WILFRID and St DUNSTAN.

R.W. Southern, *St Anselm and his Biographer* (1963).

Eck, Johann (1486–1543) Theologian and Economist. Eck was born Johann Mayr in the town of Eck in Swabia. He was educated at the Universities of Heidelberg, Tübingen and Freiberg and subsequently taught at Ingolstadt. He remained a loyal Roman Catholic and is chiefly remembered for his determined opposition to Martin LUTHER in the Leipzig debate of 1519. He also seems to have been largely responsible for securing the Reformer's excommunication. He was the author of *De Primatu Petri adversus Ludderum* (a defence of the Papacy), the *Enchiridion Locorum Communium adversus Lutherum et Alias Hostes Ecclesiae* (a treatise against the Protestant Reformers) and the confutation of the Augsburg Confession. The *Enchiridion* went through forty-six printings in fifty years. He also translated the Bible into German and defended the lending of money at up to five per cent interest. Usury had been forbidden by the Church in the Middle Ages and this liberalism towards the taking of interest made the development of modern capitalism possible.

Catholic University of America, *New Catholic Encyclopaedia* (1967).

Eckhart (*c.* 1260–1327) Mystic. Known as Meister Eckhart, he was born in Hockheim, Germany. After joining the Dominican Order, he became Prior of Erfurt and Vicar of Thuringia. In 1304 he was appointed Provincial of Saxony and in 1307 Vicar-General of Bohemia. He then taught in Paris and later lived in Strasbourg and Cologne. In 1326 he was tried and convicted of heresy before the Archbishop of Cologne. He appealed to the Pope, but died before the final judgement. In fact, JOHN XXII condemned twenty-eight of his sentences. He is remembered for his mystical writings, but because of the taint of heresy not all of his works have survived. He was influenced both by neo-Platonism and by Thomism and, in his turn, he was influential on the Romantic poets and the philosophers of the nineteenth century.

O. Davies, *Meister Eckhart: Mystical Theologian* (1991); R. Schurmann, *Meister Eckhart: Mystic and Philosopher* (1978).

Eddy, Mary Baker (1821–1910) Sect Founder. Eddy was born near Concord, New Hampshire, and she was brought up a Congregationalist. From early childhood she suffered from convulsive fits, but she was cured in 1862 after visiting a hypnotist. She was so overwhelmed by this experience that she wrote her famous volume *Science and Health*, which she claimed was dictated under divine inspiration. (She subsequently had the Almighty's grammar corrected by a local clergyman.) Her fundamental belief was that God is in everything and that there is no reality outside God's spirit. Evil, sin and death are unrealities which can and should be ignored. She married Asa Gilbert Eddy as her third husband in 1877 through whom she inherited considerable wealth. She is remembered as the founder of an international movement, Christian Science, based on *Science and Health*. She also was the author of *Unity of God and Unreality of Evil* and *Retrospection and Introspection*. Christian Science has spread throughout the world and is particularly successful in English-speaking countries.

A.F. Conant, *A Complete Concordance to Science and Health* (1916); M. Gardner, *The Healing Revelations of Mary Baker Eddy: The Rise and Fall of Christian Science* (1993); I.P. Powell, *Mary Baker Eddy* (1930).

Edward VI (1537–53) Monarch. Edward VI was the son of King HENRY VIII of England by his third wife, Jane Seymour. A sickly, scholarly boy, he succeeded to the throne at the age of ten. During his reign, the country was ruled by the Privy Council, led first by the King's uncle the Duke of Somerset, and then by the Duke of Northumberland. Between 1547 and 1553 many Protestant innovations were introduced into the Church, including the repeal of most heresy legislation and two Prayer Books of 1549 and 1552. On his deathbed, Edward was persuaded to nominate a Protestant successor, his cousin Lady Jane Grey, but his half-sister, the Roman Catholic MARY I, took the throne after only a few days.

W.K. Jordan, *Edward VI: The Young King* (1968); W.K. Jordan, *Edward VI: The Threshold of Power* (1970).

Edwards, Jonathan (1703–58) Theologian. Edwards was educated at the University of Yale where he underwent a religious conversion. He was ordained to the Congregational ministry and in 1724 he became the pastor of the Congregational Church of Northampton, Massachusetts. A devout Calvinist, he was an exceptionally powerful preacher and was a leader of the religious revival known as the 'Great Awakening'. He later became a close friend of George WHITEFIELD who led an even more extensive revival in the 1740s. Edwards described the Great Awakening in his *Faithful Narrative of the Surprising Works of God* published in 1737. As a result of various controversies within his church, he moved to Stockbridge on the frontier where he wrote dissertations on original sin, true virtue and free will. In this last, he defended CALVIN's doctrine of election and, influenced by LOCKE, he argued that the notion of freedom was 'unphilosophical, contradictory and absurd'. His commitment and dedication were undisputed and his influence has been widespread in the Churches of America. His teachings were continued by a group of disciples who evolved a 'New England Theology' which dominated Congregational schools in the nineteenth century.

E.H. Davidson, *Jonathan Edwards: The Narrative of a Puritan Mind* (1968); P.J. Tracy, *Jonathan Edwards Pastor: Religion and Society in 18th-Century Northampton* (1980); L.W. Jenson, *American Theologian* (1988).

El Greco (1541–1614) Artist. El Greco was born Domenico Theotocopoli in Crete. He is thought to have been a pupil of TITIAN in Venice. By 1577 he had moved to Spain where he lived for the rest of his life. Almost all his paintings are of religious subjects and his works include *The Disrobing of Christ* for the Church of Santo Domingo, Toledo, and the altar pieces for the Hospital of San Juan Bautista, near Toledo. His pictures are highly distinctive with dark backgrounds, austere, elongated figures and an extraordinary atmosphere of intense piety.

L. Bronstein, *The Paintings of El Greco* (1967); H.E. Wethey, *El Greco and his School*, 2 vols (1962).

Elias, John (1774–1841) Preacher and Devotional Writer. Elias was educated in Caernarvon, Wales, and was ordained to the Calvinist Methodist ministry in 1811. He was the most famous preacher of his day and the leader of his Church. He was known as the 'Anglesey Pope' for his unyielding opposition to liberalism and for his autocratic temperament. His published sermons give no hint of the extraordinary power of his voice and its devastating effect on his listeners. His eloquence and dedication are still remembered in Wales today.

John Elias, *Letters and Essays* (1847); E. Morgan, *Memoir of John Elias* (1844).

Eliot, John (1604–90) Missionary. Eliot was educated at the University of Cambridge and was ordained to the Anglican ministry in 1622. In 1631 he emigrated to America and became attached to the church at Roxbury. He taught himself various Indian dialects and organised self-governing groups of Christian Indians. He also set up a school for the education of both Indians and Negroes. He founded the first Indian church in Natick in 1660 and he was successful in raising money for all his causes. Although his mission was set back by local skirmishes, Eliot's faith never wavered. His *Bay Psalm Book*, a metrical version of the Psalms, was the first book to be published in New England. He also made translations into the Indian dialects. His translation of the Bible was printed in 1661 and he published an Indian grammar in 1666. In 1659 he produced a book on government, *The Christian Commonwealth*, which was suppressed for its republican sympathies, but his learning and charitable work were much admired by his contemporaries, including the young Cotton MATHER.

C. Mather, *Magnalia Christi Americana*, 2 vols (1820); W. Walker, *Ten New England Leaders* (1901).

Eliot, Thomas Stearns (1888–1965) Poet. Eliot was born in St Louis, Missouri, and was educated at the Universities of Harvard, Oxford and the Sorbonne. After settling in England, he worked in a bank, edited the literary magazine *The Criterion*, and in 1925 he joined the board of the publishers Faber and Faber. Although he was agnostic as a young man (and this is reflected in his *Lovesong of Alfred J. Prufrock* (1917) and *The Wasteland* (1922)), he later converted to Anglo-Catholicism. Subsequently his work was strongly informed by his Christianity and his *Ash Wednesday* (1930), *Murder in the Cathedral* (1935) and *Four Quartets* (1944) are full of allusions to the works of St JOHN OF THE CROSS, DANTE and the metaphysical poets. Besides poetry and plays, he also wrote several works of criticism. In his *Idea of a Christian Society* (1939) and his *Notes Towards the Definition of Culture* (1948), he further expounded his religious and political beliefs which he had earlier defined as being those of a 'classicist in literature, royalist in politics and Anglo-Catholic in religion'. Eliot is regarded as a leader in the Modernist movement and one of the greatest poets of the twentieth century.

T.S. Eliot, *The Complete Poems and Plays* (1969); V. Eliot (ed.), *The Letters of T.S. Eliot* (1988); T.S. Eliot, *Selected Prose*, edited by F. Kermode (1975); G. Williamson, *A Reader's Guide to T.S. Eliot*, 2nd edn (1967).

Elizabeth I (1533–1603) Monarch. Elizabeth was the daughter of King HENRY VIII of England by his second wife, Anne Boleyn. During the reign of her elder half-sister, MARY I, she conformed to the prevailing Catholicism, although for a period she was imprisoned in the Tower of London. She succeeded to the throne in 1559. The Roman Catholic Bishops refused to take the Oath of Allegiance and she was eventually crowned by the Bishop of Carlisle. In religion she tried to steer a middle course between the old Catholicism and the new Protestantism and she insisted that she disliked making 'windows into men's souls'. Rejecting her father's title of Supreme Head of the Church, she chose to be described as Supreme Governor. She reissued the 1552 Prayer Book with some conciliatory amendments and she appointed the moderate Matthew PARKER to be her Archbishop of Canterbury. Gradually, uniformity was established and the first text of the Thirty-Nine Articles defining the Anglican faith was issued in 1563. In 1570 she was excommunicated by Pope PIUS V. This effectively led to the greater harassment of Catholics, but, after the execution of her cousin Mary Queen of Scots and the defeat of King PHILIP II of Spain's Armada, the Catholic threat subsided. By the time of Elizabeth's death in 1603, England was largely united and was the leading Protestant power in Europe.

G.B. Harrison (ed.), *The Letters of Queen Elizabeth* (1935); C. Cross, *The Royal Supremacy in the Elizabethan Church* (1969); W.P. Haugaard, *Elizabeth and the English Reformation* (1968); J.E. Neale, *Queen Elizabeth I* (1934).

Elizabeth of Hungary (1207–31) Saint and Monarch. Elizabeth was the daughter of King Andrew of Hungary and she was married, at the age of fourteen, to King Ludwig IV of Thuringia. Her husband died in 1227 and she moved to Marburg where she became a member of the Franciscan Tertiary Order. Under the spiritual direction of Conrad of Marburg, she led a life of extraordinary asceticism, dedicating herself to the care of the sick and the poor. After her death, the Elizabethskirche, Germany's first Gothic cathedral, was built at Marburg to house her relics. She was canonised in 1235.

J. Ancelet-Hustache, *The Life of St Elizabeth of Hungary* (1963).

Elizabeth of the Trinity (1880–1906) Mystic. Elizabeth of the Trinity was born Elizabeth Catez in Farges-en-Seine, France. At the age of fourteen she took a vow of perpetual virginity and she was received into a Carmelite monastery in 1901. She was much influenced by the writings of TERESA OF AVILA, TERESA OF LISIEUX and JOHN OF THE CROSS. Her mystical experiences centred on the mystery of the indwelling Trinity, which she described in a famous prayer: 'O my Three, my all, my beatitude, infinite solitude, immensity, in which I lose myself, I surrender to you.'

H.U. von Balthasar, *Elizabeth of Dijon: An Interpretation of her Spiritual Mission* (1956).

Elkesai (late first century) Theologian and Sect Founder. Elkesai was the author of the *Book of Elkesai*. He seems to have been a Jewish Christian who stressed the importance of the Law and claimed to have had a special revelation from an angel, whom he identified with the Son of God, and a female spirit whom he recognised as the Holy Spirit. A vegetarian and strongly ascetic, he rejected the theology of St PAUL and he seems to have taught that although JESUS was higher than the archangels, he was not divine. This teaching seems to have spread as far as Rome and Alexandria; we know of it from fragments preserved in the works of HIPPOLYTUS and EPIPHANIUS.

J. Daniélou, *The Theology of Jewish Christianity* (1964).

Ellul, Jacques (b. 1912) Theologian. Ellul was born in Bordeaux, France. His father was a member of the Greek Orthodox Church while his mother was a Protestant. Trained as a lawyer, he taught at the University of Strasbourg until he was removed by the Vichy government. During the Second World War he was involved in the Resistance movement and after the war he accepted a position at the University of Bordeaux teaching law and sociology. A member of the French Reformed Church, he broke with the World Council of Churches over their attitude to Third World revolutionary movements. Ellul has written several important and influential books on the Church, technology and social change. Those translated into English include *The Technological Society* (1954), *Propaganda* (1965), *The Meaning of the City* (1970) and *The Ethics of Freedom* (1976).

C.G. Christians and J.M. Hook, *Jacques Ellul: Interpretation Essays* (1981).

Elmo (*c.* 1190–1246) Saint and Missionary. Elmo was born Peter González in Castile, Spain. A nephew of the Bishop of Astorga, he rejected worldly preferment and joined the Dominican Order. He served as chaplain to King Ferdinand III in his crusade against the Moors, but subsequently concentrated on preaching the gospel to the poor sailors of Spain and Portugal. He became their patron saint and when an electrical flash is seen on board ship, it is frequently described as 'St Elmo's fire'.

D.H. Farmer (ed.), *The Oxford Dictionary of Saints*, 3rd edn (1992).

Emerson, Ralph Waldo (1803–82) Philosopher and Sect Founder. Emerson was educated at Harvard University in the United States of America. Ordained into the Congregationalist ministry, he served for a time as a pastor in Boston. In 1832 he resigned his position and became a leading voice in the Transcendentalist movement. The Transcendentalists went beyond Unitarianism and, influenced by the mysticism of Samuel Taylor COLERIDGE, saw God as immanent in nature. Emerson's address to the Harvard Divinity School delivered in 1838 clarified the distinction between the two groups; in particular he advocated 'faith like Christ's' rather than 'faith in Christ'.

Today he is mainly remembered for his essays on a wide variety of subjects.

W.R. Hutchison, *The Transcendentalist Ministers: Church Reform in the New England Renaissance* (1959); R.L. Rusk, *Life of Ralph Waldo Emerson* (1957); D. Vanella, *Ralph Waldo Emerson* (1982).

Emmerick, Anna Katharina (1774–1824) Mystic. Emmerick was born in Westphalia. She joined an Augustinian convent when she was eighteen and her religious life was conspicuously intense. In 1812, while she was suffering from a serious illness, she received the stigmata. Her visions were taken down and published in three separate collections.

J.H. Crehan (ed.), *Surprising Mystics* (1955).

Ephraem Syrus (*c.* 306–73) Saint, Poet and Devotional Writer. Ephraem was born in Nisibis, Syria, and was ordained as a deacon. He is thought to have saved Nisibis from a Persian invasion, but, after 363, he moved to Edessa in the Roman Empire, which was a centre of Syriac Christianity. He was renowned for his ascetic life and, according to legend, he visited Egypt to argue with the Arians and went to Caesarea where he met St BASIL. He is remembered for his devotional writings, which included hymns, treatises against heretics, devotional manuals and biblical exegeses. In the Syriac Church, his hymns were very popular and he was known as the 'lyre of the Holy Spirit'.

A. Vööbus, *Literary, Critical and Historical Studies in Ephraem the Syrian* (1958); S. Brock, *The Harp of the Spirit* (1983).

Epiphanius (*c.* 315–403) Bishop, Saint and Theologian. Epiphanius was elected Bishop of Salamis in 367. He is remembered for his dogmatic insistence that there was no place in the Church for Greek learning or theological speculation. This contrasted sharply with the views of his contemporaries Basil of Caesarea, GREGORY OF NYSSA and

GREGORY OF NAZIANZUS. He was the author of the *Ancoratus* (a compendium of Church doctrine), an encyclopaedia of the Bible and the *Panarion* (a fulmination against various heresies). This last is particularly valuable since it contains extracts from the works of many authors which would have otherwise been lost.

P.R. Amidon (ed. and trans.), *The Panarion of St Epiphanius of Salamis: Selected Passages* (1990).

Erasmus, Desiderius (*c.* 1469–1536) Theologian. Erasmus was the illegitimate son of the Dutch priest Rogerius Gerardus. In 1486 he joined an order of Augustinian Canons at Steyn, near Gouda, and in 1492 he was ordained as a priest. He became secretary to the Bishop of Cambrai and left his monastery. He studied in Paris and then travelled to England with his pupil, Lord Mountjoy, who was to become his patron. In England he mixed with the leading scholars of the day and, after further travels in France and a second visit to England, he settled for a time in Italy. Then, in 1509, encouraged by Mountjoy, he returned to England where he stayed with Sir Thomas MORE and may have succeeded John FISHER to the Lady Margaret Chair of Divinity. In 1516 he returned to Europe where he became a councillor of the Emperor CHARLES V, but he eventually settled in Basle. He was a prolific writer. His *Praise of Folly* and *Colloquies*, satirising the abuses of the Roman Catholic Church, went through many editions. He was also responsible for splendid texts of the works of the early Church Fathers and a Greek New Testament based on early manuscripts. He entered into controversy with Martin LUTHER on the question of free will and his *Enchiridion Militis Christiani* was a defence of scholarship in Christian education. He was the most famous scholar of his day, but has been judged variously by historians. He never left the Catholic Church and this has been interpreted by some as weakness; others view him as a forerunner of the enlightened scholars of the eighteenth century. In any event his profound intelligence is revealed not only in his writings, but in the famous portrait by Holbein. He himself believed that scholarly investigation would uncover the truth of Christianity and he once declared 'I would to God that the ploughman would sing texts of the Scripture at his plough and that the weaver would hum them to the tune of his shuttle'.

A.G. Dickens, *Erasmus the Reformer* (1994), M. M. Phillips, *Erasmus and the Northern Renaissance*, revised edition (1981); R.J. Schoeck, *Erasmus of Europe: The Prince of Humanists* (1993).

Erastus, Thomas (1524–83) Theologian. Erastus was born in Baden, Switzerland. He studied medicine and was appointed to the Chair of Medicine in Heidelberg in 1558. He is remembered for his *Explicatio Gravissimae Quaestionis* in which he argued that the civil authorities should exercise authority in all matters including the religious. This position came to be known as Erastianism and was elaborated by thinkers such as Richard HOOKER and Thomas HOBBES. The modern Church of England is an example of an Erastian Church – all legislation appertaining to it has to be passed by Parliament.

J.N. Figgis, 'Erastus and Erastianism', *Journal of Theological Studies*, ii (1901).

Erigena, John Scotus (*c.* 810–*c.* 77) Theologian. Erigena was born in Ireland, and, under the patronage of Charles the Bald of France, he participated in the European doctrinal debates of the time. He is remembered for his translations of the works of Pseudo-DIONYSIUS, MAXIMUS THE CONFESSOR and GREGORY OF NYSSA. His own theology, as expressed in *De Divisione Naturae*, was an attempt to reconcile the Christian with the neo-Platonic view. In this work, although he denied that the created world was identical with God, he maintained that God was the only true reality. In his lifetime he was regarded as an important thinker, but his work was condemned in the thirteenth century by Pope HONORIUS III.

J.J. O'Meara, *Erigena* (1988).

Erskine, Ebenezer (1680–1754) Denomination Founder. Erskine was born into a Scottish non-conforming family and he was educated at the University of Edinburgh. After ordination into the Presbyterian ministry, he served a congregation in Portmoak until 1731. After moving to Stirling, he preached against the system of clerical patronage and, together with three supporters, was suspended by the General Assembly. They left the Church and founded the Secession Church of the Church of Scotland. This grew rapidly, but it later split over the issue of the burghers' oath (whether it was lawful for newly elected burghers to take an oath). Erskine sided with the burgher majority, but both groups split several times more after Erskine's death. The Secession Church rejoined the Church of Scotland in 1956.

R.S. Wright (ed.), *Fathers of the Kirk* (1960).

Erskine, Thomas (1788–1870) Theologian. Erskine was born in Linlathen, Scotland and was educated at the University of Edinburgh. A gentleman of private means, he entertained many of the leading thinkers of his day and was a personal friend of Thomas CARLYLE, Benjamin JOWETT, Charles KINGSLEY and Dean STANLEY. His books included *The Internal Evidence for the Truth of the Christian Religion, The Unconditional Freeness of the Gospel* and *The Brazen Serpent*. His letters were collected and published after his death and are considered to be minor religious classics.

H.F. Henderson, *Erskine of Linlathen* (1899).

Ethelbert (d. 616) Saint and Monarch. Ethelbert succeeded to the Kingdom of Kent in 560 and was married to BERTHA, a Christian princess from France. He is remembered for encouraging St AUGUSTINE OF CANTERBURY's mission to England in 597. Thus Ethelbert was the first Christian Anglo-Saxon King.

Bede, *Historia Ecclesiastica* [many translations and editions]; M. Deanesly, *Augustine of Canterbury* (1964).

Ethelwold (*c*. 908–84) Saint and Bishop. Ethelwold was a monk at Glastonbury. He was elected Abbot of Abingdon and from 963 he was Bishop of Winchester. He is remembered for his connection with St DUNSTAN and St OSWALD and he was largely responsible for the monastic reform of the tenth century. He is thought to have been the author of the *Regularis Concordia*, which was approved at the Synod of Winchester. Its provisions follow the Rule of St BENEDICT and were influenced by the reforms of Cluny and by the customs of the monastic houses of Ghent and Fleury.

E.S. Duckett, *St Dunstan of Canterbury: A Study of Monastic Reform in the Tenth Century* (1955); J.A. Robinson, *The Life and Times of St Dunstan* (1923).

Eugenius III (d. 1153) Pope. Eugenius was born Bernardo Pignatelli in Pisa, Italy. He joined the Cistercian community of Clairvaux and subsequently became Abbot of a house in Rome. He was elected Pope in 1145 and BERNARD OF CLAIRVAUX's ascetical treatise, *De Consideratione*, was dedicated to him. He supported the Second Crusade and was greatly involved in the European politics of his day. He negotiated the treaty of Constance with the Emperor FREDERICK BARBAROSSA; he supported Archbishop THEOBALD in England and he sent the future Pope HADRIAN IV as a legate to Scandinavia. He summoned the Council of Rheims in 1148 which heard the defence of GILBERT DE LA PORRÉE against the charge of heresy and examined the visions of HILDEGARD OF BINGEN. Eugenius also issued Canons to strengthen the decrees of the Lateran Council of 1139 which ensured the excommunication of ARNOLD OF BRESCIA.

J.N.D. Kelly (ed.), *The Oxford Dictionary of Popes* (1986).

Eugenius IV (1383–1447)   Pope. Eugenius was born Gabriele Condulmaro in Venice, Italy. He was the nephew of Pope Gregory XII, who brought him to Rome. He was appointed a Cardinal in 1408 and was elected Pope in 1431. He attempted to dismiss the Council of Basle which was setting a limit on papal power. However, the Council refused to be dismissed and eventually Eugenius was compelled to accept its principles of conciliarism. As a result of a rebellion in Rome, he was forced to flee to Florence, whereupon the Council set up an antipope, Felix V, the Duke of Savoy. However, Eugenius reasserted his authority and succeeded in effecting a temporary union between the Churches of East and West; he also excommunicated the Bishops at the Council. He encouraged a crusade against the Turks which ended in a Christian defeat at Varna. Eugenius is primarily remembered for his dealings with the Council of Basle and for his attempts to achieve reunion with the Greek Church. The principle that was established for union, diversity of rite coupled with unity of faith, remains accepted to this day.

J. Gill, *Eugenius IV: Pope of Christian Union* (1961).

Eunomius (d. 394)   Bishop and Heretic. Eunomius was born in Cappadocia. He became an extreme Arian and was forced to resign as Bishop of Cyzicus. Nevertheless, despite banishment, he continued to expound his view that the Son of God was created, rather than begotten of the Father, and that he was not of the same substance. Similarly, he maintained that the Holy Spirit was created by the Son to sanctify humanity. He was the author of

the *Apology* which elicited a response from St BASIL the Great and his teachings were also refuted by GREGORY OF NYSSA in *Contra Eunomium*. Eunomius was banished to Dakora and he died in exile.

R.P.C. Hanson, *The Search for the Christian Doctrine of God: The Arian Controversy 318–381* (1988); M.R. Barnes and D. Williams (eds), *Arianism after Arius* (1993).

Eusebius of Caesarea (c. 260–c. 340) Bishop and Historian. Eusebius was a pupil of Pamphilus who kept a theological school in Caesarea and was himself a pupil of ORIGEN. After a period of wandering, he became Bishop of Caesarea in c. 315 and attended the Council of Nicaea in 325. Initially Eusebius had been a moderate supporter of ARIUS, but by the time of the council he had rejected his doctrines. None the less he never fully supported the stance of ATHANASIUS. He was present at the Council of Tyre in 331 and acted as advisor to the Emperor CONSTANTINE on ecclesiastical affairs. Although he declined the Patriarchate of Antioch, he presided over the Council of Caesarea. He is mainly remembered, however, for his ecclesiastical history, which is the main source of our knowledge of the first three centuries of the Church and which is largely based on earlier documents. In addition he wrote a life of Constantine, a history of the martyrs of Palestine, a chronicle of world history, various apologetic treatises and a book on biblical topography. He has been called the 'Father of Church History'.

Eusebius, *The History of the Church from Christ to Constantine*, edited and translated by G.A. Williamson (1965); R.M. Grant, *Eusebius as Church Historian* (1980); C. Luibheid, *Eusebius of Caesarea and the Arian Crisis* (1981).

Eusebius of Nicomedia (d. c. 342)   Patriarch and Heretic. Eusebius was a fellow student of ARIUS at the school of LUCIAN in Antioch. After a time as Bishop of Berytus, he was consecrated Bishop of

Nicomedia and subsequently became Patriarch of Constantinople. He officiated at the baptism of the Emperor CONSTANTINE and was equally influential with the Emperor Constantius. Because of his connections, he was able to secure the deposition and exile of ATHANASIUS in 336 and again in 339. Although he put his name to the Creed of the Council of Nicaea in 325, his lack of sympathy with Nicaean views was well known.

A. Lichtenstein, *Eusebius von Nikomedien* (1903) [no English translation available]; R. Williams, *Arius: Heresy and Tradition* (1987).

Eustace (?)   Legendary Saint and Martyr. Eustace is generally portrayed as a huntsman seeing a vision of a crucifix, which appears between the antlers of a stag he is hunting. According to legend, he was a Roman general who was converted to Christianity by this vision. Subsequently he was martyred by being roasted alive. He is a popular figure in Christian art.

H. Delehaye, 'La légende de St Eustache', *Académie Royale de Belgique Bulletins* (1919) [no English translation available].

Euthalius (? fourth/fifth century)   Devotional Writer. Euthalius was the supposed author of a collection of editorial work on the New Testament. This includes a division of the books into chapters, a collection of Old Testament quotations relevant to the text, a list of names and places associated with the text and a short biography of St PAUL. Authorities disagree as to Euthalius's dates and origins. He is generally thought to have been a Deacon living in Alexandria in the fifth century, but there is no certainty about this.

J.A. Robinson, 'Euthaliana', *Texts and Studies*, 3, iii (1895).

Euthymius Zigabenus (eleventh/twelfth

century)   Theologian. Euthymius was a monk living in Constantinople who wrote commentaries on the Psalms, Gospels and Epistles. These are noteworthy for their literal understanding of the text in an age when an allegorical interpretation was more usual. However, he is remembered for his *Panoplia Dogmatica*, which was commissioned by the Emperor and was designed as a refutation of all heresies. Many early mediaeval heresies are only known to us as a result of this work.

M. Jugie, 'La Vie at les Oeuvres D'Euthyme Zigabène', *Echos d'Orient*, xv (1912) [no English translation available].

Eutyches (*c.* 378–454)   Heretic. Eutyches was Archimandrite of a monastery in Constantinople. He was a determined opponent of the heresies of NESTORIUS and he argued instead that JESUS in his manhood was not fully human. Thus Eutyches must be seen as the founder of Monophysitism, the doctrine that Christ has a single, divine, nature. He was accused of heresy at the Synod of Constantinople in 448 and was deposed. He then appealed to Pope LEO I in Rome. The 'Robber Synod' of Ephesus was summoned in 449 and Eutyches was reinstated. This decision, however, was reversed at the Council of Chalcedon in 451, which confirmed the Nicaean Creed, the two Cyrilline Letters and the Tome of Leo. The Chalcedon definition maintained that the two natures of Christ are fully God and fully man; these are united 'unconfusedly, unchangeably, indivisibly and inseparably' and are preserved eternally in the One Person. After Chalcedon, the Monophysites broke away from the Catholic Church. Monophysitism survives today as the official doctrine of the Coptic, Syrian and Armenian Churches.

W.H.C. Frend, *The Rise of the Monophysite Movement* (1972); R.V. Sellers, *The Council of Chalcedon* (1953).

Evagrius Ponticus (346–99) Devotional Writer. Evagrius was ordained by GREGORY OF NAZIANZUS and, after 382, he lived as a hermit in the Egyptian desert. His writings survive only in Latin and Syrian translations and include a treatise on the spiritual life of a monk, another on evil thoughts and a collection of sayings. Although he was criticised by St JEROME for Origenism, he was highly influential on John CASSIAN, Pseudo-DIONYSIUS, MAXIMUS THE CONFESSOR and PALLADIUS.

D.A. Chitty, *The Desert a City* (1966).

Evelyn, John (1620–1706) Historian and Theologian. Evelyn was a native of Surrey and was educated at the University of Oxford. During the English Civil War, he served in the Royalist army and then lived first abroad and then in retirement during the Commonwealth period until the restoration of King Charles II. He held several important appointments in the 1660s and 1670s and was a co-founder of the Royal Society. However, he is chiefly remembered for his diary, which is an important source for the social and religious history of his time. Although he did not approve of the lasciviousness of the court, he remained loyal to the crown and to the Church of England. He was also the author of several religious works, including treatises against the Jesuits, a history of religion and translations of works of John CHRYSOSTOM.

J. Bowle, *John Evelyn and his World* (1981).

F

Faber, Frederick William (1814–63) Devotional Writer. Faber was born in Yorkshire and was educated at the University of Oxford. He came from an Anglican family, but at Oxford he was greatly influenced by John Henry NEWMAN and followed him into the Roman Catholic Church in 1845. Initially he went with Newman to the Oratory of St Philip Neri in Birmingham, but in 1849 he was sent to found a new oratory in London. The two men subsequently quarrelled over the issue of hearing nuns' confessions. Faber was a famous and affecting preacher, but is now remembered for his devotional writings. These include *All for Jesus, Growth in Holiness, The Blessed Sacrament, The Creator and the Creature, The Foot of the Cross* and *The Precious Blood*. All achieved huge circulation, although, by today's standards, his books seem florid and overemotional. His hymns, such as 'My God, how wonderful thou art', and 'Hark! Hark my soul', are still sung.

D. Brown, *Faber: Poet and Priest*, edited by R. Addington (1974); R. Chapman, *Father Faber* (1974).

Facundus (sixth century) Bishop and Heretic. Facundus was Bishop of Hermiane in North Africa. He supported the theological views of IBAS, THEODORE OF MOPSUESTIA and THEODORET as expressed in the 'Three Chapters'. In an attempt to conciliate the Monophysites, these had been condemned by the Emperor JUSTINIAN as being too sympathetic to the opinions of NESTORIUS. Facundus justified himself in three treatises including the *Epistola Fidei Catholicae in Defensione Trium Capitolorum*. Nevertheless at the Fifth General Council (the Second Council of Constantinople) in 553, the 'Three Chapters' were condemned and in consequence Facundus was excommunicated by Pope VIGILIUS.

R.B. Eno, 'Doctrinal authority in the African ecclesiology of the sixth century', *Revue des Etudes Augustiniennes* (1976).

Faith (? third century) Saint and Martyr. Little certain is known of the life of St Faith. She is thought to have been martyred in Aquitaine in the late third century. A basilica was built over the supposed site of her death, but subsequently her relics were moved to the Abbey of Conques which became an important place of pilgrimage in the Middle Ages. St Faith is regarded as a patron of soldiers, pilgrims and prisoners. She is not to be confused with the three legendary sisters, Faith, Hope and Charity, who were martyred in the second century at the ages of twelve, ten and nine by being boiled in pitch and then beheaded.

D.H. Farmer (ed.), *The Oxford Book of Saints*, 3rd edn (1992).

Faraday, Michael (1791–1867) Scientist. Faraday was the son of a blacksmith working in London. He started his scientific career as an assistant to Sir Humphry Davy and became Professor of Chemistry at the Royal Institution in 1827. He is remembered as the maker of the first electric motor and the first dynamo. His scientific outlook was influenced by his religious stance. His parents had been followers of Robert SANDEMAN, and embraced a strongly biblical form of Christianity. Faraday himself was a member of the Sandemanian Church and he was convinced that the discoveries of science served to reveal the power and wisdom of God. He was a brilliant lecturer who attracted large audiences. His attitude to wealth was also affected by his Christian convictions. He lived modestly and gave away most of his earnings. In consequence, on his retirement he had to be granted a government pension.

G. Cantor, *Michael Faraday: A Study of Science and Religion in the Nineteenth Century* (1991); J.M. Thomas, *Michael Faraday and the Royal Institution* (1991).

Farrar, Frederic William (1831–1903) Devotional Writer. Farrar was educated at the Universities of London and Cambridge, England. Initially he became a school-master and taught at Harrow and Marlborough. Subsequently he became a Canon of Westminster Abbey and in 1895 he was installed as Dean of Canterbury Cathedral. Farrar wrote a very successfui *Life of Christ*, published in 1874, and a *Life and Works of St Paul* (1879). He is mainly remembered for his somewhat pious juvenile fiction which includes *Eric: Or Little by Little*, *Julian Home* and *St Winifred's, or the Word of the School*. These have been both enjoyed and mocked by generations of English adolescents.

F.W. Farrar, *Eric: Or Little by Little* [many editions]; R. Farrar, *The Life of Dean Farrar* (1904).

Fawkes, Guy (1570–1606) Rebel. Fawkes was a native of Yorkshire and was brought up in the Church of England. In *c*. 1593 he converted to Roman Catholicism and, under the influence of Robert Catesby, he became involved in the Gunpowder Plot of 1605. The plan was to store explosives in a cellar under the Houses of Parliament, set them alight when King JAMES I was opening Parliament and to seize control of the government. Fawkes was deputed to light the fuse. The plot was discovered before it could be executed. Fawkes was arrested in the cellar and, under torture, he revealed the names of his fellow conspirators. All the plotters were put to death. This incident intensified anti-Roman Catholic feeling in England and, to this day, the defeat of the conspiracy is celebrated with bonfires, fireworks and a ritual burning of Guy Fawkes in effigy.

H. Garnett, *Portrait of Guy Fawkes: An Experiment in Biography* (1962); H.R. Williamson, *The Gunpowder Plot* (1941).

Febronius, Justinian see **Hontheim, Johann Nikolaus von** (1701–90)

Fell, John (1625–86) Bishop and Educator. Fell was the son of a Dean of Christchurch College, Oxford, England, and he was educated at that university. As a staunch Royalist, he lost his college fellowship during the Commonwealth period, but he was reinstated with the accession of King Charles II and he became Dean of the College in his turn. In 1676 he was consecrated Bishop of Oxford. Among his writings was an important critical edition of the works of St CYPRIAN. He was successful in re-establishing loyalty to the Church of England in the university and he was instrumental in removing John LOCKE from his studentship at Christchurch. He was also a significant figure in the founding of the Oxford University Press and he attracted many famous scholars to Oxford. Thus he must be seen as an important figure in the restoration of the university as an outstanding place of learning. However, his main claim to fame is as the subject of an undergraduate rhyme, based on one of Martial's epigrams: 'I do not love thee Dr Fell,/The reason why I cannot tell,/But this I know, I know full well/I do not love thee Dr Fell!'

S. Morrison and H. Carter, *John Fell, the University Press and the 'Fell' Types* (1967).

Fénelon, François de Salignac de la Mothe (1651–1715) Archbishop, Educator and Devotional Writer. Fénelon was born in Périgord, France and was educated at the seminary of St Sulpice. After ordination, he became Superior of a house for recent converts from Protestantism and then led a mission to the Huguenots. In 1689, he was appointed tutor to the Duke of Burgundy and, from his position at court, he became acquainted with the Quietist Madame GUYON. He was consecrated Archbishop of Cambrai in 1695 and after Madame Guyon had been censured, he signed the Articles of Issy which rejected Quietism. Subsequently he was engaged in a long conflict with Jacques BOSSUET about mysticism, which led to his banishment in 1697. Twenty-three propositions from his book *Explication des Maximes des Saints* were condemned by the Pope in 1699 and Fénelon spent the rest of his life away from court in Cambrai. He is primarily remembered for his educational writings, *Traité de l'Education des Filles* and *Télémaque*, for his opposition to political absolutism as expressed in his *Lettre à Louis XIV* and for his devotional writings such as his *Traité de l'Existence de Dieu*, which was published in its final form after his death.

M. de la Bedoyere, *The Archbishop and the Lady: The Story of Fénelon and Madame Guyon* (1956); K.D. Little, *Francis de Fénelon. Study of a Personality* (1951).

Ferdinand V (1452–1516) Monarch. Ferdinand was born in Sos, Aragon, the son of King John II. In 1469, he was married to his cousin ISABELLA, who was to become Queen of Castile. Together Ferdinand and Isabella united the Kingdom of Spain. In 1492 Granada was annexed; in 1504 Naples became a Spanish possession and in 1515 Navarre was added to their territories. In addition the Pope was persuaded to divide the lands of the newly discovered Americas between Spain and Portugal. Ferdinand is often given the title 'the Catholic' because he expelled the Muslims from Granada, evicted the Jewish community from Spain and established the Spanish Inquisition. However, despite his zeal for the Church, in his personal life he was neither kind, nor modest, nor chaste.

F. Fernandaz-Armesto, *Ferdinand and Isabella* (1975); J. Vicens Vives, *Historia Critica de la Vida y Reinado de Ferdinando II de Aragon* (1962) [no English translation available].

Ferrar, Nicholas (1592–1637) Community Founder. Ferrar was born in London, England and was educated at the University of Cambridge. After a period of travel abroad, he worked for the Virginia Company and in 1624 he was elected to Parliament. However, dissatisfied with worldly success, he withdrew from the public arena. With his brother, brother-in-law and their families he established an Anglican religious house at Little Gidding. He was the spiritual director and the whole community lived a life of austere piety. King CHARLES I was much impressed when he visited, but the household was regarded as nothing short of Papist by the Puritans of the time. In 1656, after Ferrar's death, it was denounced in a pamphlet entitled *The Arminian Nunnery* and was subsequently destroyed in an armed raid. Interest in the work of Ferrar was revived by the poet T.S. ELIOT who named one of his *Four Quartets* 'Little Gidding' and described the place as one 'Where prayer has been valid.'

T.S. Eliot, 'Little Gidding', *Four Quartets* (1944); A.L. Maycock, *Nicholas Ferrar of Little Gidding* (1938).

Feuerbach, Ludwig Andreas (1804–72) Philosopher. Feuerbach was born in Landshut, Germany. He was educated at Heidelberg and then became a pupil of G.W.F. HEGEL in Berlin. For most of his subsequent life, he lived as a private scholar. In his books he taught that Christianity was an illusion that revealed more about the nature of man than it did about any form of transcendental reality. His most famous work was his *Wesen der Christentums* which was translated into English by the novelist George Eliot. Feuerbach is remembered for his influence on later thinkers, particularly on Friedrich NIETZSCHE and on Karl MARX.

W.B. Chamberlain, *Heaven Wasn't his Destination: The Philosophy of Ludwig Feuerbach* (1941); V. Harvey, *Ludwig Feuerbach* (1996); E. Kamenka, *The Philosophy of Ludwig Feuerbach* (1970).

Fey, Clara (1815–94) Order Founder. Fey was born in Aachen, Germany. In 1837 she opened a school for the poor in Aachen and this became a religious community, the Sisters of the Poor Child Jesus, in 1844. For the next fifty years, until her death, she served as Superior although she and her sisters were forced to leave Germany during the Kulturkampf. The order is dedicated to the education of the poor and the abandoned and has spread through Western Europe to the Americas and Indonesia.

J. Solzbacher (ed.), *Heaven on Earth*, translated by M. Colman (1958); I. Watterot, *The Life of Mother Clare Fey* (1923).

Fichte, Johann Gottlieb (1762–1814) Philosopher. Fichte was born in Rammenau, Saxony, and was educated at the Universities of Göttingen, Jena and Leipzig. Although he was appointed to a Chair of Philosophy at Jena in 1794, he was dismissed for atheism in 1799 and his place taken by F.W.J. SCHELLING. Ultimately he became Rector of the new University of Berlin in 1809. Fichte was a student of the philosophy of Immanuel KANT and he maintained that his idealism was implicit in Kant's work. He understood the religious life as obedience to the absolute moral order which was to be discovered through the exercise of

intellectual intuition. His ideas were expounded in a series of books, including *Anweisung zum Seligen Leben*. He is remembered both for his moral philosophy and for his famous lecture, published as *Reden an die Deutsche Nation*, which was a call for the unity of Germany and which had a profound influence on the later development of German nationalism.

R.W. Stine, *The Doctrine of God in the Philosophy of Fichte* (1945); F. Copleston, *A History of Philosophy*, Vol. 1 (1963).

Ficino, Marsilio (1433–99) Philosopher and Mystic. Ficino was born near Florence. Under the patronage of Cosimo de' Medici, he studied Greek philosophy and by 1477 he had translated all the dialogues of Plato. He was the founder of the Platonic Academy in Florence, which became an important intellectual centre. In 1473 he was ordained and in 1477 he published his *De Religione Christiana*, an original synthesis of Greek philosophy and Christian theology. He believed that philosophy and theology were parallel paths leading to ultimate reality. On one occasion he maintained that 'philosophy and religion are sisters'. Subsequently he produced his *Theologia Platonica de Immortalitate Animorum*. He also translated the works of Plotinus and Pseudo-DIONYSIUS. Ficino's influence was enormous. His translations became standard works; he conducted a correspondence with John COLET and it was largely through his efforts that the leading European scholars of his time became familiar with the writings of the Greek philosophers.

M.J.B. Allen, *The Platonism of Marsilio Ficino: A Study of his Phaedrus Commentary* (1984); P.O. Kristell, *The Philosophy of Marsilio Ficino* (1943).

Field, John (1545–88) Polemicist. Field was educated at the University of Oxford. After ordination, he became known as a leading Puritan in London. After being barred from preaching, he produced an *Admonition to Parliament* with Thomas Wilcox. In this he argued against Catholic practices in the Church of England and for a Presbyterian form of Church government. As a result of this document, he was imprisoned for a year for being in breach of the Act of Uniformity. During the archiepiscopacy of WHITGIFT, he was the corresponding secretary of the London Conference of extreme Puritan ministers and he was tireless (though ultimately unsuccessful) in his campaigns against the Bishops. He may well have been behind the MARPRELATE Tracts issued between 1588 and 1589, a series of scurrilous satirical tracts directed against the Church establishment. Field is remembered as the most effective of the Elizabethan extreme Puritans.

P. Collinson, 'John Field and Elizabethan Puritanism', in S.T. Bindoff et al. (eds), *Elizabethan Government and Society* (1961).

Finnian (*c.* 495–579)   Saint and Order Founder. Finnian was a native of Ireland. He went to Rome to be ordained and then returned home, bringing with him a Latin vulgate and a Pentateuch. He formed a monastic house at Moville and many legends are connected with him. He is now regarded as the patron saint of Northern Ireland. He is not to be confused with St Finnian of Clonard (d. 549) who is thought to have established monasticism in Ireland.

J.F. Kenney, *The Sources for the Early History of Ireland* (1929).

Fiorenza, Elisabeth Schussler (b. 1938)   Theologian. Fiorenza has taught at Notre Dame University and at Harvard Divinity School in the United States. A biblical scholar, her works include *In Memory of Her* and *Bread not Stone: The Challenge of Feminist Biblical Interpretation*. In contrast to some feminist scholars, she works within the framework of established historical criticism, but is concerned to show how the early Church encouraged the equal participation of men and women. Only later did men seize control of Christian institutions. Fiorenza believes that it is the task of feminist theologians to uncover the true heritage of women within Christianity.

D. Hampson, *Theology and Feminism* (1990); L.M. Russell (ed.), *Feminist Interpretations of the Bible* (1985).

Fisher, John (1469–1535)   Bishop, Theologian, Saint and Martyr. Fisher was born in Yorkshire and was educated at the University of Cambridge. After a period as chaplain to Lady MARGARET BEAUFORT, he was consecrated Bishop of Rochester in 1504. A dedicated, scholarly man, he was interested in the ideas of ERASMUS. Although he strongly opposed the theology of Martin LUTHER, he was not averse to moderate Church reform. As confessor to Queen Catherine of Aragon, he protested against King HENRY VIII's attempts to divorce her. His property was confiscated and he was imprisoned in the Tower of London for refusing to take the Oath required by the Act of Succession. In 1535, to the additional fury of the King, the Pope created him a Cardinal. He was put on trial in 1535 and beheaded as a traitor. His theological writings on the real presence in the Eucharist were influential on the participants of the Council of Trent later in the sixteenth century. Fisher was canonised with Sir Thomas MORE by Pope Pius XI in 1936.

E.L. Surtz, *The Works and Days of John Fisher* (1967).

Flacius, Matthias Illyricus (1520–75)   Theologian. Flacius was born in Croatia. In his youth he wanted to become a monk, but his uncle, who had Protestant leanings, tried to dissuade him from this by sending him to study at the Protestant universities of Basle, Tübingen and

Wittenberg. As a result of contact with Philip MELANCHTHON and Martin LUTHER, he was converted to an evangelical form of Christianity and became Professor of Hebrew at Wittenberg. However he fell out with Melanchthon over the provisional doctrinal formula known as The Augsburg Interim, which he strongly opposed. Subsequently he taught at Jena University (where again he aroused strong criticism), and after some time in Ratisbon, he died in Frankfurt. He was the author of *Clavis Scripturae Sacrae*, a key to the Scriptures, and he was one of the leading contributors to the *Magdeburg Centuries*, an influential and intensely anti-papal interpretation of Church history. He also published the *Missa Illyrica*, an eleventh-century order for the service of the Mass.

A.E. McGrath, *Reformation Thought: An Introduction* (1988).

Fletcher, Joseph (b. 1905)   Philosopher. Fletcher was a pastor before he was appointed to the Chair of Social Ethics at the Episcopal Theological School, Cambridge, Massachusetts. Subsequently he taught at the University of Virginia. In his influential *Situation Ethics*, published in 1966, he argued that the right ethical choice is the one informed by love in a particular situation: 'The situationist enters into every decision-making situation fully armed with the ethical maxims of his community. . . . Just the same, he is prepared in any situation to compromise them or to set them aside in the situation if love seems better served by doing so'. Although his position has been much criticised, little has since been written on Christian ethics which has so gripped the public imagination.

Joseph Fletcher, *Moral Responsibility: Situation Ethics at Work* (1967); R. Gill, *A Textbook of Christian Ethics* (1985); P. Ramsey, *Deeds and Rules in Christian Ethics* (1967).

Flew, Antony Garrard Newton (b. 1923) Philosopher. The son of a Methodist

professor, Flew was educated at the Universities of London and Oxford, and has taught philosophy at the Universities of Aberdeen, Keele, Reading and Toronto. He has been President of the Voluntary Euthanasia Society and is the author of many books. He is particularly known in Christian circles for his attack on the logic of religious belief in his article 'Theology and Falsification', first published in 1950. He asks the question what evidence could be said to count against the claim that God is love. Whatever counter-evidence is produced, such as cancer, earthquakes, cruelty or landslides, the believer will argue that the evil is merely an exception which can be accommodated within the proposition that God is love. Thus, Flew argues, religious belief 'dies the death of a thousand qualifications'. It cannot be falsified and therefore has no content as a factual proposition.

Antony Flew, *God and Philosophy* (1966); J. Hick, *The Existence of God* (1964); J. Macquarrie, *God-Talk* (1967).

Fliedner, Theodor (1800–64)   Order Founder. Fliedner was a native of Germany and was educated at Giessen and Göttingen. He served as a pastor in Kaiserswerth and came into contact with the Mennonite practice of appointing Deaconesses. In 1833 he set up the Kaiserswerth Sisters, an order for young women who wished to dedicate themselves to public service. Among his projects was a home for ex-convicts, a school and teacher-training college, and a teaching hospital. This Deaconess order of the German Lutheran Church spread throughout Germany and was also established in the United States and Palestine.

E.A. Livingstone (ed.), *The Oxford Dictionary of the Christian Church*, revised edn (1997).

Florovsky, George (1893–1979)   Theologian and Ecumenist. Florovsky was the son of a Russian Orthodox priest and was educated at the University of Odessa. After the Revolution, he left Russia and held academic positions in Sofia, Prague and Paris. After the Second World War, he moved to the United States of America, where he taught in New York, at Harvard and at Princeton. His *Ways of Russian Theology* (English translation 1972) did much to introduce Orthodox thought to the West and he was an important figure in the ecumenical movement, serving as a delegate at assemblies of the Faith and Order movement and of the World Council of Churches.

T.E. Bird, 'Russian scholar and theologian', *The American Benedictine Review* (1965); Y.N. Lelouvier, *Perspectives Russes sur l'Eglise* (1968) [no English translation available].

Foliot, Gilbert (d. 1187) Bishop and Politician. Foliot was a native of Normandy and became a monk at the monastery of Cluny. He rose in the Church to become Prior of Cluny, Abbot of Gloucester, Bishop of Hereford in 1148 and Bishop of London in 1163. An opponent of Archbishop BECKET, he supported King HENRY II and in consequence was excommunicated. Foliot appealed to the Pope, who gave permission to the Bishop of Exeter to absolve him. Foliot then took part in the coronation of Henry's son, again defying Becket, and he was excommunicated again. Although he was not involved in Becket's murder, he was connected with it in the public mind and was not absolved until 1172. Many of his letters have survived and give an interesting picture of the life of the twelfth-century English Church.

A. Morey and C.N.L. Brooke, *Gilbert Foliot and his Letters* (1965).

Forsyth, Peter Taylor (1848–1921) Theologian. Forsyth was born in Aberdeen, Scotland and was educated at Aberdeen University and at Göttingen, where he was a student of Albrecht RITSCHL. He was ordained as a Congre-

gationalist minister and in 1901 became principal of Hackney College, London. His books include *The Cruciality of the Cross*, *The Person and Place of Jesus Christ* and *The Work of Christ*. He is remembered for his kenotic christology, his argument that God's self-emptying and man's fulfilling are the two movements found in Christ which effect reconciliation between God and humanity.

G.O. Griffith, *The Theology of P.T. Forsyth* (1948); J.H. Rogers, *The Theology of P.T. Forsyth* (1965); T. Hart (ed.), *Justice the True and Only Mercy* (1995).

Fox, George (1624–91) Denomination Founder and Devotional Writer. Fox was born in Leicestershire, England and was apprenticed as a young boy to a shoemaker. In 1643 he felt called to give up all his worldly ties and he travelled around the countryside in search of enlightenment. Then, in 1646, he felt the 'inner light of the Living Christ'. He gave up attending formal Church services and he began to preach that the truth is to be found in God's voice speaking to the individual soul. His organisation came to be called the 'Friends of Truth' which was later abbreviated to the 'Friends'. He was imprisoned in 1649 for interrupting a Church service and again in 1650 as a blasphemer. It was then that the Friends were given the name of 'Quakers' because Fox had urged the judge at his trial to 'tremble at the word of the Lord'. Altogether he spent six years in prison. The rest of his life was spent in promoting his message. His famous journal was published after his death and has become a spiritual classic. By the end of the seventeenth century, Quakerism had spread throughout Great Britain and in 1682 William PENN founded the American colony of Pennsylvania to assure liberty of conscience for members of the society. To this day there is no formal ministry in the society and meetings have no formal liturgy. Members refuse to take oaths and, as pacifists, do not take part in military service.

G.H. Gorman, *The Society of Friends* (1978); E. Russell, *The History of Quakerism* (1943); H.E. Wildes, *The Voice of the Lord: A Biography of George Fox* (1965).

Foxe, John (1516–87)   Historian. Foxe was a native of Lincolnshire and was educated at the University of Oxford. He was acquainted with John BALE who encouraged his interest in history and he was ordained in 1550 by Nicholas RIDLEY. During the reign of the Roman Catholic Queen MARY, Foxe lived abroad. He occupied his time by writing a history of the Reformation and, using Edmund GRINDAL's stories of the Protestant martyrs, he began to compile his own martyrology. This was published in 1564 in the reign of Queen ELIZABETH. Popularly known as *Foxe's Book of Martyrs*, it has gone through many editions. Frequently enlivened with gruesome illustrations of tortures and burnings, it has done much to preserve and inflame anti-Catholic feeling in the English-speaking world.

J.F. Mozley, *John Foxe and His Book* (1940); W. Haller, *Foxe's Book of Martyrs and the Elect Nation* (1967).

Frances of Rome (1384–1440)   Saint, Mystic and Order Founder. Frances was born in Rome and, despite her desire for the religious life, was married at the age of thirteen to Lorenzo de' Ponziani. In 1425 she founded the Oblates of Mary, who were later called the Oblates of Tor de' Specchi. This was a society of gentlewomen who were dedicated to prayer and good works, but who neither took vows, nor gave up their property, nor lived in enclosure. The order continues today and has branches in Switzerland and the United States of America. Frances became the first Superior of the community. In her later life she was subject to a series of visions, including one of her guardian angel, which is supposed to have stayed with her for several years. It was perhaps her special awareness of

angelic guidance which led Pope PIUS XI to nominate her as the patron saint of motorists.

I. Hernaman, *Life of St Frances of Rome* (1931).

Francis Borgia (1510–72)   Saint, Missionary and Educator. Francis was the great-grandson of Pope ALEXANDER VI and the son of the Duke of Gandia. Although he was drawn to the religious life from an early age, he married and had eight children. During this period, he served as viceroy of Catalonia and did much to combat administrative corruption. On his wife's death, he was privately received into the Jesuit Order and was ordained as a priest in 1551. He was a friend of both St TERESA OF AVILA and St IGNATIUS LOYOLA. In 1554 he became Commissary General of the order in both Spain and Portugal and became responsible for the supervision of the Society's work overseas. He established many schools and colleges and was involved in the foundation of the Collegium Romanum. Then, in 1565, on the death of James Laynez, he was elected the third General of the order. An outstanding administrator, he was canonised less than a hundred years after his death.

M. Yeo, *The Greatest of the Borgias* (1936).

Francis of Assisi (*c.* 1181–1226)   Saint, Mystic, Poet and Order Founder. Francis was the son of a wealthy cloth merchant of Assisi, Italy. After a period in his father's business and as a soldier, he turned away from his old life. In obedience to an inner voice, he dedicated himself to repairing the ruined church of San Damiano. For several years he lived alone as a beggar, tending lepers and identifying with the poor. Soon others joined him and a community was established at Portiuncula from where he and his followers made regular preaching tours. In 1210 Francis drew up a rule of life, the Regula Prima, which was approved by

Pope INNOCENT III. The group called themselves friars ('fratres minor') and their ideals spread rapidly. St CLARE of Assisi set up a similar society for women based on the church of San Damiano. Francis himself travelled through France and Spain, but was prevented by illness from preaching to the Muslims of North Africa. Later he made another preaching tour to Eastern Europe. Meanwhile the organisation of the order had changed. It already had five thousand members and different administrative arrangements had become necessary. A second, more comprehensive rule was drawn up which was approved in 1223 and Francis also set up the Tertiary Order, by which lay people could dedicate themselves to God while continuing to live with their families. During the last years of his life, he held no official position. He remained a Deacon and lived quietly within the order. In 1224 he received the impression of the stigmata on his body and he died two years later at the age of forty-five. St Francis remains one of the most attractive of the Christian saints. His devotion to the Lady Poverty, his wonderful *Canticle of the Sun* and the story of his simple, holy life, have been an inspiration to generations. Assisi remains a centre of pilgrimage to this day and the Franciscan Order has produced several other saints – BONAVENTURA and ANTONY OF PADUA being the most prominent.

G.K. Chesterton, *Francis of Assisi* (1923); L. Cunningham (ed.), *An Anthology of Writings by and about St Francis of Assisi* (1973); J.R.H. Moorman, *A History of the Franciscan Order from its Origins to the Year 1517* (1968); J.H. Smith, *St Francis of Assisi* (1973).

Francis of Paola (1416–1507) Saint and Order Founder. Francis spent a year at the Franciscan friary of San Marco in Italy and, after living as a hermit in Paola, in 1436 he started the Order of Minims (Ordo Fratres Minimorum). Members of the order were dedicated to the practice of humility. They were to live on charity and were to eat neither meat, fish, nor dairy food. Francis himself was renowned for his holiness. In obedience to the Pope, he ministered to King Louis XI of France and he acted as spiritual advisor to his son, King Charles VIII. The order spread through France, Spain and Germany and there is a Tertiary Order for those who cannot live in community, in South America.

The Catholic University of America, *New Catholic Encyclopaedia* (1967).

Francis of Sales (1567–1622) Saint, Bishop, Order Founder and Devotional Writer. Francis was born in Savoy of an aristocratic family. He studied law at the Universities of Paris and Padua, but in 1593 he was ordained and he became Provost of Geneva. He preached among the Calvinists of Chablais and he is said to have converted eight thousand back to Catholicism. His sermons were simple and straightforward and he used to declare, 'Love alone will shake the walls of Geneva'. In 1599 he was appointed Bishop-Coadjutor of Geneva although he was not consecrated until 1603. With St JANE FRANCES DE CHANTEL, he founded the Order of the Visitation. This is an order of contemplative nuns who follow a rule drawn up by Francis and are dedicated to gentleness, humility and sisterly love. Francis was an important figure in the Counter-Reformation, but today he is particularly remembered for his two devotional classics, *The Introduction to the Devout Life* and *The Treatise on the Love of God*. Both have been reprinted many times. In 1923 he was named the patron saint of Catholic journalists.

R. Kleinman, *Saint François de Sales and the Protestants* (1962); E.J. Lajeunie, *Saint François de Sales: l'Homme, la Pensée, l'Action*, 2 vols (1966) [no English translation available].

Francis Xavier (1506–52) Saint and Missionary. Francis was born in Navarre of an aristocratic family. While studying theology at the University of Paris, he became acquainted with IGNATIUS LOYOLA. In 1534, Francis, Ignatius and five others vowed themselves to a life of single-minded dedication to JESUS CHRIST and all seven were ordained as priests three years later. In 1539 Francis was sent as a missionary to the East Indies where he started a preaching and healing ministry. From his base in Goa, he travelled through south-west India and in 1549 he landed in Japan where he founded a community of two thousand people. He returned to Goa in 1552, but died on his way to China. Francis is said to have brought seven hundred thousand souls to God. His methods have been criticised as insensitive and imperialistic and his use of the Inquisition to reinforce his message does not recommend itself to the modern mind. None the less his self-less dedication is undisputed and he did much to interest the Christian world in foreign missions.

J. Brodrick, *St Francis Xavier* (1952).

Frank, Jacob (1726–91) Sect Founder. Frank was born Jankiev Lebowicz of Jewish parents. He was influenced by the Donmeh cult of Turkey – a group of Jews who had followed the false messiah Shabbetai Zevi into Islam. Frank seems to have believed that he was a reincarnation of Shabbetai Zevi and also the Second Person of the Trinity. After a debate with traditional Jews, Frank and his followers were baptised into the Catholic Church. However, he still allowed himself to be worshipped as the Messiah and was imprisoned for a time. His followers were said to indulge in licentious orgies and the cult spread from Poland to Bohemia and Germany. It had died out by the middle of the nineteenth century.

G. Scholem, *The Messianic Idea in Judaism and Other Essays* (1920).

Frazer, James (1854–1941) Anthropologist. Frazer was born in Glasgow and was educated at the University of Cambridge, where he read Classics. He was a prolific writer, but he is mainly remembered for his *Golden Bough* published in 1890 with later editions in 1900 and 1915. He was particularly influenced by Edward Tylor, the first Professor of Anthropology at Oxford University, and he believed that religion was the product of evolutionary development and that it developed out of magic. He did no first-hand work in the field, relying instead on a large number of secondary sources, and he particularly studied the myths connected with sacral kingship, the dying god, the scapegoat and the eternal soul. He concluded that polytheism grew out of animism and monotheism from polytheism. Although his hypotheses were not generally accepted by other anthropologists, Frazer is a significant figure in that he introduced to the reading public the practice of explaining religion in anthropological terms.

R. Ackerman, *J.G. Frazer: His Life and Work*, (1990); R.A. Downie, *James George Frazer* (1940).

Frederick I [Barbarossa] (*c.* 1122–90) Monarch. Frederick was the nephew of Emperor Conrad III and was elected King of Germany in 1152 on his uncle's death. He was anxious to restore the rights of the German monarchy and, to this end, he issued a proclamation of peace and built up an efficient administrative organisation. In 1154 he invaded Italy, with the approval of Pope HADRIAN IV. He repressed the Lombard communes and was crowned Holy Roman Emperor. However, his alliance with the Pope disintegrated when Frederick's plans threatened the Pope's secular power. Pope Hadrian's successor, ALEXANDER III, was not recognised by Frederick, who chose to support the Antipope Victor IV. After a schism lasting seventeen years and in the face of military defeat, the Emperor submitted to Alexander, but not before he had persuaded his antipope to canonise his predecessor, the Holy Roman Emperor CHARLEMAGNE. In 1189 Frederick embarked on the Third Crusade, which was designed to drive the Sultan Saladin from Jerusalem. This was the culmination of his ambitions as ruler of the Holy Roman Empire, but he was drowned in the river Saleph in Cilicia before he could reach the Holy Land.

G. Barraclough, *The Origins of Modern Germany* (1947); P. Munz, *Frederick Barbarossa: A Study in Mediaeval Politics* (1969); M. Pacaut, *Frederick Barbarossa* (1970).

Frederick II (1194–1250) Monarch. Frederick II was the grandson of FREDERICK I (Barbarossa). He was elected German king at the age of two, but when his father died the following year, the German princes refused to accept him. However, in 1212 he was again named king and, supported by his guardian Pope INNOCENT III, his position was consolidated. In 1220 he was crowned Holy Roman Emperor. As a result of his threatening papal interests in central Italy, he was excommunicated by Pope GREGORY IX in 1227 and again in 1239. Meanwhile he reached agreement with the Sultan al Kamil and in 1228 he had himself crowned king in Jerusalem. On this occasion he declared himself to be an instrument of God, following in the footsteps of the biblical King David. Subsequently he continued with his Italian plans and in 1245 Pope INNOCENT IV declared a crusade against him, but with little effect. At the time of his death, the conflict between Pope and Emperor was still unresolved. Frederick was sceptical in religion, tolerant of Jews and Muslims, a brilliant linguist and a flamboyant diplomat: he was an outstanding figure of his age.

E. Kantorowicz, *Frederic II* (1931); D.P. Waley, *The Papal States in the Thirteenth Century* (1961).

Frederick III (1463–1525) Monarch. Frederick succeeded his father Ernst as Elector of Saxony in 1486. A cultured man, he was interested in the new learning and he was a patron of Cranach and DÜRER. In 1500 he became President of the Reichsregiment, but he refused to stand as candidate for Holy Roman Emperor in 1519. He founded the University of Wittenberg in 1502. When Martin LUTHER was required to go to Rome in 1518, Frederick intervened and had the trial take place at Augsburg. In 1520 he refused to execute the bill 'Exsurge Domine' against Luther and, after the Diet of Worms had imposed an imperial ban, he provided sanctuary for the Reformer. It has been disputed how far he accepted Protestant ideas, though it is known that he received Communion in both kinds before his death. Frederick was known as 'the Wise' because of his reputation for fairness.

J. Bossy, *Christianity in the West 1400–1700* (1985); A.E. Dickens, *The German Nation and Martin Luther* (1974).

Frederick III (1515–1576) Monarch. Frederick III became Elector of the Palatine in 1559. A devout and cultured man, he became a committed follower of the teachings of John CALVIN. After studying the question, he rejected Article 10, 'On the Lord's Supper', in the Augsburg Confession and he commissioned the Heidelberg Catechism to be imposed on all his subjects. He pursued Protestant interests abroad, actively helping the French Huguenots and the Dutch Calvinists against their Roman Catholic rulers, and he was unhappy with the Peace of Augsburg of 1555 because it recognised Lutheranism, but not Calvinism. Nicknamed 'the Pious', he introduced a Presbyterian form of Church government into the Palatine in 1570. Frederick's reign is an interesting example of the principle *cuius regio, eius religio* (whose kingdom, his religion) in practice.

C.P. Clasen, *The Palatine in European History (1559–1660)*, 2nd edn (1966).

Freud, Sigmund (1856–1939) Psychologist. Freud was born of Jewish parents in Freiberg, Moravia. He was educated at the University of Vienna where he studied medicine. He invented psychoanalysis, as a method of dealing with hysterical and psychological illness. On the ascendance of Nazism in Germany, he moved his practice to London in 1938, but died of cancer a year later. With his hypothesis of the unconscious mind, he has proved an outstandingly influential figure in modern culture. Within the history of the Christian Church, he is remembered for his hostility to religion, which he expressed in his *Totem and Taboo*, *Moses and Monotheism* and *The Future of an Illusion*. He argued that religion is the product of wish fulfilment and that it perpetuates infantile behaviour patterns since it allows the believer to retain the illusion of an omnipotent father figure. Similarly, he maintained that ethical imperatives are merely the internalisation of parental commands. Although Freud's theories remain controversial, his psychoanalytic explanations of religion have not been ignored by modern Christian apologists.

Sigmund Freud, *The Origins of Religion*, edited by A. Dickson (1985); P. Balogh, *Freud: A Biographical Introduction* (1971); A.J. de Luca, *Freud and Future Religious Experience* (1976); P. Gay, *A Godless Jew: Freud, Atheism and the Making of Psychoanalysis* (1987); H. Philp, *Freud and Religious Belief* (1956).

Froissart, Jean (*c.* 1335–*c.* 1405) Historian. Froissart was born in Valenciennes, France, but at an early age visited the English court. Queen Philippa, wife of King Edward III, was his patron and with her encouragement he travelled throughout Europe collecting material for his chronicles. These cover the history of Europe between 1325 and 1400 and are largely based on the accounts of eyewitnesses. They give a lively, if sometimes unreliable, account of the events of the fourteenth century and have been frequently reprinted.

Froissart's Chronicles, abridged by G. Beretson (1968); G.G. Coulton, *The Chronicler of European Chivalry* (1930).

Froude, Richard Hurrell (1803–36) Devotional Writer. Froude was educated at the University of Oxford where he came under the influence of John Henry NEWMAN and John KEBLE. After his early death from tuberculosis, his *Remains* was published, edited by Newman, and caused a storm of protest. He was extremely negative about the Protestant Reformers, he was devoted to the notion of celibacy and keen on strict ascetic practices. This was all foreign to mainstream Anglican opinion in the early nineteenth century and was a foretaste of the scandal that was to erupt with Newman's later defection to Rome.

P. Brendon, *Hurrell Froude and the Oxford Movement* (1974); G.C. Faber, *Oxford Apostles: A Character Study of the Oxford Movement* (1933).

Frumentius (fourth century) Saint, Bishop and Missionary. Frumentius was said to have been captured off a merchant ship by Ethiopians. He seized the opportunity to spread the gospel among his captors and was subsequently consecrated a Bishop by ATHANASIUS in Alexandria. He is much venerated as the founder of the Ethiopian Church and his see, Axum, is regarded as a sacred city.

L.E. O'Leary, *The Ethiopian Church* (1936).

Fry, Elizabeth (1780–1845) Philanthropist. Fry was born Elizabeth Gurney in Norwich, England, and married the London merchant, Joseph Fry. She was a devout member of the Society of Friends and in 1811 was admitted as a 'minister'. She is remembered as a pioneer of prison reform. In 1813 she began reading the Bible to the female prisoners in Newgate and by 1818 she was considered sufficiently expert to be giving evidence on the state of the nation's prisons to a Parliamentary committee. Despite having a large family, she continued to work for the betterment of prisons both in Britain and abroad while, at the same time, she also campaigned for hostels for the homeless. After her death a hostel for discharged prisoners was named after her in London. Her work was inspired by her religious faith and her philanthropy was combined with an active desire to spread the gospel.

Elizabeth Fry, *Memoir*, edited by two of her daughters, 2nd edn (1848); J. Kent, *Elizabeth Fry* (1962).

Fulbert (*c.* 960–1028) Saint, Educator and Bishop. Fulbert was born in Italy and studied at the schools of Rheims and Chartres. He became Chancellor of Chartres Cathedral School, making it one of the most lively in Europe. Subsequently it was to include BERNARD OF CHARTRES, THIERRY OF CHARTRES and GILBERT DE LA PORRÉE among its students. In 1007 Fulbert was consecrated Bishop of Chartres. His surviving writings include hymns and sermons. The existing crypt of Chartres Cathedral was built under his supervision.

L.C. Mackinney, *Bishop Fulbert and Education at the School of Chartres* (1957).

Fuller, Andrew (1754–1815) Theologian. Fuller was born in Cambridgeshire, England, and was ordained a Baptist minister at the age of twenty-one. He was self-educated, but he made an extensive study of the Scriptures and of the work of thinkers such as Jonathan EDWARDS. His book *The Gospel Worthy of All Acceptance*, published in 1785, created considerable controversy among the Baptists and did much to break down the extreme Calvinism among them. However, it also caused some Baptist leaders to break off and form their own Strict and Particular Baptist denomination. Fuller was an important influence on William CAREY and from 1792 until the year of his death, he was secretary of the Baptist Missionary Society.

G. Laws, *Andrew Fuller, Pastor, Theologian, Ropeholder* (1942).

G

Galgani, Gemma (1878–1903) Saint and Mystic. Galgani was born in Camigliano, Italy, of a poor family. Illness prevented her acceptance as a nun in the Passionists' congregation. Throughout her short life she had mystical experiences of various types which she recorded in her letters. She received the stigmata and offered herself as a victim for the expiation of the sins of the world. She was frequently plagued by demons, but, as she herself wrote, 'I am contented, because suffering thus and suffering ceaselessly, I am doing God's most holy will.'

A. della M. del Buon Pastore, *Life of Gemma Galgani* (1935).

Galileo Galilei (1564–1642) Scientist. Galileo was born in Pisa, Italy. He was educated at the university there and in 1589 he was appointed Professor of Mathematics. Two years later he moved first to Florence and then to the University of Padua where he remained until 1610. It was during this period that he discovered the four moons orbiting the planet Jupiter, which led him to support the Copernican theory of the solar system. In 1610 he was appointed philosopher and mathematician to the Duke of Tuscany. Galileo is remembered in Christian history for his conflict with the Church authorities. At this period, largely for theological reasons, the Church was still insisting on the Ptolemaic explanation of the universe, that all the heavenly bodies circled the earth. In 1616 Copernicus's theory – that the sun was at the centre of the solar system – was con-

demned and Galileo was forbidden to teach it. Nevertheless in 1632 he published his *Dialogo dei Due Massimi Sistemi del Mondo*, showing the inadequacies of the Ptolemaic view. He was brought to trial before the Inquisition and, under threat of torture, was forced to recant. According to legend, even at this point, he is said to have whispered that none the less the earth *does* move. He was sentenced to life imprisonment under suspicion of heresy and died while under house arrest.

M.A. Finocchiaro (ed. and transl.), *The Galileo Affair: A Documentary History* (1989); J.J. Langford, *Galileo, Science and the Church* (1966); M. Sharratt, *Galileo: Decisive Innovator* (1994).

Galla Placidia (*c.* 390–450) Ruler. Galla Placidia was the daughter of THEODOSIUS I. She became regent on the accession of her son Valentinian III and established her court at Ravenna. She was a dedicated Christian and she is remembered for her unrelenting opposition to all forms of heresy, particularly that of EUTYCHES. Several of the Ravenna churches were built under her patronage, including her own splendid mausoleum.

S.I. Oost, *Galla Placidia Augusta: A Biographical Essay* (1968).

Gardiner, Stephen (*c.* 1490–1555) Bishop and Politician. Gardiner was educated at the University of Cambridge. He was introduced to public life by Cardinal WOLSEY and became involved in the negotiations for the divorce between King HENRY VIII and Queen Catherine of Aragon. In 1532 he was consecrated Bishop of Winchester and in 1533 he presided over a court nullifying the marriage. He was a supporter of the King's supremacy in the Church, arguing in his *De Vera Obedientia* that the Pope had no jurisdiction over national Churches. None the less he was not a Protestant. He was probably the author of the Six Articles and he was imprisoned and deprived of his bishopric during the reign of the Protestant King EDWARD VI. With the accession of the Roman Catholic Queen MARY, he was reinstated and he was appointed Lord High Chancellor. He approved of the resubmission of the Church of England to Rome, but he succeeded in negotiating the very English compromise that the old monastic lands should remain in the hands of their new secular owners.

Stephen Gardiner, *Letters*, edited by J.A. Muller (1932); J.A. Muller, *Stephen Gardiner and the Tudor Reaction* (1926).

Gaunilo (eleventh century)   Theologian. Gaunilo was a Benedictine monk of the community of Marmoutiers, France. He criticised ANSELM's ontological argument for the existence of God (as expressed in his *Proslogion)*, by taking on the guise of the fool 'who says in his heart there is no God' (Psalm 14:1) and writing his *Liber pro Insipiente*. Gaunilo's intervention caused Anselm to refine the argument still further in his *Liber Apologeticus adversus Respondentem pro Insipiente*.

R.W. Southern, *St Anselm and his Biographer* (1963).

Gelasius I (d. 496)   Saint and Pope. Gelasius was probably a Roman citizen from Africa. Against the background of the Acacian Schism between the Church of Rome and that of Constantinople, Gelasius consistently upheld the supremacy of Rome. Many of his letters survive, as well as a treatise against the heretics EUTYCHES and NESTORIUS. He laid down the rule that ordinations should take place during the four groups of Ember Days and he encouraged Communion in both kinds. He is remembered for his statement to the Emperor Anastasius I that the world is ruled by two powers, the sacred authority of the priesthood and the authority of kings, both of which are bestowed by God and are independent of each other. This was to be much quoted in mediaeval political theory. The Gelasian Sacramentary and the *Decretum Gelasianium*, listing the books of the Bible, are wrongly ascribed to him.

B. Moreton, *The Eighth-Century Gelasian Sacramentary* (1976); A.K. Ziegler, 'Pope Galasius I and his teaching on the relation of Church and State', *Catholic Historical Review*, xxvii (1942).

Geneviève (*c.* 422–*c.* 500)   Saint. Little certain is known of the life of St Geneviève. She is said to have dedicated herself to God at the early age of seven. Under the direction of St GERMANUS OF AUXERRE, she became a nun when she was fifteen and between the ages of fifteen and fifty she ate only barley bread, and that only twice a week. Subsequently, in obedience to her Bishop, she added a little fish and milk to the regime. In 451 the troops of Attila the Hun were diverted from their march on Paris – supposedly as a direct result of her prayers. In consequence she is regarded as the patron saint of Paris.

D.H. Farmer (ed.), *The Oxford Dictionary of Saints*, 3rd edn (1992).

Geoffrey of Monmouth (*c.* 1100–54) Bishop and Historian. Geoffrey was a nephew of Uchtryd, Bishop of Llandaff. In *c.* 1140, he was appointed Archdeacon of St Teilo's and he became Bishop of St Asaph just before his death. He is remembered for his *Historia Britonum* which claims to be a translation of an older Celtic book. Although not historically accurate, it is the source of much later British mythology – in particular the story of King Arthur and his Knights of the Round Table, the tales of the Wizard Merlin – and it emphasised the common ancestry of Britons, Anglo-Saxons and Normans.

J.S.P. Tatlock, *The Legendary History of Britain* (1950).

George (? third/fourth century) Legendary Saint. Little is known of the life of St George, although he is believed to have died a martyr, possibly at Lydda in Palestine. He is the subject of many legends including that of the slaying of a fearsome dragon. Most authorities believe that this is a Christianised version of the tale of the Greek hero, Perseus. He became the patron saint of England in the thirteenth century when King Edward III nominated him as guardian of the new Order of the Garter. In recent years, because doubt has been cast on his existence, the Roman Catholic Church has removed George from its calendar of saints, but his flag (a red cross on a white background) remains the flag of England and a component of the Union Jack.

G.J. Marcus, *Saint George of England* (1939).

George Scholarius (*c.* 1400–*c.* 1468) Patriarch. George was a teacher of philosophy in Constantinople who spoke in favour of reunion with the Church of Rome at the Council of Florence in 1439. By *c.* 1450, however, he had become a leader of the anti-union party. He entered a monastery and, after the capture of Constantinople by the Muslims, he was appointed Patriarch under the name of Gennadius II. With Sultan Mohammed II, a concordat between the Orthodox Church and the Muslim secular power was established and this remained in force until 1923. He soon resigned his charge, however, and returned to his monastery. He was a prolific author and his works include translations of the writings of St THOMAS AQUINAS into Greek and a *Confession*, which was a dialogue with the Sultan, defending the Christian position.

J. Gill, *Personalities of the Council of Florence and Other Essays* (1964).

Gerhard, Johann (1582–1637) Theologian and Devotional Writer. Gerhard was born in Quedlingburg, Germany and was educated at the Universities of Wittenberg, Jena and Marburg. In 1616, after a period in the service of the Duke of Coburg, he became a professor at Jena. He is remembered both for his theological and for his devotional writings. His *Confessio Catholica* and *Loci Theologici* were regarded as standard statements of the Lutheran theological position, and his *Meditationes* was being reprinted as late as 1846.

A.E. McGrath, *Reformation Thought: An Introduction* (1988).

Gerhardt, Paul (1607–76) Poet. Gerhardt was born in Saxony and was educated at the University of Wittenberg. After a time as a tutor, he served as a Lutheran pastor at Mittenwalde and at St Nicolaikirche in Berlin. In 1668, he was appointed Archdeacon of Lüben. He is remembered as a prolific and popular hymn writer. His hymns are still sung in Germany and many have been translated into English, including 'The duteous day now closeth', 'Jesu thy boundless love to me' (translated by Charles WESLEY) and 'O sacred head sore wounded'. This last became a central theme in J.S. BACH's *St Matthew Passion*.

T.B. Hewitt, *Paul Gerhardt as a Hymnwriter and his Influence on English Hymnology* (1919).

Germanus of Auxerre (*c.* 378–448) Saint and Bishop. Germanus was consecrated Bishop of Auxerre in 418. There are many legends about his life, but some events are certain. He visited Britain in 429 to combat the heresy of PELAGIUS and he made a second visit some years later to lead the British against the Picts and the Saxons. Later he visited Ravenna. It is said that he was an influential teacher. St PATRICK is thought to have been instructed by him in Gaul and he is

believed to have encouraged the ascetic St
GENEVIÈVE in her holy practices.

G. Le Bras (ed.), *Saint Germain d'Auxerre et son
Temps* (1950) [no English translation available];
E.A. Thompson, *Saint Germanus of Auxerre and
the End of Roman Britain* (1984).

Germanus of Constantinople (c. 634–
c. 733) Patriarch and Liturgist. Germanus was Patriarch of Constantinople
between 715 and 730. One of his first acts
as Patriarch was to condemn the Monothelite heresy – the belief that JESUS
CHRIST, although he had two natures,
had but a single will. He came into conflict with the Emperor LEO III over the
question of icons. The Emperor legis-
lated against the veneration of pictures;
Germanus was determined in his opposition to the decree and was eventually
compelled to resign his office. He was the
author of seven homilies on the Blessed
Virgin MARY and was a promoter of her
cult. He also probably wrote the *Historia
Mystica Ecclesiae Catholicae*, an important liturgical work.

F.E. Brightman, 'The *Historia Mystagogica* and
other Greek commentaries on the Byzantine liturgy', *Journal of Theological Studies*, ix (1907–8).

Germanus of Paris (c. 496–576) Saint
and Bishop. An important saint in the
French Church, Germanus was Abbot of
St Symphorian, Autun, and in 555 he was
consecrated Bishop of Paris. He exerted
great influence on King Childebert, the
son of CLOVIS, and did much to curb his
excesses. Many legends are associated
with him and he is buried in the Church
of St Vincent in Paris, which was renamed the church of St Germain-des-
Près in his honour.

F.L. Cross (ed.), *The Oxford Dictionary of the
Christian Church*, 2nd edn (1976).

Gerson, Jean le Charlier de (1363–1429)
Devotional Writer, Mystic and Theo-
logian. Gerson was born in the Ar-
dennes, France, and was educated at the
University of Paris where he was influenced by the nominalism of WILLIAM
OF OCKHAM. In 1395 he was appointed
Chancellor of the University, but in 1397
he moved to Bruges and he returned to
Paris only in 1401. He was the author of
several mystical treatises including *The
Mountain of Contemplation*, *Mystical
Theology* and the *Perfection of the
Heart*. These were much admired by such
diverse figures as NICHOLAS OF CUSA
and Gerhard GROOTE. He argued that
the Pope did not have absolute powers
and that in an emergency, a General
Council had the right to call a Pope to
account. These views were stated in his
De Potestate Ecclesiastica. He took part
in the Council of Pisa in 1409 and in the
Council of Constance which deposed
Popes Gregory XII, BENEDICT XIII and
JOHN XXIII. Because he had incurred the
displeasure of the Duke of Burgundy by
denouncing Jean Petit's tyrannicidical
writings, he was not allowed to return to
Paris. He spent the remainder of his life
in an abbey near Vienna and in seclusion
in Lyons. Gerson is regarded as one of
the chief theorists of the Conciliar
movement and he has been described as
the father of Gallicanism.

J.L. Connolly, *John Gerson, Reformer and Mystic*
(1928); J.B. Morrall, *Gerson and the Great Schism*
(1960).

Gertrude (626–59) Saint. Gertrude was
the daughter of King Pepin the Elder.
Her mother founded a convent in
Nivelles, Belgium, and Gertrude became
its first Abbess. She is a highly popular
saint in the Netherlands and Belgium.
Her symbol is a mouse (although the legend attached to this has been forgotten)
and she is the patron saint of travellers.

F.L. Cross (ed.), *The Oxford Dictionary of the
Christian Church*, 2nd edn (1974).

Gertrude the Great (1256–c. 1302)
Saint, Mystic and Devotional Writer.
Gertrude was born in Eisleben and was
educated at the convent in Helfta in

Thuringia. In 1281, at the age of twenty-five, she had her first mystical experience and from then on she led a life of contemplation. Her *Legatus Divinae Pietatis* is a classic of mediaeval spirituality. She was one of the first exponents of the cult of the Sacred Heart, her visions of which she described. She was also responsible for a collection of prayers known as *Exercitia Spiritualia*, which have been much used in Roman Catholic circles. Known as 'Gertrude the Great', she is the patron of the West Indies.

Anon, *St Gertrude the Great* (1912); D. H. Farmer (ed.), *Oxford Dictionary of Saints*, 3rd edn (1992).

Ghéon, Henri (1875–1944) Poet and Playwright. Ghéon was the pen-name of Henri Léon Vangeon, who was born in Bray-sur-Seine, France, and who trained as a doctor. As an adolescent, he lost his faith, but in his late thirties, after the death of his niece, he rejoined the Roman Catholic Church. He is remembered as the author of the verse collection *Chanson d'Aube* and for his Christian dramas which included *La Vie Profonde de S. François d'Assisi*, *Le Mystère du Roi S. Louis* and *Mystère des Prodiges de Notre-Dame de Verdun*. He founded a theatre group of young people for the performance of his plays which had clear similarities with mediaeval mystery dramas. He also wrote successful biographies of saints including TERESA OF LISIEUX, John BOSCO, VINCENT FERRER and MARTIN OF TOURS.

M. Deléglise, *Le Théâtre d'Henri Ghéon* (1947) [no English translation available].

Gibbon, Edward (1735–94) Historian. Gibbon was born in Putney, near London, and was educated at the University of Oxford. For a short time he became a Roman Catholic, but by 1754 he had returned to Protestantism. Of private means, he dedicated himself to scholarship and he is chiefly remembered for his monumental *Decline and Fall of the Roman Empire*. This learned study is in seven volumes and it prompted the somewhat philistine King George III to remark, 'Scribble, scribble, scribble, Mr Gibbon!' Gibbon argued that the fall of the Roman Empire was the result of the 'triumph of religion and barbarism'. He was particularly scathing about the rapid acceptance of the Christian religion in the ancient world, which he believed was due to the intolerant zeal of the early Christians, their promise of a future life, the apparent miracles in the Church, the ethical standard of Church members and the internal discipline of the institution. His approach was consistently ironical, sceptical, humane and civilised. *Decline and Fall* remains a classic of English literature and historical scholarship.

Edward Gibbon, *Memoirs of my Life*, edited by G.A. Bonnard (1966); H.L. Bond, *The Literary Art of Edward Gibbon* (1960); S.T. McCloy, *Gibbon's Antagonism to Christianity* (1933); R. Porter, *Edward Gibbon: Making History* (1988).

Gibbons, James (1834–1921) Cardinal, Archbishop, Theologian and Church Leader. Gibbons was the son of Irish immigrants to the United States of America and he was born in Baltimore. He became a Roman Catholic priest and was consecrated Archbishop of Baltimore in 1877. He received his Cardinal's hat in 1886. The American Roman Catholic Church of the late nineteenth century was largely made up of hordes on non-English-speaking immigrants and the earlier Protestant settlers were intolerant of Catholicism. Gibbons was determined to show that the Catholic population could be good Americans. He dedicated himself to programmes of Americanisation and was a leading light in the foundation of the Catholic University of America and the National Catholic Welfare Conference. As the leading Catholic prelate of his day, he did much to break down prejudice and assimilate the new citizens into the 'melting pot' of American society.

J.T. Ellis, *The Life of James Cardinal Gibbons*, 2 vols (1952).

Gibbons, Orlando (1583–1625) Composer. Gibbons served as organist of the Chapel Royal and Westminster Abbey in London. He was the first composer to write music only for the English Protestant rite and many of his anthems are still sung today, particularly in English cathedrals. The best known include 'Hosanna to the Son of David' and 'Almighty and Everlasting God'.

T. Armstrong, *Orlando Gibbons* (1951); E.H. Fellowes, *Orlando Gibbons*, 2nd edn (1970).

Gichtel, Johann Georg (1638–1710) Mystic and Sect Founder. Gichtel was born in Regensberg, Germany, and was educated at the University of Strasbourg. He was brought up a Lutheran, but was influenced by the mystical writings of Jakob BOEHME and broke away from the Church. He got into difficulties with the authorities and eventually he settled in Amsterdam. There he produced the first complete edition of Boehme's works and developed his own doctrines, which involved a mystical marriage between divine wisdom and the human soul. His followers became known as the Angelic Brethren. They esteemed Boehme's writings as highly as the Bible and they renounced earthly marriage. Gottfried Arnold, the German devotional writer, was among those whom he influenced. The sect continued to exist in the Netherlands and Germany until the end of the nineteenth century.

G.C.A. von Harless, *Jakob Boehme und die Alchymisten* (1870) [no English translation available].

Gilbert de la Porrée (*c.* 1080–1154) Bishop and Theologian. Gilbert was born in Poitiers, France, and was a pupil of BERNARD OF CHARTRES and ANSELM OF LAON. He was consecrated Bishop of Poitiers in 1142. He was the author of commentaries on the Psalms and on the Epistles of St PAUL. However, he is mainly remembered for his teachings on the Trinity, which he expressed in his commentary on the work of BOETHIUS. He defended his position at the Council of Rheims in 1148 where he was opposed by PETER LOMBARD. Although there was much discussion, Gilbert's view was not condemned and his followers, known as the Porretani, continued to promulgate it. However, in 1215, at the Fourth Lateran Council, Peter Lombard's formulation was accepted as orthodox.

M.E. Williams, *The Teaching of Gilbert Porreta on the Trinity as Found in his Commentary on Boethius* (1951).

Gilbert of Sempringham (*c.* 1083–1189) Saint and Order Founder. Gilbert was born in Sempringham, now in Lincolnshire, England. After ordination, he became the parish priest of Sempringham and there he encouraged seven women to follow the Cistercian Rule. The order grew and several houses were established. However, in 1148, the authorities of Citeaux refused to accept women as members of the order, so Gilbert organised that they be supervised by the Augustinian Canons. Thus the Gilbertines, as they were called, became a mixed double order. By 1189, the year of Gilbert's death, there were nine mixed houses and by the time of the dissolution of the monasteries in the reign of King HENRY VIII, there were twenty-five. The order never spread beyond England.

R. Graham, *St Gilbert of Sempringham and the Gilbertines* (1901).

Giles (? eighth century) Saint. Little is known of the life of St Giles. He is said to have been a native of Athens who lived as a hermit on the banks of the Rhône in France. He survived on a diet of herbs and the milk of a hind. When King Flavius Wamba of the Visigoths hunted the hind and met Giles, he was so impressed by his sanctity that he had a monastery built for him. Later the town of St Giles grew up near his grave and this became an important place of pilgrimage. He is regarded as the patron saint of beggars and the lame; he was extremely popular in the Middle Ages and is regarded as one of the fourteen Auxiliary Saints.

F. Brittain, *Saint Giles* (1928); D.H. Farmer (ed.), *The Oxford Dictionary of Saints*, 3rd edn (1992).

Giles of Rome (d. 1316) Archbishop, Theologian and Philosopher. Giles was born in Rome, Italy. He was a student of St THOMAS AQUINAS at the University of Paris and he joined the order of Augustinian Hermits. He was appointed General of the order in 1292. He was tutor to King Philip IV of France and he was consecrated Archbishop of Bourges in 1295. He was a prolific writer, but he is mainly remembered for his political treatise *De Regimine Principum* and for his *De Ecclesiastica Potestate*. In this last he defended the power of the Pope as the fulfilment of the ideal promulgated by St AUGUSTINE in his *Civitas Dei*. It inspired Pope BONIFACE VIII's famous bull *Unam Sanctam*, which asserted that it was necessary for salvation for every human being to be subject to the Roman Pontiff. Giles was known as 'Doctor Fundatissimus' and his books were prescribed reading in the Augustinian schools after 1287.

R.W. Dyson, *Giles of Rome on Ecclesiastical Power* (1986).

Gill, Eric (1882–1940) Artist. Gill was the son of a Methodist minister who subsequently was ordained in the Church of England. He himself, at the age of thirty-one, was received into the Roman Catholic Church and took vows as a Dominican Tertiary. He was well known as a sculptor, letterist and wood-engraver and his art was in-tended as an expression of his Christianity. His works included the *Stations of the Cross* in Westminster Cathedral and a bas-relief of the *Creation of Adam* for the League of Nations Hall in Geneva. A committed pacifist, he was also a writer on social issues and a prolific illustrator. He formed his own family into a quasi-religious community and his private life, particularly with regard to his relationship with his daughters, was decidedly unconventional.

Eric Gill, *Autobiography* (1940); F. MacCarthy, *Eric Gill* (1989); R. Speaight, *The Life of Eric Gill* (1966).

Gillespie, Thomas (1708–74) Denomination Founder. Gillespie was minister of Carnock, Fife, Scotland. He was a friend of Jonathan EDWARDS. He was deposed from his parish by the Church of Scotland General Assembly in 1752 because he refused to take part in a forced settlement. He was supported by his congregation and in 1761, with two other ministers, he founded the Relief denomination. This was notable for its support of foreign missions and for offering Communion to all Christian believers. In 1847 the Relief joined with the United Secession Church (originally founded by Ebenezer ERSKINE) to form the United Presbyterian Church of Scotland. Later, in 1900, the United Presbyterians joined with the Free Church of Scotland to make up the United Free Church of Scotland.

R.S. Wright (ed.), *Fathers of the Kirk* (1960).

Giotto di Bondone (c. 1266–1337) Artist. Giotto worked in Florence where he was appointed head of the Florence Cathedral School in 1334. A contemporary of DANTE, his portrayal of biblical scenes was totally different from that of the existing majestic Byzantine tradition and extremely influential. Although his saints wear halos, they are portrayed as real people, living on solid ground. His best-known works are his frescos in the Arena Chapel, Padua. Although by later standards his perspective was technically faulty, his placing of figures on the ground and in the landscape emphasises their human interaction.

M. Barasch, *Giotto and the Language of Gesture* (1987); L. Schneider, *Giotto in Perspective* (1974); J. Stubblebine, *Giotto: The Arena Chapel Frescos* (1969).

Giovanni Capistrano (1386–1456) Missionary and Saint. Giovanni was born in Capistrano in Italy. He studied law at the University of Perugia and in 1412 he married and was appointed Governor of Naples. While a prisoner of war, he had a vision of St FRANCIS OF ASSISI and in 1416 he disentangled himself from his marriage and joined the Franciscan Order. He preached throughout Italy and became Vicar-General of the cismontane community. He supported BERNARDINO in his reforms of the order and defended him before Pope MARTIN V. In 1451 he was sent by Pope NICHOLAS V to preach against the teachings of John HUS in Austria, Hungary and Bohemia. He was highly effective in this mission, which was only curtailed by the capture of Constantinople by the Turks in 1453. Inspired by the danger, he travelled to Hungary to preach a crusade. He succeeded in raising an army which defeated the Turks in 1456 and which diverted them from Belgrade. He himself died of plague the same year. Giovanni is remembered as one of the early heroes of the Franciscan Order.

G. Hofer, *St John Capistran, Reformer*, translated by P. Cummins (1943).

Glas, John (1695–1773) Denomination Founder. Glas was the son of the minister of Auchtermuchty, Fife, Scotland, and was educated at the University of St Andrews. He himself was ordained a minister in the Church of Scotland and served the parish of Tealing in 1719. In 1730, however, he was deposed from his pulpit because he refused to accept that the Church should be controlled by the secular powers. These views were expressed in his *Testimony of the King of Martyrs concerning his Kingdom*. With his son-in-law, Robert SANDEMAN, he founded a series of new congregations. Members of the new sect were known as Glasites or Sandemanians and the movement eventually spread from Scotland to Yorkshire, London and the United States of America. Glas taught that creeds and catechisms should be abandoned and that the Bible should be the only spiritual guide. This he interpreted very literally and the Glasites were known for their customs of washing each other's feet and for their revival of the *agape*, or common religious meal.

H. Escott, *A History of Scottish Congregationalism* (1960).

Gordon, Lord George (d. 1793) Polemicist. Gordon was born of an aristocratic Scottish family. He was a determined opponent of Roman Catholicism and in 1779 he became President of the Protestant Association. In 1778 the British Parliament had passed a Relief Act which extended some civil liberties to Roman Catholics. Gordon was outraged. In 1780 he led a huge procession to Parliament with a petition demanding the Act's repeal. The occasion became the excuse for a serious disturbance, later known as the Gordon Riots. Roman Catholic chapels were destroyed, Newgate Prison was burnt down and the Bank of England was attacked. Eventually King George III stepped in and personally ordered the army to dispel the riots. In the ensuing mêlée, nearly three hundred people died. The riots are vividly described by the novelist Charles Dickens in his *Barnaby Rudge*. Gordon himself was arrested, but was acquitted of high treason and he subsequently converted to Judaism. He died insane in prison.

P. Colson, *The Strange History of Lord George*

Gordon (1937); C. Hibbert, *King Mob: The Story of Lord George Gordon and the Riots of 1780* (1958).

Gore, Charles (1853–1932) Bishop, Theologian and Order Founder. Gore was educated at the University of Oxford. He was ordained in 1875 and in 1883 he became the first Principal of Pusey House. He was a dedicated Anglo-Catholic, but he brought a degree of liberalism into the movement. In 1889, *Lux Mundi*, a collection of essays edited by him, caused a sensation. In the preface he argued that changing times 'required a new point of view' and that the aim of the book was to 'put the Catholic faith into its right relationship to modern intellectual and moral problems'. In his own essay on the Holy Spirit and inspiration, he accepted scientific hermeneutical principles. Gore became a Canon of Westminster in 1894, Bishop of Worcester in 1902, the first Bishop of Birmingham in 1905 and Bishop of Oxford in 1911. He was an immensely influential figure within the Church of England, not least for his founding of the Community of the Resurrection (now at Mirfield), an Anglican community dedicated to educational and pastoral work.

The Community of the Resurrection Diamond Jubilee Book (1952); J. Carpenter, *Gore: A Study in Liberal Catholic Thought* (1960); W.R. Inge, 'Bishop Gore and the Church of England', in *Outspoken Essays* (1919).

Goreh, Nehemiah (1825–95) Theologian. Goreh was born in Benares, India, of a Brahmin family. He converted to Christianity 'being much struck by the beauty of Christ's teaching in the Sermon on the Mount'. He was a prolific writer and his works include *Theism and Christianity, The Brahmos, Their Ideas of Sin* and *Proofs of the Divinity of Our Lord*. A convinced Anglican, he wrote against Roman Catholicism as well as against Hindu theological systems. He joined the Society of St John the Evangel-

ist and the last years of his life were spent in the society's house in Poona. He is primarily remembered for his conviction that, although the Hindu notion of the divine was erroneous, in some ways it was 'a presentiment of the future gift' to be found in Christianity.

C.E. Gardner, *Life of Father Goreh* (1900); A.M. Paradkar, *Theology of Nehemiah Goreh* (1969).

Gorham, George Cornelius (1787–1857) Theologian. Gorham was born in Towthorpe, Yorkshire, and was educated at the University of Cambridge. He served in various parishes, but in 1847, the Bishop of Exeter refused to institute him into his new charge of Brampford Speke on the grounds that he did not believe in baptismal regeneration. Gorham brought a case against the Bishop in the provincial ecclesiastical courts, but the court found against him. Nothing daunted, Gorham appealed to the Judicial Committee of the Privy Council. Although the Council did not feel itself to be qualified to pronounce on the truth or error of Gorham's opinions, it decreed that they did not seem to be inconsistent with Anglican doctrine. The High Church party were appalled. The judgement indicated that even Church doctrine was subject to the secular powers and it was the occasion of MANNING's secession to the Church of Rome. Many supported Gorham, however, and his legal fees were paid by public subscription.

J.C.S. Nias, *Gorham and the Bishop of Exeter* (1951).

Görres, Johann Joseph von (1776–1848) Theologian. Görres was born in Coblenz, Germany. After a period as a teacher, he dedicated himself to the cause of German independence. In 1814 he started the *Rheinische Merkur*, the first important German newspaper, which was suppressed by the authorities in 1816. He returned to the Roman Catholic

Church in 1824 and from thenceforth dedicated himself to theology. His most important work was his *Christliche Mystik*, a study of Christian mysticism. He also published several tracts demanding greater freedom for the Catholic Church in Germany. From 1827 he taught at the University of Munich where he was at the centre of a group of scholars dedicated to the revival of Catholicism. The Görres-Gesellschaft, founded on the centenary of his birth, is an important society devoted to Catholic scholarly research.

The Catholic University of America, *New Catholic Encyclopaedia* (1967).

Gorton, Samuel (*c.* 1592–1677) Denomination Founder. Gorton was born in Lancashire, England, but emigrated to Massachusetts in 1637. He quickly came into conflict with the authorities for his religious views. He taught that immortality was not a necessary attribute of the human soul, but depended for its existence on the behaviour of the individual; he also cast doubt on the nature and existence of the Trinity. He founded the colony of Shawomet, which was renamed Warwick in honour of the Earl of Warwick, who had guaranteed its religious liberty. His followers were called Gortonites and the sect survived into the eighteenth century.

A. Gorton, *The Life of Samuel Gorton* (1907).

Goscelin (d. after 1107) Historian. Goscelin was a French Benedictine monk. He moved to England in 1058 in the service of Herman, Bishop of Sherborne, and in *c.* 1090, he finally settled in Canterbury. He wrote an account of the lives of many of the early Anglo-Saxon saints, including St AUGUSTINE OF CANTERBURY, St Ives, St Werburgh, St Edith, St Wulfhilde, St Lawrence of Canterbury, St Wulsin, St Justus and St Milburg. The memory of many of these saints is only preserved as a result of his chronicle.

A. Wilmart, 'Eve et Goscelin', *Revue Bénédictine*, xlvi (1934) [no English translation available].

Gossner, Johannes Evangelista (1773–1858) Missionary and Philanthropist. Gossner was born in Augsberg, Germany, and was educated at the University of Dillinger. After ordination he served a variety of congregations in Germany and in 1829 he moved to Berlin. There he was pastor of the Bethlehem Church and was involved in numerous philanthropic activities. In particular he is remembered for the missionary society which he founded and which bears his name. Gossner missionaries have served mainly among the Khols of East India.

W. Holsten, *Johannes Evangelista Gossner: Glaube und Gemeinde* (1949) [no English translation available].

Gottschalk of Orbais (*c.* 804–*c.* 869) Theologian and Poet. Gottschalk was the son of a Saxon count. He was compelled to enter a Benedictine community and, although he seems to have been released from his vows by the 829 Synod of Mainz, this was opposed by his Abbot and he finally moved to Orbais. After studying the theology of St AUGUSTINE OF HIPPO, Gottschalk began to teach the doctrine of double predestination – that the elect are freely predestined to bliss and the damned to condemnation (on the foreknowledge of their guilt). He was opposed by RABANUS and he was condemned at the 848 Synod of Mainz and at the 849 Synod of Quiercy as denying human free will and God's universal saving rule. Although he was beaten and imprisoned, he was unrepentant and issued his *Confessio Prolixior*. He died unreconciled to the Church. His work was studied by the followers of Cornelius JANSEN in the seventeenth century. Gottschalk is also remembered as an important religious poet.

The Catholic University of America, *New Catholic Encyclopaedia* (1967).

Graf, Karl Heinrich (1815–69) Theologian. Graf was educated at the Protestant Seminary at Strasbourg and was a student of Edouard Reuss. He himself earned his living as a school-master. He came to the conclusion that the Pentateuch grew out of several earlier sources including P, a priestly document composed after the Babylonian exile. His theory was developed by Julius WELLHAUSEN, the biblical critic, who explained his 'documentary hypothesis' in his *Prolegomena to the History of Ancient Israel* published in 1883. Graf's contribution to the theory was particularly important because it showed that neither the Book of Deuteronomy nor the Deuteronomic histories had any knowledge of the Priestly Code. The whole theory is often known as the 'Graf–Wellhausen' hypothesis.

R.E. Clements, *A Century of Old Testament Study* (1983); W. Rogerson, *Old Testament Criticism in the Nineteenth Century* (1984).

Graham, William Franklin [Billy] (b. 1918) Missionary. Graham was born in North Carolina in the United States of America and he was educated at Bob Jones University, Florida Bible College and Wheaton College. He was ordained as a Southern Baptist minister and became an evangelist for the Youth for Christ movement. He achieved national fame through his Los Angeles Crusade of 1948 and he founded the Billy Graham Evangelistic Association. His adult life has been dedicated to spreading the gospel, and his crusades throughout the United States and Great Britain have attracted huge audiences. He has also contributed regularly to the newspapers; he founded the fortnightly *Christianity Today* and the monthly *Decision* and his books *Peace with God* and *World Aflame* have been best-sellers. He has been a hugely influential figure and has advised several American Presidents. Probably no evangelist has made such an impression in Britain since the time of Dwight L. MOODY and Ira D. SANKEY in the 1870s.

J. Pollock, *The Authorised Biography of Billy Graham* (1966).

Gratian (twelfth century) Historian and Legalist. Little is known of the life of Gratian. He was probably born in Chiusi, Italy, and was a professed Camaldolese monk. He is remembered for his *Concordantia Discordantium Canonum*, generally known as the *Decretum*. This is a collection of patristic texts, conciliar decrees and papal statements on the theme of Church discipline. It is presented in a commentary designed to reconcile the contradictions. It quickly became the standard text of Canon Law and forms the first part of the chief collection of Canon Law in the Roman Church before 1917, the *Corpus Iuris Canonici*.

S. Kuttner, 'The father of the science of Canon Law', *Juristi*, i (1948).

Grebel, Conrad (c. 1498–1526) Denomination Founder. Grebel was born in Zürich, Switzerland, and was educated at the Universities of Basle, Vienna and Paris. Initially he was a follower of Ulrich ZWINGLI, but became dissatisfied with his teaching. He rejected infant baptism and insisted on the primacy of Scripture, pacifism and the complete separation of Church and State. His Anabaptist group was founded when he baptised Georg Blaurock and Blaurock started the first Anabaptist congregation in Zöllikon, near Zürich. The authorities quickly took action against the new sect. Grebel was imprisoned and died soon afterwards. Blaurock became a travelling preacher. He converted many people before he was burned for heresy in 1529.

R.W. Estep, *The Anabaptist Story* (1963); R.J. Smithson, *The Anabaptists* (1935); G.H. Williams, *The Radical Reformation* (1962).

Green, Thomas Hill (1836–82) Philosopher. Green was educated at the

University of Oxford and taught at Balliol College under the mastership of Benjamin JOWETT. From 1878 he held a Chair in Moral Philosophy. He is remembered for his propagation of the views of the European philosophers Immanuel KANT and G.W.F. HEGEL. The British philosophical establishment had previous been dominated by empiricism. He was the author of the *Prolegomena to Ethics* and *Lectures on the Principles of Political Obligation* and he taught that morality and religion pointed to Spirit as the ultimate nature of reality. He was highly influential on the thinking of his students, particularly on that of Charles GORE and the *Lux Mundi* group.

W.D. Lamont, *Introduction to Green's Moral Philosophy* (1934); M. Richter, *The Politics of Conscience: T.H. Green and his Age* (1964).

Gregory I [the Great] (*c.* 540–604)   Pope, Theologian and Saint. Gregory was born in Rome and was educated as a lawyer. He was ordained Deacon by Pope Benedict I and was elected Pope in 590. At that period the city of Rome was under threat from the Lombards. Gregory was unable to persuade the imperial forces to defend the city so he sent his own troops. His administrative arrangements were an important stage in the foundation of the Papal States. In the religious sphere, he insisted that the See of Peter had universal jurisdiction and he did not hesitate to reverse a decision of the Patriarch of Constantinople. He asserted his control over the Frankish Church and he placed the Spanish Church under the care of his friend Bishop Leander. He sent St AUGUSTINE OF CANTERBURY on his mission to convert Britain and he rebuked the African Bishops' complacency over the Donatist schism. Gregory is also regarded as one of the four great doctors of the Roman Church and his theological works include the *Liber Regulae Pastoralis*, which became a standard guide for bishops, the *Dialogi* (a mystical life of St

BENEDICT), homilies on the Gospels, expositions of various books of the Bible and many letters. He was a dedicated promoter of monasticism; he encouraged the veneration of relics and he made some changes in the liturgy. Much of the Sacramentary which bears his name, however, is later. Gregory was the dominant figure of the late sixth-century Church. He did much to establish the Papacy as the supreme ecclesiastical power and he was canonised immediately after his death.

J. Richards, *Consul of God* (1980); C. Shaw, *Gregory the Great* (1991).

Gregory VII [Hildebrand] (*c.* 1023–85)   Pope and Saint. Gregory was born in Saona, Tuscany, and his original name was Hildebrand. As a young man, he was in the service of Pope Gregory VI, who was exiled in Germany. He returned to Rome with Pope LEO IX and was himself elected Pope by acclamation in 1073. This was, in fact, in violation of the law of 1059. Gregory was a reformer. He reinforced the laws against simony and clerical marriage, but he came into conflict with the German HENRY IV in 1075 over the question of lay investiture. After the Emperor was threatened with excommunication, he had a Diet at Worms declare Gregory deposed. Gregory retaliated by excommunicating Henry and releasing his subjects from their oath of allegiance. The Emperor was forced to make public penance at Canossa in 1077. During a subsequent civil war in Germany, Gregory supported Rudolf of Swabia and again excommunicated Henry. In response, at the Synod of Brixen in 1080, the Emperor negotiated the election of Antipope Clement III and in 1084 Gregory was taken into exile by the Norman prince Robert Guiscard. Despite these tempestuous events, Gregory is remembered for his reform of the Canon Law which was an important element in the regeneration of the mediaeval

Church. He was canonised in the seventeenth century.

A.J. Macdonald, *Hildebrand: A Life of Gregory VII* (1932); W. Ullman, *The Growth of Papal Government in the Middle Ages*, 2nd edn (1962).

Gregory IX (*c.* 1148–1241) Pope. Gregory was born Count Ugolino of Segni and was a nephew of Pope INNOCENT III. He was made a Cardinal in 1198, consecrated Bishop of Ostia in 1206 and was elected Pope in 1227. Earlier he had preached a crusade in north and central Italy and, as Pope, he excommunicated the Emperor FREDERICK II for insufficient enthusiasm for the project. Later he excommunicated him again for invading Lombardy and appropriating the rights of the Church in Sicily. In 1241 he summoned a General Council, but the Emperor prevented it from meeting and laid siege to Rome, during the course of which Gregory died. Gregory is remembered as the friend of St FRANCIS OF ASSISI and as a protector of his order. He entrusted the Inquisition into the hands of the Dominicans who combated the Albigensian heresy and he also supported the Cistercian and Camaldolese Orders. He encouraged RAYMOND OF PEÑAFORT to make a collection of papal decretals and he commissioned an official edition of the works of Aristotle.

J.N.D. Kelly (ed.), *The Oxford Dictionary of Popes* (1986).

Gregory X (1210–76) Pope. Gregory was born Teobaldo Visconti. In 1268, when he was elected Pope, the see of St PETER had been vacant for three years. Gregory is remembered for his confirmation of the election of Rudolf I, the first Hapsburg Holy Roman Emperor and for the agreement reached with the Greek Orthodox Church at the Second Council of Lyons in 1274/5. Unfortunately this did not last long. Gregory also tried to organise a crusade, but nothing came of it and he introduced the conclave as a device to hasten the election of a new Pope. This practice is followed to the present day.

J.N.D. Kelly (ed.), *The Oxford Dictionary of Popes* (1986).

Gregory XI (1329–78) Pope. Gregory was born Pierre Roger de Beaufort and was a nephew of Pope Clement VI. He was made a Cardinal at the age of nineteen and studied law at the University of Perugia. In 1370 he was elected Pope. He was the last of the Avignon Popes. While still in France he was compelled to wage war against the city of Florence, which led to a revolt in the Papal States. He was persuaded by St CATHERINE OF SIENA to return to Rome in 1377 to restore order, despite the hostility of the King of France and many of the Cardinals. His death was the signal for the Great Schism, with one Pope elected in Avignon and another in Rome. Gregory is also remembered as the Pope who condemned John WYCLIFFE.

J.N.D. Kelly (ed.), *The Oxford Dictionary of Popes* (1986); G. Mollat, *Les Papes d'Avignon* (1963).

Gregory XIII (1502–85) Pope. Gregory was born Ugo Buoncompagni in Bologna, Italy. After a legal training, he was appointed to a judgeship in Rome and he later became a jurist at the Council of Trent. He was ordained at the age of forty, was consecrated Bishop of Viesti, was appointed a Cardinal in 1565 and he was elected Pope in 1572. Gregory was one of the great Popes of the Counter-Reformation. Although he failed to bring back Sweden or England to the Catholic fold, he supported the Jesuits in their educational enterprises and he approved the reforms of St Charles BORROMEO. He also celebrated the news of the massacre of St BARTHOLOMEW's Day in France with a *Te Deum* in Rome. He was a tremendous builder with a clear notion of the grandeur that befitted the Papacy. As a result of his extravagance, the Vatican found itself in increasing financial difficulty. None the less he is remembered for his success in instituting the Gregorian Calendar, for founding the Gregorian University and for bringing about many reforms within the Catholic Church.

J.N.D. Kelly (ed.), *The Oxford Dictionary of Popes* (1986).

Gregory XVI (1765–1846) Pope. Gregory was born Bartolomeo Cappellari and he joined the Camaldolese Order at the age of eighteen. He was appointed a Cardinal in 1814; he became Prefect of Propaganda in 1826 and he was elected Pope in 1831. Almost immediately he faced revolution in the Papal States but, with the aid of Austrian troops, he managed to keep his hold on temporal power. In 1799 he had published *Il Trionfo della Santa Sede e della Chiesa*, in which he had argued for the infallibility of the Pope and for the Papal States being a bulwark against foreign and secular intervention. When Pope, he condemned the writings of LAMENNAIS for their liberalism and he is remembered as the last Pope who was also a secular prince. His successor, Pope PIUS IX, was to preside over the end of papal temporal power and to follow Gregory's lead in promulgating the doctrine of papal infallibility. Gregory also encouraged world-wide missionary activity; he appointed nearly two hundred missionary Bishops and he succeeded in centralising control of Catholic missions in the Vatican.

E.E.Y. Hales, *Revolution and Papacy 1769–1846* (1966); J.N.D. Kelly (ed.), *The Oxford Dictionary of Popes* (1986).

Gregory the Illuminator (c. 240–332) Saint, Missionary and Bishop. Gregory was a native of Armenia and may have been of royal descent. While in exile he became a Christian and, on his return to Armenia, he converted King Tiridates to the faith. Armenia then became the first country to adopt Christianity as its

official religion. Gregory himself was consecrated Catholicos (Bishop) in Cappadocia and for several generations this became a hereditary position. Initially the Armenian Church was under the jurisdiction of Caesarea, but between 374 and 1375 it was wholly independent.

L. Arpee, *A History of Armenian Christianity from the Beginning to our own Time* (1946).

Gregory of Nazianzus (c. 330–89) Bishop, Theologian and Saint. Gregory was the son of Gregory, Bishop of Nazianzus in Cappadocia. He was educated at Caesarea, where he became a life-long friend of St BASIL, and at the University of Athens. He was ordained priest in 362 and became Bishop of Sasima in 372. After the death of his father in 374, he retired to Seleucia. However, he was summoned to Constantinople to defend the Church against the teachings of ARIUS. He was a remarkable preacher and his five theological addresses against the Arians are masterpieces of theological reasoning. He attended the Council of Constantinople in 381, during the course of which he was consecrated Bishop of the city. Gregory is remembered as a successful and eloquent upholder of orthodoxy. Among his writings were the *Philocalia* (a selection of the works of ORIGEN), many letters and several treatises against the heresy of APOLLINARIUS.

R. Radford Ruether, *Gregory of Nazianzus: Rhetor and Philosopher* (1969).

Gregory of Nyssa (c. 330–c. 395) Bishop, Mystic, Theologian and Saint. Gregory was the younger brother of St BASIL and St MACRINA. Initially he became a teacher of rhetoric, but then he joined his brother's community and was consecrated Bishop of Nyssa. He was deposed by an Arian synod in 376, but was reinstated after the death of the Emperor Valens in 378. He took a prominent part in the Councils of Constantinople of both 381 and 394; he was much in demand as a preacher and during his lifetime he did a great deal of travelling. However, Gregory is remembered as a theologian. Influenced by ORIGEN, he maintained that the Fall was a consequence of free will and that redemption is effected through the incarnation of JESUS CHRIST and communicated through the Sacraments. He may well have been the first to compare the atonement with a fish hook on which the devil is impaled. His works include the *Sermo Catecheticus*, which expounds the doctrines of the incarnation, redemption, Sacraments and Trinity. He also wrote various exegetical and mystical works, which include a treatise on virginity. Although he lacked the practical abilities of his brother and sister, he was undoubtedly the best theologian. He was designated 'Father of Fathers' at the Seventh Ecumenical Council of 787.

A. Meredith, *The Cappadocians* (1995); E. Ferguson and A.J. Malherbe, *Gregory of Nyssa. The Life of Moses* (1978).

Gregory of Rimini (d. 1358) Philosopher. Gregory was a member of the Order of Augustinian Hermits. He was educated at the University of Paris and, after teaching at Bologna, Padua and Perugia, he was appointed a Doctor of the Sorbonne by Pope Clement VI in 1345. He became Vicar-General of his order in 1357. He is remembered as an important mediaeval philosopher. Influenced by WILLIAM OF OCKHAM and a determined Augustinian, he taught that actions performed without grace are sinful. He took this to its logical conclusion and maintained that unbaptised babies who die are condemned to eternal damnation. In consequence he was given the title 'Tortor Infantium' – the torturer of infants.

G. Leff, *Gregory of Rimini* (1961).

Gregory of Tours (c. 538–94) Bishop and Historian. Gregory was consecrated

Bishop of Tours in France in 573. He is remembered for his *Historia Francorum*, which covers the history of the Frankish people from the creation of the world to his own times. Although some of it is based on original documents, much of the history is doubtful. None the less the book gives an invaluable picture of Gaul in the sixth century. Gregory also wrote eight hagiographical works and was a dedicated Bishop, who instituted important reforms in his diocese.

J.M. Wallace-Hadrill, 'The work of Gregory of Tours in the light of modern research', *Transactions of the Royal Historical Society*, 5th series, i (1951).

Gregory Palamas (c. 1296–1359) Mystic, Theologian and Archbishop. Gregory was educated in Constantinople and in c. 1316, he joined the monastic community on Mount Athos. In 1326 he was ordained priest and in 1347 he was consecrated Archbishop of Thessalonica. Gregory is remembered as the chief defender of Hesychasm. The Hesychists devoted themselves to silent, mystical meditation through which they believed they could attain full unity with God. Mount Athos was the centre of the movement. The monks would pray with their chins pressed down on their chests, holding their breath until they fell into an ecstatic trance. It was then that they would experience the Divine Light. When the Hesychists were attacked in Constantinople, Gregory, in his 'Triads in defence of the holy Hesychists', argued that even though the essence of God was unknowable, God's energies could be perceived by human beings. In 1341 a council was summoned in Constantinople to discuss the issue and it upheld Gregory's doctrine of the Uncreated Light. Gregory is regarded as an important figure in the Orthodox mystical tradition.

J. Meyendorff, *Gregory Palamas* (1964); Gregory Palamas, *The Triads*, edited by J. Meyendorff et al. (1983).

Gregory Thaumaturgus (*c.* 213–*c.* 270) Saint, Bishop, Theologian and Missionary. Gregory was a pupil of ORIGEN in Caesarea and had trained as a lawyer. In *c.* 238, he was consecrated Bishop of Neocaesarea in Pontus. There are many legends about his miracles – hence his title Thaumaturgus ('wonder worker'). He believed that pagan learning could be used to promote Christianity, he turned traditional pagan festivals into Christian holidays and he was highly successful in bringing the pagan population of his diocese to the Church. He was the author of a treatise on the Trinity and a semi-autobiographical account of the teachings of Origen. During his time as Bishop, he combated the heresy of PAUL OF SAMOSATA and he witnessed the devastation of Pontus by the Goths. His biography was written by GREGORY OF NYSSA, whose grandmother, St Macrina the elder, was one of his students.

W. Telfer, 'The cultus of St Gregory Thaumaturgus', *Harvard Theological Review*, xxix (1936).

Griffiths, Ann (1776–1805) Poet and Mystic. Griffiths was born Ann Thomas in Wales. After an evangelical conversion in 1797, she joined the Methodist Society. In 1804 she married John Griffiths and she died the following year in childbirth. She composed her religious poems orally and she used to recite them to her servant, Ruth Evans. When Evans married the Methodist minister John Hughes, the poems were written down for the first time and published. Today they are still sung as hymns in the Welsh chapels.

Ann Griffiths, 'Memoirs', *Traethodydd* (1846).

Grignion de Montford, Louis-Marie (1673–1716) Devotional Writer, Order Founder, Missionary and Saint. Grignion de Montford was educated at the Jesuit College in Rennes, France. He was ordained in 1700 and he founded the congregation of the Daughters of Wisdom for nursing the sick and educating the

poor in Poitiers. In 1704 he embarked on his career as a missionary in western France and in 1712 he founded another congregation, the Company of Mary, this time for missionaries. He was the author of *Traité de la Vraie Dévotion à la Sainte Vierge*. This was translated by F.W. FABER in 1863 and has been popular with both French and English Catholics. He was canonised in 1947.

Dr Cruickshank, *Blessed Louis-Marie Grignion de Montford and his Devotions*, 2 vols (1892); Catholic University of America, *New Catholic Encyclopaedia* (1967).

Grimshaw, William (1708–63) Missionary. Grimshaw was born of a poor family in Lancashire and he was educated at the University of Cambridge. After ordination, he became perpetual curate of the parish of Haworth, Yorkshire (where Patrick Brontë, the father of Charlotte, Emily and Anne, was later to be incumbent). Grimshaw was an extraordinary pastor. He rounded up sinners and shirkers with the aid of his riding crop; his sermons were heartfelt and funny and he paid particular attention to the sick and the poor. He even invited George WHITEFIELD and John WESLEY to preach from his pulpit. From Haworth, he began to preach in the surrounding parishes, to the fury of their regular ministers. However, when protests were made to the Archbishop of York, Archbishop Hutton gave Grimshaw his support.

F. Baker, *William Grimshaw 1708–1763* (1963).

Grindal, Edmund (*c.* 1519–83) Archbishop and Liturgist. Grindal was born in Cumberland and was educated at the University of Cambridge. A convinced Protestant, he became chaplain to King EDWARD VI and a Canon of Westminster in 1552. He spent the years of Queen MARY's reign abroad. On the accession of Queen ELIZABETH in 1559, he became Bishop of London. He was consecrated Archbishop of York in 1570 and Archbishop of Canterbury in 1575.

While in exile he had tried to reconcile John KNOX to the Book of Common Prayer and later he was partly responsible for the revision of the Elizabethan Prayer Book. However, Grindal is remembered for his conflict with the civil authorities over the Puritans. He refused to suppress the meetings of clergy known as 'prophecyings'. As a result he was stripped of his jurisdictional functions and he was not fully reconciled with the Queen at the time of his death.

P. Collinson, *Archbishop Grindal 1519–1583* (1979).

Groote, Geert de (1340–84) Mystic, Missionary and Order Founder. Groote was born in Deventer and was educated at the University of Paris, France. In 1374 he was converted from his luxurious lifestyle and, after contact with the mystic Jan van RUYSBROECK, he became a missionary–preacher in Utrecht. Together with his friend Florentius Radewijns, he founded the Brethren of the Common Life in Deventer. Members of the community made no vows and pursued their ordinary lives. At the same time, they were dedicated to a life of prayer. Groote also wrote a Rule for a similar order for women. In 1383 his enemies ensured the removal of his licence to preach and he died before his appeal to Rome could be heard. After his death the Brethren reorganised themselves as Augustinian Canons. THOMAS À KEMPIS was perhaps the most famous member of the order and he was the author of a biography of Groote.

A. Hyma, *The Brethren of the Common Life* (1950); T.P. van Zijl, *Gerard Groote: Ascetic and Reformer 1340–1384* (1963).

Grotius, Hugo (1583–1645) Philosopher and Jurist. Grotius had a legal training at the University of Leyden. He served in various political positions and in 1613 he became Pensionary of Rotterdam. As an Arminian, he supported Oldenbarnevelt against the Calvinist Prince Maurice and he was sent to prison for life in 1618. However, in 1621 he escaped to Paris where for a period he served as an ambassador for Queen Christina of Switzerland. He is remembered for his *De Iure Belli et Pacis* and for his *De Veritate Religionis Christianae*. This last was intended as a handbook for missionaries confronted by other faiths. Grotius defended the rationality of Christianity and he maintained that the law of nature, which is derived from the will of God, can be known by human beings. His theory of the atonement anticipated that of the liberals of the nineteenth century in that he argued that JESUS's death was a penal example by which God upholds the moral order of the universe.

W.S.M. Knight, *The Life and Works of Hugo Grotius* (1925).

Grünewald, Matthias (c. 1475–1528) Artist. Little is known of the life of Grünewald. However his *Crucifixion* is world-famous. JESUS on the cross is a tortured figure while JOHN THE BAPTIST points to him and the inscription reads, 'He must increase and I must decrease'. The picture is used as an illustration by the twentieth-century theologian Karl BARTH, to demonstrate correct Christian witness. It points away from the speaker and is entirely directed towards God's objective Word.

N. Pevsner and M. Meier (eds) *Paintings and Drawings of Matthias Grünewald* (1958); A. Burckhardt, *Matthias Grünewald, Personality and Accomplishment* (1936).

Gurney, Joseph John (1788–1847) Missionary, Philanthropist and Sect Founder. Gurney was born in Norwich and was the brother of the prison reformer Elizabeth FRY. At the age of thirty he became a minister in the Society of Friends. Between 1837 and 1840, he went on a missionary journey around the United States of America and the West Indies. This was just after the period of the Second

Great Awakening. The Friends had been divided by a movement led by Elias HICKS. Gurney encouraged the new revivalist pattern; his followers, known as Gurneyites, adopted the more usual Protestant services of regular preaching and celebration of the Sacraments. He also campaigned for the abolition of the slave trade and wrote for the temperance movement.

E. Isichei, *Victorian Quakers* (1970).

Gutenberg, Johann (*c.* 1396–1468) Scientific Inventor. Gutenberg was born in Mainz, Germany, and was apprenticed to a goldsmith. In *c.* 1430 he moved to Strasbourg and, while he was there, seems to have invented a printing press with moveable type. However, no printed books survive from this period. He returned to Mainz in *c.* 1448, borrowed money, and set about printing a Bible. However, his partner, Johann Fust, foreclosed on the loan and took over the press. None the less Gutenberg is credited with the invention of the printing press. The Bible which bears his name was the first known book to be printed and it appeared in 1456. The invention transformed European learning. It enabled books to be produced quickly and cheaply and thus encouraged the spread of both literacy and scholarship.

P. Butler, *The Origin of Printing in Europe* (1940); G.P. Winship, *John Gutenberg* (1940).

Guthrie, Thomas (1803–73) Philanthropist. Guthrie was born in Brechin, Scotland, and was educated first at the University of Edinburgh and then in Paris. He served congregations in Edinburgh where he published in 1857 his *The City: Its Sins and Sorrows*. With the disruption of the Church of Scotland in 1843, he joined the Free Protesting Church and successfully organised a fund for deprived ministers. He was a well-known preacher and his book on the prophet Ezekiel was a religious best-

seller of its time. However, he is primarily remembered for his philanthropy. He worked tirelessly for the establishment of ragged schools and for the temperance movement; his funeral attracted thirty thousand mourners.

A.L. Drummond, 'Thomas Guthrie', in R.S. Wright (ed.), *Fathers of the Kirk* (1960).

Gutierrez, Gustavo (b. 1928) Theologian. Gutierrez was born in Lima, Peru, and was educated at the Universities of Louvain, Lyons and Rome. In 1959 he was ordained to the Roman Catholic priesthood and he began to teach at the Catholic University of Lima while living in the slum area of the city. Increasingly he became uneasy at the gap between the theology taught in the university and the reality of ordinary people's lives. A leading exponent of liberation theology, his writings stress that JESUS CHRIST is the liberator from political and social, as well as spiritual, oppression. His works include *A Theology of Liberation, The Power of the Poor in History, We Drink from our own Wells* and *On Job*.

R.M. Brown, *Gustavo Gutierrez: An Introduction to Liberation Theology* (1990); M. Ellis and O. Maduro, *The Future of Liberation Theology: Essays in Honour of Gustavo Gutierrez* (1989).

Guyard, Marie (1599–1672) Mystic and Missionary. Guyard was born in Tours, France. Although she wanted to be a nun, in obedience to her family she married Claude Joseph Martin. After his death, she entered an Ursuline house and, with three other sisters, she travelled to Quebec, Canada, in 1639 to open a new convent. Under her guidance, the order flourished and engaged in valuable educational and social work among both the French and the Indians. All through her life she was subject to visions and, in accordance with the wishes of her spiritual director, she wrote them down. Together with her letters they were published after her death.

Marie Guyard, *Word from New France*, edited and translated by Joyce Marshall (1967).

Guyon, Jeanne Marie (1648–1717) Mystic and Devotional Writer. Guyon was born Jeanne Marie Bouvier de la Mothe in Montargis, France. She married, at the age of sixteen, a man twenty-two years older than herself. She was always inclined to mysticism and once she became a widow in 1676, she embarked on the devotional life. She was arrested in 1687, together with her spiritual director, on the suspicion of heresy and immorality, but on the intercession of Mme de Maintenon, she was released. From 1688 she was in correspondence with François FÉNELON, who defended her against Bishop BOSSUET. She was condemned again for her supposed Quietist views at the 1695 Conference of Issy and was not released from the Bastille until 1702. Her devotional writings include an autobiography, *Moyen Court et Très Facile de Faire Oraison* and *Le Cantique des Cantiques*.

M. de la Bedoyere, *The Archbishop and the Lady: The Story of Fénelon and Madame Guyon* (1956); R.A. Knox, *Enthusiasm* (1950).

H

Hadrian IV (*c.* 1100–59)   Pope. Hadrian was born Nicholas Breakspear in St Albans, England. He became Abbot of the Augustinian monastery of St Rufus, Avignon, in 1137; he was appointed Cardinal-Archbishop of Albano by Pope EUGENIUS III and, after a successful mission to Scandinavia, he was elected Pope in 1154. He is primarily remembered as the only English Pope. During his Pontificate, he secured the execution of ARNOLD OF BRESCIA and crowned the Emperor FREDERICK BARBAROSSA. However, his insistence that the Emperor held his throne only as a gift from the Pope was to lead to a long dispute. Similarly he maintained that the territorial rights of the King of Sicily were dependent upon his paying homage to the papacy. The bull 'Laudabiliter', which gave rights to King HENRY II of England over Ireland, may have been a forgery.

E.M. Almedingen, *The English Pope* (1925); W. Ullman, 'The Pontificate of Adrian IV', *Cambridge Historical Journal*, x (1953–5).

Ham, Sok-Hon (1901–89)   Theologian. Ham is regarded as the father of Min-Jung theology, which has similarities with Latin-American liberation theology. He was imprisoned by the Japanese during their occupation of Korea in the Second World War and he was subsequently arrested by the South Korean police. In his theology, he stressed the *sse-al*, the seed of humanity which remains independent of all imposed human structures. It may be trodden down, but like JESUS CHRIST, it rises again. This concept has proved fundamental to later Min-Jung thinkers.

J.Y. Lee, *An Emerging Theology in World Perspective: Commentary on Korean Min-Jung Theology* (1988).

Hamann, Johann Georg (1730–88)   Philosopher. Hamann was a native of Königsberg, Germany. After a varied education, he became first a private tutor and then a business man. It was during a business trip that he had a conversion experience and, after nursing his dying father, he became a minor customs and excise officer, thus allowing himself time for study. He is regarded as one of the leaders of the German 'Sturm und Drang' movement and he saw himself as the rejuvenator of the German Christianity of Martin LUTHER. His most significant religious work was *Golgotha und Scheblimini*, in which he stressed the importance of personal faith over rationalist philosophy. A personal friend of Immanuel KANT, his work was to have an important influence on that of SCHLEIERMACHER and KIERKEGAARD.

R.G. Smith, *J.G. Hamann: A Study in Christian Existence* (1960).

Hamilton, Patrick (1504–28)   Martyr. Hamilton was born of an aristocratic Scottish family and, at the age of thirteen, he was appointed Abbot of Fern. He was educated at the Universities of Paris and St Andrews and was converted to Lutheran opinions. In 1527 he fled to Wittenberg where he came into contact with both LUTHER and MELANCHTHON. On his return to Scotland, he was summoned by the Roman Catholic Archbishop Beaton to St Andrews where he was tried for heresy, convicted and burned at the stake. The death of such a committed and highly born young man caused a *furor* and it was said that 'the reek of Mr Patrick Hamilton has infected as many as it did blow upon'. He is remembered as the first Protestant Scottish martyr.

A. Cameron (ed.), *Patrick Hamilton, First Scottish Martyr of the Reformation* (1929); D.M. Kay, *Patrick Hamilton, Scottish Martyr* (1929).

Hampden, Renn Dickson (1793–1868) Bishop and Theologian. Hampden was educated at the University of Oxford and became a fellow of Oriel College. He was the Bampton Lecturer of 1832 and he recommended a Christianity in which dogma played a relatively minor part. As a Broad Churchman, he was bitterly opposed by John Henry NEWMAN and his followers and the mistrust was fully reciprocated. The High Church party tried to prevent his appointment as Regius Professor of Divinity in 1837 and, ten years later, they campaigned against his consecration as Bishop of Hereford. In the event he proved to be a popular and conscientious Bishop. Hampden's own writings are no longer read, but he is remembered as typical of the liberal churchmen against whom the adherents of the Oxford Movement fulminated.

C. Dawson, *The Spirit of the Oxford Movement* (1933); H. Hampden, *Some Memorials of Renn Dickson Hampden* (1871); H. Swanston, *Ideas of Order: Anglicans and the Renewal of Theological Method in the Middle of the Nineteenth Century* (1974).

Hampson, Daphne (b. 1944) Theologian. Hampson was born in Croydon, England, and was educated at the Universities of Keele, Oxford, Harvard and Warwick. She has taught at the Universities of Stirling and St Andrews. She is known as one of Britain's most radical feminist theologians and, like the American Mary DALY, describes herself as a 'post-Christian'. In 1986, a debate was held between Hampson and Rosemary Radford RUETHER on 'Is there a place for Feminists in the Christian Church?' in which she argued that in feminism, 'Christianity has met a challenge to which it cannot accommodate itself'. She is the author of *Theology and Feminism* (1990) and *After Christianity* (1995). The latter work seeks to find a way to express spirituality beyond Christianity.

A. Loades, 'Feminist theology', in D. Ford (ed.), *The Modern Theologians*, Vol. 2 (1989).

Handel, George Friedrich (1685–1759) Composer. Handel was born and educated in Saxony, Germany. After some years in France, he settled in England in 1710 and eventually became a naturalised British citizen. A prolific composer of many sorts of music, he was much admired by Haydn, MOZART and Beethoven. Among Church people, he is mainly remembered for his choral anthems and for his religious oratorios such as the 'Messiah', 'Samson' and 'Judas Maccabaeus'. The 'Messiah' in particular is frequently performed by amateur as well as professional groups and for many English people is an essential Christmas event.

D. Burrows, *Handel* (1994); W. Dean, *Handel's Dramatic Oratorios and Masques* (1959); R.M. Myers, *Handel's Messiah: A Touchstone of Taste* (1948).

Harnack, Adolf von (1851–1930) Theologian. Harnack was the son of a German Lutheran Professor of Theology. He was educated at the Universities of Dorpat and Leipzig and he subsequently taught at the Universities of Giessen, Marburg and Berlin. This last appointment was disputed by the German Church because of his liberal interpretation of scripture. None the less he is remembered as the most influential German theologian of the late nineteenth century. He was a follower of Albrecht RITSCHL, and his works include *Lehrbuch der Dogmen Geschichte* (which traced the history of Christian dogma from the early days of the Church until the Reformation), *Das Wesen des Christentums* (a series of lectures in which he discussed the essence of the Christian religion) and *Beiträge zur Einleitung in das Neue Testament* (on the Gospels and Acts). With the New Testament scholar Emil Schürer, he founded *Theologische Literaturzeitung* in 1881. Harnack believed that the metaphysical doctrines developed by St PAUL and the Roman Catholic Church had their origin in the Hellenistic thought of the time. Once they were disregarded, the true message of JESUS would be revealed. This he identified with the Kingdom of God which he defined as the 'fatherhood of God' and the 'brotherhood of man'. Harnack's liberalism stands in sharp contrast to the 'Crisis Theology' of Karl BARTH and his followers, which denied any natural point of contact between God and human beings.

G.W. Glick, *The Reality of Christianity: A Study of Adolf von Harnack as Historian and Theologian* (1967); M. Rumscheidt (ed.), *Adolf von Harnack: Liberal Theology at its Height* (1989).

Harris, Howel (1714–73) Missionary and Denomination Founder. Harris was born in humble circumstances in Talgarth, Wales. Initially he earned his living as a school-master, but he had a conversion experience at the age of twenty-one. Planning to be an Anglican clergyman, he went to Oxford University, but left after a week to start an extensive mission in Wales. He is generally regarded as the founder of Welsh Calvinist Methodism, although he himself remained loyal to the Church of England. His preaching attracted huge crowds and there were scenes of extraordinary enthusiasm. He was not an original thinker and his ideas were drawn from a variety of sources. He was shy with his fellow evangelists and he fell out with both Daniel Rowland and with George WHITEFIELD. After his retirement in 1752, he set up a revivalist centre in

Trevecca Fach, which was supported by the Countess of Huntingdon (HASTINGS). The many chapels built throughout Wales testify to the success of his life's work.

R. Bennett, *The Early Life of Howell Harris* (1962); G.F. Nuttall, *Howel Harris* (1965).

Hartshorne, Charles (b. 1897) Philosopher. Hartshorne was born in Pennsylvania and was educated at Haverford College and at the Universities of Harvard, Freiberg and Marburg. He has taught philosophy at the University of Chicago, at Emory University and at the University of Texas. He is regarded as a leading proponent of process theology. Developing the thought of A.N. WHITEHEAD, he teaches the doctrine of panentheism, that everything is in God. This differs from Pantheism in that God's being is not identical with the being of the universe. It allows for the possibility of constant change and development within the godhead and his nature is perceived as endlessly adaptable. Even his omniscience entails foreknowledge, not of future events, but of future possibilities. Hartshorne argues that this view is closer than the classical idea to the biblical picture of the Almighty. He is the author of many books, including *Man's Vision of God, The Divine Relativity, A Natural Theology for our Time, Omnipotence and Other Theological Mistakes* and *Wisdom and Moderation: A Philosophy of the Middle Way*.

Charles Hartshorne, *The Darkness and the Light: A Philosopher Reflects on his Fortunate Career and Those who made it Possible* (1990); J.B. Cobb and H. Daly, *Process Theology: An Introductory Exposition* (1989).

Hastings, Selina [Countess of Huntingdon] (1707–91) Denomination Founder. Hastings had been attracted first to the Moravian Church and she joined John WESLEY's Society of Methodists in 1739. On the death of her husband in 1746, she dedicated herself to the evangelical cause. Although she retained her links with the Church of England, she made it her aim to convert the British upper classes to renewed religious enthusiasm. To this end, she opened chapels in Bath, Brighton, London and Tunbridge Wells. Then, in 1768, she set up Trevecca House in Talgarth, Wales, as a training college for clergy, near the community of the eminent Welsh missionary Howel HARRIS. In order to encourage the evangelical party, she appointed several clergymen, including George WHITEFIELD, as personal chaplains, but this practice was outlawed by the consistory courts. In consequence, she was compelled to register her chapels as dissenting places of worship and thus founded what was known as the Countess of Huntingdon's Connexion. She also took an interest in missions in America and, on the death of Whitefield, she became trustee of his orphanage in Georgia. She also corresponded with George Washington about the American Indians. The Connexion still survives in Britain today.

F.F. Bretherton, *The Countess of Huntingdon* (1940); S.C. Carpenter, *Eighteenth-Century Church and People* (1959).

Havergal, Frances Ridley (1836–79) Poet. Havergal was the daughter of an Anglican clergyman who served a parish in Worcestershire, England. She was well educated in the Classics, but her chief interest was in the writing of devotional poetry. She had a conversion experience at the age of fifteen, never married and dedicated herself to parish works. Among her most famous hymns is 'Take my life and let it be' which is still often sung, particularly at Confirmation services in the Church of England.

M.V.G. Havergal, *Memorials of Frances Ridley Havergal* (1880).

Hawthorne, Nathaniel (1804–64) Novelist. Hawthorne was born in Salem, Massachusetts. He was a classmate of the poet Longfellow at Bowdoin College

and, after a short period of working in a Boston customs house, he dedicated the rest of his life to his writing. He was a friend of both EMERSON and Thoreau, but did not share their transcendentalist views. In Christian circles, he is primarily remembered for his two novels, *The Scarlet Letter*, published in 1850, and *The House of the Seven Gables* (1851). Both deal with the values of the early American settlers, their moral ideals and their ultimate decadence. Hawthorne is thus perceived as the foremost interpreter of American Puritanism.

M. Bell (ed.), *New Essays on Hawthorne's Major Tales* (1993); M. J. Colacurcio, *The Province of Piety: Moral History in Hawthorne's Early Tales* (1984); E. H. Miller, *Salem is my Dwelling Place: A Life of Nathaniel Hawthorne* (1991).

Headlam, Stewart (1847–1924) Philanthropist. Headlam was born near Liverpool, England, and was educated at the University of Cambridge. There he came under the influence of Frederick Denison MAURICE and he was ordained in 1870. Throughout his life he was in constant difficulties with the Church of England establishment. His Bishop delayed his ordination because he could not bring himself to believe in eternal punishment. He advocated the abolition of the blasphemy laws. He consorted with the avowed atheist Charles Bradlaugh. In an era which regarded the theatre as a den of vice, he started the Church and Stage Guild. He founded the Guild of St Matthew, one of the early focuses for Christian Socialism. For the sake of justice, he stood bail for Oscar Wilde, even though the two men scarcely knew one another, and he publicly recommended the abolition of the House of Lords. His passion was education and he was dedicated to the spread of schooling among the poor. Today Headlam is remembered as an important philanthropist, as well as one of the most courageous and radical clergymen ever to serve the Church of England.

K. Leech, *Stewart Headlam (1847–1924)* (1968).

Heber, Reginald (1783–1826) Bishop and Poet. Heber was educated at the University of Oxford. After ordination, he served as a parish priest in Shropshire and in 1823 he was consecrated Bishop of Calcutta. The diocese included the whole of British India. Heber did not spare himself and during his short episcopate he travelled constantly. He is remembered in India for ordaining the first native Anglican clergyman. He is more generally famous for his hymns which are still frequently sung. Among the most popular are 'From Greenland's icy mountains', 'Brightest and best of the sons of the morning' and 'Holy, holy, holy, Lord God Almighty'.

D. Hughes, *Bishop Sahib: A Life of Reginald Heber* (1986).

Hecker, Isaac Thomas (1819–88) Order Founder. Hecker was born in New York City in the United States of America. He was initially a Methodist, but became involved with Transcendentalism and in 1844 he was baptised into the Roman Catholic Church. He joined the Redemptorist Order and, after studying in Belgium and Holland, he was ordained in England by Cardinal WISEMAN. In 1851 he returned to the United States. He started to work with Catholic immigrants, but he was dispensed from his vows in 1857 by Pope PIUS IX after coming into conflict with his superiors. However, he obtained permission to found the Missionary Priests of St Paul the Apostle, generally known as the Paulist Order. Its members live under a rule similar to that of the Redemptorists and the order is dedicated to mission, particularly among Protestants. Although Pope LEO XIII may have been thinking of the Paulists when he condemned 'Americanism' (that is the adaptation of the life of the Church to American norms) in 1899, there is no certain evidence of this, and the order has survived and continues its work.

J.M. Gillis, *The Paulists* (1932); V.F. Holden, *The Yankee Paul* (1958); T.T. McAvoy, *The Great Crisis in American Catholic History 1895–1900* (1957).

Hegel, Georg Wilhelm Friedrich (1770–1831) Philosopher. Hegel was born in Stuttgart, Germany, and was educated at the University of Tübingen. As a tutor in Switzerland, he wrote a life of JESUS CHRIST whom he saw as one who transcended both virtue and vice. He settled in Jena in 1801 and he collaborated with SCHELLING in producing the *Kritische Journal der Philosophie*. In 1806 he was forced to move and, after a spell as headmaster of a school in Bavaria and a period teaching in Heidelberg University, he was appointed Professor of Philosophy at the University of Berlin in 1818 in succession to Johann FICHTE. Friedrich SCHLEIERMACHER was Dean of the theological faculty at the same time and Hegel made no secret of his disapproval of his stress on the role of feeling in religion. Hegel's works include *Wissenschaft der Logik, Die Encyclopadie der Philosophischen Wissenschaften im Grundrisse* and his *Grundlinien der Philosophie des Rechts*. He taught that both realism and subjective idealism were inherently contradictory and he argued that true knowledge of the spirit of ultimate reality was derived only through a dialectical process of thesis, antithesis and synthesis. Truth lay not in individual facts or a single discipline, but in the whole dialectical evolution of the spirit. His system has been described as 'absolute idealism' and has been profoundly influential both on social philosophers such as Karl MARX, on spiritual idealists like T.H. GREEN and on radical biblical critics such as D.F. STRAUSS.

B. Cullen (ed.), *Hegel Today* (1988); P. Singer, *Hegel* (1983); P. Hodgson, *Hegel* (1988).

Heidegger, Martin (1889–1976) Philosopher. Heidegger was born in Messkirch, Germany, and was educated at the University of Freiberg. In 1923 he began his teaching career at Marburg, where he was a colleague of Paul TILLICH and Rudolf BULTMANN and in 1929 he went back to Freiberg. He is regarded as an important proponent of existentialist philosophy. In his *Sein und Zeit*, he identified the nature of being as the major concern of philosophy. Authentic, as opposed to inauthentic, existence is lived by the human being in full acceptance of death. Bultmann was to use these categories in his understanding of the death of JESUS as a challenge to humanity. In his later writings, Heidegger claimed that poetry could expose us to and help us intuitively to grasp being. He himself was a secular philosopher, but with KIERKEGAARD, he provided a metaphysic by which Christianity could be interpreted by later theologians.

M. King *Heidegger's Philosophy: A Guide to his Basic Thought* (1964); J. Macquarrie, *Martin Heidegger* (1968).

Heisenberg, Werner (1901– 76) Scientist. Heisenberg was born in Würtzburg, Germany. He was educated at the University of Munich and he taught at Göttingen and Leipzig. During the Second World War, he directed the German atomic bomb project. Today, however, he is remembered for his 'uncertainty principle'. He argued that at an atomic level, the uncertainty of our knowledge of the values of variables (such as momentum, energy or position) is always greater than Planck's constant of action. Thus we cannot know both the place and the speed of a particle. This theory has been seized upon by theologians and clergy as providing an escape from the closed cause-and-effect picture of the universe offered by traditional science.

D.C. Cassidy, *Uncertainty: The Life and Science of Werner Heisenberg* (1992).

Helena (*c.* 255–*c.* 330) Saint. Helena was the mother of the Emperor CONSTANTINE. Once her son became emperor, she was honoured at court and was converted to Christianity. In her old age she made a visit to the Holy Land where she founded basilicae at Bethlehem and on the Mount of Olives. According to legend, she also found the True Cross on which JESUS was crucified. In the chronicles of GEOFFREY OF MONMOUTH, she is described as the daughter of Coel ('Old King Cole') of Colchester, but there are no grounds for believing that she had British origins.

D.H. Farmer (ed.), *Oxford Dictionary of Saints*, 3rd edn (1992).

Helwys, Thomas (*c.* 1550–*c.* 1616) Polemicist and Denomination Founder. Helwys was born in Nottinghamshire, England. In 1608 he became a member of the 'Brownist' Church in Amsterdam, which had been founded by John SMYTH in 1606. However, both he and Smyth were expelled from the congregation because they rejected infant baptism. They formed a new Baptist congregation which, in 1611, issued a declaration of faith defining baptism as 'the outward manifestation of dying with Christ and walking in newness of life: and therefore in nowise appertaineth to infants'. In 1611 Helwys returned to England and established his headquarters in Newgate Street, London. Although this was probably the first general Baptist church in England, in fact the community followed the Mennonite practice of baptism by affusion rather than total immersion. Helwys is also remembered for his *Declaration of the Mystery of Iniquity* in which he made a plea for full freedom of individual conscience.

W.H. Burgess, *John Smith, the Se-Baptist, Thomas Helwys and the First Baptist Church in England* (1911); A.C. Underwood, *A History of English Baptists* (1947).

Henderson, Alexander (*c.* 1583–1646)

Polemicist. Henderson was born in Fife, Scotland, and was educated at St Andrews University. As an Episcopalian, he taught at the university and served a nearby parish. By 1618, however, he had been converted to Presbyterianism. He was one of the authors of the National Covenant of 1638, which bound the estimated three hundred thousand subscribers to defend the freedom of the Scottish Church and the Presbyterian religion. It was produced in response to King CHARLES I's attempt to impose episcopacy. Henderson was elected Moderator of the General Assembly and, when Charles visited Scotland in 1641, he was compelled to accept him as his chaplain. In 1643 Henderson drew up the Solemn League and Covenant which was accepted by the British Parliament and the 1644 Directory for Public Worship which was designed to replace the Book of Common Prayer. This was imposed on the English Church in 1645.

R.C. Orr, *Alexander Henderson, Churchman and Statesman* (1919).

Henry II (972–1024)   Saint and Monarch. Henry was the son of Henry the Quarrelsome, Duke of Bavaria. He succeeded Otto III as Holy Roman Emperor in 1002, but was not crowned until 1014. He is remembered for founding the See of Bamburg and for encouraging ecclesiastical renewal. In particular he strongly supported the monastic reforms of Cluny. In later Christian legend, he was regarded as the ideal king, strong and noble, just and pious. He was canonised in 1146 and his wife Kunigunde followed him into sainthood in 1200. In fact his reign was dominated by war and, as a result of his constant interference, he was in frequent conflict with Church leaders.

H. Mikoletzky, *Kaiser Heinrich II und die Kirche* (1951) [no English translation available].

Henry II (1133–89)   Monarch. Henry was the eldest son of Matilda, heiress of King Henry I of England, and Geoffrey Plantagenet. He inherited the English crown from his cousin Stephen in 1154. In Christian circles he is remembered for his conflict with Thomas BECKET over the rights of the Church. The King wished to remove certain clerical privileges. The Archbishop, despite his earlier loyal service to the King, adamantly resisted. The affair ended with Becket's murder in Canterbury Cathedral in 1170 and the King performing public penance in 1174.

F. Barlow, *Thomas Becket* (1986); T.S. Eliot, *Murder in the Cathedral* (1935); W.L. Warren, *Henry II* (1973).

Henry IV (1050–1106)   Monarch. Henry IV inherited the throne from his father, the Holy Roman Emperor Henry III, while he was still a child. During his minority, there was civil strife and, on his majority, Henry was determined to reassert royal power. He managed to subdue the Saxon princes in 1075, but Pope GREGORY VII prohibited lay investiture, thus depriving him of secular control over the German Church. Henry refused to accept this; he declared the Pope deposed and was excommunicated. Then the Saxons rose again in rebellion and, in order to forestall difficulties, he had to make a humiliating submission to the Pope at Canossa in 1077. However, in 1080, he again deposed the Pope, who died in exile, and he set up an antipope, Clement III, who crowned him Holy Roman Emperor. Meanwhile Pope URBAN II was elected in succession to Gregory. The last years of Henry's reign were fraught with civil war, family rebellion and administrative difficulty.

I.S. Robinson, *Authority and Resistance in the Investiture Contest* (1978).

Henry IV (1553–1610)   Monarch. Henry was the son of Anthony of Bourbon and Jeanne d'Albret, a niece of the French King Francis I. He was brought up a

Protestant and he inherited the throne of Navarre from his mother in 1572. It was during the celebration of his marriage to Margaret of Valois in 1572 that CATHERINE DE' MEDICI ordered the St Bartholomew's Day massacre. When King Henry III was assassinated, Henry was the heir to the French crown, but his Protestantism made him unacceptable to many French citizens as well as to the Pope and King PHILIP II of Spain. According to popular legend, he declared 'Paris vaut bien une messe' (Paris is worth a Mass) and, for reasons of political expediency, converted to Catholicism. Many scholars, however, believe that the conversion was sincere. In any event, by 1595 he was in complete control of the country and had been formally absolved by the Pope for heresy. In 1598 he issued the Edict of Nantes which gave French Protestants freedom of worship. He was assassinated by a Roman Catholic fanatic in 1610.

D. Buisseret, *Sully and the Growth of Centralised Government in France 1598–1610* (1968); M. Reinhard, *Henri IV ou la France Sauvée* (1943) [no English translation available].

Henry VI (1421–71) Monarch. Henry was the son of King Henry V of England and the French princess, Catherine of Valois. He inherited the throne of England as a baby and his reign was dominated by civil war in England (the Wars of the Roses) and the attempt to keep English possessions in France. Henry himself was a kindly, scholarly man who is primarily remembered for his contribution to education; he was the founder of Eton College and King's College, Cambridge. Eventually he was deposed and died (probably murdered) in 1471. His tomb became a place of pilgrimage and there were attempts by his Lancastrian successor, Henry VII, to have him declared a saint.

F.A. Gasquet, *The Religious Life of King Henry VI* (1923).

Henry VIII (1491–1547) Monarch. Henry was the surviving son of King Henry VII of England. In 1509 he married his elder brother's widow, Catherine of Aragon, daughter of FERDINAND and ISABELLA of Spain, which required a papal dispensation. In the same year he inherited the throne. His chief minister in the early days was Thomas WOLSEY. Always interested in theological questions, he was awarded the title Defender of the Faith by the Pope after writing a pamphlet against the sacramental teaching of Martin LUTHER. His marriage produced only one daughter, MARY, and, in order to secure the succession, Henry was determined to divorce Catherine. In 1529 a legatine court refused the divorce and Wolsey fell from office. Thomas CRANMER became Archbishop of Canterbury in 1533 and pronounced the marriage invalid. Under the guidance of Thomas CROMWELL, various bills were passed through Parliament which placed the English Church outside the control of Rome. Henry then married Anne Boleyn and dealt ruthlessly with any protesters against these arrangements. Thomas MORE, once Chancellor of England, for example, was beheaded. In 1536 the monasteries of England and Wales were dissolved and their wealth was transferred to the crown. Some of it was used to set up new sees. Queen Anne Boleyn produced another daughter, ELIZABETH, and was executed for adultery. Henry subsequently married Jane Seymour (who produced EDWARD VI) and three other wives. The Ten Articles of 1536 and his marriage to Anne of Cleves in 1540 show a measure of tolerance for Protestantism, but in the Six Articles of 1539 the King reaffirmed Catholic doctrine. Nevertheless, during the final years of the reign the seeds of English Protestantism were sown. Henry's successor, the young King Edward, was educated by Protestant tutors. Henry's reign is remembered for the establishment of a national English Church, independent of Rome.

G.R. Elton, *The Tudor Revolution in Government* (1953); R. Richard, *Henry VIII and the English Reformation* (1993); J.J. Scarisbrick, *Henry VIII* (1968); G.W.O. Woodward, *The Dissolution of the Monasteries* (1966).

Henry, Matthew (1662–1714) Devotional Writer. Henry was the son of Philip Henry (1631–96), the English Puritan diarist. He trained as a lawyer, but instead was ordained as a Presbyterian minister. He served congregations in Chester and Hackney. He is remembered for his monumental, seven-volume *Exposition of the Old and New Testaments*, a detailed, spiritualised commentary on the biblical text. It was highly influential in the eighteenth and nineteenth centuries and preachers such as Charles SPURGEON acknowledged their debt to it.

C. Chapman, *Life of Matthew Henry* (1859).

Henry Suso (*c.* 1300–66) Mystic and Devotional Writer. Henry was born in Swabia. He joined a Dominican friary in Constance at the age of thirteen and he finished his education in Cologne under Meister ECKHART. He is remembered for his mystical books, the most famous of which is *Das Büchlein der Ewigen Weisheit*. This has become a classic; it was widely read and was admired by THOMAS À KEMPIS. It is intended as a practical guide to contemplation and includes a hundred short meditations on the passion of JESUS. He spent the later part of his life as an itinerant preacher and he was much in demand as a spiritual director in Dominican convents.

J.M. Clark, *The Great German Mystics* (1949).

Henson, Herbert Hensley (1863–1947) Bishop and Popular Theologian. Henson was educated at the University of Oxford. After ordination, he served as a parish priest and hospital chaplain. He was appointed Dean of Durham in 1912, Bishop of Hereford in 1918 and Bishop of Durham in 1939. He was liberal in his views and his consecration as Bishop was questioned; Henson was forced to retract his early radical views on the virgin birth and the gospel miracles. In his early writings, he strongly believed that the Church of England should be an all-embracing national Church, but after Parliament rejected the revised Prayer Book, he became an advocate of disestablishment. His books aroused much interest in their time and included *The National Church* (1908), *Anglicanism* (1921), *Disestablishment* (1929), *Christian Morality* (1936) and *The Church of England* (1939).

Herbert Hensley Henson, *Retrospect of an Unimportant Life*, 3 vols (1942–50).

Heraclius (575–641) Monarch. Heraclius was born in Cappadocia. He became Byzantine Emperor in 610. During his reign, he reorganised the imperial army, but, despite this, Syria and Egypt were lost to the Arabs, Edessa and Antioch to the Persians and Spain to the Visigoths. He is remembered for restoring the True Cross to Jerusalem in 614 and for trying to reach a compromise with the Monophysites by proposing that JESUS CHRIST had but one divine human will (the Monothelite position). In 638 he issued a statement of faith (Ecthesis) which forbade the teaching of one or more modes of activity in the person of Christ. Two councils held in Constantinople accepted this solution, but it was rejected by the Western Church which insisted that Christ had both a divine and a human will. The Ecthesis was withdrawn in 648.

W.H.C. Frend, *The Rise of the Monophysite Movement* (1972).

Herbert, Edward [Lord Herbert of Cherbury] (1583–1648) Philosopher. Herbert was born into an aristocratic English family and was an older brother of the poet George HERBERT. He was appointed an ambassador to France in

1619 and, while there, he published *De Veritate*, an attack on empiricist philosophy. This was to be very influential on the later seventeenth-century thinker John LOCKE. He also was the author of various theological works in which he argued for the existence of God and the importance of duty. He is remembered as a forerunner of the English Deists.

Edward Herbert, *The Life of Edward, First Lord Herbert of Cherbury*, edited by J.M. Shuttleworth, (1976); R.D. Bedford, *The Defence of Truth: Herbert of Cherbury and the 17th-Century* (1979).

Herbert, George (1593–1633)   Poet and Devotional Writer. Herbert was a younger brother of the philosopher Edward HERBERT. He was educated at the University of Cambridge, where he was appointed Public Orator in 1620. Influenced by Nicholas FERRAR, he was ordained to the Church of England ministry in 1630. For the remaining years of his life he served as rector of the parish of Fugglestone, near Salisbury. His *A Priest to the Temple: Or the Country Parson* is an analysis of the ideal qualities to be found in a priest and has proved an inspiration to generations of clergy. However, he is mainly remembered as a devotional poet. Some of his verses, such as 'Teach me my God and King' and 'The God of love my Shepherd is', are still sung as hymns today. His poetry was much admired by later writers such as Henry VAUGHAN and Samuel Taylor COLERIDGE and it is generally regarded as distilling the very best in Anglican piety.

T.S. Eliot, *George Herbert* (1962); J.H. Summers, *George Herbert: His Religion and Art* (1954); H.H. Vendler, *The Poetry of George Herbert* (1975); I. Walton, *The Life of Mr George Herbert*, 1st edn (1670).

Hermann [The Lame] of Reichenau (1013–54)   Poet and Historian. Hermann was the son of Count Wolverad II of Swabia. He joined a monastic community in Reichenau in 1043. Despite his considerable physical handicaps, he was highly scholarly and attracted many students. He is remembered for his Chronicle, which begins with the birth of JESUS CHRIST and ends with the year of Hermann's own death. It was based on a variety of sources and is regarded as a considerable achievement. He is also credited with being the author of the two famous hymns 'Salve regina' and 'Alma redemptoris mater' – although not all scholars accept this.

H. Hansjakob, *Hermann der Lahme von der Reichenau* (1875) [no English translation available]; C.C. Martindale, *From Bye-Ways and Hedges* (1935); H. Thurston, 'The 'Salve Regina', *Month*, cxxviii (1918).

Hermas (late first/second century)   Apostolic Father. Hermas is known as the author of *The Shepherd of Hermas*, a New Testament apocryphal work. It consists of five visions, twelve mandates and ten similitudes and may well have been composed by more than one author. He himself says that he was a contemporary of CLEMENT OF ROME and a freed Christian slave. He became a farmer; his sons were apostates and ultimately the whole family did penance. The Muratorian Canon, however, records that the *Shepherd* was written by a brother of Pope Pius I, who died *c*. 154. The book was widely accepted as part of the Christian Canon of scripture and it was still used for the instruction of catechumens in the time of St ATHANASIUS. It stresses the importance of penance and encourages the belief in the forgiveness of sins after baptism. For this reason, TERTULLIAN described it as 'the Shepherd for the Adulterers'.

L. Pernveden, *The Concept of the Church in the Shepherd of Hermas* (1966); J. Reiling, *Hermas and Christian Prophecy* (1973); J.A. Robinson, *Barnabas, Hermas and the Didache* (1920).

Heylyn, Peter (1600–62)   Polemicist and Historian. Heylyn was born in Oxfordshire and was educated at the University of Oxford. In 1624 he was ordained and, with his High Church views, he quickly achieved recognition within the Church. In 1630 he became a chaplain to King CHARLES I and in 1631 a prebendary of Westminster. A determined opponent of Puritanism, he wrote *A History of the Sabbath*; he was involved in the case against William PRYNNE and he had a long battle with the Dean of Westminster. During the Commonwealth period, he was forced to retire from public life, but he continued to work for the full restoration of the Church of England. Among his books were a biography of William LAUD, a history of Presbyterianism and *Ecclesia Restaurata* – a history of the Reformation of the Church of England.

G. Barnard, 'Theologico-historicus or the true life of the most reverend historian Peter Heylyn', in Peter Heylyn, *Ecclesia Restaurata* (1849).

Hick, John Harwood (b. 1922)   Theologian. Hick was educated at the Universities of Edinburgh and Oxford. He has taught philosophy of religion at Cambridge and Birmingham and at the Claremont School of Graduate Studies in California and he is an ordained minister of the United Reform Church. He is a prolific writer, and his books include *Evil and the God of Love, The Second Christianity* and *The Metaphor of God Incarnate*. Probably the most significant philosopher of religion of his generation, he is remembered for his defence of 'eschatological verification' against Antony FLEW's argument that religious claims are intrinsically neither verifiable nor falsifiable (and therefore meaningless). *The Myth of God Incarnate*, of which Hick was an editor, caused a minor sensation within the Church with its suggestion that the doctrine of the incarnation may not be literally true. In recent years he has turned to the vexed question of the relationship of Christianity with other faiths and he is a leading proponent of the pluralist position – that salvation may not be exclusively found through the person of JESUS CHRIST.

John Hick and P. Knitter (eds), *The Myth of Christian Uniqueness* (1987); C. Gillis, *A Question of Final Belief: John Hick's Pluralistic Theory of Salvation* (1989); H. Hewitt (ed.), *Problems in the Philosophy of Religion: Critical Studies of the Work of John Hick* (1991).

Hicks, Elias (1748–1830)   Denomination Founder. Hicks was born in Long Island in America, of Quaker parents. From 1779 he became a popular itinerant preacher and he was particularly eloquent in his disapproval of slavery. He also insisted that the Quakers should not be bound by a formal creed and he emphasised 'the Christ within' every individual. In 1827, following his preaching, some Quakers withdrew from the Society of Friends and established their own meetings in protest against those who wanted to enforce a written doctrine. In 1902 the Hicksites, as they were called, formed their own confederation, the Friends' General Conference.

R.W. Doherty, *The Hicksite Separation* (1967); R. Forbush, *Elias Hicks, Quaker Liberal* (1956).

Hilarion (c. 291–371)   Saint and Order Founder. Hilarion was born in Thabatha in Palestine of pagan parents. During the course of his education in Alexandria, he was converted to Christianity. After spending some time with St ANTONY in the Egyptian desert, he returned to Palestine and settled in the wilderness near Gaza. According to St JEROME, who had his information from Hilarion's disciple EPIPHANIUS, he was the founder of hermit life in Palestine. He was visited by many and, to escape the crowds, he went first to Egypt and then Sicily, Dalmatia and Cyprus.

E. Coleiro, 'St Jerome's lives of the hermits', *Vigiliae Christianae*, xi (1957); D.H. Farmer (ed.), *The Oxford Dictionary of Saints*, 3rd edn (1992).

Hilary of Poitiers (c. 315–67)   Bishop, Poet, Theologian and Saint. Hilary was a native of Poitiers, Gaul, and was consecrated bishop in *c.* 353. A determined defender of orthodoxy, he was condemned at the Council of Béziers in 356 and banished by the Emperor to Phrygia. He justified his position at the Council of Seleucia, but the Emperor refused to lift the order of banishment. He is mainly remembered for his defence of the Trinity, *De Trinitate*, against the teachings of ARIUS. He also produced a polemic against the Emperor, *Contra Constantum*, poems, biblical expositions and histories. In 1851 he was proclaimed a Doctor of the Church. He is generally regarded as the leading Western theologian of his era and the first known Latin hymn-writer.

A.J. Mason, 'The first Latin Christian poet', *Journal of Theological Studies*, v (1904); G.M. Newlands, *Hilary of Poitiers: A Study in Theological Method* (1978).

Hilda (614–80)   Saint and Order Founder. Hilda was a great-niece of King Edward of Northumbria. She became a Christian at the age of thirteen and in 649 she was appointed Abbess of the Convent of Hartlepool by St AIDAN. In 657 she founded a double monastery for men and women in Whitby, which was to become a famous house. At the Synod of Whitby in 664, she argued in favour of retaining the Celtic religious customs, but, when the decision was found in favour of the Romanising party led by St WILFRID, she accepted it.

P. Hunter Blair, *The World of Bede* (1970).

Hildegard of Bingen (1098–1179)   Saint, Mystic, Poet and Devotional Writer. Hildegard was of noble German ancestry. She joined the Benedictine community of Diessenberg in *c.* 1116 and in 1136 she became Abbess. Later she moved the house to Rupertsberg near Bingen. Throughout her life she was subject to visions which were certified as authentic by both the Archbishop of Mainz and Pope EUGENIUS III. Her major

work, *Scivias*, is an account of twenty-six religious experiences. She also wrote lives of the saints, books of medicine and natural history, homilies and hymns. She conducted extensive correspondence with leading figures of her time including FREDERICK BARBAROSSA. In recent years her hymns have been revived and she has become something of a feminist heroine.

S. Flanagan, *Hildegard of Bingen: A Visionary Life* (1989); I. Ulrich, *Hildegard of Bingen: Mystic, Healer, Companion of the Angels* (1993).

Hilton, Walter (d. 1396)   Mystic and Devotional Writer. Little is known of Hilton's life. He was a member of the Augustinian Order based in Thurgarton in Nottinghamshire. His best-known work, the *Scala Perfectionis*, describes and compares the active ascetic 'life of faith' with the contemplative, mystical 'life of feeling'. His work shows the influence of AUGUSTINE OF HIPPO, GREGORY THE GREAT, Richard ROLLE and the author of the *Cloud of Unknowing*. It was first printed in 1494 and was widely read.

H.L. Gardner, 'Walter Hilton and the mystical tradition in England', in *Essays and Studies*, xxii (1936); J.E. Milosh, *The Scale of Perfection and the English Mystical Tradition* (1966).

Hippolytus (*c.* 170–*c.* 236)   Antipope, Theologian and Saint. Little definite is known of the life of Hippolytus. ORIGEN heard him preach as a presbyter in Rome; he set himself up as antipope during the Pontificate of Callistus, but he was probably reconciled with Pope Pontianus before his death. His body was brought back to Rome and many legends grew up about him – it was said that he was a soldier converted by St LAURENCE or that he was a martyred Bishop of Portus. He was generally forgotten until a headless statue of him, enthroned as a bishop, was discoved in 1551 which was engraved with a list of his writings. These include his *Refutation of all Heresies*, which had traditionally been attributed to Origen, and a treatise on the apostolic tradition. He taught that the Logos could be both immanent and eternal, and exterior and temporal. This led to his being accused of ditheism by his enemies. None the less he is generally regarded as the most important third-century theologian of the Western Church. The so-called Canons of Hippolytus are, however, not his work.

D.H. Farmer (ed.), *The Oxford Dictionary of Saints*, 3rd edn (1992); J.B. Lightfoot, *The Apostolic Fathers*, Vol. 1 (1890).

Hobbes, Thomas (1588–1679) Philosopher. Hobbes was educated at the University of Oxford, England, and acted as tutor to the Cavendish family. He spent the years 1640–51 in exile in France where he was the tutor of Charles, Prince of Wales, son of the beheaded CHARLES I. When he returned to England he submitted to Parliamentary rule, although in 1666, after the Restoration, his great work of political philosophy, *The Leviathan*, was censured in the House of Commons. Hobbes is remembered for his description of natural human life as 'solitary, poor, nasty, brutish and short'. He argued that if men did not contract to band together under an absolute sovereign, things would be intolerable. The book succeeded in offending both those who believed in the divine right of kings and those who maintained the right of human liberty. It was regarded as atheistic and immoral. Later, in his *Questions Concerning Liberty, Necessity and Chance*, he insisted that human beings are bound by a psychological determinism and he must be regarded as the first philosopher to base a theory of conduct on natural science and observed phenomena rather than on abstract principles.

D. Baumgold, *Hobbes's Political Theory* (1988); D. Boonin-Vail, *Thomas Hobbes and the Science of Moral Virtue* (1994); A. Green, *Hobbes and Human Nature* (1993).

Hodge, Charles (1797–1878) Theologian. Hodge was ordained into the Presbyterian ministry in 1821 and for most of his adult life he taught theology at the University of Princeton in America. He was the author of several New Testament commentaries, but his major work was *Systematic Theology*, a Calvinistic exposition of the doctrines of sin, election and biblical infallibility. He regarded the theory of Charles DARWIN as 'atheism to all intents and purposes, and he disapproved of the moral optimism of his age. Always he stressed religious understanding over the more fashionable and Romantic mystical experience. He had a considerable following among his students and his views were known as 'Princeton orthodoxy'. He himself rejoiced that the seminary had 'never originated a new idea'.

W. Thorp (ed.), *Reformed Theology in America* (1985).

Hofmann, Johann Christian Konrad von (1810–77) Theologian. Von Hofmann was born in Nuremburg, Germany, and was educated at the Universities of Erlangen and Berlin. For most of his career he taught at Erlangen. His books include *Weissagung und Erfüllung, Der Schriftbeweis* and *Die Heilige Schrift*. He is generally regarded as the most significant member of the Erlangen School. He denied that the atonement was effected by penal substitution – rather it was through JESUS's maintenance of oneness with God even to his death. This caused considerable controversy, but von Hoffmann regarded himself as a faithful upholder of the doctrines of Martin LUTHER.

M. Schellbach, *Theologie und Philosophie bei von Hofmann* (1935) [no English translation available].

Holland, Henry Scott (1847–1918) Theologian. Holland was educated at the University of Oxford where he came under the influence of T.H. GREEN. He was appointed a Canon of St Paul's Cathedral in 1884 and Regius Professor of Divinity at Oxford in 1910. He was a member of Charles GORE's *Lux Mundi* group, and he is primarily remembered as a prominent member of the Christian Social Union. He was the author of works such as *Logic and Life, Creed and Character* and *God's City* and his hymn 'Judge eternal, throned in splendour' is still sung today. His view of JESUS CHRIST as 'the solution of all human problems' struck a chord in many listeners, but his belief in human progress was sadly shattered by the events of the First World War.

F. Lyttleton, *The Mind and Character of Henry Scott Holland* (1926).

Honorius I (d. 638) Pope. Little is known of the early life of Honorius. He is remembered in England for his letter of congratulation to King Edwin of Northumbria when he became a Christian and also for his involvement in the Monothelite controversy. This was an attempt to reach a compromise with the Monophysites by arguing that although JESUS CHRIST had two natures, he had but one mode of activity. SERGIUS, the Patriarch of Constantinople, asked for support for this formula and Honorius replied that there should be no more discussion on the matter, but also 'we confess one will of the Lord Jesus Christ'. This notion of 'one will' was incorporated into the Ecthesis of 638, the statement of faith of the Monothelites. The Monothelite view was formally condemned and in 681, at the Council of Constantinople, Honorius himself was anathematised. His Pontificate therefore has always been a stumbling block for those who support the doctrine of papal infallibility.

J.N.D. Kelly (ed.), *The Oxford Dictionary of Popes* (1986).

Honorius III (d. 1227) Pope. Honorius

was born Censio Savelli in Rome, Italy. He became a Cardinal in 1193, was tutor to FREDERICK II and was elected Pope in 1216 in succession to INNOCENT III. He was greatly involved in the politics of Europe; he crowned Frederick II Holy Roman Emperor and Peter of Courtney, Emperor of Byzantium. He supported the boy-king Henry III of England and he arbitrated between Philip II of France and James of Aragon. His main concern, however, was to liberate Jerusalem from Muslim control, to which end he called the Fifth Crusade; this did not prove a success. More significantly he encouraged the new Dominican and Franciscan Orders and he continued a crusade against the heresy of the Albigensians, whom his forces crushed with utmost ferocity. Many of his writings survive, including an important collection of Canon Laws.

J.N.D. Kelly (ed.), *The Oxford Dictionary of Popes* (1986); J.E. Sayers, *Papal Government in England during the Pontificate of Honorius III* (1984).

Honorius of Autun (twelfth century) Theologian. Little is known of the life of Honorius of Autun except that he was a priest, a teacher and a prolific writer. His books covered a variety of subjects, but the most popular include the *Imago Mundi* on geography and cosmology, the *Elucidarium* on Christian doctrine and the *Gemma Animae*, a treatise on liturgy. All these works were widely read and circulated. He described himself as 'Augustodunensis' but scholars no longer believe that this implies that he came from Autun.

E.M. Sanford, 'Honorius, presbyter and scholasticus', *Speculum*, xxii (1948).

Hontheim, Johann Nikolaus von (1701–90) Bishop and Theologian. Hontheim was born in Trier, Germany, and was appointed Suffragan Bishop of Trier in 1748. He wrote his famous *De Statu Ecclesiae et Legitima Potestate Romani Pontificis* under the pseudonym Justinus

Febronius. This was the classic statement of Febronianism, a German and Austrian movement to limit papal power. Hontheim argued that the 'keys of the kingdom' had been given to the whole Church, not just to the Apostle PETER and his papal successors. This differed from the Gallican view since Hontheim maintained that ecclesiastical power should be held by the Bishops and not by a secular ruler. The book inspired much debate and Hontheim recanted in 1778. None the less his ideas were later used by the Emperor JOSEPH II to establish secular control over the Austrian Church.

J. Kuntziger, *Febronius et le Fébronianisme* (1891) [no English translation available].

Hooker, Richard (*c.* 1554–1600) Theologian. Hooker was born near Exeter and was educated at the University of Oxford. After ordination he served in various parishes of the Church of England. He is remembered for his monumental *Treatise on the Laws of Ecclesiastical Polity* which is a splendid defence of the Church Settlement of Queen ELIZABETH I. Arguing from natural law whose 'seat is the bosom of God, her voice the harmony of the world', he maintained that the law of the land must be made in accord with natural law. The Church must be seen as a political society, analogous to civil society, and subject to both natural law and biblical commandments. Thus he refuted the fundamentalist stance of the Puritan party and he could show that the Church of England, although reformed, was a clear development of the historical Church. Hooker is generally regarded as one of the greatest theologians ever produced by the Anglican Church.

W.S. Hill, *Studies in Richard Hooker* (1974); G. Hillerdal, *Reason and Revelation in Richard Hooker* (1962); J.S. Marshall, *Hooker and the Anglican Tradition* (1963)

Hooper, John (d. 1555) Bishop and Martyr. Hooper was educated at the University of Oxford and he became a monk. After the dissolution of the monasteries in the reign of King HENRY VIII, he went to London where he was converted to Protestantism. He was forced to live abroad between 1547 and 1549 where he became acquainted with the reformer Johann Heinrich BULLINGER. On the accession of EDWARD VI he returned to England where he was appointed chaplain to the Duke of Somerset. In 1550 he was nominated Bishop of Gloucester, but, because he objected to vestments, he was not consecrated until the following year. He proved to be an excellent, conscientious Bishop, severe on abuse and generous to the poor. He also wrote the influential *Godly Confession and Protestation of the Christian Faith*. However, with the accession of the Roman Catholic Queen MARY, he was arrested, imprisoned, tried and burnt to death for heresy. His martyrdom is recorded in John FOXE's *Book of Martyrs*.

L.B. Smith, *Tudor Prelates and Politics* (1953).

Hopkins, Gerard Manley (1844–89) Poet. Hopkins was born in Stratford, Essex, and he was educated at the University of Oxford. At the age of twenty-two he was received into the Roman Catholic Church and joined the Jesuit Order. He gave up writing poetry when he entered the religious life, but was encouraged to resume by his Superior. His poems are distinctive for their sharp and vivid language: 'That night, that year/Of now done darkness I wretch lay wrestling with (my God!) my God' ('Carrion Comfort'). They were not published until 1918 when they were issued by his literary executor, the poet Robert Bridges. Today Hopkins is recognised, with T.S. ELIOT, as one of the great devotional poets of the twentieth century.

G. Storey (ed.), *The Journal and Papers of Gerard Manley Hopkins* (1959); E. Hollahan (ed.), *Gerard Manley Hopkins and Critical Discourse* (1993); G. Storey, *A Preface to Hopkins*, 2nd edn (1992); N. White, *Hopkins: A Literary Biography* (1992).

Hort, Fenton John Antony (1828–92) Theologian. Hort was educated at Rugby School under Thomas ARNOLD and at the University of Cambridge. Subsequently he taught at the university and ultimately was appointed Lady Margaret Professor. He is known for his New Testament scholarship, particularly for his work with B.F. WESTCOTT on the Greek text which was finally published in 1881. He also prepared the Book of Wisdom and II Maccabees for the new Revised Version and was the author of *Judaistic Christianity* and the *Christian Ecclesia*, both published posthumously. Hort, together with Westcott and J.B. LIGHT-FOOT, is remembered as one of a triumvirate of remarkable Cambridge New Testament scholars.

A.F. Hort, *Life and Letters of Fenton John Anthony Hort*, 2 vols (1896); E.G. Rupp, *Hort and the Cambridge Tradition* (1970).

Hosius (c. 256–357) Bishop and Theologian. Hosius was a native of Spain. He came to prominence in the Council of Milan of 316 where he is said to have advised the Emperor CONSTANTINE against the Donatists. Subsequently he was sent to Alexandria to settle a dispute with ARIUS; it is possible that the Council of Nicaea was called on his advice. His influence in the council has been much disputed. Later, in 345, he presided over the Council of Sardica where he was condemned by the Eastern Bishops for holding communion with ATHANASIUS. Finally in 355 Constantius summoned him to Milan where he refused to condemn Athanasius, but was forced to sign the 'Blasphemy', an Arian creed. He almost certainly repudiated this before his death. His only surviving writing is a letter to Constantius.

V.C. de Clercq, *Ossius of Cordova: A Contribution to the History of the Constantinian Period* (1954).

Hosius, Stanislaus (1504–79) Cardinal and Polemicist. Hosius was born in Cracow, Poland, and was educated at the Universities of Padua and Bologna. He became Secretary to the Bishop of Cracow, was ordained in 1543 and was consecrated Bishop in 1549. A dedicated Catholic, he was determined to root out Protestantism from Poland. His *Confessio Fidei Catholicae Christianae* was hugely successful and went through many editions. Known as the 'hammer of heretics', he was a leading figure of the Counter-Reformation. In 1558 he was appointed to the College of Cardinals and, as a leading member of the Curia, he took a prominent part in the Council of Trent (1545–63).

F.J. Zdrodowski, *The Concept of Heresy according to Cardinal Hosius* (1947).

Hoskyns, Sir Edwyn Clement (1884–1937) Theologian. Hoskyns was educated at the Universities of Cambridge and Berlin, where he was influenced by the thought of Adolf HARNACK. He was ordained to the Anglican ministry in 1908 and, after the First World War, he taught at Cambridge. He is remembered for his English translation of Karl BARTH's *Commentary on Romans* and for his *Riddle of the New Testament*, written with F.N. Davey, in which he argued for the historical reality of the JESUS CHRIST of faith. He also contributed 'The Christ of the Synoptic Gospels' to *Essays Catholic and Critical* and 'Jesus the Messiah' to *Mysterium Christi*. His important commentary on the Fourth Gospel was published posthumously.

Edwyn Clement Hoskyns, *Cambridge Sermons* (1938).

Howard, John (c. 1726–90) Philanthropist. Howard was born in East London. During his travels as a young man, he was for a short time imprisoned in France. In 1758 he settled in Bedfordshire and ultimately became High Sheriff of the county. He is remembered, however, for his tireless campaign for prison reform. His book, *The State of the Prisons*, publicised the deplorable conditions under which prisoners lived and he was largely responsible for a Prison Reform Act being passed through Parliament in 1777. He also explored the prisons of Europe as well as the lazarettos (quarantine quarters). He died from camp fever, caught during the course of his researches. The Howard League for Penal Reform was founded in his memory in 1866 and continues his work today.

M. Southwood, *John Howard: Prison Reformer* (1959).

Howe, Julia Ward (1819–1910) Philanthropist and Poet. Howe was born Julia Ward in New York City and moved to Boston on her marriage to Samuel Howe. She was prominent in the movement to abolish slavery and was also involved in the campaigns for women's suffrage, for prison reform, and for children's welfare and she became a well-known Unitarian preacher. However, she is chiefly remembered for her 'Battle hymn of the Republic' which, sung to the tune of 'John BROWN's Body lies a-mouldering in the grave', is close to being an American national anthem.

M. Hetherington Grant, *Private Woman, Public Person: An Account of the Life of Julia Ward Howe from 1819–1868* (1994).

Howson, John Saul (1816–85) Theologian. Howson was educated at the University of Cambridge and he was ordained to the Anglican ministry in 1845. He had a successful career and ultimately he became Dean of Chester. He was the author of the *Life and Epistles of St Paul*, but today he is chiefly remembered for his article 'Deaconesses in the Church of England', which appeared in the *Quarterly Review* of 1861. This did much to revive the order of Deaconesses in England and paved the way for the decisions to ordain women as Deacons and priests in the 1980s and 1990s.

D.A. Johnson, *Women in English Religion 1700–1925* (1983).

Hrosvit (tenth century) Poet. Hrosvit was a Benedictine nun who lived in a community in Gandersheim, Saxony. She was well educated in the Classics and her poetry was written in the style of Terence. It particularly emphasises the chastity and courage of Christian women. Although she was well known during her life-time, she was subsquently forgotten until her verse was rediscovered by the humanist Conrad Celtes and was published in 1501. There has been a recent revival of interest in her work.

A.C. Haight (ed.), *Hroswitha of Gandersheim* (1965).

Hubbard, Lafayette Ronald (Ron) (1911–86) Sect Founder. Hubbard was born in Nebraska and little certain is known of his early life. In 1950 he published *Dianetics*, 'a system for the analysis, control and development of human thought'. Four years later, he founded the Church of Scientology based on this system. From its inception, Scientology has been the source of controversy – not least as to its religious status. Certainly the Church teaches a belief in reincarnation and is concerned with the development of the human soul and with its ultimate release from the prison of the body. L. Ron Hubbard himself wrote more than five hundred books (including works of science fiction) and the organisation claims that more than twenty-three million volumes have been sold. Adherents of the system claim that Hubbard's teaching has transformed their lives, making them more effective people. In contrast, opponents insist that the Church hierarchy is only interested in making money from its gullible and inadequate disciples. Although Hubbard described the new movement as a 'Church', his system has in general been repudiated by mainstream Christianity.

L.R. Hubbard, *Scientology: The Fundamentals of Thought* (1950).

Hubert (d. 727) Saint and Bishop. Hubert was consecrated Bishop of Maestricht in 705 and later he became Bishop of Liège. According to legend he was converted to Christianity by seeing an image of the crucified JESUS CHRIST between the antlers of a stag he was hunting. However, this story rightly belongs to St EUSTACE. None the less Hubert is still regarded as a patron of huntsmen and a hunting horn supposedly his can be seen in the Wallace Collection in London.

D.H. Farmer (ed.), *The Oxford Dictionary of Saints*, 3rd edn (1992).

Hübmaier, Balthasar (*c.* 1485–1528) Rebel and Martyr. Hübmaier was a student of Johann ECK at Freiberg University and he later taught at Ingoldstadt. Initially he was attracted to the teachings of ZWINGLI, but by 1525 he had identified himself with the Anabaptists. His *Von dem Tauf der Gläubigen*, published in that year, rejected infant baptism and insisted that a personal adult faith was necessary for valid baptism. He is also thought to have been the author of the Twelve Articles, the main charter of the Peasants' Revolt of 1525. However, he was forced to seek Zwingli's protection in Zürich and there he was compelled to recant his opinions. By 1526 he was working independently in Moravia and had returned to his Anabaptist views. Eventually the Austrian authorities caught up with him. He was arrested in 1527 and was burnt at the stake as a heretic the following year.

G.H. Williams, *The Radical Reformation* (1962).

Hugh of Cluny (1024–1109) Saint. Hugh was born of an aristocratic Burgundian family. At the age of fourteen he entered the monastery at Cluny, was chosen as Prior at an early age and succeeded ODILIO as Abbot in 1049. During his reign he presided over an extraordinary expansion in the influence of Cluny. When the new basilica was consecrated in 1095, it was the largest church in the Christian world. Hugh settled the usages of the whole order by 1068 and, in addition, he was the confidential advisor of nine Popes, including LEO IX and GREGORY VII. He was involved in the condemnation of BERENGAR; he tried to reconcile the Emperor HENRY IV with the Papacy; he served as Papal legate on different occasions in Hungary, Toulouse and Spain and he initiated the First Crusade at the Council of Clermont. He must be considered one of the most influential churchmen of the eleventh century and he was canonised only eleven years after his death.

H.E.J. Cowdrey, *The Clunaics and the Gregorian Reform* (1970); N. Hunt, *Cluny under St Hugh* (1967).

Hugh of Lincoln [Little St Hugh] (d. 1255) Martyr. As a child of nine, Hugh was murdered in the town of Lincoln and his body was thrust into a well. His murderer was unknown, but it was rumoured that a wealthy Jew named Koppin had conspired with his co-religionists to torture and crucify the boy. Although there was no firm evidence, Koppin and eight other Jews were executed for the crime. This was one of the first cases in which Jews were accused of the ritual murder of Christian children. The charge became commonplace in the Middle Ages and the 'blood libel' has been revived by anti-Semites even in modern times. It has been a frequent excuse for the persecution of whole Jewish communities and for the confiscation of Jewish property. The best-known version of the story of Little St Hugh in English is to be found in the Prioress's Tale in Geoffrey Chaucer's *Canterbury Tales*.

C. Roth, *Ritual Murder Libel and the Jews* (1935).

Hugh of Lincoln (*c.* 1140–1200) Saint

and Bishop. Hugh was a native of Burgundy. He first joined the Regular Canons, but then became a member of the Carthusian Order at Chartreuse. He was appointed the first Prior of King HENRY II's new Carthusian house at Witham, Somerset, and he was consecrated Bishop of Lincoln in 1186. He is remembered for his tireless efforts in reforming his diocese, for helping rebuild the cathedral and for his courage in standing up in the cause of justice not only to Henry II, but also to his sons King Richard I and King John. A saintly figure, he used to say that the lay-person who practised charity in his heart, truth on his lips and chastity in his body, would have in Heaven a reward equal with monks and nuns. He was canonised in 1220 and, until King HENRY VIII's Reformation, his tomb attracted almost as many pilgrims as that of Thomas BECKET in Canterbury.

D.H. Farmer, *Saint Hugh of Lincoln* (1985); H. Mayr-Harting (ed.), *St Hugh of Lincoln: Lectures delivered at Oxford and London* (1987).

Hugh of St Victor (*c.* 1096–1142)   Theologian, Mystic and Devotional Writer. Hugh was a member of the Augustinian house of Canon Regulars at St Victor in Paris, France. From 1120 he taught in the St Victor School and was Prior of the Abbey some time afer 1133. He was the author of works of philosophy, including *Epitome in Philosophiam*, theological treatises such as *Summa Sententiarum* and *De Sacramentis Christianae Fidei*, devotional books such as *De Laude Caritatis* and *De Vanitate Mundi* and various commentaries on the Scriptures. His work shows the influence of other leading theologians of the time, such as Peter ABELARD, ANSELM of Canterbury, ANSELM OF LAON and BERNARD OF CLAIRVAUX. He emphasised the historical study of the biblical books and of doctrine, and he stressed the importance of the contemplative life as the means to mystical union with God.

J.P. Kleinz, *The Theory of Knowledge of Hugh of St Victor* (1945); J. Taylor, *The Origin and Early Life of Hugh of St Victor* (1957).

Hume, David (1711–76)   Philosopher and Historian. Hume was born and educated in Edinburgh. He was the author of several important works of philosophy including *A Treatise on Human Nature, Philosophical Essays Concerning Human Understanding* (which contains his essay on miracles), *An Enquiry Concerning the Principles of Morals* and, perhaps most interesting of all to the student of religion, his *Dialogues Concerning Natural Religion*. He also compiled a six-volume history of England. He is remembered for his sceptical attitude towards miracles – he argued that it was always more reasonable to reject a witness's testimony about a miracle than to accept it, since 'it is contrary to experience that a miracle should be true, but not contrary to experience that testimony should be false'. His dismissal of the teleological argument for the existence of God in the *Dialogues* is also masterly. Hume's philosophy has been immensely influential and he must be seen as the forerunner of the modern logical positivists.

A.J. Ayer, *Hume* (1980); J.C.A. Gaskin, *Hume's Philosophy of Religion* (1978); S. Tweyman (ed.), *David Hume: Critical Assessments* (1995).

Hung, Hsiu-Ch'uan (1813–64)   Rebel. As a young scholar in Canton, China, Hung was introduced to the beliefs of Christianity and began to teach a syncretistic faith combining Christian ideas with traditional Chinese doctrines. In 1851 he and his peasant followers rebelled against the rule of the Manchu emperors and dedicated themselves to setting up the 'Heavenly Kingdom of Great Peace'. Initially the insurrection was successful, but it was eventually put down by foreign troops led by Lieutenant Colonel C.G. Gordon. Hung himself commited suicide in 1864. The whole episode did little to recommend Christianity to the Chinese authorities.

W. Franke, *A Century of Chinese Revolution 1851–1949* (1970).

Huntingdon   see Hastings

Hus, John (1373–1415)   Theologian and Martyr. Hus was born in humble circumstances in Husinec, South Bohemia. He was educated at the University of Prague and was ordained a priest in 1402. While he was still teaching at the university, he was appointed Rector of Bethlehem Chapel in Prague and was regarded as the leader of the Czech reform party. In 1409 he was excommunicated by Archbishop Zbynek for continuing to preach and for supporting Pope Alexander V over Pope Gregory XII. King Wenceslas agreed with Hus, however, and made him Rector of the Czech University. In 1411 he was exiled from Prague. He had opposed the papal sale of Indulgences and in retaliation, the Roman Curia had placed the city of Prague under interdict. He spent the next two years in South Bohemia preaching and writing his most important book *De Ecclesia*, which was influenced by the theology of John WYCLIFFE. In 1414 he was lured to the Council of Constance. There he was summarily imprisoned in a Dominican monastery and put on trial for heresy. He refused to recant on the grounds that he did not hold the views that were ascribed to him – and thus recantation would amount to perjury. Consequently he was defrocked as a priest and burned at the stake outside the city.

H. Kaminsky, *A History of the Hussite Revolution* (1967); M. Spinka, *John Hus: A Biography* (1968).

Hutten, Ulrich von (1488–1523)   Polemicist. Hutten was born in Steckelberg, Germany. As a child he was placed in a monastery, but he rejected the vocation and travelled as a young man from university to university. He settled finally in Germany in 1517 and entered the service of the Elector of Mainz. He had, by that stage, established a reputation as a poet and satirical writer. After 1519 he became an ardent supporter of Martin LUTHER's Reformation and, as a result of a series of ironical attacks on the Pope, he was dismissed from the Elector's household and was under order of arrest from Rome. He was refused sanctuary by the towns of Schlettstadt and Basle and was eventually rescued by ZWINGLI who provided a home on the island of Ufenau until his death. Hutten's role in the Reformation is a matter of scholarly debate. In general he seems to have been more interested in the political freedom of Germany than in a religious revival. None the less his later books show signs of genuine piety.

H. Holborn, *Ulrich von Hutten and the German Reformation* (1978).

Hutter, Jacob (d. 1536)   Denomination Founder and Martyr. Hutter was the leader of an Anabaptist group which established settlements in Moravia. These were based on the ideals of pacifism and the common ownership of property. As Anabaptists they also refused to accept infant baptism and reintroduced the practice of believer's baptism. The sect was much persecuted and Hutter himself died a martyr's death three years after he had assumed the group's leadership. It was forced to move from Moravia to Transylvania, then to the Ukraine and finally to the United States of America. Small colonies still exist in South Dakota and more recently in Canada, where they are known as Hutterites.

J.W. Bennett, *Hutterian Brethren* (1967); R. Friedman, *Hutterite Studies* (1961); G.H. Williams, *The Radical Reformation* (1962).

Huxley, Thomas Henry (1825–95)   Scientist and Educator. Huxley was born in Ealing, West London, and trained as a physician. As a naval doctor, he pursued his biological studies in the South Seas and, at the early age of twenty-six, he was elected a fellow of the Royal Society. A fervent disciple of Charles DARWIN, he was the author of *Collected Essays, Zoological Evidences in Man's Place in Nature* and a study of David HUME. He also delivered an important lecture in 1868 on 'The physical basis of life' in which he described himself by his own newly coined term as an 'agnostic'. His final views were summarised in lectures on 'Ethics and evolution' delivered in 1893. Huxley was one of the most prominent English unbelievers of his day. A man of impeccable integrity, he worked tirelessly in several public offices and he did much to lay down the foundation for systematic scientific education in schools. In the history of the Church, however, he is mainly remembered as the man who was asked by the Bishop of Oxford, Samuel WILBERFORCE, at a meeting of the British Association in 1860, whether he traced his descent from an ape on his grandfather's or his grandmother's side.

C. Bibby, *Scientist Extraordinary: The Life and Scientific Work of Thomas Henry Huxley* (1972); W. Irvine, *Apes, Angels and Victorians: The Story of Darwin, Huxley and Evolution* (1963), J.G. Paradis, *T.H. Huxley: Man's Place in Nature* (1978).

I

Ibas (d. 457) Bishop and Theologian. Ibas was Bishop of Edessa from 435 to 449 and again from 451 to 457. In 433 he wrote a letter to Bishop Mari in Persia in which he took a mediating line between the doctrines of NESTORIUS and those of CYRIL OF ALEXANDRIA. He was associated with THEODORET, who was himself a close friend of Nestorius and had translated the works of THEODORE OF MOPSUESTIA into Syriac. Because of his supposed heretical views, he was deposed at the 'Robber Synod' of Ephesus, but was reinstated at the Council of Chalcedon. A hundred years later, the Fifth Ecumenical Council condemned Ibas's letter together with the writings of Theodoret and Theodore. Today only a Greek translation of the letter survives.

J.N.D. Kelly (ed.), *Early Christian Doctrines* (1958).

Ignatius of Antioch (*c*. 35–*c*. 107) Bishop, Theologian and Saint. Ignatius was the author of seven letters written in Smyrna and Troas when travelling on his way to execution in Rome. The letters were addressed to the Churches of Ephesus, Magnesia, Tralles, Rome, Philadelphia and Smyrna, and to St POLYCARP. They emphasise the three-fold ministry of Bishops, priests and Deacons and attack a Judaistic docetic heresy, stressing the full humanity as well as the divinity of JESUS CHRIST. Ignatius expresses himself anxious for martyrdom, believing that he will thus 'attain God' and he describes the Eucharist as 'the bread that is the flesh of Jesus Christ'. According to ORIGEN, Ignatius succeeded PETER as the Bishop of Antioch after Euodius and

Polycarp records that his wish for martyrdom was fulfilled. The letters were much quoted by early Church Fathers, but there has been considerable scholarly debate about their authenticity. Largely as a result of the work of James USSHER and J.B. LIGHTFOOT, they are now accepted as genuine.

V. Corwen, *St Ignatius and Christianity in Antioch* (1960); J.B. Lightfoot, *The Apostolic Fathers*, Part II (1885).

Ignatius, Father [Joseph Leycester Lyne] (1837–1908) Order Founder. After serving curacies in Plymouth and London, Lyne determined to revive the Rule of St BENEDICT in the Anglican Church. As Father Ignatius, he started one community in Claydon and another in Norwich and finally he started building a monastery on a site in Capel-y-ffin in Wales. Despite his ritualism, he was a fervent evangelical preacher and attracted large audiences. He remained in Deacons' orders until 1898 when he was irregularly ordained by the Old Catholic 'Bishop', Mar Timotheos (Joseph René VILATTE). After his death, Capel-y-ffin passed to the community of Anglican Benedictines on Calding Island.

A. Calder-Marshall, *The Enthusiast: An Enquiry into the Life, Beliefs and Character of the Rev. Joseph Leycester Lyne alias Father Ignatius OSB* (1962).

Ignatius Loyola (? 1491–1556) Saint and Order Founder. Ignatius was born of a noble family in Loyola, northern Spain. After a short career as a soldier, he was wounded in the leg which led him to reassess his life. After a period of withdrawal from the world in Manresa, he travelled first to Rome and then to Jerusalem as a pilgrim before returning to Spain. He studied in Barcelona, Alcalá and Salamanca before spending seven years at the University of Paris. By this stage he had written his famous *Spiritual Exercises*. These are a series of meditations on sin, the Kingdom of Christ, the Passion and the risen Lord. He gathered round him a band of six followers, who included FRANCIS XAVIER, and together they vowed themselves to lives of poverty, chastity and service to the Church. In 1540 the new order, known as the Society of Jesus, was approved by Pope Paul III. Ignatius was chosen as its first General. He drew up the constitution of the society and dedicated the rest of his life to its establishment. Within the order stress was laid on obedience, discipline and efficiency. The Jesuits, as members of the society were called, quickly established a reputation for effective missionary and educational work. They were strong supporters of the Papacy at the Council of Trent and their theologians have continued to lead the attack against Protestantism in all its forms. Even today the order is regarded as a powerful force in Catholic education.

J. Brodrick, *The Origin of the Jesuits* (1940); M.P. Harney, *The Jesuits in History*, 2nd edn (1962); P. van Dyke, *Ignatius Loyola: The Founder of the Jesuits* (1968).

Ildefonsus (*c.* 607–67) Archbishop, Devotional Writer, Historian and Saint. As a young man, lldefonsus may have been a pupil of ISIDORE OF SEVILLE. He entered the Benedictine monastery of Agalia, Spain, and rose to be its Abbot. Then in 657 he was consecrated Archbishop of Toledo. He was a prolific writer and his surviving works include *De Virginitate S. Mariae*, two devotional works, *Annotationes de Cognitione Baptismi* and *De Itinere Deserti quo Pergitur Post Baptismum*, and an important history *De Viris Illustribus*. He was de-

voted to the cult of the Blessed Virgin MARY and he is often portrayed being presented with the chasuble by the Virgin herself.

Sr Athanasius Braegelmann, *The Life and Writings of St Ildefonsus of Toledo* (1942).

Illich, Ivan (b. 1926) Educationalist and Social Theorist. Illich was born in Austria and was educated at the Gregorian University in Rome and the University of Salzburg. After moving to the New World, he founded the Center for Intercultural Documentation in Mexico which became the focus for seminars on alternative societies. Among his books were *Deschooling Society* and *Limits to Medicine*. In both he argued for more openness, less mystifying technology and the right of ordinary people to be involved in decisions affecting their own lives. His work was highly influential in the 1970s although his ideas are now generally considered to be more practical for developing countries than for the rich Western world.

P. Lund, *Ivan Illich and his Antics* (1978); I. Lister (ed.), *Deschooling: A Reader* (1974); J. Ohlinger, *Lifelong Learning or Lifelong Schooling? A Tentative View of the Ideas of Ivan Illich* (1971).

Inge, William Ralph (1860–1954) Popular Theologian and Devotional Writer. Inge was born in Yorkshire and was educated at the University of Cambridge. He had a successful career within the Church of England, becoming Lady Margaret Professor of Divinity at Cambridge in 1907, and he was Dean of St Paul's Cathedral from 1911 to 1934. His works included *Christian Mysticism, Personal Idealism and Mysticism* and *Faith and its Psychology*. Platonic in outlook, he was best known for his series of *Outspoken Essays* in which he defined God as the 'supreme value' and faith as 'belief in the reality of absolute value'. He also contributed a regular, but not always cheerful, column to a London newspaper and was thus perhaps the most widely read churchman of his generation.

R.M. Helm, *The Gloomy Dean. The Thought of William Ralph Inge* (1962).

Innocent I (d. 417) Pope and Saint. Innocent made greater claims for the Papacy than any of his predecessors. Thirty-six of his letters survive and in them he argued forcefully that the Western Bishops should follow Rome's lead since their Churches were formed through the agency of St PETER. During his Pontificate, Alaric the Goth sacked Rome and this increased his secular influence. In addition he attempted to extend his jurisdiction over the Eastern Churches by supporting St JOHN CHRYSOSTOM and by bringing East Illyricum under his direct control. His letter to Decentius throws light on the liturgical practices of his time; it describes Confirmation as a Sacrament reserved for Bishops and mentions the Eucharistic prayer of consecration and the Sacraments of penance and unction. Innocent's reign is generally regarded as an important stage in the development of the power of the Papacy.

J.N.D. Kelly (ed.), *The Oxford Dictionary of Popes* (1986).

Innocent III (1160–1216) Pope. Innocent was born Giovanni Lotario de' Conti and was educated at the Universities of Paris and Bologna. In 1190 he was made a Cardinal-Deacon and, at the age of thirty-seven, he was unanimously elected Pope. He is generally regarded as one of the greatest of the mediaeval Popes. He was the author of the widely read ascetical treatise *De Miseria Humanae Conditionis*. He reorganised the administration of the city of Rome and expanded the Papal States. He launched the Fourth Crusade in 1202 and managed to establish the Latin Kingdom of Constantinople. He did not succeed, however, in uniting the Eastern and Western Churches. He supported Otto of Bruns-

wick in his quest to become Holy Roman Emperor. Then when Otto invaded Sicily, he excommunicated him and put his weight behind FREDERICK II. He reconciled King Philip Augustus of France to his wife and he excommunicated John, King of England, for refusing to accept Stephen LANGTON as Archbishop of Canterbury. However, he is mainly remembered for summoning the Fourth Lateran Council in 1215. The suppression of the Albigensian heresy, the approval of the term 'transubstantiation', the necessity of the payment of tithes and the encouragement of the foundation of schools, were among its many decrees. The Council thus did much to shape the policy of the Church in the later Middle Ages.

C.R. Chesney, *Pope Innocent III and England* (1976); S.R. Packard, *Europe and the Church under Innocent III* (1968); H. Tillman, *Pope Innocent III* (1980).

Innocent IV (*c.* 1200–54) Pope. Innocent IV was born in Genoa, Italy, and was educated at the University of Bologna. He was made a Cardinal in 1227 and succeeded to the Papacy in 1243 after an eighteen-month vacancy. At this point the Emperor FREDERICK II was trying to extend his power in Italy. In 1245 at the Council of Lyons, Innocent excommunicated him and preached a crusade against him. Pope and Emperor were only reconciled in 1254 after the death of the Emperor Conrad IV. Innocent was a notable Canon Lawyer and his *Commentaria* on the Decretals was much respected. However, he is primarily remembered as the Pope who issued a Bill permitting the Inquisition to use torture.

J.N.D. Kelly (ed.), *The Oxford Dictionary of Popes* (1986).

Innocent XI (1611–89) Pope. Innocent was born Benedetto Odescalchi at Como, Italy, and was educated at the University of Naples. A man of the highest principles and great saintliness, he was made a Cardinal in 1645 and became Bishop of Novara in 1650. He was elected Pope in 1676. His reign was distinguished for the reform of abuses. In particular he is remembered for his opposition to the absolutism of King LOUIS XIV of France. Eventually he excommunicated the King. He also encouraged daily Communion; he opposed the revocation of the Edict of Nantes and he condemned Quietism. However, he seems to have encouraged Jansenism to some extent and, for this reason, the Church hesitated to beatify him. His beatification was only achieved in 1956.

J.N.D. Kelly (ed.), *The Oxford Dictionary of Popes* (1986).

Irenaeus (*c*. 130–*c*. 200) Bishop, Theologian and Saint. Irenaeus is thought to have been born in Smyrna since, as a boy, he heard St POLYCARP. He became a Presbyter in Lyons, Gaul, and was commissioned to ask Bishop Eleutherus of Rome for toleration for the Montanists. In *c*. 177 there was a persecution against the Christians of Lyons during which the Bishop died. On his return from Rome, Ilrenaeus was appointed to succeed him. He was the author of *Adversus Omnes Haereses* against the Gnostics. Although a complete version only survives in a Latin translation, it gives a valuable account of the various Gnostic beliefs of the time. Another work, *The Demonstration of the Apostolic Preaching*, was only found, in an Armenian translation, in the modern period. Irenaeus is regarded as an important early link between the theologies of the Eastern and Western Churches and between the ideas of the Apostolic Church and those of the developed ecclesiastical tradition. He stressed the unity of the Three Persons of the Trinity in the works of creation and redemption and he defended the canon of the Four Gospels. He also developed the doctrine of 'recapitulation' and understood the incarnation of JESUS CHRIST to be the summation of God's

dealings with humanity, thus giving positive value to Christ's humanness.

G. Wingren, *Man and the Incarnation: A Study in the Biblical Theology of Irenaeus* (1959); D. Minns, *Irenaeus* (1995); R.M. Grant, *Irenaeus* (1997).

Irving, Edward (1792–1834) Reputed Sect Founder. Irving was born in Annan, Scotland, and was educated at the University of Edinburgh. After serving as an assistant to Thomas Chalmers in Glasgow, he moved to London. First he ministered at the Caledonian Chapel, but his sermons attracted so many that a new church was built in 1827 in Regent Square. He was a friend of COLERIDGE and CARLYLE and was one of the best-known churchmen of his time. However, his preaching became wilder and as the more spectacular manifestations of the Spirit became evident, disorder grew. From the pulpit, he deplored Catholic emancipation and any form of political reform. The congregation split. Irving was deprived of his position by the London Presbytery and many of those who remained faithful to him subsequently joined the new Catholic Apostolic Church. Irving, unlike his friend Henry Drummond, was not recognised among their twelve latter-day apostles, so he cannot be regarded as a founder of the movement. In 1833 he was formally excommunicated from the Church of Scotland as his book *The Orthodox and Catholic Doctrine of Our Lord's Human Nature* was deemed heretical. He took up a new career as an itinerant preacher, but he died the following year in Glasgow.

A.L. Drummond, *Edward Irving and His Circle* (1938); H.C. Whitley, *Blinded Eagle: An Introduction to the Life and Teaching of Edward Irving* (1955); C.G. Flegg, *Gathered Under Apostles: A Study of the Catholic Apostolic Church* (1992).

Isaac of Nineveh (seventh century) Bishop and Devotional Writer. Isaac was a monk living in Bethabe, Kurdistan. For a short time he was Bishop of Nineveh, but he soon retired to a monastery at Rabban Shappur. He was a Nestorian in his theology, but his writings on the ascetic life, originally written in Syriac, were frequently translated and were influential in the development of the monastic life.

S. Brody, 'Isaac of Nineveh and Syriac spirituality', *Sobornost*, ii (1975).

Isaac the Great (*c.* 350–440) Patriarch, Poet and Saint. Isaac was the son of the sixth Armenian Patriarch (Catholicos). He was educated at Constantinople, married, and, once widowed, became a monk. In 390, he himself became Catholicos and he negotiated the independence of the Armenian Church from the See of Caesarea. He was very popular, and he encouraged the development of an Armenian literature. He is venerated as a hymn writer and two days in the Armenian Church calendar are set aside to his memory.

F.L. Cross (ed.), *The Oxford Dictionary of the Christian Church*, 2nd edn (1974).

Isabella of Castile (1451–1504) Monarch. Isabella was the daughter of John II, King of Castile, and she married FERDINAND, heir to the throne of Aragon. She became Queen of Castile in her own right in 1474. Although the two countries remained separate, she and her husband became known as the 'Catholic Sovereigns' and did much to unite Spain. A woman of real personal piety, in the history of the Church she is remembered for instigating the Inquisition in Spain in 1478, for expelling the Jews in 1492 and the Muslims in 1502 and for supporting Archbishop XIMÉNEZ, her confessor, in his reforms. She also encouraged Christopher Columbus in his explorations and supported LAS CASAS in his efforts to convert the Indians of the New World.

F. Fernandez-Armesto, *Ferdinand and Isabella* (1975).

Isidore of Seville (*c.* 560–636) Archbishop, Educator and Saint. Isidore was a younger brother of Leander, Archbishop of Seville. He succeeded his brother as Archbishop in *c.* 600 and he presided over the Councils of Seville in 619 and Toledo in 633. However, he is mainly remembered for his writings. His *Sententiarum Libri Tres* was the first Latin manual of doctrine; his *Etymologiarum sive Originum Libri Viginti* was a twenty-volume encyclopaedia of human knowledge; his *Historia de Regibus Gothorum, Vandalorum et Suevorum* was a history of the Visigoths and he also produced several books on the Bible. He was a man of great generosity and sanctity and has been described as the 'schoolmaster of the Middle Ages'. In 1722 he was named a Doctor of the Church.

E. Bréhaut, *An Encyclopaedist of the Dark Ages* (1912).

Ivo of Chartres (*c.* 1040–1115) Bishop, Legalist and Saint. Ivo was educated first in Paris and then as a pupil of LANFRANC at Bec. He was consecrated Bishop of Chartres in 1090. For a short time he was imprisoned, after opposing King Philip I's determination to remarry. However, he is remembered as a formidable Canon Lawyer. His *Panormia* and *Decretum* brought together a wide variety of ecclesiastical laws, laid down principles of interpretation and laid the groundwork for a synthesis. Meanwhile the Cathedral School of Chartres was flourishing and Ivo's surviving letters and sermons throw interesting light on the religious life of the period.

J. Leclercq (ed.), *Correspondence of St Ivo, Bishop of Chartres* (1949); The Catholic University of America, *New Catholic Encyclopaedia* (1967).

J

Jacob Bardaeus (d. 578) Bishop and supposed Sect Founder. Jacob was a native of Tella, near Edessa. He became a monk at the monastery of Phesilta. From there he visited Constantinople to plead the cause of the Monophysites with the Empress THEODORA. In about 542 he was consecrated Bishop of Edessa and spent the rest of his life as an itinerant preacher. He was nicknamed Bardaeus ('ragged') because, to avoid arrest, he disguised himself as a beggar. For nearly forty years he travelled between the rivers Nile and Euphrates, founding independent churches and monasteries. The Monophysites of Syria, who rejected the doctrine of the two natures of JESUS CHRIST, were described as Jacobites in commemoration of Jacob's work. Led by the Monophysite Patriarch of Antioch, the Jacobite Church still exists.

W.H.C. Frend, *The Rise of the Monophysite Movement* (1972).

Jacob of Nisibis (fourth century) Theologian, Bishop and Saint. Jacob was Bishop of Nisibis, but, apart from the fact that he took a leading part in the Council of Nicaea, little is known of his life. Traditionally he is thought to have been a hermit, to have suffered in the persecution of Maximus, to have befriended EPHRAEM SYRUS, to have organised a week of public prayer against ARIUS (which seems to have resulted in the heretic's sudden death) and to have saved Nisibis from Persian invasion. To this day he is revered for his learning and sanctity, particularly in the Syriac and Armenian Churches.

A. Vööbus, *History of Asceticism in the Syrian Orient* (1958).

Jacob of Surug (*c.* 451–521) Bishop, Theologian and Poet. Jacob was a native of Kurtnam on the River Euphrates and he was educated in Edessa. After his ordination, he did much to help his people during the Persian occupation of his country. In 519 he was consecrated Bishop of Batnae, the chief town of Surug. He is remembered for his series of homilies on biblical themes and for several hymns. He was nicknamed the 'flute of the Holy Ghost'. His theological opinions remain a matter for debate; some scholars believe him to have been orthodox while others insist that he was a Monophysite.

J.M. Hussey, *The Orthodox Church in the Byzantine Empire* (1986).

Jacob of Voragine (*c.* 1230–*c.* 1298) Archbishop and Historian. Jacob was born near Genoa. He joined the Dominican Order and in 1292 he was consecrated Archbishop of Genoa. He is remembered as the author of the *Legenda Aurea*, a delightful collection of lives of the saints based on the liturgical year. It was exceptionally popular and was translated into many languages. Among his other works was a chronicle of Genoese history and a collection of sermons.

E.C. Richardson, *Materials for a Life of Jacobo da Varagine* (1935); Jacobo da Varagine, *Golden Legend*, translated by W.G. Ryan, 2 vols (1993).

Jacopone da Todi (*c.* 1230–1306) Mystic and Poet. Jacopone was probably educated as a lawyer in Bologna. On the death of his wife, he withdrew from the world and enrolled as a Franciscan lay-brother. In 1294 he was one of a group given permission to follow the original strict Rule of St FRANCIS, but this permission was withdrawn by Pope BONIFACE VIII in 1498 and Jacopone, along with his brother friars, was imprisoned until 1303. He is remembered for his mystical piety, in particular for his hymns 'Laude' and 'Stabat mater'. Although there have been moves to have him beatified, these have been rejected by the authorities – probably as a result of his satirical attack on Boniface in 'Laude'. He is, however, the focus of a local cult in Todi.

E. Underhill, *Jacopone da Todi, Poet and Mystic* (1919).

James 'The Great' (first century)   Apostle. James was the son of Zebedee and the brother of the apostle JOHN. According to the Gospels, JESUS called him away from his occupation as a fisherman to be his disciple. Together with his brother, he was given the nickname Boanerges ('son of thunder'). With PETER, the two sons of Zebedee seemed to have formed an inner circle of the Twelve. They were present at the raising of Jairus's daughter from the dead, at Jesus's transfiguration and in the garden of Gethsemane just before Jesus was arrested. In addition they asked on one occasion whether they should call down fire on a Samaritan village and they demanded the place of honour when Jesus came into his Kingdom. James was among the Twelve when they received the Holy Spirit on the first Whitsunday and, according to Acts, he was put to death by King Herod Agrippa in AD 44. There is a tradition dating from the seventh century that James preached the gospel in Spain before his martyrdom and that his body rests in Compostela. The shrine of St James in Spain remains an important place of pilgrimage, but

the legend behind it is generally regarded as unhistorical.

The Four Gospels; The Acts of the Apostles; J.S. Stone, *The Cult of Santiago* (1927).

James 'The Less' (first century) Apostle. James is described in the list of the twelve disciples as the son of Alphaeus. The title 'The Less' comes from MARK 15:40, but there is no definite evidence that this James is the same as the son of Alphaeus. There have been attempts to identify him with JAMES THE LORD'S BROTHER, but this seems unlikely. Nothing further is known of him.

The Four Gospels.

James the Lord's Brother (first century)   Apostle. James is mentioned in MARK 6:3, along with Simon, Jude and Joses, as being the brother of JESUS. The obvious interpretation is that James was a younger son of JOSEPH and MARY. However, because the Church believes in the perpetual virginity of Mary, it has been suggested either that James was a son of Joseph by an earlier marriage or that he was a cousin, rather than a brother, of Jesus. He played little part in the Gospel story (unless he is to be numbered among the twelve as JAMES (The Less) the son of Alphaeus), but he is mentioned in I Corinthians 15 as having seen the resurrected Jesus. Certainly he was an early leader of the Church in Jerusalem and, according to Acts 15, he presided over the Council of Jerusalem. EUSEBIUS maintained on the authority of CLEMENT OF ALEXANDRIA that he was a bishop in Jerusalem. Various writings have been ascribed to him, such as the Gnostic Epistle of St James, the Liturgy of St James and the Infancy Gospel of St James. The New Testament Epistle bearing his name was traditionally ascribed to him. It is believed that he was martyred by the Jewish Council in AD 62.

The Acts of the Apostles; I Corinthians; Epistle of James; W. Patrick, *James the Lord's Brother* (1906).

James I and VI (1566–1625) Monarch. James was the son of Mary Queen of Scots and her second husband Lord Darnley. He inherited the throne of Scotland from his mother and the throne of England from his cousin Queen ELIZABETH I. A man of considerable theological learning and a believer in the doctrine of the divine right of kings, he was the author of the *Trew Law of Free Monarchies* and *Basilikon Doron* on the subject. Against the Presbyterians, he made arrangements to impose an episcopal structure on the Scottish Church. Once he was proclaimed King of Great Britain in 1603, the English Puritans presented him with the Millenary Petition, in response to which James convened the Hampton Court Conference. He determined, however, to support the Bishops (famously declaring 'No Bishop, no King!') but he did authorise a new translation of the Bible (the Authorised, or King James, version of 1611). He also raised the hopes of his Roman Catholic subjects, but subsquently disappointed them – this leading to the famous gunpowder plot of Guy FAWKES. Among his other theological books was a work on demonology and a meditation on the Lord's Prayer.

K. Fincham, *Prelate as Pastor: The Episcopate of James I* (1990); M. Lee, *Great Britain's Solomon: James VI and I and his Three Kingdoms* (1990); D.H. Willson, *James VI and I* (1959).

James VII and II (1633–1701) Monarch. James was the son of King CHARLES I of England and Princess Henrietta Maria of France. He succeeded to the English throne on the death of his brother King Charles II. A committed Roman Catholic, he had spent much of his youth abroad. There had been attempts to exclude him from the succession on the grounds of his Catholicism, but these had been rejected by the House of Lords. In the event, he alienated influential members of the Church of England by appointing Catholics to high office. He

even imprisoned the Archbishop of Canterbury William SANCROFT and six other Bishops, when they refused to publish his *Declaration of Liberty of Conscience* from the pulpit. He was deposed in 1688 by his son-in-law, William of Orange. William with his wife Mary ruled jointly in his place and Parliament passed an Act declaring that no future British monarch could either be or marry a Roman Catholic.

J. Miller, *James II: A Study in Kingship* (1978); D. Ogg, *England in the Reigns of James II and William III* (1955).

James, William (1842–1910) Philosopher. James grew up in a Swedenborgian household and was a brother of the novelist Henry James. For most of his career he taught at the University of Harvard. He is remembered for his writings, which included *The Varieties of Religious Experience* in which he discussed the whole phenomenon of religious conversion, *The Will to Believe* and *Pragmatism*. James insisted that there was no certainty that God existed, but that human beings were 'better off' believing in a divine being.

G.W. Allen, *William James: A Biography* (1967); G. Myers, *William James: His Life and Thought* (1986).

Jane Frances de Chantel (1572–1641) Order Founder and Saint. She was born Jeanne Françoise Frémiot and was the daughter of the President of the Burgundian Parliament. After the death of her husband, the Baron de Chantel, in 1601, she took a vow of chastity. Guided by her spiritual director, FRANCIS OF SALES, in 1610 she founded the Congregation of the Visitation of Our Lady. The order was initially dedicated to the care of the sick and the poor, but was not so ascetic in its regime as most religious houses. By the time of her death, eighty-six houses were in existence, following an adaptation of the Augustinian Rule. Today the order is mainly contemplative. Mother Jane Frances was canonised in 1767.

F.A. Gasquet, *The Order of the Visitation* (1910); E. Stopp, *The Life of Mother Jane Frances* (1962).

Jansen, Cornelius Otto (1585–1638) Movement Founder, Theologian and Bishop. Jansen was educated at Louvain and Paris. With SAINT-CYRAN, he also studied at Bayonne and Champré. In 1617 he became Director of the new college at Louvain and was known to be a public opponent of the Jesuits. He was the author of *Augustinius*, a treatise on human nature and grace, strongly influenced by the thought of St AUGUSTINE, and in 1636 he was consecrated Bishop of Ypres. Jansen is primarily remembered for giving his name to Jansenism, a movement within the Roman Catholic Church. It emphasised the importance of God's grace in the efficacy of the Sacraments and was frequently seen to be anti-papal. Although the Five Propositions of the Jansenists, together with the *Augustinius*, were condemned by Pope Innocent X in 1653, the movement continued to be influential within the Church until the eighteenth century.

N.J. Abercrombie, *The Origins of Jansenism* (1936).

Januarius (third/fourth century) Bishop and saint. Little certain is known of the life of St Januarius. He was a Bishop of Benevento, Italy, who was martyred during the Diocletian persecutions. A small quantity of his blood is said to be preserved in Naples Cathedral and on eighteen occasions every year, it is thought to liquefy. This phenomenon draws huge crowds to the cathedral.

D.H. Farmer (ed.), *The Oxford Dictionary of Saints*, 3rd edn (1992); H. Thurston, 'The blood miracles of Naples', *Month*, cxlix (1927).

Jaspers, Karl (1883–1969) Philosopher. Jaspers was educated at the University of Heidelberg, Germany. He stayed on at the university to teach until he was forced to resign by the Nazis. Although he was reinstated after the Second World War, he ended his career at the University of Basle. He is remembered as a Christian existentialist. Influenced by the writings of both KIERKEGAARD and NIETZSCHE, he described philosophy as a 'way of thought by which man seeks to become himself' and as a means of illuminating 'the Ground within us and beyond us, where we can find meaning and guidance'. He did not accept that JESUS CHRIST was the sole means of salvation, but he insisted that religious myths serve the function of bringing humanity in touch with the transcendent. Among his works translated into English are *Myth and Christianity* (written with Rudolf BULTMANN), *Truth and Symbol* and *Philosophical Faith and Revelation*.

A.M. Olson, *Transcendence and Hermeneutics: An Interpretation of the Philosophy of Karl Jaspers* (1979); P.A. Schlipp (ed.), *The Philosophy of Karl Jaspers* (1957); C.F. Wallraff, *Karl Jaspers: An Introduction to his Philosophy* (1970).

Jefferson, Thomas (1743–1826) Philosopher and Politician. Jefferson was born in Shadwell, Virginia, and was educated at the College of William and Mary. He had a distinguished career and was appointed Governor of Virginia in 1779, Minister to France in 1785, Secretary of State in 1790 and Vice President of the new Republic in 1797. He was elected the third President of the United States of America in 1801 and served until 1809. He was one of the authors of the Declaration of Independence and is thus remembered for his insistence that 'life, liberty and the pursuit of happiness' are inalienable human rights. He also founded the University of Virginia in Charlottesville and campaigned for religious freedom. In his own religious beliefs he was a Deist and in his edition of the Gospels, *The Life and Morals of*

Jesus of Nazareth, he eliminated all references to the miraculous and supernatural. Jefferson's must be regarded as an influential voice in the founding of the United States and in the shaping of its philosophy of religious liberty for all.

H.S. Commager, *Jefferson, Nationalism and the Enlightenment* (1975); D. Malone, *The Sage of Monticello* (1981); H. Wellenbrand, *The Unfinished Revolution: Education and Politics in the Thought of Thomas Jefferson* (1990).

Jeremias, Joachim (1900–79) Theologian. Jeremias was born in Dresden, Germany, and taught at the Universities of Greifswald and Göttingen. He was the author of a range of studies on JESUS's life and teaching, based on his knowledge of the history and culture of first-century Judaism, as well as the Aramaic language. His *Die Verkundigung Jesu*, translated as *New Testament Theology: The Proclamation of Jesus*, has been influential on later New Testament scholars, particularly in the English-speaking world.

S. Neill and N.T. Wright, *The Interpretation of the New Testament 1861–1986* (1988).

Jerome (*c.* 342–420) Historian, Theologian, Translator and Saint. Jerome was born Eusebius Hieronymus of a Christian family in Stridon, Italy. He was educated in Rome, travelled in Gaul and embarked on the ascetic life. Then, in *c.* 374, he set out for the Holy Land, spending some time as a hermit near Chalcis and in Antioch, where he was ordained priest. Subsequently he studied with GREGORY of NAZIANZUS in Constantinople, and then, in 382, journeyed to Rome where he became secretary to Pope Damascus. Finally he settled in Bethlehem in 386 where he supervised a monastery and acted as a spiritual advisor. Jerome is primarily remembered for his translation of the Bible into Latin (the Vulgate) from the original languages. This translation has been used up to the present day and has

been enormously influential within the Church. In addition he wrote many biblical commentaries; he distinguished between the Hebrew canon of Scripture and the Apocrypha; he translated the works of EUSEBIUS OF CAESAREA and ORIGEN into Latin; he engaged in theological controversy against the ideas of ARIUS, PELAGIUS, Origen and Helvidius and compiled a bibliography of ecclesiastical writers. He must be seen as the most outstanding scholar of his day. In Christian art he is often portrayed in a red hat (presupposing that Pope Damascus made him a Cardinal) and with a lion at his feet.

J.N.D. Kelly, *Jerome: His Life, Writing and Controversies* (1975); F.X. Murphy (ed.), *A Monument to St Jerome: Essays on his Life, Work and Influence* (1952); H.F.D. Sparks, 'Jerome as biblical scholar', in P.R. Ackroyd and C.F. Evans (eds), *The Cambridge History of the Bible*, Vol. 1 (1970).

Jerome Emiliani (1481–1537) Order Founder, Philanthropist and Saint. Jerome was born of a noble family in Venice. After a short career as a soldier, he was ordained. He opened a hospital in Verona in 1518 and in 1532 he founded a society in the village of Somascia. This was to be an order of clerks who would dedicate themselves to the care of orphans. The Somaschi, as the members of the society were called, still carry out their work in Italy. Jerome himself was canonised in 1767 and nominated patron saint of abandoned children in 1928.

D.H. Farmer (ed.), *The Oxford Dictionary of Saints*, 3rd edn (1992).

Jerome of Prague (*c.* 1370–1416) Theologian and Martyr. Little is known of the early life of Jerome. He was educated at the Universities of Prague and Paris; he was a close friend of John HUS and he was strongly influenced by the works of John WYCLIFFE. He spread his reforming doctrines in Paris, Heidelberg and Prague and was excommunicated in 1409 by the Archbishop of Prague. Later he taught in Hungary, Vienna and Cracow and in Russia and Lithuania. Everywhere he aroused the suspicions of the authorities. In 1415 he went to the Council of Constance, where he was put on trial. He was forced to recant and to reject the views of Hus and Wycliffe, but in the following year the trial was resumed. Jerome fearlessly stated his true opinions and was condemned to be burnt at the stake. He died reciting prayers to the Blessed Virgin MARY.

P.P. Bernard, 'Jerome of Prague, Austria and the Hussites', *Church History*, xxviii (1958); R.R. Betts, 'Jerome of Prague', *University of Birmingham Historical Journal*, i (1947).

Jesus Christ (*c.* 4 BC–*c.* AD 30) Founder of Christianity. Jesus's life is known only from the accounts given in the Four Gospels. According to St LUKE and St MATTHEW, he was born in Bethlehem of MARY, who was at the time betrothed but not married to JOSEPH. The Gospels indicate that Joseph was not his father, but that he was of divine origin. He grew up in the town of Nazareth on the Sea of Galilee with brothers and sisters, one of whom, JAMES, became a leader in the early Church. He did not begin his ministry until he was approximately thirty, when he was baptised by JOHN in the River Jordan. At his baptism he experienced a divine call; he was anointed with the Holy Spirit and hailed as God's Messiah and suffering servant. After spending a short time in the wilderness of Judaea, he returned to the region of Galilee. There he recruited twelve disciples, including PETER, JAMES and JOHN, and dedicated himself to preaching the arrival of God's Kingdom on earth. His ministry was accompanied by healings and exorcisms and he attracted large crowds in the Galilean countryside. He spoke of God as father and he stressed the virtues of generosity, unselfishness, mercy and love – 'Be ye perfect even as your Father in Heaven is perfect'. Even though his activities fulfilled the Old Testament prophecies about the role of the Messiah, he was at pains to emphasise that he was not the nationalistic Messiah the Jews were expecting. Instead he would have to 'suffer many things'. Even though his miracles demonstrated that the Kingdom of God was already present, he still instructed his followers to pray 'Thy Kingdom come'. At the end of his ministry, he turned his face to Jerusalem, knowing the fate that awaited him there. He deliberately fulfilled the prophecy of the Messiah coming to the city 'meek and riding upon an ass' and he was recognised by the crowds with much rejoicing. He preached in the Temple and aroused the hostility of the authorities by 'cleansing' its outer courts of traders and moneychangers with the memorable words 'My house shall be called a house of prayer for all nations, but you have made it a den of thieves'. He was arrested one night and, according to the Gospels, was first tried before the High Priest. His accusers found it difficult to prove their charges, but finally, when Jesus seemed to accept the title of Messiah, he was handed over to the Roman governor as a political rebel. The Roman authorities condemned him to death by crucifixion and the accusation 'The King of the Jews' was nailed above the cross. Christians believe that through Jesus's suffering and death, atonement was effected for the sins of humanity. He himself had spoken of 'giving his life as a ransom for many'. He died just before the start of the Jewish Sabbath and he was buried by JOSEPH OF ARIMATHAEA in a nearby tomb. Two days later, on the Sunday morning, the tomb was found to be empty and, after seeing him again, his disciples believed that he had risen from the dead and was now exalted in Heaven. They preached this message, beginning in Jerusalem and it has spread to all corners of the earth. Jesus's earthly life is commemorated in the Christian year.

Christmas celebrates his birth, Good Friday his death, Easter Sunday his resurrection and Whitsunday the birthday of the Church. The title 'Christ' attached to his name signifies that he is the long-awaited Messiah and the Church teaches that, as second person of the Trinity, he is a co-equal, co-eternal person within the Godhead, 'God of God, Light of Light, Very God of Very God'.

The Four Gospels; The Acts of the Apostles; H. Carpenter, *Jesus* (1980); G. Vermes, *Jesus the Jew* (1973); B. Chilton and C.A. Evans, *Studying the Historical Jesus; Evaluations of the Current Research* (1994).

Jewel, John (1522–71) Bishop and Theologian. Jewel was educated at the University of Oxford where he was influenced by the reformer PETER MARTYR. During the reign of Queen MARY, he fled to Frankfurt, where he defended the moderate 1552 Prayer Book against the radical John KNOX. Later he travelled to Strasbourg and Zürich. He was appointed Bishop of Salisbury by Queen ELIZABETH I and proved to be a conscientious Bishop. He was the author of *Apologia pro Ecclesia Anglicana*, a defence of the Church of England against the Church of Rome. The book was officially approved by Archbishop BANCROFT in the reign of King JAMES I and was influential on the work of Richard HOOKER.

J.E. Booty, *John Jewel as Apologist of the Church of England* (1963).

Joachim of Fiore (*c.* 1132–1202) Mystic and Philosopher. Joachim was a Cistercian monk who was at one stage Abbot of Corazzo, Italy. Later he lived at Casamari and then at Fiore. He was the author of *Liber Concordiae Novi et Veteris Testamenti, Expositio in Apocalypsim* and *Psalterium Decem Cordarum*. In these works he argued that the whole of history can be divided into three periods: the first was the age of the Father in which humanity lived under law; the second was the age of the Son, which was

lived under grace and the third would be the age of the Spirit. Joachim believed that this would begin in about 1260 and would be characterised by a rise of religious orders which would spiritualise the world. This teaching was highly popular in the Middle Ages and the Fraticelli and the Spiritual Franciscans saw themselves as the fulfilment of Joachim's prophecies.

M.W. Bloomfield, 'Recent scholarship on Joachim of Fiore', in A. Williams (ed.), *Prophecy and Millenarianism* (1980); M. Reeves, *The Influence of Prophecy in the Later Middle Ages: A Study in Joachimism* (1969).

Joan (ninth/twelfth centuries) Legendary Pope. According to a later legend, a woman was chosen as Pope either in the early twelfth century or in the ninth century. She was said to have given birth during a Lateran procession and died immediately afterwards. The story was widely believed and first appears in the work of the Dominican chronicler Jean de Mailly.

The Catholic University of America, *New England Encyclopaedia* (1967).

Joan of Arc (1412–31) Rebel and Saint. Joan was born in humble circumstances in Domrémy, France. From an early age she heard the voices of Saints MICHAEL, CATHERINE and MARGARET, urging her to go to the rescue of France. At that stage, much of the country was occupied by the forces of the English King, who also claimed to be King of France. The French Dauphin, Charles, was convinced by her and, after being examined by theologians at Poitiers, she was allowed to lead the army. Here she was notably successful. She defeated the English at the siege of Orléans and, after clearing the route to Rheims, she encouraged the Dauphin to be crowned King in 1429. However, the following year she was captured by the Burgundians who sold her to the English. She was charged with witchcraft before the

Bishop of Beauvais, and the guilty verdict was confirmed by the University of Paris. At the age of nineteen she was burnt at the stake in the marketplace of Rouen. Pope Callistus III ordered a retrial and she was found innocent in 1456. In 1920 she was canonised and she has become a French national heroine.

R. Pernoud, *Joan of Arc* (1965); M. Warner, *Joan of Arc and the Image of Female Heroism* (1981).

Joasaph [Josaphat] Legendary Saint. Joasaph was the son of a heathen Indian king; he was protected throughout his youth from all knowledge of human misery. On escaping from the palace, he was converted to Christianity by St BARLAAM. After ruling the kingdom for a time, he became a monk. Most authorities believe that the story is derived from Buddhist sources and it is thought that the name Josaphat is a corruption of 'Bodisatva', a title of the Buddha.

D.M. Lang, *The Wisdom of Balahvar: A Christian Legend of the Buddha* (1957); R. Wolff, 'Barlaam and Joasaph' *Harvard Theological Review*, xxxii (1939).

John (first century) Saint and Apostle. John was the son of Zebedee and the brother of JAMES. Before he was called to discipleship, he was a fisherman. JESUS nicknamed the two brothers Boanerges ('sons of thunder') and, with PETER, they seem to have formed an inner group of disciples. As one of the three, John was present at the raising of Jairus's daughter from the dead, at the transfiguration and at the agony in the garden. In addition, with Peter, he prepared the final Passover meal for Jesus and the Twelve. He is not mentioned by name in the Fourth Gospel, but he has traditionally been identified with the 'disciple Jesus loved'. If this is correct, John lay next to Jesus at the Last Supper, was entrusted with Jesus's mother MARY at the crucifixion and was one of the earliest witnesses to the empty tomb.

In Acts, he is mentioned on three separate occasions, always in conjunction with Peter. According to IRENAEUS, John lived at Ephesus and died naturally. EUSEBIUS OF CAESAREA stated that he was exiled on Patmos during the reign of Domitian. Traditionally he is believed to have been the author of the Fourth Gospel, the Johannine epistles and the Book of Revelation. There is also a theory that he was martyred with his brother James. Both the question of the identity of the beloved disciple and that of the authorship of the Johannine corpus have been subjects of much scholarly controversy.

C.H. Dodd, *The Interpretation of the Fourth Gospel* (1957); M.W.G. Stible, *John's Gospel* (1994); J. Ashton, *Understanding the Fourth Gospel* (1991).

John XII (d. 964) Pope. John was born Octavian, the son of Alberic II of Spoleto, the ruler of Rome. He became Pope at the age of eighteen and his dissolute behaviour caused considerable scandal. He asked OTTO I for help against the Italian ruler and crowned him Emperor in Rome in 962 in return for the Emperor gaining rights in the papal elections. Later, regretting this, John negotiated with Otto's enemy Berengar II. In 963 Otto returned to Rome. He called a synod which deposed John and had another Pope chosen. The following year John came back to the city, reasserted his authority and called another synod. He died before Otto could come back and he left the Papacy at a very low ebb.

J.N.D. Kelly (ed.), *The Oxford Dictionary of Popes* (1986); W. Ullmann, 'The origin of the Ottoniarium', *Cambridge Historical Journal*, xi (1953–5).

John XXII (1249–1334) Pope. John was born Jacques Duèse in Cahors, France. He was educated at the University of Paris and was appointed Bishop of Fréjus in 1300, Bishop of Avignon in 1310, Cardinal Bishop of Porto in 1312, and was elected Pope in 1316. He was the first of the Avignon Popes and is remembered as an excellent administrator. None the less his reign was troubled by a variety of conflicts. He ruled against the thesis that the poverty of JESUS and his disciples was absolute and he supported the order of Friars Minor in an acrimonious dispute with the Franciscan Spirituals. He excommunicated the Emperor Lewis of Bavaria in 1324, in retaliation for which Lewis organised the Ghibelline League. The allies seized Rome and set up the Spiritual Franciscan Nicholas V as antipope between 1328 and 1330. Lewis also encouraged MARSIGLIO OF PADUA who had written his *Defensor Pacis* against papal power. At the end of his life, John XXII was involved in a doctrinal controversy on the nature of the beatific vision. This was only finally settled in the reign of BENEDICT XII.

J.N.D. Kelly (ed.), *The Oxford Dictionary of Popes* (1986).

John XXIII (*c.* 1370–1419) Antipope. John was born Baldassare Cossa in Naples, and was educated at the University of Bologna. He presided over the Council of Pisa in 1409 in an attempt to bring the papal schism to an end. Both existing Popes were deposed (though neither accepted deposition) and after the sudden death of Pope Alexander V, Cossa was elected as John XXIII in 1412. At this stage there were, then, three Popes. To end this undesirable situation, John was persuaded to convoke a General Council which met at Constance. The Council deposed John in 1415 and elected MARTIN V. John submitted to the new Pope in 1418 and was appointed Cardinal Bishop of Tusculum. He is remembered for his condemnation of both HUS and WYCLIFFE at the Synod of Rome in 1412.

E.J. Kitts, *Pope John XXIII and Master John Hus of Bohemia* (1910); J.H. Mundy and K.M. Woody (eds), *The Council of Constance* (1961).

John XXIII (1881–1963) Pope and Ecumenist. John was born Angelo Giuseppe Roncalli. In 1953 he was appointed Cardinal and Patriarch of Venice, and, after a long conclave, he was elected as an elderly 'interim' Pope in 1958. To the amazement of everyone, he announced that he intended to summon an ecumenical council to promote the unity of all Christians. The last council had met a hundred years previously in the reign of PIUS IX and was summoned to declare the infallibility of the Papacy. This was to be a different affair. In his opening speech, John urged the participants to respond to the needs of the twentieth century. During the course of the first session he gave active encouragement to those who were in favour of change. In addition he created a commission to revise the Code of Canon Law and he did a great deal to promote good relationships with leaders of other Churches. During his reign, for the first time the Roman Catholic Church was represented at the World Council of Churches and non-Catholic observers were invited to the Second Vatican Council. In addition, adherents of other faiths ceased to be described as 'schismatic heretics', but became 'separated brethren'. John did not live to see the end of the Council, but it must be regarded as a landmark in the history of the Western Church. He himself was a genial, kindly man, much given to good works; his death was universally mourned.

John XXIII, *Journey of a Soul* (1965); P. Johnson, *Pope John XXIII* (1975); P. Hebblethwaite, *John XXIII: Pope of the Council* (1984).

John of Avila (1500–69) Missionary, Mystic and Saint. John was born near Toledo, Spain, and was educated at Salamanca and at Alcalá. Although he had initially wanted to go to America, he was persuaded to do his missionary work in Andalusia. A powerful preacher, he was fearless in his denunciations and was brought before the Inquisition in 1533. After his innocence was established, he helped found the University of Granada and did much to reform the Spanish Church. A friend of JOHN OF GOD, TERESA OF AVILA and FRANCIS BORGIA, he is today remembered for his *Audi Filia* (a treatise on spiritual perfection) and for his *Spiritual Letters*, which are now regarded as classics.

L. degli Oddi, *Life of John of Avila*, translated by J.G. Macleod (1898); The Catholic University of America, *New Catholic Encyclopaedia* (1967).

John the Baptist (*c.* 4 BC–AD 28) Missionary and Saint. John was the son of the priest Zachariah and Elizabeth, a relative of the Virgin MARY. In the Gospel of LUKE, his birth was seen as a miracle since his mother was beyond the age for bearing children. John was portrayed as an ascetic preacher, drawing crowds into the wilderness and preparing the people for the coming Kingdom of God. He dressed in the same garb as the Old Testament prophet Elijah and his mission was seen as the fulfilment of Malachi's prophecy that Elijah would return before the 'great and terrible day of the Lord'. He encouraged his listeners to be baptised as a sign of repentance. Jesus was amongst those who were cleansed in the River Jordan under John's guidance. John indicated that he was not himself the Messiah, but that one would come after him who would be greater than he. He was eventually arrested for preaching against King Herod's marriage and, according to the Gospel story, Herod was tricked into having him executed. In the Christian tradition John is seen as the last of the prophets. Various scholarly conjectures have been offered as to his relationship with the monastic community of Qumran, but no firm conclusions have been reached.

E. Bammel, 'The Baptist in the Early Christian tradition', *New Testament Studies*, xviii (1971–

2); C.H.H. Scobie, *John the Baptist* (1964); W. Wink, *John the Baptist in the Gospel Tradition* (1968).

John Baptist de la Salle (1651–1719) Educator, Order Founder and Saint. John Baptist was born in Rheims into a noble family and he was ordained in 1678. He was appalled by the lack of educational facilities for the poor. He set up the order of the Brothers of the Christian Schools in 1684 and the first Rule was written in 1693. Although he met with considerable opposition, he had established schools in twenty-two French towns before he died. He was the author of several educational manuals and his methods were revolutionary for the time. He used French rather than Latin; he encouraged class teaching; great emphasis was placed on silence and according to the Rule 'the Brothers should be careful to punish their pupils but rarely'.

W.J. Battersby, *St John Baptist de la Salle* (1957).

John Colombini (*c.* 1300–67) Order Founder and Philanthropist. John was a rich merchant in Siena, Italy. After reading a life of MARY OF EGYPT, he determined to change his life. First he cared for the sick and the old in his own home, but in *c.* 1360 he formed a society of laymen who were dedicated to philanthropy. The group was constituted as the Clerici Apostolici S. Hieronymi in 1367 by Pope URBAN V, but the brothers were generally known as the Gesuati. John's cousin Catherine founded a similar order for women known as the Sisters of the Visitation of Mary (the Jesuatesses). The Gesuati spread throughout Italy, but the order was finally dissolved in the seventeenth century. John himself was beatified by Pope GREGORY XIII.

The Catholic University of America, *New Catholic Encyclopaedia* (1967).

John of the Cross (1542–91) Mystic, Poet, Devotional Writer, Order Founder and Saint. John was born Juan de Yepez y Alvarez in Old Castile, Spain. He joined the Carmelites at the age of twenty-one and, after studying in Salamanca, he joined the new Discalced Order of Friars at Duruelo. From 1571 to 1572 he was master of the Discalced Carmelite College at Alala de Henares and then he became the spiritual advisor of the Convent of the Incarnation at Avila until 1577, where TERESA was Prioress. He was imprisoned for nine months in Toledo by the opponents of reform and, after his escape, he became the first Rector of the College at Baeza, then Prior, first of Granada and then of Segovia. In 1591 he was banished to Andalusia and he died at Ubeda. He was a victim of the controversy over the severity of the Carmelite Rule and he and Teresa must be regarded as the founders of the reformed Discalced Order. However, he is mainly remembered for his mystical poems which are regarded as religious classics. They include 'The dark night of the soul', 'The spiritual canticle' and 'The living flame of love'. They are accompanied by commentaries and describe the stages of purgation, illumination and union through which the soul achieves oneness with God.

E.W.T. Dicken, *The Crucible of Love: A Study of the Mysticism of St Teresa of Jesus and St John of the Cross* (1963); E.A. Peers, *Handbook of the Life and Times of St Teresa and St John of the Cross* (1954).

John of Damascus (c. 675–c. 749) Theologian, Poet and Saint. Little is known of the life of John of Damascus. He served as chief representative of the Christians at the court of the Caliph of Damascus; he entered the monastery of St Sabas near Jerusalem and he participated in the Iconoclastic Controversy, defending the use of icons in churches. He is remembered for his great three-part work, the *Fount of Wisdom*, which dealt with philosophy, heresy and the Orthodox faith. The last part has always been used as a textbook of doctrine in the Orthodox Church, but his work was not known in the West until the twelfth century. It was used by both PETER LOMBARD and THOMAS AQUINAS and must be regarded as a foundation document of mediaeval theology. It is a work of immense learning and was influenced by the writings of Aristotle, MAXIMUS THE CONFESSOR, EPIPHANIUS, GREGORY OF NAZIANZUS and Pseudo-DIONYSIUS. John was also a considerable poet and some of his hymns have been incorporated into the Orthodox liturgy. He was declared a Doctor of the Church in 1890.

D.H. Farmer (ed.), *The Oxford Dictionary of Saints*, 3rd edn (1992).

John the Elder [Presbyter] (? first century) Devotional Writer. John the Elder was named by EUSEBIUS OF CAESAREA as the author of the New Testament Book of Revelation. This was followed by Dionysius of Alexandria who pointed to the existence of two Johannine tombs in Ephesus, arguing that one belonged to JOHN The Apostle and the other to John the Elder. PAPIAS referred to a John the Elder, and the author of the Second and Third Epistles of John describes himself as an elder. None of this evidence is conclusive proof of John's existence, since the title 'Elder' may well have been used of the apostle.

'John St, Apostle' and 'John, Epistles of St', in F.L. Cross (ed.), *The Oxford Dictionary of the Christian Church*, 2nd edn (1974).

John the Faster (d. 595) Patriarch. As John IV, John the Faster served as Patriarch of Constantinople from 582. His cognomen derives from his austere ascetic practices. He is remembered for assuming the title 'Ecumenical (universal) Patriarch' in 588 which, despite the protests of Pope Pelagius II and, later, GREGORY THE GREAT, was handed down to his successors. Thus John not only established the supremacy of Constantinople over the other Eastern sees, he gave it a claim to be of at least equal standing with Rome. John is also the attributed author of a *Penitential*, but it was in fact written long after his death.

G. Every, *The Byzantine Patriarchate 451–1204*, revised edition (1962).

John of God (1495–1550) Philanthropist, Order Founder and Saint. John was a native of Portugal and, as a young man, he served as a soldier. When he was about forty he turned back to religion and, guided by JOHN OF AVILA, he dedicated his life to the care of the sick and the poor. He is generally regarded as the founder of the Brothers Hospitallers' Order, which developed out of his work. The order was formally approved in 1572 by Pope PIUS V and today it runs hospitals in Italy, Spain and France. John was canonised in 1690.

D.H. Farmer (ed.), *The Oxford Dictionary of Saints*, 3rd edn (1992); N. McMahon, *The Story of the Hospitallers of St John of God* (1958).

John Gualbert (*c.* 990–1073) Order Founder and Saint. John was a Benedictine monk, first at San Miniato, Italy and then at Camaldoli. Later in Vallumbrosa, he formed his own community based on a modified form of the Rule of St BENEDICT, but with a greater emphasis on austerity and penance. The Vallumbrosian monks spread throughout Italy and the order still exists. Members lead a hermit-like existence and it is essentially a contemplative order. Laybrothers were introduced to do manual work and perpetual silence is observed. At one stage GALILEO was a Vallumbrosian novice.

The Catholic University of America, *New Catholic Encyclopaedia* (1967).

John of Leyden (1509–36) Rebel. John was born Jan Beukelszoon. He was con-

verted to militant Anabaptism in the late 1520s. With Jan Mattheys, he took control of the city of Haarlem and, after Mattheys was killed, he was crowned king of the 'New Zion'. He instituted a system of common ownership, introduced polygamy and executed his opponents. In 1536, Protestant and Catholic forces besieged the city and John was killed in the battle. Leaders such as John gave Anabaptism a reputation for revolutionary lawlessness.

G.H. Williams, *The Radical Reformation* (1962).

John of Matha (?1160–1213) Order Founder and Saint. Little is known of the life of John of Matha. He was born in Provence, France, and he dedicated his life to the redemption of Christians captured by the Turks. To this end he founded the Trinitarian Order, with Felix of Valois. Members of the order followed a version of the Augustinian Rule. Today the only branch which survives is a reformed group called the Barefoot Trinitarians who engage in medical and educational work. There is a parallel order of nuns.

The Catholic University of America, *New Catholic Encyclopaedia* (1967).

John of Nepomuk (1340–93) Saint and Martyr. Little is known of the life of John of Nepomuk. He was Vicar-General of the Archdiocese of Prague and he defied King Wenceslas IV. Whether the issue was the diminution of clerical privileges, or his refusal to break the seal of the confessional to give evidence against the Queen, is not clear. Whatever the reason, the King ordered him to be drowned in the River Moldau. His cult was highly popular and he was canonised in 1729.

A.H. Wratislaw, *St John of Nepomuk* (1873).

John Paul I (1912–78) Pope. John Paul was born Albino Luciani in Forno di Canale, Italy. He was educated at the Gregorian University in Rome and he was ordained in 1935. Consecrated as a Bishop in 1958, he became Patriarch of Venice in 1969 and was appointed Cardinal in 1973. On his election as Pope in 1978, he incorporated the names of his two immediate predecessors, JOHN XXIII and PAUL VI, indicating that he intended to build on their work. He died suddenly thirty-three days after his election. His death gave rise to various conspiracy theories, none of which have been proved.

S. Dean, *Pope John Paul I* (1978).

John Paul II (b. 1920) Pope. John Paul was born Karol Jozef Wojtyla in Wadowice, Poland. He was educated at the Jagiellonian University and was a member of the resistance during the Nazi occupation of Poland. He was ordained in 1946 and, after a career as a parish priest and university professor, he was made a Bishop in 1958, Archbishop of Cracow in 1964 and Cardinal in 1967. After the thirty-three-day Pontificate of Pope JOHN PAUL I, he was elected, as the first Polish Pope, in 1978. He has made a series of visits world-wide, but, perhaps because of his experience of Poland under Communism, he has remained unbending in his opposition to liberation theology and the politicisation of the priesthood. In addition, he is a staunch traditionalist in ethical matters; he is uncompromising in his condemnation of artificial contraception and abortion and he is unenthusiastic about the idea of women priests. He survived an assassination attempt in 1981 and is increasingly seen as a bastion of conservative values in a transitional world.

John Paul II, *Word of Certitude* (1984); P. Johnson, *Pope John Paul II and the Catholic Restoration* (1982); M. Walsh, *John Paul II* (1994).

John of Ragusa (d. *c.* 1443) Bishop and Theologian. John was born John Stojković in Ragusa. He was a member of a Dominican Order and by 1420 he was

teaching at the University of Paris. As papal theologian, he preached the opening sermon at the Council of Basle and debated with the followers of John HUS. Later he was sent by Pope MARTIN V to Constantinople to try to bring about the union between the Eastern and Western Churches. He successfully persuaded John Palaeologus of Constantinople to send a delegation to the Council. He became Bishop of Ardijsek in 1438 and possibly a Cardinal in 1440. However, he is mainly remembered for his writings against the Hussites and for the Greek manuscripts he brought back from Constantinople to Basle. These were used by ERASMUS in his edition of the Greek New Testament and for his work on the early Church Fathers.

The Catholic University of America, *New Catholic Encyclopaedia* (1967).

John of Salisbury (*c.* 1115–80) Philosopher and Bishop. John was born in Salisbury and he was a student of ABELARD and GILBERT DE LA PORRÉE at the University of Paris. After serving as a papal clerk, he became part of the household first of THEOBALD, Archbishop of Canterbury, and then of Thomas BECKET. He was present in Canterbury when Becket was murdered. Subsequently he became Bishop of Chartres. He was the author of *Policraticus*, a political treatise, and *Metalogicon*, a defence of the study of logic. He was one of the leading men of letters of his day and his own correspondence is an important source for the history of the conflict between Becket and King HENRY II.

M.A. Brown, 'John of Salisbury', *Franciscan Studies*, xix (1959); M. Wilks (ed.), *The World of John of Salisbury* (1984).

Johnson, Samuel (1709–94) Literary Figure. Johnson is famous in the history of English literature for his *Dictionary of the English Language* and as the subject of James Boswell's biography. He was a highly influential writer in his own time. He was born in Lichfield, and, after an unsuccessful career as a school-master, he settled in London and earned his living by his pen. He wrote regular essays between 1750 and 1752, under the title of the *Rambler*, which led him to be known as the 'Great Moralist', and from 1758 to 1760 he wrote similar essays for the *Universal Chronicle*. He was a typical eighteenth-century high churchman, tolerant of Roman Catholicism and scornful of all forms of nonconformity.

J. Boswell, *Life of Dr Johnson* [many editions]; W.T. Cairns, *The Religion of Dr Johnson and Other Essays* (1946); C.F. Chapin, *The Religious Thought of Dr Johnson* (1968).

Jones, Bob (1883–1968) Missionary and Educator. Jones was born in Alabama and found his vocation early, holding his first evangelistic meeting at the age of fifteen. He was educated at Southern University in Greensboro, North Carolina, and became a Methodist preacher. In 1924 he determined to found a new university based on a fundamentalist understanding of the Bible. Today the Bob Jones University in Greenville, South Carolina, is highly successful, with a modern campus and a dedicated student body. In the past it has been associated with highly conservative politics, racial segregation and conservative evangelical theology. Jones himself pursued his career as an evangelist and it was estimated that during his lifetime he preached more than twelve thousand sermons.

J.D. Hunter, *American Evangelicalism* (1983); G. Marsden, *Fundamentalism and American Culture* (1980).

Jones, Griffith (1683–1761) Educator and Missionary. Jones was born into a non-conformist family, but he was ordained into the ministry of the Church of England at the age of twenty-five. As well as serving a parish, he made long preaching tours around the Welsh valleys. Then in 1730 he started organising 'circulating schools' for both children and adults. Making use of travelling teachers, the instruction was given mainly in reading the Welsh Bible. By the time of his death, more than three thousand of these 'schools' had been opened. Daniel Rowland, one founder of Welsh Methodism, was converted through Jones's efforts.

T. Kelly, *Griffith Jones, Llanddowror: Pioneer in Adult Education* (1950); W.M. Williams, *The Friends of Griffith Jones: A Study in Educational Philanthropy* (1939).

Jones, Rufus Matthew (1863–1948) Theologian and Mystic. Jones was born in south China of a Quaker family. He was educated at Haverford College and Harvard University in the USA and in Europe. In 1887 he had a mystical experience which prompted him to dedicate his life to religion. He was Principal of Oak Grove Seminary from 1889 to 1893 and then taught philosophy at Haverford. Among his many books were *Studies in Mystical Religion*, *The Faith and Practice of the Quakers* and *The Testimony of the Soul*. During the First World War he was a founder of the American Friends' Services Committee and he was recognised as the most prominent Quaker of his time.

H.H. Brinton (ed.), *Children of Light: In Honour of Rufus M. Jones* (1938); E.G. Vining, *Friend of Life: The Biography of Rufus M. Jones* (1958).

Joseph (first century) Saint. Joseph was the husband of the Virgin MARY. In the Gospels he is described as a carpenter and as a descendant of King David. He was betrothed to Mary at the time of JESUS's conception, but was encouraged by God in a dream to stay with her. Jesus grew up in Joseph's house in Nazareth with brothers and sisters. According to Christian legend, he was considerably older than Mary. His cult grew up in the Eastern Church, based largely on the apocryphal Infancy Gospel of JAMES, and it appeared in the West only in the fifteenth century. In 1870 PIUS IX declared Joseph to be the Patron of the Universal Church. Today he is a popular saint and is constantly represented in Nativity plays and crib scenes.

F.J. Filas, *The Man Nearest to Christ: Nature and Historic Development of the Doctrine of St Joseph* (1944); B.M. Metzger and M.D. Coogan (eds), *The Oxford Companion to the Bible* (1993).

Joseph II (1741–90) Monarch. Joseph was Holy Roman Emperor from 1765. He pursued a policy of state control for the Church with the aim of 'rationalising' society through an 'enlightened' programme of centralisation. The policy was first instituted in 1767; it included religious toleration for all, the restriction of the powers of the Pope within the Austrian Empire and the right of the secular government to correct ecclesiastical abuse. The most important measures included the Law of Toleration of 1781, the suppression of several religious orders, the introduction of a new form of 'rationalist' censorship and the obligation of Bishops to swear loyalty to the State. The new system was closely identified with the Emperor himself and was known as Josephinism.

T.C.W. Blanning, *Joseph II* (1994); M.C. Goodwin, *The Papal Conflict with Josephinism* (1938); S.K. Padover, *The Revolutionary Emperor: Joseph II of Austria*, revised edition (1967).

Joseph of Arimathaea (first century) Saint. According to the Gospels, Joseph was a member of the Jewish Council, 'a good and upright man' who was 'waiting for the Kingdom of God'. After JESUS's crucifixion, having asked the Roman Governor, Pontius PILATE, for permission, he buried Jesus's body in his own tomb. No more is known of him. According to legend, he was a tin merchant who visited England in the course of

business with the young Jesus. He is also said to have returned to Glastonbury after Jesus's death with the Holy Grail. This story is the inspiration behind William BLAKE's famous hymn 'Jerusalem'.

B.M. Metzger and M.D. Coogan (eds), *The Oxford Companion to the Bible* (1993); R.F. Treherne, *The Glastonbury Legends* (1967).

Joseph Calasanctius (1556–1648) Philanthropist, Order Founder and Saint. Joseph was born near Petralta de la Sal, Spain, and was educated at Lerida, Valencia and Alcalá. After ordination he settled in Rome where he devoted himself to the education of the poor. He founded the first free elementary school in Europe in 1597 and in 1602 he organised the Piarist Order of teachers. This was recognised as a congregation in 1617 and an order in 1621. However, in 1643 Joseph was put on trial, suspected of subversive activity and in 1646 the order was temporarily reduced to a federation of religious houses. Joseph himself was canonised in 1767 and was later declared 'the heavenly patron of all Christian schools'.

The Catholic University of America, *New Catholic Encyclopaedia* (1967).

Joseph of Cupertino (1603–63) Mystic and Saint. Joseph was born Joseph Desa in humble circumstances in south-east Italy. He joined the Franciscan Order as a stable-boy and lived a life of extreme asceticism. Despite his awkwardness and poor education, he was ordained in 1628. He became notorious for swooning in ecstasy and levitating when immersed in prayer. The religious authorities, disturbed by these phenomena, kept him in isolation and he was even, on one occasion, brought before the Inquisition. Many eye-witnesses testified to these events. John Frederick of Brunswick, the Lutheran patron of the philosopher LEIBNIZ, was so impressed that he converted to Roman Catholicism. Joseph was canonised in 1767.

The Catholic University of America, *New Catholic Encyclopaedia* (1967).

Joseph the Hymnographer (*c.* 810–86) Poet and Saint. Joseph was born in Sicily and initially joined a monastery in Thessalonica. For a time he lived in Constantinople and Rome before being captured by pirates and sold as a slave in Crete. He founded a monastery in Constantinople in *c.* 850, but suffered two further periods of exile. He is remembered for his hymns. In the *Menaion*, the twelve liturgical books of the Eastern Church, there are more than two hundred of his Canons. He also produced the final form of the *Octoechos*, the book containing the variable parts of the services.

F.L. Cross (ed.), *The Oxford Dictionary of the Christian Church*, 2nd edn (1974).

Joseph of Volokolamsk (*c.* 1439–1516) Order Founder and Saint. Joseph was the founder of the important monastery of Volokolamsk, near Moscow, Russia. It was a well-endowed, disciplined and educated community and many of its members attained high office in the Russian Church. The order expanded in the sixteenth century and many monasteries were found on the Volokolamsk pattern.

I. Smolitsch, *Russisches Mönchtum* (1953) [no English translation available].

Jowett, Benjamin (1817–93) Theologian. Jowett was educated at the University of Oxford. He was ordained a priest in the Church of England in 1845, was appointed Regius Professor of Greek at the University of Oxford in 1855 and in 1870 he was elected Master of Balliol College. He was the author of a liberal commentary on the Epistles of St PAUL and, even more controversially, a piece on the interpretation of scripture in

Essays and Reviews. This was denounced in no uncertain terms by Bishop Samuel WILBERFORCE. After the furore, Jowett turned away from theology and concentrated his attention on the Classics. He took an active part in the affairs of the university and perhaps is most readily remembered as the subject of the undergraduate verse: 'I am the master of this College, And what I don't know isn't knowledge!'

G. Faber, *Jowett* (1957); P. Hinchcliff, *Benjamin Jowett and the Christian Religion* (1987).

Judas Iscariot (first century) Apostle. Judas was one of the twelve disciples of JESUS. Unlike most of the others, he seems to have come from Judaea in the south and he was the treasurer of the group. He is remembered as the disciple who betrayed Jesus with a kiss for thirty pieces of silver. According to the Gospels, he led the soldiers to the Garden of Gethsemane where Jesus was away from the crowds. His motives were obscure. His subsequent remorse and suicide are recorded in the Gospel of MATTHEW. In the Christian tradition, Judas has always been regarded as the worst of all sinners and, all too often, as the archetypal Jew.

R.B. Halas, *Judas Iscariot* (1946); H. Maccoby, *Judas* (1995).

Jude (first century) Apostle. Jude is listed as an apostle in the Gospel of LUKE and in Acts. MATTHEW and MARK, however, list the twelfth disciple as THADDAEUS. He is traditionally regarded as the author of the New Testament Epistle of Jude, where he is described as the 'brother of JAMES'. One of JESUS's brothers (and also therefore brother of James) was also called Jude, so that is a possible identification. According to the apocryphal *Passion of Simon and Jude*, he was martyred in Persia while preaching the gospel. Traditionally Simon and Jude are commemorated together and Jude is best known as the patron saint of lost causes.

A. Chester, *The Theology of the Letters of James, Peter and Jude* (1994); J.N.D. Kelly, *Commentary on the Epistles of Peter and of Jude* (1969).

Judson, Adoniram (1788–1850) Missionary. Judson was born in Malden, Massachusetts, and was educated at Brown University. He was one of the founders of the American Board of Commissioners for Foreign Missions and was ordained to the Congregational ministry in 1812. However, on their journey out to the mission field in Burma, he and his wife became Baptists. He settled first in Rangoon where he learnt Burmese and began his Burmese translation of the Bible. Imprisoned for over a year by the British in 1824/5, he moved to Moulmein and also travelled among the Karen tribe. Between 1842 and 1849, he worked on a Burmese dictionary, but his health broke down and he died during the course of a sea voyage.

B.R. Pearn, *Adoniram Judson* (1962).

Julian the Apostate (332–63) Monarch. Julian was the nephew of the Emperor CONSTANTINE I and he became the Emperor Flavius Claudius Julianus in 361, succeeding his cousin Constantius II. He had had an eventful childhood and had resisted Christianity. Despite being a schoolfellow in Athens of GREGORY OF NAZIANZUS, he was a convinced neo-Platonist. After he inherited the imperial title, he was determined to promote paganism at the expense of Christianity. To this end he removed the financial and legal privileges of Christians; he published treatises against Christian theology: he imprisoned prominent Christians and he ordered paganism to be taught in all the imperial schools. He himself was a man of high moral principles and led an austere and disciplined life. He died in 363 on a military campaign and, according to legend, pronounced as his last words, 'Vicisti,

Galilaee' (You have conquered O Galileean!). He was the author of satires, epigrams and orations. In the history of Christianity, his most important work was *Adversus Christianos* which survives only in CYRIL OF ALEXANDRIA's refutation.

G.W. Bowersock, *Julian the Apostate* (1978).

Julian of Norwich (*c.* 1342–*c.* 1415) Mystic and Devotional Writer. Little is known of the life of Julian. She lived in a cell attached to the Church of St Julian in Norwich. She is remembered for her *Revelations of Divine Love*, a classic of mysticism. It is an account of a series of sixteen visions which took place on 8 and 9 May 1373 and it was written twenty years later. She taught that divine love is revealed through the suffering of JESUS CHRIST. Jesus's followers must share in that suffering and through prayer and contemplation they will achieve union with God.

G. Jantzen, *Julian of Norwich: Mystic and Theologian* (1987); E.I. Watkin, *On Julian of Norwich* (1979).

Juliana of Liège (1192–1258) Mystic and Saint. Juliana was orphaned at an early age and grew up in the Convent of Mont Corrillon, near Liège, France. She experienced mystical visions which led her to devote herself to the establishment of the Feast of Corpus Christi. She met with considerable opposition, but, through the support of the Archbishop of Liège, the feast was proclaimed in 1246. However, once Juliana lost her patron, the festival was not celebrated again during her lifetime and she herself was forced into exile, first near Namur and later at Fosses. Pope Urban IV reinstated the feast in 1264. It commemorates the institution of the Eucharist and in the Western Church it is celebrated on the first Thursday after Trinity Sunday. Juliana was canonised in 1869.

The Catholic University of America, *New Catholic Encyclopaedia* (1967).

Julius I (d. 352)   Pope and Saint. Julius was elected Pope in 337, the year of the death of the Emperor CONSTANTINE. He was a firm advocate of orthodoxy and stood against the teachings of ARIUS at the Synod of Rome in 341 and at the Council of Sardica in 343. As a result of the disciplinary Canons of the Council, the Bishop of Rome was seen as the final Court of Appeal for accused Bishops. Julius was a supporter of ATHANASIUS and he sheltered him when he was exiled between 339 and 346. Two of his letters survive.

J. Chapman, *Studies on the Early Papacy* (1929); H. Hess, *The Canons of the Council of Sardica* (1958).

Julius II (1443–1513)   Pope. Julius was born Giuliano della Rovere in Abissola, Italy. He joined the Franciscan Order and, when his uncle was elected Pope SIXTUS IV, he was appointed a Cardinal and collected a clutch of profitable benefices. He was influential in the election of Pope Innocent VIII in 1484, but, with the accession of his rival, the Borgia ALEXANDER VI, he fled to shelter with King Charles VIII of France in 1492. When Alexander died in 1503, he returned to Rome. Then, after the month-long reign of Pius III, with the aid of bribery and promises which he had no intention of keeping, he negotiated his own election. By making alliances with France and the Holy Roman Emperor, he extended the Papal States at the expense of Perugia, Bologna and Venice. Then he founded the Holy League with Spain, England, Venice and Switzerland to drive the French out of Italy. In response, Louis XII of France called for the Pope to be deposed at the Council of Pisa. Julius in his turn, with the aid of the Emperor, called the Fifth Lateran Council in 1511. Julius is remembered as the subject of ERASMUS's satire and as the patron of MICHELANGELO and RAPHAEL. He was a generous supporter of the arts and during his reign, the cornerstone was laid for the Basilica of St Peter. Later, it was the selling of Indulgences to finance the building work that led Martin LUTHER to nail his theses against the practice on the door of Wittenberg Church. Julius is also known as the subject of a remarkable portrait by Raphael.

L.W. Partridge, *A Renaissance Likeness: Art and Culture in Raphael's Julius II* (1980); C. Shaw, *Julius II: The Warrior Pope* (1993).

Julius Africanus Sextus (*c.* 160–*c.* 240) Historian. Julius was born in Palestine and, as a young man, travelled widely. After settling in Emmaus, he led an embassy to the Emperor Heliogabulus which enabled the town to be rebuilt. He met ORIGEN in Alexandria and supervised the building of a public library in Rome. He is remembered for his five-volume *Chronographia*, a history of the world, in which he argued that the world had existed for 5,700 years and would last approximately three hundred more. He also wrote the twenty-four-volume *Cesti*, an encyclopaedia of medicine, science and natural history. Both works survive only in fragments.

F. Granger, 'Julius Africanus and the Library of the Pantheon', *Journal of Theological Studies*, xxxiv (1933); F. Thee, *Julius Africanus and the Early Christian View of Magic* (1984).

Jung, Carl Gustav (1875–1961)   Psychologist and Philosopher. Jung was born in Kessivil, Switzerland. He trained as a doctor in Basle and studied psychiatry in Zürich and Paris. For many years he collaborated with FREUD, but formed his own school of analytical psychology in 1914. He travelled widely in order to study ancient mythology and he developed a theory of the collective unconscious. He focused on the universal ideas, images and archetypes which could be discovered in religion and mythology and surfaced in the symbolism of dreams. He insisted that modern secularism has led to a lack of awareness of the powers within human nature and that this is the cause of much psychological disorder. Although Jung never succeeded in proving the existence of the collective unconscious, subsequent generations of philosophers of religion have found it impossible to ignore.

W.B. Clift, *Jung and Christianity: The Challenge of Reconciliation* (1988); M. Stein and R.L. Moore, *Jung's Challenge to Contemporary Religion* (1987); A. Stevens, *Jung* (1994).

Jurieu, Pierre (1637–1713) Polemicist and Theologian. Jurieu was the son of a Protestant minister in Mer, France, and he was educated at Saumur and Sedan and in England. After serving the congregation at Mer, he was appointed Professor of Hebrew at Sedan. When the Sedan Academy was dissolved by King LOUIS XIV, he became Minister of the Walloon Church in Rotterdam in the Netherlands. Jurieu is remembered as the most prominent apologist for the French Protestant Church in the late seventeenth century, during the period of the revocation of the Edict of Nantes. He was the author of the *Histoire du Calvinisme et du Papisme*, in which he demanded freedom of conscience for all citizens. In his *L'Accomplissement des Prophéties ou la Délivrance de l'Eglise*, he argued from the Book of Revelation that Protestantism would triumph in the year 1689. Disappointed in this, he later maintained that because the French King had used military force to coerce religious belief, violent revolution against the secular power was justifiable. He also inveighed against Bishop BOSSUET and against the Jansenists in his *Histoire Critique des Dogmes et des Cultes*.

G.H. Dodge, *The Political Theory of the Huguenots of the Dispersion with Special Reference to the Thought and Influence of Pierre Jurieu* (1947).

Justinian I (483–565) Monarch. Justinian was the adopted son of the Emperor Justin I and the husband of THEODORA. He succeeded as Emperor of Byzantium in 527. As Emperor he reconquered North Africa from the Vandals in 534 and Italy from the Goths in 535. He is remembered for having built the great church of Hagia Sophia in Constantinople and for the establishment of a famous legal code. Devoutly orthodox in his religious beliefs, he persecuted the Montanists, closed down the philosophical schools of Athens and forced many pagans into baptism. However, he failed to reconcile the Monophysites and his condemnation of the writings of THEODORE OF MOPSUESTIA, those of THEODORET against CYRIL OF ALEXANDRIA and the letter of IBAS, led to a fifty-year schism with the Western Church. None the less Justinian is regarded as the most effective and energetic of the early Byzantine Emperors.

R. Browning, *Justinian and Theodora* (1971); J. Moorhead, *Justinian* (1994).

Justin Martyr (*c.* 100–*c.* 165) Saint, Martyr and Theologian. Justin was born into a pagan family in Nablus, Samaria, and was converted to Christianity in 132, having studied the pagan philosophies. He taught first in Ephesus and then in Rome. Finally he was denounced as a Christian and he died a martyr's death. He is remembered for his two apologies for Christianity. In the first, he argued that Christianity, of all the philosophies, had the only rational creed. The Word of God became human in order to teach his people the truth and to save them from the power of demons. However, he insisted that all human beings share in divine reason, but it is only in JESUS CHRIST that the full Logos resides. He also described the Sacraments of Baptism and the Eucharist. The second apology, which is much shorter, rebutted particular charges against

Christians and fulminated against their persecution. He was also the author of the *Dialogues with Trypho* in which he discussed the place of Jew and Gentile in God's plan. Justin is generally recognised as the most outstanding of the early apologists.

L.W. Barnard, *Justin Martyr: His Life and Thought* (1967); E. Osborn, *Justin Martyr* (1973).

K

Kagawa, Toyohiko (1888–1960) Philanthropist and Devotional Writer. Kagawa was an illegitimate son of a Japanese high official and he was born in Kobe. At the age of fifteen, he converted to Christianity and, in consequence, was disinherited by his family. He was educated at the Presbyterian College in Tokyo, at Kobe Theological College and at Princeton University in the United States. On his return to Japan, he decided to dedicate himself to alleviating the dreadful conditions of the Japanese poor. He founded the first Japanese labour union in 1921; in 1928 he organised the Anti-War League and in 1930 he began the missionary Kingdom of God movement. He was the author of many books including (in their English translations) *Before the Dawn*, *Christ and Japan* and *Love the Law of Life*. He achieved many reforms within Japan and is regarded as the most prominent Japanese Christian of his time.

W. Axling, *Kagawa* (1932); J.M. Trout, *Kagawa: Japanese Prophet* (1959).

Kähler, Martin (1835–1912) Theologian. Kähler was born in Neuhausen, East Prussia, and was educated at the Universities of Heidelberg, Tübingen and Halle. For most of his career he taught systematic theology at the University of Halle. He was the author of *Die Wissenschaft der Christlichen Lehre* and a collection of essays *Der Sogenannte Historische Jesus und der Geschichtliche Biblische Christus*. Today his writings are seen as anticipating the works of WEISS, SCHWEITZER and BULTMANN in that he was sceptical of the nineteenth-century quest for the historical JESUS.

C.E. Braaten, 'Martin Kahler on the historic, biblical Christ', in R.A. Harrisville (ed.), *The Historical Jesus and the Kerygmatic Christ* (1964).

Kant, Immanuel (1724–1804) Philosopher. Kant was born in Königsberg, Germany; he was educated at Königsberg University and he spent most of his career as Professor of Logic there. Despite this circumscribed existence, his influence on the philosophy of religion cannot be overstated. Among his books were *Der Kritik der Reinen Vernunft*, *Der Kritik der Praktischen Vernunft*, *Prolegomena zu Einer Jeden Kunftigen Metaphysik* and *Religion Innerhalb der Grenzen der Blossen Vernunft*. Influenced by the thought of David HUME, Kant argued that given the structure of human reason, metaphysical knowledge is an impossibility. The traditional proofs for the existence of God must be abandoned, but, none the less, the moral law demands the existence of the (unknowable) God. His ethical thought was equally important. He emphasised the role of duty; an action is moral only if it is performed out of a sense of duty and is in accordance with the Categorical Imperative. The Categorical Imperative can be determined through practical reason. Kant did not invent a new philosophical system, but, by defining the limits of human thought, he closed the door on traditional theological speculation. Among the very many later thinkers who were influenced by him must be included

SCHLEIERMACHER, HEGEL, SCHELL-
ING, FICHTE and GREEN.

C.D. Broad, *Kant: An Introduction* (1978); B.M.G.
Reardon, *Kant as Philosophical Theologian* (1988);
R. Scruton, *Kant* (1982).

Karlstadt, Andreas Bodenstein von (*c.*
1477–1541) Theologian. Karlstadt was
born in Bavaria and attended the
Universities of Erfurt, Cologne and
Wittenberg. He settled in Wittenberg and
initially opposed the stand of Martin
LUTHER, but, after studying the teachings of AUGUSTINE, he became a determined Reformer. In 1519 he debated
against Johann ECK and he later described the experience in his tract
*Against the Dumb Ass and Stupid Little
Doctor Eck*. He rapidly became more
radical than Luther in his views. After
moving to Orlamünde, he took to
wearing peasant's dress and demanding
social equality. He insisted that Communion must be offered in both kinds,
that music should have no place in services and that the direct revelation of the
Holy Spirit was much to be preferred
over theological reasoning. He is remembered as the celebrator of the first
Protestant Communion service (in
1521).

E.G. Rupp, 'Andrew Karlstadt and Reformation
Puritanism', *Journal of Theological Studies*, x
(1959); R.J. Sider, *Andreas Bodenstein von Karlstadt: The Development of his Thought* (1974).

Kasatkin, Ivan (**Nicolai**) (*c.* 1835–
1912) Archbishop and Missionary. Kasatkin was an Orthodox monk who took
the name of Nicolai. He volunteered to
act as chaplain to the Russian Consulate
at Hakodate in Hokkaido, Japan, and he
landed in Japan in 1861. At that time
Christianity was forbidden in Japan, and
he did not baptise anyone until 1868. In
1869 he formed the Orthodox Mission in
Russia and, when the laws against
Christianity were repealed, he settled
permanently in Tokyo. In 1880 he was
consecrated Bishop and in 1906 Arch-

bishop of Tokyo. By the time of his
death, he had made more than thirty
thousand converts.

R.H. Drummond, *A History of Christianity in
Japan* (1971).

Käsemann, Ernst (b. 1906) Theologian.
Käsemann was born in Bochum-
Dalhausen, Germany, and he was a student of BULTMANN at Marburg. During
the Nazi period, he was a leading member
of the Confessing Church and was imprisoned for a short time in 1937. After
the Second World War, he taught at
Mainz, Göttingen and Tübingen. One of
the most eminent New Testament spe-
cialists of his day, he was the author of
Exegetische Versuche und Besinnungen,
which arguably started a new 'quest' for
the historical JESUS. His commentary on
St PAUL's Epistle to the Romans was both
scholarly in its methods and radical in its
conclusions. Käsemann's work has been
influential on generations of students
both in Germany and in the English-
speaking world.

Ernst Käsemann, *Jesus Means Freedom: A Polemical Survey of the New Testament* (1969); N.T.
Wright, *A New Tübingen School? Ernst Käsemann
and his Commentary on Romans* (1982).

Keble, John (1792–1866) Theologian,
Poet and Devotional Writer. Keble was
the son of a Church of England parson
and he was educated at the University of
Oxford. After teaching at the university,
he served as parish priest at Hursley,
Hampshire, until his death. In 1833, he
preached a sermon on national apostasy
at the Oxford University Assize. His
friend John Henry NEWMAN always pin-
pointed that sermon as the start of the
Oxford Movement. The aim of the
movement was to restore to the Church
of England its seventeenth-century High
Church ideals. Keble contributed to the
Tracts for the Times and, after Newman's defection to the Roman Catholics,
he continued to lead the movement with

PUSEY. Keble College, Oxford, was named in his honour. Today he is chiefly remembered as a hymn writer. His *Christian Year*, published in 1827, contained 'New every morning is the love' and 'Blest are the pure in heart' which are still sung today.

G. Buttiscombe, *John Keble: A Study in Limitations* (1963); O. Chadwick (ed.), *The Mind of the Oxford Movement* (1960); B.W. Martin, *John Keble: Priest, Professor and Poet* (1976).

Kelly, William (1821–1906) Sect Founder. Kelly was a native of Ulster and was educated at Trinity College, Dublin. At the age of twenty, he joined the Plymouth Brethren, as a follower of John DARBY, whose collected works he later edited. For much of his life he edited two Brethren periodicals, *The Prospect* from 1848 to 1850 and the *Bible Treasury* from 1856 until the time of his death. In 1879 there was a split among the Exclusive Brethren, with Kelly leading the more moderate group. Today the Kelly Assemblies still exist as a separate body.

F.R. Coad, *A History of the Brethren Movement* (1968); H.H. Rowdon, *The Origin of the Brethren* (1967).

Kempe, Margery (c. 1373–c. 1433) Mystic. Kempe was born Margery Burnham, the daughter of the Mayor of Bishop's Lynne, England. She married John Kempe and was the mother of fourteen children. She is remembered for her *Book of Margery Kempe* in which she recorded the story of her life. She had several visions. She and her husband made a vow of chastity in 1413 and she was a great traveller, visiting Canterbury, the Holy Land in 1413, Compostela in 1417 and Norway and Danzig in 1433. There is some evidence that she was encouraged in her spirituality by JULIAN OF NORWICH. Margery Kempe's book is an extraordinary record of an ordinary life illumined by mystical experience. In recent years she has become something of a feminist heroine.

L.S. Johnson, *Margery Kempe's Dissenting Fiction* (1994); S.J. McEntire (ed.), *Margery Kempe: A Book of Essays* (1992); M.S.F. Thornton, *Margery Kempe: An Example in the English Pastoral Tradition* (1960).

Ken, Thomas (1637–1711) Bishop, Poet and Devotional Writer. Ken was educated at the University of Oxford. In 1679 he was appointed chaplain to Princess Mary in the Hague and in 1683 he became Chaplain to King Charles II. Despite being part of the royal household, he refused to allow Nell Gwynn, the King's mistress, to stay in his house. The King admired his stand and in the following year he was nominated to the See of Bath and Wells. In 1685 he was summoned to minister to the King when he lay on his death-bed. With six other Bishops, in 1688, he refused to read out King JAMES II's Declaration of Indulgence, as he viewed it as contrary to the doctrines of the Church of England. A man of great principle, he also refused to take the Oath of Allegiance to King William and Queen Mary in 1689 on the grounds that, by doing so, he would be breaking his oath to James. As a result, he was deprived of his bishopric. Today Ken is mainly remembered as the author of the famous hymns 'Awake my soul, and with the sun' and 'Glory to Thee, my God, this night'.

E. Marston, *Thomas Ken and Izaak Walton* (1908); H.A.L. Rice, *Thomas Ken* (1958).

Kensit, John (1853–1902) Polemicist. Kensit was born in London, England, in humble circumstances. A committed and fervent Protestant, he founded the City Protestant Bookshop in London in 1885 and in 1890 he became the Secretary of the Protestant Truth Society. He was appalled by the activities of the ritualists in the Church of England. He organised demonstrations against them and established the Wycliffe Preachers. He met his end while conducting a Protestant crusade in Liverpool. He was assaulted by a largely Roman Catholic mob and he died in hospital soon afterwards.

J.C. Wilcox, *John Kensit: Reformer and Martyr* (1903).

Kentigern (Mungo) (d. 603) Bishop, Missionary and Saint. Kentigern was born of a noble family and grew up in Culross, Scotland. He became Bishop of Strathclyde, but was later driven out by the anti-Christian party. He then conducted missions in Cumbria and Wales, before returning to Glasgow. He is said to have met St COLUMBA. St Mungo's Cathedral in Glasgow is named in his honour.

D.H. Farmer (ed.), *The Oxford Dictionary of Saints*, 3rd edn (1992); K.H. Jackson, 'The sources for the life of St Kentigern', in N.K. Chadwick (ed.), *Studies in the Early British Church* (1958); J.W. James, *A Vindication of St Kentigern's Connection with Llanelwy* (1960).

Kepler, Johann (1571–1630) Scientist. Kepler was born near Stuttgart, Germany, and was educated at the University of Tübingen. In 1601 he was appointed Court Astronomer in Prague and imperial mathematical aide to Rudolph II. He was the discoverer of the three laws of planetary motion, to which he was led by his neo-Platonist philosophy. A determined supporter of Pope GREGORY XIII's reform of the calendar, he suggested that the star which led the wise men to the baby JESUS was a conjunction of the planets Mars, Saturn and Jupiter which occurred in 6 BC. He accepted the authority of the Bible, although he was pantheistic in his religious views, believing that the order of the universe was an expression of the Being of God.

C. Baumgarten, *Johannes Kepler: Life and Letters* (1952); M. Caspar, *Johann Kepler* (1959); A. Koestler, *The Watershed: A Biography of Johannes Kepler* (1961).

Kettlewell, John (1653–95) Devotional Writer. Kettlewell was born in Yorkshire

and was educated at the University of Oxford. He served the parish of Coleshill in Warwickshire, but was a determined opponent of the Protestant Revolution of 1689. In consequence he was deprived of his living and settled in London. There he attempted to set up a fund for other deprived clergy who had shared in his stand, but he was prevented by the government. He was the author of several devotional manuals including *The Measure of Christian Obedience*, *The Practical Believer* which went through many editions and *The Companion for the Persecuted*, which was meant to comfort others in his predicament.

T.T. Carter (ed.), *The Life and Times of John Kettlewell* (1895).

Kevin (d. *c.* 618) Saint. Little certain is known of the life of Kevin. He is said to have been born in Leinster, Ireland, into a noble family. He was the founder and Abbot of Glendalough, County Wicklow, which was to become the parent house of other Irish monasteries and a centre of pilgrimage. Many miracles are ascribed to him, not the least remarkable of which is that he is thought to have died at the age of one hundred and twenty. He is a popular saint in Ireland.

D.H. Farmer (ed.), *The Oxford Dictionary of Saints*, 3rd edn (1992); D.P. Mould, *The Irish Saints* (1964).

Khama III (*c.* 1838–1923) Monarch. Khama III became Chief of the Ngwato tribe of Southern Africa in 1875. He had been converted to Christianity in 1862 and, once Chief, he supported missions among his people and tried to rule his lands by Christian standards. In particular, he controlled the sale of alcohol, he outlawed many tribal customs and he was determined to dispense justice as fairly as possible. In general he was remarkably successful. In 1885 he accepted the protection of the British and his grandson Seretse Khama became the first President of Botswana when the country achieved independence.

A.J. Dachs, *Khama of Botswana* (1971).

Khomyakov, Aleksei Stepanovich (1804–60) Philosopher and Theologian.

Khomyakov was born in Moscow, Russia, into an aristocratic family. After finishing his course at the University of Moscow, he joined the army, but by 1830 he had retired to his estates where he tried to improve the condition of his serfs. At the same time he participated in the intellectual life of the capital. He was a leader of the Slavophil movement and he saw the Russian Orthodox Church as the only bastion of true Christianity. He believed that the Protestants had over-emphasised freedom at the expense of unity and the Catholics had insisted on unity, but had lost sight of freedom. His key concept was 'Sobornost', signifying both Catholicity and Conciliarity. He argued that the individual within the Orthodox Church shared in a common life, but at the same time retained his individual liberty. He was particularly critical of post-Enlightenment Western civilisation which he condemned as decadent and materialistic. During the last years of his life, he contributed to *Russkaia Beseda*, a review promoting the Sobornost ideal. His writings were occasional and covered many topics, but his view of the Church has been highly influential on later Orthodox ecclesiology.

S. Bolshakoff, *The Doctrine of the Unity of the Church in the Works of Khomyakov and Moehler* (1946); A. Schmemann (ed.), *Ultimate Questions: An Anthology of Modern Russian Religious Thought* (1965).

Kierkegaard, Søren Aabye (1813–55) Philosopher.

Kierkegaard was born into a Lutheran family in Copenhagen, Denmark. By normal standards, he did not have a successful life. He was twenty-seven before he finished his university course; he broke off his engagement and never married; he was lampooned in the Copenhagen comic papers and he was of an exceptionally uncheerful disposition. None the less, today he is regarded as one of the most important of the modern philosophers. His books include (in their English translation) *Either – Or*, *Fear and Trembling*, *The Concept of Dread*, *Philosophical Fragments* and *Sickness unto Death*. He insisted that there was a great gulf between the transcendental realm of God and the immanent world of humanity, and that therefore God must remain hidden from man. Even in the incarnation, the divinity of JESUS CHRIST was hidden so man can only commit himself unequivocally and existentially in faith. Because Kierkegaard wrote in Danish, his work was unknown outside Denmark for many years. Once it was translated, it was profoundly influential both on the Crisis Theologians who followed Karl BARTH and on the existentialists such as Martin HEIDEGGER.

J.A. Bain, *Søren Kierkegaard: His Life and Religious Teaching* (1971); R. Bretall (ed.), *A Kierkegaard Anthology* (1947); L. Dupré, *Kierkegaard as Theologian*, (1963); A. Hannay, *Kierkegaard* (1982).

Kilham, Alexander (1762–98) Sect Founder.

Kilham was born in Epworth, England, into a Methodist family. As a young man, he acted as an aide to the preacher Robert Carr and he himself was admitted as a preacher in 1785. He became deeply involved in controversy about the relationship of the Society to the Church of England and he was expelled from the Conference in 1796. In consequence, in the following year, he founded the 'New Connexion' which was based on complete separation from the established Church and on greater lay participation. The Connexion grew rapidly despite Kilham's death in 1798. In 1907, it joined with the United Methodist Free Churches and the Bible Christians to form the United Methodist Church. This in its turn reunited in 1932 with the Wesleyan Church and the

Primitive Methodist Churches to form a single Methodist Church.

R.E. Davies and E.G. Rupp (eds), *A History of the Methodist Church in Great Britain* (1965); W.J. Townsend, *Alexander Kilham* (1889).

Kilian (*c. 640–c. 689*) Bishop, Missionary, Saint and Martyr. Kilian was an Irish Bishop who, with eleven companions, set out to preach the gospel in Franconia. He established headquarters in Würtzburg and converted the local ruler, Duke Gozbert. However, he aroused the enmity of the Duchess and, when the Duke was away, she had him put to death. Kilian is the patron saint of Würtzburg and he was a popular saint in the Middle Ages.

D.H. Farmer (ed.), *The Oxford Dictionary of Saints*, 3rd edn (1992); A. Gwynn, 'New light on St Kilian', *Irish Ecclesiastical Records*, lxxxviii (1957).

Kim, Chi-Ha (*b. 1941*) Theologian and Rebel. Kim was educated at the Seoul National University in Korea. As a political activist in the 1960s, he was imprisoned and tortured. Many of his writings were produced in response to that experience and have become important texts of Min-Jung theology. Min-Jung is an indigenous theology which has similarities to Latin American liberation theology.

Commission on Theological Concerns of the Christian Conference of Asia (ed.), *Minjung Theology* (1983); J.Y. Lee, *An Emerging Theology in World Perspective: Commentary on Minjung Theology* (1988).

Kim, Jai-Jun (b. 1901) Theologian and Denomination Founder. Kim is remembered as the first systematiser of Korean political theology. The early Protestant missionaries to Korea were strict fundamentalists and they had discouraged involvement in political activity. Despite this, Korean Christianity became a focus of radical protest against Japanese domination. Kim himself believed that the Christian scriptures must be interpreted

politically and he inveighed against fundamentalism. In consequence he was expelled from the Korean Presbyterian Church and founded a new group known as the Kitokyo Presbyterian Church. He is thus seen as an anticipator of the Min-Jung theology which emerged in the 1970s. Min-Jung is the indigenous Korean theology which shares some of the characteristics of liberation theology in Latin America.

S.H. Moffet, *The Christians of Korea* (1962); H.A. Rhodes, *History of the Korean Mission: Presbyterian Church* (1934).

King, Edward (1829–1910) Bishop and Devotional Writer. King was educated at the University of Oxford. He was appointed Regius Professor of Pastoral Theology in 1873 and Bishop of London in 1885. A high churchman, he was a friend of both PUSEY and LIDDON. He is remembered as a man of great pastoral gifts; his lectures on pastoral theology and a series of spiritual letters to individuals were published after his death. In 1888, however, he was prosecuted for 'ritualism' in his celebration of the Eucharist. For example, he mixed water with wine in the chalice, had lighted candles on the altar and read the service facing to the east. Despite earlier decisions in these matters, the Archbishop of Canterbury found in King's favour and this proved to be an important landmark in the development of Anglo-Catholic ritual.

O. Chadwick, *Edward King: Bishop of Lincoln* (1968); B.W. Randolph (ed.), *The Spiritual Letters of Edward King* (1910).

King, Martin Luther (1929–68) Philanthropist and Polemicist. King was born in Atlanta, Georgia, in the United States of America and he was educated at the Afro-American Morehouse College and at Boston University. After becoming a Baptist minister, he served a congregation in Montgomery, Alabama, from 1954. At this period black Americans were campaigning against segregation and King organised a boycott of buses which resulted in a desegregation order from the Supreme Court. From 1960 he worked full time for the Civil Rights Movement. In 1964 the Civil Rights Bill was passed and he was awarded the Nobel Peace Prize. Influenced by the Indian leader Gandhi, he was committed to non-violent methods. He is perhaps best remembered for his great speech for integration which began 'I have a dream . . .'. He was the author of several books, including *Stride Toward Freedom* and *Why We Can't Wait*. In general, he won over the white liberal establishment to his cause. He also aroused a great deal of opposition both from white reactionaries and from more radical blacks. He was assassinated in 1968.

T. Branch, *Parting the Waters: Martin Luther King and the Civil Rights Movement* (1988); D.L. Lewis, *Martin Luther King: A Critical Biography* (1970); K. Smith, *Search for the Beloved Community: The Thinking of Martin Luther King Jnr* (1986).

Kingsley, Charles (1819–75) Philanthropist and Novelist. Kingsley was born in Devon, England, and was educated at the Universities of London and Cambridge. For most of his life he served a country parish in Hampshire, but for a time he was Professor of Modern History at Cambridge. He was a prominent leader of the Christian Socialist movement. Influenced by F.D. MAURICE, he contributed to both *Politics for the People* and the *Christian Socialist*. His novels *Yeast*, *Alton Locke*, *Hypatia* and *Westward Ho!* were also popular in their day. Today he is remembered as an advocate of 'muscular Christianity' and for his decidedly unpuritanical views about sex. His children's book, *The Water Babies*, is still read.

S. Chitty, *The Beast and the Monk: A Life of Charles Kingsley* (1974); G. Kendall, *Charles Kingsley and his Ideas* (1946).

Knibb, William (1803–45) Missionary. Knibb arrived in Jamaica as a Baptist minister in 1824 and he remained in the West Indies for the rest of his life. During this period the slaves revolted, emancipation was granted and the economy of the islands underwent radical change. He was a tremendous campaigner, championing the black slaves and he was largely responsible for the decision to declare the Jamaica churches independent of the Baptist Missionary Society. He did much to found the Calabar Training College and he organised a mission to Africa from the West Indies. He is perhaps the best known of the early Baptist missionaries.

P. Wright, *Knibb the Notorious: Slaves' Missionary* (1973).

Knox, John (*c.* 1513–72) Theologian and Polemicist. Knox was born in Haddington, Scotland, and was educated at the University of Glasgow and perhaps at St Andrews. He took orders in the Roman Catholic Church, but soon became an enthusiastic supporter of the Protestant Reformation. In 1547 he was taken prisoner by the French, but was released and came to England in 1549. He was appointed chaplain to the boy-king EDWARD VI and made an important, and radical, contribution to the 1552 Prayer Book. With the accession of Queen MARY, he fled to the continent and for a time he lived in Frankfurt. He became pastor of the English church in Geneva in 1556 and it was here that he published his *First Blast of the Trumpet against the Monstrous Regiment of Women*. This was directed against the Catholic Mary of Guise, Regent of Scotland, but it did not endear him to the Protestant ELIZABETH I who had just succeeded her sister to the throne of England. In 1560, with the death of Mary of Guise, Knox returned to Scotland where he was responsible for the *Scottish Confession*, a strongly Calvinistic document, which was accepted by the Scottish Parliament. When the Catholic Mary Queen of Scots returned to her kingdom, Knox was fearless in his confrontations with her and frequently preached against the worldliness of her court. When she abdicated, he was the preacher at the coronation of the young King JAMES VI and he supported the Regent, the Earl of Moray. Knox must be seen as the prime architect of the Scottish Reformation. The *First Book of Discipline*, detailing Church organisation, was largely his work and he was also the author of *The History of the Reformation of Religion within the Realm of Scotland*.

J.A.S. Burleigh, *A Church History of Scotland* (1960); S. Lamont, *The Swordbearer: John Knox and the European Reformation* (1991); J. Ridley, *John Knox* (1968).

Knox, Ronald Arbuthnot (1888–1957) Devotional Writer. Knox was the son of the Anglican Bishop of Manchester. He was educated at the University of Oxford and was initially a dedicated Anglo-Catholic. His satire on the modernist position *Absolute and Abitofhell* brought him immediate acclaim, but in 1917 he was received as a Roman Catholic and subsequently he was ordained. Between 1926 and 1939, he held the position of Roman Catholic chaplain to the undergraduates of Oxford. Subsquently he concentrated on translating the Vulgate into modern English. This version proved extremely popular. Among his other works were an early autobiography, *Some Loose Stones*, *Enthusiasm* and several detective stories. He was a highly influential figure in England in the middle years of the twentieth century and was the subject of numerous reminiscences.

T. Corbishley, *Ronald Knox the Priest* (1964); R. Speaight, *Ronald Knox the Writer* (1966); E. Waugh, *The Life of the Right Reverend Ronald Knox* (1959).

Koyama, Kosuke (b. 1929) Theologian. Koyama was born in Tokyo in 1929 of a Christian family. He was educated at

Tokyo Theological Seminary, Drew University and Princeton Theological Seminary in the United States of America and at the Ecumenical Institute of the World Council of Churches in Switzerland. He has taught in Thailand and New Zealand and since 1980 has been at the Union Theological Seminary in New York. His works include *Waterbuffalo Theology*, *No Handle on the Cross* and *Mount Fuji and Mount Sinai*. His theology is seen as a meeting of East and West, Buddhist and Christian, rich and poor. It has no overarching system, but is a prophetic response to the complexities of the modern situation in which 'a broken Christ heals a broken world'. He attempts to offer an agenda for Asian theology and he is an important figure in the development of a global Christianity.

D. Ford, *The Modern Theologians*, Vol. 2 (1989).

Küng, Hans (b. 1928) Theologian and Ecumenist. Küng was born in Lucerne, Switzerland, and was educated at the Gregorian University and at the Sorbonne. As an ordained priest, he taught at the Roman Catholic faculty in Tübingen. He became known as a champion of reform in the Church. He called for more emphasis on scripture and less on ecclesiastical tradition and papal infallibility. As a result of the greater conservatism of the Church under Pope JOHN PAUL II, his position as approved teacher within the Church was withdrawn and he moved to the Institute for Ecumenical Research at Tübingen. Among his many books are *Council, Reform and Reunion*, *Infallible?*, *On Being a Christian*, *Does God Exist?* and *Structures of the Church*. In recent years he has widened his ecumenical interests still further and he has turned his attention to the world religions and their relationship with Christianity.

H. Haring and K.-J. Kuschel (eds), *Hans Küng: His Work and Way* (1979); P. Hebblethwaite, *The New*

Inquisition (1980); Hans Küng, *Why I am Still a Christian* (1987).

Kuyper, Abraham (1837–1920) Theologian, Denomination Founder and Politician. Kuyper was educated at the University of Leyden in the Netherlands and became a minister in the Dutch Reformed Church. A committed Calvinist and opponent of all forms of liberalism, he joined Groen Van Prinsterer's Anti-Revolutionary Party and was elected to the Dutch Parliament in 1874. Central to his platform was the demand for State aid for Church schools and a revitalisation of national life. Among many other activities, he started a Calvinist University in Amsterdam; he formed a new denomination known as the Gereformeerde Kirk and in 1901 he became Minister for the Interior. During the four years he was in office, he was prepared to use legislation to break a railway strike and he campaigned for the Dutch to mediate in the South African war between the British and the Boers. He was also a prolific writer and is perhaps best known for his *Calvinism*, which was originally produced as a series of lectures delivered in the United States of America. His Anti-Revolutionary Party still exists and he was an important figure in the revival of traditional Calvinism in the Netherlands.

F. Vandenberg, *Abraham Kuyper* (1960).

L

LaBadie, Jean de (1610–74) Mystic and Order Founder. Labadie was born near Bordeaux, France. He was ordained as a Roman Catholic priest, but he later became a Protestant minister serving congregations in Geneva and the Netherlands. He formed a community in Middleburg based on holding everything in common and living a simple life. His principles were expounded in Anna Maria von Schurman's book *Eucleria*. The community was forced to move from the Netherlands and it finally settled in Altona. Known as the Labadists, the group had died out by the middle of the eighteenth century.

The Catholic University of America, *New Catholic Encyclopaedia* (1967).

Lactantius (*c.* 240–*c.* 320) Theologian and Historian. Lactantius was a native of North Africa. He was appointed by the Emperor Diocletian to teach Latin oratory in Nicomedia, but he resigned on becoming a Christian. Later he became the tutor of the Emperor CONSTANTINE's son Crispus. He is remembered for his masterful apology for Christianity, *Divinae Institutiones*, in which he argued that paganism was an inadequate philosophy and that the moral improvement Christianity brought about in its adherents argued for its truth. He also produced *De Mortibus Persecutorum*, a gory account of the recent persecutions. Its primary thesis was that good emperors live happily, while persecuting emperors suffer horrible fates. It was based on sound historical traditions and has become an important source for the period.

'The life and literary activity of Lactantius', in K. Aland and F.L. Cross, *Studia Patristica I*, lxiii (1957).

Ladislaus (1040–95) Monarch and Saint. Ladislaus was chosen as King of Hungary in 1077. He expanded his kingdom into Croatia and Dalmatia and he worked tirelessly for the spread of Christianity within his realm. He was a great builder of churches and passed a series of religious laws at the Synod of Szabolcs of 1092. Although he had supported the Pope against the Holy Roman Emperor in the matter of the lay investiture of Abbots and Bishops, he refused to accept Pope URBAN II as his temporal lord when Urban claimed some of his territory. His piety, however, was never in question and he was canonised in 1192.

I.S. Robinson, *Authority and Resistance in the Investiture Contest* (1978).

Lambert of Hersfield (*c.* 1027–*c.* 1085) Historian. Little is known of the life of Lambert. He was a Benedictine monk in the Abbey of Hersfeld. He is remembered for his *Annales*, a chronicle which starts with the creation of the world and finishes in his own time. The period from 1067 to 1077 is very detailed and, until the middle of the nineteenth century, it was the main historical source for the story of the struggle between Pope GREGORY VII and the Emperor HENRY IV.

I.S. Robinson, *Authority and Resistance in the Investiture Contest* (1978).

Lamennais, Félicité Robert de (1782–1854) Theologian, Philosopher and

Politician. Lamennais was born in St Malo, France. Despite his early loss of faith, he returned to the Church and was ordained a Roman Catholic priest in 1816. He became the centre of a religious circle and in 1818 produced the first volume of his *Essai sur l'Indifférence en Matière de Religion*. In this and in subsequent volumes, he argued that the Church should be free from the State and that the Pope should be regarded as the supreme leader of all kings. In order to promote his ideas, he founded a religious congregation in 1828, an agency for the defence of religious liberty and in 1830 a newspaper, *L'Avenir*. In 1832 he went to Rome to try to persuade Pope GREGORY XVI to lead a crusade on behalf of religious and political freedom. The Pope rejected the suggestion and, in response, Lamennais produced his *Paroles d'un Croyant* in 1834 in which he outlined his vision of the ideal society. The book generated huge enthusiasm, but was unequivocally condemned by the Pope, whereupon Lamennais left the Church. Subsequently he dedicated himself to the promotion of political liberty and his religious philosophy became increasingly Pantheistic. He became a member of the French Parliament in the Revolutionary government of 1848 and he died unreconciled to the Church. Lamennais is regarded as an important forerunner of the French Catholic Modernist movement.

J.J. Oldfield, *The Problem of Tolerance and Social Existence in the Writings of Félicité Lamennais, 1809–1831* (1973); W.G. Roe, *Lamennais and England: The Reception of Lamennais's Religious Ideas in England* (1966); A.R. Vidler, *Prophecy and Papacy: A Study of Lamennais, the Church and the Revolution* (1954).

Lanfranc (*c.* 1010–89) Theologian and Archbishop. Lanfranc was born in Pavia, Italy. He was a student of BERENGAR of Tours and became a Benedictine monk at the Abbey of Bec in 1042. Under his guidance, Bec became one of the most famous schools of Europe and Lanfranc was the teacher, among others, of ANSELM OF CANTERBURY. In 1063 he moved to Caen and then, in 1070, he was consecrated Archbishop of Canterbury. Among his theological writings was *De Corpore et Sanguine Domini*, an important treatise on the Eucharist. He is chiefly remembered, however, as a superb administrator. He was a trusted advisor of both King William I and King William II of England; he rebuilt Canterbury Cathedral and began the Cathedral library and he established the priority of the Archdiocese of Canterbury over that of York.

M.T. Gibson, *Lanfranc of Bec* (1978); R.W. Southern, 'Lanfranc of Bec and Berengar of Tours', in R.W. Hunt, W.A. Pantin and R.W. Southern (eds), *Studies in Mediaeval History Presented to Frederick Maurice Powicke* (1948).

Lang, [William] Cosmo Gordon (1864–1945) Archbishop. Lang was born of Presbyterian parents in Scotland and was educated at the Universities of Glasgow and Oxford. In 1890 he was ordained a priest in the Church of England. He had a highly successful career and after serving as a parish priest, he was consecrated Bishop of Stepney in 1901, Archbishop of York in 1908 and Archbishop of Canterbury in 1928. Today he is mainly remembered for his role in the abdication crisis of 1936. In fact he was not in consultation with Edward VIII and had little to do with the final decision. It was when Edward finally announced that he would abdicate the throne rather than give up the twice-divorced Mrs Simpson, that the Archbishop made an unfortunate broadcast to the nation. This elicited the memorable lines: 'My Lord Archbishop, what a scold you are!/And when your man is down, how bold you are!/Of Christian charity how scant you are!/And, auld Lang swine, how full of Cantuar!'

J.G. Lockhart, *Cosmo Gordon Lang* (1949).

Langton, Stephen (d. 1228) Theologian and Archbishop. Langton was born in England, but was educated and later taught in Paris. He was made a Cardinal by Pope INNOCENT III in 1206 and was consecrated Archbishop of Canterbury in the following year. However, King John would not receive him in England until 1213. He was a signatory of the Magna Carter and mediated between the King and the barons. Between 1215 and 1218, he was suspended from his duties by the Pope, who supported John, but, on his return to England, he upheld the Regency during the minority of King Henry III against the ambitions of the barons. He also established the right of the Archbishop of Canterbury to be the Pope's legate in England. In 1222 at the Synod of Oseney, he issued special conditions for the English Church as well as promulgating the decrees of the Fourth Lateran Council. His most important theological works were commentaries on the scriptures; he is also believed to have divided the biblical text into the chapters which are still in use today.

F.M. Powicke, *Stephen Langton* (1928).

Las Casas, Bartolomé de (*c.* 1475–1566) Missionary, Bishop and Polemicist. Las Casas was born in Seville, Spain, and was educated at the University of Salamanca. His father had accompanied Christopher Columbus on his second voyage. After he was ordained in 1510, he concentrated on improving the conditions of the native Indians in the New World and he made several journeys across the Atlantic Ocean. In 1521 the Indians in his Indian settlement revolted against the organisation. Las Casas went into retreat and subsequently joined the Dominican Order. When he returned to his work, he campaigned for new laws to improve the lot of the native Americans. Although these were passed in 1542/3, there was much opposition from the colonists. Las Casas was consecrated Bishop of Chiajia, Mexico, in 1544. Then, in 1551, he returned to Spain and continued to work for his cause near the centre of government. He was the author of several works including *Brevísma Relacion de la Destrucción de las Indias* in which he inveighed against colonial exploitation. Today he is a controversial figure in that he encouraged the importing of African slaves. None the less he fearlessly and tirelessly worked for the betterment of the Indians and has been described as the 'Apostle of the Indies'.

J. Fried and B. Keen (eds), *Bartholomew de las Casas in History* (1972); H.R. Wagner, *The Life and Writings of Bartolomé de las Casas* (1967); G. Guttierez, *Las Casas* (1993).

Latimer, Hugh (*c.* 1485–1555) Bishop and Martyr. Latimer was born in Leicestershire and was educated at the University of Cambridge. He was consecrated Bishop of Worcester in 1535, having advised King HENRY VIII during the break with Rome. However, as a Reformer, he was compelled to resign his see in opposition to the Catholic teaching contained in the Six Articles imposed in 1539. During the reign of King EDWARD VI, he was a popular court preacher and his series of sermons 'On the plough', preached against ecclesiastical abuse, became famous. He accused the more worldly bishops of 'pampering their paunches . . . munching in their mangers and moiling in their gay manors and mansions'. He is primarily remembered as a martyr. He was burnt at the stake as a Protestant in Oxford during the persecutions of Queen MARY. As the fire was lit, he said to his companion Nicholas RIDLEY, 'Be of good cheer, Master Ridley, and play the man. We shall this day light a candle by God's grace in England as I trust shall never be put out!'

A.G. Chester, *Hugh Latimer, Apostle to the English* (1954); H.S. Darby, *Hugh Latimer* (1953).

Laubach, Frank Charles (1884–1970) Missionary and Educator. Laubach was born in Benton, Pennsylvania, and was educated at the Universities of Princeton and Columbia. He was ordained into the Congregational ministry in 1914 and first went as a missionary to the Philippines. Later he worked in other countries including India. He is remembered for his literacy project in which reading and writing were taught through the medium of phonetic symbols and pictures. His methods were particularly suitable for underdeveloped countries and he numbered the Indian leader, Gandhi, among his admirers. His writings included *India Shall be Literate* and *Teaching the World to Read*.

Frank Charles Laubach, *Teaching the World to Read* (1947).

Laud, William (1573–1645) Archbishop and Politician.

Laud was born in Reading, as the son of a tailor. He was educated at the University of Oxford and was ordained in 1601. A determined high churchman, he became Dean of Gloucester in 1616, Bishop of St David's in 1621, Bishop of Bath and Wells in 1626, Bishop of London in 1629 and Archbishop of Canterbury in 1633. His religious views accorded with those of King CHARLES I and he played an important part in the King's government. As Chancellor of the University of Oxford, he introduced several important reforms. He aroused the hostility of the Puritans by his attempts to enforce uniformity of liturgical practice on the English Church. He also tried to impose a new liturgy in Scotland and he introduced new Canons to Convocation proclaiming the divine right of kings. In 1641, he was impeached by the Long Parliament and imprisoned. He was brought to trial in 1644 and was executed for treason the following year. Laud was an able administrator, but, like his royal master, he lamentably failed to read the mood of the times.

C. Carlton, *Archbishop William Laud* (1987); H. Trevor-Roper, *Archbishop Laud 1573–1645* (1962).

Laurence (d. 258) Saint and Martyr.

Laurence was one of seven Deacons in Rome during the reign of Pope SIXTUS II, who died during the persecution of Valerian. According to legend, he was asked to give up the Church's treasure. In response, he assembled together the poor of Rome and declared 'These are the Church's treasure!' As a result, he was roasted to death on a gridiron. Most scholars do not hold this tale to be historical, but none the less Laurence with his gridiron is one of the most popular of the saints.

D.H. Farmer (ed.), *The Oxford Dictionary of Saints*, 3rd edn (1992); V.L. Kennedy, *The Saints of the Canon of the Mass* (1938).

Law, William (1686–1761) Devotional Writer and Polemicist.

Law was born in Northamptonshire, and he was educated at the University of Cambridge. In 1711 he was ordained into the Church of England ministry, but he refused to take the oath of allegiance to the Hanoverian King George I and, as a result, could not hold a position within the Church. For several years he served as tutor to Edward Gibbon, father of GIBBON the historian. Among his writings were various polemical works including *Three Letters to the Bishop of Bangor*, which made fun of the Bishop's conviction that sincerity was all that was required in the profession of religion. Today, however, he is remembered for his *Serious Call to a Devout and Holy Life*, which remains a classic of English spirituality. It was widely read and was influential on such diverse figures as Samuel JOHNSON and John WESLEY.

A.K. Walker, *William Law: His Life and Thought* (1973); P. Stanwood (ed.), *William Law, Classics of Western Spirituality Series* (1978).

Lawrence, Brother (c. 1605–91) Mystic and Devotional Writer.

Brother Lawrence was born Nicholas Herman in

humble circumstances in Lorraine. Before entering a Carmelite monastery at the age of more than fifty, he held a variety of jobs as a soldier and a personal servant. In the monastery, he took the name Brother Lawrence and he worked in the kitchens – an occupation he is said to have detested. He is remembered for his devotional classic, *The Practice of the Presence of God*, in which he described how God's presence could be felt as acutely in work as in prayer. It was much quoted by François FÉNELON; it has been translated into many languages and is still read today.

Brother Lawrence, *The Practice of the Presence of God*, translated by D. Attwater (1926).

Lazarus (first century) Disciple. According to the Gospel of JOHN, Chapter 2, Lazarus was the brother of MARY and MARTHA and he lived with his sisters at Bethany. Three days after he died, he was raised by JESUS. Later legend has it that he subsequently became a Bishop in Cyprus and that his personal relics were preserved in Constantinople. He has been a subject of veneration in the Church from early times and recently there have been attempts to identify him with the 'disciple Jesus loved' in the Fourth Gospel.

R. Dunkerley, 'Lazarus', *New Testament Studies*, (1959); J.N. Sanders, 'Who was the disciple Jesus loved?', in F.L. Cross (ed.), *Studies in the Fourth Gospel* (1957).

Lee, Ann (*c.* 1736–84) Sect Founder. Lee lived near Manchester, England. After an unfortunate marriage and losing four children, she became involved in a local dissenting group and became its leader. The principles of the society (known as the United Society of Believers in Christ's Second Appearing) included confession, celibacy, pacifism and the common ownership of property. As Mother Ann, Lee believed she was a manifestation of the female principle of Christ (JESUS being the male principle) and that therefore she was a fulfilment of the promise of a Second Coming. Worship in the sect involved dancing, leaping, singing, barking and shaking – hence the group came to be known as the Shakers. As a result of persecution, Lee and seven followers emigrated to America in 1774 where the society rapidly increased in numbers. In 1787, three years after Lee's death, the first settlement was established in New Lebanon, New York and later other settlements were founded in Kentucky, Pennsylvania, Ohio and Indiana. Numbers declined from the middle of the nineteenth century and today very few remain. None the less the Shakers are well known and admired for their elegant and economical furniture design, which is much reproduced.

E.D. Andrews, *The People Called Shakers*, 2nd edn (1963); M.F. Melcher, *The Shaker Adventure* (1941); R.E. Whitson (ed.), *The Shakers: Two Centuries of Spiritual Reflection* (1983).

Lefebvre, Marcel (1905–91) Archbishop and Sect Founder. Lefebvre was born near Lille, France, and was ordained into the Roman Catholic priesthood in 1929. He served as a missionary in Gabon, was consecrated a Bishop in 1947 and became Archbishop of Dakar in 1948. He is remembered for his rejection of both the spirit and the letter of the edicts of the Second Vatican Council. Believing that democratisation was the work of the devil, he founded the ultraconservative Priestly Confraternity of St PIUS X with its own seminary. In defiance of the Council, the order continued to celebrate the Latin Tridentine Mass and by 1976, Lefebvre had been suspended from his priestly functions. Although the quarrel was patched up with Pope PAUL VI, the movement continued to grow. New seminaries were founded in Argentina, France, Germany and the United States of America. Then, in 1988, Lefebvre consecrated four Bishops and in a sermon castigated the Church for the sins of 'liberalism, socialism, modernism and Zionism'. He went so far as to maintain that the throne of St PETER was occupied by an Anti-Christ. That afternoon Lefebvre and the four new Bishops were excommunicated and pronounced schismatic. Lefebvre's rebellion was the most serious challenge within the Church to the reforms of the Second Vatican Council.

P. Nichols, *The Pope's Divisions: The Roman Catholic Church Today* (1982).

Leibniz, Gottfried Wilhelm (1646–1716)

Philosopher, Theologian and Ecumenist. Leibniz was born in Leipzig, Germany, and was educated at the Universities of Leipzig and Jena. After ten years in the service of the Duke of Mainz, he was appointed librarian and historiographer of the Duke of Brunswick. Among his philosophical works was *Monadology*, in which he argued that the universe was composed of an infinite series of simple substances which form a continuous ladder from the lowest to the highest. It is not clear whether he believed God was the highest of the monads or whether He was outside the system altogether. He also produced theological works such as *Systema Theologicum* and *Essais de Théodicée*. He was a correspondent of Bishop BOSSUET and was a believer in the possibility of Church reunion. He also produced a lengthy critique of John LOCKE's *Essay Concerning Human Understanding*. He accepted the validity of the classical proofs for the existence of God and he was convinced that the findings of reasons and the maxims of faith could be reconciled.

N. Jolley (ed.), *The Cambridge Companion to Leibniz* (1995); G.J. Jordan, *The Reunion of the Churches: A Study of G.W. Leibniz and his Great Attempt* (1927); G.M. Ross, *Leibniz* (1984); B. Russell, *A Critical Exposition of the Philosophy of Leibniz*, 2nd edn (1937).

Lenshina, Alice (c. 1919–78)

Sect Founder. Lenshina was born in Kasomo, Northern Rhodesia (Zambia), and was baptised as a member of the Presbyterian Church. After a near-death experience, she believed she had a special mission. In her preaching and prophesying, she emphasised the sanctity of marriage and home and she was bitterly opposed to polygamy and traditional African sorcery. In 1955 she started her own separate congregation, known as the Lumpa ('excelling') Church. They believed that the End was at hand, and conflict soon arose with the local chiefs since the adherents of the new sect wanted to live separately and independently. During the skirmishes more than seven hundred people were killed, while Lenshina herself died in prison after eleven years of captivity. At its height, her movement is estimated to have attracted one hundred thousand people. The Church continued to exist underground after her death, but it is still repressed by the government of Zambia as a threat to law and security.

G. Bond, 'A prophecy that failed: the Lumpa Church of Uyombe, Zambia', in S. Walker (ed.), *African Christianity* (1979).

Leo I (d. 461)

Pope and Saint. Leo was born in Tuscany. He succeeded Pope Sixtus III in 440. His Pontificate is remembered for Leo's establishment of strong Church government. He sent representatives to the Council of Chalcedon in 451 and his doctrine of the Person of Christ, as expressed in his letter to Flavian, Patriarch of Constantinople, was finally adopted by the Council. He defended orthodoxy against the Pelagian, Monophysite and Manichaean heresies and he managed to persuade both Attila the Hun in 452 and the Vandals in 455 to refrain from destroying Rome. His jurisdiction was recognised in all the Western provinces and he was also respected in the East. Many of his letters and sermons have survived, giving us an interesting picture of the liturgical traditions of the time. He was declared a Doctor of the Church by Pope BENEDICT XIV.

J.N.D. Kelly (ed.), *The Oxford Dictionary of Popes* (1986); W. Ullman, 'Leo and the theme of papal primacy', *Journal of Theological Studies*, n.s.xi (1960).

Leo III (*c.* 680–741) Emperor. Leo III was elected Byzantine Emperor in 717. He is remembered for defeating the Arabs and for initiating the Iconoclastic Controversy. He believed that the use of icons hindered the conversion of Jews and Muslims to Christianity and in 726 he issued an edict ordering the destruction of all images. When the Patriarch GERMANUS appealed to the Pope, he was deposed; JOHN OF DAMASCUS wrote strongly against the edict and Pope Gregory III condemned Leo's actions. None the less the policy was continued by Leo's son Constantine V.

J.N.D. Kelly (ed.), *The Oxford Dictionary of Popes* (1986); D.J. Sahas, *Icon and Logos* (1986).

Leo III (d. 816) Pope and Saint. Leo was elected Pope in 795, but was compelled to put himself under the protection of CHARLEMAGNE after he was attacked by his predecessor's relations. Charlemagne escorted him back to Rome where Leo crowned him Holy Roman Emperor on Christmas Day 800. Although he accepted that the Holy Ghost proceeded from the Father and the Son, he discouraged the use of the 'filioque' formula, in order to keep peace with the Eastern Church. He acted firmly against adherents of the Adoptionist heresy and he is remembered as a beautifier of churches. He was canonised in 1673.

J.N.D. Kelly (ed.), *The Oxford Dictionary of Popes* (1986); L. Wallach, 'The Roman Synod of December 800 and the alleged trial of Leo III', *Harvard Theological Review*, xlix (1956).

Leo IV (d. 855) Saint, Pope and Liturgist. Leo IV succeeded Sergius II as Pope in 847. Among many activities, he built a great wall round much of Rome and he restored several of the city's churches. His reputed quenching of a fire in the Borgo is portrayed in a fresco by RAPHAEL. He is chiefly remembered, however, as the founder of Asperges, the ceremony of sprinkling holy water over the altar and the congregation at the Sunday Mass. This is accompanied by the singing of 'Asperges me, Domine, hyssopo' from Psalm 51.

J.N.D. Kelly (ed.), *The Oxford Dictionary of Popes* (1986).

Leo IX (1002–54) Saint and Pope. Leo was born Bruno in Alsace and he was consecrated Bishop of Toul in 1027. He was elected Pope in 1048 and, inspired by the reforms initiated by the monastery of Cluny, he set himself to reform the Church. He held councils at Bari, Pavia, Mainz and Rheims at which he issued decrees against simony and he imposed clerical celibacy. He numbered among his advisors Hildebrand (who was to become Pope GREGORY VII) and PETER DAMIAN. In 1050 the eucharistic doctrine of BERENGAR of Tours was condemned and this prompted the development of official Catholic teaching.

J.N.D. Kelly (ed.), *the Oxford Dictionary of Popes* (1986).

Leo X (1475–1521) Pope. Leo was born Giovanni de' Medici and was the son of Lorenzo the Magnificent. He became a Cardinal at the age of thirteen, but travelled extensively before settling in Rome in 1500. He was elected Pope in 1511 when he was thirty-eight. He was a great patron of scholarship and the arts, but such tastes did little to improve the finances of the Papacy. As a result he encouraged the sale of Indulgences to support the building of St Peter's. This was to lead to the revolt of Martin LUTHER and the Protestant Reformation. Leo ex-communicated Luther in 1520, but there is little evidence to indicate that he understood the gravity of the protest.

A.G. Dickens, *Reformation and Society in Sixteenth Century Europe* (1966); H.J. Hillerbrand, *Christendom Divided: The Protestant Reformation* (1971); B. Mitchell, *Rome in the High Renaissance: The Age of Leo X* (1973).

Leo XIII (1810–1903) Pope. Leo was born Vincenzo Gioacchino Pecci in Carpineto, Italy. He was ordained into the Roman Catholic priesthood in 1837, was consecrated Bishop of Perugia in 1846, was created a Cardinal in 1853 and was elected Pope in succession to PIUS IX in 1878. He made it his aim to reconcile the Papacy with modern civilisation and to that end he established an apostolic delegation in Washington; he established good relations with Belgium and Germany; he made contact with Russia and Japan and he sent an Apostolic Letter to the English. However, he failed to regain the Papal States, anti-clericalism in France grew ever stronger and he condemned the 'Americanism' movement associated with Isaac HECKER. He is remembered for his encyclical *Rerum Novarum* of 1891 which encouraged social legislation and the formation of trade unions, for his opening of the Vatican Archives to scholars and for giving some encouragement to biblical critics. Although he was anxious to create friendly relations between the Churches, his commission rejected the validity of Anglican Orders and his idea of Church Union was that the Protestants and the Orthodox should all join Rome. Within his own Church, he promoted spirituality in several encyclicals and in 1900 he consecrated all humanity to the Sacred Heart of JESUS.

E. Soderini, *Leo XIII, Italy and France* (1935); L.P. Wallace, *Leo XIII and the Rise of Socialism* (1966).

Leodegar (Leger) (*c.* 616–79) Bishop, Saint and Martyr. Leodegar was Bishop of Autun, France, and he did much to reform his diocese. He also became involved in the politics of his time and he was eventually tortured, blinded and put to death by one of the rivals for the Frankish throne. Although he was killed for political reasons, he was soon regarded as a martyr and his cult spread throughout France to England. The famous horse race, the St Leger, was named after a Colonel of that name.

D.H. Farmer (ed.), *The Oxford Dictionary of Saints*, 3rd edn (1992).

Leonard (sixth century) Saint. Little certain is known of the life of St Leonard. He was said to have been a nobleman in the time of CLOVIS. He was converted to Christianity and became a hermit near Limoges, France. He is supposed to have helped deliver Clovis's wife of a child when she went into labour when out hunting near his cell. There is nothing recorded of him before the eleventh century, but he became highly popular throughout Western Europe and is regarded as the patron saint of pregnant women and prisoners.

D.H. Farmer (ed.), *The Oxford Dictionary of Saints*, 3rd edn (1992).

Leonardo da Vinci (1452–1519) Artist and Scientist. Leonardo was a pupil of the artist Verrocchio in Florence, Italy. Between 1483 and 1499 he lived in Milan; he then wandered for several years and finally settled in France. He was a passionate investigator into the workings of nature and his surviving notebooks contain observations on every branch of science as well as plans for the invention of guns and flying machines. As a religious painter, he is remembered for works such as *The Virgin of the Rocks* and the fresco of the *Last Supper* painted on the walls of a Dominican convent. He was a man of extraordinary genius, and his portrayals of the Virgin MARY, JESUS and his disciples have imprinted themselves on Western consciousness.

K. Clark, *Leonardo da Vinci* (1939); I.B. Hart, *The World of Leonardo de Vinci* (1961).

Leontius of Byzantium (sixth century) Theologian. The identity of Leontius is confused. There was a Scythian monk of that name who was involved in the controversy about the suffering of the Godhead in the crucifixion. Most scholars believe he was different from the Leontius who defended ORIGEN mentioned by the hagiographer Cyril of Scythopolis. Cyril's Leontius has been identified as the author of *Libri III Contra Nestorianos et Eutychianos, Triginta Capitula adv. Nestorium* and two works directed against SEVERUS of Antioch. He is remembered as a staunch defender of the Chalcedon formula and for introducing the idea of Enhypostasia. This was the doctrine that the humanity of JESUS CHRIST was included within the substance of the Godhead. This idea was also defended by JOHN OF DAMASCUS.

B. Daley, 'The Origenism of Leontius of Byzantium', *Journal of Theological Studies* n.s.xxvii (1976); D.B. Evans, *Leontius of Byzantium: An Origenist Christology* (1970).

Lessing, Gotthold Ephraim (1729–81) Dramatist and Theologian. Lessing was the son of a Lutheran pastor and was born in Saxony. He became a well-known literary critic and playwright and was regarded as a leading figure of the German Enlightenment. A personal friend of the important Jewish scholar Moses Mendelssohn (on whom his dramatic poem *Nathan der Weise* was based), he did much to encourage the integration of Jewish intellectuals into the cultural life of Germany. In his study of the Gospel origins, he argued for there having been an Aramaic original behind the Gospel of MATTHEW which was also known by LUKE and MARK. In his *Die Erziehung des Menschengeschlects*, he argued that Christianity could not be regarded as an historical religion, but that its truth could only be discovered through personal experience and objective enquiry. He became the centre of controversy when he published the *Wolfenbüttel Fragments*, extracts from the writings of REIMARUS which argued that the disciples had invented the story of JESUS's resurrection in order to explain why his prophecies on the immediate arrival of the Kingdom of God had not been fulfilled. Lessing himself took a neutral position, but the controversy itself opened the door to disinterested investigations of the origins of the Christian faith.

H.E. Allison, *Lessing and the Enlightenment* (1966); H.B. Garland, *Lessing: The Founder of Modern German Literature*, 2nd edn (1962).

Levi (first century) Apostle. All that is known of Levi is that he was the son of Alphaeus and was a tax collector. Jesus called him to be his disciple and he is identified with MATTHEW, of whom an identical story is told.

St Mark's Gospel, Chapter 2; St Matthew's Gospel, Chapter 9.

Lewis [Louis] I (778–840) Emperor. Lewis was the third son of the Emperor CHARLEMAGNE. He was appointed joint Emperor in 813, but his reign was troubled as a result of the rivalry between his four sons. He was deposed in 833, but reinstated in 835. He is remembered as 'the Pious' as well as 'the Weak-Hearted'. He helped ANSKAR in his Scandinavian mission; he built a model abbey near Aachen and he encouraged monastic reform. He also patronised many of the scholars of the Carolingian renaissance.

E.S. Duckett, *Carolingian Portraits* (1962); F.L. Ganshof, 'Louis the Pious reconsidered', *History*, lxii (1957).

Lewis, Clive Staples (1898–1963) Novelist and Devotional Writer. Lewis was born in Belfast, Northern Ireland, and during the course of his career as a teacher of English Literature, he held chairs at both Oxford and Cambridge Universities. He is primarily remembered for his Narnia books, which are allegorical children's novels, and for his works of simple theology. In particular, his *Screwtape Letters* (imaginary letters from a senior to a junior devil), his *Mere Christianity* and his *Letters to Malcolm Chiefly on Prayer* are still read. Late in life, he married Joy Davidman, an American divorcee. His reaction to her early death from cancer is agonisingly recorded in *A Grief Observed* which was later turned into a successful Hollywood film. Lewis himself has been criticised as theologically naive and as patronising towards women. None the less his books remain popular.

C.S. Lewis, *Surprised by Joy* (1955); A. Arnott, *The Secret Country of C.S. Lewis* (1974); R.L. Green and W. Hooper, C.S. *Lewis: A Biography* (1974); A.N. Wilson, *C.S. Lewis* (1990).

Li, Florence (twentieth century) Order Founder. Li served as an Anglican Deaconess in Macao. During the Second World War, while the Japanese occupied Hong Kong, it was nearly impossible for an ordained priest to bring the Sacrament to the people of Macao. In response to this extreme situation, the Bishop of Hong Kong ordained Li a priest – the first woman priest ever in the Anglican Communion. He was criticised for his action by the Lambeth Conference and after the war was over, Li agreed to retire from the priesthood. None the less her ordination was an important precedent and, since 1971, Anglican Churches throughout the world have started accepting women as priests. Despite considerable opposition, including the threat of schism, in an historical vote of the General Synod in 1992, the Church of England itself agreed to ordain women on equal terms with men.

R.B. Edwards, *The Case for Women's Ministry*

(1989); M. Furlong, *Feminine in the Church* (1984).

Liddell, Eric (1902–45) Athlete and Missionary. Liddell was born in Tientsin, China, and was educated at the University of Edinburgh. He was an outstanding runner and an Olympic gold medallist. Subsequently he returned to China to join the staff of the Anglo-Chinese Christian College. He was interned by the Japanese during the Second World War and he died of a brain tumour in the inhumane conditions of the camp. He has become well known as a result of a highly successful film, *Chariots of Fire*. This tells the story of how he refused to run in the race for which he had trained because the race took place on a Sunday and he was a strong believer in Sabbath observance. In the event, another athlete offered to change places with him; he ran a much longer race, but virtue was rewarded and he won anyway.

C. Swift, *Eric Liddell: God's Athlete* (1986); D.P. Thompson, *Eric Liddell: Athlete and Missionary* (1970).

Liddon, Henry Parry (1829–90) Theologian and Historian. Liddon was born in London, and was educated at the University of Oxford. A committed high churchman, he became a Canon of St Paul's Cathedral where he was known as one of the most powerful preachers of his day. He was conservative in his theology, as was illustrated in his Bampton lectures on *The Divinity of Our Lord and Saviour Jesus Christ* and he was distressed by the publication of *Lux Mundi*, edited by fellow high churchman Charles GORE. Today he is mainly remembered for his monumental four-volume biography of the Tractarian E.B. PUSEY.

J.O. Johnston, *Life and Letters of Henry Parry Liddon* (1904).

Lightfoot, Joseph Barber (1828–89) Bishop, Historian and Theologian.

Lightfoot was born in Liverpool, England, and was educated at the University of Cambridge, where he was a student of B.F. WESTCOTT. He had a distinguished career as first Hulsean and then Lady Margaret Professor of Divinity. In 1879 he was consecrated Bishop of Durham. Today he is primarily remembered for his New Testament scholarship. He wrote commentaries on St PAUL's Epistles to the Galatians, Philippians and Colossians with PHILEMON. In addition, he produced work on CLEMENT OF ROME and IGNATIUS and he defended the historicity of the Christian religion in nine famous articles in the *Contemporary Review*.

G.R. Eden and M.C. Macdonald (eds), *Lightfoot of Durham* (1931).

Lilburne, John (?1614–57) Rebel. Lilburne was born of an interesting family. His father was one of the last people in England to demand settlement by single combat in a civil suit and his brother, Robert, was one of the signatories of the death warrant of King CHARLES I. He was born in Greenwich, England, and, as a young man, was whipped and pilloried for circulating unlicensed books. He is remembered as the most prominent of the Levellers, a radical party of the Commonwealth period. The Levellers demanded that sovereignty be transferred to the House of Commons and that the House be elected by universal suffrage. They also campaigned for freedom of religion and equality before the law. Eventually most of the party leaders were arrested. Lilburne himself was banished in 1652 and, when he returned to England, he was put on trial and imprisoned until 1655. He was released after it was known he had converted to Quakerism and would cause no more trouble. He was the author of *The Case of the Army Truly Stated*, which was published in 1647. After 1651, the Levellers ceased to be a significant political force.

J. Frank, *The Levellers: A History of the Writings of Three Seventeenth-Century Social Democrats, John Lilburne, Richard Overton and William Walwyn* (1955); P.E. Gregg, *Free-Born John: A Biography of John Lilburne* (1961).

Lingard, John (1771–1851) Historian and Devotional Writer. Lingard was born in Winchester into a Roman Catholic family. He was educated at the English College at Douai and at Crook Hall, Durham. He was ordained a priest in 1795. He is remembered for his eight-volume *History of England*, which tells the story from a Catholic viewpoint. As the historian Thomas Macaulay put it, he worked from the first principle that any Protestant opinion must, by definition, be wrong. It was much approved by the Roman Catholic hierarchy and there is some evidence that Lingard was created a Cardinal in 1826. Subsequently he produced *A New Version of the Four Gospels* which was based on the Greek original rather than on St JEROME's Vulgate text.

M. Haile, *Life and Letters of John Lingard, 1771–1851* (1911); D. Shea, *The English Ranke: John Lingard* (1969).

Linzey, Andrew (b. 1952) Theologian. Linzey was born in Oxford, England, and was educated at the University of London. An ordained priest of the Church of England, he is known for his championing of the rights of animals. In his *Christianity and the Rights of Animals*, he argued that 'Spirit-filled, breathing creatures, composed of flesh and blood, are subjects of inherent value to God' and 'where we speak of animal rights, we conceptualize what is objectively owed to animals as a matter of justice by virtue of their Creator's right'. Going on from this, in his later work, he has maintained that humanity should do more than respect the rights of animals; given animal vulnerability, they should be morally generous. Linzey is standing against the entrenched Christian humano-centric attitude towards animals (as exemplified by THOMAS AQUINAS who argued that animals are created solely for the use of man). None the less, there is no doubt that his view is gaining ground within the Churches.

Andrew Linzey, *Animal Theology* (1984); T. Regan, *The Case for Animal Rights* (1988); K. Thomas, *Man and the Natural World: A History of Modern Sensibility* (1983).

Lipsius, Richard Adelbert (1830–92) Theologian. Lipsius was educated at the University of Leipzig and spent much of his career as Professor of Systematic Theology at the University of Jena. He is remembered for his attempt at reconciling the principles of scientific and religious method. He insisted that it was through science that the externals of the empirical world were understood, but it was through the religious experience of God as unity that a true understanding could be found. His works included *Die Apokryphen Apostelgeschichten und Apostellegenden*, an edition of the apocryphal New Testament material, *Lehrbuch der Evangelisch-Protestantischen Dogmatik* and *Philosophie und Religion*.

H. Weinel, *Richard Adelbert Lipsius* (1930) [no English translation available].

Liudhart (d. *c.* 602) Saint. Liudhart was the chaplain of Queen BERTHA of Kent. He is thought to have done much to prepare the King and Queen for the mission of St AUGUSTINE OF CANTERBURY.

M. Deansley, *Augustine of Canterbury* (1964); H.D. Farmer (ed.), *The Oxford Dictionary of Saints*, 3rd edn (1992).

Livingstone, David (1813–73) Missionary. Livingstone was born in Blantyre, Scotland. He worked long hours in a factory as a child and he was largely self-educated. After a conversion experience at the age of seventeen, he studied theology and medicine in Glasgow. In 1841 he was sent to Africa as a medical missionary. He was a great traveller and is remembered for his historic journey across Africa, during the course of which he discovered (and named) the Victoria Falls. He was the author of *Missionary Travels and Researches in South Africa*, which aroused great enthusiasm for African mission in England. He also did much to expose the Arab slave trade. After 1870, it seemed as if he had disappeared. An American newspaper sent H.M. Stanley to find him. The two finally met in Ujiji, where Stanley is said to have made the famous introductory remark, 'Dr Livingstone, I presume . . .'.

J.I. Macnair, *Livingstone's Travels* (1954); G. Seaver, *David Livingstone: His Life and Letters* (1957); H.M. Stanley, *How I found Livingstone* (1872).

Locke, John (1632–1704) Philosopher. Locke was born in Wrington, England, and was educated at the University of Oxford. He is remembered as the author of the famous *Essay Concerning Human Understanding*, in which he argued that all knowledge is derived from ideas, which emerge either from self-awareness or from sense-experience. Thus he rejected the Platonism of many earlier philosophers as well as the radical doubt of DESCARTES. He also produced *The Reasonableness of Christianity* in which he maintained that reasonableness was the only correct basis for belief. This aroused the disapproval of Jonathan EDWARDS and paved the way for the later Deists. In his *Letters Concerning Toleration*, he made a plea for religious toleration for all (except for Roman Catholics and atheists, who were seen as a threat to religious stability). Locke was an important figure in the development of the English empirical philosophical tradition.

J. Yolton, *Locke: An Introduction* (1985); J. Dunn, *Locke* (1984).

Loisy, Alfred Firmin (1857–1940) Theologian. Loisy was born in Ambrières, France, and was educated at the

Institut Catholique in Paris. He was ordained to the priesthood in 1879 and, after serving in a parish, he returned to Paris where he worked on the critical study of Scripture. In 1893, he was dismissed from the Institut because he had ceased to believe in the inerrancy of the Bible. He became chaplain to the Dominican nuns of Neuilly and subsequently taught at the Ecole Pratique des Hautes Etudes. His best-known book, *L'Evangile et l'Eglise*, was published in 1902. This was intended as a response to HARNACK's *Wesen des Christentums* and it argued that Christianity was not based on the actual teachings of JESUS, but on the faith of the Catholic Church as developed by the Holy Spirit. It was condemned by the Archbishop of Paris and Pope PIUS X put it (and Loisy's later books) on the Index of Prohibited Books. In 1906 Loisy resigned his priestly functions and in 1908 he was excommunicated. He is remembered as the founder of Catholic Modernism in France and was in close touch with Baron VON HÜGEL. His later years were spent in teaching the history of religions at the Collège de France.

A.R.Vidler, *A Variety of Catholic Modernists* (1970); G. Daly, *Transcendence and Immanence* (1980); M.R. O'Connell, *Critics on Trial* (1994).

Longinus (first century) Legendary Saint. Longinus was the name given either to the soldier who pierced JESUS's side with a spear at the crucifixion, or to the centurion who declared 'Truly this man was the Son of God!' According to BEDE, he died a martyr's death.

D.H. Farmer (ed.), *The Oxford Dictionary of Saints*, 3rd edn (1992); R.J. Peebles, *The Legend of Longinus in Ecclesiastical Tradition and English Literature* (1911).

Longley, Charles Thomas (1794–1868) Archbishop. Longley had a distinguished career in the Church of England. After serving as headmaster of Harrow School, he was consecrated Bishop of

Ripon in 1836, Bishop of Durham in 1856, Archbishop of York in 1860 and Archbishop of Canterbury in 1862. He is remembered both as the Archbishop who proceeded against Bishop COLENSO and as the instigator of the Lambeth Conferences. These are regular assemblies of all the Bishops of the Anglican Communion, which take place every ten years.

A.M.G. Stevenson, *The First Lambeth Conference 1867* (1967).

Lopez, Gregory (1611–91) Bishop. Lopez was born A-Lou in Fogan, China. He was converted to Christianity and in 1651 he joined the Dominican Order. In 1656, under his new name, he was ordained a priest and in 1690 he became the first native Chinese to be consecrated a Bishop. He had initially been very reluctant to accept such preferment and no further native Chinese became a Bishop until 1918. He was sympathetic towards Matteo RICCI's attempt to explain Christianity in Chinese terms and his toleration of the Confucian practice of honouring ancestors. This was to anticipate later missionary strategy, but was condemned by Pope Clement XI early in the eighteenth century.

P.M. d'Elia, *The Catholic Mission in China* (1934).

Lossky, Vladimir (1903–58) Theologian. Lossky was educated at the University of St Petersburg, Russia, at Prague and at the Sorbonne. He had been expelled from Russia by the Soviet government in 1922 and he finally settled in Paris and the United States of America. He is remembered as a leading Orthodox theologian and as an opponent of the wisdom theology of BULGAKOV, who also settled in Paris. Among his works were *Essai sur la Théologie Mystique de l'Eglise d'Orient*, *Vision de Dieu* and *A l'Image et à la Ressemblance de Dieu*.

D. Ford, *The Modern Theologies* (1997); R. William, 'The via negativa and the foundations of theology: An introduction to the thought of V.N. Lossky', in S. Sykes and D. Holmes (eds), *New Studies in Theology I* (1980).

Lou Tseng-Tsiang (1871–1949) Politician and Theologian. Lou was born in Shanghai, China, and was educated in Shanghai and Peking. He was born into a Protestant family and he was baptised Jean-Jacques. He had a distinguished career as a diplomat, as Foreign Minister and from 1922 to 1927 he was Chinese Minister in Berne. He had converted to Roman Catholicism in 1911 and in 1926 he joined a Benedictine community near Bruges, in Belgium. As Dom Pierre Celestin Lou, he was made Abbot of St-Pierre-de-Grand. He is remembered as both a Christian statesman in China and one who saw Christianity as the fulfilment of traditional Chinese religions. His *Souvenirs et Pensées* was translated as *Ways of Confucius and of Christ*.

E. Neut, *Jean-Jacques Lou, Dom Lou* (1962).

Louis IX (1214–70) Monarch and Saint. Louis IX was a grandson of King Philip II of France and he inherited the throne at the age of twelve. In French history he is often regarded as the ideal king. He was intensely pious and he was committed to justice. He reformed the French administration; he controlled his nobles and he negotiated a fair treaty with King Henry III of England. He also was determined to free the Holy Land from Muslim domination and, to that end, he launched first the unsuccessful Seventh Crusade (when he was taken prisoner) and then the Eighth Crusade (during the course of which he died of dysentery). Today he is perhaps most frequently remembered as the builder of the Sainte-Chapelle in Paris, a masterpiece of gothic architecture, which was constructed to house the relic of JESUS's crown of thorns. He was

canonised by Pope BONIFACE VIII in 1297.

M.W. Labarge, *Louis IX* (1968).

Louis XIV (1638–1715) Monarch. Louis inherited the French throne while he was still a child and he did not begin his personal reign until 1661. At that point France was the most powerful nation in Europe. Louis centralised power around himself, building a huge palace at Versailles and extending the boundaries of France by war. In the history of Christianity, he is remembered for his determination that the French Church should be autonomous. To that end, he initially encouraged Bishop BOSSUET and the Gallican party. In addition, he persecuted the Jansenists and he revoked the Edict of Nantes, which had guaranteed toleration for Protestants. Thus Louis managed to ensure uniformity, to retain Catholicism, but, at the same time, to keep control of the Church within his realm.

W.F. Church (ed.), *The Greatness of Louis XIV: Myth or Reality* (1959); J.B. Wolf, *Louis XIV* (1968).

Lucaris, Cyril (1572–1638) Patriarch and Theologian. Lucaris was born in Crete and was educated in Verona and Padua. He became Patriarch of Alexandria in 1601, after serving the Orthodox Church for a time in Poland. This experience seems to have turned him against Roman Catholicism and both in Alexandria and Constantinople (where he succeeded in 1620), he showed decided favour towards the Protestant Churches. He maintained good relations with several Protestant leaders: his own theology was influenced by that of CALVIN and he encouraged the translation of the Bible into the vernacular for his own people. As Patriarch, he was deposed several times, but was restored largely through the intervention of the British and the Dutch. However, in 1638 he was put to death on the order of the Sultan Murad. Lucaris's theology was finally condemned within the Orthodox Church at the Synod of Jerusalem in 1672.

G.A. Hadjiantoniou, *Protestant Patriarch: The Life of Cyril Lucaris* (1961).

Lucian of Antioch (*c*. 240–312)   Educator, Saint and Martyr. Lucian was a native of Samosata and served as a presbyter in Antioch. He became head of the theological school at Antioch and his students included ARIUS and EUSEBIUS OF NICOMEDIA. He seems to have taught that although Christ was pre-existent, he did not exist from all eternity. Thus Lucian has been described as the father of Arianism. He was opposed to the allegorical interpretation of the Bible and he produced an important text of the Scriptures, known as the Lucian version. He died a martyr's death in Nicomedia.

D.H. Farmer (ed.), *The Oxford Dictionary of Saints*, 3rd edn (1992); B.M. Metzger, 'The Lucianic recension of the Greek Bible', in *Chapters in the History of New Testament Criticism* (1963).

Lucifer of Cagliari (d. *c*. 370)   Bishop, Theologian, and Sect Founder. Lucifer was Bishop of Cagliari and an envoy of Pope Liberius to the Emperor Constantius asking for a Council. This took place in Milan in 355. Because he refused to condemn ATHANASIUS, he was exiled by the Emperor. On his release, he consecrated Paulinus as Bishop of Antioch, thus creating a schism within the Church at Antioch.

E.A Livingstone (ed.), *The Oxford Dictionary of the Christian Church*, revised edition (1997).

Lucius (? second century)   Legendary King. As King of Britain, Lucius is said to have asked Pope Eleutherus for Christian missionaries to his people. He is said to have died in Gloucester and even to have been the son of SIMON OF CYRENE

and a student of TIMOTHY. Although he is mentioned by BEDE, there is no historical evidence for his existence.

V. Berther, 'Der H. Lucius', *Zeitschrift der Schweizerischen Kirchengeschichte*, xxxii (1938) [no English translation available].

Lucy (d. *c*. 303)   Saint. Lucy was martyred in the Diocletian persecutions. She is said to have demonstrated her Christianity by giving all her possessions to the poor; she was then denounced to the authorities by her fiancé. She was a popular saint in the early Church.

D.H. Farmer (ed.), *The Oxford Dictionary of Saints*, 3rd edn (1992).

Ludlow, John Malcolm Forbes (1821–1911)   Philanthropist and Educator. Ludlow was educated in France and then returned to England for legal training. A friend of F.D. MAURICE, he was in Paris during the 1848 Revolution and he declared in a letter 'the new socialism must be Christianised'. With Maurice, he edited the journal *Politics for the People* and later, by himself, the *Christian Socialist*. Today he is remembered as the founder of the Christian Socialist movement. He was involved in the setting up of the Working Men's College in London and he taught there for many years. Throughout his life, he was convinced that political emancipation must be accompanied by spiritual education and, as a result of his work, many of the clergy became interested in social welfare issues.

J.F.C. Harrison, *A History of the Working Men's College, 1854–1954* (1954); N.C. Masterman, *John Malcolm Ludlow* (1963); A.R. Vidler, *F.D. Maurice and Company* (1966).

Ludolf of Saxony (*c*. 1300–78)   Devotional Writer. Little is known of the life of Ludolf. He was a Carthusian monk in Strasbourg, Germany; he became Prior of the Charterhouse of Coblenz in 1343 and he retired to Mainz in 1348. His *Vita*

Christi, which was a meditation on the life of JESUS CHRIST, was highly popular. It has been frequently translated and has gone through many editions. It includes prayers, moral maxims and commentaries by the Church Fathers; among many others, IGNATIUS LOYOLA knew it and was influenced by it.

M.I. Bodenstedt, *The Vita Christi of Ludolfus the Carthusian* (1955).

Luis of Granada (1504–88) Devotional Writer and Mystic. Luis was born Luis Sarriá in Granada, Spain. He joined the Dominican Order in 1525 and, after studying in Valladolid, he spent eleven years in Córdoba restoring a dilapidated convent and reading mystical works. In 1547 he became Prior of Badajoz. For much of the rest of his life, he lived in Portugal, where he was elected Provincial of the Order. A follower of JOHN OF AVILA, he was a famous preacher in his day and he was the confessor of Queen Catherine and the Duke of Alva. Today he is remembered for his books of spiritual guidance, particularly his *Libro de la Oración y Meditación* and his *Guía de Pecadores*. In these he stressed the importance of the inward life. Through the practice of virtue, he believed that the individual could be liberated from the burden of sin and his life would be illumined by the influx of the Holy Spirit. These works were widely read and they influenced among others FRANCIS OF SALES and VINCENT DE PAUL.

E.A. Peers, *Studies of the Spanish Mystics,* Vol 1 (1927); R.L. Oeschslin, *Louis of Granada* (1962).

Luke (first century) Historian, Missionary and Saint. According to IRENAEUS and TERTULLIAN, Luke was the author of the Third Gospel and the Acts of the Apostles. He seems to have accompanied St PAUL on some of his missionary journeys (since the pronoun used is 'we') and, according to the Epistle to the Colossians, he was a physician.

According to good Church tradition, he was a Gentile and a member of the Church at Antioch. Later tradition has it that he died unmarried at the age of eighty-four; that he was a painter who painted a portrait of the Virgin MARY and that he was one of the unnamed disciples to whom the risen JESUS appeared on the road to Emmaus. From the internal evidence of Luke and Acts, the author was a careful historian, who wrote in idiomatic Greek and who insisted that the salvation offered in Christ was available to everyone – Gentile as well as Jew, woman as well as man, the outcast as well as the Pharisee. It is from the Third Gospel that we have the stories of the miraculous births of both JOHN THE BAPTIST and JESUS, the visit of the shepherds and Jesus's encounter with the wise men of the Temple at the age of twelve.

C.K. Barrett, *Luke the Historian in Recent Study* (1961); B.M. Metzger and M.D. Coogan (eds), *The Oxford Companion to the Bible* (1993).

Lull, Ramón (*c.* 1232–*c.* 1316) Missionary, Mystic and Philosopher. Lull was born in Majorca and was educated as a knight. At the age of thirty he had a religious experience and was determined to dedicate the rest of his life to the conversion of the Muslims and Jews. To this end he learnt Arabic. In 1276 he organised the setting up of a Franciscan monastery in which the friars could study Arabic and prepare for missionary work. Then, from 1287, he travelled constantly around Europe raising support for his projects and he also made three missionary journeys to North Africa. He wrote a huge number of books including his *Ars Generalis Ultima* which showed strong neo-Platonist leanings. As a mystic, he defended the doctrine of the Immaculate Conception and he is today appreciated as a forerunner of TERESA OF AVILA and JOHN OF THE CROSS.

E.A. Peers, *Ramón Lull: A Biography* (1929); J.N. Hillgarth, *Ramón Lull and Lullism in Fourteenth Century France* (1971).

Luther, Martin (1483–1546) Theologian and Denomination Founder. Luther was born in Eisleben, Germany, and was educated at the University of Leipzig. According to his own account, he became a monk to fulfil a vow made in a terrified moment during a thunderstorm. He was ordained a priest in 1507 and moved to Wittenberg where he continued to study at the university. He was subsequently appointed to a Chair in Bible Studies there. The turning point of his career came in 1517. In order to finance the building of the basilica of St Peter in Rome, Pope LEO X had licensed the sale of Indulgences. On 31 October Luther nailed on to the door of Wittenberg Church ninety-five theses against this practice. The ecclesiastical authorities hoped to silence the protest, but Luther refused to recant and converted others, such as Martin BUCER, to his position. Under the protection of Elector FREDERICK III of Saxony, he fled from Wittenberg. In 1519, in a formal debate with Johann ECK, he went so far as to deny the primacy of the Pope and the infallibility of General Councils. In 1521 he was summoned to the Diet of Worms, but again he refused to recant and was declared an outlaw; he had already, earlier in the year, been excommunicated. He continued to be protected by Frederick and he returned to Wittenberg in 1522, from where he directed the new movement. During the Peasants' Revolt of 1524–5, he urged the princes to put down the rebellion, thus ensuring the support of the German secular authorities. In 1524 he finally discarded the religious habit and the following year he married Katharina von Bora, who had herself been a nun. Among his many books were *An den Christlichen Adel Deutscher Nation*, in which he urged the German princes to embark on the reform of the Church themselves; *De Captivitate Babylonica Ecclesiae*, in which he argued that only Baptism and the Eucharist were true Sacraments; and *Von der Freiheit eines Christenmenschen*, in which he proclaimed the doctrine of justification by faith alone. Among his other writings were a magnificent translation of the Bible into German; a stream of pamphlets against particular church abuses; *De Servo Arbitrio*, which was a response to ERASMUS's *De Libero Arbitrio*; a small and a large catechism intended to propagate his teaching among the people and a bitter diatribe against the Papacy, *Wider das Papsttum zu Rom, vom Teufel Gestiftet*. He himself was a conservative by temperament. Although he abolished many Catholic practices, he strongly disapproved of the Anabaptists and he disagreed with ZWINGLI's understanding of the Eucharist. His own liturgical writings retained many of the old patterns, although his talents as a writer of German prose and poetry (particularly in his Bible translation and his famous hymn 'Ein' Feste Burg') did much to develop the modern German language. His own theological position was expressed in the *Augsburg Confession* of 1530. He stressed that scripture must be seen as the sole rule of belief and that justification was by faith alone. Churches which describe themselves as Lutheran may have episcopal, congregational or presbyterian organisation; what they share is a strong Christocentric theology. It is through faith in the redemptive death and resurrection of JESUS, that salvation is to be found, as is revealed in Scripture. Today Lutheran churches can be found all over the world, with the highest concentration in Germany, Scandinavia and the United States of America.

J. Bodensieck (ed.), *The Encyclopaedia of the Lutheran Church*, 3 vols (1965); A.G. Dickens, *Martin Luther and the Reformation* (1967); H.G. Haile, *Luther: A Biography* (1981).

Luwum, Janani (1922–77) Bishop and Martyr. Luwum was born in Mucwini, Acholi, Uganda. His parents were converts to Christianity and he himself was ordained in the Anglican Church in 1955.

He was consecrated Bishop of North Uganda in 1969 and Archbishop of Uganda, Rwanda, Burundi and Boga-Zaire in 1974. During the tyrannical regime of Idi Amin in Uganda, Luwum tried to co-ordinate Church protests with the Roman Catholics and made every effort to protect his people. However, in 1977, at a Bishops' meeting, he was taken outside and shot. He is generally regarded as a modern martyr for the faith.

P. Mutibwa, *Uganda Since Independence* (1992).

Lyell, Charles (1797–1875) Geologist. Lyell was born in Forfarshire, Scotland, and he was educated at the University of Oxford. As a young man he travelled a great deal which gave him the opportunity to study rock formation. In 1823 he was made Secretary of the Geological Society and he was elected a Fellow of the Royal Society in 1826. He is remembered for his *Principles of Geology*, published between 1830 and 1833 and which went through many editions. Inevitably his findings called into question the traditional Mosaic cosmogeny that the world was created in 4004 BC. Later Lyell was to be a firm supporter of DARWIN's views on the transmutation of species. At that period, the Church was still teaching that the creation story in the Book of Genesis was literal historical truth; both the *Principles* and the *Origin of Species* were highly disturbing to that comfortable view.

E. Bailey, *Charles Lyell* (1962); L.G. Wilson, *Charles Lyell: The Years to 1841: Revolution in Geology* (1972).

M

Macarius (d. c. 333) Saint and Bishop. Macarius was Bishop of Jerusalem and a strong opponent of the doctrines of ARIUS. He was present at the Council of Nicaea where he is thought to have played an important part in the drafting of the Creed. He may also have been in conflict with EUSEBIUS OF CAESAREA over the primacy of the See of Jerusalem over that of Caesarea. Today he is remembered for his part in the building of the Church of the Holy Sepulchre after St HELENA's discovery of the True Cross.

C. Coüason, *The Church of the Holy Sepulchre in Jerusalem* (1974); A.P. Stanley, *History of the Eastern Church*, revised edition (1974).

Macarius of Egypt (d. c. 390) Mystic, Saint and Order Founder. Macarius was an ascetic who founded a monastery in Upper Egypt, which was to become an important centre. His activities are described by PALLADIUS. Since the sixteenth century, he is thought to have been the author of fifty homilies, a mystical (and arguably heretical) work. Today many scholars doubt this ascription. Another miracle-working, ascetic Macarius is known as Macarius of Alexandria or Macarius the Younger. The Alexandrian Macarius may have been the author of a monastic Rule of thirty regulations.

C. Butler, *The Lausiac History of Palladius*, Vol. 2 (1904); E.A. Livingstone (ed.), *The Oxford Dictionary of the Christian Church*, revised edition (1997); G.L. Marriott, 'The Messalians and the discovery of their ascetic book', *Harvard Theological Review*, xix (1926).

Macarius of Moscow (1816–82) Theologian, Historian and Metropolitan. Macarius was born Michael Bulgakov and was educated at Kurst and Kiev. He became Bishop of Tamboy in 1857, Bishop of Kharkov in 1859, Bishop of Vilna in 1868 and Metropolitan of Moscow in 1879. He was the author of two works of dogmatic theology, which reflect mainstream Russian Orthodox thought of the nineteenth century. He also produced an important twelve-volume history of the Russian Church.

T. Titor, *Russian Life*, 2 vols (1895–8) [no English translation available].

Macdonald, George (1824–1905) Poet and Novelist. Macdonald was born in Aberdeenshire, Scotland, and was educated at King's College, Aberdeen, and Highbury Theological College. He became a minister of the Congregational Church, but after serving a congregation in Sussex, his (slightly) unorthodox views induced him to leave the ministry in 1853. Subsequently he earned a living by writing and teaching. He was the author of several novels set in Scotland, popular children's books such as *The Princess and Curdie* and religious fiction such as *Phantasies*. Although he is no longer widely read, his work had a considerable influence on C.S. LEWIS, who always maintained that it was Macdonald's books that persuaded him that goodness need not be dull.

J. Johnson, *George Macdonald: A Biographical and Critical Appreciation* (1906); C.S. Lewis, *George Macdonald: An Anthology* (1946); G. Macdonald, *George Macdonald and his Wife* (1924).

Macedonius (d. *c.* 362) Bishop and possible Sect Founder. Macedonius was Bishop of·Constantinople. He seems to have supported the Semi-Arians at the Council of Seleucia in 359 and was subsequently deposed in 360. He is remembered as the founder of the Pneumatomachi sect, which denied the full godhead of the Holy Spirit. Although they were described as the Macedonians, today most scholars believe that Macedonius had died before the sect emerged.

E.A. Livingstone (ed.), *The Oxford Dictionary of the Christian Church*, revised edition (1997).

Mack, Alexander (1679–1735) Sect Founder. Mack was born in Schriesheim, Germany, of humble parents. After a time spent accompanying the Pietist E.C. Hochmann von Hochenau, he moved to Schwarzenau. There he set up the first Church of the New Baptists or Brethren. As a result of their Anabaptist inclinations, they were persecuted in Germany and eventually, under Mack's leadership, they settled in Pennsylvania in America. Mack was the author of *Basic Questions* and *Rights and Ordinances*, which outlined the principles of the new community. In 1871 the group took the title German Baptist Brethren. Today they are known as the Church of the Brethren and have about two hundred thousand members. They are known for their pacifism and sober way of life.

D.F. Durnbaugh (ed.), *European Origins of the Brethren* (1959); H.A. Kent, *250 Years Conquering Frontiers: A History of the Brethren Church* (1958).

Mackintosh, Hugh Ross (1870–1936) Theologian. Mackintosh was educated at the Universities of Edinburgh, Freiburg and Marburg. He was ordained into the ministry of the Church of Scotland and, after several years serving a congregation, he was appointed to a Chair of Systematic Theology at Edinburgh. In 1932, he was elected Moderator of the General Assembly of the Church of Scotland. He is remembered for his *Doctrine of the Person of Christ*, which clearly showed the influence of German Protestant theology and his *Types of Modern Theology*, published after his death.

J.W. Leitch, *A Theology of Transition: H.R. Mackintosh as an Approach to Barth* (1952).

McPherson, Aimee Semple (1890–1944) Missionary and Sect Founder. McPherson was born Aimee Kennedy in Canada. She experienced an evangelical conversion through the preaching of Robert J. Semple and she subsequently married him. Together they went as missionaries to China where he swiftly died of malaria. On her return with her new baby to Canada, she married Harold McPherson, whom she eventually divorced. McPherson was arguably the most famous evangelist of her day. She preached throughout the United States and by 1922 she had built the huge Angelus Temple in Los Angeles, California. There she taught her 'four-square gospel' of JESUS CHRIST, the baptism of the Holy Spirit and the expectation of the Second Coming. In 1922 she preached what was probably the first radio sermon and in 1927 her chuch became formally known as the International Church of the Four-Square Gospel. Today it is one of the best known of the Pentecostalist Churches; it has over seven hundred congregations and more than a hundred thousand members. After an eventful life (on one occasion she claimed to have been kidnapped), McPherson died of a heart attack after a visit to the Holy Land.

K. Kendrick, *The Promise Fulfilled: A History of the Modern Pentecostalist Movement* (1961); A.S. McPherson, *This is That: Personal Experiences: Sermons and Writings* (1923); J.T. Nichol, *Pentecostalism* (1966).

Macquarrie, John (b. 1919) Theologian. Macquarrie was educated at the University of Glasgow, Scotland. After serving in a parish, he returned to teach at Glasgow. Subsequently he held a Chair in Systematic Theology at the Union Theological Seminary, New York, and he was appointed Lady Margaret Professor of Divinity at Oxford in 1970. Initially influenced by existentialism, he translated HEIDEGGER's *Being and Time* into English. Among his other works are *Principles of Christian Theology, In Search of Deity* and *Jesus Christ in Modern Thought*. He is known as an academic theologian whose work remains accessible to the ordinary Christian lay-person.

John Macquarrie, *The Faith of the People of God: A Lay Theology* (1972).

Macrina (*c.* 328–*c.* 380) Saint and Order Founder. Macrina was born in Cappadocia and she was the elder sister of BASIL and GREGORY OF NYSSA. She exerted considerable influence on her brothers, particularly on Basil, and she also founded an order of women ascetics. We owe our knowledge of her to Gregory's *Vita Macrinae Junioris*. (She was known as Macrina Junior to distinguish her from her grandmother, another saintly Macrina.)

W.K.L. Clarke (ed.), *Life of Macrina Junior* (1916).

Magnus (d. 1116) Saint and Martyr. Magnus was the Earl of Orkney, Scotland. After a short career as a pirate, he was converted to Christianity. Captured by the King of Norway, he escaped to the court of King Malcolm III of Scotland. There he led a life of penance and austerity. Eventually he returned to rule Orkney, but was killed by his cousin Haakon. He died heroically, praying for his enemies. Although he was executed for political reasons, he was regarded as a martyr and became an important Scottish saint. In particular, he is said to have appeared in 1314 in a vision to Robert Bruce, promising him victory in the Battle of Bannockburn.

D.H. Farmer (ed.), *The Oxford Dictionary of Saints*, 3rd edn (1992); J. Mooney, *St Magnus, Earl of Orkney* (1935).

Major, Georg (1502–74) Theologian. Major was a professor at the University of Wittenberg. He aroused the wrath of the Lutheran Matthias FLACIUS by arguing that good works were necessary for salvation. The Reformers, headed by Nicholas von Amsdorf, a close friend of LUTHER, were insistent that salvation was by faith alone. Amsdorf indeed went so far as to argue that good works were positively harmful. Ultimately the Formula of Concord of 1577 maintained that although a Christian was, in fact, sure to do good works, his salvation was entirely independent of them.

A.E. McGrath, *Reformation Thought: An Introduction* (1988).

Malachy (1094–1148) Saint and Archbishop. Malachy was Archbishop of Armagh, Ireland. He became a close friend of BERNARD OF CLAIRVAUX who later wrote his biography. After staying with Bernard, he was determined to establish his order in Ireland and the first Cistercian monastery was built in Mellifont, County Louth, in 1142. He was involved in the struggle to bring the traditional Celtic Church under the supervision of Rome. To this end, he made two journeys to Rome to receive the pallium, the traditional sign of office. He died in Clairvaux before he could complete the second journey. The *Prophecies of Malachy*, which supposedly gave a suitable motto for every future Pope, was a later document and, despite its ascription, had no connection with Malachy.

A. Gwynn, 'St Malachy of Armagh', in *Irish Ecclesiastical Record*, lxx (1948), lxxi (1949); H.J. Lawlor, *St Malachy of Armagh* (1920).

Mamertus (d. *c.* 475) Saint, Archbishop and Liturgist. Mamertus was Archbishop of Vienne and the elder brother of the neo-Platonist theologian Claudianus

Mamertus. His diocese was disturbed by various volcanic eruptions and he is remembered for instituting special prayers for protection from such dangers on the days before Ascension Day. These were to become Rogation Days, which were days sets apart in the Church calendar for intercession. The Major Rogation was on 25 April and Minor Rogations were the three days before Ascension Day. They survived in the Roman Catholic Church until 1969.

F.L. Cross (ed.), 'Rogation days', in *The Oxford Dictionary of the Christian Church*, 2nd edn (1974).

Mani (216–276/7)   Sect Founder. Mani was born into an aristocratic family in South Babylon. In 204, he embarked on a mission, preaching throughout the Persian Empire and even spending time in India. During the reigns of King Shapur I and Hormizd I, he enjoyed royal protection, but, with the accession of Bahram I, he was imprisoned and eventually executed. His religious system was dualistic. The two forces, light and darkness, God and matter, were eternal. Particles of light had been imprisoned by darkness and JESUS, the Buddha, the Prophets and Mani himself had been sent to help release the light. In order to contribute to the process, the Manichaean believer embarked on a hierarchical life of austerity. AUGUSTINE OF HIPPO was one of several Christian theologians who wrote against these doctrines. The Manichaeans were much persecuted, but none the less Manichaean documents have survived in Coptic, Greek, Persian and even Chinese. Scholars disagree as to the extent of Buddhist, Christian and Gnostic elements within Manichaeism and also as to the extent of its influence on later heresies such as that of the Bogomiles of the tenth-century Balkans and the Albigensians of late twelfth-century France. Recently an early biography of Mani himself has been discovered in Egypt which fills in the details of his early life.

S. Lieu, *Manichaeism* (1985); L.J.R. Ort, *Mani* (1967).

Manning, Henry Edward (1808–92) Archbishop and Philanthropist. Manning was the youngest son of a member of the British Parliament. He was educated at the University of Oxford and subsequently entered the Anglican ministry. In 1841 he was appointed Archdeacon of Chichester. He was influenced by the Oxford Movement and contributed to the *Tracts for the Times*. After the GORHAM judgement, he felt he could no longer remain within the Church of England and he converted to Roman Catholicism. He was ordained a priest and in 1865 he was consecrated Archbishop of Westminster. An authoritarian by temperament, he was a strong supporter of the doctrine of papal infallibility and he was made a Cardinal in 1875. He is remembered for his work among the poor of London and for his support of the dockers in their strike of 1889.

R. Gray, *Cardinal Manning* (1985); D. Newsome, *The Convert Cardinals: John Henry Newman and Henry Edward Manning* (1993).

Marcellus (d. *c.* 374)   Bishop and Theologian. Marcellus was Bishop of Ancyra in Anatolia. He was the author of a treatise directed against the teachings of Asterius, EUSEBIUS OF NICOMEDIA and EUSEBIUS OF CAESAREA. He was a determined supporter of the 'homoousion' (of the same substance) formula of the Council of Nicaea, but he seems to have thought that the persons of the Trinity only became independent for the duration of the incarnation. In consequence he was deposed from his See in 336, restored temporarily and then deposed again. To combat his position, the clause 'Whose Kingdom shall have no end' was put into the Nicene Creed. A letter he wrote to Pope Julius I also survives. It contains the oldest Greek text of the Old Roman Creed, an earlier version of the Apostles' Creed.

J.N.D. Kelly, *Early Christian Creeds* (1950).

Marcion (second century)   Heretic and
Sect Founder. Marcion was a native of
Pontus. He was a shipbuilder by trade
and he had settled in Rome by 140. After
he was excommunicated by the Church,
he set up an alternative movement which
spread to many parts of the Roman Empire. Marcion taught that there was no
continuity between the God of the Hebrew Scriptures and the God revealed as
the Father of JESUS CHRIST. The Jewish
God was an inferior being who had created the physical world, but who had no
spiritual understanding. Marcion recognised only the Epistles of St PAUL and the
Gospel of LUKE (all carefully edited) as
canonical. His own writings, none of
which have survived, included the *Anti-
theses*, which contrasted flesh and spirit,
law and gospel, slavery and freedom.
His theology was attacked by TERTUL-
LIAN, IRENAEUS, CLEMENT OF ALEX-
ANDRIA and ORIGEN, among others,
but his movement survived for several
centuries. Today he is primarily remembered as the one who compelled the
Church to decide which Scriptures were
canonical. The short introductory pro-
logues which are found in many manuscripts of JEROME's Vulgate are generally agreed to have come from Mar-
cionite circles.

E.C. Blackman, *Marcion and his Influence* (1948).

Marcus (second century)   Heretic and
Sect Founder. Marcus was a follower of
VALENTINUS. According to IRENAEUS,
he used magic to deceive gullible women
and he taught that by calculating the
numerical value of God's names, all sorts
of esoteric wisdom could be found. His
followers formed an independent sect in
the Rhone valley. They had their own
forms of baptism and regarded the Gospel of THOMAS as canonical. The group
survived into the fourth century.

F.C. Burkitt, *Church and Gnosis* (1932).

Margaret [Marina] of Antioch (late
second/early third century)   Saint and
Martyr. Little is known of Margaret, although someone of that name seems to
have suffered in the Diocletian persecutions. Many legends surround her, including that she jumped off a building to
preserve her virginity (the same tale is
told of St PELAGIA). Hers was one of the
voices heard by JOAN OF ARC; she is frequently portrayed leading a dragon and
she has recently been included among the
fourteen Auxiliary Saints – as a patron of
childbirth.

D.H. Farmer (ed.), *The Oxford Dictionary of Saints*,
3rd edn (1992).

Margaret of Scotland (*c.* 1045–93)
Queen and Saint. Margaret was the
grand-daughter of King Edmund Iron-
side of England and the wife of King
Malcolm III of Scotland. She was famous
for her piety and charity. She was determined that the Scottish Church should
follow the practices of Rome and, under
her guidance, many reforms took place.
Her biography was written by Turgot,
Bishop of St Andrews, and records both
her public successes and her private aus-
terities. She was the mother of two Scottish kings and the great-grandmother of
King HENRY II of England. She was canonised in 1250, and remains an important saint in Scotland.

D.H. Farmer (ed.), *The Oxford Dictionary of
Saints*, 3rd edn (1992); A.J. Wilson, *St Margaret of
Scotland* (1993).

Margaret Beaufort, Lady (1443–1509)
Educational Patron. Margaret was the
daughter of the Duke of Somerset and
the wife first of the Earl of Richmond,
then of Lord Henry Stafford and finally
of the Earl of Derby. By her first husband
she was the mother of the first Tudor
king, Henry VII. Under the spiritual
guidance of John FISHER, she led a life
of piety and charity. Today she is remembered for her many educational
foundations. These include the Lady

Margaret Chairs of Divinity at the Universities of Oxford and Cambridge; Christ's College, Cambridge; and St John's College, Cambridge.

E.M.G. Routh, *Lady Margaret Beaufort* (1924).

Maritain, Jacques (1882–1973) Philosopher and Theologian. Maritain was born in Paris, of a Protestant family. He was educated at the Sorbonne and as a young man came under the influence of Henri BERGSON. However, in 1906, he converted to Roman Catholicism and he became an expert on the writings of THOMAS AQUINAS. For many years he continued to teach in Paris. Then in 1933 he moved to Toronto and between 1945 and 1948 he was the French Canadian Ambassador to the Vatican. From 1948 to 1956 he taught at Princeton University and, on his retirement, he joined the Community of the Little Brothers of Jesus in Toulouse. A prolific writer, he applied Thomist doctrines to metaphysics and to moral, political, educational and social philosophy. He even added a sixth to the traditional five ways to God's existence – arguing that intuition and self-consciousness pointed to a pre-personal existence with God.

Jacques Maritain, *The Countryman of Garonne* (1968) [English translation]; J. Macquarrie, *Twentieth Century Religious Thought* (1963).

Mark (first century) Disciple and Historian. Mark is identified with the author of the Second Gospel. He may have been the same person as John Mark, whose mother's house was a centre for the early Jerusalem Church and who accompanied PAUL and BARNABAS on the first missionary journey and, later, Barnabas on a preaching tour of Cyprus. Another (or maybe the same) Mark is mentioned in the Epistles to the Colossians, PHILEMON and TIMOTHY as a useful companion to St Paul. Also a Mark is with PETER in 'Babylon' in Peter's First Epistle. According to PAPIAS, Mark in his Gospel was

the 'interpreter of Peter' and EUSEBIUS OF CAESAREA recorded that he became the first Bishop of Alexandria. The Gospel is generally believed to have been the earliest of the four to be written and to have been known by both MATTHEW and LUKE. It has been suggested that the young man present at JESUS's arrest in the Garden of Gethsemane who ran away naked (an incident recorded only in the Second Gospel) was Mark himself.

R.P. Martin, *Mark: Evangelist and Theologian* (1972); B.M. Metzger and M.D. Coogan, *The Oxford Companion to the Bible* (1993).

'Marprelate, Martin' (1588–89) Polemicist. Marprelate was the pseudonymous author of eight scurrilous Puritan tracts, attacking the English episcopate. They caused a sensation and there was much conjecture as to their true authorship. They may have been produced in response to Archbishop WHITGIFT's insistence in 1586 that all publications must be approved by the Church authorities. Several churchmen, including the Bishop of Winchester, attempted to respond to them.

L.H. Carlson, *Martin Marprelate Gentleman: Master Job Throkmorton Laid open his Colours* (1981); D.J. McGinn, *John Penry and the Marprelate Controversy* (1966).

Marsden, Samuel (1764–1834) Missionary. Marsden was educated at the University of Cambridge, but, influenced by William WILBERFORCE, in 1794 he decided to go as a missionary to New South Wales, Australia. Initially he worked with Richard Johnson, but after Johnson returned to England in 1800, he was the only chaplain in the colony. Besides his pastoral duties, he became a successful farmer and a harsh magistrate. Under the auspices of the Church Missionary Society, he also organised a mission to New Zealand and he visited that colony seven times. He is a controversial figure in Australian history, but there is no doubt that he did much to establish the Anglican Church in the new country.

J.L. Nicholas, *Narrative of a Voyage to New Zealand ... in company with the Rev. Samuel Marsden*, 2 vols (1970).

Marsiglio [Marsilius] of Padua (*c.* 1275–1342) Political Philosopher. Marsiglio was a native of Padua, Italy, and was educated there and in Paris. He is remembered as the author of *Defensor Pacis* in which he argued that the Church must be subordinate to the State. He maintained that because JESUS himself submitted to the secular powers, the Papacy had no business to interfere in the temporal world. The Church's powers were of human origin, dating back to the Donation of CONSTANTINE. The State, on the other hand, was the unifying element in society and it derived its powers ultimately from the people, who had the right to depose an unjust ruler. This was a radical doctrine for the fourteenth century and, after Marsiglio was identified as the author, he was compelled to seek the protection of the Emperor. He was formally excommunicated in 1327 and, after a short period as Imperial Vicar of Rome (while the Emperor had seized the city), he lived quietly for the rest of his life in Munich.

E. Emerton, *The Defensor Pacis of Marsiglio of Padua: A Critical Study* (1920); N. Rubinstein, 'Marsilius of Padua and Italian political thought of his time', in J.R. Hale (ed.), *Europe in the Late Middle Ages* (1965).

Martensen, Hans Lassen (1808–84) Bishop and Theologian. Martensen was born in Flensburg, Denmark, and was educated at the University of Copenhagen where he became Professor of Systematic Theology in 1840. In 1854, he was consecrated Bishop of Zealand. He is remembered primarily for his *Den Christelige Dogmatik* and his *Den Christelige Ethik*. Influenced by SCHLEIERMACHER, HEGEL and the Roman Catholic thinker von Baader, he attempted to produce a synthesis between philosophy and theology, and religion and secular culture. He was a highly successful teacher and preacher. While he was a Bishop, he engaged in controversy with KIERKEGAARD, who insisted that there was no synthesis, but rather a radical gap, between reason and faith. He also wrote against both the Baptists and the Roman Catholics. Unusually for his time, he had some sympathy with the socialist aspirations of the Danish workers, but he was an authoritarian in religious matters and went so far as to insist on baptising the children of Baptists. In all he must be regarded as the most significant Danish churchman of his day.

Martensen's autobiographical reflections were published in Danish (1882/3) and translated into German, 3 vols (1883/4).

Martha (first century) Disciple and Saint. Martha was the sister of MARY and LAZARUS, with whom she lived in Bethany, Judaea. She appears on two occasions in the Gospels: firstly when she asked JESUS to make her sister help her with the domestic work and Jesus responded that Mary had chosen the better part in listening to the word of God and, secondly, when Lazarus was raised from the dead. Martha is thus regarded in the Christian tradition as the epitome of the busy woman who receives little thanks. According to later legend, she and her brother and sister founded churches in the south of France.

Luke 10:38–42; John, Chapter 11; D.H. Farmer (ed.), *The Oxford Dictionary of Saints*, 3rd edn (1992).

Martin of Tours (*c.* 335– *c.* 400) Saint, Order Founder and Bishop. Martin was born in Sabaria in what is now Hungary, to a pagan family. He joined the Roman army at the age of fifteen and it is during this period that he is said to have divided his cloak with a beggar. He was baptised after seeing a vision in which JESUS appeared wearing the half-cloak. He became a disciple of HILARY OF POITIERS and founded a monastery at Ligugé. It was a community of hermits and Martin lived quietly until he was appointed Bishop of Tours. He set himself to convert the unchurched of his diocese and to encourage the growth of monasticism. In 386 he pleaded unsuccessfully for the life of the heretic PRISCILLIAN who was subsequently executed by the Emperor. Martin himself left no writings, but his life was recorded by Sulpicius Severus and this volume was highly influential on later hagiography.

N.K. Chadwick, *Poetry and Letters in Early Christian Gaul* (1955); P. Monceaux, *St Martin* (1928); C. Stancliffe, *St Martin and his Hagiographer* (1983).

Martin I (d. 655)   Pope, Saint and Martyr. Martin was born in Tuscany, Italy. He was elected Pope in 649. Even before his election had been confirmed by the Eastern Emperor, Martin, with MAXIMUS THE CONFESSOR, had encouraged the condemnation of Monethelitism (the heresy that the God–Man possessed but a single will) at the Lateran Synod. Subsequently the Synod condemned the Emperor's 'Typos' which forbade discussion of both Monothelitism and Diothelitism (the orthodox opinion that the God–Man had both a divine and a human will). In consequence the Emperor tried to persuade his Exarch, Olympius, to arrest Martin. Olympius refused, but his successor Theodore Calliopias imprisoned him in Naxos and then brought him to Constantinople. There he was formally disgraced and banished. He died soon afterwards and is venerated within the Roman Catholic Church as a martyr.

J.N.D. Kelly (ed.), *The Oxford Dictionary of Popes* (1986).

Martin V (1368–1431)   Pope. Martin was born Otto Colonna. He was elected Pope at the Council of Constance in 1417 in an attempt to heal the Great Schism.

Gregory XII had abdicated in 1416; JOHN XXIII had been deposed the same year and BENEDICT XIII was deposed in 1417. The last possible claimant, Clement VIII finally submitted in 1429. Martin himself entered Rome in 1420 and during his reign he did much to restore the city. He is remembered for strengthening the power of the Papacy and for re-establishing its influence after the disastrous years of the Great Schism.

J.N.D. Kelly (ed.), *The Oxford Dictionary of Popes* (1986); P. Partner, *The Papal State under Martin V* (1958).

Martyn, Henry (1781–1812)   Missionary. Martyn was born in Cornwall, and was educated at the University of Cambridge. As curate to Charles SIMEON, he was encouraged to offer himself as a missionary. In 1805 he was appointed Chaplain to the East India Company and he initially settled in Calcutta. He is primarily remembered for his translation of the New Testament and the Book of Common Prayer into Hindustani. Later he travelled to Persia to work on his Persian New Testament translation. He died at the early age of thirty-one in Toket, while returning from Persia. The pathos of his life story and his intensely spiritual journals caused him to be regarded as a religious hero in England.

C.E. Padwick, *Henry Martyn: Confessor of the Faith* (1922).

Marx, Karl (1818–83)   Political Philosopher. Marx was born in Trier, Germany. He was of Jewish origin, but was baptised a Protestant at the age of six. After a period as editor of the Cologne newspaper *Rheinische Zeitung*, he moved first to Paris and then to Brussels. In 1848, with Friedrich Engels, he published *The Communist Manifesto* and in 1849 he settled in London where he wrote *Das Kapital*. He maintained that the human spirit was alienated from self-realisation through the conditions of modern capitalism. However, as a result of the inevitable development of history, the proletariat would triumph over the bourgeoisie, Communism would be established and alienation would be overcome. He was particularly hostile to religion, openly declaring that it was the 'opium of the people'. His work has been hugely influential, not only in inspiring political revolutions such as that of Russia in 1917, but even within the Churches. Latin American liberation theology, for example, largely rests on a Marxist analysis of society and history.

G.A. Cohen, *Karl Marx's Theory of History* (1978); D. McLellan, *Karl Marx: His Life and Thought* (1973).

Mary (first century) The Mother of JESUS CHRIST. According to the Gospels of MATTHEW and LUKE, while Mary was still a virgin, she conceived Jesus through the Holy Spirit. His future birth was announced by the Angel Gabriel and Mary willingly accepted her role as the mother of the Son of God. She visited her cousin Elizabeth who recognised her as the 'mother of my Lord' and Mary sang the Magnificat, a hymn glorifying God for his great works. Subsequently she visited Bethlehem with JOSEPH, her betrothed husband, and Jesus was born in a stable. As a result of heavenly visitations, shepherds came to see the new-born baby. Then, when Mary and Joseph presented Jesus in the Temple in Jerusalem, SIMEON prophesied that a sword would pierce Mary's soul. Matthew's Gospel records the visit of the wise men to Bethlehem and Mary and Joseph's flight to Egypt to escape the jealousy of King Herod. Mary was mentioned in the context of Jesus's visit to Jerusalem at the age of twelve; she appeared as a wedding guest in Cana when Jesus turned water into wine and, according to the Fourth Gospel, she was present at the crucifixion. Although the Gospels recorded that Jesus had several brothers and sisters, Mary's perpetual virginity was first mentioned in the apoc-

ryphal Gospel of JAMES; this was generally accepted from the fifth century and has become an important article of faith in the Eastern Orthodox and Roman Catholic Churches. In order to combat the teachings of NESTORIUS, she was described as *Theotokos* (Bearer of God) also in the fifth century. Subsequently the doctrine of her Assumption into heavenly glory was formulated by GREGORY OF TOURS and became official dogma of the Roman Catholic Church in 1950. In 1854 Pope PIUS IX had already proclaimed the dogma of her Immaculate Conception (that she was born without stain of original sin). She has been the subject of intense devotion within the Church and the inspiration for many artists. The legendary story of her birth was recorded in the mediaeval *Gospel of the Birth of Mary*.

Luke, Chapters 1–2; Matthew, Chapters 1–2; H.C. Graef, *Mary: A History of Doctrine and Devotion*, 2 vols (1963–5); J. McHugh, *The Mother of Jesus in the New Testament* (1975).

Mary (first century) Disciple. Mary was the sister of LAZARUS and MARTHA. She lived at Bethany and when JESUS visited the house, she stayed listening to him while her sister bustled about doing the domestic chores. On occasion she has been identified with MARY MAGDALENE. According to legend, with her brother and sister, she founded churches in the south of France.

Luke, Chapter 10.

Mary I (1516–58) Queen. Mary was the daughter of HENRY VIII of England by Catherine of Aragon. She was thus a grand-daughter of FERDINAND and ISABELLA of Spain. After her father divorced her mother, she was declared illegitimate, but in 1544 she was restored and placed second in the succession after her half-brother, EDWARD VI. She was intensely Roman Catholic, and on the death of Edward, there was an unsuccessful attempt to place the Protestant Lady Jane Grey on the throne in her place, but Mary was crowned Queen in 1553. She is remembered for the persecution of Protestants which took place during her reign. Thomas CRANMER, Hugh LATIMER and Nicholas RIDLEY were among many who were burnt at the stake for their religious beliefs. Their deaths were recorded in John FOXE's popular *Book of Martyrs*. This persecution, coupled with her marriage to PHILIP II of Spain, made her extremely unpopular and earned her the soubriquet 'Bloody Mary'. In fact she was kind and gentle by nature, but she grossly misunderstood the mood of the times. She was succeeded by her Protestant half-sister ELIZABETH I.

D.M. Loades, *The Reign of Mary Tudor* (1979).

Mary of Egypt (*c.* 344–421) Saint. Little certain is known of the life of Mary. She is said to have enjoyed an immoral existence in Alexandria, North Africa, before being converted to Christianity outside the Holy Sepulchre in Jerusalem. Subsequently she lived as a solitary penitent east of Jordan until her death forty-one years later. She was the subject of many popular legends.

D.H. Farmer (ed.), *The Oxford Dictionary of Saints*, 3rd edn (1992).

Mary Magdalene (first century) Disciple and Saint. Mary is mentioned in LUKE's Gospel as someone from whom seven devils had been exorcised. She witnessed JESUS's death on the cross and she was the first to discover that his tomb was empty on Easter morning. In the Fourth Gospel, she was the first human being to see the resurrected Jesus. Initially she thought he was the gardener, but after he said her name, she recognised him and was told to tell the good news to the other disciples. Although there is no biblical evidence for this, she has been identified with the woman who

was a sinner, and who anointed Jesus's feet, and also with MARY, the sister of MARTHA and LAZARUS. In Christian mythology, she is therefore regarded as the prototype of the sinning woman who repents. She was also a major character in the Gnostic *Gospel of Mary*.

Luke, Chapter 8; Mark, Chapters 15–16; John, Chapter 20; D.H. Farmer (ed.), *The Oxford Dictionary of Saints*, 3rd edn (1992).

Mary Magdalene de' Pazzi (1566–1607) Saint and Mystic. Mary Magdalene was a member of the Carmelite Convent in Florence. She is remembered for her intense spiritual experience. She suffered both spiritual desolation and periods of ecstasy and she endured long periods of illness. Her sayings were written down by her sisters and published posthumously. She was canonised in 1669.

O. Carm, *Mary Magdalene de' Pazzi* (1958).

Mather, Cotton (1663–1728) Theologian and Philanthropist. Mather was born in Boston in the American colonies and was educated at the University of Harvard. He was Senior Pastor of the Second Church of Boston and was elected a fellow of Harvard in 1690. A prolific writer, he produced works of theology, history and ethics. Among his best-known books were *Magnalia Christi Americana* and *Essays to do Good*, both of which were widely read. He conducted a large correspondence and among his many philanthropic activities founded a school for Afro-American slaves.

R.A. Bosco (ed.), *The Autobiography of Cotton Mather* (1976); C. Felker, *Reinventing Cotton Mather in the American Renaissance* (1993); K. Silverman, *The Life and Times of Cotton Mather* (1984).

Mathew, Arnold Harris (1853–1919) Putative Archbishop. Mathew was ordained a Roman Catholic priest in 1878, but, after his marriage in 1892, was allowed to serve as a Church of England minister. In 1908 the Old Catholic

Church of Holland (which had separated from the Church of Rome in 1724) consecrated him Archbishop of Great Britain – apparently in the belief that he had a considerable personal following. When the real situation came to light, the Dutch Church repudiated the consecration. None the less Mathew continued to describe himself as an Archbishop and went so far as to consecrate several other Bishops. Thus in the 1920s and 1930s, several Bishops existed in England who presumably stood in the Apostolic Succession, but whose jurisdiction was recognised by no one except themselves.

H.R.T. Brandreth, *Episcopi Vagentes and the Anglican Church*, revised edition (1961); Arnold Harris Mathew, *An Episcopal Odyssey* (1915).

Matthew (first century)   Apostle and Historian. The name Matthew appears in the Gospel lists of the twelve Apostles of JESUS. According to the First Gospel, Matthew was a tax-collector who left his livelihood to follow Jesus. However, in the Gospels of MARK and LUKE, the same story is told of LEVI. Since the time of IRENAEUS, the First Gospel has been ascribed to the Apostle Matthew. PAPIAS wrote that Matthew wrote the 'logia' (sayings) in Hebrew and this may perhaps refer to the Gospel. In any event, most modern scholars believe that the author of the First Gospel knew Mark's Gospel and it does seem unlikely that one of the original apostles would be so dependent on a secondary historical work. The Gospel emphasises how Jesus fulfilled the prophecies of the Hebrew scriptures and it contains a full summary of Jesus's ethical teaching in the Sermon on the Mount. There are various legends about Matthew the Apostle. According to EUSEBIUS OF CAESAREA, he preached to the Jews and, according to the Roman martyrology, he died for his faith in Ethiopia.

J.C. Fenton, *The Gospel According to St Matthew* (1963); R.T. France, *The Gospel according to Matthew: An Introduction and Commentary* (1985);

B.M. Metzger and M.D. Coogan (eds), *The Oxford Companion to the Bible* (1993).

Matthew Paris (*c.* 1199–1259)   Historian. Matthew was a Benedictine monk at the Abbey of St Alban, England. He is remembered for his extraordinary chronicles, which included *Chronica Majora*. This was a history of the world and the early part was largely based on the work of Roger Wendover. The section relating to his own times was far more lively. Matthew did not hesitate to criticise the Papal Court, King Henry III of England and the general avarice of the age. It seems to have been based on information gleaned from visitors to the Abbey as well as on his own travels. His manuscripts were decorated with heraldic devices and illustrations of the events recorded. Matthew is an important figure in that he realised the moral responsibilities of the historian and was not content to remain a mere chronicler of events.

R.Vaughan, *Matthew Paris* (1958); R.Vaughan (ed.), *Chronicles of Matthew Paris: Monastic Life in the 13th Century* (1984).

Matthias (first century)   Apostle. After the death of JUDAS ISCARIOT, the eleven apostles chose Matthias by lot to replace him. He was not mentioned again in the New Testament, but, according to legend, he later preached Christianity in Ethiopia. ORIGEN mentioned a lost Gospel, supposedly written by him.

Acts of the Apostles, Chapter 1; D.H. Farmer (ed.), *The Oxford Dictionary of Saints*, 3rd edn (1992).

Mauriac, François (1885–1970)   Novelist. Mauriac was born in Bordeaux, France, and was educated in Bordeaux and Paris. He was a devout Roman Catholic and his novels reflected his acute moral and religious seriousness. He used to maintain that the justification for writing fiction was to throw light on the evil that lurks in even the noblest of human beings and, conversely, to show the sanctity which can be found in the most loathsome and pitiable. Among his many books were *Le Noeud de Vipères* and *La Pharisienne*. During the occupation of France, he worked tirelessly and with immense courage against the Nazis. He was awarded the Nobel Prize in 1952.

J.E. Flower and B.C. Swift (eds), *François Mauriac: Visions and Reappraisals* (1989); M.F. Moloney, *François Mauriac: A Critical Study* (1958).

Maurice, Frederick Denison (1805–72) Theologian, Philanthropist and Educator. Maurice was born in Suffolk, the son of a Unitarian minister. He was educated at the University of Cambridge, but was not awarded a degree because he refused to subscribe to the Anglican Thirty-Nine Articles. Subsequently he did join the Church of England and, after a period at Oxford University, he was ordained into the Anglican ministry. In 1838 he published *The Kingdom of God* in which he argued that universal fellowship was only to be found in JESUS CHRIST. In 1848, stirred by the European revolutionary movements of the time, he formed the Christian Socialist movement with Charles KINGSLEY and J.M.F. LUDLOW, strongly believing that Christianity stood for a structure of society in which people could co-operate rather than compete. He had been appointed Professor of Theology at King's College, London, in 1846, but he was expelled from his post in 1853 after questioning the doctrine of eternal punishment. Later, in 1866, he became Professor of Moral Philosophy at the University of Cambridge. Besides his role as a Christian Socialist, Maurice is remembered as an educational innovator. He was closely involved both in the founding of Queen's College, London, in 1848, which was the first place of higher education for women in England and in 1854, he started the Working Men's College in London.

W.M. Davies, *An Introduction to F.D. Maurice's Theology* (1964); A.M. Ramsey, *F.D. Maurice and the Conflict of Modern Theology* (1951); A.R. Vidler, *F.D. Maurice and Company* (1966).

Maurus (d. 565) Saint. Little is known of the life of St Maurus except that he was a follower of St BENEDICT of Nursia. He is said to have founded the Abbey of Glanfeuil in France and to have lived a life of great sanctity. The Benedictines of the Abbey of Saint-Vanne chose him as their patron when they founded the new Congregation of St Maur in 1621. The Maurists were largely dedicated to scholarship and produced a considerable number of literary and historical works. Many within the congregation showed Jansenist sympathies in the seventeenth and eighteenth centuries and the order was finally dissolved in 1818.

D.H. Farmer (ed.), *The Oxford Dictionary of Saints*, 3rd edn (1992).

Maximus the Confessor (*c.* 580–662) Mystic, Theologian and Saint. As a young man, Maximus served as secretary to the Byzantine Emperor. However, in *c.* 615, he became a monk at the monastery of Chrysopolis. In 626, when the Persians invaded, he fled to North Africa. There he combated the Monothelite heresy and in 645 he worsted the exiled Patriarch of Constantinople in a debate on the subject. In 649, the Monothelites were condemned at the Lateran Council. Maximus refused to accept the 'Typos' of the Emperor Constans II. This was an edict forbidding the assertion of either Monothelite or orthodox Diothelite beliefs. In consequence, Maximus was tried in Constantinople and exiled to Thrace. Later he was summoned again and his tongue and right hand were cut off. Many of his theological works survive, including *Quaestiones ad Thalassum* and expositions on the works of GREGORY OF NAZIANZUS and Pseudo-DIONYSIUS. He was also the author of mystical volumes such as *Mystagogia*, a spiritual understanding of the liturgy.

L. Thurnberg, *Microcosm and Mediator: The Theological Anthropology of Maximus the Confessor* (1965); A. Louth, *Maximus the Confessor* (1995).

Mazarin, Jules (1602–61) Politician and Cardinal. Mazarin was born in Piscina, Abruzzi, and he was educated in Rome and in Acalá, Spain. After a military and diplomatic career, he entered the service of the Church. He became a naturalised Frenchman in 1639 and a Cardinal in 1641. In 1642, with the death of Cardinal RICHELIEU, he became chief minister of France. He enjoyed the favour of the King's mother, Anne of Austria (court rumour had it that they were married), and became all powerful. Among his many achievements was the Peace of Westphalia. He secured the marriage of the young King LOUIS XIV with Maria Theresa of Spain and, despite civil war and a short period of banishment, he enormously enhanced the prestige of France in Europe. In the religious sphere, he pursued a policy of toleration towards the Huguenots, but he supported Pope Innocent X's condemnation of Jansenism. He also found the Collège Mazarin, to which he donated his magnificent library.

R. Bonney, *Society and Government in France under Richelieu and Mazarin* (1988).

Mbiti, John S. (b. 1931) Theologian and Ecumenist. Mbiti was born in Kitui, Kenya, and he was educated in Uganda, the United States of America and England. After ordination in the Anglican Church, he taught at the University of Makerere and was Director of the World Council of Churches Ecumenical Institute in Switzerland. Among his books are *African Religions and Philosophy* and *Bible and Theology in African Religion*. His theology is remarkable in that he argues that God can be found in the old African ways as well as in the Judaeo-Christian tradition.

John S. Mbiti (ed.), *Akamba Stories* (1966); John S. Mbiti, *The Prayers of African Religion* (1975).

Mechitar (1676–1749) Order Founder. Mechitar was an Armenian priest who joined the Roman Catholic Church. In 1701 he founded the Mechitarist Order with sixteen others. They initially lived in Constantinople under a modified Benedictine Rule, using the Armenian liturgy. After being driven from the city, they settled in Venetian territory and in 1717 they were granted the island of St Lazzaro. This has remained the headquarters of the order. The monks work as missionaries and educators and their presses have published several important Armenian works.

The Catholic University of America, *New Catholic Encyclopaedia* (1967).

Mechthilde (c. 1210–c. 1280) Mystic and Saint. Mechthilde was born into an aristocratic family in Saxony. In c. 1230 she joined an austere convent in Magdeburg. She is remembered for her mystical visions which she recorded in *Das Fliessende Licht der Gottheit*. During the last few years of her life, she lived in a Cistercian convent in Helfta. The original version of her work has been lost, but it survived in Latin and High German translations. Her revelations greatly influenced later German mystics and they included a vision of the Sacred Heart of JESUS.

L. Menzies (ed.), *Mechthilde's 'Light of the Godhead'* (1953).

Melanchthon, Philip (1497–1560) Theologian. Menlanchthon was born Philip Schwarzerd in Bretten, Germany. His name was changed by his great-uncle because of his aptitude for academic learning. He was educated at the Universities of Heidelberg and Tübingen and he was appointed Professor of Greek at Wittenberg in 1518. He became a firm supporter of the Reformation cause and he took part in the Leipzig disputations. After the Diet of Worms Melanchthon emerged as the leader of the movement and he later participated in the 1529 Colloquy of Marburg and the 1530 Diet of Augsburg. Among his works were *Loci Communes* (the first systematic exposition of LUTHER's theology), the Augsburg Confession, the Wittenberg Concord of 1536 and various biblical commentaries. He is remembered as perhaps the most learned of the early Reformers and as one who was essentially conciliatory in his views. Although his work has been the subject of scholarly controversy, his writings were highly influential on the development of Protestantism.

A. McGrath, *Reformation Thought: An Introduction* (1988); M. Rogness, *Melanchthon: Reformer without Honor* (1969).

Melitius (late third/early fourth century)   Bishop and Sect Founder. Melitius was Bishop of Lycopolis, Egypt. He insisted that Christians who had lapsed during the Diocletian persecutions had been allowed to return to the Church too easily. Eventually he founded his own separate Church and ordained his own clergy. ARIUS is said to have been one of Melitius's ordinands. There was an attempt to bring the Melitians back to the mainstream Church at the Council of Nicaea in 325, but once ATHANASIUS became Bishop of Alexandria, the agreed arrangement broke down. The sect seems to have survived into the eighth century.

'Melitian schism', in F.L. Cross (ed.), *The Oxford Dictionary of the Christian Church*, 2nd edn (1974).

Melitius (d. 381)   Saint and Bishop. Melitius was Bishop of Sebaste and then was consecrated Bishop of Antioch. In Antioch he was sent back to Armenia for preaching a sermon against the doctrines of ARIUS. Although he returned in 362, ATHANASIUS supported a rival orthodox leader, Paulinus, while an Arian Bishop

had also been appointed. Melitius was banished twice more, but as a result of the efforts of BASIL of Caesarea, he finally returned to his see in 379. He presided over the Council of Constantinople in 381 – during the course of which he died. Melitius is remembered as the much admired teacher of John CHRYSOSTOM as well as for his part in the controversies of his time.

W.A. Jurgens, 'A letter of Meletius of Antioch', *Harvard Theological Review*, liii (1960); J.N.D. Kelly, *Golden Mouth: The Story of John Chrysostom* (1995).

Melville, Andrew (1545–1622)   Theologian and Denomination Founder. Melville was born near Montrose, Scotland. He was appointed to a Chair at the University of Geneva (where he had come under the influence of Theodore BEZA). On his return to Scotland, he became the Principal of the University of Glasgow and later he was appointed Rector of St Andrews. A determined Presbyterian, he refused the offer of the Archbishopric of St Andrews and he was elected Moderator of the General Assembly of the Scottish Church in 1582. Under his leadership, the Assembly ratified his Presbyterian 'Second Book of Discipline'. His stand incurred the wrath of King JAMES VI and he was, on one occasion, compelled to live outside Scotland for nearly two years. Later, in 1606, when James had also inherited the English throne, he was summoned to explain himself in London and this led to four years' confinement in the Tower of London. He spent the remainder of his life as Professor of Biblical Theology at the University of Sedan. Melville's influence must be seen as second only to that of John KNOX in the setting up of the Church of Scotland.

R.S. Wright (ed.), *Fathers of the Kirk* (1960).

Menas (d. 552)   Saint and Patriarch. In 536 Menas succeeded the Monophysite

Anthimos as Patriarch of Constantinople and he was consecrated by Pope Agapetus. He supported the Emperor JUSTINIAN's stand against the followers of ORIGEN, THEODORE OF MOPSUESTIA, THEODORET and IBAS. In consequence he was excommunicated by Pope VIGILIUS in 547 and again in 551. However, relations with Rome were fully restored by the time of his death. His reign was significant in that it showed the extent of the influence of the Papacy on the Eastern Church in the mid sixth century.

R. MacMullen, *Christianizing the Roman Empire* (1984); R.A. Markus, *Christianity in the Roman World* (1974).

Menno Simons (1496–1561) Sect Founder and Theologian. Menno was born in Dutch Friesland and he was ordained into the Roman Catholic priesthood. He was subsequently influenced by the teachings of Martin LUTHER and he joined the Anabaptists in 1536. He spent the remainder of his life travelling through West Germany and the Netherlands, preaching the Anabaptist gospel. His doctrines were based on scripture alone; he believed that the Second Coming was imminent and taught that believers should live together in a close-knit community, separated from the secular world. He gave his name to the Mennonite communities. Today the majority of Mennonite groups live in the United States of America, Canada and South America. They are descended largely from Swiss and Russian immigrants and they practise a strict New Testament faith.

C.J. Dyck (ed.), *Introduction to Mennonite History* (1968).

Merton, Thomas (1915–68) Mystic and Devotional Writer. Merton was born in Prades, France, of a New Zealand mother and an American father. He was educated at Columbia University in the United States of America and, as a student, he converted to Roman Catholicism. Subsequently he entered the Trappist monastery of Our Lady of Gethsemane in Kentucky. He was the author of a large number of devotional works including his autobiography, *Elected Silence*, which made a huge impact. In his writings, Merton addressed the pressing social issues of the day as well as describing his own path to the realisation of a loving union with JESUS CHRIST. Towards the end of his life, he became interested in Zen Buddhism and Eastern spirituality. Merton's writings have proved very popular and have led many ordinary Christians to the mystical path.

Thomas Merton, *The Asian Journeys of Thomas Merton* (1973); M. Furlong, *Merton: A Biography* (1995).

Mesrob (*c.* 345–440) Patriarch, Historian and Saint. Mesrob succeeded Sahak as Patriarch of Armenia. He is remembered for his ardent devotion to Armenian culture. He composed the Armenian alphabet; he translated the New Testament and the Book of Proverbs into Armenian and he encouraged the development of Armenian monasticism. He is thus an important figure in the history of Armenian Christianity. Many of the sermons and hymns supposedly written by GREGORY THE ILLUMINATOR may have been composed by Mesrob. His biography was written by his pupil Korium.

L. Arpée, *A History of Armenian Christianity from the Beginning to our own Time* (1946).

Methodius (*c.* 815–85) Saint, Missionary and Bishop. Methodius was the brother of St CYRIL. The two brothers were sent in 862 by the Emperor Michael to convert the Slavs in what is now Moravia. After his brother's death, Methodius was consecrated a Bishop in Rome to give papal authority for his work. In 1980, Pope JOHN PAUL II designated the brothers 'Patrons of Europe'.

F. Dvornik, *Byzantine Missions Among the Slavs* (1970).

Meyendorff, John (b. 1926) Theologian and Historian. Meyendorff was awarded a doctorate from the Sorbonne, Paris. He has spent his career in the United States of America, where he has taught at both Harvard and Fordham Universities. He is regarded as an international authority on Eastern Orthodox Christianity and is himself an Orthodox priest. He has made the work of St GREGORY PALAMAS his special study and he has been instrumental in the revival of interest in Palamite theology. His other books include *The Orthodox Church*, *Christ in Eastern Thought* and *Byzantine Theology*.

John Meyendorff, *St Gregory of Palamas and Orthodox Spirituality* (1974).

Michelangelo Buonarroti (1475–1564) Artist. Michelangelo was the son of a minor Italian nobleman. He studied both painting and sculpture in Florence and in 1534 he settled permanently in Rome. He was subject to two major influences: on the one hand that of the sensuous beauty of the Classical world and, on the other, the austere religious vision of SAVONAROLA. He was inspired by biblical subjects and his sculptures included *David*, *Moses*, *St John in the Wilderness* and the famous *Pieta*. Among his paintings were the frescos for the Sistine Chapel on which he worked for a total of eleven years. The subjects included both the Creation and the Last Judgement. As an architect, he was responsible for the Medici Memorial Chapel and a reworking of the plan of St Peter's Cathedral in Rome. Michelangelo must be reckoned, with LEONARDO, as one of the greatest artists of the Italian Renaissance – and indeed of all time.

J.S. Ackerman, *The Architecture of Michelangelo*, 2

vols (1961); L. Goldscheider (ed.), *The Paintings of Michelangelo* (1939); L. Goldscheider (ed.), *The Sculptures of Michelangelo* (1940); J.A. Symonds, *The Life of Michelangelo Buonarroti*, 2nd edn (1983).

Miller, William (1782–1849) Cult Founder. Miller was born in Pittsfield, Massachusetts, and spent much of his life as a farmer. He was licensed as a Baptist preacher in 1833 and he was the author of *Evidence from Scripture and History of the Second Coming of Christ about the Year 1843*. This was the beginning of the American Adventist movement which was to produce several Churches. The most prominent of these was that of the Seventh Day Adventists. They believe that the end of the age will come when the Church has reached a predetermined size. At that point the righteous, both living and dead, will be taken to spend a thousand years in Heaven while Satan will rule the Earth. Then, JESUS CHRIST and the Saints will destroy the wicked and a New Earth will be created. Adventists celebrate the Sabbath on Saturdays; they follow the Old Testament food laws; they do not smoke or drink and they try to avoid all 'worldly entertainments'. Miller himself abandoned the movement he started when his deadline for the Second Coming had passed.

H.C. Sheldon, *Studies in Recent Adventism* (1915); A.W. Spalding, *Origin and History of Seventh Day Adventists*, 4 vols (1961–2).

Milton, John (1608–74) Poet. Milton was born in London and was educated at the University of Cambridge. During the English Civil War, he supported the Parliamentary cause and he wrote various pamphlets, urging Church reform, freedom of the press and a more liberal attitude towards divorce. He defended the execution of King CHARLES I and, with the accession of King Charles II, he was imprisoned for a short time. By this stage he was blind and his friends secured his release. Today he is remembered for his poetry. One of his earliest works, 'On the Morning of Christ's Nativity', was a hymn to the incarnation. The masque *Comus* presented the conflict between chastity and vice, while *Lycidas* was a lament for a dead friend. His best-known works are *Paradise Lost* and *Paradise Regained*, glorious epic poems describing the Fall and the redemption of humanity. His avowed intention was to 'justify the ways of God to man'. They are written in blank verse and have the same scale and grandeur as DANTE's *Divina Commedia*. In the final period of his life, he also produced *Samson Agonistes*, a dramatic poem portraying the final episode in the life of the blind Israelite judge Samson. Milton was an independent thinker. He set out his religious views in *De Doctrina Christiana*, published after his death. He inclined towards Arianism and he seems to have believed that matter was inherent in the Godhead. His poetry, however, remains an essential element in the canon of English literature.

C.C. Brown, *John Milton: A Literary Life* (1995); M.H. Nicolson, *John Milton: A Reader's Guide to his Poetry* (1963); C.A. Patrides, *Milton and the Christian Tradition* (1966); C.A. Patrides, *An Annotated Critical Bibliography of John Milton* (1987).

Moffat, Robert (1795–1883) Missionary. Moffat was born in East Lothian, Scotland, where he was apprenticed as a boy to a gardener. He was sponsored by the London Missionary Society, and sent to South Africa in 1817. He eventually settled in Kuruman, which remained his headquarters until 1870. His mission involved establishing African congregations led by African ministers, exploration, the translation of the Bible into Sechwana and the introduction of modern methods of agriculture. Moffat's achievements were remarkable. By the time he left South Africa, the whole area around Kuruman had been Christianised and his methods were generally recog-

nised to be highly successful. He is also remembered as the father-in-law of David LIVINGSTONE.

J.S. Moffat, *The Lives of Robert and Mary Moffat* (1885); W.C. Northcott, *Robert Moffat* (1961).

Moffatt, James (1870–1944) Biblical Scholar and Historian. Moffatt was born and educated in Glasgow, Scotland. He was ordained into the ministry of the Church of Scotland and subsequently he taught in Oxford, Glasgow and at the Union Theological Seminary in New York. He is remembered for his translation of the Bible. The New Testament appeared in 1913, and the Old in 1924. The whole was revised in 1935. It was written in a colloquial style and proved highly popular. In addition he edited a seventeen-volume commentary on the books of the New Testament and he produced works on Church history and translations of HARNACK's writings.

E.F. Scott, 'James Moffatt', in L.G. Wickham Legg and E.T. Williams (eds), *Dictionary of National Biography 1941–1950* (1959).

Mogila, Peter (1597–1646) Metropolitan and Theologian. Mogila was born in Moldavia and was educated in Poland and at the University of Paris. He became a monk and was elected Abbot of a monastery in Kiev in 1627. He was appointed Metropolitan of Kiev in 1633. He is remembered for his *Orthodox Confession of the Catholic and Apostolic Eastern Church*, in which he outlined the beliefs of the Orthodox. This was approved by the Four Patriarchs in 1643 and was endorsed by the Synod of Jerusalem in 1672. Mogila was also responsible for an important catechism. Both documents have become standard statements of the faith of the Eastern Church.

J.J. Overbeck (ed.), Peter Mogila, *Confession*, translated by P. Lodvel (1898); T. Ionesco, *La Vie et l'Oeuvre de Pierre Mogila, Métropolite de Kiev* (1944) [no English translation available].

Möhler, Johann Adam (1796–1838) Historian and Theologian. Möhler was born in Igersheim, Germany, and he was educated at Ellwangen and Tübingen. After ordination as a Roman Catholic priest, he taught at the Universities of Tübingen and Munich and, before his death, he was appointed Dean of Würtzburg Cathedral. He is remembered particularly for his *Symbolik* in which he took account of the theological contributions of SCHLEIERMACHER, HEGEL and SCHELLING. This caused offence among his more conservative Roman Catholic colleagues, but today he is considered to have been an important Catholic apologist.

S. Bolshakoff, *The Doctrine of the Unity of the Church in the Works of Khomyakov and Moehler* (1946); J. Fitzer, *Moehler and Baur in Controversy 1832–1838* (1974).

Molina, Luis de (1535–1600) Theologian. Molina was a member of the Jesuit Order. He is remembered as the author of *Concordia Liberi Arbitrii cum Gratiae Donis*. In this he put forward a theory of grace which became known as 'Molinism'. He argued that the grace of God was effective because God already knew that a particular human being would co-operate with it. The more traditional position was that God's grace is in and of itself effective, but, according to the Molinists, this leaves no room for the activity of human free will. In general, Molinism was accepted by the Jesuits, but rejected by the Dominicans. In 1597, Pope Clement VIII appointed a special congregation to discuss the question. The congregation rejected Molina's view, but the Pope refused to act on the decision. Ultimately, in 1607, Pope PAUL V declared that just as Molina's position was not Pelagian, so the Dominican view was not Calvinist and neither could be regarded as heretical.

B. Hamilton, *Political Thought in Sixteenth-century Spain* (1963).

Molinos, Miguel de (*c.* 1640–97) Mystic and Devotional Writer. Molinos was born in Muniesa, Spain. He was ordained into the Roman Catholic priesthood and he spent most of his life in Rome. He was the author of the *Guida Spirituale*, in which he traced the path to spiritual perfection through the total annihilation of the individual will. Although Molinos was a personal friend of Pope INNOCENT XI, the guide was quickly attacked as 'Quietist' by the Jesuits and it must be admitted that members of religious orders who followed its advice all too often neglected the precepts of their Rules and caused severe disruptions within their communities. On the initiative of King LOUIS XIV of France, Molinos was arrested in 1685 and two years later he was put on trial. Although he was prepared to recant, he was accused of immorality and was kept in captivity for the rest of his life. He seems to have borne his imprisonment with remarkable patience. The guide was an important influence on Protestant Pietist circles amongst whom its author was both admired and pitied.

R.A. Knox, *Enthusiasms* (1951).

Moltmann, Jürgen (b. 1926) Theologian. Moltmann was born in Hamburg, Germany. He fought in the Second World War, was captured in Belgium and spent some time as a prisoner-of-war in England. Subsequently, he went to Göttingen University and, after serving in a country parish, he has taught systematic theology at Wuppertal, Bonn and Tübingen. A highly influential figure in modern theology, he is the author of many books including (in their English titles) *Theology of Hope*, *The Crucified God* and *The Church in the Power of the Spirit*. He grounds his Christianity in a theology of the Trinity and his doctrine of God in the cross of JESUS CHRIST. He sees the essential theological task as working out the implications of his theology for Christian living.

R. Bauckham, *Theology of Jürgen Moltmann* (1995); A.J. Conyers, *God, Hope and History: Jürgen Moltmann and the Christian Concept of History* (1988).

Monica [Monnica] (*c.* 331–87) Saint. Monica was the mother of St AUGUSTINE OF HIPPO. According to the *Confessions*, she was a woman of strong character who pursued her son in his unregenerate days to Carthage and Milan. She was born into a Christian family, but she married the somewhat dissolute Patricius of Tagaste, Numidia. She had at least two other children besides Augustine – Navigius, who was also converted to Christianity, and Perpetua, who became Abbess of a convent in Hippo. In Milan, she was influenced by St AMBROSE and she appears in the Augustinian dialogues *De Ordine* and *De Beata Vita*. She died in Ostia accompanying Augustine home to North Africa.

St Augustine, *Confessions*, Book 9 [many editions]; P.L.R. Brown, *St Augustine of Hippo* (1965).

Montaigne, Michel de (1533–92) Philosopher. Montaigne was born into a noble French Périgord family. He was educated in Bordeaux and he studied law in Toulouse. By 1571 he had retired from public life and it was in this period that he wrote the majority of his essays. In 1580 he travelled extensively and between 1581 and 1585 he was Mayor of Bordeaux. His essays on moral philosophy were widely read and were influential on writers such as BACON and PASCAL. He himself was a practising and conventional Roman Catholic, but his sceptical intelligence, his self-sufficient moral system, his wide knowledge of Classical philosophy and his appealing writing style make his work very attractive.

Michel de Montaigne, *Essays*, translated by M.A. Screech (1991); D.M. Frame, *Montaigne: A Biography* (1965).

Montanus (second century) Sect Founder. Montanus was a preacher of Phrygia. He taught that the New Jerusalem was about to appear, heralded by a great outpouring of the Holy Spirit. He regarded himself and his immediate followers as the bringers of this new era and he urged withdrawal from the world, fasting and the anticipation of renewed persecution. Prominent among his early disciples were two women, Maximilla and Prisca. The movement spread through the African Churches and TERTULLIAN was a prominent convert. It was condemned, however, by the mainstream Church and by 230 AD it had been driven underground. Montanism is interesting in that it foreshadowed many later millenarian groups which tried to return to the simplicity and enthusiasm of the Primitive Church.

T.D. Barnes, 'The chronology of Montanism', *Journal of Theological Studies*, n.s. xxi (1971); J.M. Ford, 'Was Montanism a Jewish-Christian heresy?', *Journal of Ecclesiastical History*, xvii (1966); C. Trevett, *Montanism* (1996).

Monteverdi, Claudio (1567–1643) Composer. Monteverdi was the organist of St Mark's Cathedral in Venice. He was the foremost musician of his day and he has been described as the 'father of modern music'. He composed both secular and sacred pieces. His Church music, both in the older Renaissance style and in the new Baroque mode, is frequently enjoyed to this day.

D. Arnold and N. Fortune (eds), *The Monteverdi Companion* (1968); P. Fabbri, *Monteverdi* (1994).

Moody, Dwight Lyman (1837–99) Missionary and Educator. Moody was born in Northfield, Massachusetts. He had a scanty education, but experienced an evangelical conversion and was received into membership of a Boston Congregational Church in 1856. After moving to Chicago, he began to organise a Sabbath school and he established the

Illinois Street Church. With his associate, Ira D. SANKEY, he became a highly successful travelling evangelist. His 1873 tour of the British Isles was a triumph. More than two and a half million people heard him preach. He also travelled round the major cities of the United States – Philadelphia, New York, Chicago, Boston, Baltimore, St Louis, Cleveland and San Francisco. His campaigns were heralded by considerable publicity and he made a practice of co-operating with the local Churches. Altogether it has been estimated that he addressed more than a hundred million people and travelled over a million miles. He also founded educational institutions – Northfield Seminary for girls, Mount Hermon School for boys and the Chicago Evangelization Society (which became the Moody Bible Institute). He was one of a series of successful American evangelists whose tradition continues today with the various television and broadcasting ministries. Moody himself died during the course of a mission in Kansas City.

J.F. Findlay Jnr, *Dwight L. Moody: American Evangelist* (1969).

Moon, Sun-Myung (b. 1920) Sect Founder. Moon was born in Korea. The story of his origins and early life is obscure, but he claims to have had a vision of JESUS CHRIST in 1936. This was the first of several visitations and, at the end of the Second World War, he started his own Church. He was arrested on several occasions and served time in a labour camp, but in 1954, the Holy Spirit Association for the Unification of World Christianity was founded. The Unification Church, as it is called, is based on Moon's *Divine Principle*. He teaches that the fallen nature of humanity can only be restored through the purification of blood lineages which takes place at the sect's mass marriage ceremonies. In the 1970s, Moon moved his headquarters to the United States, where he was sub-

sequently imprisoned for tax evasion. Undaunted, the Church sustains a theological seminary, the Washington Institute, the *Washington Times* newspaper and various other organisations. Moon and his followers have been accused of using brainwashing techniques on new recruits, but this has never been substantiated. The Church is known to be virulently anti-Communist and it supports (and is supported by) a range of right-wing causes.

E. Barker, *The Making of a Moonie* (1984); Sun-Myung Moon, *The Divine Principle* [many editions].

More, Hannah (1745–1833) Philanthropist and Devotional Writer. More was born in Stapleton, near Bristol, England. Financially independent, she became part of the London literary world and was a personal friend of Samuel JOHNSON, the artist Joshua Reynolds and the actor/manager David Garrick. During this period she wrote a series of *Sacred Plays* which Garrick helped to produce. Later she became involved in the activities of the Clapham Sect and she was much influenced by William WILBERFORCE and John NEWTON. She organised a Sunday School in Cheddar in the Mendip Hills which was attached to a school of industry. This extended into a series of schools and adult educational institutes throughout the area. In addition, she wrote a series of religious tracts (known as the Cheap Repository Tracts), many of which urged the poor to be content with their lot and rejoice in the thought of their reward in Heaven. Her most popular work was *Coelebs in Search of a Wife*. She faced considerable mockery and criticism – for example, she was described by the Radical, William Cobbett, as 'an old Bishop in petticoats', but within her limitations, her educational work was both progressive and effective.

M.G. Jones, *Hannah More* (1952); C.M. Yonge, *Mrs Hannah More* (1888).

More, Henry (1614–87) Philosopher. More was educated at the University of Cambridge, England, and he remained at Cambridge for the rest of his life. He was a prominent member of the Cambridge Platonist group, which sought to apply the doctrines of neo-Platonism to the Christian religion. His writings included *An Antidote against Atheism*, *Conjectura Cabbalistica*, the *Grand Mystery of Godliness* and *An Antidote against Idolatry*. He believed that by subduing the natural self and by striving towards moral perfection, it was possible to grasp divine wisdom – a 'principle more noble and inward than reason itself'. The Cambridge Platonists were highly influential on their own generation.

R.A. Hall, *Henry More: Magic, Religion and Experiment* (1990); C.A. Patrides, *The Cambridge Platonists* (1969).

More, Sir Thomas (1478–1535) Statesman, Political Philosopher, Saint and Martyr. More was educated at the University of Oxford, England, and trained as a lawyer. He became a Member of Parliament in 1504 and rose to be Lord Chancellor, succeeding Cardinal WOLSEY in 1529. He was a personal friend of humanists such as COLET and ERASMUS and members of his household were painted by the artist Holbein. He was the author of *Utopia*, a description of an ideal state governed by natural law; this is still read today. He was a devout Roman Catholic and went so far as to compose a theological refutation of the ideas of Martin LUTHER. However, he incurred the displeasure of King HENRY VIII by opposing his plans for the divorce of his first wife, Catherine of Aragon. In 1532 he resigned the Lord Chancellorship and in 1534 he was imprisoned in the Tower of London for refusing to take the oath of the Act of Succession. In the following year he was accused of high treason on the (untrue) grounds that he had opposed the Act of Supremacy and, after his conviction, he was executed. He

was canonised in 1935. More remains a significant figure in English mythology. In recent times his life has been successfully dramatised by Robert Bolt as *A Man for all Seasons*, which became a popular film.

Thomas More, *Utopia* [many editions]; A.J.P. Kenny, *Thomas More* (1983); M.J. Moore (ed.), *Quincentennial Essays on St Thomas More* (1978); G. Rupp, *Thomas More: The King's Good Servant* (1978).

Morison, James (1816–93) Sect Founder. Morison was born in Bathgate, Scotland, and he was educated at the University of Edinburgh. He became a licensed minister of the United Secession Church (the denomination originally founded by Ebenezer ERSKINE), but he was suspended from his duties in 1841 because he was teaching that JESUS CHRIST made atonement for all, not just for the Elect. In response, he founded the Evangelical Union in 1843 in Kilmarnock where his preaching attracted huge congregations. In 1851, he moved his headquarters to the Dundas Street Church in Glasgow and he founded a theological hall in the city. Among his works were commentaries on the Gospels of MATTHEW and MARK and an exposition on the ninth chapter of St PAUL's Epistle to the Romans. The Union became an association of independent theological Churches, most of which joined the Congregational Union of Scotland in 1897.

H. Escott, *A History of Scottish Congregationalism* (1960); W.H.O. Smeaton, *The Life of James Morison* (1901).

Morrison, Robert (1782–1834) Missionary. Morrison was born in Northumberland, England, and was largely self-educated. He was sponsored by the London Missionary Society to translate and distribute the Bible in China. He was ordained and sailed for Canton in 1807. At that period, China was almost completely closed to the West, but Morrison set about learning the language thoroughly and he was employed as an interpreter by the East India Company. By 1818 he had translated the entire Bible and his Chinese Dictionary was published in 1821. This remained the standard work for many years. He sent his assistant, William Milne, to found the Anglo-Chinese College in Malacca and, on his return to England in 1824, he promoted greater understanding of the Chinese people. Even at the time of his death, China was still closed to Westerners, but none the less Morrison's work provided the foundation for later Protestant missions in that country.

M. Broomhall, *Robert Morrison* (1935); L. Ride, *Robert Morrison: The Scholar and the Man* (1957).

Moschus, John (*c.* 550–*c.* 619) Devotional Writer. Moschus was a monk who lived at the monastery of St Theodosius in the Holy Land. He travelled widely, however, and he is remembered for his *Deimon* ('The meadow') which was a collection of monastic stories. It was extremely popular.

H. Chadwick, 'John Moschus and his friend Sophronius the Sophist', *Journal of Theological Studies*, n.s xxv (1974).

Mott, John Raleigh (1865–1955) Ecumenist. Mott was born in New York and he was educated at Upper Iowa University and at Cornell. He became the General Secretary of the World Student Christian Federation and subsequently in 1901, assistant General Secretary of the YMCA. He was a tremendous campaigner for missions and largely as a result of his efforts, the Edinburgh Missionary Conference was convened in 1910. He was Chairman of the International Missionary Council in 1921, Chairman of the second Life and Work Conference in 1937, Vice-Chairman of the provisional committee of the World Council of Churches in 1938 and a Co-President of the World Council of Churches in 1948. He himself was a Methodist, but he was totally committed to the ecumenical movement and was perhaps its most influential figure in the years between 1910 and 1948.

R.C. Mack et al., *Layman Extraordinary: John Mott 1865–1955* (1965); R. Rouse and S.C. Neill (eds), *A History of the Ecumenical Movement 1517–1948*, 2nd edn (1967).

Mowinckel, Sigmund Olaf Plytt (1884–1965) Biblical Scholar and Theologian. Mowinckel was born in Kjernrigøy, Norway, and was educated at the Universities of Oslo, Copenhagen, Marburg and Giessen. Subsequently he was appointed to teach at the University of Oslo, where he remained for his whole career. Among his works were books on the Psalms, on the Messiah, on Ezra and Nehemiah and on the problem of the Hexateuch. He is mainly remembered for his thesis that the liturgical psalms were regularly used at an annual pre-exilic festival, in which the enthronement of God was ritually celebrated. The themes of the festival were later incorporated into the post-exilic hope of the Messiah. His work has been highly influential in the field of Old Testament studies.

S. Mowinckel, *The Psalms in Israel's Worship*, 2 vols (1962); D.R. Ap-Thomas, 'An appreciation of Sigmund Mowinckel's contribution to biblical studies', *Journal of Biblical Literature*, lxxxv (1966).

Mozart, Wolfgang Amadeus (1756–91) Composer. Mozart was born in Salzburg, Austria; he was the son of Leopold Mozart, the Archbishop's court composer. An extraordinary child prodigy, he embarked on extensive tours, playing in all the major courts of Europe. In 1782 he moved to Vienna, but dogged by debt and poverty, he died at the age of thirty-five. He is now recognised as one of the greatest musical geniuses who has ever lived. Among his Church music was his Coronation Mass, two settings for Vespers, the 'Miseracordias Domini', an unfinished Mass in C Minor and a

Requiem. In the nineteenth century, his music was regarded as frivolous and inappropriate for sacred settings, but today his sacred music is as much played as his operas, symphonies and concerti.

A.H. King, *Mozart in Retrospect: Studies in Criticism and Bibliography* (1955); H.C. Robbins Landon (ed.), *The Mozart Compendium* (1990); W. Hildesheimer, *Mozart* (1983).

Muggleton, Ludowicke (1609–98) Sect Founder. As a young man, Muggleton worked in London and came under the influence of various Puritan mystical and millenarian groups. With his cousin, John Reeve, he came to believe that he was one of the two witnesses mentioned in Chapter 11 of the Book of Revelation, who were to seal the Elect immediately before the Day of Judgement. Spurred on by this conviction, he issued a series of tracts in which he argued that his was the final message from God, that reason was the creation of the Devil, that matter and God were the two ultimate realities and that the unforgivable sin was to ignore his (Muggleton's) teaching. He was unafraid of controversy and had many debates with the Quakers and other groups. His followers were known as Muggletonians and the sect survived into the nineteenth century.

C. Hill et al., *The World of the Muggletonians* (1983); A. Jessopp, 'The prophet of Walnut Tree Yard', in *The Coming of the Friars and Other Historical Essays* (1889).

Münzer, Thomas (*c.* 1490–1525) Rebel. Münzer was born in Stolberg, Germany, and he was educated at the Universities of Leipzig and Frankfurt. He met Martin LUTHER at the disputation with ECK in Leipzig in 1519 and, as a Reformer, he settled in Zwickau in 1520. There he came under the influence of the three radical 'Zwickau prophets' (Nicholas Storch, Thomas Drecksel and Marcus Stubner) and he began to teach that he was directly inspired by the Holy Spirit and had no need of intermediary priests or an institutional Church. Expelled from Zwickau, he moved first to Prague and then to Allstedt. His wild preaching attracted attention and, as a danger to public order, he was again evicted from the town. Eventually in Mühlhausen, he encouraged his followers to become involved in the Peasants' Revolt. Luther himself was totally opposed to the peasants and Münzer and his army were defeated at Frankenhausen in 1525. Subsequently he was captured and put to death. He was one of the most effective of the Anabaptist preachers. He turned against Luther when the Reformer refused to countenance a social revolution, describing him as 'Brother Soft-Life' and 'Dr Liar'. He has been the subject of much recent historical interest as the forerunner of later, radical leaders.

E.W. Gritsch, *Reformer Without a Church: The Life and Thought of Thomas Muentzer* (1967); E.G. Rupp, 'Thomas Münzer: Prophet of radical Christianity', *Bulletin of the John Rylands Library*, xlviii (1966); G.H. Williams, *The Radical Reformation* (1962).

Muratori, Lodovico Antonio (1672–1750) Historian, Theologian and Liturgist. Muratori was born near Modena, Italy. He was ordained as a Roman Catholic priest and in 1700 he was appointed archivist and librarian to the Duke of Modena. He was the author of several works of theology, liturgy and Italian history, but he is chiefly remembered for publishing the earliest list of New Testament writings. He found the eighty-five-line document in an eighth-century manuscript. It was thought to date from the second century and was written in bad Latin. In fact, it may well be a translation. Included in the list were the Gospels, Acts, all PAUL's Epistles except Hebrews, the Johannine Epistles and Revelation. The Epistles of JAMES and PETER were omitted. Also included were the Apocalypse of Peter and the Wisdom of Solomon. The Shepherd of HERMAS and Paul's Epistles to the Laodiceans and the Alexandrians, which were regarded as canonical by MARCION, were rejected. This important find is now known as the Muratorian Canon, named after Muratori.

E. Cochrane, 'Muratori: The vocation of a historian', *Catholic Historical Review*, li (1965); G.M. Hahneman, *The Muratorian Fragment and the Development of the Canon* (1972).

N

Nathaniel (first century) Disciple. Nathaniel only appears in the Fourth Gospel. He was a native of Cana in Galilee; he accepted the call to follow JESUS and he was described as being without guile. He is frequently identified with BARTHOLOMEW, one of the twelve Apostles.

John, Chapters 1 and 21.

Nayler, James (*c*. 1618–60) Sect Founder. Nayler was born in Yorkshire and he fought on the Parliamentary side in the Civil War. In 1615, he was converted by George FOX to Quakerism and became a travelling preacher. He suffered several terms of imprisonment and became involved with the Ranters, an antinomian sect which appealed solely to personal religious experience. After it was rumoured that Nayler had raised a woman from the dead, he was heralded as the new Messiah. He initially seems to have resisted this, but subsequently, in 1656, he entered Bristol in triumph with his followers. The authorities arrested him and he was whipped and pilloried. He was eventually released from prison in 1659 and seems to have been reconciled with Fox and the Quakers before his death.

G.F. Nuttall, *James Nayler: A Fresh Approach* (1954).

Neale, John Mason (1818–66) Order Founder and Hymn Writer. Neale was born in London, and was educated at the University of Cambridge. A devoted high churchman, he founded the Cambridge Camden Society in 1839 for the study of ecclesiastical art. This was to become the Ecclesiological Society and was highly influential in the ceremonial and liturgical revival of the nineteenth-century Church of England. From 1846 he was Warden of Sackville College, East Grinstead, which was a charity hospital for old men. He also founded the Sisterhood of St Margaret, an Anglican version of VINCENT DE PAUL's Sisters of Charity, who were dedicated to educational and charitable work. This was to become one of the leading orders of the Church of England. Neale himself was constantly embattled with his Bishop over his ritualism. Always in delicate health, he died young. Today he is primarily remembered for his hymns, many of which are translations from early Greek and Latin originals. Among those which are still sung are 'All glory, laud and honour', 'Good King Wenceslas', 'O come, O come Emmanuel', 'Jerusalem the golden' and 'O happy band of pilgrims'.

M. Donovon, 'John Mason Neale', *Church Quarterly Review*, clxvii (1966); A.G. Lough, *John Mason Neale* (1975).

Neander, Joachim (1650–80) Hymnwriter. Neander was born in Bremen, Germany. He was converted to Pietism as a student and he became the Rector of Dusseldorf Lateinschule. Today he is remembered for his hymns, of which he wrote more than sixty. They are still often sung in the German Protestant Churches and two, translated, are well known in England: 'Praise to the Lord, the Almighty' and 'All my hope on God is founded'.

J. Mearns, 'Neander', in J. Julian (ed.), *A Dictionary of Hymnology*, 2nd edn (1907).

Nerses (*c.* 326–73) Patriarch and Saint. Nerses was a descendant of GREGORY THE ILLUMINATOR and he was educated in Caesarea, Cappadocia. After his wife died, he became a priest and was elected Catholicos (Patriarch) of the Armenian Church in *c.* 363. He instituted a number of reforms within the Church and was known for his charity. Fearless in his duty, he did not hesitate to castigate both King Arshak III and King Pap for their immorality. He was eventually poisoned in consequence. He is remembered as a notably virtuous Patriarch and as the father of St ISAAC.

A.S. Atiya, *A History of Eastern Christianity* (1968).

Nestorius (d. *c.* 451) Patriarch and Heretic/Saint. Nestorius was born in Germanicia in Syria Euphratensis. He was probably a student of THEODORE OF MOPSUESTIA in Antioch and in 428 he was appointed Patriarch of Constantinople. He was unhappy about the term 'Theotokos' (Bearer of God) as a title for the Virgin MARY since it did not give full expression to the humanity of JESUS CHRIST. CYRIL OF ALEXANDRIA spoke out against his views and in 430, at a Council in Rome, Nestorius's teachings were condemned. In 431, the Emperor THEODOSIUS II summoned the Council of Ephesus which deposed Nestorius from his see. His books were condemned in 435 and he finally died in banishment in Egypt. Only fragments of his writings survive, so his theological position remains a matter for scholarly dispute. The term 'Nestorian' came to mean the belief that Jesus had two distinct persons, one human and born of Mary and the other divine. The Council of Ephesus had confirmed the orthodoxy of the title *Theotokos* and, in consequence, several Bishops broke away to form a separate Nestorian Church based in Persia. Nestorian theology was taught first at Edessa under IBAS, and later at Nisibis, at a school founded by BARSUMAS. The new Church had its own Patriarch, first at Seleucia-Ctesiphon and later at Baghdad. Today the Nestorian Church (or the Assyrian Church) calls itself the 'Church of the East' and regards Nestorius as a saint. It uses a Syriac liturgy and survives as a small group in the Middle East and the United States of America.

A. Grant, *History of the Nestorians* (1955); W.A.Wigram, *An Introduction to the History of the Assyrian Church* (1910); F. Young, *From Nicaea to Chalcedon* (1983).

Neumann, Thérèse (1898–1962) Mystic. Neumann was born in Konnersreuth, Bavaria. She became bedridden and blind in 1919. However, she miraculously regained her sight on the day that TERESA OF LISIEUX was beatified in 1923 and she walked again when Teresa was canonised in 1925. She received the stigmata, which bled every Friday; she was subject to visions; and she was reputed to have eaten nothing except Holy Communion from 1922. The town of Konnersreuth rapidly became a place of pilgrimage and Neumann herself has been the subject of great interest.

H.C. Cornef, *The Case of Theresa Neumann* (1951).

Nevius, John Livingston (1829–93) Missionary. Nevius was educated at Princeton Seminary in New Jersey, and he served as a Presbyterian missionary in China from 1854. He is remembered as the author of the 'Nevius method' of mission which involved self-support, lay-witness, self-government and the building of churches in indigenous styles. This approach was used particularly in Korea where a highly successful church network was constructed which survives to this day.

K.S. Latourette, *A History of Christian Missions in China*, 2 vols (1929); L.G. Pack, *The History of Protestant Missions in Korea*, 2nd edn (1971).

Newman, John Henry (1801–90) Theologian and Cardinal. Newman was educated at the University of Oxford, and was ordained into the Church of England ministry. In 1828 he was appointed vicar of the University Church. He came to the notice of the public with his contribution to the *Tracts for the Times*. With E.B. PUSEY, John KEBLE and Hurrell FROUDE, he was a leader of the Oxford Movement, believing that the Church of England was a middle way between the excesses of Rome and the errors of Protestantism. The final tract, number 90, in particular, caused a sensation in its attempt to reconcile the doctrines of the Church of Rome with the Anglican Thirty-Nine Articles of Religion. During this period, Newman also wrote the *Arians of the Fourth Century*. He was having increasing doubts about the validity of Anglicanism; in 1843 he resigned from the University Church and in 1845 he was received as a Roman Catholic. Subsequently he established the Oratory of St PHILIP NERI in Birmingham; he was Rector of the short-lived Catholic University in Dublin from 1854 until 1858 and he fell out with MANNING over a book review in the *Rambler* periodical. He seemed doomed to a succession of failures. However, as a result of a personal attack from Charles KINGSLEY, in 1864 he produced his *Apologia pro Vita Mea* in which he explained his religious odyssey. His obvious sincerity and his mellifluous prose style won him a host of admirers. Among his other books were the *Essay on the Development of Doctrine*, the *Idea of a University* (which contains the most devastating description of that nineteenth-century ideal, the gentleman) and *A Grammar of Assent*. Although the rift with Manning was never healed, his merits were recognised within the Church and he was made a Cardinal in 1879. Newman's ideas on the development of doctrine have influenced many later thinkers and he himself has become something of a cult figure. With his 'silvery voice', his final sermon on the 'parting of friends' and his melancholy career as a Roman Catholic, he has been the inspiration for numerous monographs.

John Henry Newman, *Autobiographical Writings*, edited by H. Tristram (1955); D. Newsome, *The Convert Cardinals* (1993); D. Nicholls and F. Kerr (eds), *John Henry Newman: Reason, Rhetoric and Romanticism* (1991); T.R. Wright (ed.), *John Henry Newman: A Man for our Time?* (1983).

Newton, Sir Isaac (1642–1727) Scientist. Newton was born in Lincolnshire and was educated at the University of Cambridge. A committed member of the Church of England, he none the less had fairly unconventional religious views, rejecting the notion of the Trinity. He was the most eminent scientist of his day and is remembered for his formulation of the law of gravity, for the separation of white light into colours through a prism and for his discovery of differential calculus. He believed that the findings of science revealed the perfect transcendence and omnipotence of God. Among his works were *Philosophiae Naturalis Principia Mathematica* and a work of apocalyptic speculation, *Observations on the Prophecies of Daniel and the Apocalypse of St John*.

F.E. Manuel, *The Religion of Isaac Newton* (1974); R.S. Westfall, *The Life of Isaac Newton* (1993).

Newton, John (1725–1807) Hymn-Writer and Philanthropist. Newton was the son of an English sea-captain and, at a young age, Newton himself joined the Royal Navy where he was involved in the slave trade. After series of traumatic events, and being on a ship that nearly sank in the North Atlantic in 1748, he was converted to Christianity. Influenced by George WHITEFIELD, he was ordained into the Anglican ministry in 1764 and he served congregations in Buckinghamshire and London. With William COWPER, he produced the *Olney*

Hymns, many of which are still sung today. Among the best known are 'How sweet the name of Jesus sounds', 'Amazing grace' and 'Glorious things of thee are spoken'. In his later years he became a famous evangelical preacher and, as a friend of William WILBERFORCE, he became involved in the campaign to abolish the slave trade.

B. Martin and M. Spurrell (eds), *John Newton: Journal of a Slave Trader* (1962); B. Martin, *John Newton: A Biography* (1950).

Nicephoras (*c.* 758–829) Patriarch, Historian, Polemicist and Saint. Nicephoras was a strong defender of icons in the Iconoclastic Controversy and, as a secretary to the Emperor, he was present at the Second Council of Nicaea in 787. Soon afterwards he retired to a monastery, but he was appointed Patriarch of Constantinople in 806. However, in accepting the position, he exonerated the priest Joseph who had blessed the adulterous marriage of the Emperor Constantine VI. This aroused great resentment among the influential Studite monks. With the resumption of the Iconoclastic Controversy, Nicephoras was exiled in 815 and he returned to his monastery. Here he continued to inveigh against the iconoclasts and he produced an important history of Byzantium, the *Historia Syntomos*, in which he tried to find an explanation for the military success of Islam. Despite his weakness in the Adulterine Controversy (as it came to be called), he was regarded as a saint soon after his death.

P.J. Alexander, *The Patriarch Nicephorus of Constantinople* (1958).

Nicholas (? fourth century) Legendary Bishop and Saint. Nicholas is said to have been the Bishop of Myra in Lycia. He is one of the most popular saints, being the patron of Russia, of sailors and of children. Various legends are told of him. He is thought to have provided the dowries for three poor girls and pawnbrokers commonly work under the sign of three gold balls commemorating those gifts. He is also believed to have saved three little boys from being pickled by a murderous butcher. Today, as Santa Claus, he is expected to provide annual gifts for the world's children – either on 6 December or on Christmas Eve.

C.W. Jones, *St Nicholas* (1978).

Nicholas I (d. 867) Saint and Pope. Nicholas was born into a noble Roman family and he was elected Pope in 858. His reign was dominated by the question of the primacy of Rome. The Eastern Emperor Michael III had deposed Ignatius from the See of Constantinople and had promoted PHOTIUS. Nicholas refused to sanction this; he anathematised Photius and restored Ignatius. He also tried to win the Bulgars to allegiance to Rome rather than to Constantinople. In response, Photius declared Nicholas deposed in 867, but was himself removed the same year. In the West, Nicholas removed the Archbishops of Trier and Cologne from their sees when they supported the bigamous marriage of Lothair II of Lorraine. He deposed Archbishop John of Ravenna for violating papal property rights and he made use of the False Decretals in 865, knowing them to be false. These upheld his authority; they were attributed to St ISIDORE, but were, in fact, compiled in France in *c.* 850. He is also remembered for supporting the endeavours of the missionaries CYRIL and METHODIUS. Nicholas emerges as one of the more imperious of the early mediaeval Popes. His success in increasing the prestige of Rome was a large factor in his canonisation.

F. Dvornik, *The Photian Schism* (1948); J. Haller, *Nikolaus I und Pseudo-Isidor* (1936) [no English translation available].

Nicholas V (1397–1455) Pope. Nicholas was born Tommaso Parentucelli and he was educated in Bologna and Florence, Italy. He was consecrated Bishop of Bologna in 1444 and elected Pope in 1447, succeeding EUGENIUS IV. He is remembered for securing the abdication of Antipope Felix V and for the dissolution of the Council of Basle – thus ending the Schism. As a result of his declaring a Jubilee in 1450, many pilgrims visited Rome and in 1452 he crowned Frederick III Holy Roman Emperor. This was to be the last imperial coronation in Rome. He was a great patron of the Renaissance. He did much to rebuild the city of Rome and Fra ANGELICO was among the artists employed. In addition, he was a notable collector of books and he laid the foundations of the Vatican Library. The fall of Constantinople to the Turks in 1453 was a tremendous blow to the whole of Christendom. It is said that the news hastened his death; certainly he was unsuccessful in rousing the European princes to crusade against the Muslim invasion.

K. Pleyer, *Die Politik Nikolaus V* (1927) [no English translation available]; C.W. Westfall, *In This Most Perfect Paradise: Alberti, Nicholas V and the Invention of Conscious Urban Planning in Rome* (1974).

Nicholas of Cusa (1401–64)   Cardinal and Philosopher. Nicholas was born in Kues, Germany and was educated in Heidelberg, Prague and Cologne. He attended the Council of Basle and was created a Cardinal in 1448. As Bishop of Brisen, he served as papal legate throughout Germany and he worked tirelessly for the reform of abuses. His efforts, however, were opposed by Duke Sigismund of Austria and he was forced to flee to Rome. He was supported throughout by the Pope and he died as Camerarius of the Sacred College in Rome. He is remembered for his *De Docta Ignorantia*, in which he argued that truth is unknowable. Only in God are all contradictions resolved and it is through intuition (*docta ignorantia*) that God can be found. Among his other works were *De Concordantia Catholica* (a defence of the authority of Church Councils), *De Coniecturis, De Quaerendo Deum, De Non Aliud* and a final summary of his position, *De Apice Theoriae*. His writings were influenced by those of AUGUSTINE, BONAVENTURA, Pseudo-DIONYSIUS and Meister ECKHART and, within the Western Church, he is regarded as a significant thinker.

H. Bett, *Nicholas of Cusa* (1932); E.F. Jacob, 'Nicholas of Cusa', in F.J.C. Hearnshaw (ed.), *The Social and Political Ideas of Some Great Thinkers of the Renaissance and Reformation* (1925); P.E. Sigmund, *Nicholas of Cusa and Mediaeval Political Thought* (1963).

Nicholas, Henry (c. 1502–c. 1580)   Sect Founder and Mystic. Nicholas was born in Münster, Germany. From an early age, he claimed to have had visions from God. He became a merchant and, in c. 1540, he founded a new sect, the Family of Love or Familists. Among the beliefs of the new group were an emphasis on mystical, Pantheistic communion with God, the imminent Second Coming of JESUS and salvation only available to members of the sect. Nicholas spent much of his adult life at Emden, but he was constantly harassed by the religious authorities and he spent his final years as a fugitive. There were Familist groups throughout the Low Countries and the sect had a strong following in England. However, it had disappeared by the end of the seventeenth century.

C.W. Marsh, *The Family of Love in English Society* (1994); A.C. Thomas, *The Family of Love or the Familists* (1893).

Nicodemus (first century)   Disciple. Nicodemus was a member of the Jewish Council who came to visit JESUS in secret. According to Chapter 3 of the Fourth Gospel, this encounter prompted Jesus's famous discourse on spiritual rebirth. Later Nicodemus was described as helping JOSEPH OF ARIMATHAEA bury

Jesus. An apocryphal gospel is attributed to him.

John, Chapters 3 and 19; M. de Jonge, *Nicodemus and Jesus: Some Observations on Misunderstanding and Understanding in the Fourth Gospel* (1971); S. Mendrer, 'Nikodemus', *Journal of Biblical Literature*, lxxvii (1958) [English synopsis].

Nicodemus of the Holy Mountain (*c.* 1749–1809) Saint and Devotional Writer. Nicodemus was born on the Greek island of Naxos and he joined the monastic community on Mount Athos. He is remembered for his *Philocalia*, a collection of mystical writings connected with Hesychasm. He compiled this in conjunction with St Macarius Notares. He also produced the *Pidalion*, a commentary on the Canon Law of the Orthodox Church, and he published a Greek edition of IGNATIUS LOYOLA's *Spiritual Exercises*. He is regarded as a saint in the Eastern Church.

E. Kadloubovsky and G.E.H. Palmer (eds), *Unseen Warfare* (1952).

Nicolas (first century) Sect Founder. The Nicolaitans were a sect mentioned in Chapter 2 of the Book of Revelation. They seem to have retained various pagan practices and later they were mentioned by IRENAEUS, CLEMENT OF ALEXANDRIA and TERTULLIAN. Irenaeus recorded that the sect was founded by Nicolas of Antioch, who was listed in Acts Chapter 6 as being appointed a Deacon in the Apostolic Church. In any event the sect seems to have disappeared by the end of the second century. The term 'Nicolaitan' was sometimes used disparagingly of a married priest by a celibate in the Middle Ages.

M. Goguel, 'Les Nicolaites', *Revue d'Histoire des Religions*, cxv (1937) [no English translation]; A. von Harnack, 'The sect of Nicolaitans and Nicolaus the Deacon in Jerusalem', *Journal of Religion*, iii (1923).

Nicole, Pierre (1625–95) Theologian. Nicole was born in Chartres, France.

After studying at the University of Paris, he taught at the Convent of Port-Royal where he collaborated with Antoine ARNAULD. His early works were written from a moderate Jansenist position. Later he defended Catholic doctrines against the Calvinists and his final work was written at the instigation of Bishop BOSSUET against the Quietism of Mme GUYON and de MOLINOS. His most important book was perhaps his *Essais de Morale*, a series of essays applying the teachings of Christianity to the problems of everyday existence.

E.D. James, *Pierre Nicole: Jansenist and Humanist* (1972).

Niebuhr, Reinhold (1893–1971) Theologian. Niebuhr was born in Missouri. He was the elder brother of Richard Niebuhr, another important theologian. From 1928 until 1960 he taught at the Union Theological Seminary, New York. Influenced by both BARTH and BRUNNER, he was none the less critical of Barth's lack of interest in society. As a young man he had served an evangelical congregation and had been a member of the American Socialist Party. Among his many books were *Moral Man and Immoral Society*, *The Nature and Destiny of Man* and *Christian Realism and Political Problems*. His aim was to propound a 'vital prophetic Christianity' and he famously taught that 'Man has always been his most vexing problem. How shall he think of himself?' He taught both the absolute sovereignty of God and the possibility of reforming human institutions. With his boundless energy, he exerted enormous influence on the religious and political thinking of educated Americans in the mid twentieth century.

R.M. Brown (ed.), *The Essential Reinhold Niebuhr* (1986); K. Durkin, *Reinhold Niebuhr* (1989); G. Harland, *The Thought of Reinhold Niebuhr* (1960); N.A. Scott (ed.), *The Legacy of Reinhold Niebuhr* (1975).

Niemöller, Martin (1892–1984) Rebel. Niemöller was born in Lynstadt, Germany, and he was educated at the University of Münster. He served in the German navy in the First World War and he was ordained to the Lutheran ministry in 1924. A successful pastor, he joined BONHOEFFER and others in their protests against Nazi policies. He became President of the Pastors' Emergency League in 1933 and he was an active member of the Confessing Church. He opposed Bishop Marahren's decision to co-operate with the Ministry of Church Affairs and in 1937 he was arrested. He refused to compromise his principles and spent the years from 1937 until 1945 in Sachsenhausen and then in Dachau concentration camps. He thus became a symbol of Christian opposition to the barbarities of the Nazi regime. After the war, he held various positions within the Evangelical Church and between 1961 and 1968, he was a President of the World Council of Churches.

J. Bentley, *Martin Niemöller* (1984); K. Robbins, 'Martin Niemöller, the German Church struggle and English opinion', *Journal of Ecclesiastical History*, xxxi (1970); D. Schmidt, *Martin Niemöller* (1959).

Nietzsche, Friedrich Wilhelm (1844–1900) Philosopher. Nietzsche was born in Rocher, Prussia. He was the son of a Lutheran minister and he was educated at the Universities of Bonn and Leipzig. On the recommendation of RITSCHL he was appointed to a Chair at the University of Basle in 1869, but was compelled to resign on grounds of ill-health ten years later. He became insane in 1889. He is remembered for his prophetic books which included *Also Sprach Zarathustra*, *Jenseits von Gut und Böse* and *Der Antichrist*. Influenced by SCHOPENHAUER and profoundly disturbed by the evolutionary theories of DARWIN, he taught that the 'Superman' must go beyond good and evil and transcend the traditional teachings of Christianity. In a single-minded drive for power, through self-discipline and strength, he will achieve success, order and power in the world. Nietzsche's vision and his scorn of the 'weak' and 'pitiful' values of the Christian Church were adopted as part of the fascist creed of Adolf Hitler.

F. Copleston, *Friedrich Nietzsche: Philosopher of Culture*, revised edition (1975); W.A. Kaufmann, *Nietzsche; Philosopher, Psychologist, Antichrist* (1974); P.R. Sedgwick (ed.), *Nietzsche: A Critical Reader* (1995); M. Tanner, *Nietzsche* (1994).

Nightingale, Florence (1820–1910) Philanthropist. Nightingale was born into an aristocratic English family in Florence. In the face of strong disapproval, she insisted on studying nursing and she visited the Sisters of Charity in Alexandria in 1849 and FLIEDNER's Deaconesses at Kaiserswerth in 1851. An opportunity came with the outbreak of the Crimean War in 1854: with the support of the Secretary of State for War and in the teeth of innumerable obstructions from the military establishment, she completely transformed the chaotic hospital in Scutari, in the process becoming a household name. On her return to England, she was personally commended by Queen Victoria and the Nightingale School for Nurses was founded in St Thomas's Hospital in 1860. Her *Notes on Nursing* remained a standard text book for many years and went through many editions. Her powerful social connections and her indomitable will totally changed the image and nature of the nursing profession.

M.E. Baly, *Florence Nightingale and the Nursing Legacy* (1986); L. Strachey, *Eminent Victorians* (1918); C. Woodham-Smith, *Florence Nightingale* (1950).

Nikon (1605–81) Patriarch and Liturgist. After a brief marriage, Nikon became a monk first at Solovietski and then at Kojeozerski. In 1646 he was appointed Archimandrate of the Novospaski monastery; in 1649 he became Metropolitan of Novgorod and in 1652, with the support of the Czar, he was elected Patriarch of Moscow. He is remembered for his reforms of the Russian liturgy which brought it into line with that of Greece and the Ukraine. This aroused considerable opposition and caused the 'Old Believers', such as AVVAKUM, to form a separate sect. A man of great ability, but little tact, Nikon had fallen from royal favour by 1658 and in 1667 he was finally deposed and banished. None the less his liturgical reforms were confirmed and, after his death, all the decrees against him were revoked and he was buried with full Patriarchal honours. Today he is regarded as one of the greatest of the Russian Patriarchs.

F.C. Conybeare, *Russian Dissenters* (1921); R. Thornton, *Lives of Eminent Russian Prelates* (1854).

Norbert (*c.* 1080–1134) Saint, Archbishop and Order Founder. Norbert was born in Xanten, Germany, and he led a worldly life until he had a conversion experience at the age of thirty-five. He was then ordained as a priest and, after an unsuccessful attempt at reforming his brother Canons in Xanten, he became an itinerant preacher. In 1120 he founded a community in Prémontré in Northern France which was to become the Premonstratensian Order. The order was formally recognised by Pope Honorius II in 1126 and Norbert himself was appointed Archbishop of Magdeburg in the same year. The Premonstratensians follow an austere version of the Augustinian Rule and, known as the 'White Canons' or 'Norbertians', they quickly spread throughout Europe. They were dedicated to preaching and to parish work and still survive, in greatly depleted numbers, to this day. Norbert himself was a friend of St BERNARD OF CLAIRVAUX; he was much respected as a clerical reformer and

he ended his life as Chancellor of Italy. He was canonised in 1582.

O. Praem, *St Norbert* (1886).

Noth, Martin (1902–68) Theologian and Biblical Scholar. Noth was born in Dresden, Germany, and he was educated at the Universities of Erlangen, Rostock and Leipzig. He subsequently taught at Königsberg, Bonn and Jerusalem. He is remembered for his radical theses on the origin and organisation of the early Israelite tribes, which he expounded in his *Geschichte Israels* and his *Die Welt des Alten Testaments*. In addition, he argued that the Book of Deuteronomy must be seen as a preamble to the 'Deuteronomic histories' (the Books of Joshua, Judges, Samuel and Kings) rather than as a conclusion to the Pentateuch. He was also the author of several biblical commentaries. His ideas have been highly influential and have transformed the pattern of Old Testament Scholarship.

Martin Noth, *The Laws in the Pentateuch*, edited by H.W. Wolff and with a memoir by R. Smend (1966).

Novatian (d. 257/8) Antipope, Sect Founder and Martyr. Little is known of the life of Novatian. He was a Roman presbyter who was elected Bishop of Rome in opposition to Pope Cornelius in 251. He was the author of an important work on the doctrine of the Trinity and he was martyred in the Valerian persecutions. The cause of the quarrel was that Novatian believed that those who had fallen away in the Decian persecutions should not freely be welcomed back into the Church. The new sect was orthodox in its theology; it was intensely disciplined and it survived well into the fifth century.

W.H.C. Frend, *The Rise of Christianity* (1984); J.N.D. Kelly, *Early Christian Doctrines* (1958).

O

Oates, Titus (1649–1705) Conspirator. Oates was born in Rutland, England. He was the son of a Baptist minister, but in 1673 he was ordained as an Anglican clergyman. Subsequently he converted to Roman Catholicism. While pursuing his studies in Spain, he claimed to have heard of a plot to replace the Protestant King Charles II with his brother, the Catholic James (who was later to become JAMES II). The case became a cause célèbre. Oates was regarded as a national hero and many innocent people were harassed and persecuted (including Oliver PLUNKET, Archbishop of Armagh). It turned out, however, that there was no evidence of such a plot and Oates was convicted of perjury in 1685. The incident did much to revive anti-Catholic feeling in England.

J. Lane, *Titus Oates* (1949).

Occom, Samson (1723–92) Missionary. Occom was born in Mohegan, Connecticut. As a young man, during the course of the 'Great Awakening', he had a conversion experience. He determined to dedicate his life to the care of the American Indians. Between 1749 and 1764 he ministered to the Montauk Indians on Long Island. He then spent three years in Great Britain and raised ten thousand pounds, then an enormous sum, for his missions. He returned to America in 1768 to continue his work. He is remembered for establishing the Indian town of Brotherstown in New York and for producing an Indian hymnal. Occom was perhaps the best-known of the eighteenth-century Indian missionaries.

R.F. Bekhofer, *Salvation and the Savage* (1965).

O'Connell, Daniel (1775–1847) Politician and Rebel. O'Connell was born in Ireland. He dedicated himself to the causes of Catholic Emancipation and the Repeal of the Irish Union with Great Britain. In 1823 he formed the Catholic Association to agitate for emancipation. He became a Member of Parliament in 1828 and after the Roman Catholic Emancipation Act was finally passed in 1829, he continued to fight for Irish freedom. In 1840 he founded the Repeal Association and, after organising several mass meetings, he was imprisoned for a year in 1844. Although released on appeal, his health was broken by the experience. O'Connell was an immensely influential orator, but, unlike later Irish republicans, he rejected the use of violence in gaining his political objectives.

R.D. Edwards, *Daniel O'Connell and his World* (1975); M. Tierney, *Daniel O'Connell: Nine Centenary Essays* (1949).

Odilia (d. *c.* 720) Saint and Order Founder. Odilia was born blind. She was the daughter of Aldaric, a nobleman of Alsace. When she miraculously regained her sight, she founded a convent in Odilienberg in the Vosges Mountains. This became an important centre of pilgrimage in the Middle Ages, particularly for those with eye disease. Odilia is the patron saint of Alsace.

M. Barth, *Die Heilige Odilia* (1938) [no English translation available].

Odilio (*c.* 962–1049) Saint. Odilio entered the monastery of Cluny in 991 and in 994 he was elected its fifth Abbot. He presided over a period of enormous expansion for the order. Not only were twenty-eight new daughter houses founded, but the whole organisation was centralised around the mother-house at Cluny. In addition he was a councillor of the Emperor HENRY II and an influential figure in European politics. He is particularly remembered for introducing the commemoration of All Souls' Day at Cluny. This spread throughout the whole Western Church. A man of enormous compassion as well as phenomenal administrative ability, he was canonised only fourteen years after his death.

Catholic University of America, *New Catholic Encyclopaedia* (1967).

Odo (879–942) Saint, Devotional Writer and Order Founder. Odo was the son of Lord Abbo of Déols and he was educated in Aquitaine and Paris. In 901 he joined the religious community at Baume where he supervised the monastery school. In 927 he was elected Abbot of Cluny and, under his leadership, the influence of the monastery was greatly extended. Many monasteries in the south of France and even Monte Cassino (founded by St BENEDICT himself) reformed themselves along Clunaic lines. Odo also took part in the diplomatic affairs of his time and was the author of several devotional works. In the eleventh and twelfth centuries, Cluny was to exercise a decisive influence on the life of the Church, but the foundation of this pre-eminence was laid by Odo a hundred years earlier.

G.B. Sitwell, *St Odo of Cluny* (1958).

Offa (d. 796) Monarch. Offa succeeded Ethelbald as King of Mercia in 757 and by 779 he controlled the whole of the south of England. He even went so far as to describe himself as 'King of the whole English land'. In the history of the English Church, he is remembered as the founder of the Archbishopric of Lichfield (which was suppressed in 803) and of the Abbeys of St Albans and Bath. He conducted diplomatic negotiations with CHARLEMAGNE and was anxious to support the authority of the Church in his kingdom.

F.M. Stenton, *Anglo-Saxon England* (1943).

Olave (995–1030) Monarch and Saint. Olave fought against the Danes in England and Normandy and was converted to Christianity during this period. After winning the battle of Nesje, he became King of Norway in 1016. Known as Olave the Fat, his rule was not popular and he was finally deposed by his chieftains aided by King Canute of England in 1025. He died trying to regain his kingdom at the Battle of Stiklestad. Subsequently his death was regarded as a martyrdom. Miracles took place at his grave and, after his son Magnus became King, the cult grew rapidly. Today Olave is regarded as the patron saint of Norway.

S. Sturluson, *Heimskringla*, translated by E. Monsen and A.H. Smith (1938); G. Turville-Petre, *The Heroic Age of Scandinavia* (1951).

Oldcastle, Sir John (*c.* 1378–1417) Rebel. Oldcastle was born in Herefordshire and he later became Lord Cobham. He was known to be a follower of John WYCLIFFE and in 1413 he was accused of heresy. He escaped from imprisonment in the Tower of London and he led a Lollard rebellion against the government. When this proved unsuccessful, he went into hiding until he was finally caught and executed in 1417. He was believed to have been a drinking companion of the young Prince Henry and, as such, was the inspiration for Shakespeare's Falstaff.

M.E. Ashton, 'Lollardy and sedition', *Past and Present*, xvii (1960); M. Dominik, *A Shakespearean*

Anomaly: Shakespeare's Hand in 'Sir John Oldcastle' (1991); W.T. Waugh, 'Sir John Oldcastle', *English Historical Review*, xx (1905).

Oldham, Joseph Houldsworld (1874–1969) Ecumenist and Missionary. Oldham was born in India of an army family and was educated at the Universities of Oxford, Edinburgh, and Halle, Germany. He was appointed organising secretary of the World Missionary Conference which met in 1910. Subsequently he edited *The International Review of Missions* and was joint secretary of the International Missionary Conference from 1921 until 1938, during which time he worked closely with John MOTT. He organised the 1938 Life and Work Conference in Oxford and it was at this conference that the first provisional committee for the World Council of Churches was convened. He is also remembered for his work in Africa. A natural leader, he acted as unofficial missionary representative to the colonial government for many years.

K. Bliss, 'Joseph Oldham', in *Dictionary of National Biography 1961–1971* (1995).

Olier, Jean-Jacques (1608–57) Community Founder and Devotional Writer. Olier was born in Paris, and was educated at the Sorbonne. Under the influence of VINCENT DE PAUL, he was ordained into the Roman Catholic priesthood. In 1641 he founded a seminary for priests at Vaugirard. The following year it moved to St Sulpice, Paris, where Olier was parish priest. This was to become a model for other seminaries. It was a community of secular priests sharing a common life, who were dedicated to mission and social reform. In 1657 Olier sent a group of his priests to the new Canadian colony of Montreal to continue their work in the New World. He was the author of several devotional works including *Catéchisme Chrétien pour la Vie Intérieure* and *Introduction à la Vie et aux Vertus Chétiennes*, both of which were influential on generations of clergy.

C. Letourneau, *La Mission de Jean-Jacques Olier et la Fondation des Grands Séminaires en France* (1906) [no English translation available].

Olivi, Petrus Johannis (*c.* 1248–98) Theologian. Olivi was born in Sérignan, France and in *c.* 1260 he joined the Franciscan community at Béziers. He soon became regarded as a leader of the Spiritual Franciscans, but in 1282 he was accused of heresy. His orthodoxy was established at the General Chapter of Montpellier in 1287 and in Paris in 1292. He was the author of *Postilla super Apocalypsim* (which was to be condemned in 1326) and various biblical commentaries. Influenced by JOACHIM OF FIORE, he taught a neo-Platonic doctrine of plurality of forms.

C. Partee, 'Petrus John Olivi: Historical and doctrinal study', *Franciscan Studies*, xx (1960).

Onesimus (first century) Saint and possibly Bishop. Onesimus was a slave who was returned to his master PHILEMON by St PAUL. In the Epistle, Paul urged Philemon to treat Onesimus as 'no longer a slave, but more than a slave, as a beloved brother'. His name means 'useful' and Paul made a play on this when he wrote: 'Formerly he was useless to you, but now he is indeed useful to you and to me'. Onesimus has tentatively been identified with Onesimus, Bishop of Ephesus, mentioned by IGNATIUS.

Epistle of Paul to Philemon.

Optatus (fourth century) Bishop and Theologian. Optatus was Bishop of Milevis in Numidia. Nothing is known of his life, but he is remembered for his treatise *De Schismate Donatistarum*. He argued that the Donatists could not be the true Church because they lacked catholicity (worldwide extension) and he attacked their claim to holiness. These arguments were later used to great effect by St AUGUSTINE. *De Schismate* also has an attached appendix of useful historical documents.

R.B. Eno, 'The Works of Optatus as a turning point in the African ecclesiology', *The Themist*, xxxvii (1973); J. Merdringer, 'Optatus reconsidered', *Studia Patristica*, xxii (1989).

Origen (*c.* 185–*c.* 254) Theologian. Origen was born in Egypt. He was a student of CLEMENT OF ALEXANDRIA and his father was martyred in the Severine persecutions of 202. He supervised the Catechitical School at Alexandria for twenty-eight years, during which time thousands came to hear his lectures. During the persecution of Caracella in 215, he travelled to Palestine and, on his second visit in 230, he was ordained by the Bishops of Caesarea and Aelia. Bishop DEMETRIUS of Alexandria, however, objected to this and exiled Origen from his diocese. The reasons for Demetrius's stand are not clear. EUSEBIUS OF CAESAREA insists that it was a result of jealousy. There may have been canonical objections; as a young man Origen may have castrated himself (taking literally the words of JESUS in MATTHEW 19:12) and Demetrius may have objected to the ordination of a eunuch. In any event, Origen established an equally successful school in Caesarea. During the persecution of Decius in 250 he was imprisoned and tortured and he died soon afterwards. He was a highly prolific writer and his surviving works include the *Hexpla* (a comparison of six versions of the Old Testament), *De Principiis* (a systematic theology which dealt with God and his relationship with the universe, the place of humanity, good and evil and the interpretation of Scripture) and an important treatise on prayer. In this he argued that prayer is not a matter of asking for things, but of participating in the life of God. Much of what we know of his life comes from Eusebius's history, from JEROME (who accused him of subordinationism) and from his devoted follower,

GREGORY THAUMATURGUS. Although his teachings were admired by ATHANASIUS, BASIL and GREGORY OF NAZIANZUS, a council at Alexandria in 400 condemned his ideas on the Trinity in *De Principiis*, and the controversy continued to smoulder until the sixth century when his teaching was condemned at the Council of Constantinople. Despite the ultimate rejection of his speculative theology, Origen is an exceptionally important figure in the history of the Church. In his biblical scholarship, he recognised that Scripture could be interpreted literally, morally and allegorically. His stress on the symbolic meaning of the text has been profoundly influential on the later history of biblical understanding.

H. Crouzel, *Origen* (1989); R.P.C. Hanson, *Allegory and Event: A Study of the Sources and Significance of Origen's Interpretation of Scripture* (1959).

Orosius Paulus (early fifth century) Historian. Orosius was a native of Spain, but in the face of the Vandal invasions of 414, he fled to Hippo in North Africa. He acted as a messenger for St AUGUSTINE to recruit JEROME's support against the Pelagians. When the teachings of PELAGIUS were upheld at a council in Diospolis, Orosius was compelled to defend his own position. Then, in 417, encouraged by Augustine, he wrote his *Historia Adversus Paganos*, which rebuts the pagan charge that Rome was sacked by the Goths in 410 because the people had deserted the gods. The material from 378 to 417 has important historical value because its sources have not survived.

I.W. Raymond (ed.), *The 'Historia' of Orosius* (1936).

Ortlieb of Strasbourg (early thirteenth century) Sect Founder. Little is known of the life of Ortlieb. He was the leader of an ascetic sect known as the Ortlibarii who were condemned by Pope INNOCENT III. They seem to have rejected the

authority of the Church and to have re-
lied on the guidance of the inner spirit.
Similarities have been detected between
them and the Waldensians, the Cathari
and the Amalricians, but there is no
historical evidence of any connection.

G. Leff, *Heresy in the Later Middle Ages* (1967).

Osmund (d. 1099) Saint, Bishop and
?Liturgist. Osmund was King William I
of England's Chancellor. He is primarily
remembered as a compiler of the
Domesday Book. In 1078 he was consecrated Bishop of Salisbury. An able
administrator, his constitution of the
cathedral chapter became a model for
several other foundations. He is also
credited wth establishing the Sarum Rite,
a modification of the Roman liturgy,
but most scholars date it to the early
thirteenth century.

R.W. Pfaff, *New Liturgical Feasts in Later Mediaeval England* (1970); W.J. Torrance, *St Osmund*
(1919).

Oswald (*c.* 605–42) Saint and Monarch. Oswald was the son of Ethelfrith of
Northumbria. He was converted to
Christianity by the monks of Iona and he
became King after defeating the British
monarch Cadwalla in 634. It was he who
invited St AIDAN to establish his headquarters on Lindisfarne and he did a
great deal to support the mission. He
was eventually killed at the battle of Ma-
serfield against the pagan King Penda of
Mercia. He was generally regarded as a
martyr and his reign was long regarded
as a golden age of co-operation between
Church and State.

P. Clemoes, *The Cult of St Oswald on the Continent* (1983); E. Grierson, *The Story of the North-
umbrian Saints* (1913).

Otterbein, Philip William (1726–1813)
Denomination Founder. Otterbein was
born in Prussia. He was the son of a minister and was himself ordained. In 1752
he travelled to America as a missionary.

Initially he served a German Reformed
congregation in Lancaster, Pennsylvania.
His ministry was highly successful and
in 1800, with Martin BOEHM, he
founded the Church of the United Brethren in Christ. This was a sect of the
Methodist type, Arminian in theology
and episcopal in organisation. In 1946
it merged with the Evangelical Church
to form the Evangelical United
Brethren. This subsequently joined with
the Methodist Church to form the United
Methodist Church in 1948.

T. Shaw, *The Bible Christians* (1965).

Otto (*c.* 1060–1139) Bishop, Missionary and Saint. Otto was born into a
noble family in Swabia. He entered the
service of the Emperor HENRY IV and he
was consecrated Bishop of Bamberg in
1106. He proved to be a dedicated Bishop
and is credited with building several new
churches and monasteries and with com-
pleting Bamberg Cathedral. Although he
tried to take a neutral position in the Investiture Controversy, for a short time he
was suspended from his duties in 1118.
The conflict was only finally resolved
with the Concordat of Worms of 1122.
He is mainly remembered today for his
highly successful missionary journey
among the people of Pomerania. He was
canonised fifty years after his death.

I.S. Robinson, *Authority and Resistance in the
Investiture Contest* (1978).

Otto I (912–73) Monarch. Otto inherited the throne of Saxony from his
father, Henry I, in 936. He was anxious
to restore the alliance of Church and
State that apparently existed in the time
of CHARLEMAGNE and, to this end, he
insisted on his right to appoint new
Bishops and Archbishops. He did much
to establish new dioceses and he supported the cultural initiatives of the
Church. He extended his territory to the
east and in Italy and he was crowned
Holy Roman Emperor by Pope JOHN XII

in 962. The Pope also confirmed his rights in papal elections. Subsequently, however, John schemed against Otto who deposed him and appointed a layman as Pope Leo VIII. Although John later disposed of Leo, the Papacy itself was left in a less than satisfactory position. Otto's determination to control the Papacy set a precedent for many later conflicts.

W. Ullmann, 'The origin of Ottonianum', *Cambridge Historical Journal*, xi (1953/5).

Otto, Rudolf (1869–1937) Theologian. Otto was born in Hanover, Germany, and was educated in Erlangen and Göttingen. He then taught theology at Göttingen, Breslau and Marburg. He is primarily remembered for his *Das Heilig*, translated into English as 'The Idea of the Holy'. Drawing on his knowledge of oriental religions and psychology as well as on the Christian tradition, he coined the term 'numinous' to describe the feeling of awe and attraction evoked by an encounter with the Divine.

P.C. Almond, *Rudolf Otto: An Introduction to his Philosophical Theology* (1984); R.F. Davidson, *Rudolf Otto's Interpretation of Religion* (1947); H.W. Turner, *Rudolf Otto, The Idea of the Holy: A Guide for Students* (1974).

Ozanam, [Antoine] Frédéric (1813–53) Historian and Order Founder. Ozanam is remembered as the founder of the Society of St VINCENT DE PAUL. This is a society for laymen who volunteer for work among the poor. It started as a student organisation at the Sorbonne, Paris, France. Two years earlier Ozanam had written a pamphlet criticising the socialism of SAINT-SIMON and he later was to give a series of lectures expounding a new Catholic social theory. In 1848, with the well-known orator Lacordaire, he founded the periodical *Ere Nouvelle* as an organ of Catholic socialism. Then in 1849 he published his *Civilisation Chrétienne chez les Francs*, a study of the influence of the Church on the education of the early Frankish tribes. He also wrote important books on DANTE and on early Franciscan poetry. Although subject to much criticism, the Society was hugely successful and, at the time of Ozanam's death, had nearly three thousand chapters in Europe, the Near East, North America and Africa.

G. Goyau et al., *Frédéric Ozanam* (1925) [no English translation available]; E. Rermer, *The Historical Thought of Frédéric Ozanam* (1959).

P

Pachomius (*c.* 290–346) Saint and Order Founder. Little certain is known of the life of Pachomius. He was born into a pagan family in Egypt, but was converted to Christianity after serving for a time as a soldier. In *c.* 320 he settled in Tabennisi and he is remembered as the founder of community monastic life. By the year of his death, eleven monasteries were in existence under his supervision (including two for women). His Rule has survived only in a Latin translation, but it was influential on BASIL, John CASSIAN and on BENEDICT.

D. Knowles, *From Pachomius to Ignatius: A Study in the Constitutional History of the Religious Orders* (1966); P. Rousseau, *Pachomius: The Making of a Community in Fourth-Century Egypt* (1985).

Pacian (*c.* 310–*c.* 390) Devotional Writer, Bishop and Saint. Pacian was an early Bishop of Barcelona, Spain. He is mentioned in JEROME'S *De Viris Illustribus* and his surviving works include three letters and a short treatise on the forgiveness of sins. He is chiefly remembered, however, for the epigram '*Christianus mihi nomen est, Catholicus vero cognomen*' (my personal name is Christian; my surname is Catholic).

E.A. Livingstone (ed.), *The Oxford Dictionary of the Christian Church*, revised edition (1997).

Paine, Thomas (1737–1809) Political Philosopher. Paine was brought up in Thetford, England. Although he was baptised into the Church of England, his father was a member of the Society of Friends and the young Thomas was influenced by Quaker ideas. After a varied career, he moved to America in 1774 where he published his pamphlet *Common Sense*, in which he argued for the colonies' independence. This sold in huge numbers and gave him a certain notoriety. In 1787 he returned to England and in 1791 and 1792 both parts of his *Rights of Man* were published. He was indicted on a charge of treason and had to make a hasty escape to France. There he wrote the *Age of Reason*, for which the French imprisoned him for a year. He spent the final years of his life in America. Deist in their orientation, his books are still read for their radical commitment to individual freedom.

A.O. Aldridge, *Man of Reason: The Life of Thomas Paine* (1960); I. Dyck (ed.), *Citizen of the World: Essays on Thomas Paine* (1988); J. Keane, *Tom Paine: A Political Life* (1995); I.M. Thompson Jr, *The Religious Beliefs of Thomas Paine* (1965).

Palestrina, Giovanni Pierluigi da (*c.* 1525–94) Composer. Palestrina was born in the Italian town of Palestrina (hence his name), but was educated in Rome. In 1551 he was appointed Master of the Capella Giulia of St Peter's by Pope Julius III and later he moved first to the Capella of St John Lateran and later to Santa Maria Maggiore. In 1570 he became the composer of the Papal Chapel and in 1571 Choirmaster of St Peter's. He is remembered as the author of over a hundred settings for the Mass and more than two hundred and fifty motets. He is generally regarded as the most prominent composer of the Counter-Reformation.

H.K. Andrews, *An Introduction to the Technique of Palestrina* (1958); J. Roche, *Palestrina* (1971).

Paley, William (1743–1805) Philosopher and Theologian. For much of his early career Paley taught at the University of Cambridge. Subsequently he served a parish in Cumbria and he was appointed Archdeacon of Carlisle in 1782. He is remembered for his works of philosophical theology, in particular his *View of the Evidences of Christianity* and his *Natural Theology*. His exposition of the teleological argument for the existence of God, which involves the illustration of a watch found on the sea shore, is still studied by students today.

M.L. Clarke, *Paley: Evidences for the Man* (1974).

Palladius (c. 365–425) Bishop and Historian. Palladius is thought to have been born in Galatia, but he spent time as a student of EVAGRIUS PONTICUS in Egypt. He was consecrated Bishop of Heliopolis in Asia Minor in c. 400, but, because of his connection with John CHRYSOSTOM, he was exiled in 406. He returned to his diocese in 412 and in 417 he became Bishop of Aspuna. He is remembered as an important historian of early monasticism. Although he was somewhat uncritical of some of the tales of the early Egyptian monks, his *Historia Lausiaca* is a valuable source of information.

R.T. Meyer (ed.), *Palladius' Historia* (1965).

Pallotti, Vincent (1795–1850) Order Founder. Pallotti was born into an Italian noble family. He is remembered as the founder in 1835 of the Pious Society of Missions, who are more generally known as the Pallottini Fathers. The society is composed of priests, lay-brothers and associates. It is a missionary order and is primarily dedicated to preserving and nurturing the faith of emigrants. Pallotti founded a similar order for women in 1843.

F. Frank, *The Life of Vincent Pallotti*, 2 vols (1952, 1963).

Pancras (d. 304) Saint and Martyr. Little is known of the life of St Pancras. He is said to have been martyred in Rome at the age of fourteen during the course of the Diocletian persecution. His cult was particularly popular in Rome. He is well known to the English since an important London railway station is named after him.

D.H. Farmer (ed.), *The Oxford Dictionary of Saints*, 3rd edn (1992).

Pannenberg, Wolfhart (b. 1928) Theologian. Pannenberg was born in Stettin, Germany, and he was educated at the Universities of Berlin, Göttingen, Basle (where he studied with Karl BARTH) and Heidelberg. Subsequently he has taught at Wuppertal, Mainz and Munich. He is the author of several important books, including (in their English titles) *Jesus – God and Man, Theology and the Philosophy of Science, Anthropology* and a multi-volume systematic theology. He is notable for his determination to integrate theology with other disciplines and, in contrast to Barth, he insists that God has revealed himself in and through the course of human history.

S. Grenz, *Reason for Hope: The Systematic Theology of Wolfhart Pannenberg* (1990); D. McKenzie, *Wolfhart Pannenberg and Religious Philosophy* (1980); D.P. Polk, *On the Way to God: An Exploration into the Theology of Wolfhart Pannenberg* (1989).

Pannikar, Raimundo (b. 1918) Theologian and Ecumenist. Pannikar was born in Barcelona, Spain, of a Hindu father and a Roman Catholic mother. As a child he studied both the Hindu and the Christian scriptures. He was educated in Spain, Germany and Italy and he was ordained as a Roman Catholic priest in 1946. He has spent most of his career in India, teaching at the Universities of Mysore and Benares. In his writings, he emphasises the role that Hinduism can play in enriching the Christian tradition, and he compares it with the way the categories of Greek philosophy were incorporated into mediaeval theology. His best-known book is *The Unknown Christ of Hinduism*.

D. Ford, *The Modern Theologians*, revised edition (1997).

Pantaleon (late third/early fourth century) Saint and Martyr. Little certain is known of the life of St Pantaleon. His name means 'all-merciful' and he is thought to have been the court physician of the Emperor Galerius in Nicomedia. Despite apostasy in middle life, he suffered martyrdom as a Christian in the Diocletian persecutions and his cult remains popular in the Eastern Church. With St LUKE, he is regarded as the patron saint of doctors. His blood, like that of St JANUARIUS, is said to liquefy from time to time.

D.H. Farmer, *The Oxford Dictionary of Saints*, 3rd edn (1992).

Papias (*c.* 60–*c.* 130) Bishop and Devotional Writer. Little certain is known of the life of Papias. He was Bishop of Hieropolis in Asia Minor and, according to IRENAEUS, was a disciple of JOHN (which John is not specified) and a companion of POLYCARP. He is remembered as the author of *Logion Kyriakon Exegeses* (Expositions of the words of the Lord) which were quoted both by Irenaeus and by EUSEBIUS OF CAESAREA. In particular he maintained that he had heard from 'the Elder' that MARK was the interpreter of PETER and in his Gospel he set down accurately, but not in order, all that he had been told of the words and actions of JESUS. MATTHEW's 'logia' (words) were written in Hebrew and everyone interpreted them as best they could.

U.H.J. Körtner, *Papias von Hieropolis* (1983) [no English translation available]; J.Munck, 'Presbyters and disciples of the Lord in Papias', *Harvard Theological Review*, lii (1959).

Paracelsus [Theophrastus Bombastus von Hohenheim] (1493–1541) Mystic

and Scientist. Paracelsus (his own name for himself) was the city physician of Basle, Switzerland. In 1528, however, as a result of his insistence on the empirical basis of medical knowledge, he was compelled to leave the city and he spent the rest of his life wandering from place to place. Although he is an important figure in the history of medicine, he is remembered in the Church for his mysticism. He believed that just as we understand nature because we are part of it, so we understand God, because we ourselves are God. Paracelsus has become a popular figure for study in the last century.

J. Ferguson, *Contributions Towards a Knowledge of Paracelsus and his Writings*, 2 vols (1890, 1892); C.G. Jung, *Paracelsia. Zwei Vorlesungen über den Arzt und Philosophen Theophrastus* (1942) [no English translation available].

Parker, Matthew (1504–75) Archbishop and Historian. Parker was educated at the University of Cambridge. He was known as a moderate Protestant and when Queen ELIZABETH I inherited the English throne in 1559, she chose him to be her Archbishop of Canterbury. He was consecrated by four of King EDWARD VI's Bishops (Queen MARY's, being Roman Catholic, had been deprived of their sees) and he dedicated the rest of his life to the setting up of a moderately reformed established Church. He aroused the opposition of the Puritans because he allowed the retention of several Catholic rituals, and the Thirty-Nine Articles, published in 1563 during his Archiepiscopate, are remarkable for their mediating tone. A gentle, scholarly man, Parker was interested in the history of the English Church and he edited the work of several mediaeval chroniclers.

W. Haugaard, *Elizabeth and the English Reformation* (1968).

Pascal, Blaise (1623–62) Mathematician and Theologian. Pascal was born in Clermont-Ferrand, France, and from an early age showed a remarkable talent for mathematics. In 1646 he first came into contact with Jansenism and in 1651 his sister Jacqueline entered the convent of Port-Royal, the Jansenist headquarters. Then, in 1654, Pascal himself had a conversion experience and he became a regular visitor to Port-Royal. In his *Lettres Ecrites à un Provincial*, he attacked the theology of the Jesuits and caused violent controversy in France. He is chiefly remembered, however, for his *Pensées*, which were not published until after his death. He insisted that God was not to be found through human reason, but through faith and in his famous 'wager', he pointed out how much was to be gained and how little to be lost in putting one's trust in the Almighty. Thus his belief was in the 'God of Abraham, the God of Isaac and the God of Jacob', not in the god of the philosophers and scientists. Although his views were regarded with derision in the eighteenth century, Pascal has been the subject of considerable scholarly interest for the last one hundred and fifty years.

D. Adamson, *Blaise Pascal: Mathematician, Physicist and Thinker about God* (1995); J.H. Broome, *Pascal* (1965); R.J. Nelson, *Pascal: Advocate and Adversary* (1981); C.C.J. Webb, *Pascal's Philosophy of Religion* (1929).

Paschasius Radbertus (*c.* 790–865) Theologian and Saint. Paschasius was a member of the Benedictine monastery in Corbie, France, but he resigned in 849 to dedicate himself to study. As well as for an important commentary on St MATTHEW's Gospel, he is remembered for his *De Corpore et Sanguine Domini* in which he expounded his doctrine of the Eucharist. He argued for the real presence of JESUS CHRIST in the bread and the wine and he is regarded as an early advocate of the doctrine of transubstantiation.

D. Stone, *A History of the Doctrine of the Holy Eucharist* (1909).

Patrick (*c.* 390–*c.* 460) Saint and Missionary. Patrick was born into a British Christian family. As a young man he was captured by Irish pirates and taken as a slave to Ireland. After six years he managed to make his escape and he returned to his family. These years left a deep impression on him and he decided to train as a missionary and go back to Ireland to convert the Irish to Christianity. He spent the rest of his life preaching the gospel, founding religious houses and educating the young. In his final years he wrote a *Confession* in which he told the story of his spiritual journey. The precise chronology of his life and death is not known, but he is revered as the patron saint of Ireland and as the 'apostle of the Irish'. Many later legends grew up about him, but these have little historical value. It is also unlikely that the hymn known as St Patrick's Breastplate ('I bind unto myself this day, the strong name of the Trinity . . .') was his composition.

J. Carney, *The Problem of St Patrick* (1961); D.N. Dumville, *St Patrick AD 493–1993* (1995); R.P.C. Hanson, *St Patrick: His Origin and Career* (1968).

Patteson, John Coleridge (1827–71) Missionary and Bishop. Patteson was educated at the University of Oxford. After ordination he served as a curate for a short time in Devonshire, but was persuaded by Bishop SELWYN to go as a missionary to Melanesia. He was consecrated Bishop of Melanesia in 1861 and his work was highly successful. However, in 1871 he was murdered by natives in an act of revenge against white traders, who had captured the local inhabitants for forced labour in Australia. His death caused a sensation in England and led to a surge of interest in foreign missions.

J. Gutch, *John Coleridge Patteson* (1961); C.M. Yonge, *The Life of Bishop J.C. Patteson*, 2 vols (1873).

Paul (d. *c.* 65) Apostle. According to
the Acts of the Apostles in the New Testament, Paul's Jewish name was Saul. Although a Roman citizen, he was brought
up as a pharisee and had been a student
of Gamaliel, the most eminent Jewish
teacher of the day. As a young man, he
had been strongly opposed to the teachings of Christianity. He was present at
the martyrdom of STEPHEN and he embarked on a journey to Damascus to
round up and arrest the adherents of the
new sect. During the course of the journey, however, he had an experience of the
resurrected JESUS. In consequence he was
baptised and he determined to spend the
rest of his life serving his new master. It
is not easy to reconcile the events of Acts
with Paul's own account in the Epistle to
the Galatians. He seems to have spent
some time in Arabia preparing himself
for his mission; he was introduced to the
Church in Jerusalem by BARNABAS; he
then visited Caesarea, Syria and Cilicia
and finally made his headquarters in Antioch. Acts describes three missionary
journeys. Everywhere Paul preached first
in the local synagogue to the Jews, but he
also encouraged Gentile believers to be
baptised. This raised the difficult issue as
to whether the Gentile Christians should
be compelled to keep the full Jewish law.
Paul strongly argued against this at the
first Council of the Church, the Council
of Jerusalem, and he won his point. He
preached throughout Asia Minor, Macedonia and went as far as Athens. Everywhere he planted new churches. Eventually he was arrested in Jerusalem and was
first brought before the Sanhedrin, the
Jewish council. Protected by the Romans,
he was imprisoned in Caesarea for two
years and eventually demanded, as was
his right as a Roman citizen, to be tried
before the Emperor in Rome. The Book
of Acts ends with Paul preaching openly
and unhindered in Rome. We learn more
about his life from the Epistles and from
later Church tradition. He is said to have
been martyred in Rome during the per-

secution of Nero. Arguably Paul can be
described as the founder of Christianity.
It was he who established the network of
churches throughout the Roman Empire
and his Epistles, as collected in the New
Testament, laid the groundwork for subsequent Christian theology. He taught
that the sacrificial death and resurrection
of Jesus ushered in a new era in which sin
and death no longer hold sway over humanity. Through baptism and faith,
Christians can share in the new age of
love and joy in the Holy Spirit. Collectively all believers form the body of Christ
here on earth; each individual has a different function, but all (Jew and Gentile
alike) are animated by the one Spirit;
they are nourished by the one food and
they are all inheritors of the promises
outlined in the Hebrew Scriptures. They
can look forward in perfect confidence to
Christ's return in glory, when the dead
shall be raised, Christ shall receive the
homage of all creation and God will be
all in all.

Acts of the Apostles; Epistles of Paul to the Ro-
mans, Corinthians, Galatians and Thessalonians;
W.D. Davies, *Paul and Rabbinic Judaism* (1948);
E.P. Sanders, *Paul* (1991).

Paul III (1468–1549) Pope. Paul was
born Alessandro Farnese. He became a
Cardinal-Deacon in 1493; he was dean of
the Sacred College under Pope LEO X
and he was elected Pope in 1534. He cannot be described as a saintly figure. Despite the injunction to clerical celibacy, he
was the father of three sons and a daughter and he was much given to promoting
his own relations to senior positions
within the Church. None the less he is
primarily remembered for the significant
reforms which took place within the
Church during his reign. He restored the
Inquisition; he approved the setting up of
new orders such as the Jesuits and the
Ursulines and, as a result of his determination, the first session of the
Council of Trent opened in 1545.
Although he failed to stem the tide of

Protestantism, he must be regarded as a preliminary architect of the Counter-Reformation. In addition he was a great patron of art and learning. He appointed MICHELANGELO as architect-in-chief to St Peter's Cathedral and he did much to improve the Vatican Library.

A.G. Dickens, *The Counter Reformation*, 2nd edn (1989).

Paul IV (1476–1559) Order Founder and Pope. Paul IV was born Giovanni Pietro Caraffa in Naples, Italy. In 1504 he was consecrated Bishop of Theate and in 1524, with St CAJETAN, he founded the Theatine Order as a means of ridding the Church of its scandals and abuses. Then in 1536 he became Cardinal-Archbishop of Naples and he was elected Pope in 1555. He is remembered as the first of the Counter-Reformation Popes. He promoted the Inquisition and he codified the list of forbidden books, known as the Index. Despite this, his anti-Spanish foreign policy and his fanatical anti-Protestant stance may have promoted the Reformed cause.

A.G. Dickens, *The Counter Reformation*, 2nd edn (1989).

Paul V (1552–1621) Pope. Paul V was born Camillo Borghese in Rome, Italy. He was made a Cardinal in 1596; he was appointed Vicar of Rome in 1603 and he was elected Pope in 1605. He is primarily remembered for his political struggle with the City of Venice, for his condemnation of the teachings of GALILEO and for his support of the Jesuits in their bitter dispute with the Dominicans over the question of grace and free will. He was an intelligent and holy man and he did much to enforce the decrees of the Council of Trent. He also supported the work of teaching and missionary orders.

J.N.D. Kelly (ed.), *The Oxford Dictionary of Popes* (1986).

Paul VI (1897–1978) Pope. Paul VI was born Giovanni Battista Montini. He was ordained in 1920 and for more than thirty years he served in the Papal Secretariat of State. In 1954 he was consecrated Archbishop of Milan and he was created a Cardinal by Pope JOHN XXIII. He was elected Pope in 1963. During his reign the second, third and fourth sessions of the Second Vatican Council took place. As a result of its activities, both the liturgy and the Canon Law of the Church were very much changed. Paul VI himself is chiefly remembered for his ecumenical efforts and for his attitude towards artificial methods of birth control. Together with Patriarch ATHENAGORAS, he expressed his regret for the rift which had taken place between the Eastern and Western Churches in 1054. The previous year he had made a pilgrimage to the Holy Land, during the course of which he had publicly embraced the Patriarch of Constantinople. Despite his support of the Vatican Council, his own encyclicals were not always forward-looking. In particular, in *Humanae Vitae*, issued in 1968, against the advice of the majority of the Papal Commission appointed by his predecessor, Paul condemned all forms of contraception except the rhythm method. This stance alienated many Roman Catholics, particularly in the developed world.

B.C. Butler, *The Theology of Vatican II*, enlarged edn (1981); P. Hebblethwaite, *Paul VI: The First Modern Pope* (1993).

Paul of the Cross (1694–1775) Order Founder and Saint. Paul was born Paolo Francesco Danei in Ovado, Italy. At the age of twenty-six, he became a hermit and he drew up the Rule for a new order which became known as the Passionists. The first house opened in 1737 and the Rule was approved by Pope BENEDICT XIV. Paul himself was regarded as one of the most impressive preachers of his age and he was much sought after as a spiritual director. The Passionists are known for their mission work and for their conducting of retreats. There is also an order of Passionist nuns who lead a strictly enclosed contemplative life.

Father Edmund (J.E. Burke), *St Paul of the Cross* (1946); F. Ward, *The Passionists* (1923).

Paul of Samosata (third century) Bishop, Heretic and Sect Founder. Paul was consecrated Bishop of Antioch in *c.* 260, but he was deposed in 268 because of his heretical views. He seems to have taught that the divine Word of God was to be distinguished from the human JESUS and that during the incarnation, the Word descended on the human being. Paul is seen as a forerunner of NESTORIUS. His followers were known as Paulianists and they survived at least until the Council of Nicaea in 325. The Paulician sect which was still in existence in the eleventh century may also have taken its name from Paul of Samosata. Adherents taught a dualistic doctrine in which the Good God created Heaven and the human soul and the Evil God made the material universe. They denied the reality of Jesus's body; they rejected the orthodox doctrine of the cross and they revered Jesus only as a great teacher.

N.G. Garsoian, *The Paulician Heresy* (1967); H. de Riedmatten, *Les Actes du Procès de Paul de Samosate* (1952) [no English translation available].

Paul of Thebes (early fourth century) Saint Paul is known only through the writings of St JEROME. He was born in Thebaid and he escaped the Decian persecution by living as a hermit in a cave by the Red Sea. He is remembered as the first Christian hermit and St ANTONY is said to have paid him a visit when he was one hundred and thirteen years old. He is often portrayed with two lions who were thought after his death to have dug his grave.

D.H. Farmer (ed.), *The Oxford Dictionary of Saints*, 3rd edn (1992).

Paulinus of Nola (*c.* 353–431) Saint, Bishop and Poet. Paulinus was born in Bordeaux into a rich family. He was converted to Christianity in 390 and he was ordained a priest in 394. He finally settled in Nola in Campania. With his wife Theresa, he led an austere life and built a hospital for monks and the poor. In 409 he was consecrated Bishop of Nola. Many of his letters survive and, among others, he was a correspondent of AMBROSE, AUGUSTINE and MARTIN OF TOURS. He is mainly remembered, however, for his poetry. Much of his verse was composed for the annual festival of St Felix. He wrote in Latin and he is regarded as one of the most important Christian poets of the period. He is also supposed to have been the first to introduce bells into Christian worship (hence the Latin words for bell, *nola* and *campana*).

J.T. Lienhard, *Paulinus of Nola and Early Christian Monasticism* (1977); J.R. Nichols, *Bells thro' the Ages* (1928).

Paulinus of York (d. 644) Missionary, Bishop and Saint. Paulinus was sent by Pope GREGORY THE GREAT to Britain in 601 to be an assistant to St AUGUSTINE OF CANTERBURY. In 625, after he had been consecrated a Bishop, he went to the north as Chaplain to Queen Ethelberga, the wife of King Edwin, King of Northumbria. In 627 Edwin himself was baptised and Paulinus established the See of York. However, five years later, Edwin was killed in battle by the pagan Cadwallon and Paulinus returned to Kent. There he became Bishop of Rochester. York became the most important see in the British Church after Canterbury.

Bede, *The History of the English Church* [many editions]; H.M.R.E. Mayr-Harting, 'Paulinus of York', in G.J. Cuming (ed.), *Studies in Church History* (1967).

Peake, Arthur Samuel (1865–1929) Biblical Scholar and Ecumenist. Peake was born in Leek, England, the son of a Primitive Methodist minister. He was educated at the University of Oxford and, after a period of teaching there, he moved to Manchester to be tutor of the Primitive Methodist College. Later, he also held a chair at Manchester University. He is remembered for his many works of popular biblical scholarship, in particular his one-volume commentary on the whole Bible. This has gone through many editions and, in a new revision, is still used by students today. He was also very committed to and worked hard for the reunion of the Methodist Churches.

A.J. Grieve (ed.), *Supplement to Peake's Commentary* (1936); J.T. Wilkinson (ed.), *Arthur Samuel Peake 1865–1929. Essays in Commemoration* (1958).

Péguy, Charles Pierre (1873–1914) Mystic and Devotional Writer. Péguy was born in Orléans, France. For a while he attended the Sorbonne, but he left to manage a bookshop. Initially he was a determined socialist and was appalled by the anti-semitism displayed by the Church in the Dreyfus affair. Although he retained his sense of social justice and his anti-clericalism, he later became a mystical nationalist. He is remembered as the author of *Cahiers de la Quinzaine*, a highly successful play on JOAN OF ARC, *Le Mystère des Saints Innocents* and *Eve*, a long religious poem. He exerted an enormous influence on French Catholic young people, although he himself remained estranged from the Church. He was killed in the Battle of the Marne at the start of the First World War.

M. Villiers, *Charles Péguy: A Study in Integrity* (1965).

Pelagia (d. *c.* 311) Legendary Saint. There are several St Pelagias. One is said to have thrown herself from a high window into the sea to preserve her chastity during the Diocletian persecutions. A

similar tale is told of St MARGARET. Another was a reformed actress who led an intensely austere life on the Mount of Olives in the fourth century and the third was a virgin who lived in Tarsus and who was burnt to death for refusing to become the mistress of the Emperor. All three illustrate the sort of female virtues which were venerated in the Early Church.

F.L. Cross (ed.), *The Oxford Dictionary of the Christian Church*, 2nd edn (1974).

Pelagius (d. *c.* 418) Heretical Theologian. Pelagius was a native of Britain. He was trained as a lawyer and he taught in Rome in the late fourth and early fifth centuries. He seems to have believed that human beings, of their very nature, are capable of choosing good over evil. In the face of the threat from the Goths, he left Rome for Africa and then he went to Palestine where he attracted a group of followers. After his expulsion from Palestine, he disappears from view. Pelagianism, the doctrine with which he is associated, was developed by his disciple CELESTIUS. He denied that the guilt of original sin was passed down through the human generations. Largely as a result of the efforts of St AUGUSTINE OF HIPPO, Pelagianism, together with Nestorianism, was condemned at the Council of Ephesus in 431. However, it survived in various forms, particularly in Gaul and Britain, for many years. The issues it raises (original sin, grace, moral responsibility, predestination) have constantly been areas of controversy within the Church.

R.F. Evans, *Pelagius: Inquiries and Reappraisals* (1968); J. Ferguson, *Pelagius* (1956); P. Brown, *Augustine of Hippo* (1967).

Penn, William (1644–1718) State Founder and Devotional Writer. Penn was born in London. He failed to complete his course at the University of Oxford because of his non-conformist convictions. He joined the Quakers in 1665 and was the author of many religious works including *The Sandy Foundation Shaken, No Cross, No Crown* (written in prison), *The Fruits of Solitude* and *Primitive Christianity*. He is remembered as the founder of the American colony of Pennsylvania. With his help, eight hundred Quakers had settled in New Jersey in 1678 and in 1682 he secured a new charter for the colony from King Charles II. From the first, the colony was to be a refuge for those in search of religious freedom. He himself travelled to the colony that same year, but he returned to England in 1684. His supposed support of King JAMES II resulted in his being deprived of the governorship. In 1699 he returned to Pennsylvania, intending to stay, but he went back to England in 1701 to ensure that the province would receive the status of Crown Colony. Penn's insistence on religious freedom was to become an important influence on the makers of the American constitution.

E.B. Bronner, *William Penn's Holy Experiment: The Founding of Pennsylvania* (1962); M.M. Dunn, *William Penn: Politics and Conscience* (1967); J.R. Soderlund (ed.), *William Penn and the Founding of Pennsylvania: A Documentary History* (1983).

Pepin III (714–68)   Monarch. Pepin was the son of Charles Martel and, with his brother Carloman, succeeded his father as Mayor of the Palace of the Kingdom of the Franks in 741. After Carloman retired to a monastery, Pepin was elected King in 751 and he was anointed to the office by St BONIFACE. Then, in 754, he was anointed by Pope STEPHEN III. Pepin's son, CHARLEMAGNE, was to become the first Holy Roman Emperor, but Pepin had already established the interdependence of Western political power and the authority of the Western Church. In the 'Donation of Pepin' of 754, he had promised to restore to the Pope the Exarchate of Ravenna and the territories of the Roman Republic. This he succeeded in doing in 756, thus laying the founda-

tion for the temporal power of the Pope. He also closely involved himself with the ecclesiastical reforms instituted by St Boniface.

P. Laski, *The Kingdom of the Franks* (1971); L. Levillain, 'L'avènement de la dynastie carolingienne et les origines de l'état pontifical', *Bibliothèque de l'Ecole de Chartres*, xciv (1933) [no English translation].

Perkins, William (1558–1602)   Theologian. Perkins was born in Warwickshire and was educated at the University of Cambridge. He was a fellow of Christ's College until 1594 and subsequently became the St Andrew's lecturer. He was well known as a determined Puritan and was a highly influential and much respected figure within the Church of England. Among his writings were *A Golden Chain, An Exposition of the Lord's Prayer, An Exposition of the Symbol or Creed of the Apostles* and *De Praedestinationis Modo et Ordine*. This last elicited a response from Jacob ARMINIUS. In his theology, Perkins has been seen as a forerunner of seventeenth-century Pietism.

T.F. Merrill, *William Perkins* (1966); R.A. Sisson, 'William Perkins, apologist for the Elizabethan Church', *Modern Language Review*, xlvii (1952).

Peter (first century)   Apostle. According to the Gospel story, Peter was a Galilean fisherman who was called by JESUS to follow him and to become a fisher of men. His original name was Simon; Peter was a nickname meaning 'rock'. He was the brother of ANDREW and, in the Fourth Gospel, it is implied that he was formerly a disciple of JOHN THE BAPTIST. He quickly emerged as one of the leaders of the Twelve. Together with JAMES and JOHN, the sons of Zebedee, he was present at the raising of Jairus's daughter. He was the first openly to recognise Jesus as the long-awaited Messiah, 'the son of the living God'. On this occasion, Jesus made the famous declaration, 'You are Peter (rock) and on this rock will I build my Church'. Again with James and John, he saw the transfiguration of Jesus on Mount Carmel and he was taken apart from the others in the Garden of Gethsemane, when Jesus waited for his arrest. At the Last Supper, Jesus had predicted that he would deny his master three times that very night. This indeed occurred in the High Priest's courtyard while Jesus was being tried. On the first Easter Sunday, he was among the first to find Jesus's tomb empty and it is implied both in the Gospels and in PAUL's First Epistle to the Corinthians that Jesus made a special resurrection appearance to him. In the twenty-first chapter of the Fourth Gospel (possibly a later addition to the original text), after making a three-fold declaration of loyalty, he was instructed by Jesus to 'feed my sheep'. After the Ascension, Peter continued to lead the twelve. It was he who preached on the first Whitsunday and, according to the Acts of the Apostles, it was he who baptised the first Gentile converts – the centurion Cornelius and all his household. He took a prominent part in the Council of Jerusalem, when he seems to have supported Paul's stance. Traditionally he is believed to have been the first Bishop of Rome and to have met his death by crucifixion, probably in the persecutions of Nero in c. 64. The New Testament contains two epistles written under his name, of which only the first is generally regarded as genuine. A large amount of pseudo-Petrine literature, including a gospel and an apocalypse, circulated in the second century. PAPIAS maintained that he was the main source for the Gospel of MARK. In any event, Peter was the outstanding figure in the primitive Church and as the 'rock' on which the Roman Church was supposedly founded, has been held in much reverence through the ages.

The Four Gospels; The Acts of the Apostles; O. Cullmann, *Petrus* (1953); J. Lowe, *St Peter* (1956); K. Quest, *Peter and the Beloved Disciple: Figures for a Community in Crisis* (1989).

Peter of Alcántara (1499–1562) Saint and Order Founder. Peter was born of a noble family in Alcántara, Spain. He was educated in Salamanca and he joined the Observantist Franciscans in 1515. From 1538 until 1541 he was Provincial of the Extremaduran province of St Gabriel and he was known for his austere interpretation of the Rule. In 1541, he retired to a hermitage and established a group of communities. In 1557, he founded the convent of El Pedroso del Acém which was to become the first congregation of the new Alcantarine order, the Spanish Discalced Franciscans. He was well known as a spiritual director and he greatly encouraged St TERESA OF AVILA in her reform of the Carmelites. He was also supposedly the author of the *Tratado de la Oración y Meditación*, which went through many editions. However, some scholars have attributed it to LUIS OF GRANADA. He was canonised little more than a hundred years after his death and today he is the patron saint of Brazil.

A. Barrado Manzano, *San Pedro de Alcántara* (1965) [no English translation available].

Peter of Bruys (d. *c.* 1140) Heretic and Sect Founder. Peter is mentioned in the writings of ABELARD and PETER THE VENERABLE. He had been a priest, but he seems to have rejected the authority of the Church, infant baptism, the necessity for formal church buildings, prayers for the dead and clerical celibacy. He preached doctrines throughout Provence and Dauphiné. His followers were known as the Petrobrusians and they were condemned at the Second Vatican Council of 1139. He himself seems to have been lynched by an infuriated mob. He disapproved of the veneration of the cross and, on one occasion near Nîmes, he built a huge fire to burn the offending articles. Instead, the crowd turned on him and threw him bodily into the flames.

J.C. Reagan, 'Did the Petrobrusians teach salvation by faith alone?', *Journal of Religion*, vii (1927).

W.H.C. Frend, *The Rise of the Monophysite Movement* (1972).

Peter Damian (1007–72) Bishop and Church Reformer. Peter Damian was born in Ravenna, Italy, of a poor family. He entered a Benedictine monastery in 1035 and became Prior about eight years later. He was well known as a zealous, reforming preacher and, much against his own desires, he was appointed Cardinal Bishop of Ostia in 1057. He became involved in European diplomacy and was very active in supporting Pope ALEXANDER II against Antipope Honorius II. During his lifetime he enjoyed enormous prestige within the Church and many of his writings survive today. These include a dissertation against clerical marriage and another confirming the validity of simoniacal ordinations. Although he was never formally canonised, he has been recognised as a Doctor of the Church since 1828.

J.J. Ryan, *St Peter Damiani and his Canonical Sources* (1956); J.P. Whitney, *Hildebrandine Essays* (1932).

Peter the Fuller (d. 488) Patriarch and Theologian. Peter is said to have been a monk in Constantinople. He was expelled from his monastery for his Monophysite opinions, but was appointed Patriarch of Antioch by ZENO the Isaurian in 470. However, the following year he was expelled and imprisoned in his monastery. Nothing daunted, he was restored in 475, deposed again in 477 and was restored for the last time in 482 as a result of his consenting to Zeno's 'Henoticon'. He is primarily remembered for his addition of the words 'who was crucified for us' to the formula 'Holy God, Holy Mighty, Holy Immortal'. He is also said to have introduced the recitation of the Nicene Creed at the Eucharist and the commemoration of the Virgin MARY's title *Theotokos* (Bearer of God) at every service.

Peter the Great (1672–1725) Monarch. Peter became Czar (Emperor) of Russia in 1689. He was determined to modernise all the institutions of that vast country and, inevitably, he turned his attention to the Orthodox Church. In order to secure complete power in the ecclesiastical realm, he abolished the office of Patriarch and in his 'Spiritual Regulation' of 1721, Church government was put into the hands of the Holy Synod, whose members were all nominated by the Czar. The synod remained in existence until 1917. After the Bolshevik revolution of 1917 it was abolished and a token Patriarchate was restored.

M. Smith Anderson, *Peter the Great* (1978); J. Cracraft, *The Church Reform of Peter the Great* (1971); R.K. Massie and R. Kinloch, *Peter the Great: His Life and Work* (1981).

Peter the Hermit (c. 1050–1115) Polemicist. Many legends are told of Peter the Hermit, most of them apocryphal. He was born near Amiens, France, and he lived for much of his life as a hermit. He was inspired by Pope URBAN II's call for a crusade against the Muslims and in 1096 he led about twenty thousand people, mostly peasants, across Europe and Asia Minor towards the Holy Land. Eventually most were massacred by the Turks at Civitot. Peter himself was in Constantinople at the time and thus escaped. He rallied the survivors and, although he seems to have deserted his men at the siege of Antioch, he was present at the triumphal entry into Jerusalem by the Crusaders in 1099. In his final years, he founded and was Prior of a monastery at Neufmoutier. In popular lore, Peter is often regarded as the inspiration behind the whole Crusade movement.

Y. Le Febvre, *Pierre l'Ermite et la Croisade* (1946) [no English translation available]; J. Riley-Smith,

The First Crusade and the Idea of Crusading (1984).

Peter Lombard (*c.* 1095–1160) Bishop and Theologian. Peter was born in Lombardy, Italy, and he was educated at Bologna. He was appointed a Canon of the Cathedral of Notre Dame and was consecrated Bishop of Paris in 1159. He is primarily remembered for his *Libri Quatuor Sententiarum*, generally referred to as the 'Sentences' in English. It is divided into four sections covering the Trinity, the creation, the incarnation and the Sacraments. It contains a host of quotations from the early Church Fathers and from Peter's own contemporaries and it attempts to summarise the Christian doctrines. Although it was attacked as heretical by such authorities as WALTER OF ST VICTOR, GILBERT DE LA PORRÉE and JOACHIM OF FIORE, it was pronounced orthodox in 1215 at the Fourth Lateran Council. Subsequently it became a standard theological text and was studied in universities throughout Europe until the seventeenth century. It was the basis of numerous commentaries and perhaps only the *Summa Theologica* of THOMAS AQUINAS has had such success as an educational manual.

S.J. Curtis, 'Peter Lombard, a pioneer in educational methods', *Miscellanea Lombardiana* (1957); P. Delhaye, *Pierre Lombard, Sa Vie, Ses Oeuvres, Sa Morale* (1961) [no English translation available].

Peter Martyr (*c.* 1205–52) Saint. Peter was born into a Cathar family in Verona, Italy. He was educated at Bologna and was there converted to Roman Catholic orthodoxy. He joined the Dominican Order in 1221, possibly under the influence of DOMINIC himself and he dedicated himself to the eradication of the Cathari heresy. He was a famous preacher and was so effective in his self-appointed task that he was appointed Inquisitor for North Italy by Pope GREGORY IX. The following year he was attacked by two assassins while he was journeying from Como to Milan. According to legend, before he died he wrote 'Credo in Deum' (I believe in God) in his own blood. He is immortalised in paintings by Fra ANGELICO and TITIAN. He was canonised almost immediately after his death and he was regarded as the patron saint of Inquisitors.

A. Dondaine, 'Saint Pierre Martyr' *Archivum Fratrum Praedicatorum*, xxiii (1953) [no English translation available].

Peter Martyr (1500–62) Theologian. Peter was named after PETER MARTYR the Inquisitor. He was born in Florence, Italy, and he joined the Augustinian Order at an early age. Elected Abbot of the Abbey of Spoleto in 1530 and Prior of St Petrus-ad-Aram, Naples, in 1533, he was a highly successful preacher. However, he was also studying the writings of the Reformers BUCER and ZWINGLI and his less than orthodox views caused him to be transferred to Lucca. In 1542 he left Italy and travelled to Zürich, Basle and finally Strasbourg, where he married and was appointed a Professor of Theology. He was then invited by Archbishop CRANMER to settle in England. He became Regius Professor of Theology at the University of Oxford. He was consulted in the deliberations over the 1552 version of the Book of Common Prayer; he took part in debates on the Eucharist and he was a member of the commission for the reform of Canon Law. With the accession of Queen MARY, he was imprisoned for six months, but was allowed to return to his old position in Strasbourg. He finally moved to Zürich where he became Professor of Hebrew. He was an important influence in the making of the Reformed English Church.

J.C. McLelland, *The Visible Words of God: An Exposition of the Sacramental Theology of Peter Martyr Vermiglii* (1957); P. McNair, *Peter Martyr in Italy: An Anatomy of Apostasy* (1967).

Peter Nolasco (*c.* 1189–*c.* 1256) Saint and Order Founder. Little certain is known of the life of St Peter Nolasco. He is thought to have been born in either Barcelona or Languedoc and to have taken part in the crusade against the Albigensians. He is remembered as the founder, with RAYMOND OF PEÑAFORT, of the Mercedarian Order (the Order of Our Lady of Mercy). The purpose of the new order was to tend the sick and to ransom Christians who had been captured by the Muslims. It was approved by Pope GREGORY IX in 1235 and Peter himself is said to have been imprisoned in Algiers and to have ransomed four hundred captives. The order spread from Europe to the New World and today members work in parishes, schools and charities.

F.D. Gazulla Galve, *La Orden di Nuestra Señora de la Merced* (1934) [no English translation available].

Peter the Venerable (*c.* 1092–1156) Monastic Reformer and Devotional Writer. Peter was born in the Auvergne, France, and, at the age of seventeen, he joined the congregation at Cluny under HUGH OF CLUNY. In 1122 he was elected Abbot of the whole community (which included two thousand dependent houses). He introduced several important reforms and his emphasis on intellectual work brought him into conflict with BERNARD OF CLAIRVAUX, who believed that monastic life should be dedicated only to prayer and manual labour. He took a full part in the ecclesiastical affairs of his time, supporting Pope Innocent II against Antipope Anacletus II and providing a refuge for Peter ABELARD. The author of several devotional works, he combated the heresy of PETER OF BRUYS and wrote against the Jews and the Muslims. He also was the first to have the Koran translated into Latin. Much respected in his day, he was given the title 'Venerable' both by Bernard and by FREDERICK BARBAROSSA.

M.D. Knowles, 'Peter the Venerable', *Bulletin of the John Rylands Library*, xxxix (1957); M.D. Knowles,

Cistercians and Cluniacs: The Controversy between St Bernard and Peter the Venerable (1963); J. Kritzeck, *Peter the Venerable and Islam* (1964).

Petrarch, Francesco (1304–74) Poet, Scholar and Devotional Writer. Petrarch was educated at Montpellier and Bologna and was trained as a lawyer. However, he abandoned the law for a life of scholarship and journeyed through France, Germany and Italy, searching for and editing classical manuscripts. He finally settled in Vaucluse. He is mainly remembered for his poetry, particularly his sonnets to Laura. His many prose writings include *De Contemptu Mundi* (an imaginary dialogue between himself and St AUGUSTINE), *De Otio Religioso*, on the virtues of the monastic life, and *De Vita Solitaria* in praise of solitude. He has been a highly influential figure in Italian literature and has been described as the 'father of Humanism'.

K. Foster, *Petrarch: Poet and Humanist* (1984); C. Trinkaus, *The Poet as Philosopher: Petrarch and the Formation of Renaissance Consciousness* (1979); J.H. Whitfield, *Petrarch and the Renascence* (1943).

Philaret, Theodore Nikitich Romanov (*c.* 1553–1633) Patriarch. Philaret was a cousin of Theodore I, the last Ruvik Czar of Russia. He had a successful military career in the war against Sweden, but, after Theodore's death, he was imprisoned by his successor, Boris Godunov. He was appointed the Metropolitan of Rostov by the impostor Pseudo-Dmitri in 1609. Although his son Michael Romanov was elected Czar in 1613, Philaret, who had been imprisoned by the Poles in 1609, was not released until the Truce of Deulino in 1619. That year he was enthroned as Patriarch of Moscow and was, in effect, a ruler of Russia for the rest of his life. In the history of the Russian Church, he is remembered for his energetic reorganisation of every diocese and for the establishment of the Patriarchal Library.

R.N. Bain, *The First Romanovs* (1905).

Philaret Drozdov (1782–1867) Metro-politan and Theologian. Philaret was the son of a church cantor. He took monastic vows in 1808 and, in the same year, was appointed Professor of Philosophy at the Ecclesiastical Academy of St Petersburg. In 1820 he was consecrated Bishop of Jaroslav and in 1821 he became Archbishop of Moscow. This title was changed to 'Metropolitan' in 1826. Among his theological works was his *Christian Catechism of the Orthodox Catholic Eastern Greco-Russian Church.* Although this was criticised for being influenced by Protestantism, it was much used in the Russian Church throughout the nineteenth century. He is particularly remembered as the Metropolitan who encouraged the reforming Czar Alexander II in his determination to abolish serfdom in Russia.

C. Kern, 'Pilarète, Métropolite de Moscou: Cinquante ans de gloire épiscopale', *Istina*, v (1958) [no English translation available],

Philemon (first century) Martyr and Correspondent of St PAUL. Philemon is known as the recipient of an epistle of Paul. His slave ONESIMUS had run away to Paul and Paul sent him back to his master with instructions to receive him not as a slave, but as a 'beloved brother'. According to a later Church tradition, he died as a martyr in Colossae.

The Epistle of Paul to Philemon; G.B. Caird, *Paul's Letters from Prison* (1976); K.P. Donfried, *The Theology of the Shorter Pauline Letters* (1993).

Philip (first century) Apostle. Philip was one of JESUS's twelve disciples. According to the Fourth Gospel, he was a native of Bethsaida and introduced NATHANIEL to Jesus. He is described as being present at the feeding of the five thousand and as bringing a group of Greeks to Jesus. He also prompted Jesus's discourse on the Holy Spirit by asking his master to 'show us the Father'. Little is known of his life after the Ascen-sion, but he is thought to have died by crucifixion.

John, Chapters 1, 6, 12 and 14.

Philip (first century) Deacon. Philip was one of the seven Deacons chosen by the Apostles to organise the distribution of charity. According to the Book of Acts, he preached in Samaria. Among his converts were SIMON MAGUS and an Ethiopian eunuch. He settled in Caesarea where he provided accommodation for PAUL. Little more is known of him except that Church tradition has it that he became Bishop of Tralles in Lydda.

Acts of the Apostles, Chapters 6, 8, and 21; S.F. Spencer, *The Portrait of Philip in Acts: A Study in Roles and Relations* (1992).

Philip II (1527–98) Monarch. Philip II was the son of the Emperor CHARLES V and in 1556, on his father's abdication, he became King of Spain, Naples, Milan and the Netherlands, as well as having considerable possessions in the New World. At this point in his life he was married to MARY I of England where he was widely hated as a representative of a repressive Roman Catholic power. After Mary's death in 1559, he wanted to marry her half-sister ELIZABETH I. When it eventually became clear that England was to be a Protestant power, he sent his 'invincible Armada' to capture the island in 1588. This proved to be an unmitigated disaster. In addition, revolt in the Netherlands led to the establishment of the Protestant Dutch republic in 1579. Many of his policies, however, were successful. He defeated the French at St Quentin in 1557 and the Turks at Lepanto in 1571 and he was undoubtedly the most powerful monarch in Europe of his day. A devout Roman Catholic, he made use of the Inquisition in Spain and supported the Jesuits. Under his leadership Spain became the intellectual and political centre of the Counter-Reformation.

J. Buckler, *Philip II and the Sacred War* (1989); H.G. Koenigsberg, 'The statecraft of Philip II', *European Studies Review*, i (1971); J. Lynch, 'Philip II and the Papacy', *Transactions of the Royal Historical Society*, 5th series, xi (1961); G. Parker, *Philip II* (1979).

Philip IV [The Fair] (1268–1314) Monarch. Philip inherited the throne of France in 1285. In the history of the Church, he is remembered for his feud with Pope BONIFACE VIII, initially over the question of the taxation of the clergy. Subsequently he rejected the Papal bull 'Unam Sanctam' which defended the jurisdiction of the Pope over all creatures. The dispute ended with Philip's forces capturing the Pope in 1303 and holding him prisoner in Anagni. With the election of Pope CLEMENT V in 1305, Philip effectively controlled Papal policy. During his reign the papal court was moved from Rome to Avignon, thus inaugurating the seventy years of 'Babylonian captivity'. One of Philip's most notorious ecclesiastical achievements was the abolition of the hugely rich Order of Knights Templar.

J.R. Strayer, *The Reign of Philip the Fair* (1981); C.T. Wood (ed.), *Philip the Fair and Boniface VIII: State versus Papacy* (1967).

Philip Neri (1515–95) Saint and Order Founder. Philip Neri was born in Florence, but at the age of eighteen, he settled in Rome. There he led a highly disciplined life, supporting himself by tutoring, but dedicating his spare time to prayer, study and works of charity. In 1544 he had a significant religious experience and in 1548 he became a co-founder of the Confraternity of the Most Holy Trinity, which provided a refuge for pilgrims. He was ordained as a priest in 1551 and went to live in a clergy house at San Girolamo. This was the beginning of the Congregation of the Oratory. The Oratorians remain a congregation of secular priests, living without vows, but in community. They support themselves and provide services, sermons and guidance for those who seek them out. The congregation was formally approved by Pope GREGORY XIII in 1575. Philip himself was a delightful person, gentle, kind and amusing. He was the best-known spiritual director of his day and was regarded as a saint even in his lifetime.

A. Capecelatro, *The Life of St Philip Neri, Apostle of Rome*, 2 vols (1882); M. Trevor, *St Philip Neri* (1966).

Philip Sidetes (early fifth century) Historian. Philip was born in Side, Pamphylia, but he later settled in Constantinople. He was the author of a large history, *Christianike Historia*, which seems to have covered the period from the creation of the world until AD 430. Only a small section still survives. He was a friend of John CHRYSOSTOM and he is primarily remembered for his claim that both JAMES, the apostle, and his brother JOHN were martyred by the Jews. Although the Book of Acts reports James's death, the majority of authorities claim that John survived to a great age and died naturally.

E. Honigmann, 'Philip of Side and his "Christian History", *Patristic Studies*, clxxiii (1953).

Philomena Legendary Saint. Philomena was thought to have been a martyred virgin. She was discovered in 1802 when a tomb was found near Rome on which were written the letters LUMENA PAX TE CUM FI. Rearranged this could read PAX TECUM FILUMENA ('Peace to you Philomena'). Her cult became very popular and her relics were reported to have effected several miracles. However, doubt was cast on the connection between the relics and the inscription and the saint's feast day was suppressed in 1960.

D.H. Farmer (ed.), *The Oxford Dictionary of Saints*, 3rd edn (1992).

Philoxenus (c. 440–523) Bishop and Theologian. Philoxenus was born in Tahal, Persia. He was educated in Edessa where IBAS was the Bishop. As a Monophysite, Philoxenus defended ZENO's 'Henoticon' and he was appointed Bishop of Hierapolis by PETER THE FULLER. His writings include thirteen discourses on the Christian life and he commissioned an important Syriac version of the New Testament. Although little of the original survives, the revision is known as the Philoxenian version.

R.C. Chestnut, *Three Monophysite Christologies* (1972).

Photius (c. 810–c. 895) Patriarch, Theologian and Saint. Photius was born of a noble family in Constantinople. He quickly became known for his learning and administrative abilities and in 858, while still a layman, he was elected Patriarch. His predecessor, Ignatius, had been deposed as a result of a palace intrigue and in order to regularise his position, Photius summoned a synod at Constantinople. This included legates from Pope NICHOLAS I. Although the synod confirmed Ignatius's deposition, in 863 a synod in Rome annulled its proceedings. Photius and all the clergy he had promoted were declared deposed. Although there were signs of a possible reconciliation, the quarrel re-emerged after Photius, in an encyclical letter, condemned the practices of the Western Church and, in particular, rejected the 'filioque' in the Nicene Creed. Subsequently in 867 a Council in Constantinople excommunicated and deposed the Pope. The situation was complicated still further by the accession of a new Emperor who deposed Photius and reinstated Ignatius, with the result that at the Council of Constantinople in 869, reconciliation was effected with Rome. Ignatius died in 877 and Photius was again appointed Patriarch and seems to have been accepted as such by the papal legates. None the less conflict arose again when an-

other new Emperor, Leo VI, deposed Photius in 886 and he may have been excommunicated by Pope Formosus in 892. His last years are obscure. Photius himself was an outstanding scholar. Among his surviving works are the *Amphilochia*, the *Bibliotheke* and the *Lexicon*. He also produced several treatises against the Manichaeans and an important work on the Holy Spirit. In the Eastern Church he is regarded as a saint.

F. Dvornik, *The Photian Schism* (1948).

Pilate, Pontius (first century) Procurator. Pilate was governor, or procurator, of Judaea between 26 and 36. He is remembered as the Roman ruler who condemned JESUS to death by crucifixion. According to the Gospels, he was reluctant to pass the death sentence, but was pressurised into it by the Jewish crowd. This scenario is highly unlikely. We know from the works of the Jewish historian, Josephus, that Pilate was a harsh and cruel man who did not hesitate to execute any possible rebels against the Roman Empire. According to EUSEBIUS OF CAESAREA, he committed suicide in remorse and in the Coptic Church he is regarded as a saint. The apocryphal *Acts of Pilate* probably dates back only to the fourth century.

The Four Gospels; S. Brock, 'A fragment of the *Acta Pilati* in Christian Palestinian Aramaic', *Journal of Theological Studies*, n.s. xxii (1971); G. Schofield, *Crime before Calvary: Herodias, Herod Antipas and Pontius Pilate: A New Interpretation* (1960); P. Winter, *On the Trial of Jesus*, 2nd edn (1974).

Pithou, Pierre (1539–96) Theologian. Pithou was trained as a lawyer in Paris and he converted from Protestantism to Roman Catholicism in 1573. He is remembered as the author of *Les Libertés de l'Eglise Gallicane*, the first formulation of the essential principles of Gallicanism.

L. de Rosanbo, 'Pierre Pithou', in *Revue du Seizième Siècle*, xv (1928) [no English translation available].

Pius I (d. *c.* 154)   Pope and Saint. Little is known of Pius I. He is thought to have been born in Aquileia on the Adriatic coast and another tradition has it that he was the brother of the author of *The Shepherd of Hermas*. He was Bishop of Rome from *c.* 140. There is no real evidence that he died a martyr's death.

J.N.D. Kelly (ed.) *The Oxford Dictionary of Popes* (1986).

Pius II (1405–64)   Pope. Pius was born Enea Silvio de Piccolomini in Corsignano, Italy. He had a considerable influence at the Council of Basle (1431–49) and supported Antipope Felix V against Pope EUGENIUS IV. At this stage he believed that the supreme authority in the Church lies with a General Council and his book *Libellus Dialogorum de Concilii Auctoritate* is an important exposition of conciliar theory. He became the secretary of Emperor Frederick III in 1442, and in 1445 he threw his support behind Pope Eugenius. The following year, he renounced his dissolute life and was ordained. His rise in the ecclesiastical hierarchy was spectacular. He was consecrated Bishop of Trieste in 1447 and Bishop of Siena in 1450; he became a Cardinal in 1456 and he was elected Pope in 1458. In 1453 Constantinople had fallen to the Muslims. Pius proclaimed a Crusade. He received little support from the kings of Europe, particularly after 1460 when, in the bull 'Execrabilis', he rejected the practice of appealing to a General Council. When taxed with inconsistency, he famously declared, in the bull 'In Minoribus Agentes', '*Aeneam rejicite, Pium suscipite*' (Reject Enea, Accept Pius). In 1464 he decided to lead a Crusade personally, but he died of a fever before the expedition left Italy. Pius was a highly intelligent and talented writer. In his younger days he was the author of the love story *Euryalus and Lucretia*; he also produced several histories and an important commentary on the events of his own time.

Pius II, *Memoirs of a Renaissance Pope*, edited by L.C. Gabel (1960); R.J. Mitchell, *The Laurels and the Tiara: Pope Pius II* (1962).

Pius IV (1499–1565)   Pope. Pius was born Gian Angelo Medici in Milan, Italy. He became Archbishop of Ragusa in 1545 and a Cardinal in 1549. He was elected Pope in 1559 in succession to PAUL IV. He is remembered as the uncle of Charles BORROMEO and as the Pope who brought the Council of Trent to a reasonably successful conclusion. Among several measures, Pius published a new Index in 1564 and prepared a new edition of the Roman Catechism. Also, as a compromise with the Emperor, and to discourage the spread of Protestantism, he allowed the laity to receive the wine as well as the bread at the Eucharist. This concession, however, was revoked by his successors.

L. Pastor, *The History of the Popes from the Close of the Middle Ages*, Vols 15 and 16 (1928).

Pius V (1504–72)   Pope and Saint. Pius was born Michele Ghislieri and, at an early age, joined the Dominican Order. He became Commissary-General of the Inquisition in 1551, Bishop of Nepi and Sutri in 1556 and a Cardinal and the General Inquisitor of Christendom in 1557. He was elected Pope in 1566 in succession to PIUS IV. He is remembered as a determined reformer. He enforced the recommendations of the Council of Trent; he revised the liturgy; he named THOMAS AQUINAS as a Doctor of the Church and commissioned a new edition of his works and, with the aid of St Charles BORROMEO, he reformed the papal household. Although he successfully halted the advance of the Reformation in Italy and Spain, he was less successful in England where he excommunicated Queen ELIZABETH I and caused widespread anti-Catholic feeling. He did, however, succeed in defeating the Turks at the decisive sea battle of Lepanto in 1571, after forging an alliance between Spain and Venice. He was canonised in 1712.

L. Pastor, *The History of the Popes from the Close of the Middle Ages*, Vols 17 and 18 (1929.)

Pius VI (1717–99) Pope. Pius was born Giovanni Angelico Braschi in Cesana, Italy. After a legal training and ordination, he became treasurer of the Roman Church in 1766 and a Cardinal in 1773. He was elected Pope in 1775 in succession to CLEMENT XIV. He is remembered for his struggle against Febronianism in Germany, against the ecclesiastical reforms of the Emperor JOSEPH II and against the secular Revolutionaries in France. Although HONTHEIM, the leader of Febronianism, recanted, Pius only achieved partial success in reasserting his authority in the Empire. In France he excommunicated the Revolutionaries and suspended all clerics who had taken the secular authorities' oath. None the less the French troops occupied the Papal States of Avignon and the Venaissin and in 1798 they seized Rome itself. The Pope was taken prisoner, was harried from place to place and eventually died in captivity. Despite the increased secularism of the age, the plight of the old man in his last year excited widespread sympathy.

J.M. Gendry, *Pius VI*, 2 vols (1906); E.E.Y. Hales, *Revolution and Papacy* (1960).

Pius VII (1740–1823) Pope. Pius was born Gregorio Barnaba Chiaramonti. A member of the Benedictine Order, he was consecrated Bishop of Tivoli in 1782, Bishop of Imola in 1785 and, in the same year, was made a Cardinal. He was elected Pope in 1800. His Pontificate was dominated first by the grandiose claims of Napoleon and secondly by the re-organisation of Europe after the Treaty of Vienna of 1815. By nature conciliatory, Pius was present at Napoleon's coronation, but, despite papal protest, the new Emperor systematically took control of the Church. In 1809 Pius was in effect taken prisoner and he was not released until 1814. After the Treaty of Vienna, the Papal States were restored and reorganised. Despite the political turmoil, the Pope did succeed in promoting missions to Asia and to Latin America; he restored the Jesuit Order and his dedication and piety were admired by his contemporaries.

E.E.Y. Hales, *Napoleon and the Pope* (1962); J. Leflon, *Pie VII* (1958) [no English translation available].

Pius IX (1792–1878) Pope. Pius was born Giovanni Maria Mastai-Ferretti. He was consecrated Archbishop of Spoleto in 1827, Bishop of Imola in 1832 and he was appointed a Cardinal in 1840. In 1846, in succession to GREGORY XVI, and as a reputed liberal, he was elected Pope. Initially he seemed true to his liberal ideals and he released all political prisoners. However, in 1848 he was forced to flee from Rome in the face of revolution. He was restored by the French, who continued to occupy the Papal States until 1870. In effect the temporal power of the Papacy was over. King Victor Emmanuel of Italy took possession of Rome in 1870 and, under the Law of Guarantees, only the Vatican and the Lateran palace remained in the Pope's possession. These experiences turned Pius away from liberalism once and for all. He issued a series of encyclicals against rationalism, democratisation and anti-clericalism. In addition, he encouraged the ultramontane party. He defined the doctrine of the Immaculate Conception of the Blessed Virgin MARY, and issued the Syllabus of Errors. He imposed a new diocesan structure on the Netherlands and England and he

established many new dioceses throughout the Roman Catholic world. Then, in
1869, he called the First Vatican Council
which formally declared the doctrine of
papal infallibility. It was not unanimous;
the Old Catholics broke away and the
new dogma gave rise to the Kulturkampf
movement in Germany. None the less,
despite opposition and the loss of temporal power, Pius IX succeeded in placing the Papacy on the highest possible
spiritual plane. He was the longest serving of all the Popes and he is particularly
remembered for his famous reply to one
dissident critic: 'Tradition? I am
tradition'.

C. Butler, *The Vatican Council* (1962); A.B. Hasler,
Pius IX 1846–78, 2 vols (1977) [no English transla-
tion available]; E.E.Y. Hales, *Pope Pius IX* (1954);
H. Küng, *Infallible? An Enquiry* (1971).

Pius X (1835–1914)   Saint and Pope.
Pius was born Giuseppe Melchior Sarto
in Riese, Italy. In 1884 he was consecrated Bishop of Mantua; he was appointed Patriarch of Venice and a Cardinal in 1893 and he was elected Pope in
1903. He is remembered for laying down
the principles for Catholic Action –
namely, social action effected under
hierarchical control. He condemned the
theological modernism of LOISY and his
followers and he insisted in 1910 that all
clergy take an oath against the new
movement. He also was anxious to bol-
ster the faith of ordinary people by encouraging frequent Communion, more
effective religious education and a new
devotion to the Virgin MARY. Although
he was primarily concerned with his role
as a religious leader, he was also forced to
concern himself with maintaining the
independence of the French Church from
State control. His holiness was recognised even in his lifetime and he was
canonised in 1954.

G. Del Gal, *Pius X: The Life Story of the Beatus*
(1954); L Von Matt, *St Pius X: A Pictorial Biography* (1955).

Pius XI (1857–1939)   Pope. Pius was
born Achille Ambrogio in Damiano,
Italy. He became titular Archbishop of
Lepanto in 1919, Cardinal and Archbishop of Milan in 1921 and he was
elected Pope in 1922. He is primarily remembered as achieving agreement with
the Fascist dictator Mussolini in the Lateran Treaties of 1922, which resulted in
the creation of the Vatican City. Although he did condemn the principles of
Fascism, Nazism and Communism, he
was more concerned with the encouragement of religious devotion. To
that end, the Feast of Christ the King was
instituted in 1922 and he canonised many
popular figures such as TERESA OF
LISIEUX.

P. Hughes, *Pope Pius XI* (1937); R.J. Miller, *Forty
Years After: Pius XI and the Social Order* (1947).

Pius XII (1876–1958)   Pope. Pius was
born Eugenio Pacelli. An experienced
diplomat for the Vatican, he was appointed Cardinal and Papal Secretary of
State in 1930. Among his many achievements was the signing of a concordat
with the Nazi government of Germany in
1933. He succeeded PIUS XI in 1939 and
is a figure of enormous controversy. He
has been strongly criticised for his refusal
to speak out against the atrocities which
were occurring in Germany, particularly
against the Jews. His admirers argue that
he was silent because he knew that a protest would have aggravated the situation.
He himself when asked whether he
would protest against the extermination
of the Jews, is said to have replied, 'Dear
friend, do not forget that millions of
Catholics serve in the German armies.
Shall I bring them into conflicts of conscience?' There is no doubt, however, that
he did try to relieve the distress of
prisoners. Among his many encyclicals,
'Divino Afflante Spiritu' seemed to open
the way towards a more liberal attitude
to biblical criticism, and he also introduced various liturgical reforms. In 1950

he defined the doctrine of the Assumption of the Blessed Virgin MARY; he appointed a large number of new Cardinals, thus creating a more international Curia, and he made an attempt to improve relations with the Eastern Orthodox Churches.

K. Burton, *Witness of the Light: The Life of Pope Pius XII* (1958); C. Falconi, *The Silence of Pius XII* (1970); S. Friedlander, *Pius XII and the Third Reich* (1966).

Plotinus (c. 205–70)   Philosopher. Plotinus established an independent school of philosophy in Rome, Italy. He was himself of Egyptian origin, but he taught in Greek. He is remembered as the originator of the neo-Platonist system. He believed in a single indivisible being, who was the ultimate cause of the universe. This One stood at the top of a hierarchy of being – each stage proceeding from the one above. Thus the One was said to produce the Divine Mind and the Divine Mind produced the Soul, on which the entire created world depended for its existence. The soul of the individual, like its heavenly counterpart, must strive to know the truth through contemplation. Through reincarnation and ascetic living, each individual soul has the potential to achieve union with the One. Plotinus himself was not a Christian, but his philosophy was highly influential on theologians such as AUGUSTINE and Pseudo-DIONYSIUS, and has thus become part of the mystical heritage of the Church.

P. Merlan, *From Platonism to Neo-Platonism* 2nd edn (1960); J.M. Rist, *Plotinus: The Road to Reality* (1969).

Plunket, Oliver (1629–81)   Archbishop and Saint. Plunket was born in Meath, Ireland, and was educated in Dublin and Rome. He was ordained as a Roman Catholic priest in 1654 and was appointed Archbishop of Armagh in 1669. A thoroughly conscientious Archbishop, he was arrested as a result of the Titus

OATES plot. Despite his complete innocence, he was executed for treason in London. He has continuously been venerated in Ireland and he was canonised in 1975.

A. Curtayne, *The Trial of Oliver Plunkett* (1953).

Pole, Reginald (1500–58)   Cardinal and Archbishop. Pole was the great-nephew of King Edward IV of England. He was educated at the University of Oxford and for several years he corresponded with Thomas MORE and ERASMUS. He refused King HENRY VIII's invitation to be either Archbishop of York or Bishop of Winchester and in 1534 he openly condemned Henry's conduct in the matter of his divorce. He was created a Cardinal in 1536 and in 1540, as a result of his treason in encouraging France and Spain to break with England, an Act of Attainder was passed against him. None the less he rose in the hierarchy of the Church and he was nearly elected Pope in 1549. Then, in 1552, the Roman Catholic MARY I inherited the English throne from her half-brother the Protestant EDWARD VI. Pole was sent as papal legate to England; he absolved Parliament from schism with Rome and, after the martyrdom of CRANMER, he was appointed Archbishop of Canterbury. He did not succeed in bringing back the English people to the Catholic fold and, indeed, the torture and burning of Protestants made the Church an object of hatred. None the less he was a dedicated and pious man and he died only twelve hours after the Queen.

W. Schenk, *Reginald Pole: Cardinal of England* (1950).

Polycarp (c. 69–c. 155)   Saint and Bishop. Little is known of the life of Polycarp. He was the Bishop of Smyrna in Asia Minor and was a determined opponent of heresy. He is remembered as an important link between the world of the first-generation apostles and that of the writers and theologians of the late second century. According to IRENAEUS, he knew JOHN (whether the Apostle or the Elder is unclear) and spoke 'with the rest of those who had seen the Lord'. A letter to him from Irenaeus survives. In addition a letter (or possibly two) which Polycarp wrote to the Philippians is still in existence. He died as a martyr in Smyrna during a pagan festival and this is described in the second-century *Martyrium Polycarpi*, the earliest surviving acts of a martyr.

T. Camelot (ed.), *Acts of the Martyrs*, 4th edn (1969); C.P.S. Clarke, *St Ignatius and St Polycarp* (1930).

Porphyry (232–*c.* 303) Philosopher. Porphyry was born in Tyre of a pagan family. There is some dispute as to whether he ever converted to Christianity, although the general consensus is that he did not. After travelling through Syria, Palestine, Egypt and Greece, he became a student of PLOTINUS in Rome. He was responsible for the preservation and editing of his master's work and was himself a prolific writer. He produced fifteen works which attacked Christianity and which were condemned at the Council of Ephesus in 431. He also wrote several works on ethics and his introduction to the categories of Aristotle was much studied in the mediaeval schools.

T. Whittaker, *The Neo-Platonists* (1918).

Prester John (? twelfth century) Legendary Monarch. Prester (Presbyter) John was a priestly king who was said to have conquered the Muslims and who would eventually liberate the Holy Land. The story first appears in the Chronicle of Otto of Freising and Pope ALEXANDER III's letter 'to the most holy prince, the King of India', written in 1177, may have been written to him. Other scholars have identified Prester John with the Chinese Prince, Gor Khan, who did defeat the

Persian Sultan in 1141 or, alternatively, with a King of Ethiopia.

L.N. Gumilev, *Searches for an Imaginary Kingdom: The Legend of the Kingdom of Prester John* (1987); A.P. Newton (ed.), *Travel and Travellers in the Middle Ages* (1926); C.E. Nowell, 'The historical Prester John', *Speculum*, xxviii (1953); E. Ullendorf, *The Hebrew Letters of Prester John* (1982).

Priscilla [Prisca] (first century) Saint. Priscilla was the wife of Aquila, a Jew of Pontus, but her name is always listed first. According to the Book of Acts, they were forced to leave Rome in obedience to the decree of the Emperor Claudius. PAUL met them in Corinth and took them with him as far as Ephesus. They are also mentioned in the Epistle to the Romans, in I Corinthians and in II Timothy and were clearly important members of the Church. Although the name 'Prisca' appears on one of the catacombs and there is a church dedicated to the martyred St Prisca, there is no evidence that either of these was the New Testament Priscilla. HARNACK argued that Priscilla and Aquila were the authors of the Epistle to the Hebrews, but there are no real grounds for this conjecture.

Acts of the Apostles, Chapter 18; 'Prisca' in D.H. Farmer (ed.), *The Oxford Dictionary of Saints*, 3rd edn (1992).

Priscillian (d. *c.* 385) Bishop and Heretic. Priscillian was a Spaniard of noble birth. He seems to have taught Gnostic beliefs and to have attracted many followers. These doctrines were condemned at the Council of Saragossa in 380. In retaliation, Bishops who had supported Priscillian consecrated him Bishop of Avila. In 381 he was driven into exile, but, after a series of appeals, he was allowed to return to Spain. Eventually the Emperor MAXIMUS ordered him to be tried by a synod in Bordeaux. Priscillian appealed directly to the Emperor and he was put on trial for sorcery in Trier. Despite the intervention of St MARTIN OF

TOURS, he was condemned to death. Priscillian is remembered as the first Christian to be put to death for heresy. His followers continued in their enthusiasms until the middle of the fifth century.

H. Chadwick, *Priscillian of Avila: The Occult and the Charismatic in the Early Church* (1976).

Proclus (d. *c.* 446)   Saint and Patriarch. Proclus was known as a famous preacher and he is particularly remembered for giving a sermon on the *Theotokos* in front of NESTORIUS. He became Patriarch of Constantinople in 434 and was much respected. Several of his letters and sermons have survived, but the formula *'Unus ex Trinitate passus est'* (one of the Trinity suffered) is falsely ascribed to him. This was to become a slogan of the Monophysites in the Theopaschite controversy of the sixth century.

'Theopaschites' and 'Theotokos', in F.L. Cross (ed.), *The Oxford Dictionary of the Christian Church*, 2nd edn (1974).

Prynne, William (1600–69)   Polemicist. Prynne was born in Somerset, and he was educated at the University of Oxford. A determined Puritan, he was a prolific pamphlet writer. His *Histriomastix*, directed against the immorality of play-acting, was understood as an attack on the court of King CHARLES I and, in consequence, Prynne was imprisoned, fined and lost both his ears in the pillory. He was imprisoned again after campaigning against the *Book of Sports*, a list of certain recreations which the Church permitted on Sundays. He also did not hesitate to lead the attack against Archbishop LAUD. He won a seat in the House of Commons in 1648, but he opposed the execution of the King. Subsequently he was imprisoned yet again, this time for attacking Parliament. He was a supporter of the restoration of King Charles II, but his uncompromising Presbyterianism put him out of sympathy with the high Anglicanism of the new reign. However, he continued to write his pamphlets and participate in Parliamentary debates for the rest of his life. Prynne is remembered for his independence of mind, his courage and relentless persistence in promoting what he believed to be right.

W.M. Lamont, *Marginal Prynne* (1963).

Pugin, Augustus Welby Northmore (1812–52)   Artist, Architect and Designer. Pugin was the son of a French refugee aristocrat, who had settled in England. In *c.* 1835, he converted to Roman Catholicism and he is remembered as the main proponent of the gothic style in nineteenth-century England. He regarded gothic as the only truly Christian architecture and he promulgated his views in works such as *The True Principles of Pointed or Christian Architecture*. Among his surviving buildings are St George's Roman Catholic Cathedral in Southwark and the chapel of St Edmund's College, Ware. He also helped Barry with the design of the new Houses of Parliament.

P. Atterbury and C. Wainwright, *Pugin: A Gothic Passion* (1994); P.B. Stanton, *Pugin* (1971).

Pulcheria (399–453)   Saint and Monarch. Pulcheria was the daughter of the Emperor Arcadius and the elder sister of the Emperor THEODOSIUS II. She was a determined upholder of orthodoxy and condemned both Nestorianism and Monophysitism. She encouraged the Patriarch PROCLUS to bring back the body of St John CHRYSOSTOM to Constantinople and she ensured that life at court was conducted on strict Christian principles. On the death of her brother in 450 she became Empress and she is chiefly remembered for arranging the Ecumenical Council of Chalcedon which met in 451.

A. Grabar, *Byzantium from the Death of Theodosius to the Rise of Islam* (1966); R.V. Sellers, *The Council of Chalcedon* (1953).

Purcell, Henry (1659–95) Composer. Purcell was born in London and he became organist of Westminster Abbey in 1680 and organist of the Chapel Royal in 1682. In the history of Church music, he is remembered for his many anthems which include 'My heart is inditing', 'Rejoice in the Lord alway' and 'O praise God in his holiness'. Many of his compositions are still sung today.

I. Holst (ed.), *Henry Purcell: Essays on his Music* (1959); R. King, *Henry Purcell: 'A Greater Musical Genius England Never Had'* (1994); F.B. Zimmerman, *Henry Purcell: His Life and Times* (1967).

Pusey, Edward Bouverie (1800–82) Theologian. Pusey was educated at the University of Oxford and in Germany and in 1828 he was appointed Regius Professor of Hebrew at Oxford. Encouraged by KEBLE and NEWMAN, he contributed to the *Tracts for the Times* and quickly became regarded as a leader of the Oxford Movement. He remained in the Church of England after Newman's defection to Rome and dedicated the rest of his life to combating liberal theology, to the study of the Church Fathers, to the foundation of Anglican religious orders and to working for Anglican and Roman Catholic reunion. In many of these enterprises he was disappointed, but he remained, until the time of his death, an important figure in the English Church. Pusey House at Oxford was named in commemoration of him.

P. Butler (ed.), *Pusey Rediscovered* (1983); D.A.R. Forrester, *Young Doctor Pusey: A Study in Development* (1989); H.P. Liddon, *Life of Pusey*, 4 vols (1893–7) A.G. Lough, *Dr Pusey: Restorer of the Church* (1981).

Pym, Barbara (1913–80) Novelist. Pym was born in Oswestry, England, and she was educated at the University of Oxford. She served in the British navy during the Second World War and then worked for the Institute of African Studies until retirement. She is remembered for novels such as *Some Tame Gazelle, Excellent Women, Jane and Prudence* and *An Unsuitable Attachment*. In them she created a hilarious but recognisable picture of the Church of England, staffed by well-meaning but ineffectual clergymen, who are ministered to by adoring groups of capable, but ultimately superfluous, 'excellent women'.

H. Holt, *A Lot to Ask: A Life of Barbara Pym* (1992); R. Liddell, *A Mind at Ease: Barbara Pym and her Novels* (1989); D. Salwak (ed.), *The Life and Work of Barbara Pym* (1987).

Q

Quesnel, Pasquier (1634–1719) Theologian. Quesnel was a member of the Congregation of the Oratory in Paris, France. He is remembered for his *Réflexions Morales*, a verse-by-verse commentary on the New Testament. Then, in 1675, his edition of the works of St LEO was placed on the Index because of its supposed Gallican tone. He was accused of holding Jansenist opinions and in 1684 he moved to Brussels where he stayed with Antoine ARNAULD. Arrested at the instigation of LOUIS XIV, he escaped to Holland. In 1708 the *Réflexions* was formally condemned by Pope Clement XI. Although Quesnel continued to defend himself, his theology was rejected in the papal bull 'Unigenitus' of 1713.

N.J. Abercrombie, *The Origins of Jansenism* (1936); A. le Roy, *Un Janséniste en Exil* (1900) [no English translation available].

R

Rabanus Maurus (*c.* 776–856) Archbishop, Theologian and Devotional Writer. Rabanus was born in Mainz, Germany. He was educated at Fulda and Tours (under ALCUIN) and he subsequently became Master of the Fulda monastery school, making it one of the most important in Europe. He became Abbot of Fulda in 822 and Archbishop of Mainz in 847. Among his many works were an important devotional manual for clergy, commentaries on the Scriptures, two penitentials, a martyrology, a study on grammar and a collection of sermons. He was also an important poet and the famous hymn 'Veni creator' is often attributed to him. These efforts did much to further the evangelisation of Germany and he was known as the 'Praeceptor Germaniae'.

D. Bullough, *The Age of Charlemagne* (1965).

Rad, Gerhard von (1901–71) Theologian and Biblical Scholar. Von Rad was born in Nuremburg, Germany, and was educated at the Universities of Erlangen and Tübingen. Subsequently he held chairs at Jena, Göttingen and Heidelberg. He is remembered as an important scholar of the Old Testament. Among his books were works on the origin of the Book of Deuteronomy, on the Hexateuch and on the theology of the Old Testament. His analyses were largely based on form-critical study (the study of different forms of narrative) and have been highly influential both in Germany and in the English-speaking world.

J.L. Crenshaw, *Gerhard von Rad* (1978); D.G.

Spriggs, *Two Old Testament Theologies: A Comparative Evaluation of the Contributions of Eichrodt and Von Rad to our Understanding of Old Testament Theology* (1974).

Rahner, Karl (1904–84) Theologian. Rahner was a member of the Jesuit Order and he taught theology at the Universities of Innsbruck and Munich. He was strongly influenced by the philosophy of Martin HEIDEGGER and he attempted to interpret traditional Roman Catholic theology, particularly the work of THOMAS AQUINAS, in existential terms. Among his works was *Geist im Welt* (translated as *Spirit in the World*) and his *Theological Investigations*. He was one of the most influential theologians of his day; he acted as an advisor to the Second Vatican Council and he was one of the editors of the widely used *Lexikon für Theologie und Kirch*.

W.V. Dych, *Karl Rahner* (1992); L. Roberts, *The Achievement of Karl Rahner* (1967).

Raikes, Robert (1735–1811) Educator and Philanthropist. Raikes was born in Gloucester. He was the owner of the *Gloucester Journal* in which he recommended several philanthropic causes. In 1780 he set up a Sunday School in his own parish which was a huge success and in 1783 he wrote about it in his paper. His methods were imitated all over the country and by 1786 more than two hundred thousand children were receiving a Sunday School education. Raikes's school was not the first, but his promotion of the idea led to it spreading throughout England. Hannah MORE was amongst those influenced by him.

F. Booth, *Robert Raikes* (1980); J. Ferguson (ed.), *Christianity, Society and Education: Robert Raikes: Past, Present and Future* (1981); C. Newby, *The Story of Sunday Schools: Robert Raikes and After* (1930).

Ramabai, Pandita (1858–1922) Educator and Missionary. Ramabai was born of high-caste Hindu parents near Mangalore, India. She became interested in Christianity in Bengal and then went to England in 1883 to further her education. There she was baptised and in 1886 she travelled to the United States to study educational methods. She was the author of the *High-Caste Hindu Woman* which did much to waken the Western world to the plight of Indian women. On her return to India, she opened a boarding school in Bombay, which later moved to Poona. She then established the Mukti mission which provided shelter for women and which grew into a highly successful evangelical mission. Among her many other activities, she also made a Marathi translation of the Bible.

Pandita Ramabai, *Testimony* (1917); P. Sengupta, *Pandita Ramabai* (1970).

Ramsey, [Arthur] Michael (1904–88) Archbishop and Theologian. Ramsey was educated at the University of Cambridge. He was ordained to the Anglican ministry in 1928 and he taught theology at the Universities of Durham and Cambridge. He was consecrated Bishop of Durham in 1952, Archbishop of York in 1956 and he was Archbishop of Canterbury between 1961 and 1974. He was regarded as one of the most eminent English theologians of his day and his books include *The Gospel and the Catholic Church*, *The Resurrection of Christ* and *God, Christ and the World*. During his time at Canterbury, the Church of England changed over to synodical government. Although the scheme for Anglican and Methodist reunion failed, under his leadership there was a notable im-

provement in relationships between the various Christian denominations.

O. Chadwick, *Michael Ramsey: A Life* (1990); R. Gill and L. Kendall (eds), *Michael Ramsey as Theologian* (1995).

Raphael Sanzio (1483–1520) Artist. Raphael was born in Urbino, Italy. He studied first with Perugino and later with LEONARDO DA VINCI and MICHELANGELO in Florence. In 1508 he moved to Rome at the invitation of Pope JULIUS II. There he painted a series of pictures for the Vatican. Then in 1514, Pope LEO X appointed him chief architect of St Peter's. Among his many paintings are a variety of biblical and religious scenes, as well as the famous *School of Athens*. His Madonnas are particularly admired.

L Bortolon, *The Life and Times of Raphael* (1968); J. Pope-Hennessy, *Raphael* (1970); D. Thompson, *Raphael: The Life and the Legacy* (1983).

Rashdall, Hastings (1858–1924) Philosopher and Theologian. Rashdall was educated at the University of Oxford, where he subsequently taught. He was a Canon of Hereford from 1909 to 1917 and he became Dean of Carlisle in 1917. Among his books was the important *Theory of Good and Evil* in which he tried to steer a middle course between idealist and utilitarian theories of ethics. He is also remembered for his *Idea of the Atonement* in which, like ABELARD, he explained JESUS's death as an example of faithful obedience rather than as a means of penal substitution. Determinedly rational, he was Vice-President of the Modern Churchman's Union and he was highly critical of any form of mystical theology.

P.E. Matheson, *Hastings Rashdall* (1928).

Ras Tafari [Haile Selassie] (1892–1975) Cult Focus. Haile Selassie was the Emperor of Ethiopia between 1930 and 1974 and during that period he did much to modernise the country. He was driven into exile by the Italians between 1934 and 1941, but, on his return, he revived the Ethiopian Patriarchate and he established relations with the Pope. He was finally deposed by a military coup in 1974 and he died while under house arrest. He has become a Messianic figure for the Rastafarian movement. This originated among the black population of Jamaica. It was inspired by Marcus Garvey's 'Back to Africa' movement and by the magnificent enthronement ceremony of the Emperor. Haile Selassie (or Ras (Lord) Tafari) is regarded as the Messiah of all black people, the descendant of King Solomon and the Queen of Sheba and the fulfilment of all biblical prophecies. Although the Rastafarians reject traditional Christianity as a white aberration, they continue to use the Bible for proof texts and sing a selection of hymns from the MOODY and SANKEY hymn book.

E.E. Cashmore, *Rasta Man: The Rastafarian Movement in Britain* (1983); L. Sandford, *The Lion of Judah hath Prevailed* (1972); Haile Selassie, *My Life and Ethiopia's Progress* (1976).

Rauschenbusch, Walter (1861–1918) Theologian. Rauschenbusch was born in Rochester, New York. His parents were of German origin and he was educated in Germany and at the University of Rochester. He was called to the Baptist ministry and became Pastor of the Second German Baptist Church in New York from 1886. Subsequently he taught at Rochester Seminary. He is remembered as a strong advocate of Christian socialism and has been described as 'the father of the social gospel in America'. Among his books were *Christianizing the Social Order* and *A Theology for the Social Gospel*.

R.T. Handy (ed.), *The Social Gospel in America* (1966).

Raymond Nonnatus (*c.* 1204–40) Saint, Missionary and Cardinal. Little certain is known of the life of Raymond Nonnatus. His name means 'not born' and it is thought that his mother died in childbirth. He grew up in Portello, Catalonia, and he is said to have been admitted to the Mercedarian order by PETER NOLASCO himself. He worked in North Africa, redeeming slaves and preaching the gospel and he was made a Cardinal by Pope GREGORY IX in 1239. He is remembered as the patron saint of midwives.

Acta Sanctorum, August 6 (1743) [no English translation available].

Raymond of Peñafort (*c.* 1185–1275) Canon Lawyer, Order Founder and Saint. Raymond was born near Barcelona, Spain. He taught first at the Barcelona Cathedral School and later at the University of Bologna. In 1222 he joined the Dominican Order and then, with PETER NOLASCO, he founded the Mercedarian Order. The new foundation was dedicated to the redemption of Christians captured by Muslims. In 1230, Pope GREGORY IX commissioned him to revise the papal decretals (papal letters which have the force of law). This was a huge task, but Raymond finished it in four years. He also wrote the *Summa de Casibus Poenitentiae*, which was highly influential on the later practice of the Sacrament of penance. In 1638 he became General of the Dominican Order in Spain and then, after resigning, he dedicated himself to missionary work among the Muslims and Jews. He is particularly remembered for encouraging THOMAS AQUINAS to write his *Summa Contra Gentes*.

T.M. Schwertner, *St Raymond of Peñafort* (1935).

Reimarus, Hermann Samuel (1694–1768) Theologian. Reimarus was born in Hamburg, Germany, and was educated at Jena. Subsequently he taught at Wittenberg, Wismar and Hamburg. He is remembered for his huge Deist treatise, most of which was never published. However, after his death, G.E. LESSING issued a selection from it, known as the *Wolfenbüttel Fragments*. This caused a sensation. Reimarus had rejected the miraculous, supernatural element in Christianity and had argued that JESUS was preaching an immediate, eschatological message. This analysis was to be highly influential on the thought of D.F. STRAUSS and Albert SCHWEITZER.

A.C. Lundsteen, *Hermann Samuel Reimarus und die Anfänge der Leben-Jesu-Forschung* (1939) [no English translation available]; A. Schweitzer, *The Quest for the Historical Jesus*, 3rd edn (1954).

Reinkens, Joseph Hubert (1821–96) Bishop. Reinkens was born in Burtscheid near Aachen and he was appointed Rector of Breslau University in 1865. Strongly opposed to the decree of papal infallibility passed at the First Vatican Council in 1870, he joined DÖLLINGER in protest and was excommunicated. In 1873 he became the first Bishop of the German 'Old Catholics'. He was consecrated by Bishop Hermann Heykamp of the Old Catholic Church of Utrecht and in 1876 in his turn, he consecrated Edward Herzog as the first Old Catholic Bishop of Switzerland. He dedicated the rest of his life to the new organisation.

C.B. Moss, *The Old Catholic Movement: Its Origins and History* (1948).

Rembrandt van Rijn (1606–69) Artist. Rembrandt was born in Leyden, Holland. He achieved early fame as a portrait painter and he moved to Amsterdam in 1631. In the history of Christian art, he is remembered for his dark paintings, from which the figures glow with an extraordinary inner light. He frequently treated biblical themes and altogether he produced ninety versions of the Passion stories in paintings and etchings. Although he fell out with the Dutch Church after fathering an illegitimate child, Rembrandt has long been recognised as a profoundly religious painter and he has been described as the 'artist of the soul'.

C. Brown, *Rembrandt: The Master and his Workshop* (1991); M. Lepore, *The Life and Times of Rembrandt* (1968); W.A. Visser'Hooft, *Rembrandt and the Gospel* (1957).

Remigius (c. 438–c. 533) Archbishop and Saint. Remigius was from an aristocratic Frankish family and he became Archbishop of Rheims at the age of twenty-two. He is remembered primarily as the one who baptised King CLOVIS. According to legend, the vessel which held the anointing oil used at the coronation of the French kings had been brought to Remigius by a dove and he is traditionally believed to have bestowed on the King the power of healing 'the King's evil' or scrofula. He is also associated with the foundation of several sees.

F. Oppenheimer, *The Legend of the Sainte Ampoule* (1953) [no English translation available]; G. Tessier, *Le Baptême de Clovis* (1964) [no English translation available].

Renan, Joseph Ernest (1823–92) Philosopher and Theologian. Renan was born in Tréguier, France. He was a student of semitic languages and German theology and he was also an expert archaeologist. Initially drawn to the Roman Catholic priesthood, he lost his faith in c. 1845. He is remembered for his *Vie de Jésus*, which caused a sensation. He portrayed JESUS as a delightful Jewish teacher, but he entirely removed the supernatural elements from the Gospel story. Because of the outcry, he was dismissed from his position at the Collège de France and he went on to write a five-volume *Histoire du Peuple d'Israël* and the popular *Souvenirs d'Enfance et de Jeunesse*.

R.M. Chadbourne, *Ernest Renan* (1968); M. Weiler, *La Pensée de Renan* (1945) [no English translation available].

Ricci, Matteo (1552–1610) Missionary. Ricci was a member of the Jesuit

Order. He went to Macao in 1582 where he learnt the Mandarin language. Then, in 1583 he settled in mainland China, living successively in Chao-ching, Shaochow, Nanking and finally, after a period of imprisonment, in Peking. He impressed the Chinese with his Western instruments, such as clocks and a map of the world. He translated the Ten Commandments and a catechism into Chinese and he taught Christianity in such a way that it was compatible with the Chinese world view. He was respected by the Chinese aristocracy and he even made contact with the Emperor. However, after Ricci's death, his tolerant attitude towards Confucian ancestor worship aroused controversy in the Roman Catholic Church and in the early eighteenth century Pope Clement IX formally condemned the rites. None the less, Ricci's practice of explaining the Christian religion in his listeners' own terms was to become common missionary strategy.

V. Cronin, *The Wise Man from the West* (1955); O. Gentili, *L'Apostolo della Cina: Matteo Ricci* (1963) [no English translation available].

Richard of Chichester (*c.* 1197–1253) Saint and Bishop. Richard was born in Droitwich, England. He was appointed Chancellor of Oxford in *c.* 1235 and later of Canterbury. In 1244 he was chosen to be Bishop of Chichester, but he had to be consecrated in France because King Henry III preferred another candidate. The King only withdrew his opposition after being threatened with excommunication. Richard proved to be an excellent Bishop and, after his death, his tomb quickly became a place of pilgrimage.

E.F. Jacob, 'St. Richard of Chichester', *Journal of Ecclesiastical History*, vii (1956).

Richard of St Victor (d. 1173) Mystic and Theologian. Richard was born in Scotland. He became Prior of the Abbey of St Victor in Paris in 1162. He is re-

membered for his philosophical treatise *De Trinitate* and for his description of the six stages of contemplation as explained in his *De Praeparatione Animi ad Contemplationem, seu Liber Dictus Benjamin Minor* and *De Gratia Contemplationis seu Benjamin Maior*.

C. Kirchberger (ed.), *Selections from the Writings of Richard of St Victor* (1957).

Richelieu, Armand Jean du Plessis (1585–1642) Cardinal and Politician. Richelieu was born into an aristocratic family in Paris, France. He was consecrated Bishop of Luçon in 1607 and he was appointed Secretary of State to the young King Louis XIII in 1616. For a time he was out of favour, but he was recalled in 1619 and became a Cardinal in 1622. He was made President of the Council of Ministers in 1625 and Chief Minister in 1629. From then until his death he was, in effect, the ruler of France. In the history of the Church, he is remembered for his support of Gallicanism, his defeat of the Huguenots, his rejection of Jansenism and his alliance with the Protestant princes which largely ensured the destruction of Hapsburg influence in Europe. As a result of his efforts, France emerged as the leading power. Despite his ruthlessness and opportunism, he was genuinely religious and he is remembered for his *Défense des Principaux Points de la Foi Catholique* and his important catechism, *Instruction du Chrétien*.

J. Bergin, *Cardinal Richelieu: Power and the Pursuit of Wealth* (1985); R.J. Knecht, *Richelieu* (1991); G.R.R. Treasure, *Cardinal Richelieu and the Development of Nationalism* (1972).

Ridley, Nicholas (*c.* 1500–55) Bishop and Martyr. Ridley was educated at the Universities of Cambridge, the Sorbonne and Louvain. In 1537 he was appointed chaplain to Archbishop CRANMER and in 1547 he was consecrated Bishop of Rochester. He became Bishop of London in 1550. A convinced Protestant, he contributed to the 1549 Book of Common Prayer. With the death of the young King EDWARD VI, he supported the claims of Lady Jane Grey to ensure the Protestant succession. When the Roman Catholic Queen MARY I succeeded, he was deprived of his see and excommunicated. In 1555 he was burnt at the stake for heresy at Oxford, together with Hugh LATIMER. These martyrdoms did much to turn the ordinary people of England against the Church of Rome.

G.W. Bromiley, *Nicholas Ridley: Scholar, Bishop, Theologian* (1950); J.G. Ridley, *Nicholas Ridley* (1957).

Ritschl, Albrecht (1822–89) Theologian. Ritschl was born in Berlin, Germany, the son of a Protestant pastor. He was educated at Bonne, Halle, Heidelberg and Tübingen and he subsequently became a Professor of Theology first at Bonn and then at Göttingen. He was initially a disciple of F.C. BAUR and a member of the Tübingen school. Later, he came to believe the Christian doctrines were not statements of fact, but of value. He abandoned the metaphysical bases of Christianity and he insisted that the purpose of JESUS's mission was to establish God's ethical Kingdom in the world so that humanity could live together in mutual love. Among his more important books were *Die Christliche Lehre von der Rechtfertigung und Versöhnung, Theologie und Metaphysik* and *Geschichte des Pietismus.* He was a hugely influential figure and the 'Ritschlian school' spawned at least three theological journals. Among his followers must be numbered Adolf HARNACK and Ernst TROELTSCH.

K. Barth, *From Rousseau to Ritschl* (1959); D.W. Lotz, *Ritschl and Luther: A Fresh Perspective on Albrecht Ritschl's Theology* (1978).

Robert of Arbrissel (*c.* 1055–1117) Order Founder. Robert was a pupil of ANSELM OF LAON in Paris, France. At the urging of Pope URBAN II, he became a travelling preacher and in 1100 he founded a monastery at Fontevrault. This was to be an order of both monks and nuns, living in two separate houses, but under one Abbess, following a strict version of the Rule of St BENEDICT. The order prospered, but was abolished in the French Revolution. It was revived in the early nineteenth century as an order for women only. Although Robert himself had a reputation for holiness and several miracles were ascribed to him, he has never been formally canonised.

R. Niderst, *Robert d'Arbrissel et les Origines de l'Ordre de Fontevrault* (1952) [no English translation available].

Robert of Molesne (*c.* 1027–1111) Order Founder and Saint. Robert was born into a noble family in Champagne, France. He joined the abbey of Moutier-la-Celle at the age of fifteen. After a short time at St-Michel-de-Tonnerre, he founded a monastery at Molesne which was to be based on the strictest Benedictine principles. However, after a disagreement in 1098, Robert left to found the famous house at Citeaux. This was to become the mother house of the Cistercian Order, and it is remembered as the monastery of BERNARD OF CLAIRVAUX in the twelfth century. The Cistercians interpret the Rule of St BENEDICT very austerely, emphasising manual labour, plain living and secluded communal prayer. Robert himself returned to Molesne in 1100.

J.A. Lefèvre, 'Saint Robert de Molesne dans l'opinion monastique du XIIe et du XIIIe siècle', *Analecta Bollandiana*, lxxiv (1956) [no English translation available]; L.J. Lekai and S.O. Cist, *The White Monks: A History of the Cistercian Order* (1953).

Roberts, Evan John (1878–1951) Missionary Revivalist. Roberts was born in Glamorgan, Wales, in very humble circumstances. After a short career as a miner and blacksmith, he was accepted for training as a Calvinist Methodist minister in 1904. That year Roberts had a deep spiritual experience and he felt inspired to return home to conduct a mission. There was an extraordinary religious revival throughout Glamorgan with many manifestations of the more spectacular gifts of the Spirit. Roberts and his friends then took the message to Liverpool, Anglesey and Caernarvonshire. Altogether it has been estimated that one hundred thousand people were converted as a result of his work. By 1906, however, Roberts himself was exhausted and he retired from his preaching career.

E. Evans, *The Welsh Revival of 1904* (1969).

Robinson, John (*c.* 1575–1625) Sect Founder and Polemicist. Robinson was probably educated at the University of Cambridge. He was ordained into the Anglican ministry, but, as a strict Puritan, he joined a separatist group in Norfolk. In 1609 he was forced to flee with the group to Holland where he became the leader of the congregation in Leyden. He encouraged emigration and in 1620 part of his flock left the Netherlands and, in the *Mayflower*, eventually landed in Plymouth, Massachusetts. Robinson himself stayed in the Netherlands, but he continued to exert an important influence on the Pilgrim Fathers through letters and sermons.

F.J. Powicke, *A Life of John Robinson* (1920).

Robinson, John Arthur Thomas (1919–83) Bishop and Theologian. Robinson was the son of a Canon of Canterbury Cathedral and was a student of C.H. DODD at Cambridge University. After teaching at the university, he became Anglican Bishop of Woolwich in 1959. A New Testament scholar, he is primarily remembered for his *Honest to God*, published in 1963. This questioned the conventional supernatural image of a 'God out there' and asked whether JESUS should be regarded as God 'dressed up'

as a human being. It was serialised in a Sunday newspaper and caused a sensation. He was unfairly accused of atheism and was seen by many as symbolising the uncertainties of the 1960s.

E. James, *The Life of Bishop John A.T. Robinson* (1987); A. Kee, *The Roots of Christian Freedom: The Theology of John A. T. Robinson* (1988); R.P. McBrien, *The Church in the Thought of Bishop John Robinson* (1966).

Roch (*c.* 1295–*c.* 1327) Saint. Little is known of the life of St Roch. He is said to have been born in Montpellier, France, and to have lived as a hermit. He is remembered for effecting miraculous cures of the bubonic plague at Aquapendente, Cesaria, Mantua and Parma. After his death he was frequently invoked in times of plague and he was mentioned by Martin LUTHER in his denunciation of saint-worship.

D.H. Farmer (ed.), *The Oxford Dictionary of Saints*, 3rd edn (1992).

Rogers, John (*c.* 1500–55) Biblical Scholar and Martyr. Rogers was born near Birmingham, England, and was educated at the University of Cambridge. He served as a chaplain in Antwerp, became a committed Protestant and married. Under the name of Thomas Matthew, he published an English translation of the Bible using the manuscripts of William TYNDALE and the translation of Miles COVERDALE. This was to be hugely influential on later English versions. In 1548, in the reign of King EDWARD VI, he returned to England and in 1550 he became a Prebendary of St Paul's Cathedral in London. With the accession of the Roman Catholic Queen MARY I, he was arrested and tortured. He was finally burnt at the stake for heresy in 1555 and is remembered as the first of the Marian martyrs.

J.L. Chester, *John Rogers the Compiler of the First Authorised English Bible: The Pioneer of the English Reformation and its First Martyr* (1861); J.F. Mozley, *William Tyndale* (1937).

Rolle of Hampole, Richard (*c.* 1295–1349) Mystic and Devotional Writer. Rolle was born in Yorkshire and studied for a time at the University of Oxford. Subsequently he became a hermit and he ended his life in a Cistercian convent at Hampole. He is remembered for his mystical works *Incendium Amoris* and *Emendatio Vitae*, for his lyric poetry and for his letters of spiritual guidance. His writings were widely read in the Middle Ages and the Latin treatises were translated into Middle English. They have an appealing directness and were probably influential on John WYCLIFFE and the Lollards.

M.D. Knowles, *The English Mystical Tradition* (1961); M.A. Knowlton, *The Influence of Richard Rolle and of Julian of Norwich on Middle English Lyrics* (1973); N. Watson, *Richard Rolle and the Invention of Authority* (1991).

Romanos (d. 556) Poet and Saint. Romanos was born in Syria. After serving as a Deacon in Beirut, he lived for the rest of his life in Constantinople. He is remembered as the author of over a thousand hymns, of which about eighty survive. Perhaps the most famous of these was 'On the Nativity', which used to be sung every Christmas Eve in the Emperor's palace. He was known as 'Melodus'.

E.A. Livingstone (ed.), *The Oxford Dictionary of the Christian Church*, revised edition (1997).

Romauld (*c.* 950–1027) Saint and Order Founder. Romauld was born of noble parents in Ravenna, Italy. As a result of his father killing another man in a duel, he entered the Abbey of Sant'Apollinare in Classe. Although he was elected Abbot in 998, he resigned the following year to become a hermit. He travelled throughout Italy and his new monastery at Campus Moldoli became the mother house of the Camaldolese Order. He left no written Rule so the different congregations follow different patterns.

Catholic University of America, *New Catholic Encyclopaedia* (1967).

Roscellinus (*c.* 1050–1125) Philosopher. Roscellinus was probably born in Compiègne, France. He was educated at Soissons and Rheims and then he returned to Compiègne. As early as 1102 he was accused of teaching that the three persons of the Trinity were three separate divinities (tritheism). He denied the charge and subsequently became a Canon at Bayeux Cathedral and he taught at Loches, Besançon and Tours. Again he was accused of tritheism and among his detractors were ANSELM, ABELARD and JOHN OF SALISBURY. Little of his own writings survives so it is impossible to assess the truth of these accusations. He also seems to have insisted that universals have no independent existence of their own and that reality can only be ascribed to particular things or instances. This position is known as nominalism and emerged as a reaction to realism. Roscellinus is generally regarded as the father of mediaeval nominalism.

Catholic University of America, *New Catholic Encyclopaedia* (1967).

Rose of Lima (1586–1617) Saint. Rose was born in Lima, South America. She led an extraordinarily austere existence and, at the age of nineteen, she joined the Tertiary Order of St Dominic. Largely as a result of her mortifications and inner distress, she died young. She was the first person born in the New World to be canonised and she is the patron saint of South America and the Philippines.

F. Parkinson Keyes, *The Rose and the Lily* (1962).

Rosenkreutz, Christian Mythical Sect Founder. In the early seventeenth century, the Lutheran pastor J.V. Andreae published anonymously the *Chymische Hochzeit Christiani Rosenkreutz* and *Confessio Fraternitatis*. They were probably intended as a spoof and purported to be an account of the founding of an esoteric secret society by one Christian Rosenkreutz. The society was dedicated to learning about the wisdom of the East and the mysteries of nature. The books were taken seriously and several Rosicrucian societies were started including the Viennese Gold-und-Rosen-Kreuzer which only admitted senior Freemasons. Rosicrucian ideas were to become influential and, through the Freemason network, they spread through the upper and middle classes of Europe and the United States of America. Together with Theosophy, they were particularly fashionable in the 1920s and 1930s.

F. de P. Castells, *Our Ancient Brethren: The Originators of Freemasonry* (1932); A.E. Waite, *The Brotherhood of the Rosy Cross* (1924); F.A. Yates, *The Rosicrucian Enlightenment* (1972).

Rosmini-Serbati, Antonio (1797–1855) Philosopher and Order Founder. Rosmini-Serbati was born in Rovereto Trentino, Italy. He was ordained to the Roman Catholic priesthood in 1821. He was the author of several important philosophical works including the *Nuovo Saggio sull'Origine delle Idee,* which incurred the displeasure of the Jesuits. He also proposed various reforms of the clergy and Church organisation, with the result that his *Constituzione Secondo la Giusticia Sociale* and his *Cinque Piaghe della Chiesa* were put on the Index in 1849. He founded the Order of the Fathers of Charity, with an order for women, the Sisters of Providence. Both are dedicated to the cultivation of personal holiness and to works of charity, particularly education. They are famous in England for introducing the clerical or Roman collar.

D. Cleari, *Antonio Rosmini: Introduction to his Life and Teaching* (1992); C.J. Emery, *The Rosminians* (1960).

Rossetti, Christina Georgina (1830–94) Poet and Devotional Writer. Rossetti was the sister of the Pre-Raphaelite painter and poet, Dante Gabriel Rossetti. She published several books of poetry in her lifetime, many with strong Christian themes, and she was the author of devotional works such as *Lost and Found,* which are now no longer read. She is remembered in the history of the Church for her carols 'Love came down at Christmas' and 'In the bleak mid-winter', both of which are still great favourites.

D. A. Kent (ed.), *The Achievement of Christina Rossetti* (1987); J. Marsh, *Christina Rossetti: A Literary Biography* (1994); F. Thomas, *Christina Rossetti* (1994); F. Winnar, *The Rossettis and their Circle* (1934).

Rousseau, Jean-Jacques (1712–78) Philosopher. Rousseau was born in Geneva into a Calvinist family, but he converted to Roman Catholicism in 1728. He moved to Paris in 1742 where he became a member of the 'philosophe' circle and led a somewhat unconventional private life. Then, in 1754, he returned to both Geneva and Protestantism and, two years later, he moved to Montmorency. He had already come to the attention of the public with his essay *Discours sur les Sciences et les Arts.* In 1761 he published *Julie ou la Nouvelle Heloïse,* which caused a sensation since he condemned the artificial nature of society and advocated a natural religion based on reason and the beauties of nature. The following year, he produced *Emile ou de l'Education* in which he took up a gentle Deist position. Finally, his *Du Contrat Social* recommended that the laws of a country should express the general will of the people. He also rejected all forms of religious intolerance and suggested that some sort of civil religion was necessary to ensure social stability. These works were put on the Index in 1762. Rousseau spent the next few years wandering through Europe (for a time he stayed with David HUME). His *Confessions* were published in 1772. Rousseau's ideas became hugely influential after his death and his political works were used by the

French and the German Revolutionaries. With his emphasis on subjectivism, he is regarded as an important forerunner of Romanticism and, by emphasising the role of human reason in religion and in his advocacy of tolerance, he must be seen as anticipating modern liberal humanism.

R. Grimsley, *Rousseau and the Religious Quest* (1968); T. McFarland, *Romanticism and the Heritage of Rousseau* (1995); M. Viroli, *Jean-Jacques Rousseau and the 'Well-Ordered Society'* (1988); R. Wokler, *Rousseau* (1995).

Rowntree, Joseph (1836–1925) Philanthropist. Rowntree was born in Yorkshire of an eminent Quaker family; his father had had a life-long interest in education and had founded several schools. As a boy, the young Rowntree joined the family grocery business and later became head of the Rowntree cocoa works. He was known as an enlightened business man who did much to improve workplace conditions. He is particularly remembered for founding the model village of New Earswick, which demonstrated how a caring employer could both ensure decent conditions for his workers and run a profitable enterprise. He remained a prominent member of the Society of Friends and is one of a long line of English Quaker philanthropists.

A. Vernon, *A Quaker Business Man: The Life of Joseph Rowntree* (1958).

Ruether, Rosemary Radford (b. 1936) Theologian. Ruether was born in St Paul, Minnesota, and she was educated at Scripps College and Claremont Graduate School. She subsequently has taught theology at Garrett Seminary and North-Western University in Illinois. A member of the Roman Catholic Church, she has produced several important books including *Faith and Fratricide, Sexism and God-Talk* and *Gaia and God: An Eco-feminist Theology of Earth Healing*. Her work reflects many of the theological preoccupations of the late twentieth century – the disavowal of racism and a concern with gender and language, and the place of human beings in the environment.

I. Diamond and G. Orenstein, *Reweaving the World: The Emergence of Eco-Feminism* (1990); A. Loudes, 'Feminist theology', in D. Ford (ed.), *The Modern Theologians* (1997); D. Hampson, *Theology and Feminism* (1991).

Russell, Charles Taze (1852–1916) Sect Founder. Russell was the owner of a chain of drapery shops in Allegheny, Pennsylvania. He had been brought up in the Congregational Church, but after extensive Bible study, he became convinced that the Second Coming of JESUS CHRIST would occur in 1874 and that the end of the world was scheduled for 1914. By 1878 he was pastor of a small church in Pittsburgh and in the following year *The Watchtower* magazine was launched. Among his books were *The Object and Manner of Our Lord's Return, Food for Thinking Christians* and the six-volume *Studies in the Scriptures*. Various scandals dogged his career. His wife left him in 1897; he attempted to sell 'miracle wheat' in aid of church funds and he was involved in two libel suits. None the less the new group, the Jehovah's Witnesses, flourished. (In Russell's time they were known as the International Bible Students.) Russell's theology was developed by Joseph Franklin RUTHER-FORD and today the sect boasts more than a million active members. They have stood firm against considerable prejudice in such places as Australia and downright persecution in the countries of the former Communist bloc.

G.D. McKinney, *The Theology of the Jehovah's Witnesses* (1962); A. Rogerson, *Millions Now Living will Never Die: A Study of Jehovah's Witnesses* (1969).

Rutherford, Joseph Franklin (1869–1941) Sect Founder. Rutherford succeeded RUS-SELL as head of the Jehovah's Witnesses. A lawyer by profession, he was a native of Missouri in the United States of

America. When JESUS failed to return as predicted in 1914, he argued that he had come back invisibly and that the last battle between Satan and Jehovah was to take place in the near future. Under his leadership the sect took the name of Jehovah's Witnesses. He taught that the Elect owed allegiance only to the Messianic Kingdom and that all other commitments to Church or country should be abandoned. When the sect grew to number more than the promised 144,000 Chosen, he decided that a second class of 'other sheep' would also be saved. He was the author of many books and tracts and, like Russell, he was the subject of considerable scandal. For example, in 1918 he was sent to prison for propaganda against military service and on several occasions he was accused of fraudulent practice. None the less there are groups of Jehovah's Witnesses in many countries.

A. Rogerson, *Millions Now Living Will Never Die:* *A Study of Jehovah's Witnesses* (1989); H. Thurston, *'Judge' Rutherford* (1940).

Ruysbroeck, Jan van (1293–1381) Mystic and Devotional Writer. Ruysbroeck was born in Ruysbroeck, Flanders, and he was educated in Brussels. In *c.* 1317 he was ordained to the Roman Catholic priesthood and, after serving a parish, in 1343 he retired to a hermitage. This was to become the Augustinian monastery of Groenendael. He is remembered for his mystical writings, the best-known of which is *Die Chierheit der Gheest elijke Brulocht* ('The spiritual espousals'). His works were translated into Latin and, with their exalted goal of attaining the beatific vision, were highly influential on such later mystics as JOHN OF THE CROSS.

S. Axters, *La Spiritualité des Pays-Bas* (1954); M. d'Asbeck, *La Mystique de Ruysbroeck l'Admirable* (1928) [no English translation available]; E. Underhill, *Ruysbroeck* (1915).

S

Sabellius (third century) Theologian. Little is known of Sabellius. He seems to have been a teacher in Rome, but he may have been an African from Libya. He has given his name to Sabellianism. This was an influential movement in which it was taught that the three persons of the Trinity were merely different modes of being of the One God. It was opposed by TERTULLIAN in North Africa and HIPPOLYTUS in Rome. Detractors called the theory Patripassianism since if God the father became, in another mode of being, a human person, then he must have experienced human suffering.

J.N.D. Kelly, *Early Christian Doctrines* (1958).

Saint-Cyran, Abbé de (1581–1643) Devotional Writer and Theologian. Saint-Cyran was born Jean Duvergier de Hauranne. He was educated in Paris and Bayonne where Cornelius JANSEN was a fellow-student. After acting as secretary to the Bishop of Poitiers, he became Abbot of Saint-Cyran in 1620 and from then on he lived in Paris. He was in correspondence with Jansen from 1617 to 1635; he knew VINCENT DE PAUL, Jean-Jacques OLIER and Pierre de BÉRULLE and in 1633 he was chosen to be spiritual director of the Convent of Port-Royal, the intellectual centre of Jansenism. He was the author of several books advocating reform in the Church and was, in his day, a highly influential figure. Cardinal RICHELIEU strongly disapproved of his theology and saw him as a dangerous man. In 1638 he was imprisoned and it was during this period that he wrote his *Lettres Chrétiennes et Spirituelles*. After

his death he was revered as a martyr by his supporters.

Catholic University of America, *New Catholic Encyclopaedia* (1967).

Saint-Simon, Claude Henri de Rouvroi (1760–1825) Philosopher. Saint-Simon was born into a noble family in Paris. He led an adventurous life and he fought with the rebels in the American War of Independence. He is remembered for his belief that it was the industrial working class who were the main contributors to the good of the State. He propounded this thesis in his periodicals *L'Industrie* and *L'Organisateur* in which he argued for the complete transformation of society. Later, in his *Nouveau Christianisme*, he maintained that the Church should concentrate on teaching the Christian message of the brotherhood of man and thus work for the improvement of the world, rather than being preoccupied with theology. Saint-Simon's ideas were influential on a generation of European intellectuals in the early nineteenth century.

E. Durkheim, *Socialism* (1958), F.E. Manuel, *The New World of Henri Saint-Simon* (1956).

Salesbury, William (c. 1520–c. 1584) Biblical Scholar. Salesbury was born in Llansannan, Wales. He was educated at the University of Oxford and he trained as a lawyer. For most of his life he lived in Plas Isa in Denbighshire. He is remembered for his translation of the Book of Common Prayer and the New Testament into Welsh. He seems to have used ERASMUS's edition of the Greek text,

JEROME's Vulgate, TYNDALE's English version and LUTHER's German translation. Salesbury's version proved to be the foundation for all later Welsh translations and was an important factor in the spread of Protestantism in Wales.

I. Thomas, *William Salesbury and his Testament* (1967).

Sancroft, William (1617–93) Archbishop and Sect Founder. Sancroft was educated at the University of Cambridge. In 1662 he was appointed to be a chaplain to King Charles II and in 1665 he became Dean of St Paul's Cathedral. He was thus closely involved with Christopher WREN in rebuilding the cathedral after the Great Fire of London of 1666. He was consecrated Archbishop of Canterbury in 1678. During the reign of the Roman Catholic JAMES II, in 1688, he refused to read the King's declaration of indulgence which suspended all penalties incurred by Roman Catholics and other non-conformists. In consequence, he was imprisoned in the Tower of London with six other Bishops. All were found not guilty at their trial, amidst scenes of Protestant jubilation. However, Sancroft then refused to accept the Protestant William III as King after James had abdicated, on the grounds that he would be breaking his oath of loyalty. Together with eight other Bishops and about four hundred priests, he was deprived of his position and he became the unofficial leader of the Non-Jurors (as they were called). The Non-Jurors continued as a separate party outside the Church of England throughout the eighteenth century.

LM. Hawkins, *Allegiance in Church and State: The Problem of Non-Jurors in the English Revolution* (1928); R. Thomas, 'The seven bishops and their petition', *Journal of Ecclesiastical History*, xii (1961).

Sandeman, Robert (1718–71) Sect Founder. Sandeman was the son-in-law of John GLAS and he gave his name to the Sandemanian sect. This group's doctrines were strictly based on the Bible and it exerted strict discipline on its members. Sandeman himself was the author of *Some Thoughts on Christianity* and *Discourses on Passages in Scripture*. He had his headquarters in Perth, but he left Scotland in 1764 to found new churches in the American colonies.

H. Escott, *A History of Scottish Congregationalism* (1960).

Sankey, Ira David (1840–1908) Essayist and Hymn-Writer. Sankey was a native of Pennsylvania. He fought on the Union side in the Civil War and in 1870 he was recruited by Dwight L. MOODY to join his organisation in Chicago. He accompanied Moody on his famous mission to Britain in 1873 for which he provided the musical accompaniment. He is primarily remembered for the extraordinarily popular *Sankey and Moody Hymnbook* published in 1874.

J. Findlay Jr, *Dwight L. Moody: American Evangelist* (1969).

Santos, Lucia (b. 1907) Visionary. Santos was one of three children who claimed to have seen the Virgin MARY on several occasions in the little town of Fatima, Portugal. The other two died soon afterwards, but Santos became a Carmelite nun. She wrote two accounts of the visions, in which the Virgin is said to have recommended penance, the recitation of rosary prayers and devotion to the immaculate heart of Mary. Fatima has become an important centre of Roman Catholic pilgrimage.

E. Dhanis, 'A propos de Fatima et la critique', *Nouvelle Revue Théologique*, lxxiv (1952); W.T. Walsh, *Our Lady of Fatima* (1949).

Sartre, Jean-Paul (1905–80) Philosopher. Sartre was born in Paris. He was a nephew of Albert SCHWEITZER. He was educated in Paris and Berlin and it was there that he discovered German philosophy, particularly the works of HEGEL, HEIDEGGER and Husserl. With his lover, the feminist philosopher, Simone de Beauvoir, he was at the centre of French intellectual life from the late 1920s onwards. He is remembered not only for his atheistic, communistic existentialism which he expressed in novels and plays such as *La Nausée*, as well as in his philosophical works, but also for his circle of personal relationships. Like KIERKEGAARD and Heidegger, he emphasised the burden of individual personal freedom and he was a highly influential figure in the cultural life of mid-twentieth-century Europe.

A.C. Danto, *Sartre*, 2nd edn (1991); K. Fulbrook, *Simone de Beauvoir and Jean-Paul Sartre: The Remaking of a Twentieth-Century Legend* (1993); C. Howells (ed.), *The Cambridge Companion to Sartre* (1992); M. Warnock, *The Philosophy of Sartre* (1965).

Sava (*c.* 1175–*c.* 1235)   Saint and Archbishop. Sava was the third son of King Stephen Nemanya, the first monarch of a united Serbia. He retired to the monastery of Mount Athos in 1191 and then, with his father, he founded the monastery of Hilanda which was later to become an important centre of Serb culture. Then in 1208 he returned to political life and in 1219 he established an independent Serbian Church of which he was the first Archbishop. Today he is venerated as the patron saint of Serbia.

A. Butler, 'Sava', in H. Thurston (ed.), *The Lives of the Saints*, Vol. 1 (1926).

Savonarola, Girolamo (1452–98) Preacher and Reformer. Savonarola was born in Ferrara, Italy. He joined the Dominican Order in 1475 and in 1490 he settled in Florence. He was a famous and inspiring preacher, calling for the reform of corruption and justice for the poor. After the invasion of King Charles VIII of France, who left without sacking the city, he encouraged the Florentine citizens to found a republic. This was to be a reformed community, intensely moral and upright. In consequence, Savonarola made many enemies and, after he had denounced the worldliness of the papal court, he was excommunicated by Pope ALEXANDER VI and forbidden to preach. In response, Savonarola demanded a General Council to depose the Pope. He was challenged to an ordeal by fire by the Franciscans, but a rainstorm put out the fire before it could take place. Finally the people of Florence turned against him: they imprisoned and tortured him and finally had him publicly hanged. After his death a few continued to venerate him, but he was generally regarded as a tiresome, self-important fanatic.

D. Weinstein, *Savonarola and Florence* (1970).

Sayers, Dorothy Leigh (1893–1957) Novelist, Playwright and Devotional Writer. Sayers was born in Oxford, the daughter of an Anglican clergyman. She was educated at the University of Oxford and is primarily remembered as the creator of the aristocratic detective, Lord Peter Wimsey. She abandoned that form of fiction in the 1940s and concentrated on translating DANTE's *Divina Commedia*. She also wrote a series of religious radio plays, *The Man Born to be King*, and a play for Canterbury Cathedral, *The Zeal of thy House*. She was a highly intelligent apologist for Christian doctrine and did much to explain the Church's message in a way that was attractive to her contemporaries.

J. Brabazon, *Dorothy L. Sayers: The Life of a Courageous Woman* (1981); B. Reynolds, *The Life and Soul of Dorothy Sayers* (1993).

Schelling, Friedrich Wilhelm Joseph von (1775–1854) Philosopher. Schelling was born in Württemberg, the son of a pastor. He was educated in Tübingen and he subsequently taught at Jena, Würtzburg, Erlangen, Munich and Berlin. A personal friend of HEGEL, FICHTE and Goethe, he is primarily remembered in Christian circles for his *Philosophische Untersuchungen über das Wesen der Menschlichen Freiheit*, in which he attempted to reconcile his Christianity with his idealist philosophy. Over the years his position moved from abstract Pantheism to modified neo-Platonism. Influenced by KANT and BOEHME, he maintained that consciousness is the only immediate object of knowledge. Many elements of his thought were taken up by later German philosophers.

E.D. Hirsch, *Wordsworth and Schelling: A Typological Study of Romanticism* (1960); F.G. Nauen, *Revolution, Idealism and Human Freedom: Schelling, Holderlin and Hegel and the Crisis of Early German Idealism* (1971).

Schillebeeckx, Edward Cornelis Florentius Alfons (b. 1914)   Theologian. Schillebeeckx was born in Antwerp, Belgium, and he was educated in Louvain and Paris. He became Professor of Theology at Nijmegen and was an advisor at the Second Vatican Council. Among his books are *Jesus*, *Christ* and *Church*. As a result of his dissatisfaction with the increased conservatism of the Roman Catholic Church, he has come under the suspicion of the Vatican. Both his and KÜNG's difficulties in this area are often used to demonstrate the more authoritarian climate of the Church under Pope JOHN PAUL II.

J. Bowden, *E. Schillebeeckx: A Portrait of a Theologian* (1983); D. Ford (ed.), *The Modern Theologians*, revised edition (1997); P. Kennedy, *Schillebeeckx* (1992).

Schleiermacher, Friedrich Daniel Ernst (1768–1834)   Theologian. Schleiermacher was born in Breslau, Germany. His parents were members of a Pietist sect and he was educated at Halle. After ordination, he served as minister of the Charité Hospital in Berlin. Subsequently he became involved in the founding of the new university in Berlin. He became the first Dean of the theological faculty and he was for a time Rector of the university. He is remembered for his important books, *Religion: Speeches to its Cultured Despisers* and *The Christian Faith*. He located human knowledge of God in a 'sense of absolute dependence' and he defined religion as a 'sense and taste for the infinite'. On this understanding, sin is explained as an inappropriate desire for independence and JESUS is described as a man whose sense of dependence on God is complete. Schleiermacher's work has been described as the 'theological expression of Romanticism'. It was highly influential throughout the nineteenth century but it was roundly condemned by Karl BARTH after the First World War as being about man rather than about God.

K.W. Clements, *Friedrich Schleiermacher: Pioneer of Modern Theology* (1987); R.R. Niebuhr, *Schleiermacher on Christ and Religion* (1965); S. Sykes, *Friedrich Schleiermacher* (1971).

Scholastica (*c.* 480–*c.* 543)   Saint and Order Founder. Scholastica was the sister of St BENEDICT. She founded a convent near Monte Cassino and the monks and nuns met annually to discuss spirituality. She is mentioned in St GREGORY THE GREAT's 'Dialogues'; this is our only source of knowledge of her.

D.H. Farmer (ed.), *The Oxford Dictionary of Saints*, 3rd edn (1992).

Schopenhauer, Arthur (1788–1860) Philosopher. Schopenhauer was born in Danzig, Germany, and he was educated at Göttingen and Berlin, where he was a student of FICHTE and SCHLEIERMACHER. He is mainly remembered for his *Die Welt als Wille und Vorstellung*, in which he argued that striving was the ultimate reality. Overcoming striving through the control of the passions was the only remedy of life's evils. His teaching was thus influenced by Buddhism but he himself claimed that it was no different from that of the great Christian mystics. NIETZSCHE, in his early years, was much attracted to this world view.

F. Copleston, *Arthur Schopenhauer: Philosopher of Pessimism* (1946); R.A. Gonzales, *An Approach to the Sacred in the Thought of Schopenhauer* (1992); C. Janaway, *Schopenhauer* (1994); B. Magee, *Misunderstanding Schopenhauer* (1989).

Schutz, Roger (b. 1915) Order Founder. Schutz was educated at the University of Lausanne, Switzerland. He came to believe that some form of monasticism was needed within Protestantism and, to that end, after the Second World War he founded a community at Taizé. The Taizé monks are a truly ecumenical community and are drawn from a variety of denominational backgrounds including Roman Catholic and Eastern Orthodox. The monks recite the office three times a day and run a farm, a printing press and an extensive guest house. They are known for their work with young people and Taizé itself has become a place of pilgrimage.

P.L. Moore, *Tomorrow is Too Late: Taizé, An Experiment in Christian Community* (1970).

Schweitzer, Albert (1875–1965) Theologian and Missionary. Schweitzer was born in Kaiserberg, Alsace, and he was educated at Strasbourg, Berlin and Paris. As a theologian, he is chiefly remembered for his *Von Reimarus zu Wrede*, translated into English as the *Quest for the Historical Jesus*. It caused a sensation. He argued that the attempt of the nineteenth-century theologians to reconstruct the evidence and discover the historical JESUS was merely a sophisticated exercise in narcissism. The real Jesus was an eschatological figure, making radical demands because he was convinced that the world was soon to come to an end. This was far removed from the delightful teacher and compassionate healer of the liberal Protestant imagination. After medical training, he left Germany in 1913 to settle in French Equatorial Africa as a medical mission-

ary. He established a hospital and, with a few interuptions, he dedicated the rest of his life to it. During this period, he developed an ethical philosophy of reverence for life and in 1952 he was awarded the Nobel Peace Prize. Although he has been criticised as being too paternalistic, he is generally regarded as a twentieth-century saint.

J. Brabazon, *Albert Schweitzer: A Biography* (1976); H. Clark, *The Philosophy of Albert Schweitzer* (1964); G. McKnight, *Verdict on Schweitzer* (1964); Albert Schweitzer, *My Life and Thought* (1933).

Schwenckfeld, Kaspar von Ossig (1489–1561) Theologian and Sect Founder. Schwenckfeld was born into an aristocratic family in Silesia. He was converted to the principles of the Protestant Reformation, but he held individual opinions on such matters as the Eucharist and Church order. In 1540 he produced his *Grosse Confession* in which he argued that the humanity of JESUS CHRIST was, in some sense, divine. As a result he was ostracised by LUTHER and the mainstream Protestant leaders. A small group of his followers survived in Silesia until the early nineteenth century and there is still a small Schwenckfeldian community in Philadelphia, Pennsylvania.

E.L. Lashlee, *The Via Regia: A Study of Caspar Schwenckfeld's Ideas of Personal Renewal and Church Reform* (1969); P.L. Maier, *Caspar Schwenckfeld on the Person and Work of Christ* (1959); S. Schultz, *Caspar Schwenckfeld von Ossig* (1946).

Scopes, John Thomas (b. *c.* 1895) Scientific Educator. Scopes was a young high school teacher in Dayton, Tennessee. In 1925 he was charged with teaching DARWIN's theory of evolution in his science lessons. This was forbidden by Tennessee state law. The case gave rise to a sensational trial. On one side was the fundamentalist William Bryan, a congressman from Nebraska and three times an unsuccessful contender for the Democratic nomination, and on the other, a well-known sceptical lawyer, Clarence Darrow. Although in the end, Scopes was found guilty and was fined one hundred dollars, Bryan's arguments were felt to be ill-informed and specious. The Scopes trial, as it was called, did much to discredit fundamentalism with the American public.

W.G. Gatewood Jr (ed.), *Controversy in the Twenties: Fundamentalism, Modernism and Evolution* (1969); R. Ginger, *Six Days or Forever? Tennessee v. John Thomas Scopes* (1958).

Scott, George Gilbert (1811–78) Architect. Scott was the grandson of Thomas Scott, the author of the *Calvinist Commentary on the Bible*. He was committed to the gothic style of ecclesiastical architecture and he is remembered for designing the Martyrs' Memorial in Oxford (commemorating CRANMER, LATIMER and RIDLEY), the Albert Memorial (commemorating Queen Victoria's husband) and for substantial restoration work in Westminster Abbey, Ely, Hereford, Salisbury and Gloucester Cathedrals. Largely as a result of his determination to impose his own designs on old buildings, the Society for the Protection of Ancient Buildings was founded to preserve original fabric and concepts.

George Gilbert Scott, *Personal and Professional Recollections* (1879).

Sebastian (late third century) Saint. Sebastian is thought to have been a native of Milan, Italy, and to have been martyred in the Diocletian persecutions. He is traditionally portrayed standing in the middle of a group of archers, being shot through with arrows. In fact, he is supposed to have recovered from this onslaught as a result of the ministrations of a kindly widow and eventually he had to be clubbed to death. He became the patron saint of archers and, in recent years, transfixed with arrows, he has become an unofficial icon for many in the homosexual community.

D.H. Farmer (ed.), *The Oxford Dictionary of Saints*, 3rd edn (1992).

Seeley, John Robert (1834–95) Historian. Seeley was educated at the University of Cambridge and he subsequently taught Latin at London University and then History at Cambridge. He is remembered for his *Ecce Homo*, a popular life of JESUS which became a best-seller. The book was an attempt to present the historical Jesus and it emphasised his ethical teaching at the expense of the supernatural elements in the Gospels. When it first appeared it was disliked by John Henry NEWMAN and Arthur STANLEY, and it was exactly the sort of work which was later condemned so effectively in Albert SCHWEITZER's *Quest for the Historical Jesus*.

W. Sanday, *The Life of Christ in Recent Research* (1907); D. Wormell, *Sir John Seeley and the Uses of History* (1980).

Segundo, Juan Luis (b. 1925) Theologian. Segundo is a native of Uruguay. He was educated in Argentina, Louvain and Paris and has taught at Harvard, Chicago, Toronto, Montreal, Birmingham and São Paulo. A prominent exponent of liberation theology, his works include *The Liberation of Theology* and the five-volume *Jesus of Nazareth, Yesterday and Today*. In his books he argues that in order to understand the Bible, it must be read through the eyes of the oppressed, since God is the God of the oppressed.

R.S. Chopp, 'Latin American liberation theology', in D. Ford (ed.), *The Modern Theologians*, Vol. 2 (1989); B. Mahan and L. Dale Richesen (eds), *The Challenge of Liberation Theology* (1981); A.J. Tambasco, *The Bible for Ethics: Juan Luis Segundo and First World Ethics* (1981).

Sellon, Priscilla Lydia (*c.* 1821–76) Order Founder. Sellon was the daughter of an English naval officer. With the help and encouragement of E.B. PUSEY, she set up the first Church of England religious community since the Reformation. It was initially called the Devonport

Sisters of Mercy and the nuns were dedicated to nursing the sick and to setting up schools and orphanages. Later the community was to amalgamate with the Sisters of the Holy Cross and Sellon became Abbess of the Society of the Most Holy Trinity. She was always in delicate health, and her last days were wracked by pain, but none the less the community prospered under her leadership.

T.J. Williams, *Priscilla Lydia Sellon*, revised edition (1965).

Selwyn, George Augustus (1809–78) Bishop and Missionary. Selwyn was educated at the University of Cambridge. In 1841 he was consecrated Missionary Bishop of New Zealand, which diocese initially included Melanesia. The prosperity of the Episcopal Church in New Zealand was largely due to his enthusiasm and diligence. He ensured that the Church should have a large measure of independence; he succeeded generally in working harmoniously with other missionaries and, by the time he left, the New Zealand Church had four separate bishoprics. He returned to England in 1867 and was appointed Bishop of Lichfield. Selwyn College, Cambridge, was founded in his memory in 1881.

J.H. Evans, *Churchman Militant: George Augustus Selwyn, Bishop of New Zealand and Lichfield* (1964).

Seraphim of Sarov (1759–1833) Saint. Seraphim was born in Kursk, Russia. He entered a monastery at the age of nineteen and subsequently lived as a hermit. He became the most famous spiritual director of his time in the Orthodox Church and people came to see him from all over Russia. He was canonised in 1903.

G.P. Fedotov (ed.), *A Treasurer of Russian Spirituality* (1950); V. Zander, *St Seraphim of Sarov* (1975).

Sergius (d. 638) Patriarch, Poet and Theologian. Sergius was a native of Syria. He became Patriarch of Constantinople in 610. He is remembered for his attempts to reconcile the Monophysites with the Orthodox. To this end he propounded Monothelitism, the theory that although there was both a divine and a human nature in the person of JESUS CHRIST, there was only one energy or will. He outlined this position in his *Ecthesis* in 638 and it was initially accepted in two synods in Constantinople. However, it was never agreed by the Western Church and it was finally rejected at the Council of Constantinople in 681. Sergius is also thought to have composed the 'Akathiston', a hymn to the Virgin MARY sung during Lent.

W.H.C. Frend, *the Rise of the Monophysite Movement* (1972).

Sergius of Radonezh (c. 1314–92) Saint, Order Founder and Mystic. Sergius was born in Rostov, Russia, but his family made their home in Radonezh. With his brother Stephen, he founded the important Orthodox monastery of the Holy Trinity. He was a hugely influential figure, founding forty monasteries, negotiating between warring Russian princes and encouraging Prince Dmitri against the Tartar invasions. Today he is regarded as the greatest of the Russian saints and as an architect of the Russian nation.

G.P. Fedotov (ed.), *A Treasury of Russian Spirituality* (1950); P. Kovalevsky, *Saint Sergius and Russian Spirituality* (1976); N. Zemov, *St Sergius: Builder of Russia* (1939).

Servetus, Michael (1511–53) Theologian. Servetus was born in Tudela, Navarre, and was educated at Saragossa and Toulouse. Subsequently he travelled to Basle and Strasbourg where he met Martin BUCER. He came to believe that the doctrine of the Trinity should be abandoned and he expressed this view in his *De Trinitatis Erroribus Libri VII* and, later, in his *Christianismi Restitutio*. In the meantime he had become a distinguished doctor and between 1541 and 1553 he was physician to the Archbishop of Vienna. However, as a result of his religious convictions, he was arrested by the Inquisition in Vienna. He managed to escape to Geneva, but CALVIN turned out to be no more merciful or tolerant than the Roman Catholic authorities. Servetus was burnt at the stake by the Genevan authorities after refusing to recant. Calvin has been much criticised for his part in this affair.

R.H. Bainton, *Hunted Heretic: The Life and Death of Michael Servetus* (1953); J. Friedman, *Michael Servetus: A Case Study in Total Heresy* (1978); J.F. Fulton, *Michael Servetus: Humanist and Martyr* (1953).

Severus (*c.* 465–538)   Patriarch. Severus was born in Pisidia and was educated in Alexandria and Berytus. He became a Christian in 488 and soon after joined a monastic order. In *c.* 508 he went to Constantinople where he was consecrated Patriarch in 512. He was deposed as a Monophysite with the accession of the Emperor Justin I and he was eventually excommunicated in 536. He was a prolific writer and many of his works survive, mainly in Syriac translations.

I.R. Torrance, *Christology after Chalcedon: Severus of Antioch and Sergius the Monophysite* (1988).

Shaftesbury, Anthony Ashley Cooper, Earl of (1801–85)   Philanthropist. Shaftesbury was educated at the University of Oxford and he subsequently entered Parliament. He was of an aristocratic family and was a nephew of Lord Palmerston, who served several terms as Prime Minister. He is remembered as a notable social reformer. Among his many achievements was the Ten Hour Act of 1847 (which limited working hours in a factory to ten hours a day), the establishment of a permanent Lunacy Commission, acts regulating child and female labour, the Factory Act of 1874 and the Chimney Boys' Act of 1875. His philanthropy was largely inspired by his devout evangelical faith. He was president of the British and Foreign Bible Society and an enthusiastic supporter of the Church Missionary Society, the Church Pastoral Aid Society and the London City Mission.

G.F.A. Best, *Shaftesbury* (1964); G.B.A.M. Finlayson, *The Seventh Earl of Shaftesbury* (1981); J. Pollock, *Shaftesbury: The Poor Man's Earl* (1985).

Shembe, Isaiah (*c.* 1870–*c.* 1960)   Sect Founder. Shembe was born in Natal, South Africa. As a young man he was converted to Christianity and he was baptised in the African Native Baptist Church. He embarked on a career of teaching and healing and soon founded his own organisation based at Ekuphakamen ('the high place') near Durban. Known as the Ama-Nazaretha, his followers believed that he was sent from God and born of the Spirit and they followed the Nazarite rules of the Old Testament. Their doctrines were a mixture of traditional African beliefs and Christianity. After Shembe's death, it was thought that he would rise again and his son succeeded him as leader of the movement.

G. Oosthuizen, *The Theology of a South African Messiah* (1967).

Shenoute (d. *c.* 450)   Order Consolidator. Shenoute was a nephew of Pgôl who had founded a monastery based on the Rule of St PACHOMIUS, near Schag, Egypt. Under his leadership, the community greatly expanded. He was highly authoritarian by temperament and he established the monastery on a sound organisational basis. Many of his writings survive in their original Coptic. He accompanied CYRIL OF ALEXANDRIA to the Council of Ephesus in 431 where he proved to be a determined opponent of the teachings of NESTORIUS. He is venerated as a saint in the Coptic Church.

O.F.A. Meinardus, *Monks and Monasteries of the Egyptian Deserts* (1961).

Sheppard, Hugh Richard Lawrie [Dick] (1880–1937) Devotional Writer and Broadcaster. Sheppard was educated at the University of Cambridge and was ordained into the Anglican ministry in 1907. He became well known as the Vicar of St Martin in the Fields, London. He was quick to realise the possiblilities of broadcasting as a means of propagating the Gospel and he was the author of *The Human Parson* and *The Impatience of a Parson*, both of which achieved large sales. He was a determined promoter of ecclesiastical reform and a convinced pacifist. In 1929 he was appointed Dean of Canterbury Cathedral, but ill-health prompted his resignation.

R. Ellis Roberts, *H.R.L. Sheppard: Life and Letters* (1942); W. Paxton et al., *Dick Sheppard: An Apostle of Brotherhood* (1938).

Sickingen, Franz von (1481–1523) Rebel. Sickingen was born in Ebernburg, Germany. He and his band of knights supported the election of the Emperor CHARLES V and in 1519 he became an Imperial Counsellor. However, he was converted to Protestantism and he offered the use of his castle to any fugitive Reformer. In 1521 his troops were ranged outside Worms, ostensibly to protect LUTHER during the Diet and the following year Luther dedicated a treatise on confession to him. In 1522 he campaigned against the Archbishop of Trier and his castle was besieged. During the battle to defend it, he was killed. Sickingen was one of the most colourful figures of the Reformation, but, despite his support of the Protestant cause, his ideas were rooted in an earlier, feudal age.

W.R. Hitchcock, *The Background of the Knights' Revolt 1522–1523* (1958).

Silas (first century) Missionary and Bishop. Silas went with PAUL to Macedonia and Corinth on his second missionary journey. In the Epistles to the Thessalonians, he is called by the name Silvanus. This has led some commentators to distinguish between Silas who supposedly became the first Bishop of Corinth and Silvanus, who became Bishop of Thessalonia.

The Acts of the Apostles, Chapter 15; I Thessalonians, Chapter 1; II Thessalonians, Chapter 1; D.H. Farmer (ed.), *The Oxford Dictionary of Saints*, 3rd edn (1992); B.M. Metzger and M.D. Coogan (eds), *The Oxford Companion to the Bible* (1993).

Simeon (first century) Poet. Simeon was a devout elderly Jew who encountered the infant JESUS in the Temple in Jerusalem. He took him in his arms and pronounced the words of the song which is now known as the 'Nunc Dimittis': 'Lord, now lettest thou thy servant depart in peace, according to thy word; for mine eyes have seen thy salvation'. This has been part of the Church's liturgy since at least the fourth century.

Luke, Chapter 2.

Simeon the New Theologian (949–1022) Mystic, Devotional Writer and Saint. Simeon was a monk, first at Studios, the famous monastery in Constantinople, and then at St Mamas. Between 981 and 1005 he was Abbot, but his teachings aroused such hostility that he was sent into exile in 1005 and he remained in retirement for the rest of his life. He produced many ethical and theological treatises as well as hymns. His style was direct and vivid and he stressed his vision of the divine light. Influenced by MACARIUS OF EGYPT, ISAAC OF NINEVEH and BASIL the Great, he was an important figure in the history of Hesychasm, the Eastern tradition of inner mystical prayer. He is probably known as the 'New' theologian in contrast with GREGORY OF NAZIANZUS who was known as 'the Theologian'.

G.A. Maloney, *The Mystic of Fire and Light: St Symeon the New Theologian* (1975); B. Krivocheine, *The Light of Christ: St Symeon the New Theologian*, Eng. trans. (1987).

Simeon, Charles (1759–1836) Revivalist. Simeon was educated at the University of Cambridge and he was ordained into the ministry of the Church of England. For the rest of his life he served a parish in Cambridge. He was an important leader of the Evangelical Revival and laid stress on personal conversion and salvation through faith in the saving death of JESUS CHRIST. At this period, the Anglican Church was largely sleeping the sleep of the complacent and Simeon did much to awaken the religious spirit in the university; he also worked diligently for missions abroad. He was one of the founders of the Church Missionary Society and the Church Mission to the Jews and he was an enthusiastic supporter of the British and Foreign Bible Society. Henry MARTYN, the important missionary to India, was one of his curates. He also founded the Simeon Trust which tried to place like-thinking evangelical clergymen in parishes. He was a hugely influential figure, and his sermons were collected and published after his death.

H.C.G. Moule, *Charles Simeon* (1892); A. Pollard, *Charles Simeon* (1959); C. Smyth, *Simeon and Church Order* (1940).

Simeon Stylites [the Elder] (*c.* 390–459) Saint. Simeon was the most famous of the pillar hermits. He was born in Cilicia and, after finding monastic life too distracting, he retired to Telanissos where he lived on top of a pillar. It was about sixty feet high and on it Simeon dedicated himself to prayer and contemplation. He attracted numerous sightseers and from his vantage point, he seems to have exerted a considerable influence on his contemporaries. He lived like this until his death – a period of some thirty-six years. Subsequently a church and a monastery were built on the site.

E.A. Livingstone (ed.), *The Oxford Dictionary of the Christian Church*, new edn (1997).

Simon (first century) Apostle. Simon was one of JESUS's twelve original apostles. He is called the Canaanite by MATTHEW and MARK and the Zealot by LUKE. This may imply that he was a member of the Jewish freedom fighters who were to lead the rebellion against Rome later in the first century. Little is known of his life. With St JUDE, he is supposed to have been martyred in Persia and the two saints share the same patronal day.

Acta Sanctorum Oct. XII (1867); J.S. Hoyland, *Simon the Zealot* (1941).

Simon of Cyrene (first century) Gospel Figure. Simon was forced by the Roman guard to carry JESUS's cross before his crucifixion. His sons, Alexander and Rufus, may have been members of the early Church since Simon's only identification is as their father. The Cyrenians, an organisation which looks after the homeless, is named after him.

Mark, Chapter 15.

Simon Magus (first century) Magician and possible Sect Founder. Simon appears in Acts. He is described as a sorcerer who claimed to be the Power of God 'called Great'. He was baptised by PHILIP in Samaria and he then offered PETER and JOHN money in exchange for the power to bestow the Holy Spirit. In consequence, he was sternly rebuked. JUSTIN MARTYR claimed that he was a native of Gitta and was the founder of a Christian Gnostic sect. According to HIPPOLYTUS, he again came into conflict with Peter in Rome and he is also mentioned in the Pseudo-Clementine literature. Simon has been the inspiration for many later legends, including possibly the Faust story. The sin of simony (selling Christian offices for money) is named after him.

The Acts of the Apostles, Chapter 8; J.M.A. Salles-Dabadie, *Recherches sur Simon le Mage* (1969) [no English translation available].

Simon of Sudbury (d. 1381) Archbishop. Simon was born in Sudbury, Suffolk. He was educated at the University of Paris and he was consecrated Bishop of London in 1361. Then in 1375 he became Archbishop of Canterbury. He took a prominent part in the political life of his time and in 1380 he was appointed Chancellor of England. The imposition of a poll tax inspired the Peasants' Revolt of 1381, led by Wat Tyler and John BALL. Simon was captured by the mob and was summarily executed. In consequence, he was regarded as a martyr by his supporters.

W.L. Warren, 'A reappraisal of Simon Sudbury, Bishop of London and Archbishop of Canterbury', *Journal of Ecclesiastical History*, x (1959).

Sixtus II (d. 258) Pope and Saint. Sixtus was elected Pope in 257. He is remembered for resuming relations with the African and Asia Minor Churches which had been broken off in the time of Pope STEPHEN I. He was martyred under the Second Edict of the Emperor Valerian while he was conducting services and he was highly venerated.

J.N.D. Kelly (ed.), *The Oxford Dictionary of Popes* (1986).

Sixtus IV (1414–84) Pope. Sixtus was born Francesco della Rovere. He was a member of the Franciscan Order and was appointed a Cardinal in 1467. He was elected Pope in 1471. He is remembered as a patron of the arts and scholarship; he built the Sistine Chapel and enriched the Vatican Library. He also practised nepotism on a grand scale (the later Pope JULIUS II was his nephew) and his finances were chaotic. In the early years of his Pontificate, he embarked on an unsuccessful crusade and, as a result of his nephew's activities, the Papal States were embroiled in a war with Florence between 1478 and 1480. Later commentators have judged him to be a kindly, virtuous man, but he did little to enhance the spiritual prestige of the Papacy.

E. Lee, *Sixtus IV and Men of Letters* (1978).

Slessor, Mary (1848–1915) Missionary. Slessor was born of a poor family in Aberdeen, Scotland, and she was brought up in the Presbyterian Church. She was accepted for mission training and joined the Calabar mission in Nigeria in 1876. She achieved extraordinary success in reforming evils such as witchcraft, ritual sacrifice and twin-murder and she was trusted by the native peoples. As arbiter of their disputes, she became the first woman Vice-Consul to the British Empire and she established the Hope-Waddell Training Institute. Known universally as 'Ma Slessor', she established a strong Christian presence among the Ibo people.

W.P. Livingstone, *Mary Slessor of Calabar, Pioneer Missionary* (1916); C.C.-G. Plummer, *God and One Redhead: Mary Slessor of Calabar* (1970).

Smith, Hanna Whitall (1832–1911) Devotional Writer and Conference Founder. Smith was born Hanna Whitall in Philadelphia, Pennsylvania. She and her husband Robert Pearsall Smith were members of the Society of Friends. In the United States of America, she was a well-known speaker at interdenominational Higher Christian Life meetings, which were dedicated to Bible study and testimony. Today she is remembered as the author of *The Christian Secret of Happiness* and as a founder of the Keswick Convention. This is an annual gathering of evangelical Christians. It was started in England in 1875 with the aim of promoting 'practical holiness' and it continues to attract a wide attendance.

S. Barabas, *So Great Salvation: The History and Message of the Keswick Convention* (1952); C.F. Harford (ed.), *The Keswick Convention* (1907).

Smith, Joseph (1805–44) Denomination Founder. Smith was born in Vermont, in the United States of America, and in 1816 he moved to Palmyra, New York. In 1820 he had a conversion experience in which he claimed that God had revealed to him a series of golden plates. These were written in a strange language and were supposedly composed by descendants of Jewish exiles who had fled from the besieged city of Jerusalem in 586 BC and settled in America. Under the inspiration of the Angel Morani, Smith translated these plates and they were then taken up into Heaven. He published this document as *The Book of Mormon.* Later he produced *Doctrine and Covenants*, which was to be the fundamental basis for later Mormon theology. He moved to Illinois, where he infuriated his neighbours by his practice of polygamy. With his brother, he was arrested and he was murdered in Carthage Gaol. Leadership of the movement was taken over by Brigham YOUNG who guided the faithful over the Rocky Mountains to their final destination in Salt Lake City. The Church Smith founded is now known as the Church of God of Latter Day Saints.

F.M. Brodie, *No Man Knows my History: The Life of Joseph Smith, the Mormon Prophet* (1945); R.L Bushman, *Joseph Smith and the Beginnings of Mormonism* (1984); J. Shipps, *Mormonism: The Story of a New Religious Tradition* (1985).

Smyth, John (*c.* 1565–1612) Sect Founder. Smyth was educated at the University of Cambridge and he was ordained to the Church of England ministry. He was appointed lecturer of Lincoln Cathedral in 1600, but was dismissed for his unorthodox views. He then served a Brownist group and, in order to avoid persecution, went to live in Amsterdam. There he formed his own congregation, of which Thomas HELWYS was a member. Smyth was Arminian in theology, but advocated believer's baptism. He baptised himself in 1608 and subsequently baptised Helwys and others. The community was called the Brotherhood of the Separation of the Second English Church at Amsterdam and it is regarded as the first General Baptist Church.

W.T. Whitley (ed.), *The Works of John Smyth* (*with Life*) (1915).

Sobrino, Jon (b. 1938) Theologian. Sobrino was born in Spain and was trained first as an engineer at St Louis University and then studied theology in Frankfurt. Since then he has taught philosophy in El Salvador and he is known as a prominent proponent of liberation theology. He is the author of several influential books including *Christology at the Crossroads* and the *True Church of the Poor*. He believes that there is a close parallel between the situation in Latin America today and the historical context in which JESUS lived and he argues that the role of the Church is to extend the liberating action of Christ.

L. Boff, *Introducing Liberation Theology* (1987); D.W. Ferm, *Third World Liberation Theologies* (1986).

Sölle, Dorothee (b. 1929) Theologian. Sölle was educated in Cologne, Freiburg and Göttingen. She has subsequently taught at the Union Theological Seminary in New York. She defines God as Loving Solidarity and she rejects the traditional theistic beliefs as infantile and dependent. Influenced by Marxist thought, she sees religion as a means of effecting social and ecological change, rather than as a matter of private conscience. She has appeared frequently on television and radio and her books include *To Work and to Love* and *Beyond Dialogue*.

Dorothee Sölle, *Thinking about God* (1990).

Soloviev, Vladimir Sergeevich (1853–1900) Theologian and Ecumenist. Soloviev was educated at the University of Moscow and he taught there and at the University of St Petersburg. He was compelled to retire in 1881, after he had recommended mercy for the assassins of Czar Alexander II. He is remembered for his doctrine of 'Godmanhood', the union of the Godhead with humanity through man's identification with JESUS CHRIST. He was a close friend of DOSTOIEVSKY and was an important influence on him. Towards the end of his life, he advocated the reunion of the Western and Eastern Churches. He conducted a long correspondence with the Roman Catholic Bishop Strossmayer and he outlined his ecumenical views in *La Russie et l'Eglise Universelle*. He has been described as the Russian NEWMAN and his work was much studied by White Russian émigrés after the Russian Revolution.

E. Munzer, *Solovyev: Prophet of Russian–Western Unity* (1956); N. Zernov, *Three Russian Prophets* (1944).

Song, Choan-Seng (b. 1929) Theologian. Song was the principal of a theological college in Taiwan and he later taught at the Pacific School of Religion in California. He advocates a transposition of the 'Israel-centred' view of Christian history and argues that Asian symbols from non-Christian religions can aid understanding. He goes as far as to say: 'The Word has to assume Asian flesh and plunge into the agony and the conflict of the mission of salvation'. Among his many books are *Third-Eye Theology* and *Theology from the Womb of Asia*.

K. Koyama, 'Asian theology', in D.F. Ford (ed.), *The Modern Theologians*, Vol. 11 (1989).

Southcott, Joanna (1750–1814) Prophet and Devotional Writer. Southcott was born in Devon in humble circumstances. She became a Methodist in 1791 and in the following year she issued her first book of prophecies. She believed that she was the woman described in Revelation, Chapter 12 and, despite her lack of education or coherence, she attracted a large following. She supported her work by issuing 'seals' to the faithful to guarantee their place among the Elect. This practice fell into disrepute when one of her customers was subsequently hanged for murder. In 1814 she claimed that she would give birth to the Prince of Peace, but she died before the prediction could be fulfilled. Many of her disciples still believed in her, but faith was shaken when her 'sealed box' was opened in 1927 and found to contain objects such as a lottery ticket and a night-cap.

G.B. Balleine, *Past Finding Out: The Tragic Story of Joanna Southcott and her Successors* (1956); J.K. Hopkins, *A Woman to Deliver her People: Joanna Southcott and English Millenarianism in an Era of Revolution* (1982).

Sozzini [Socinius], Fausto (1539–1604) Theologian and Sect Founder. Sozzini was born in Siena, Italy. He was the nephew of Lelio Sozini who had been an acquaintance of MELANCHTHON, CALVIN and BULLINGER. Fausto published a treatise on St John's Gospel which denied the divinity of JESUS CHRIST, in 1562. He eventually settled in Rocov, Poland, where he drew up the Racovian Catechism, the first statement of Socinian or Unitarian principles. It described salvation as 'knowledge and a holy life', God as 'the Supreme Lord of all things' and Jesus as 'a man, by his marvellous life and resurrection raised to divine power'. Unitarianism has had a chequered history; it was driven out of Poland by the middle of the seventeenth century, but has been influential in Britain and, more notably, in the United States of America.

G. Pioli, *Fausto Socinio. Vita, Opere, Fortuna* (1952) [no English translation available]; E.M. Wilbur, *A History of Unitarianism*, 2 vols (1965–9).

Spencer, John (1630–93) Hebraist and Theologian. Spencer was born in Kent and was educated at the University of Cambridge. He is remembered for his *De Legibus Hebraeorum* in which he pointed out the similarities between the traditions of the Jews and those of their semitic neighbours. His work made little impression at the time (though it caused some to question his orthodoxy), but it was used by WELLHAUSEN and the theologians of the Tübingen school. Today Spencer is regarded as an important pioneer in the study of comparative religion.

T. Cooper, 'John Spencer', in *Dictionary of National Biography*, Vol. 53 (1898); D. Pailin, *Attitudes to Other Religions: Comparative Religion in the 17th and 18th Centuries* (1984).

Spener, Philip Jakob (1635–1705) Devotional Writer. Spener was born in Rappoltsweiler, Alsace, and he was educated at the University of Strasbourg. He travelled widely through Protestant Europe and in 1666 was appointed to a pastorate in Frankfurt-am-Main. He emerged as an important influence within the Pietist movement. He was an originator of the Collegia Pietatis (a regular meeting of pastors and laymen for study and prayer) and he was the author of the *Pia Desideria*. This sets out the fundamentals of his Pietist doctrines. Towards the end of his life he was regarded as a controversial figure. He had moved to Dresden in 1686, but he fell out with the Elector and was forced to move to Brandenberg in 1691. None the less he had a substantial following and is regarded as a significant figure in the history of German Lutheranism.

F. Stoeffler, *The Rise of Evangelical Pietism* (1965).

Spurgeon, Charles Haddon (1834–92) Preacher and Devotional Writer. Spurgeon was a native of Essex. He was converted into the Baptist Church and in 1850 he became a minister. He established his headquarters in Southwark in 1854 and so successful was his preaching that the New Metropolitan Tabernacle had to be built to accommodate his following. Among his other activities, he founded a Pastors' College, which is still known as Spurgeon's College, and an orphanage, and he was one of the instigators of the London Baptist Association. He is remembered for causing controversy within the Church of England by accusing evangelical clergymen in 1864 of committing perjury when they used the Book of Common Prayer (since they did not believe in baptismal regeneration). He also came into conflict with more liberal fellow-Baptists with the result that he was publicly censured by the Baptist Union in 1887. However, he refused to found another denomination. He was one of the most famous preachers of his day and his collected sermons were widely circulated.

E.W. Bacon, *Spurgeon: Heir of the Puritans* (1967).

Spyridon (d. *c.* 348) Saint and Bishop. Little certain is known of the life of St Spyridon. He was a shepherd who suffered in the Diocletian persecutions and, after he became a Bishop, is said to have been present at the Council of Nicaea and the Council of Sardica. Many legends were told of him and he is credited with the conversion of the pagan philosopher Eulogius, having recited the Creed to him.

F.L. Cross (ed.), *The Oxford Dictionary of the Christian Church*, 2nd edn (1974).

Stanislaus (1030–79) Saint, Bishop and Martyr. Stanislaus was born into a Polish noble family. He was consecrated Bishop of Cracow in 1072. He was successful in reforming the diocese, but he came into conflict with King Boleslaw II, whom he excommunicated. According to legend, the King murdered him while he was celebrating Mass. Many stories were told of him; he was canonised by Pope

INNOCENT IV and is venerated as the patron saint of Poland.

The Catholic University of America, *New Catholic Encyclopaedia* (1976).

Stanley, Arthur Penrhyn (1815–81) Historian. Stanley was educated at Rugby School under Thomas ARNOLD and at the University of Oxford. He had a successful career within the Church of England, becoming Professor of Ecclesiastical History at Oxford in 1856 and Dean of Westminster in 1863. Known for his liberal Broad Church views, he wanted the Church of England to embrace a wide spectrum of Christian opinion. Today he is mainly remembered for his *Lectures on the History of the Eastern Church* and his *Lectures on the History of the Jewish Church*.

A.V. Baillie and H. Bolitha (eds), *A Victorian Dean* (1930); F.J. Woodward, *The Doctor's Disciples: A Study of Four Pupils of Arnold of Rugby* (1954).

Stanley, Henry Morton (1841–1904) Explorer and Missionary. Stanley was an American journalist, who is remembered for finding David LIVINGSTONE in the depths of Central Africa and greeting him with the impeccable 'Dr Livingstone, I presume?' Subsequently he made several other journeys in Africa which enabled the Church Missionary Society to establish an important mission in Uganda.

W. Hoffmann, *With Stanley in Africa* (1938); F.J. McLynn, *Stanley: The Making of an African Explorer* (1991).

Stanton, Elizabeth Cady (1815–1902) Philanthropist and Feminist Biblical Scholar. Stanton was closely involved in the American anti-slavery movement and she was a veteran campaigner for women's rights. When she was in her eighties, she and a team of colleagues produced *The Women's Bible*, which has proved to be an important milestone in the history of feminist theory. Published in 1895 and 1898, it was a collection of comments on verses of the Bible which referred to women. It pointed out that the traditional understanding of the text has been used to reinforce notions of women's inferiority. From this pioneering work, many later feminist scholars have attempted to show that this negative attitude has its roots in later biblical interpretation rather than in the text itself.

L.W. Banner, *Elizabeth Cady Stanton: A Radical for Women's Rights* (1980); E. Griffith, *In Her Own Right: The Life of Elizabeth Cady Stanton* (1984); M.D. Pellauer, *Towards a Tradition of Feminist Theology: The Religious and Social Thought of Elizabeth Cady Stanton, Susan B. Anthony and Anna Howard Shaw* (1991); L.M. Russell, *Feminist Interpretation of the Bible* (1985).

Stein, Edith (1891–1942) Martyr. Stein was born of a Jewish family in Breslau, Germany, and she was educated in Göttingen and Freiburg. In 1922 she was converted to Christianity and was baptised as a Roman Catholic. She was a significant figure in the phenomenological school of Edmund Husserl and she published several philosophical papers. In 1934 she was received as a Carmelite nun and in 1938 was moved to Holland. Despite her religious habit, she was arrested by the Nazis as a Jew and she died in a Polish concentration camp. She is regarded as a modern-day martyr.

H.C. Graef, *The Scholar and the Cross: The Life and Work of Edith Stein* (1955).

Steiner, Rudolf (1861–1921) Sect Founder. Steiner was the son of a station master in Kaljevec, Yugoslavia, and he was educated at the University of Vienna. Initially he was attracted to Mme BLAVATSKY's Theosophical Society, but he was unhappy with its orientation towards Eastern spirituality. Consequently he founded the Anthroposophical Society with its first institute in Dornach. His aim was to 'raise the faculties of the soul to develop organs of spiritual insight'.

He taught that it was through the intervention of JESUS CHRIST that humanity, made in God's image, could regain contact with the spiritual world. His followers maintain Rudolf Steiner schools which, through the use of music, light and quiet contemplation, do much to help difficult and maladjusted children. Steiner himself explained his system in several books, including *Die Philosophie der Freiheit*.

G. Ahern, *Sun at Midnight: The Rudolf Steiner Movement and the Western Esoteric Tradition* (1984); A.W. Harwood (ed.), *The Faithful Thinker: Centenary Essays on the Work and Thought of Rudolf Steiner* (1961); A.P. Shepherd, *A Scientist of the Invisible: An Introduction to the Life and Work of Rudolf Steiner* (1954).

Stephen (first century)   Saint and Martyr. Stephen was one of the seven Deacons listed in the Acts of the Apostles. He debated with Jewish officials with the result that he was taken out of the city of Jerusalem and was stoned to death. Scholars debate whether his execution was sanctioned by the authorities or whether it was a public lynching. PAUL was present and witnessed his death. According to EUSEBIUS OF CAESAREA, he was the first Christian martyr and his feast is celebrated on 26 December, the day after Christmas.

The Acts of the Apostles, Chapters 6–7; M.H. Scharlemann, *Stephen: A Singular Saint* (1968); M. Simon, *St Stephen and the Hellenists in the Primitive Church* (1958).

Stephen I (975–1038)   Monarch and Saint. Stephen was the son of Duke Geza and he became a Christian with his father in 985. He was crowned as the first King of Hungary by Pope Sylvester II. He established sees throughout his kingdom and he made every effort to convert his subjects to Christianity. Although much of his work was undone after his death, he was canonised in 1083.

LC. Kronf, 'Pope Sylvester II and Stephen I of Hungary', *English Historical Review*, xiii (1898).

Stephen II [III] (d. 757)   Pope. Stephen was born in Rome, Italy, and in 752 he replaced another Pope Stephen II who died before his consecration. He is remembered for seeking the protection of the Frankish King, PEPIN III, against the Lombards, turning away from the traditional papal ally, the Emperor of Constantinople. Pepin's campaigns were successful and, as a result of his 'Donation' of 754, the Papal States were established. These were to be the basis of the Pope's temporal powers until the reign of Pope PIUS IX in the nineteenth century.

J.N.D. Kelly (ed.), *The Oxford Dictionary of Popes* (1986).

Stephen Harding (d. 1134)   Order Founder and Saint. Stephen was born in Dorset. He became a monk at Molême, Burgundy, but did not find the regime strict enough. With twenty others, he established a new house at Citeaux and was elected successively Sub-Prior, Prior and Abbot. In 1112 St BERNARD joined the community with thirty others and new houses had to be founded. Stephen drew up much of the *Carta Cantatis*, the constitution of the Cistercian Order, which was presented to Pope Callistus II in 1119. He is also thought to have been responsible for introducing the famous white habit.

A.W. Hutton, *The Life of St Stephen Harding* (1900); M.D. Knowles, *The Monastic Orders of England*, 2nd edn (1963).

Sternhold, Thomas (d. 1549)   Poet. Sternhold was educated at the University of Oxford and, after entering the service of King HENRY VIII, was elected a Member of Parliament. He is remembered for his metrical version of fifty-six of the Psalms. These were hugely popular, particularly when John Hopkins (d. 1570) and others added several more to the collection. Their psalter, commonly called the *Old Version*, has gone through many editions and is still used.

J. Holland, *The Psalmists of Great Britain*, Vol. 1 (1843).

Stillingfleet, Edward (1635–99) Bishop, Devotional Writer and Historian. Stillingfleet was born in Dorset and was educated at the University of Cambridge. He became Archdeacon of London in 1677, Dean of St Paul's in 1678 and Bishop of Worcester in 1689. He was known for his tolerance. In his *Irenicum*, he recommended that the Episcopalians and the Presbyterians join forces. At the same time he produced three pamphlets replying to LOCKE's *Essay Concerning Human Understanding* and he wrote his *Rational Account of the Grounds of the Protestant Religion* in response to a Roman Catholic polemic. He is chiefly remembered, however, for his *Origines Britannicae* on the sources of the British Church and for the popular collection of his sermons.

J.W.H. Nankivell, 'Edward Stillingfleet, Bishop of Worcester', *Transactions of the Worcestershire Archaeological Society* (1946).

Stowe, Harriet Beecher (1811–96) Philanthropist and Polemicist. Stowe was born Harriet Beecher in Litchfield, Connecticut. Her father became president of the Lane Theological Seminary, Cincinnati, in 1832 where her future husband was one of the professors. The couple were committed abolitionists. They sheltered runaway slaves in their house and worked doggedly for the cause. Stowe was a prolific author, but she is mainly remembered for her *Uncle Tom's Cabin*, which was first published in serialised form in 1851–2. It did much to turn public opinion against slavery and was thus an important factor in stiffening the resolution of the Union side in the American Civil War. Today her portrayal of the slave characters is regarded as sentimental and patronising and, in the black

community, 'Uncle Tom' is a gross insult. None the less, in its day, it was a highly influential and important book.

A.C. Crozier, *The Novels of Harriet Beecher Stowe* (1969); J.D. Hedrick, *Harriet Beecher Stowe: A Life* (1994); M.I. Lowance Jr, E.E. Westbrook and R.C. de Prospo (eds), *The Stowe Debate: Rhetorical Strategies in Uncle Tom's Cabin* (1994); F. Wilson, *Crusader in Crinolines: The Life of Harriet Beecher Stowe* (1942).

Strauss, David Friedrich (1808–74) Theologian. Strauss was born in Ludwigsburg, Germany. He was a student of F.C. BAUR in Blaubeuren and he also studied in Tübingen and Berlin. He is primarily remembered for his *Leben Jesu*, in which he argued that the supernatural elements in the Gospels were created myths, designed to fulfil the prophecies of the Old Testament. Its publication led to the termination of his career as a teacher of theology. None the less he persisted and produced a sequel, *Die Christliche Glaubenslehre*, in which he maintained that Christian teaching should be replaced by Hegelian philosophy. Later he turned to biography and he also attacked SCHLEIERMACHER for his attempt to reconcile the Christ of dogma with the JESUS of history. Strauss's ideas proved to be very influential on later nineteenth-century theologians.

H. Harris, *David Friedrich Strauss and his Theology* (1973); E. Lawler, *David Friedrich Strauss and his Critics* (1986); A. Schweitzer, *Quest for the Historical Jesus* (1910).

Streeter, Burnett Hillman (1874–1937) Biblical Scholar. Streeter was educated at the University of Oxford and spent his career teaching there. Towards the end of his life, he was influenced by Frank BUCHMAN and the Oxford Group and he also became interested in Buddhism. He is remembered, however, for his New Testament scholarship, in particular *The Four Gospels*. In this he argued that

MARK's Gospel was the first to be written and that MATTHEW and LUKE had access both to Mark's Gospel and to a sayings source, now lost, but known as Q. This has become the received wisdom for students of the New Testament today.

W.R. Farmer, *The Synoptic Problem: A Critical Analysis* (1976); L. Grensted, 'B.H. Streeter', in *Dictionary of National Biography 1931–1940* (1946).

Studd, Charles Thomas (1862–1931)

Missionary. Studd was educated at the University of Cambridge where he emerged as a top-rank cricketer. His father, a rich man, had experienced an evangelical conversion as a result of the mission of D.L. MOODY, and he encouraged his son to become a missionary. Sponsored by the East China Mission, Studd sailed for China in 1885. Nine years later, illness compelled him to return home and he subsequently went to America where he was involved in the founding of the Student Volunteer Union. Then, in 1900, he travelled to India where he became pastor of the undenominational church at Ootacamund. Again he became ill and he went back to England in 1906. Four years later, against medical advice, he went to Africa where he founded the 'Heart of Africa' Mission. Later he was involved in the setting up of the Worldwide Evangelisation Crusade which sent missionaries to remote areas of the world. Studd was a significant figure in that his family position and his cricketing prowess enabled him to attract considerable publicity for all his activities.

E. Buxton, *Charles Thomas Studd* (1968); N.P. Grubb, *After C.T. Studd* (1939).

Studdert Kennedy, Geoffrey Anketell [Woodbine Willy] (1883–1929)

Army Chaplain and Devotional Writer. Studdert Kennedy was educated in Dublin and Oxford. He became known to the general public for his work as an army chaplain during the First World War. Nicknamed 'Woodbine Willie' (from the cigarettes he distributed), he was the subject of many anecdotes. After the war, he served a parish in London and he became involved in the work of the Industrial Christian Fellowship. He wrote several books of popular theology, such as *Rough Rhymes* and *The Word and the Work*, which attracted a large readership.

J.K. Mozley (ed.), *G.A. Studdert Kennedy: By his Friends* (1929); W. Purcell, *Woodbine Willie* (1962).

Suarez, Francisco de (1548–1617)

Theologian. Suarez was a native of Granada, Spain, and was educated at Salamanca. Subsequently, as a member of the Jesuit Order, he taught in several Spanish universities. His theology was mainly influenced by THOMAS AQUINAS and DUNS SCOTUS, and he wrote several important books, including *De Legibus*. This was an exposition of the principles behind national and international law and it was to be highly influential in America as well as Europe. He also produced his *Defensio Fidei* which was directed against the Church of England and repudiated the theory of King JAMES I on the divine right of kings. He also attempted to arbitrate in the bitter dispute between the Jesuits and the Dominicans on the activity and efficacy of grace.

T. Cronin, *Objective Being in Descartes and Suarez* (1987); J.H. Fichter, *Man of Spain* (1940); B. Hamilton, *Political Thought in Sixteenth-Century Spain* (1963); J.J. O'Brian, *Reparation for Sin: A Study of the Doctrine of Francis Suarez* (1960).

Suh Nam-Dong (b. c. 1920)

Theologian. Suh Nam-Dong is a former professor of Systematic Theology at Yonsei University, Korea, and he is known as an important proponent of Min-Jung theology. Central to his thinking is the concept of *han*. He defines this as the underlying feeling of both despair and hope, which he perceives in the consciousness of the Korean people. He sees *han* as the language of the *minjung*, the oppressed, and he suggests it as a basis for a developed Asian liberation theology.

The Commission on Theological Concern of the Christian Conference of Asia (ed.), *Minjung Theology: People as the Subject of History* (1983); J.C. England (ed.), *Living Theology in Asia* (1982).

Sundar Singh (1889–?1929) Mystic. Sundar Singh was born of Sikh parents in Rampur, North Punjab. After seeing JESUS CHRIST in a vision, he became a Christian and, having been rejected by his family, he adopted the life of a travelling preacher. He wore the saffron robe of a sadhu, an Indian holy man, and he travelled widely through India and beyond. He finally disappeared after embarking on a mission to Tibet. In his day he aroused enormous interest, particularly in the West.

C.J. Davey, *The Yellow Robe: The Story of Sadhu Sundar Singh* (1950); B.H. Streeter and A.J. Appasamy, *The Sadhu* (1921).

Surin, Jean-Joseph (1600–65) Mystic and Devotional Writer. Surin was born in Bordeaux and he was educated there and in Paris. He joined the Jesuit Order and, in response to a request from Cardinal RICHELIEU, he went to act as an exorcist to a community of Ursuline nuns in 1636. For the next twenty years, he believed himself to be diabolically possessed and he underwent a variety of torments. This was followed by a period of religious exaltation when he wrote his *Catéchisme Spirituel*. When this was translated into Italian after his death, it was put on the Index as Quietist. He also was the author of *Les Fondements de la Vie Spirituelle* and *Dialogues Spirituels*, in both of which he stressed the role of suffering as a means of achieving purification.

M. de Certeau, 'Jean-Joseph Surin', *Month*, ccx (1960).

Swedenborg, Emanuel (1688–1772) Philosopher, Mystic and Sect Founder.

Swedenborg was born in Stockholm, the son of a distinguished clergyman. He was educated at the University of Uppsala and, after a period of travel in Europe, he became an official in the Swedish Board of Mines. He held this position until his retirement in 1747. Initially he was interested in the nature of the soul and his early works include *A Philosophical Argument on the Infinite and Final Cause of Creation*. After experiencing a mystical conversion, which included a vision of JESUS CHRIST, he dedicated himself to spreading his own version of Christianity. This was expressed in many works, including *The True Christian Religion*, which appeared the year before his death. His doctrines were influenced by neo-Platonism; God is described as invisible, spaceless and timeless; the world is sustained by spirits and angels and Jesus is God the Father manifest on earth. In 1787 his followers formed the New Jerusalem Church and there are congregations of Swedenborgians today in Europe, the United States of America and Australia.

C.U. Sigstedt, *The Swedenborg Epic: The Life and Works of Emanuel Swedenborg* (1952); S. Toksvig, *Emanuel Swedenborg* (1949).

Swift, Jonathan (1667–1745) Satirist and Churchman. Swift was ordained into the ministry of the Church of Ireland and he rose to become Dean of St Patrick's Cathedral in 1713. He took part in both the political and religious life of his time, but he is remembered for his satires, *A Tale of a Tub*, *The Battle of the Books* and, most famously, *Gulliver's Travels*. In this he illustrated a wide spectrum of folly and it is clear that he took a less than optimistic view of human nature. *Gulliver's Travels* is still read and enjoyed today and has been filmed several times.

J.A. Downie, *Jonathan Swift: Political Writer* (1984); D. Nokes, *Jonathan Swift: A Hypocrite reversed* (1985); P. Reilly, *Jonathan Swift: The Brave Desponder* (1982).

Swithin (d. 862) Saint and Bishop. Little is known of the life of Swithin. He was a Bishop of Winchester and seems to have been an advisor of King Egbert of Wessex. He is known for the legend that if it rains on St Swithin's Day (15 July), then it will continue to rain for the following forty days.

F. Bussby, *Saint Swithin* (1971); Aelfric, *Lives of Three English Saints*, edited by G.I. Needham (1966).

Sylvester (d. 335) Pope and Saint. Sylvester was Pope between 314 and 335. Although this was the era of the Emperor CONSTANTINE, when Christianity became a recognised religion of the Empire, little is known about him. However, according to legend, he healed Constantine of leprosy by baptising him (this is certainly unhistorical) and he was given the 'Donation of Constantine'. This document, giving the Bishop of Rome primacy over the Eastern Patriarchs and dominion over Italy, was in fact forged in the eighth or ninth century.

N.H. Baynes, *Constantine the Great and the Christian Church* (1929); J.N.D. Kelly (ed.), *The Oxford Dictionary of Popes* (1986).

Symmachus (d. 514) Pope and Saint. Symmachus was born in Sardinia and he was elected Pope in 498. An alternative candidate, Laurentius, was also elected and the matter was only settled by the intervention of Theodoric, King of the Goths, in 501. Laurentius's claim, however, continued to be asserted in Rome until 506. Symmachus is remembered as a determined opponent both of the Manichaeans, whom he expelled from the city, and of the 'Henoticon' of the Emperor ZENO. Among his more important innovations was the singing of the 'Gloria' on Sundays and certain feast days. He is also known for the 'Symmachian Forgeries', a collection of doubtful canons compiled by DIONYSIUS EXIGUUS, designed to show that the Pope could not be judged by his fellow human beings, but only by God.

J.N.D. Kelly (ed.), *The Oxford Dictionary of Popes* (1986).

T

Tait, Archibald Campbell (1811–82) Archbishop. Tait was born of Scottish Presbyterian parents, but after studying at Glasgow University, he went to Oxford where he conformed to the Articles of the Church of England. In 1836 he was ordained. He first came to the notice of the public when he protested against NEWMAN's Tract 90. In 1842 he succeeded Thomas ARNOLD as headmaster of Rugby School; he was appointed Archdeacon of Carlisle in 1848, Bishop of London in 1856 and Archbishop of Canterbury in 1868. He was known as a Broad Churchman, but, as Archbishop, he was a determined opponent of all forms of ritualism. He is remembered as a strong leader who ensured the continued existence of the Lambeth Conference, the regular ten-yearly meeting of all the Bishops of the Anglican Communion.

P.T. Marsh, *The Victorian Church in Decline: Archbishop Tait and the Church of England* (1969).

Tallis, Thomas (c. 1505–85) Composer. Tallis was organist of Waltham Abbey, England, until its dissolution under King HENRY VIII in 1540. For the rest of his life he was a Gentleman of the Chapel Royal. Much of his Church music is still played. He is remembered for his office hymns and, in particular, for his motet *Spem in Alium*, written for eight choirs. In his latter years, he worked closely with William BYRD.

P. Doe, *Tallis* (1968).

Tarasius (d. 806) Patriarch and Saint. Tarasius was either the uncle or the great-uncle of PHOTIUS. He enjoyed the patronage of the Empress Irene, and, as a result of her influence, he was elected Patriarch of Constantinople in 784. He worked hard for better relations between the Eastern and Western Churches and, under his presidency, a General Council was successfully summoned in Nicaea in 787. Among other business, this Council anathematised the iconoclasts. Later in his reign, he was attacked for being too lenient by THEODORE OF STUDIOS and, in consequence, he refused to recognise the marriage of Irene's divorced son, Constantine VI. Later he crowned the Emperor Nicephoras who had usurped the throne.

P. Henry, 'Initial Eastern assessments of the Seventh Oecumenical Council', *Journal of Theological Studies*, n.s. 25 (1974).

Tarsicius (third/fourth century) Legendary Saint. Tarsicius is said to have been martyred by a pagan mob while he was carrying the consecrated bread of the Eucharist. He accepted death rather than allow the host to be defiled. In 1920, a fraternity in his name was approved. This fosters devotion to the Eucharist.

Catholic University of America, *New Catholic Encyclopaedia* (1967).

Tatian (c. 110–c. 172) Devotional Writer and Supposed Sect Founder. Tatian was born in Assyria and was converted to Christianity in Rome, where he was a pupil of JUSTIN MARTYR. Later, he moved to Syria where he is said to have founded an ascetic, Gnostic sect. He was the author of the *Oratio ad Graecos*, a defence of Christianity, and the *Diatessaron*, an edition of the Four Gospels in one continuous narrative. This became the standard text of the Gospels in the Syrian Church until the fifth century. Tatian has been identified with Addai, the traditional founder of the Church of Edessa.

L.W. Barnard, 'The heresy of Tatian', *Studies in Church History*, 26 (1978); M. Whittaker (ed.), *Tatian: Oratio ad Graecos* (1982).

Tauler, Johann (*c.* 1300–61) Mystic. Tauler entered the Dominican Order in Strasbourg in 1315. He was known as a famous preacher and spiritual director. Of his devotional writings, only two letters and a few sermons survive. They are straightforward recommendations of practical Christianity, using images drawn from everyday life. The mystical quest was to be pursued by the practice of traditional values and, through the indwelling of God in the human soul, the individual could be empowered to lead a life of greater virtue and self-sacrifice. Tauler practised what he preached. During the period of the Black Death, he was selfless in his care of the ill. Martin LUTHER both admired him and was influenced by his sermons.

J.M. Clark, *The Great German Mystics* (1949).

Taylor, James Hudson (1832–1905) Missionary. Taylor was born in Yorkshire and, after a basic medical training, he volunteered for mission work in China. He arrived in Shanghai in 1854 and in 1865 he founded the China Inland Mission. Despite poor health, he made several forays into the interior. He adopted Chinese dress and he faced a great deal of opposition from more conventional missionaries, but, by the end of his career, he headed the largest Protestant organisation in the country. His work was known to the Western public through his books, which included *China: Its Spiritual Needs and Claims* and *A Retrospect*.

M. Broomhall, *The Man who Believed in God: Hudson Taylor* (1936); H. Taylor and G. Taylor, *Biography of James Hudson Taylor*, abridged edition (1965).

Taylor, Jeremy (1613–67) Bishop and Devotional Writer. Taylor was born and educated in Cambridge. After ordination he came to the attention of Archbishop LAUD who nominated him to a fellowship at All Souls', Oxford, and he was appointed to be a chaplain to King CHARLES I. After the defeat of the Royalists in the English Civil War, he retired to Wales as a chaplain to Lord Carbery. There he wrote several books including the famous *Rule and Exercise of Holy Living* and *The Rule and Exercise of Holy Dying*. Today these are regarded as classics of Anglican spirituality. He also was the author of various polemical works, defending the institution of Bishops and attacking Roman Catholic doctrine. With the Restoration, he was made Bishop of Down and Vice Chancellor of the University of Dublin. Then, in 1661, he became Bishop of Dromore. Taylor's devotional writing has been much admired; it was influential on John WESLEY and he was described by COLERIDGE as the 'Spenser of prose'.

H.T. Hughes, *The Piety of Jeremy Taylor* (1960); C.J. Stranks, *The Life and Writings of Jeremy Taylor* (1952); H.R. Williamson, *Jeremy Taylor* (1952).

Teilhard de Chardin, Pierre (1881–1955) Scientist and Theologian. Teilhard was born near Clermont in France and he joined the Jesuit Order in 1899. For much of his career he worked in China as a palaeontologist and he spent his final years in the United States of America. During his lifetime, he was primarily regarded as a scientist and he published more than a hundred and seventy articles on palaeontology. Today, however, he is remembered for his theological work *The Phenomenon of Man* (published in the year of his death) and the devotional *Divine Milieu*. He attempted to relate theology to science by arguing that God is part of the evolutionary process of the universe; it is centred on Christ and it is moving towards the omega point. Although he was regarded with suspicion by the Roman Catholic hierarchy, his work has proved popular.

T. Corbishley, *The Spirituality of Teilhard de Chardin* (1974); U. King, *Towards a New Mysticism: Teilhard de Chardin and Eastern Religions* (1980); C.F. Mooney, *Teilhard de Chardin and the Mystery of Christ* (1966); C.E. Raven, *Teilhard de Chardin: Scientist and Seer* (1963).

Temple, William (1881–1944) Archbishop and Theologian. Temple was the son of Frederick Temple, Archbishop of Canterbury between 1896 and 1902. He was educated at the University of Oxford, but his ordination was delayed because his views on the virgin birth of JESUS were not regarded as sufficiently sound. He rose steadily in the Anglican Church to become Bishop of Manchester in 1921, Archbishop of York in 1929 and Archbishop of Canterbury in 1942. Concerned with social and economic questions, he was president of the Workers' Education Association, an inaugurator of the ecumenical British Council of Churches and he chaired the Malvern Conference of 1941, which urged the economic and administrative reorganisation of the Church of England. Among his books were *Nature, Man and God*, the scholarly *Readings in St John's Gospel* and *Christianity and the Social Order*. Despite his early death, he is generally regarded as the outstanding English Archbishop of the twentieth century – as Prime Minister Winston Churchill described him, he was a 'sixpenny article in a penny bazaar'.

F.A. Iremonger, *William Temple* (1948); J. Kent, *William Temple: Church, State and Society in Britain* (1992); A.M. Suggate, *William Temple and Christian Social Ethics* (1987).

Tenison, Thomas (1636–1715) Archbishop. Tenison was educated at the University of Cambridge. As Rector of St

Martin in the Fields, London, he came to public notice as an excellent preacher and as the author of *An Argument for Union with the Dissenters*. He supported the revolution against King JAMES II in 1688 and was appointed Archdeacon of London in 1689. In 1692 he became Bishop of Lincoln and he was consecrated Archbishop of Canterbury in 1695. He is remembered as a founder member of the Society for the Propagation of the Gospel and for establishing the first public library in London. He was much admired by John EVELYN, but was described by Jonathan SWIFT as 'a very dull man'.

E.F. Carpenter, *Thomas Tenison: Archbishop of Canterbury* (1948).

Teresa, Mother (1910–1997) Missionary and Order Founder. Mother Teresa was born Agnes Gonxha Bojaxhiu in Yugoslavia. In 1928 she travelled to India as a Roman Catholic missionary teacher. Twenty years later she founded the Order of the Missionaries of Charity to serve the medical and educational needs of the poorest of the poor in the slums of Calcutta. Her nuns wear white saris with blue stripes and are now well known for their work with the under-privileged in many countries. Mother Teresa achieved international recognition for her work; she was the first recipient of the Pope JOHN XXIII Prize and she also won the Nobel Peace Prize. In recent years she has been criticised for her uncompromising stand against abortion and contraception

M. Muggeridge, *Something Beautiful for God* (1971).

Teresa of Avila (1515–82) Saint, Mystic, Devotional Writer and Monastic Reformer. Teresa was of part-Jewish descent and she was born in Avila, Spain. She entered a Carmelite monastery at the age of twenty, but another twenty years were to pass before she began to seek the life of perfection. She was subject to visions which included hearing words and being pierced with a mystical spear of divine love. In 1562 she founded the convent of St JOSEPH at Avila, in which a primitive and strict form of the Carmelite Rule was observed. She was guided by her spiritual advisor PETER OF ALCÁNTARA and her most famous book, *The Way of Perfection*, was written for the guidance of her nuns. She also wrote an autobiography and the mystical classic *The Interior Castle*. Despite opposition from the Calced Carmelites, she founded several Discalced convents throughout Spain, aided by St JOHN OF THE CROSS. The later part of her life was dedicated to placing the new foundations on a secure footing and many of her convents survive to this day. She is primarily remembered, however, for her vivid depictions of mystical prayer and as the ecstatic subject of a statue by Bernini.

V. Lincoln, *Teresa: A Woman: A Biography of Teresa of Avila* (1984); R.T. Petersson, *The Art of Ecstasy: Teresa, Bernini and Crashaw* (1970); R. Williams, *St Teresa of Avila* (1992).

Teresa of Lisieux (1873–97) Saint, Mystic and Devotional Writer. Teresa was born Marie Françoise Thérèse Martin into an intensely religious family. She was determined to join the Carmelite Order and, after a personal appeal to the Pope, she was allowed to enter at the age of fifteen. She died of tuberculosis nine years later. She achieved fame through her autobiography *L'Histoire d'une Ame*. This was described by Pope Benedict XV as 'containing the secret of sanctity for the entire world'. Lisieux became a place of pilgrimage; miracles occurred and Teresa herself was beatified in 1923 and canonised in 1925. Known in the English-speaking world as 'the Little Flower of Jesus' from the subtitle of her book, she has a huge popular following. Despite her somewhat saccharine image, she has endeared herself even to feminists by her avowed desire to be a priest. In 1947 she was named

patron saint of France, together with another inspiring French virgin, Joan of Arc.

H. von Balthasar, *Thérèse of Lisieux: the Story of a Mission* (1953).

Tertullian, Quintus Septimus (*c.* 160–*c.* 225) Theologian. Tertullian grew up as a pagan in Carthage, North Africa. He was converted to Christianity and he eventually joined the Montanist sect, but little is known of the details of his life. He is known for his theological and apologetic works. These included the *Apologeticum*, which is an appeal for the official toleration of Christians and Christianity. In *De Praescriptione Haereticorum*, he argued that only the one true Church possesses authority since her doctrines were handed down from JESUS, through the Apostles to the Bishops. He produced several polemics against MARCION and other heretics and these were to provide the vocabulary and conceptual categories by which orthodoxy was later to be defended. He was also the author of the first surviving treatises on the Lord's Prayer and baptism. Influenced by the pagan philosophy of stoicism, his works are all brilliantly argued and he has been described as the father of Latin theology. Today he is particularly remembered for his rhetorical question, 'What has Athens to do with Jerusalem?' and his statement, '*Credo quia impossibile est*' (I believe because it is impossible).

T.D. Barnes, *Tertullian: A Historical and Literary Study* (1971); T.P. O'Malley, *Tertullian and the Bible* (1967).

Tetzel, Johann (*c.* 1465–1519) Preacher. Tetzel is remembered as the Dominican friar who was commissioned to sell Indulgences for the rebuilding of St Peter's Cathedral, Rome, in the regions of Magdeburg and Halberstadt. LUTHER heard him peddling his wares in Jüterbog in 1517 and was so outraged that he issued his ninety-five theses against the sale of Indulgences.

J.E. Campbell, *Indulgences* (1953); H.A. Oberman, *Luther: Man between God and Devil* (1985).

Thaddaeus (first century) Saint and Apostle. Thaddaeus is mentioned in the Gospels of MATTHEW and MARK as one of the twelve disciples chosen by JESUS. LUKE, however, names the twelfth disciple as the 'other Judas, not Iscariot'. He has also been identified with Addai, the traditional founder of the Church of Edessa – though Addai also has been equated with TATIAN.

Mark, Chapter 3.

Thecla (first century) Saint. The story of Thecla is told in the apocryphal book *Paul and Thecla*. Paul is said to have persuaded the young Thecla to lead a life of total chastity. In consequence, she was condemned to be burnt to death in Iconium, but she miraculously escaped and eventually died in Selucia. The popularity of this tract indicates the value in which virginity, particularly female virginity, was held in the early Church in the late second and early third centuries.

M.R. James, *The Apocryphal New Testament* (1924).

Theobald (d. 1161) Archbishop. Theobald was Abbot of the Benedictine monastery of Bec, Normandy. He was consecrated Archbishop of Canterbury in 1139 and he took a full part in the political and religious life of his time. As a result of defying King Stephen, he was forced into exile and Pope EUGENIUS III put England under an interdict. After Stephen's death he crowned HENRY II and was instrumental in introducing him to Thomas BECKET. Theobald is remembered as a strong and able Archbishop under whom the English Church prospered.

A. Saltman, *Theobald of Canterbury* (1956).

Theodora I (*c.* 500–48) Monarch. In her early years, Theodora was an actress and was said to have led a thoroughly dissolute life. Then she was converted to Christianity and she married JUSTINIAN I. In 527 she was crowned Empress and she took a full part in governing the Empire. She herself was a Monophysite and, as a result of her influence, she encouraged JUSTINIAN to condemn the 'Three Chapters', namely the writings of THEODORE OF MOPSUESTIA, those of THEODORET against CYRIL OF ALEXANDRIA and the letter of IBAS. This led to serious controversy with the Western Church. Her portrait in a mosaic can be seen in San Vitale Church, Ravenna.

R. Browning, *Justinian and Theodora* (1971).

Theodore of Mopsuestia (*c.* 350–428) Bishop and Theologian. Theodore was born in Antioch and he was educated in Tarsus with John CHRYSOSTOM. He was ordained in *c.* 383 and was consecrated Bishop of Mopsuestia in 392. He was a highly successful Bishop and it was only after his death, at the Council of Ephesus in 431, that his orthodoxy came to be questioned. NESTORIUS had been one of his students and his works were attacked as heretical by CYRIL OF ALEXANDRIA. Subsequently they were condemned as part of the 'Three Chapters' of JUSTINIAN and at the Second Council of Constantinople. Little of his controversial writing survives, but in his *Disputations with Macedonians*, he refuted the theology of APOLLINARIUS. In recent years, it has been argued that his position on the incarnation was misunderstood.

R.A. Norris, *Manhood and Christ: A Study in the Christology of Theodore of Mopsuestia* (1963).

Theodore of Studios (759–826) Saint and Monastic Reformer. Theodore was born in Constantinople. He was a nephew of St Plato and in 794 he succeeded his uncle as Abbot of Saccudium. As a result of his determined opposition to the Emperor Constantine VI's adulterous marriage, he was exiled to

Thessalonica in 796. After Constantine had been deposed, he was recalled and in 799 his community moved to Studios in the face of Islamic raids. Because of Theodore's efforts, Studios rapidly became an important monastic centre. However, he was banished again in 809 because he quarrelled with the Emperor Nicephoras I over the restitution of a priest who had blessed Constantine's marriage, and again in 815 because he protested against the Emperor Leo V's iconoclastic policy. Theodore is remembered for his determined defence of the independence of the Church from State control and for his contribution to the Iconoclastic Controversy.

I. Hausherr, 'Saint Théodore Studite, l'homme et l'ascète', *Orientalia Christiana*, vi (1926) [no English translation available].

Theodore of Tarsus (*c.* 602–90)   Archbishop. Theodore was educated in Tarsus and Athens. As a refugee from Muslim invaders, he eventually settled in England and was appointed Archbishop of Canterbury in 669. He did much to improve the organisation of the English Church and he presided over its first important council in Hertford in 673. Later he summoned another council to Hatfield. As a result of his efforts, the city of Canterbury became an important centre of scholarship and the authority of the archiepiscopal see was much reinforced. Nevertheless he had serious differences with WILFRID, Archbishop of York, which were reconciled only a few years before Theodore's death.

M. Lapidge (ed.), *Archbishop Theodore: Commemorative Studies on his Life and Influence* (1995).

Theodoret (*c.* 393–*c.* 466)   Theologian and Bishop. Theodoret was born in Antioch. He was consecrated Bishop of Cyrrhus in 423 where he was widely respected. A friend of NESTORIUS, he became involved in the controversy with CYRIL OF ALEXANDRIA, arguing that

JESUS CHRIST had two natures which were united in one person, but were not of one essence. He was deposed at the 'Robber Synod' of Ephesus in 449. Subsquently he attended the Council of Chalcedon in 451 where he was reinstated, but only at the cost of anathematising Nestorius. The controversy flared up again during the reign of JUSTINIAN I and his writings were condemned at the Council of Constantinople in 553. His surviving works include the apology *Graecarum Affectionum Curatio*, a treatise against Monophysitism and various historical and exegetical works.

E.A. Livingstone (ed.), *The Oxford Dictionary of the Christian Church*, revised edition (1997).

Theodosius I (*c.* 346–95)   Monarch. Theodosius was born into an aristocratic family in Spain and he served with distinction in the imperial army. In 379 he was appointed co-Roman Emperor and he successfully restored order in the East. He outlawed paganism and heretical sects and he convened the First Council of Constantinople in 381. In Christian circles, he is primarily remembered for his public submission to St AMBROSE, after ordering a massacre in Thessalonica.

N.Q. King, *The Emperor Theodosius and the Establishment of Christianity* (1961).

Theodosius II (401–50)   Monarch. Theodosius II was the grandson of THEODOSIUS I. On the death of his father, he became Eastern Roman Emperor in 408. He is remembered in the history of the Church for appointing NESTORIUS Patriarch of Constantinople in 428, for summoning the Council of Ephesus in 431 and for codifying all the general constitutions enacted since the time of CONSTANTINE I. The Theodosian Code, as it was called, did much to regularise the relation between Church and State. Somewhat unsound in his judgements, for a period he used SIMEON STYLITES as a regular advisor.

J.B. Bury, *History of the Later Roman Empire from the Death of Theodosius I to the Death of Justinian* (1923).

Theodulf (*c.* 750–821) Bishop, Poet and Theologian. Theodulf was born in Spain and he was made Bishop of Orleans by the Emperor CHARLEMAGNE. He took a full part in the political and religious life of his time. After Charlemagne's death he was deposed, accused of conspiring with King Bernard of Italy against the Emperor LEWIS I. He is remembered as an important theologian of the Carolingian renaissance. He wrote treatises on baptism and the Holy Spirit and he sponsored the production of a new text of JEROME's Vulgate. In addition, many of his poems survive, including 'Gloria, laus et honor', which became part of the regular Western liturgy for Palm Sunday, the Sunday before Easter.

H. Liebeschütz, 'Theodulf of Orleans and the problem of the Carolingian renaissance', in D.J. Gordon (ed.), *Fritz Saxl 1890–1948* (1957).

Theophilus (first century) Dedicatee. Both the Gospel of LUKE and the Acts of the Apostles are dedicated to Theophilus. Various conjectures have been made as to his identity, but it is also possible that he was a fictional person. His name means 'lover of God' and perhaps stands for all the earnest seekers after faith reading Luke's work.

Luke, Chapter 1; The Acts of the Apostles, Chapter 1.

Theophilus of Antioch (second century) Theologian, Bishop and Saint. Theophilus was the author of an early Christian apologia, addressed to the pagan Autolycus. He contrasts the Christian doctrine of creation with the myths of the gods and he was the first known writer to describe the godhead as triune. He also produced a treatise against MARCION, which is now lost.

R.M. Grant, *The Great Apologists of the Second Century* (1988).

Thielicke, Helmut (1908–66) Theologian. Thielicke was educated at Griefswald, Erlangen, Marburg and Bonn. As a Lutheran minister, he was a prominent opponent of Nazism. After the Second World War, he taught theology at the University of Tübingen and later at Hamburg. He was an outstanding preacher, presenting Christianity as a creed for a time of crisis. He was the author of the monumental *Theologische Ethik* and a dogmatic theology, *Der Evangelische Glaube*. Although clearly influenced by Karl BARTH, he presented his evangelical message within the listener's own personal situation and he saw the gospel as the one stay against the nihilism of the modern age.

R. Higginson, 'Thielicke: Preacher and theologian', *Churchman*, xc (1976); R. Klann, 'Helmut Thielicke appraisal: A review essay', *Concordia Journal*, vi (1980).

Thierry of Chartres (d. *c.* 1152) Philosopher and Theologian. Thierry was a younger brother of BERNARD OF CHARTRES. He taught first in Chartres, France, and then in Paris. Later he succeeded GILBERT DE LA PORRÉE as Chancellor of Chartres. He is remembered for his interpretation of Christian doctrines in Platonic terms. So, in his *De Sex Dierum Operibus*, he identified God's form as the form of everything and he saw the Holy Spirit as the same as Plato's world-form. He also wrote commentaries on the work of BOETHIUS and made an important anthology of texts for students.

Catholic University of America, *New Catholic Encyclopaedia* (1967).

Thomas (first century) Apostle. Thomas was one of JESUS's twelve disciples. In the Fourth Gospel, he is known as Thomas Didymus ('the twin'). In the text he offers to die with Jesus, he prompts the final discourse and he is the central figure in a resurrection appearance: having missed seeing the risen Jesus with the others, he declared that he would not believe until he had seen with his own eyes and touched with his own hands. After Jesus appeared in front of him, he declared 'My Lord and my God'. According to different traditions, he preached the gospel in Parthia and in India. The *Acts of Thomas* is an apocryphal Gnostic work describing his mission adventures and martyrdom. It dates from the early third century and is probably Syrian in origin. The *Gospel of Thomas*, another apocryphal work, contains a collection of Jesus's sayings, and an apocalypse and an infant gospel also survive.

John, Chapters 11, 14 and 20; L.W. Brown, *The Indian Christians of St Thomas* (1980); G.E. Medlycott, *India and the Apostle Thomas* (1905); H.E.W. Turner and H. Montefiore, *Thomas and the Evangelists* (1962).

Thomas Aquinas (1225–74) Theologian, Philosopher and Saint. Thomas was born of a noble family in Roccasecca, Italy. He was educated at the famous Benedictine monastery of Monte Cassino and in Naples. Despite family opposition, he joined the Dominican Order in 1244 and then settled in Paris. There he was introduced to the philosophy of Aristotle by ALBERTUS MAGNUS. Although he spent some time in Cologne and taught in Italy from 1249 to 1259, most of the rest of his life was spent in Paris. He is regarded as the most outstanding and influential theologian of the Middle Ages and among his many works were commentaries on the books of Aristotle, BOETHIUS and Pseudo-DIONYSIUS. He produced his *Summa Contra Gentiles* as a text book for missionaries and his great *Summa Theologica* remains the fundamental text of Roman Catholic theology. Thomas was living at a time when the works of Aris-

totle were being rediscovered through the writings of the Arabic philosophers. He took the fundamental concepts of Aristotle and explained Christian doctrines in their light. Most famous are his 'five ways' to establish by natural reason the existence of God. At the same time he drew a distinction between the findings of reason and the knowledge that is only revealed by faith (such as the incarnation, the Trinity and the future resurrection), but he stressed that faith doctrines were in no way contrary to reason. Thomas was declared a Doctor of the Church in 1567 and, as late as 1923, the Vatican declared that the study of his work was mandatory for all students of philosophy and theology. Known as 'Doctor Angelicus', he is the patron saint of all Roman Catholic universities.

B. Davies, *An Introduction to the Thought of Thomas Aquinas* (1992); E. Gilson, *The Christian Philosophy of Thomas Aquinas* (1957); J.P. Torrell, *Saint Thomas Aquinas* (1996).

Thomas of Celano (c. 1190–1260) Historian. Thomas joined the Order of FRANCIS OF ASSISI in c. 1214. He is remembered as the first biographer of the saint. Altogether he produced two lives, an account of the miracles and a life of St CLARE. Although they were extremely popular, their accuracy has been questioned in recent times.

J.R.H. Moorman, *The Sources for the Life of St Francis of Assisi* (1940).

Thomas à Kempis (c. 1380–1471) Devotional Writer. Thomas was born in Kempen, Germany, and he joined the Canons-Regular at Agnietenberg in 1399. He was a well-known preacher and a prolific writer. He is remembered for his *Imitatio Christi*. In this, he instructs his readers how to seek perfection by following the example of JESUS CHRIST. It was circulated anonymously and various other suggestions have been made as to its author – such as St BONAVENTURA and Pope INNOCENT III. However, most authorities accept that it owes its origin to Thomas and it remains one of the most popular spiritual classics of all time.

D. Butler, *Thomas à Kempis: a Religious Study* (1908); S. Kettlewell, *Thomas à Kempis and the Brothers of the Common Life*, 2 vols (1882).

Thompson, Francis (1859–1907) Poet. Thompson was born into a Roman Catholic family in Preston, Lancashire. After an unsuccessful period in medical school, he moved to London where he lived in great poverty. He was discovered as a poet by Alice Meynell, then editor of the Catholic periodical *Merry England*. He published three volumes of poetry and several other prose works on religious themes. Today he is mainly remembered for his much anthologised poem 'The hound of heaven', a graphic description of God's pursuit of the soul.

R.M. Gantry, *The Tremendous Lover: An Exposition of Francis Thompson's Poetry* (1932); E. Meynell, *The Life of Francis Thompson* (1913); J. Walsh, *Strange Harp: Strange Symphony: The Life of Francis Thompson* (1967).

Tikhon (1866–1925) Patriarch. Tikhon was born Basil Ivanovitch Belavin, the son of a village priest. He was educated in St Petersburg and was ordained. He rose rapidly in the hierarchy of the Russian Church, becoming Bishop of Lublin in 1897, North America in 1898, Yaroslav in 1907 and Vilna in 1914. He was consecrated Metropolitan of Moscow in 1917 and in the same year, he was elected the first Patriarch of the Russian Church since 1700. He lived in difficult times. In the Revolution, he imposed neutrality on the clergy; later he was arrested for his protest against the confiscation of Church property and in 1923 a schismatic alternative Church was set up by the Soviet government. Despite almost insuperable problems, he continued to conduct services in Moscow and he was held in great affection.

M. Spinka, *The Church in Soviet Russia* (1956);

Prince P.M. Volkonsky, 'La reconstitution du Patriarcat en Russie: Mgr Tykhon Patriarche de Moscou et de toute la Russie', *Echos d'Orient*, xx (1921) [no English translation available].

Tikhon of Zadonsk (1724–83) Saint, Bishop and Devotional Writer. Tikhon was born into a poor family and he was educated in Novgorod, Russia. He became Bishop of Voronezh in 1763, but he resigned four years later and retired to the monastery in Zadonsk. He was the author of a large number of devotional works, many of which are considered to be classics of Eastern Orthodox spirituality.

N. Gorodetzsky, *Saint Tikhon of Zadonsk, Inspirer of Dostoevsky* (1951).

Tilak, Narayan Vaman (*c.* 1862–1919) Poet and Order Founder. Tilak was born into a high-caste Hindu family in Ratnagiri, India. He was converted to Christianity as a young man – apparently after being given a New Testament by a stranger on a train, and he was baptised in 1895. Subsequently he joined the American Marathi mission and he was ordained in 1904. He is remembered as a poet; he produced a large number of Indian songs of praise and he started a life of JESUS CHRIST in verse. Two years before his death, he started his own community, the Baptised and Unbaptised Disciples of Christ, which was based in Satara.

J.E. Orr, *The Light of the Nations* (1965).

Tillich, Paul Johannes (1886–1965) Theologian. Tillich was the son of a Lutheran pastor and was born in Starzeddal, Germany. He was educated at the Universities of Berlin, Tübingen, Halle and Breslau and his doctorate was on the work of SCHELLING. Subsequently he taught at the universities of Berlin, Marburg, Dresden, Leipzig and Frankfurt, but he was dismissed from his post in 1933 because of his opposition to Hitler's National Socialism. He moved to the United States of America where he taught at Union Theological Seminary, Columbia, Harvard and Chicago. Influenced by the philosophy of HEIDEGGER and the psychology of JUNG, his writings have been highly influential on Protestant theology in the second half of the twentieth century. His most famous work was his *Systematic Theology*, in which he defined God as 'Ground of Being' and the object of 'ultimate concern'. JESUS was the 'New Being' and his death on the cross made him 'transparent' to the 'Ground of Being'.

K. Hamilton, *The System and the Gospel: A Critique of Paul Tillich* (1963); C.W. Kegley and R.W. Bretall (eds), *The Theology of Paul Tillich* (1952); D. Ford, *The Modern Theologians* (1997).

Tillotson, John (1630–94)   Archbishop. Tillotson was educated at the University of Cambridge. A committed Protestant, he advised the seven Bishops who refused to read King JAMES II's declaration of indulgence in 1688 and in the following year, he was appointed Dean of St Paul's Cathedral in London. In 1691 he succeeded SANCROFT as Archbishop of Canterbury. He was a determined opponent of Roman Catholicism and he was a friend to all Protestants, however non-conforming. However, he is mainly remembered for his preaching; he himself described his style as 'plain and unaffected', but it was widely imitated throughout the eighteenth century.

L.G. Locke, *Tillotson: A Study in 17th-Century Literature* (1954).

Timothy (first century)   Missionary, Bishop and Saint. According to the Acts of the Apostles, Timothy was a native of Lystra, Asia Minor, and was the son of a Jewish woman and a pagan man. In order to placate the Jews, PAUL circumcised him and he accompanied Paul on the second missionary journey. Later he preached to the Thessalonians and the Corinthians and became Paul's representative in Ephesus. Two letters written by

Paul to him are collected in the New Testament. EUSEBIUS OF CAESAREA recorded that he was the first Bishop of Ephesus and, according to one tradition, he was martyred when he protested against the excesses of the pagan festival of Diana.

The Acts of the Apostles, Chapter 16; I Timothy; II Timothy; A.T. Hanson, *Studies in the Pastoral Epistles* (1968); F. Young, *The Theology of the Pastoral Epistles* (1994).

Timothy (d. 517)   Patriarch. Timothy became Patriarch of Constantinople in 511. He was a Monophysite and in 515 he condemned the Chalcedonian formula at a synod. Previously he had tried to introduce SEVERUS's formula 'who was crucified for us' into the Trisagion prayer 'Holy God, Holy and Mighty, Holy and Immortal, have mercy on us'. According to the historian, Theodore the Lector, he also introduced the Nicene Creed into the Constantinople liturgy, but this has been disputed.

W.H.C. Frend, *The Rise of the Monophysite Movement* (1972).

Timothy (728–823)   Patriarch. Timothy was elected Patriarch of Ctesiphon, Arabia, in 780 and he transferred the Patriarchate to Baghdad. He is remembered as an outstanding Church leader; he created several new sees and he was on good terms with the Muslim Caliphs, particularly with the famous Haroun-al-Rashid. He was the author of the *Dialogue with al-Mahdi*, an apology for Christianity which was much used in later Christian–Islamic apologetic. He sent out missionaries to evangelise the pagans in Turkey and on the silk route to China and several of his letters to the new Christian centres have survived.

J.W. Sweetman, *Islam and Christian Theology* (1945–55).

Timothy Aelurus (d. 477)   Patriarch and Saint. Timothy became Patriarch of

Alexandria in Egypt in 457. His name, 'Aelurus', means weasel-like and may refer to his small stature. He was a Monophysite and, because he was unacceptable to many Bishops, he was banished by the Emperor LEO I in 460. Later he was recalled by the Emperor Basilicus. Several of his letters survive. He taught that JESUS was essentially God, but not essentially man; he became human by divine dispensation. At the same time he anathematised EUTYCHES for maintaining that Jesus's body was not really a human body. In the Coptic Church he is regarded as a saint.

W.H.C. Frend, *The Rise of the Monophysite Movement* (1972).

Tindal, Matthew (1655–1733) Theologian. Tindal was the son of an Anglican clergyman and was educated at the University of Oxford. For a short time during the reign of King JAMES II he became a Roman Catholic, but by 1688 he had recognised 'the absurdities of Popery'. He is remembered as the author of three important Deist treatises, the last of which, *Christianity as Old as the Creation*, has been described as the Deist Bible. He argued that there is a fundamental law of nature, which is discernible to all rational people and that the purpose of the Christian gospel was to free humanity from superstition, not in any way to supersede the natural law. Many writers took up the challenge and wrote responses to it. It went through many editions and, in German translation, took Deist ideas to Europe.

L. Stephen, *History of English Thought in the Eighteenth Century*, i (1876).

Titian (1477–1576) Artist. Titian learnt painting in Venice under Giovanni Bellini. Giorgione was a fellow-student and became a life-long friend. During his long life (he lived to be ninety-nine), Titian painted many pictures with religious themes, accepting commissions for altar pieces as well as secular portraits and historical scenes. His technique was to influence Tintoretto and the Baroque masters. Among his many achievements must be numbered *Christ Crowned with Thorns*, painted in his old age, which glows, despite the horror of the subject, with a peculiar religious calm.

R. Goffen, *Piety and Patronage in Renaissance Venice: Bellini, Titian and the Franciscans* (1986); D. Rosand, *Titian* (1978).

Titus (first century) Disciple and Bishop. Titus is mentioned in PAUL's Epistle to the Galatians, in his second letter to the Corinthians and in his second letter to TIMOTHY. He was also the recipient of one of Paul's letters, in which he was described as 'my true child after a common faith'. It has been conjectured, but on little evidence, that he was LUKE's brother. He aided Paul in his mission campaigns and EUSEBIUS OF CAESAREA records that he was the first Bishop of Crete. Today his head is venerated as an important relic in St Mark's Cathedral, Venice.

The Epistle of Paul to Titus; A.T. Hanson, *Studies in the Pastoral Epistles* (1968); F. Young, *The Theology of the Pastoral Epistles* (1994).

Toland, John (1670–1722) Theologian. Toland was born in Ireland of Roman Catholic parents, but he converted to Protestantism at the age of sixteen. He was educated in Glasgow and Leyden His first book, *Christianity not Mysterious*, in which he argued that reason rather than revelation is the source of true Christian knowledge, was condemned by the Irish Parliament and he was forced to flee to England. Among his other books were a life of MILTON, a defence of the Hanoverian succession, a study of the early Jewish Church, several collections of essays and *Pantheisticon*. This was a parody of Christian liturgy, designed for the use of Pantheists (a word he seems to have coined). Today Toland is considered to have been one of the most significant of the English Deists.

F.H. Heinemann, 'John Toland and the Age of Enlightenment', *Review of English Studies*, xx (1944); J.G. Simms, 'John Toland: A Donegal Heretic', *Irish Historical Studies*, xvi (1969); R.E. Sullivan, *John Toland and the Deist Controversy* (1982).

Tolstoy, Leo (1828–1910)   Novelist and Philanthropist. Tolstoy was born into a Russian aristocratic family. He was educated at the University of Kazan and he fought in the Crimean War. After travelling through Europe, he returned to his estate in Tula where he freed the serfs and established schools. Today he is primarily remembered for his two novels (in their English titles) *War and Peace* and *Anna Karenina*. These are regarded as masterpieces of Russian literature. Later he turned away from fiction and he concentrated on religious and ethical subjects. He lived a life of simplicity, identifying with the poor and emphasising the moral teachings of Christianity. He rejected the doctrine of the divinity of JESUS CHRIST and ultimately he was excommunicated from the Russian Church. In his final years he took up the cause of the Doukhobors, a peasant sect; adherents believed that the Trinity appeared in the human soul as memory, reason and will and they organised their communities on communist lines. Tolstoy's last novel, *Resurrection*, was written in their defence.

E.J. Simmons, *Introduction to Tolstoy's Writings* (1969); G. Steiner, *Tolstoy or Dostoevsky: An Essay in Contrast* (1960); S. Tolstoy, *Tolstoy Remembered* (1961); A.N. Wilson, *Tolstoy* (1988).

Torquemada, Tomas de (1420–98) Inquisitor. Torquemada was a nephew of the Spanish theologian Juan de Torquemada. He joined the Dominican Order and in 1452 he became the Prior of Santa Cruz Convent in Segovia, Spain. He was appointed Confessor to King FERDINAND and Queen ISABELLA and in 1483

he became Grand Inquisitor of Spain. Ruthless in his determination to root out heresy, he was the author of the *Compilación de las Instrucciones de la Santa Inquisición*, in which he described his methods. He did not hesitate to employ torture to extract confessions and about two thousand people were burnt to death for their religious opinions. He was also largely responsible for the expulsion of the Jews from the Spanish realms in 1495. He was an ascetic, devout man, but, judged by the values of today, he seems the personification of cruelty and intolerance.

T. Hope, *Torquemada, Scourge of the Jews* (1939); R. Sabatini, *Torquemada and the Spanish Inquisition* (1913).

Tremellius, John Immanuel (1510–80) Biblical Scholar. Tremellius was born of Jewish parents in Ferrara, Italy. He was converted to Christianity by Reginald Pole in 1540 and he became a Protestant under the influence of PETER MARTYR. After a period of teaching in Strasbourg, he was invited by Thomas CRANMER to settle in England where he became the King's Reader in Hebrew at the University of Cambridge. With the accession of Queen MARY, he left England and he taught Hebrew first at Heidelberg and then at Sedan. He is remembered for his important translations of the Old Testament from Hebrew and of the New Testament from Syriac, both into Latin. For many years his was the standard translation used by Protestants.

W. Becker, *Immanuel Tremellius, ein Proselytenleben im Zeitalter der Reformation* (1887) [no English translation available].

Trimmer, Sarah (1741–1810)   Educator. Trimmer was born Sarah Kirby in Ipswich, England, and as a young woman she was an acquaintance of Dr JOHNSON. After her marriage in 1762, she settled in Brentford and she was the mother of twelve children. She is remembered as an important figure in the Sunday School movement, which had been pioneered by Robert RAIKES. She was the author of a great many improving books, mainly designed for the instruction of the poor. In particular, *The History of the Robins* went through many editions.

E. Lee, 'Sarah Trimmer', in *Dictionary of National Biography* (1899).

Troeltsch, Ernst (1865–1923) Theologian. Troeltsch was born in Augsburg, Germany, and he taught at the Universities of Göttingen, Bonn, Heidelberg and Berlin. He also served for a time in the Ministry of Education. He is remembered for his *Die Absolutheit des Christentums*, his *Der Historismus und seine Probleme* and his *Die Soziallehren der Christlichen Kirchen und Gruppen*. Influenced by Albrecht RITSCHL and also by the neo-Kantians, he maintained that religious claims must be understood relative to their cultural contexts. He also is remembered in his sociological work for making the classic distinction between Church and Sect. He was highly influential on later thinkers such as Baron VON HÜGEL.

R.H. Bainton, 'Ernst Troeltsch – thirty years after', *Theology Today*, viii (1950); S. Coakley, *Christ Without Absolutes: A Study of the Christology of Ernst Troeltsch* (1988); B.A. Reist, *Towards a Theology of Involvement* (1966).

Trophimus (first century)   Saint. There are several saints of this name. Trophimus is mentioned in the Acts of the Apostles as an early Gentile follower of St PAUL. Paul was accused of taking him into the Temple in Jerusalem, thus causing the riot which precipitated his arrest. A Trophimus is also mentioned in Paul's Second Epistle to TIMOTHY and, according to Church tradition, he is identified with one of the seventy 'missionaries' described in the Gospel of LUKE. Another early Trophimus was a missionary Bishop in Gaul. His activities are outlined by GREGORY OF TOURS.

The Acts of the Apostles, Chapter 20.

Trotter, Isabella Lilian (1853–1928) Missionary. Trotter was born in London and she was a talented artist. However, she was converted to evangelical Christianity by the mission of Hanna SMITH and her husband, and she sailed as a missionary to Algeria in 1888. She was the founder of the Algiers Mission Board, later incorporated into the North Africa Mission, and she was the author of an Algerian translation of the New Testament. She led a perilous and heroic life and she was much admired both in Algeria and in England.

B.A.F. Pigott, *I, Lilian Trotter* [no date].

Tutu, Desmond (b. 1931) Archbishop and Rebel. Tutu was born in South Africa. He studied in England and was ordained into the Anglican ministry. On his return to Africa, he was appointed Secretary-General of the South African Churches and in 1984 he was the first black to be elected Bishop of Johannesburg. For many years he was a major annoyance to the white apartheid government, which he did not hesitate to condemn as 'evil, immoral and therefore unChristian'. He has been relentless in his championship of human dignity and he is a determined proponent of liberation theology. In 1984 he was awarded the Nobel Peace Prize for his defence of human rights and he subsequently was consecrated as Archbishop of Cape Town. Several collections of his speeches and sermons have been published, including *The Rainbow People of God*.

S. du Boulay, *Tutu, Voice of the Voiceless* (1988); P. Walshe, *Church versus State in South Africa* (1983); J. Webster, *Crying in the Wilderness* (1982).

Tyndale, William (*c.* 1494-1536) Biblical Scholar. Tyndale was born in Gloucestershire and he was educated at both Oxford and Cambridge Universities. He became convinced that the only way to dispel the ignorance of lay people was to translate the New Testament into English, but he received no encouragement from the Church authorities. Consequently he moved to Germany and, despite continual harassment, the project was completed in 1525. It was promptly attacked in England by such eminent figures as Archbishop Warham and Thomas MORE. He spent the rest of his life in Antwerp, where he embarked on a translation of the Old Testament and produced treatises such as *The Parable of the Wicked Mammon* and *The Obedience of a Christian Man*. Today his style is much admired, but in his own time the persecution continued. Eventually he was arrested in Vivorde where he was strangled and burnt at the stake.

F.F. Bruce, *The English Bible: A History of Translations*, 2nd edn (1970); G. Carey, *William Tyndale: Reformer and Rebel* (1994); C.H. Williams, *William Tyndale* (1966).

Tyrrell, George (1861–1909) Theologian. Tyrrell was born in Dublin of Protestant parents. He converted to Roman Catholicism and joined the Jesuit Order in 1880. After ordination he wrote a succession of articles and books and he became a well-known spiritual director. However, his orthodoxy was called into question in 1899 and, after the publication of his *Much Abused Letter* of 1906, he was dismissed from his order. He died three years later and, since he had been excommunicated, he was refused a Roman Catholic burial. Tyrrell was an important friend of Baron VON HÜGEL (who persisted in addressing him as Father Tyrrell to the end) and he is regarded as one of the most important of the Catholic Modernists. The liberal tendencies of the movement were condemned in Pope PIUS X's encyclical *Pascendi*. In his final work, *Christianity at the Crossroads*, Tyrrell went so far as to suggest that Christianity did not represent the ultimate truth, but was merely a germ of a universal religion. Thus he must be seen as a forerunner of the modern pluralists.

R.G. Chapman, 'The thought of George Tyrrell', in *Essays and Poems presented to Lord David Cecil* (1970); E. Leonard, *George Tyrrell and the Catholic Tradition* (1982); J.L. May, *Father Tyrrell and the Modernist Movement* (1932); J. Ratte, *Three Modernists* (1968).

U

Ubaghs, Gerhard Casmir (1800–75) Theologian. Ubaghs was Professor of Philosophy at the University of Louvain, Belgium. He was the editor of the *Revue Catholique* and the author of several books propounding traditionalist ontologism. These included *Logicae seu Philosophiae Rationalis Elementa* and *Ontologiae seu Metaphysicae Generalis Elementa*. The traditionalists, such as F.R. de LAMENNAIS, taught that all knowledge of God is based on an ancient revelation handed down in an unbroken tradition and thus human reasoning has no real part in the process. Ubaghs and the Louvain school combined this with ontologism, taught by ROSMINI and others, that human knowledge of God is derived from an immediate intuition of Absolute Being. The 'Errores Ontologistarum' were condemned by the Papacy in 1861 and Ubaghs' own teaching was censured in 1864. Ubaghs submitted to the decree and retired from academic life.

Catholic Encyclopaedia of America, *New Catholic Encyclopaedia* (1967).

Ulphilas (*c.* 311–*c.* 381) Missionary, Bishop and Biblical Scholar. Little is known of the life of Ulphilas. He is thought to have been born in Cappadocia and to have been consecrated Bishop by EUSEBIUS OF NICOMEDIA, the Arian Bishop of Constantinople. He did much to convert the Visigoths to Christianity and he dedicated the rest of his life to their spiritual welfare. He was responsible for translating much of the Bible into Gothic and, for that purpose, inventing a new Gothic script. Because of his own orientation Arian opinions remained widespread among the Goths for several centuries.

E.A. Thompson, *The Visigoths in the Time of Ulfilas* (1966).

Ulrich (*c.* 890–973) Saint and Bishop. Ulrich was a Bishop of Augsburg, Germany, and he was a supporter of the reforms of the Emperor OTTO I. He is remembered as the first person formally to be canonised as a saint.

E.W. Kemp, *Canonization and the Western Church* (1948).

Unamuno, Miguel de (1864–1937) Philosopher. Unamuno was born in Bilbao, Spain. He was educated in Madrid and for much of his life was Professor of Greek at Salamanca. In 1924, however, he was exiled to the Canary Islands for his political views, which were out of harmony with those of the current dictatorship. He was the author of a variety of works, mainly advocating distrust and doubt and demonstrating the less than adequate nature of dogmatic theology. He regarded himself as a Roman Catholic, but two of his books were placed on the Index. His best-known works, in their English titles, were *The Tragic Sense of Life in Men and Peoples* and *The Agony of Christianity*. As he himself put it: 'My painful duty is ... to sow in men the seeds of doubt, of distrust, of disquiet, even of despair'.

J. Marias, *Miguel de Unamuno* (1967).

Underhill, Evelyn (1875–1941) Mystic. Underhill was born and educated in

London. She was the author of many works of mystical theology including *Mysticism, The Mystic Way* and *Worship*. For many years she was influenced by Baron VON HÜGEL and she was highly regarded as a conductor of spiritual retreats. She also translated and edited various classics such as *The Cloud of Unknowing*, Walter HILTON's *Scale of Perfection* and the works of RUYSBROECK. A committed member of the Church of England, she was also interested in the worship and liturgies of the Eastern Churches.

C.J.R. Armstrong, *Evelyn Underhill* (1975); D. Greene, *Evelyn Underhill: Artist of the Infinite Life* (1991).

Urban II (*c.* 1042–99) Pope. Urban was born Odo in Lagery, France. He was a student of BRUNO at the school of Rheims and he then entered the monastery of Cluny. He was appointed Cardinal Bishop of Ostia in 1080; as papal legate, he was responsible for the anathematisation of the Antipope Clement III, who was supported by the Emperor HENRY IV. Then in 1088 he was elected Pope, but, because of the presence of Clement in Rome, he could not finally take possession of the Lateran until 1094. In general, Urban followed the policies of his predecessor GREGORY VII and he was successful in reforming the Church in matters such as enforcing celibacy and outlawing simony. He also tried to heal the breach between the Western and Eastern Churches, but the 'filioque' clause (defended by St ANSELM) proved a stumbling block. He is primarily remembered for calling the First Crusade against the Turks; this proved to be the start of the great crusading movement of the Middle Ages. Although Jerusalem was recaptured, Urban died before the news could reach him. He was beatified in 1881.

J.N.D. Kelly (ed.), *Oxford Dictionary of Popes* (1986).

Urban V (1309–70) Pope. Urban was born Guillaume de Grimoard in Languedoc, France. He joined the Benedictine Order, was appointed Abbot of St Germain d'Auxerre in 1352 and Abbot of St Victor in 1361. The following year he was elected Pope. The Papacy was based in Avignon at the period. Urban led a monastic life within the palace and dedicated himself to Church reform. In 1367, at the urging of the Emperor, he established himself in Rome and set about establishing his authority there. However, he was forced to return to Avignon in 1369 as a result of the revolt in Perugia and the resumption of hostilities in the Hundred Years War. St BRIDGET predicted that he would soon die if he left Rome and this indeed came to pass the following year. Urban is remembered as perhaps the most effective of the Avignon Popes and as the only one to be beatified.

J.N.D. Kelly (ed.), *The Oxford Dictionary of Popes* (1986); G. Mollat, *The Avignon Popes* (1963).

Urban VI (1318–89) Pope. Urban was born Bartolommeo Prignano. He became Archbishop of Acerenza in 1363, Archbishop of Bari in 1377 and he was elected Pope in 1378, on the death of Pope GREGORY XI. The French members of the conclave felt they had been pressurised into electing an Italian and they were distressed by his unfortunate manner. In consequence they declared his election null and void and put up CLEMENT VII as antipope – thus initiating the Great Schism which was to last until 1417. According to the dictates of political expediency, the princes of Europe were almost equally divided in their support for the two candidates and the whole episode called the Church into disrepute. Towards the end of his life, Urban himself showed definite signs of insanity. He became involved in the machinations of Italian politics; he was captured on one occasion by the King of Naples and, after his escape, he had five

Cardinals tortured and executed for their supposed complicity in the plot. It was rumoured that he died from poisoning.

L. Macfarlane, 'An English account of the election of Urban VI', *Bulletin of the Institute of Historical Research*, xxvi (1953); W. Ullmann, *The Origins of the Great Schism* (1948).

Urban VIII (1568–1644) Pope. Urban was born Maffeo Barberini in Florence, Italy, and he was educated there and in Pisa. He was created a Cardinal in 1606, consecrated Bishop of Spoleto in 1608, Legate of Bologna in 1617 and he was elected Pope in 1623. During his Pontificate, much was done to fortify the Papal States and he pursued an active role diplomatically in order to preserve papal temporal power. In particular he worked against the Imperial interests in Italy, thus effectively lending support to France and Sweden in the Thirty Years War. He unashamedly promoted the careers of his relations, but at the same time he worked actively for reform in the Church. He was a great supporter of missionaries, founding the Urban College of Propaganda in 1627. He revised the Breviary and his decree on canonisation largely remains in force today. He was a tremendous builder; he was largely responsible for the Barbarini Palace and he encouraged Bernini in his plans for St Peter's Basilica. He did much to enforce the guidelines laid down in the Council of Trent and he approved several new orders, including that of St VINCENT DE PAUL. He is chiefly remembered, however, as the Pope who condemned GALILEO for a second time and as the author of the first bull against the theology of Cornelius JANSEN.

W.N. Weech, *Urban VIII* (1903).

Ursula (? third century) Legendary Saint. The story of St Ursula goes back to the fourth century and has its origin in Cologne, Germany. According to one version, she was a British princess who made a pilgrimage to Rome accompanied by eleven thousand virgins. They were all massacred in Cologne by the Huns (alternatively in the persecution of Maximinus in 235). She was the favourite saint of St ANGELA MERICI, who founded the Ursuline teaching order in her honour. Today the Ursulines are the largest teaching order in the Roman Catholic Church.

M. Aron, *The Ursulines* (1947); T.F. Tout, 'The legend of St Ursula and the eleven thousand virgins', in *Historical Essays by Members of Owen's College, Manchester* (1902).

Ussher, James (1581–1658) Archbishop and Historian. Ussher was educated at Trinity College, Dublin. He was ordained in 1601. He was appointed Professor of Divinity at Dublin in 1607; he became Bishop of Meath in 1621 and Archbishop of Armagh in 1625. After the Irish rebellion of 1641, he lived in England but he did his best to preserve the independence of the Irish Church. He is remembered, however, for his great scholarship. He was the author of many historical works, but he is chiefly known for his *Annales Veteris et Novi Testamenti*. The dates from this work were printed in many editions of the King JAMES Authorised Version of the Bible.

J.A. Carr, *The Life and Times of James Ussher, Archbishop of Armagh* (1895); R.B. Knox, *James Ussher, Archbishop of Armagh* (1967).

V

Valdés, Juan de (*c.* 1500–41) Theologian. Valdés was born in Cuenca, Spain, and was educated at Alcalá University. Influenced by both ERASMUS and LUTHER, he recognised the need for reform in the Church, but nevertheless he remained a Roman Catholic. He was the author of the *Diálogo de Doctrina Cristiana* and *Las Ciento Diez Divinas Consideraciones*, which was later translated into English from the Italian version by Nicholas FERRAR. He was forced to flee to Italy in 1531 where he became the centre of a reforming group based on the household of Giulia Gonzaga, a Cardinal's sister. After his death, several of his associates, including PETER MARTYR, joined the Protestants. Juan's twin brother, Alfonso, was another important humanist. He was the author of the *Diálogo de Lactancio y un Arcediano*, which was highly critical of the Papacy.

J.E. Longhurst, *Erasmus and the Spanish Inquisition: The Case of Juan de Valdes* (1950); J.C. Nieto, *Juan de Valdes and the Origin of the Spanish and Italian Reformation* (1970).

Valdes, Peter (late tenth/early eleventh centuries) Sect Founder. Little is known of Valdes. He was a rich merchant of Lyons, France, who, having provided for his family, gave up everything to become an itinerant preacher. He attracted a group of equally high-minded people, both men and women, but, despite their orthodoxy and virtue, they were forbidden by the Church establishment to spread their message. In consequence, they set up their own separate community outside the Church. Their lives were based on Scripture and they refused to participate in war or to take oaths. Known as the Waldensians, the sect spread through southern Europe, although there was no formal leadership after Valdes's death. They were greatly persecuted by the Inquisition from the time of Pope INNOCENT III, but none the less a small group still survives in Piedmont.

J.A. Wylie, *History of the Waldenses* (1880).

Valentine (? third century) Legendary Saint(s) and Martyr(s). There are two possible St Valentines. One was a priest martyred in the time of the Emperor Claudius and the other was a martyred Bishop of Terni. Today Valentine is one of the best-known saints as his day, 14 February, is traditionally associated with romantic love. Most authorities consider these customs stem from an early spring, pagan festival and have little to do with either of the saints.

'Sts Valentine', *Analecta Bollandiana*, xi (1892); H.A. Kelly, *Chaucer and the Cult of St Valentine* (1986).

Valentinus (second century) Theologian and Sect Founder. Valentinus was born in Egypt and he was said to be a pupil of Theodas, a student of PAUL. He lived in Rome in the middle years of the second century, but, after failing to become a Bishop, he left the Church. Although it is now lost, he was the author of an influential systematic theology. He taught that only his followers, the 'spiritual men', can have true knowledge of JESUS and the spiritual world: ordinary, unenlightened Christians merely achieve a shadowy glimpse of reality and the majority of human beings are simply consigned to perdition. According to TERTULLIAN and IRENAEUS, he had a large following who were known as Valentians, amongst whom was the heretic MARCUS.

H. Jones, *The Gnostic Religion* (1963); G. Quispel, 'The original doctrine of Valentinus', *Vigiliae Christianae*, i (1947); G. Stead, 'The Valentinian myth of sophia', *Journal of Theological Studies*, n.s. xx (1969).

Vaughan, Charles John (1816–97) Dean and Educator. Vaughan was a pupil of Thomas ARNOLD at Rugby School. After graduating from the University of Cambridge and ordination, he became headmaster of Harrow School until 1859, when he refused a bishopric and was appointed Vicar of Doncaster. There he organised a very successful ordination course and among his students was the future Archbishop of Canterbury, Randall Davidson. Evangelical in orientation, he was known as an excellent preacher. He became Master of the Temple in 1869 and Dean of Llandaff ten years later. Among his publications were collections of sermons and biblical commentaries.

F.D. How, *Six Great Schoolmasters* (1904); R.R. Williams, 'A neglected Victorian divine, Vaughan of Llandaff', *Church Quarterly Review*, cliv (1943).

Vaughan, Henry (1622–95) Poet and Mystic. Vaughan was born in Brecon, Wales, and he was educated at the University of Oxford. After medical training, he returned to Wales. He is remembered for his religious poetry, which was influenced by George HERBERT and was published as *Silex Scintillans* and *The Mount of Olives*. He seems to have held the Platonic view that before birth the human soul dwells with God.

E. Blunden, *On the Poems of Henry Vaughan: Characteristics and Innovations* (1927); S. Davies, *Henry Vaughan* (1995); R.A. Durr, *On the Mystical Poetry of Henry Vaughan* (1962); J.F.S. Post, *Henry Vaughan: The Unfolding Vision* (1982).

Vaughan Williams, Ralph (1872–1958) Composer. Vaughan Williams was born in Gloucestershire, the son of a clergyman. He was educated in Cambridge, London and Berlin. He was agnostic but he wrote a large corpus of religious music. Perhaps most significant for ordinary English Christians, he was the musical editor of *The English Hymnal* and he shared in the preparation of *Songs of Praise* and *The Oxford Book of Carols*. In addition he produced splendid settings of the Te Deum, several hymn tunes, organ pieces, anthems and choral works.

J. Day, *Vaughan Williams* (1961); M. Kennedy, *The Works of Ralph Vaughan Williams* (1964); W. Mellers, *Vaughan Williams and the Vision of Albion* (1989).

Veronica (first century) Legendary Saint. Veronica was said to be a woman of Jerusalem who wiped the blood and sweat off the face of JESUS as he made his way to his place of execution. The handkerchief returned with the imprint of the divine face on it. This incident is regularly portrayed in 'Stations of the Cross' series of devotional pictures. Veronica's handkerchief was one of the most venerated relics in the Roman Catholic Church and examples were preserved in Rome, Milan and Jaen. The apocryphal *Acts of Pilate* identified Veronica with the woman Jesus healed of a haemorrhage (MATTHEW, Chapter 9).

E. Kitryluk, *Veronica and her Cloth* (1991); H. Thurston, *The Stations of the Cross* (1906).

Vianney, Jean-Baptiste Marie [Curé d'Ars] (1786–1859) Saint. Vianney was born near Lyons, France. From an early age he was determined to become a priest, but his progress was hindered by compulsory military service and by his lack of Latin. Eventually he was ordained in 1815 and three years later he was appointed to the remote parish of Ars. There he became a famous spiritual director and he attracted a huge number of followers. Towards the end of his life, he spent almost all his time hearing confessions. He was canonised in 1925 and is now the patron saint of parish priests.

M. Trouncer, *The Curé d'Ars* (1959).

Vico, Giovanni Battista (1668–1744) Historian and Philosopher. Vico was born near Naples, Italy, and for much of his life he taught rhetoric at Naples University. He is remembered for his *Principii di Una Scienza Nuova d'Intorno alla Natura Comune delle Nazioni*. This was one of the first modern philosophies of history. Vico argued that by studying the nature of ancient languages and by examining the myths and rituals of the ancient world, much could be learnt of the organisation of society. He showed that the 'natural law' postulated by the philosophers of his time was not compatible with these early writings and he distinguished between mathematical and scientific knowledge and the knowledge that comes from imaginative empathy. Thus he must be regarded as an important figure in the development of the academic discipline of anthropology.

I. Berlin, *Vico and Herder: Two Studies in the History of Ideas* (1976); G. Tagliacozzo (ed.), *Gianbattista Vico: An International Symposium* (1969); L. Pompa, *Vico: A Study of the New Science* (1990); P. Burke, *Vico* (1985).

Victor I (d. 198) Saint and Pope. Victor was a native of Africa who was elected Pope in 189. JEROME maintained that he was the first Pope to write in Latin. He is primarily remembered for his part in the Quatrodeciman controversy. Some Churches used to celebrate Easter on the Jewish festival of Passover, irrespective of the day of the week on which it fell. This was condemned by Victor who insisted that Easter must be celebrated on a Sunday and he excommunicated the Bishop of Ephesus for doing otherwise. This drew a sharp reaction from St IRENAEUS. However, the Quatrodeci-

mans continued to exist and they eventually formed their own Church. This incident is generally seen as an important stage in the history of papal supremacy.

C.W. Dugmore, 'A note on the Quatrodecimans', in F.C. Cross (ed.), *Studia Patristica*, Vol. 4 (1961); J.N.D. Kelly (ed.), *The Oxford Dictionary of Popes* (1986).

Vigilius (d. 555) Pope. Vigilius was born of a noble family in Rome, Italy. In 531 he was nominated Pope by Boniface II, but this was pronounced uncanonical. He went to Constantinople where he was said to have promised the Empress THEODORA that he would condemn the Council of Chalcedon and restore the Monophysite Patriarch Anthimus. With Byzantine military aid, he was made Pope in 537, but he kept neither of his promises. Then, during the 'Three Chapters' controversy, he initially rejected JUSTINIAN's condemnation of the writings of THEODORE OF MOPSUESTIA, THEODORET and IBAS. However, when summoned to Constantinople, he issued the 'Iudicatum' accepting the condemnation. The Western Church was horrified. Vigilius was excommunicated at a synod in Carthage and, in consequence, he withdrew the 'Iudicatum' and later he refused to preside over the Council of Constantinople in 553. Vigilius's case was much cited by the opponents of papal infallibility in the time of Pope PIUS IX, but to no avail.

J.N.D. Kelly (ed.), *The Oxford Dictionary of Popes* (1986).

Vilatte, Joseph René (1854–1929) Bishop. Vilatte had a chequered religious history, but he eventually joined the Old Catholics. He was consecrated Old Catholic Bishop of America in 1892 and became Mar Timotheos. In his turn, he consecrated many other Bishops, amongst whom was Father IGNATIUS. None of them was recognised by any other Christian Church.

H.R.T. Brandreth, *Episcopi Vagentes and the Anglican Church*, 2nd edn (1961).

Vincent (fourth century) Saint and Martyr. According to AUGUSTINE OF HIPPO, Vincent was a Deacon of Saragossa, Spain, who was martyred in the Diocletian persecutions. Many legends were told of him. He was said to have been racked, roasted on a gridiron (like St LAURENCE) and imprisoned in the stocks. He is regarded as the first martyr of Spain and his cult spread throughout Europe.

D.H. Farmer (ed.), *The Oxford Dictionary of Saints*, 3rd edn (1992).

Vincent de Paul (1581–1660) Saint and Order Founder. Vincent was born in Ranquine, France, and he was educated in Toulouse. He was ordained in 1600. After an extraordinary period when he was captured by pirates, sold as a slave in North Africa and escaped, he settled in Paris in 1609. Influenced by Pierre de BÉRULLE, he founded the Lazarite Order (the Congregation of the Mission), which was dedicated to preaching and conducting retreats. In 1633, together with Louise de Marillac, he founded the Sisters of Charity, who were to become an important teaching and nursing order. During the minority of King LOUIS XIV, he attained considerable political influence, which he used to encourage poor relief and to oppose the Jansenists. He was canonised in 1737. The Vincent de Paul Society was founded in 1737 by Frédéric OZANAM to encourage lay people to work among the poor.

P. Coste, *La Congrégation de la Mission dite de Saint-Lazare* (1927) [no English translation available]; A. Foucault, *La Société de Saint Vincent de Paul* (1933) [no English translation available]; M. Purcell, *St Vincent de Paul* (1963).

Vincent Ferrer (c. 1350–1419) Saint, Devotional Writer and Preacher. Vincent was born in Valencia, Spain, and after studying at Tarragona, Barcelona and Toulouse, he joined the Dominican

Order. He was the author of *De Vita Spirituali* and he was famous throughout Europe for his preaching mission which inspired excesses of enthusiasm. Although he was a close associate of Antipope BENEDICT XIII, he strongly disapproved of the latter's prolongation of the Great Schism. Many miracles were ascribed to him; he was known as the 'Angel of Judgement' and he was canonised thirty-five years after his death.

H. Ghéon, *Saint Vincent Ferrer* (1939).

Vincent of Lérins (early fifth century) Theologian. Little is known of the life of Vincent. He was a monk on the island of Lérins off the south of France and he was the author of *Commonitorium*, which included the 'Vincentian canon'. This was the famous test of orthodoxy – '*Quod ubique, quod semper, quod ab omnibus creditum est*' (What has been believed everywhere, always and by everyone). In his writings he emphasised that scripture was the final source of authority, but its interpretation depended on this principle of tradition.

J. Peliha, *Emergence of Catholic Tradition (100–600)* (1971).

Vitoria, Francisco de (c. 1485–1546) Philosopher and Theologian. Vitoria was born in the Basque country. He joined the Dominican Order in 1504 and he was a student in Burgos and Paris. Subsequently he taught philosophy, first at Valladolid and then at Salamanca. He is remembered as a pioneer of international law and in his published lectures *De Indis*, *De Iure Belli* and *De Potestate Civili*, he argued that there was a natural law of nations. He criticised the conduct of the Spanish in their conquest of the New World and he went further than THOMAS AQUINAS in arguing that no war is just which brings serious evil to the world. These ideas were further developed by SUAREZ and GROTIUS. He is also regarded as a forerunner of the

Salmanticenses, a group of seventeenth-century Carmelites, who produced a huge commentary on the *Summa Theologica* of Thomas Aquinas. Vitoria used the *Summa*, rather than the 'Sentences' of PETER LOMBARD, as his prime theological text book and, after his death, Salamanca became the most important centre of Thomist study in Europe.

R.C. Gonzales, *Francisco de Vitoria* (1946) [no English translation available]; B. Hamilton, *Political Thought in Seventeenth-Century Spain* (1963); J.B. Scott, *Francisco de Vitoria and his Law of Nations* (1934).

Vitus (d. *c.* 303)   Saint and Martyr. According to legend, Vitus was born into a pagan family in Lucania, Italy, and he was secretly brought up a Christian by his nurse. He was martyred in the Diocletian persecutions. He is famous for giving his name to St Vitus Dance, a convulsive disease. He is often invoked in cases of illness and is regarded as the patron saint of actors and comedians.

D.H. Farmer (ed.), *The Oxford Dictionary of Saints*, 3rd edn (1992).

Vladimir (956-1015)   Monarch and Saint. Vladimir was a grandson of St Olga, but he was brought up a pagan. He came into power in Kiev in 980 and he later married the sister of the Emperor. According to legend, he studied the claims of Judaism and Islam before converting to Orthodoxy and he is remembered as the main Christianiser of Russia. Force was an important element in the conversion process. He is often described as the Apostle of Russia.

N. Zernov, *The Russians and their Church* (1945).

Voltaire [François Marie Arouet] (1694–1778)   Philosopher. Voltaire was educated by the Jesuits and he became one of the most celebrated of the French '*Philosophes*'. A determined critic of the Roman Catholic Church, which he regarded as a hotbed of superstition and corruption, he was a committed Deist. Between 1726 and 1729, he was exiled in London and he regarded England as a model of rationality and tolerance. He was influenced by LOCKE and NEWTON and despised the views of Blaise PASCAL. As a proponent of humanitarian justice, he set up a model village on his country estate in Ferney, in south-east France, complete with small industries and himself as a paternalistic landlord. He was a prolific letter-writer and he also produced more than twenty plays, a blasphemous epic based on the life of JOAN OF ARC and various philosophical treatises. Today his best-known work is *Candide*, a satirical story of a simpleton who believes in ultimate goodness. Voltaire was a hugely influential figure and, although many of his works were placed on the Index, his views and attitudes were shared by many educated people of his time.

W.F. Bottiglia, *Voltaire's Candide: Analysis of a Classic*, 3rd edn (1964); J.H. Brumfitt, *Voltaire, Historian* (1970); R. Pomeau, *La Religion de Voltaire*, revised edition (1969) [no English translation available]; N. Torrey, *The Spirit of Voltaire*, revised edition (1968).

Von Balthasar, Hans Urs (1905–87)   Theologian. Von Balthasar was born in Lucerne, Switzerland. He was educated in Vienna, Berlin and Zürich and he joined the Jesuit Order. He left the Jesuits in 1950 to form a secular institute and subsequently he directed his own publishing house. Early in his career he wrote a sympathetic study of the theology of Karl BARTH, but he is mainly remembered for his multi-volume study of theological aesthetics (in its English translation) *The Glory of the Lord*. In it he tried to demonstrate how the biblical vision of God's glory, as revealed in the crucified and resurrected JESUS, reflects and goes beyond the traditional Western metaphysical concept of Being.

H. von Balthasar, *Why I am Still a Christian* (1973); D. Ford (ed.), *The Modern Theologians*, revised edition (1997); J. O'Donnell, *Hans Urs Von Balthasar* (1991).

Von Hügel, Friedrich (1852–1925) Ecumenist, Philosopher and Theologian. Von Hügel was born in Florence and was of Austrian-Scottish ancestry. For most of his life he lived in England where he was regarded as an important figure in the Catholic Modernist movement. A personal friend of LOISY and TYRRELL, he was the author of works such as the *Mystical Element in Religion, Eternal Life* and *The Reality of God*. He accepted the findings of biblical criticism and constantly wrestled with the problem of the relationship of Christianity and history. Although his activities were regarded with suspicion by the Roman Catholic hierarchy, he was an influential figure in his time. A prolific letter writer, he was a committed ecumenist and was a founder member of the London Society for the Study of Religion, which brought Jewish and Christian scholars together.

L.F. Barmann, *Baron von Hügel* (1972); M.D. Petre, *Von Hügel and Tyrrell: The Story of a Friendship* (1937).

Vorstius, Conradus (1569–1622) Theologian. Vorstius was born Konrad von der Vorst in Cologne, Germany. He was a student of BEZA in Geneva and he subsequently taught at Steinfurt near Heidelberg. There he was accused of Socinianism, but was cleared of the

charge. After the death of ARMINIUS in 1609, he was invited to take his place in Leyden. Meanwhile Arminius's followers had issued the Remonstrance in an attempt to soften the rigid Calvinism of the Dutch Church. At the same time Vorstius published his *Tractatus Theologicus de Deo, sive de Natura et Attributatis Dei*, which provoked a storm of controversy from the Calvinist Counter-Remonstrants. Even King JAMES I of England felt obliged to draw up a list of its theological mistakes. Vorstius was forced to resign in 1612. He went on to translate works of SOZZINI and was condemned at the Synod of Dort.

A.W. Harrison, *The Beginnings of Arminianism to the Synod of Dort* (1926).

Voysey, Charles (1828–1912) Sect Founder. Voysey was educated at the University of Oxford and he was ordained into the Anglican ministry. After serving in a series of parishes, he was indicted for heresy and he was deprived of his orders in 1871. One of the teachings that aroused suspicion was his denial of the doctrine of eternal punishment (see also Bishop COLENSO). In consequence, Voysey organised his own group in London, known as the Theistic Church. After his death this body split to create the Free Religious Movement.

'Charles Voysey', in *Dictionary of National Biography 1912–1921* (1927).

W

Walburga (*c.* 710–79) Saint. Walburga was a native of England. She helped her kinsman, St BONIFACE, with his German mission and, on the death of her brother St Winnebald, she became Abbess of the double monastery at Hildersheim. Her feast on 1 May, often called Walpurges Night, is inappropriately connected with early summer pagan revels.

F.M. Steele, *The Life of St Walburga* (1921).

Walter of St Victor (late twelfth century) Theologian. Walter was Prior of the Augustinian Canons of St Victor. He is remembered as the author of *Contra Quatuor Labyrinthos Franciae*, which was an attack on the dialectical method of ABELARD, PETER LOMBARD, Peter of Poitiers and GILBERT DE LA PORRÉE.

P. Glorieux, 'Mauvaise action et mauvais travail', *Recherches de Théologie Ancienne et Médiévale*, xxi (1954) [no English translation available].

Walton, Brian (*c.* 1600–61) Bishop and Biblical Scholar. Walton was educated at the University of Cambridge and he was ordained to the Anglican ministry. A supporter of Archbishop LAUD, he was imprisoned by the Commonwealth Government for a short time and, with the Restoration, he became Bishop of Chester in 1660. He is remembered as the editor of the *Biblia Sacra Polyglotta*, which provided versions of the Bible in nine languages. A notable work of scholarship, it has never been superseded.

D.S. Margoliouth, 'Brian Walton', in *Dictionary of National Biography*, Vol. 59 (1899).

Warburton, William (1698–1779) Bishop and Polemicist. Warburton was consecrated Bishop of Gloucester in 1759. He is remembered for his *The Divine Legation of Moses*, in which he argued, against the Deists, that the Law of Moses was of divine origin. His argument was that the doctrine of eternal reward and punishment was essential for human order: there was no mention of the doctrine in the Law of Moses and this was so odd that it must have been of divine inspiration. He also produced *The Doctrine of Grace* directed against the theology of John WESLEY.

A.W. Evans, *Warburton and the Warburtonians* (1932); R.W. Greaves, 'The working of the alliance: A comment on Warburton', in G.V. Bennett and D. Walsh (eds), *Essays in Modern English Church History* (1966).

Ward, Mary (1585–1645) Order Founder. Ward was born in Yorkshire. A Roman Catholic, she joined the Order of Poor Clares at St Omer in 1606. Three years later she started her own order, the Institute of English Ladies (the Institute of the Blessed Virgin Mary), which was not enclosed and which was to be dedicated to education. Although she opened several houses, the order was suppressed by Pope PIUS V who insisted that all female orders should be enclosed. For a time she was imprisoned in a Poor Clares' convent in Munich. Eventually Pope URBAN VIII allowed the founding of a house on slightly different lines, but the new order was not fully approved until 1703.

M. Oliver, *Mary Ward* (1960); M. Philip, *Companions of Mary Ward* (1939).

Warfield, Benjamin Breckinridge (1851–1921) Theologian. Warfield was born in Kentucky and was educated at Princeton and in Leipzig. He became a Presbyterian minister and he subsequently taught at Pittsburgh, before returning to Princeton Theological Seminary in 1887. There he succeeded the son of Charles HODGE. He wrote a number of books including *The Lord of Glory*, *The Plan of Salvation* and *Counterfeit Miracles*. A man of great learning, he held rigidly to the doctrine of the verbal inerrancy of Scripture and he wrote constantly against those who accepted the findings of biblical criticism. His works enjoyed a wide circulation.

H.T. Kerr, *Sons of the Prophets* (1963).

Watts, Isaac (1674–1748) Hymn Writer. Watts was born in Southampton, of a non-conforming family. He was educated at the Dissenting Academy at Stoke Newington and he became the pastor of an independent congregation in London. Because of bad health he retired early and, later in life, his views seem to have veered towards Unitarianism. Today he is remembered for his hymns, many of which are still sung; these include 'When I survey the wondrous cross' and 'Jesus shall reign where'er the sun'.

H. Escott, *Isaac Watts Hymnographer* (1962); B.L. Manning, *The Hymns of Wesley and Watts* (1942).

Weatherhead, Leslie Dixon (1893–1975) Devotional Writer and Broadcaster. Weatherhead was the minister of the City Temple, London. For forty years, from the 1930s to the 1970s, he was well known in Britain as a religious broadcaster and also as a pastoral counsellor. The author of several books, he used the findings of the new science of psychiatry to throw light on his clients' problems. For much of his career he wrote in the liberal tradition, but after the Second World War and with the changes that took place in the 1950s and 1960s, his

work also reflected the secularisation and doubt that was gripping late twentieth-century society.

L. Weatherhead, *The Christian Agnostic* (1965).

Weber, Karl Emil Maximilian [Max] (1864–1920) Sociologist and Historian. Weber was born in Erfurt, Germany, and for much of his career he taught political economy at the Universities of Freiburg and Heidelberg. A friend of Ernst TROELTSCH, he is primarily remembered for his argument that Calvinist beliefs were an important element in the growth of capitalism. This he expressed in his *Protestant Ethic and the Spirit of Capitalism* (English title). He also classified different types of religious leaders and it was he who coined the term 'charismatic'.

A. Giddens, *Politics and Sociology in the Thought of Max Weber* (1972); B. Turner, *Max Weber: From History to Modernity* (1992); S. Whimster and S. Cash (eds), *Max Weber, Rationality and Modernity* (1987).

Weil, Simone (1909–43) Philosopher. Weil was born in Paris to a non-religious Jewish family. After she graduated from university, she served on the republican side in the Spanish Civil War and she also worked as a manual worker in an attempt to identify with the labouring classes. With the arrival of the Nazis in France, she and her family escaped to the United States, but Weil herself went to England where she worked for the Free French. She insisted on eating no more than the standard ration in occupied France and she died at the age of thirty-four of tuberculosis and starvation. Passionately engaged in religion, she was interested in Roman Catholicism, but was never baptised. Her book *Waiting on God* has become a modern classic.

J.P. Little, *Simone Weil: Waiting on Truth* (1988); D. MacLellan, *Simone Weil: Utopian Pessimist* (1990); P. Winch, *Simone Weil: 'The Just Balance'* (1989).

Weiss, Johannes (1863–1914) Biblical Theologian. Weiss was the son of

Bernhard Weiss, the conservative German New Testament critic. He was educated at the Universities of Marburg, Berlin, Göttingen and Breslau. Subsequently he taught at Göttingen, Marburg and Heidelberg. He maintained that JESUS's mission should be understood in eschatological terms, that it was a proclamation of the immanence of the Kingdom of God and his own Messiahship. Weiss's best-known work was *Die Predigt Jesu vom Reiche Gottes*. His work, together with that of SCHWEITZER and WREDE, is considered to mark the end of the liberal interpretation of the Christian message, commonly characterised as 'the fatherhood of God and the brotherhood of Man'. Weiss also produced *Die Religion in Geschichte und Gegenwart*, which outlined the principles of biblical form criticism and *Das Urchristentum*, a history of early Christianity. BULTMANN was one of his students.

F.C. Burkitt, 'Johannes Weiss: In Memoriam', *Harvard Theological Review*, viii (1915); H. Palmer, *The Logic of Gospel Criticism* (1968).

Wellhausen, Julius (1844–1918) Biblical Scholar. Wellhausen was born in Hamelin, Germany, and was educated in Göttingen. Subsequently he taught in Halle, Marburg and Göttingen. He is primarily remembered for his *Prolegomena zur Geschichte Israels* in which he outlined the theory that the Pentateuch, rather than being written by Moses, was the product of several earlier sources. This is generally known as the GRAF–Wellhausen hypothesis and it completely transformed Old Testament scholarship. Wellhausen himself has been described as the DARWIN of biblical studies.

R.E. Clements, *A Century of Old Testament Study* (1976); I. Engnell, 'The Pentateuch', in *Critical Essays on the Old Testament* (1970).

Wenceslas (*c*. 907–29) Monarch, Saint and Martyr. Wenceslas was the son of Duke Wratislaw of Bohemia and he was a grandson of St Ludmila. He took over the government in *c*. 922, but was murdered by his brother in 929. His death was soon regarded as martyrdom; he became the patron saint of Bohemia and his crown has become the symbol of Czech independence. He is well known in the English-speaking world through J.M. NEALE's Christmas hymn 'Good King Wenceslas'.

C. Parrott, 'St Wenceslas of Bohemia', *History Today*, xvi (1966).

Wesley, Charles (1707–88) Hymn Writer. Wesley was the eighteenth child of the Reverend Samuel Wesley, Rector of Epworth, England, and he was the brother of John WESLEY. He was educated at the University of Oxford and, after ordination to the Anglican ministry, he spent time in the American colonies. He had a conversion experience in 1738 and, influenced by the Moravians, he became an itinerant preacher in 1739. He finally settled in London. Today he is primarily remembered as a hymn-writer. Among his many compositions were 'Hark, the herald angels sing', 'Love divine, all loves excelling' and 'Lo! He comes with clouds descending', all of which are still frequently sung. He was the grandfather of the composer Samuel Sebastian Wesley (1810–76).

F. Baker, *Charles Wesley's Verse: An Introduction* (1964); F.C. Gill, *Charles Wesley* (1964); B.L. Manning, *The Hymns of Wesley and Watts* (1942).

Wesley, John (1703–91) Denomination Founder. Wesley was the fifteenth child of the Rector of Epworth, in Humberside, England. He was educated at the University of Oxford and he was ordained to the Church of England ministry. He took over the leadership of the 'Holy Club' at Oxford, an earnest society dedicated to spiritual growth founded by his brother Charles WESLEY and George WHITEFIELD. In 1735 he went with Charles and Whitefield to the American colonies to convert the Indians, but the project was not a success and he returned to England in 1738. That same year he underwent a conversion experience. After spending time with the Moravians and Count ZINZENDORF, he began his career 'to reform the nation and to spread scriptural holiness over the land'. The rest of his life was dedicated to preaching – frequently out of doors at mass meetings. He covered an average of eight thousand miles a year on horseback. In 1744 he held a conference of lay preachers which was to become the annual Methodist Conference. He himself remained within the Church of England but in 1784 he ordained without episcopal authority Thomas COKE to work for the new Methodist organisation in America. His organisation was initially a private society, but in 1784 he formally established 'the Conference of the People called Methodists' which included all preachers. Then, in 1787, Methodist Chapels were registered as Dissenting Meeting Houses. Today there are Methodist Churches throughout the world, although there have been several subsequent splits in the movement.

W.R. Cannon, *The Theology of John Wesley* (1946); R.E. Davies, *Methodism* (1963); A.C. Outler (ed.), *John Wesley* (1964); H.D. Rack, *Reasonable Enthusiast: John Wesley and the Rise of Methodism* (1989); A.S. Wood, *The Burning Heart* (1967).

Westcott, Brooke Foss (1825–1901) Theologian and Bishop. Westcott was born in Birmingham, England, and he was educated at the University of Cambridge. In 1870 he was appointed Regius Professor of Divinity and he is remembered as one of a triumvirate of Cambridge biblical scholars, the others being LIGHTFOOT and HORT. Between them they did much to establish the best Greek text of the New Testament. Westcott was also involved in founding the Cambridge Clergy Training School (which came to be called Westcott House). In 1890 he was consecrated Bishop of Durham.

H. Chadwick, *The Vindication of Christianity in Westcott's Theology* (1961); O. Chadwick, *Westcott and the University* (1963); D.O. Fuller, *True or False? The Westcott–Hort Textual Theory Examined* (1973).

Weston, Frank (1871–1924) Missionary and Bishop. Weston was educated at the University of Oxford. After ordination he worked in several slum parishes and in 1901 he was sent as a missionary to East Africa. In 1908 he was consecrated Bishop of Zanzibar. He is primarily remembered for his opposition to the unification of Protestant Churches in East Africa and for his disapproval of the appointment of the liberal B.L. STREETER as a Canon of Hertford. In both cases he went so far as to demand the arraignment of his episcopal opponents for heresy. Despite his excesses he was a selfless and devoted ecclesiastic.

H.M Smith, *Frank, Bishop of Zanzibar* (1926).

White, Ellen Gould (1827–1915) Sect Founder. White was born Ellen Gould in Maine, in the United States of America, of a Methodist family. In the 1840s they joined William MILLER's new Adventist sect. At the age of nineteen she married Elder James White and she herself became a prominent Adventist leader. She and her husband moved to Battle Creek, Michigan, which became the new Church's headquarters. She was a prolific writer and a charismatic personality and, with Miller, she must be regarded as a founder of the Seventh Day Adventist Church. Members live a strictly temperate life; alcohol and tobacco are forbidden and they pay tithes on their income. The Sabbath is celebrated on Saturday rather than Sunday and they practise baptism by total immersion. The movement has spread around the world.

E.E. Howell, *Movement of Destiny* (1971); F.D.N. Nicol, *The Midnight Cry* (1944).

Whitefield, George (1714–70) Preacher. Whitefield was born of a poor family in Gloucester. He was educated at the University of Oxford where he met the WESLEY brothers. He was ordained to the Anglican ministry in 1736 and he shared in the Wesleys' mission to America. On his return, he embarked on lengthy evangelistic tours and his travels included seven journeys to America where he finally died. As time went on differences emerged with the Wesleys – Whitefield's theology of salvation following CALVIN while the Wesleys followed ARMINIUS. So Whitefield became part of the Countess of Huntingdon's (HASTINGS) Connexion and he opened several meeting houses. He is remembered as the most significant orator of the Methodist revival. It was said that 'No preacher has ever retained his hold on his hearers so entirely as he did for thirty-four years'.

A.A. Dallimore, *George Whitefield*, 2 vols (1970, 1980); F. Lambert, *Pedlar in Divinity* (1994).

Whitehead, Alfred North (1861–1947) Philosopher. Whitehead taught philosophy and mathmatics at the Universities of Cambridge and London, and in 1924 he was appointed to a Chair at Harvard. He is remembered for his attempt at integrating science and religion by arguing that God contains within his nature all the occurrences within the universe, the whole being a dynamic forward process. Many theologians were influenced by him, including Charles HARTSHORNE and a whole school of 'process theology' has emerged. Among his books were *Process and Reality* and *Religion in the Making*.

J.B. Cobb, *A Christian Natural Theology based on the Thought of Alfred North Whitehead* (1966); G. Kline (ed.), *Alfred North Whitehead: Essays on his Philosophy* (1963); N. Pittenger, *God in Process* (1967).

Whitgift, John (*c.* 1530–1604) Archbishop. Whitgift was educated at the University of Cambridge. He became Lady Margaret Professsor of Divinity in 1563, Regius Professor in 1567, Dean of Lincoln in 1571, Bishop of Worcester in 1577 and Archbishop of Canterbury, succeeding Edmund GRINDAL, in 1583. He had been a determined opponent of the extreme Puritanism of Thomas CARTWRIGHT, which had brought him into favour with Queen ELIZABETH I. As Archbishop, he continued to suppress Puritanism, dealing severely with the authors of the MARPRELATE Tracts. He himself was the author of the strongly episcopal Six Articles of 1583 and the Calvinist Articles of 1595, and he is remembered as an important influence in the establishment of the Elizabethan Church.

V.J.K. Brook, *Whitgift and the English Church* (1957); P. Lake, *Anglicans and Puritans? Presbyterianism and the English Conformist Thought from Whitgift to Hooker* (1988).

Wichern, Johann Heinrich (1808–81) Philanthropist. Wichern was born in Hamburg, Germany, and he was educated in Göttingen and Berlin, where he came under the influence of SCHLEIERMACHER. In 1833 he founded the Rauhes Haus, an organisation to help poor children in Hamburg. The institution grew and in 1844 he started the monthly periodical *Die Fliegenden Blätter aus dem Rauhen Haus* which publicised his activities. Then in 1848 he founded the Innere Mission, a single agency which embraced all voluntary charitable work within the German Protestant Churches. Later he became involved in prison reform. The Innere Mission has continued its work and in the Second World War it took a stand against the Nazi policy of euthanasia.

'Innere Mission', in F.L. Cross (ed.), *The Oxford Dictionary of the Christian Church*, 2nd edn (1974); K.S. Latourette, *Christianity in a Revolutionary Age*, Vol. 2 (1960).

Wilberforce, Samuel (1805–73) Bishop. Wilberforce was a son of William

WILBERFORCE. He had a successful career in the Church of England, becoming chaplain to Prince Albert in 1840, Dean of Westminster in 1845, Bishop of Oxford in 1845 and Bishop of Winchester in 1869. He was a pioneer in the modern style of episcopacy and the pastoral organisation of his diocese was widely imitated. He also was a founder of Cuddesdon Theological College for the training of clergy. He is remembered for his famous debate with the scientist Thomas HUXLEY on the vexed question of evolution.

S. Meacham, *Lord Bishop: The Life of Samuel Wilberforce* (1970); D. Newsome, *The Parting of Friends* (1966).

Wilberforce, William (1759–1833) Philanthropist. Wilberforce was born in Hull, England, and he was educated at the University of Cambridge. In 1780 he was elected a Member of Parliament. Soon afterwards he was converted to a strict evangelical style of living and he became associated with the Clapham Sect – a group which tried to promote evangelical ideals in public life. He is mainly remembered for his determined efforts to abolish the slave trade. A close friend of both the Prime Minister, William Pitt, and the hymn-writer John NEWTON, he used his considerable oratorical powers to gain his end. The Abolition Bill finally became law in 1807 and the final Emancipation Act, freeing all slaves in the British Empire, was achieved just before his death. Among other activities, he helped found the Church Missionary Society and the British and Foreign Bible Society; he contributed to the charities of Hannah MORE and he was the author of the much read *Practical View of the Prevailing Religious System of Professed Christians*. Of his sons, Samuel WILBERFORCE became an Anglican Bishop, Robert was prominent in the Oxford Movement, but eventually became a Roman Catholic, and Henry also converted to Catholicism and for several

years was editor of the *Catholic Standard*.

R.T. Anstey, *The Atlantic Slave Trade and British Abolition* (1975); R. Coupland, *Wilberforce*, 2nd edn (1945); R. Furneaux, *William Wilberforce* (1974).

Wilfrid (634–709) Saint and Bishop. Although educated at the Celtic monastery of Lindisfarne, Northumbria, Wilfrid studied Roman practices and he spent three years in Lyons. He was elected Abbot of Ripon where he introduced the Rule of St BENEDICT and at the Synod of Whitby in 664 he strongly supported the victorious Roman party. Subsequently he was consecrated Bishop of York in France, but, when he arrived at the see, he found CHAD already in residence. Although Archbishop THEODORE found for Wilfrid, Theodore and Wilfrid soon quarrelled and Wilfrid was imprisoned and then spent time as a missionary in Sussex. He was reinstated in 686, but then came into conflict with King Aldfrith. In 703 Archbishop Brihtwold insisted that he should resign from York and retire to his monastery. Wilfrid appealed to Rome who found in his favour, but none the less he did hand over the diocese to John of Beverley. Wilfrid is remembered as an important figure in leading the Church in England to obedience to Rome.

E.S. Duckett, *Anglo-Saxon Saints and Scholars* (1948); A. Warin, *Wilfrid: The Biography of an Outstanding Personality in Church and State* (1992).

William of Champeaux (*c.* 1070–1121) Theologian, Order Founder and Bishop. William was a student of ANSELM OF LAON and possibly ROSCELLINUS. He taught in Paris where he was reckoned the most famous teacher of his day. None the less he was mocked by ABELARD for his determined conviction that abstract concepts have a real existence apart from their individual examples. Later he seems to have modified his position. In 1113 he founded the Victorines, the Canons-Regular of the Abbey of St Victor. He was consecrated Bishop of Chalons in the same year.

The Catholic University of America, *New Catholic Encyclopaedia* (1967).

William of Conches (*c.* 1080–*c.* 1154) Philosopher. William was a student of BERNARD OF CHARTRES and he also taught at the Cathedral School at Chartres, France. However, he was accused of assimilating the ideas of ABELARD by WILLIAM OF ST THIERRY and he withdrew from public life to become the tutor of the future King HENRY II of England. He is remembered for his *Philosophia Mundi* and his *Dragmaticon* which reveal strong Platonic tendencies.

The Catholic University of America, *New Catholic Encyclopaedia* (1967).

William of Ockham (*c.* 1285–1347) Philosopher and Polemicist. William was born in Surrey. A member of the Franciscan Order, he studied and taught at the University of Oxford. In 1323 he was summoned to Avignon to answer charges of heresy before Pope JOHN XXII and five years later he was compelled to flee from the Papal Court. From then on he lived under the protection of Louis of Bavaria and was probably never reconciled to the Church. He was the author of a variety of theological texts and several polemics against the Papacy. Today he is remembered for 'Ockham's razor' – the principle of economy that demands that entities should not be posited unnecessarily. He also insisted that universals have no separate existence and there are only individual examples in reality. He believed that knowledge can only be derived from experience and therefore he argued that the existence of God is a matter of faith and cannot be proved from first principles. Thus he undermined the whole basis of scholasticism and his concentration on individual examples rather than universal ideas

paved the way for modern scientific investigation.

M.M. Adams, *William Ockham*, 2 vols (1987); M.H. Carre, *Realists and Nominalists* (1946).

William of Paris [or Auvergne] (*c.* 1180–1249) Bishop and Theologian. William was Bishop of Paris from 1228 and he was an influential figure at the court of King LOUIS IX. He is mainly remembered for his encyclopaedic *Magisterium Divinale* which covered topics such as the Trinity, the soul, atonement, faith and the sacraments. His system made use of both neo-Platonic and Aristotelian ideas and he was among the first to recognise the important philosophical distinction between essence and existence.

S. Marrone, *William of Auvergne and Robert Grosseteste: New Ideas of Truth in the Early Thirteenth Century* (1983).

William of St Thierry (*c.* 1085–1148) Theologian and Mystic. William was born in Liège, France; he joined the Benedictine Order and became Abbot of St Thierry in *c.* 1120. He was a close friend of St BERNARD OF CLAIRVAUX and in 1135 he resigned his position to join the contemplative Cistercians in Signy. He was the author of several mystical works as well as careful theological refutations of the ideas of ABELARD and WILLIAM OF CONCHES. His best-known writing was his *Epistola ad Fratres de Monte Dei de Vita Solitaria*, which was a summary of his religious experience and ideas. This has also been attributed to Bernard.

D.N. Bell, *The Image and Likeness: The Augustinian Spirituality of William of St Thierry* (1984); B. McGinn, *The Growth of Mysticism* (1996).

William of Wykeham (1324–1404) Bishop and Educator. William was born in Wickham in Hampshire. He had an important public career, becoming Bishop of Winchester in 1366 and Chancellor of England in 1367. Although he was deprived of the Chancellorship in

1371 and was accused before Parliament of misconduct, he was restored to favour in 1377 and became Chancellor again in 1389. He is remembered as a great patron of education. He founded New College in the University of Oxford which opened in 1386 and a school for poor scholars in Winchester. This was the first independent foundation of its kind and was the model for several others. Its motto, remembered and perhaps acted upon, is 'Manners makyth man'.

W.G. Hayter, *William of Wykeham* (1970).

Williams, Charles Walter Stansby (1886–1945) Poet, Novelist and Theological Writer. Williams was born in London and he was educated at the University there. He is remembered for his religious writings. He described his novels as 'metaphysical thrillers'; they include *War in Heaven* and *Descent into Hell*. He wrote the play *Thomas Cranmer of Canterbury* for the Canterbury festival; his non-fiction included *The Descent of the Dove*, a history of the activity of the Holy Spirit, and among his poetry was *Taliessin through Logres*, which was based on the Arthurian legend. He was influenced by the mystical writings of Evelyn UNDERHILL and, like C.S. LEWIS, Dorothy SAYERS and T.S. ELIOT, he did much to make Christianity palatable to educated twentieth-century sensibility.

G. Cavaliero, *Charles Williams: Poet of Theology* (1983); A.M. Hadfield, *An Introduction to Charles Williams* (1959); M. McD. Shideler, *The Theology of Romantic Love* (1962).

Williams, George (1821–1905) Association Founder. Williams was born in Dulverton, Somerset, and he earned his living as a draper. He is remembered as the founder of the Young Men's Christian Association (YMCA) which grew out of his prayer meetings in London. His idea was to win young men to the Christian way of life by encouraging them to share wholesome leisure activities. Today there are YMCA hostels and leisure centres throughout the world and the organisation has done extensive work among prisoners-of-war as well as providing a variety of leadership courses. There is a parallel organisation for women, the YWCA. Williams was knighted in recognition of his work.

C. Binfield, *George Williams and the YMCA* (1973); J.E.H. Williams, *The Life of Sir George Williams* (1906).

Williams, John (1796–1839) Missionary. Williams was born in London. In 1817 he was sent by the London Missionary Society to Polynesia. He worked diligently and by 1834 it was said that no significant island within two thousand miles of Tahiti had not been visited. He publicised his efforts in a British lecture tour in 1838 and by his *Narrative of Missionary Enterprises in the South Sea Islands*. On his return he was murdered and eaten by natives of Erromanga, in retaliation for earlier white cruelty. He was widely mourned and his death aroused a burst of enthusiasm for missions.

G. Daws, *A Dream of Islands* (1980); B. Mathews, *John Williams* (1947).

Willibrord (658–739) Missionary, Saint and Archbishop. Willibrord was a native of Northumbria and he was a student at WILFRID's monastery in Ripon. In 690 he led a missionary expedition to Frisia and in 695 he was consecrated Archbishop of the area. He was granted land to build a cathedral in Utrecht and he founded the famous monastery at Echternach. Although his work recieved a setback with the military success of the North Frisians led by the pagan Radbod, he was helped by St BONIFACE and by the year of his death, most of South Frisia had been Christianised.

A. Grieve, *Willibrord, Missionary in the Netherlands* (1923); W. Levison, 'St Willibrord and his place in history', *Durham University Journal*, xxxii (1939–40).

Winifred [Gwenfrewi] (d. *c.* 650) Saint. According to legend, Winifred was a beautiful young woman who was courted by Prince Caradon of Hawarden. She refused his advances and, in his anger, he killed her. She was miraculously restored to life by her uncle St BEUNO and she founded the monastery at Holywell, Clwd, Wales. This became a place of pilgrimage and healing. Winifred is the patron saint of North Wales.

P. Metcalf, *Life of St Winifred*, edited by H. Thurston (1917).

Wiseman, Nicholas Patrick Stephen (1802–65) Cardinal and Archbishop. Wiseman was of Anglo-Irish descent and between 1828 and 1840 he was Rector of the English College in Rome. He returned to England as Coadjutor of the Vicar Apostolic of the Midland District. In 1850, amid demonstrations of hostility, Pope PIUS IX restored the Roman Catholic hierarchy in England with Wiseman as Cardinal Archbishop of Westminster. Even the Prime Minister, Lord John Russell, regretted what he described as 'papal aggression'. Wiseman was ultramontane by conviction; he established branches of religious orders and he did much to organise a pastoral ministry for the hordes of Irish immigrants seeking work in England. Among his writings was the popular novel *Fabiola*.

B. Fothergill, *Cardinal Wiseman* (1963).

Wittgenstein, Ludwig Josef Johann (1889–1951) Philosopher. Wittgenstein was born in Vienna, Austria, and he was a student of engineering at the Universities of Berlin and Manchester. He served in the Austrian army in the First World War and he eventually settled in England. The only book which appeared in his lifetime was the *Tractatus Logico Philosophicus*,

which attempted to define the limits of language and made the famous statement: 'Whereof one cannot speak, thereon one must remain silent'. In 1939 he was appointed Professor of Philosophy at the University of Cambridge where he became a hugely influential figure. After his death, his *Philosophical Investigations* was published. Although he had no personal connection with the Christian Church, many philosophical theologians make use of Wittgenstein's notion of 'language games' in attempting to explain the nature and rules of religious discourse.

J.W. Cook, *Wittgenstein's Metaphysics* (1994); N. Malcolm, *Wittgenstein: A Religious Point of View* (1993); S. Teghrarian (ed.), *Wittgenstein and Contemporary Philosophy* (1994); F. Kerr, *Theology After Wittgenstein* (1986).

Wolsey, Thomas (*c.* 1474–1530) Cardinal and Politician. Wolsey was born in Ipswich and he was educated at the University of Oxford. He enjoyed a meteoric rise in both the Church and the State. He became chaplain to King Henry VII in 1507, a Privy Counsellor to King HENRY VIII in 1511, Bishop of Lincoln and Archbishop of York in 1514 and a Cardinal and Chancellor of England in 1515. He even had ambitions to be elected Pope and at one stage this did not seem an impossibility. He enjoyed the King's trust and favour until he proved unable to obtain the dispensation necessary to dissolve the royal marriage. Henry's ruthlessness proved greater even than his own. In 1529 he was forced to resign the Chancellorship and give up his property (which included the newly built palace of Hampton Court) and he was only spared from answering a charge of high treason by dying on the road to London. Wolsey is remembered for successfully establishing Tudor absolutism, for effectively holding the balance of power between France and the Holy Roman Empire and as the founder of Christ Church College, Oxford.

G.R. Elton, *The Tudor Revoluton in Government* (1953); S.J. Gunn and P.G. Lindley, *Cardinal Wolsey and the Church* (1991); J.J. Scarisbrick, *Henry VIII* (1968).

Woodard, Nathaniel (1811–91) Educator. Woodard was born in Essex and he was educated at the University of Oxford. He is remembered as the founder of a series of schools. He outlined his plans in his *Plea for the Middle Classes* and among his foundations were Lancing, Hurstpierpoint and Denstone. Although educational ideas have changed since the mid nineteenth century, these schools still reflect a strong High Church ethos.

B. Heeney, *Mission to the Middle Classes: The Woodard Schools 1848–1891* (1969); K.E. Kirk, *The Story of the Woodard Schools* (1937).

Woodbine Willy see **Studdert Kennedy, Geoffrey Anketell**

Wrede, William (1859–1906) Biblical Scholar. Wrede taught New Testament at the University of Breslau, Germany, and was a prominent member of the History of Religions school. He wrote several important books including *Das Messiasgeheimnis im den Evangelien* in which he argued that MARK's Gospel was not a straightforward historical narrative, but carried a strong theological agenda and *Paulus* in which he maintained that PAUL was the real founder of Christian doctrine. His works have been highly influential on later New Testament scholarship.

R. Morgan, *The Nature of New Testament Theology: The Contribution of William Wrede and Adolf Schlatter* (1973).

Wren, Christopher (1632–1723) Architect and Scientist. Wren was the son of a clergyman and he was educated at the University of Oxford. He became Professor of Astronomy at the university as well as a founder member of the Royal Society. Today, however, he is remembered as an architect. After the Great Fire

of London in 1666, he was commissioned to undertake much of the rebuilding. Altogether he designed fifty-two churches, thirty-six company halls and several other public buildings. His greatest achievement was his plan for the magnificent Cathedral of St Paul's which was built under his supervision. This still stands today and is generally perceived as the heart of the City of London.

K. Downes, *Christopher Wren* (1971); H.F. Hutchinson, *Sir Christopher Wren: A Biography* (1976); P. Waterhouse et al., *Sir Christopher Wren* (1923).

Wulfstan (d. 1023) Archbishop and Political Philosopher. Wulfstan was elected Bishop of London in 996 and Archbishop of York in 1002. A correspondent of AELFRIC, he was an important royal counsellor. He is remembered as the author of many homilies as well as the *Institutes of Polity, Civil and Ecclesiastical*, which discussed the duties of the various classes in society. He is not to be confused with St Wulfstan (*c.* 1009–95), a friend of LANFRANC who, as Bishop of Worcester, did much to suppress the slave trade between England and Ireland.

J.W. Lamb, *Saint Wulfstan, Prelate and Patriot* (1933); E. Mason, *Saint Wulfstan of Worcester* (1990).

Wycliffe, John (*c.* 1330–84) Theologian and Polemicist. Wycliffe was probably born in Yorkshire and he was educated at the University of Oxford. He was a highly influential figure in the university and became an advisor to John of Gaunt, the Regent of England. He openly criticised the wealth of the Church and by 1377 he was being condemned by the ecclesiastical establishment. Later he was to develop his own doctrine of the Eucharist which denied transubstantiation. He was the author of a *Summa Theologica* and innumerable pamphlets, and he encouraged his followers to make an English translation of JEROME's Vulgate. By 1381 he was condemned by the university and, after Wat Tyler and John BALL's Peasants' Revolt, for which he was partially blamed, he retired from public life. Forty-four years after his death, his body was exhumed and burnt as a heretic. Wycliffe has been described as the 'Morning Star of the Reformation'. He insisted that Scripture was the ultimate guide to faith and he was critical of current ecclesiastical abuses. His followers were known as Lollards, but they were not perceived as a separate party until after Wycliffe's death. They were successfully suppressed by the Parliamentary statute of *De Heretico Cumburendo* which drove the movement underground. However, Wycliffe's disciples took their ideas abroad and, through the activities of Jan HUS, they were very influential in Bohemia.

J.H. Dahmus, *The Prosecution of John Wycliffe* (1952); L.J. Daly, *The Political Theory of John Wyclif* (1962); K.B. McFarlane, *John Wycliffe and the Beginning of English Non-Conformity* (1952); J. Stacey, *Wyclif and Reform* (1964).

X

Ximénez de Cisneros, Francisco (1436–1517)   Cardinal and Statesman. Ximénez was born in Torrelaguna, Castile, and he studied in Alcalá, Salamanca and Rome. He joined the order of Observantine Friars in Toledo and became well known for his ascetic mode of living. In 1492 he became the Confessor of Queen ISABELLA and was an important influence at court. In 1494 he was elected Provincial of the Spanish Franciscans and in 1495 he was consecrated Archbishop of Toledo. Throughout he continued to lead an austere life. He made every attempt to convert the Muslims of Granada to Christianity; he reformed the Spanish Franciscans; he founded the University of Alcalá and he sponsored the *Complutensian Polyglot*, the first polyglot edition of the whole Bible. He continued to play an active role in political life even after Queen Isabella had died and he was Regent in Castile after King FERDINAND's death in 1516 and during the minority of CHARLES V. He was a significant figure in the history of Spain. When he died, it was suspected that he had been poisoned.

R. Merton, *Cardinal Ximénez and the Making of Spain* (1934); W. Starkie, *Grand Inquisitor* (1940).

Y

Yonge, Charlotte Mary (1823–1901) Novelist. Yonge was born and lived throughout her life in a village near Winchester. John KEBLE was her parish priest and, under his influence, she produced a series of novels recommending the High Anglican way of life. These include *The Heir of Redclyffe* (which is still read today), *The Daisy Chain* and *Pillars of the House*. She was also the editor of *The Monthly Packet*, an improving periodical for young women. She taught Sunday School for seventy-one years and is a remarkable example of an influential figure who led a very private and circumscribed life.

G. Battiscombe et al., *A Chaplet for Charlotte Yonge* (1965); A.C. Percival, *A Victorian Best Seller: The World of Charlotte M. Yonge* (1947).

Young, Brigham (1801–77) Sect Founder. Young was born in Whitingham, Vermont, in the United States of America. He became a follower of Joseph SMITH, the founder of the Church of Jesus Christ of the Latter Day Saints (the Mormons) in 1832. In 1835 he was raised to the rank of Apostle and in 1838 he became Chief of the Twelve Apostles. After Smith's death in 1844, he led the Mormons from Independence, Missouri, to Nauvoo, Illinois, and from there they trekked over the Rocky Mountains to establish themselves finally in Salt Lake City, Utah. Young was a brilliant organiser; he became Governor of the Utah territory in 1850 and the splendid temple and city owe much to his dedication and planning.

K.J. Hansen, *Mormonism and the American Experience* (1981); T.F. O'Dea, *The Mormons* (1957).

Z

Zabarella, Francisco (1360–1417)
Cardinal and Lawyer. Zabarella taught
Canon Law at Florence and Padua. He
first came to public notice when he was
invited by the Pope to participate in the
Council of Pisa in 1409 in an attempt to
end the Great Schism. He was appointed
a Cardinal by Antipope JOHN XXIII. He
is remembered for his *De Schismate*,
which put forward the theory that an
ecumenical council was the supreme
source of authority in the Church. This
was eventually put on the Index, as
undermining papal power. He worked
tirelessly at the Council of Constance
and, although he died before its end, his
was an important voice in the final election of Pope MARTIN V.

B. Tierney, *Foundation of the Conciliar Theory*
(1955).

Zacchaeus (first century)   Disciple. Zacchaeus was a tax collector from Jericho,
a member of a group notorious for their
dishonesty. In his desire to see JESUS, he
climbed a tree. Jesus called him down
and caused a scandal by going to stay at
his house. As a result of this encounter,
Zacchaeus promised henceforth to lead a
moral life. This incident is recorded in
the Gospel of LUKE and illustrates the
continuous possibility of repentance and
a new life.

Luke, Chapter 19.

Zeno (*c.* 450–91)   Monarch. Zeno was
Emperor of the East from 474. He did
not achieve many successes, but he is remembered for his 'Henoticon', which
was an attempt to find a compromise between the orthodox and the Monophysites. Since it did not define the number of natures in JESUS, it was regarded
as too great a concession to the Monophysites and it was never accepted by the
Western Church.

W.H.C. Frend, *The Rise of the Monophysite
Movement* (1972).

Zinzendorf, Nikolaus Ludwig, Graf von
(1700–60)   Bishop,   Ecumenist   and
Order Founder. Zinzendorf was born of
an aristocratic family in Dresden, Germany. After serving in a government post
in Saxony, he resigned his position in
1727 to concentrate his energies on the
Herrnhuter, a community of Moravian
Brethren, whom he invited to settle on
his estate. His activities were regarded
with suspicion by the Lutheran establishment, his beliefs were formally
examined in 1734 and he was exiled from
Saxony in 1736. The following year he
received episcopal ordination in the
Moravian Church. He spent the next few
years founding Moravian communities in
Europe and America and he spent his last
years in Herrnhut. His aim had been to
create a Church based on an emotional
experience of religion, which was ecumenical and missionary in outlook.
Although he failed to incorporate the
Lutherans, he was profoundly influential
on important figures such as SCHLEIER-
MACHER and the WESLEY brothers.
Herrnhut has since become the headquarters of the German Moravian Church.

J.E. Hutton, 'The Moravian contribution to the
evangelical revival in England 1742–1755', in T.F.
Tout and J. Tait (eds), *Historical Essays by Members of the Owen College, Manchester* (1902); E.

Langton, *A History of the Moravian Church* (1956); A.J. Lewis, *Zinzendorf, the Ecumenical Pioneer* (1962).

Zita (1218-72)   Saint. Zita was a serving maid in the Fatinelli household of Lucca, Italy, from the age of twelve until her death. Initially she had a very hard life, but gradually, by her devotion, she won the respect of her employers. Many stories were told of miraculous occurrences surrounding her. She was quickly the subject of a popular cult which spread throughout Europe. She is the patron saint of domestic servants and is a splendid illustration of the virtues and rewards of humility.

D.H. Farmer (ed.), *The Oxford Dictionary of Saints*, 3rd edn (1992).

Zizka, John (d. 1424)   Sect Founder. Zizka was the leader of the Taborites, the most radical of the followers of Jan HUS. The group was based in South Bohemia and they were fundamentalist in their interpretation of the Bible. Not only did they reject transubstantiation and the sacramental priesthood, they were convinced that JESUS would soon return and they agitated for social and economic reform. Zizka himself was a brilliant soldier and his army defeated the Imperial troops. However, the group disintegrated after his death; the less radical rejoined the Roman Catholic Church while the remainder were crushed in battle in 1434.

F.C. Heymann, *John Zizka and the Hussite Revolu-*

tion (1955); J. Macek, *The Hussite Movement in Bohemia* (1965).

Zwingli, Ulrich (1484–1531)   Theologian and Reformer. Zwingli was born in Wildhaus, Switzerland, and he was educated at Berne, Vienna and Basle. He was ordained to the Catholic priesthood in 1506 and he served as a parish priest and as an army chaplain. In 1518 he moved to Zürich which became his headquarters. Strongly influenced by ERASMUS, he came to the opinion that Scripture was the sole source of truth and he rejected the authority of the Papacy. The citizens of Zürich fully supported his stand. The Church was declared independent of episcopal authority; the Mass was abolished and images were removed from churches. By 1524, Zwingli was teaching that the Eucharist was a purely symbolic act and that no change in the elements took place. Over this issue, he clashed with LUTHER and the matter was not resolved at the Colloquy of Marburg in 1529. However, he was also antipathetic towards the Anabaptists. His teachings spread throughout Switzerland and caused great dissension. War broke out between the Zwinglian and the Roman Catholic cantons in 1531 and Zwingli himself was killed in a skirmish at Cappel. Zwingli's teaching on the Eucharist is generally regarded as the extreme Protestant position.

R.C. Walton, *Zwingli's Theocracy* (1967); W.P. Stephens, *Zwingli: An Introduction to his Thought* (1992).

Glossary

Adoptionism The heretical belief that JESUS CHRIST is the adopted rather than the begotten Son of God.

Advent The season in which Christians look forward to the coming of JESUS CHRIST.

Agnosticism The belief that it is impossible to have knowledge of the supernatural world.

Albigensianism A heretical, dualistic form of Christianity which was strong in the south of France in the twelfth and thirteenth centuries.

Americanism The attempt by American Roman Catholics such as Isaac Thomas HECKER to adapt the external life of the Church to modern cultural ideals.

Anabaptism The beliefs held by various extreme Protestant groups characterised by their refusal to allow their children to be baptised.

Anathema The cutting off of offenders from the body of the Church.

Anchorite Hermit.

Anglicanism The beliefs and practices of the Church of England.

Anglo-Catholicism The beliefs and practices of the High Church party of the Church of England.

AntiChrist The leader of the enemies of JESUS CHRIST.

Antipope One who claims to be Pope in opposition to the lawfully elected Pope.

Anti-Semitism Prejudice against the Jewish (and less frequently Arab) people.

Apocalypse A revelation or unveiling, generally of the end of time.

Apocrypha Biblical books which are not accepted as part of the canon of Hebrew Scripture or the New Testament.

Apollinarianism The beliefs associated with APOLLINARIUS, that JESUS CHRIST had a human body and soul, but his spirit was replaced by the divine Logos.

Apology A reasoned defence of faith.

Apostasy The abandonment of the Christian faith.

Apostle One of the original twelve followers of JESUS CHRIST or an outstandingly significant missionary.

Apostolic Succession The handing down of the ministry of the Church in an unbroken line from the Apostles.

Archbishop   A senior Bishop who has jurisdiction over an ecclesiastical province. See also Metropolitan.

Archimandrite   Originally used for the Superior of a community in the Eastern Church, it is now used as an honorary title for any senior monastic clergyman.

Arianism   The beliefs associated with the heretic ARIUS, that JESUS CHRIST was not God by nature, and was created rather than begotten.

Aristotelianism   The philosophy of Aristotle, particularly his science of logic and postulation of a 'First Cause'.

Armenian Church   The ancient independent Church of Armenia (Turkey).

Arminianism   The doctrines associated with ARMINIUS, in particular the belief in human free will, the rejection of predestinarianism and the belief that JESUS CHRIST died for everyone, not just the Elect.

Ascension Day   The day on which JESUS CHRIST's return to Heaven is celebrated.

Asceticism   A programme of strict self-denial.

Atheism   The conviction that God does not exist.

Atonement   The reconciliation of humanity with God brought about by the death and resurrection of JESUS CHRIST.

Augustinians   Monks and nuns who follow the Rule of St AUGUSTINE OF HIPPO.

Auricular Confession   The confession of sin to God in the presence of an authorised priest who forgives the sinner in God's name.

Avignon Popes   The Popes who had their headquarters at Avignon between 1305 and 1377.

Baptism   The initiation ceremony of the Church.

Baptismal Regeneration   The belief that through baptism, the new Christian is born again in the Holy Spirit.

Baptist Church   A large Protestant denomination which stresses the rite of baptism as a means of initiation for adult conscious believers.

Beatific Vision   The final vision of God, which is the goal of the Christian life.

Beatification   The authorisation of public veneration of a particularly admirable Christian. It is often the first stage in canonisation.

Benedictines   Monks and nuns who follow the Rule of St BENEDICT of Nursia.

Benefice   An ecclesiastical office, which prescribes particular duties in exchange for reward.

Bible   The canonical Scriptures, the Old and New Testament.

Bishop   The highest order of ministers in the Church; Bishops are distinguished from priests by their power to ordain other ministers and administer the rite of Confirmation.

Breviary   A liturgical book containing the divine office of the Roman Catholic Church.

Broad Church   The liberal party in the Church of England.

Brownism   The doctrines of the Puritan separatist Robert BROWNE.

Buddhism   The religion first taught by Prince Siddhartha Gautama in India in the fifth century BC.

Bull   A written document issued by the Pope.

Calvinism   The doctrines associated with the Protestant Reformer John CALVIN.

Camaldolese   The religious order founded by St ROMAULD.

Canon   The books which make up the Bible; the title of secular clergy attached to a cathedral.

Canon Law   The body of ecclesiastical regulations amassed through the centuries.

Canonisation   The process by which particularly meritorious individuals are declared to be saints by the Roman Catholic Church.

Canon of the Mass   The prayer of consecration in the Eucharistic liturgy.

Canons Regular   A group of canons living under the Augustinian Rule.

Capuchins   Members of a strict Franciscan Order originally founded in the sixteenth century.

Cardinals   Members of the governing college of the Roman Catholic Church who have the privilege of electing the Pope.

Carmelites   Members of the Order of Our Lady of Mount Carmel, an order founded in the twelfth century.

Cathechesis   Instruction given to those preparing for baptism.

Catechism   A formal manual of Christian doctrine.

Catechumens   Those preparing for Christian baptism.

Categorical Imperative   The ethical imperative expounded by Immanuel KANT as a necessary postulate of practical reason.

Cathari   The adherents of various sects, particularly a heretical dualistic group in twelfth- and thirteenth-century Germany. In France they were known as the Albigensians.

Cathedral   The church which contains the seat of the Bishop of the diocese.

Catholic   General or universal; often used to mean orthodox as opposed to heretical; of the Western Church.

Catholic Modernism   A late nineteenth-century movement within the Roman Catholic Church which aimed to reconcile the Church's doctrine with modern philosophy, sociology and history.

Catholicos   The title of the two Patriarchs of the Nestorian and Armenian Churches.

Celibacy   The state of being unmarried. The Roman Catholic Church insists on the celibacy of the clergy.

Chalcedon Formula   The statement of faith made by the Council of Chalcedon in

451, that in JESUS CHRIST, the human and divine nature were united unconfusedly, unchangeably, indivisibly and inseparably.

Chapter The assembly of the members of a monastery or convent; the governing body of a cathedral.

Christ Literally the Greek translation of the Hebrew 'messiah' or 'anointed one'. It quickly became used in the Church as a proper name for JESUS, and emphasised his fulfilment of the Old Testament prophecies.

Christian A follower of JESUS CHRIST, a member of the Church.

Christian Science The beliefs propounded by Mary Baker EDDY.

Christian Socialists A nineteenth-century movement within the Church of England, advocating social reform.

Christmas The day on which the birth of JESUS CHRIST is celebrated.

Christology Doctrines of the person of JESUS CHRIST.

Church The body of all Christian believers; the building in which Christian worship takes place.

Church Fathers Early ecclesiastical authorities; the patristic age is generally defined as the era from the death of the Apostles until the time of St ISIDORE OF SEVILLE and St JOHN OF DAMASCUS.

Cistercians Members of the order founded in the eleventh century by St ROBERT OF MOLESNE.

Clapham Sect A group of evangelical Anglicans flourishing in the late eighteenth and early nineteenth centuries.

Communion The service of the Eucharist or Mass.

Conciliar Movement The movement associated with the theory that the supreme authority of the Church lies with the General Council.

Conclave The closed room in which the Cardinals vote on who is to become the next Pope.

Confession A profession of faith; an acknowledgement of sin made either collectively to a congregation or privately to a priest.

Confirmation The service in which a Bishop strengthens the faith of the individual who is already baptised by the laying on of hands.

Confucian A follower of the philosophy of Confucius, the Chinese ethical leader.

Congregation A group of Christians who meet together for worship; a religious society of people bound by simple vows.

Congregationalism Church organisation which gives each congregation absolute autonomy.

Consecration The separation of something from the secular sphere and its dedication to divine service.

Convocation The traditional assemblies of the Church of England. They have now been replaced by local and national synods.

Copernican Theory   The astronomical theory propounded by Nicolas Copernicus that the sun was the centre of the solar system.

Coptic Church   The ancient Church of Egypt.

Council   A formal meeting of Church leaders convened to define doctrine or arbitrate in some dispute.

Counter-Reformation   The revival of the Roman Catholic Church in the sixteenth century in response to the Protestant Reformation.

Covenant   An agreement between two parties in which both agree to do something for the other.

Creed   A formal statement of Christian belief, the best known being the Apostles, the Nicene and the Athanasian Creeds.

Crisis Theology   The theology associated with Karl BARTH which emphasised the gulf between God and humanity.

Cross   The symbol of Christianity, derived from the instrument of JESUS CHRIST's crucifixion.

Crusade   The series of attempts by Western Christendom to expel the Muslims from the Holy Land from the eleventh to the fourteenth centuries.

Cult   A small, usually heretical, religious group.

Curia   The Papal establishment through which the Roman Catholic Church is governed.

Day of Judgement   The final judgement of humanity after the general resurrection of the dead.

Deacon   The third rank in Christian ministry below that of Bishop and priest.

Decretal   Papal letters answering particular questions which have the force of law.

Deists   Individuals who believe in the existence of a Supreme Being who created the world but who takes little subsequent interest in it.

Demythologise   A term popularised by Rudolf BULTMANN as a method of removing the mythological framework in which the biblical stories are couched.

Denomination   Established group which shares a common set of Christian beliefs.

Determinism   The belief that the entire universe is rigorously subject to the immutable laws of cause and effect.

Diocese   The administrative area governed by a Bishop.

Discalced   Unshod, wearing sandals.

Disciple   Follower, pupil.

Disestablish   To remove the Church from its official, privileged position within the secular state.

Dissenters   Those individuals and churches which are not part of the Established Church.

Ditheists   Those who believe in two gods.

Dogma   A religious truth accepted and defined by the Church.

Dominican   The order of friars founded by St DOMINIC in the thirteenth century.

Dominican Tertiary   Lay-person who is attached to the Dominican Order, but who lives in the world.

Donatism   The beliefs of a schismatic group in North Africa in the fourth century who rejected the election of Caecilius as Bishop of Carthage and supported DONATUS.

Double Predestination   The belief, associated with John CALVIN, that the saving death of JESUS CHRIST was offered for the Elect alone and that salvation is denied for all eternity to the damned.

Easter   The day on which the resurrection of JESUS CHRIST is celebrated.

Eastern Church   A family of Churches all of which acknowledge the primacy of the Patriarch of Constantinople.

Eastern Orthodoxy   The beliefs and practices of the Eastern Church.

Ecclesiology   The science of the construction and decoration of churches.

Ecumenical Councils   Assemblies of Church leaders from the whole world whose decisions are regarded as binding. According to the teachings of most Churches (except the Roman Catholic) the last ecumenical council was the Second Council of Nicaea in 787 before the split between the Western and Eastern Churches.

Ecumenical Movement   The twentieth-century movement towards Church unity which may be dated from the Edinburgh Conference of 1910.

Ecumenism   The movement towards Church unity.

Elder   An official in the Presbyterian Church: a translation of the New Testament term Presbyter.

Elect   Those chosen by God for salvation.

Ember Days   Four groups of three days in the Church's year which have been set aside for abstinence.

Empiricism   The belief that human beings can only have certain knowledge of matters which are perceived by the five senses.

Enclosure   The practice of religious orders of confining their members to an enclosed area.

Enhypostasia   The doctrine associated with LEONTIUS of Byzantium and St JOHN OF DAMASCUS, that within the Godhead the personal humanity of the man JESUS was not lost.

Epiphany   The day on which the visit of the wise men to the baby JESUS is celebrated.

Episcopal   Governed by Bishops.

Episcopalianism   The belief that the Church should be governed by Bishops.

Epistle   Letter.

Erastianism   The doctrine associated with Thomas ERASTUS, that the Church should be under the control of the civil authorities.

Established Church   The Church designated the official Church of the nation.

Eucharist   The central act of Christian worship, the sharing of bread and wine as a participation in the life of the resurrected JESUS CHRIST. Also known as Holy Communion, the Lord's Supper, the Mass.

Eutycheanism   The doctrines associated with EUTYCHES who taught that before the incarnation, there were two natures in Christ; these subsequently coalesced into one – thus diminishing the humanity of JESUS.

Evangelicalism   Christian belief based primarily on Scripture.

Evangelist   Gospel writer; missionary/preacher.

Excommunication   Exclusion from the body of the Church imposed by the ecclesiastical authorities.

Exegesis   The explanation of a sacred text.

Existentialism   The philosophical position associated with Søren KIERKEGAARD which stresses the practical concerns of the individual as opposed to the emphases of objective philosophy and natural science.

Fall   The disobedience of the first human beings which led to sin and hard work being the natural lot of humanity.

Febronianism   The movement within the eighteenth-century Roman Catholic Church in Germany which rejected papal claims, particularly in the secular sphere.

Franciscans   Members of the order of friars founded by St FRANCIS OF ASSISI in the thirteenth century.

Franciscan Spirituals   Members of the order of friars who interpret FRANCIS OF ASSISI's rule most strictly.

Franciscan Tertiaries   Lay-people who are attached to the Franciscan Order, but who live out in the world.

Free Will   The freedom to make moral choices; often contrasted with predestination.

Friars   Members of one of the mendicant orders founded in the Middle Ages. Unlike monks, friars are not bound by enclosure or vows of stability and they work or beg for their living.

Friars Minor   The official name of the Franciscan Order.

Fundamentalism   The conviction that the Scriptures are verbally inerrant. The fundamentalist movement arose in various Protestant denominations at the start of the twentieth century in reaction to biblical criticism and Charles DARWIN's theory of evolution.

Gallicanism   The belief that the French Roman Catholic Church should be free from the ecclesiastical authority of the Papacy.

General Council   see Ecumenical Councils.

Gentile   Non-Jew.

Gnosticism   A complex set of beliefs current in the ancient world in which special, esoteric spiritual knowledge was revealed to the chosen few. Such teaching frequently involved a distinction between the unknowable Supreme God and a 'Demiurge' or creator god.

Good Friday   The day on which JESUS's crucifixion is commemorated.

Gospel   The good news of JESUS CHRIST and the imminent Kingdom of God; the written books in which the good news was set out – the canonical Gospels being those of Sts MATTHEW, MARK, LUKE and JOHN.

Grace   The free gift of God which blesses and sanctifies human beings.

Habit   Religious dress worn by members of religious orders.

Hagiography   Writing of the lives of the saints.

Heaven   The dwelling place of God and the ultimate destination of all redeemed Christian souls.

Hell   The waiting place of the dead: the ultimate place of punishment for those cast out from God's presence.

Henoticon   The theological formula sponsored by the Emperor ZENO which was designed to reconcile the Monophysites to the Church. It omitted the question of the number of natures in JESUS CHRIST.

Heresiarch   The founder of an heretical sect, such as ARIUS, NESTORIUS or PELAGIUS.

Heresy   The denial of an established doctrine of the Universal Church. The opposite of orthodoxy.

Hermeneutics   The formally prescribed rules of interpreting a sacred text.

Hesychasm   The tradition of mystical, inner prayer as practised in the Eastern Church.

High Church   The party within the Church of England which stresses that Church's historical links with the Catholic Church. Since the nineteenth century high churchmen have been associated with ritualism.

Holy Spirit   The Third Person of the Trinity. The Holy Spirit manifests himself in the ongoing life of the Church; according to the Western Church He proceeds from the Father and the Son, whereas in the Eastern tradition He proceeds from the Father alone.

Homoousion   Of one substance: term expressing relationship of Father to Son in the Trinity.

Huguenots   French Protestants.

Humanism   Beliefs emphasising common human needs and looking for purely rational ways of solving human problems; the literary culture of the Renaissance.

Hymn   Religious poetry set to music and sung during the course of church worship.

Hypostasis   Substance or person. The Hypostatic Union is the union of the divine and human natures in the single person (hypostasis) of JESUS CHRIST.

Icon Pictures of JESUS CHRIST, the Virgin MARY and the saints which are venerated in the Eastern Church.

Iconoclastic Controversy The controversy over the veneration of icons which raged in the Eastern Church in the eighth and ninth centuries.

Idealism The belief that the object of external perception consists of ideas: the representation of things in their ideal form.

Immaculate Conception The belief that the Virgin MARY was born without the stain of original sin.

Immanence The immediate presence of God in the Universe.

Incarnation The doctrine that the eternal Son of God became a human being. Thus the belief that JESUS CHRIST is fully God and fully human.

Index The list of books prohibited to the faithful by the Roman Catholic hierarchy.

Indulgence The remission of the temporary penalty for sin pronounced by the Church in exchange for particular good works (such as going on a crusade) or (regrettably) for money.

Infallibility The Church's inability to err in the promulgation of official doctrine.

Infant Baptism The practice of baptising the children of Christian parents in infancy.

Inquisition The official rooting out of heresy by specially constituted ecclesiastical courts.

Investiture Controversy The mediaeval dispute arising out of the claim of the Emperor or other prince to invest an Abbot or Bishop with his staff and ring before his actual consecration, thus giving the lay authority considerable powers of patronage.

Islam The religion founded by the prophet Mohammed in the early seventh century.

Israelite A member of the ancient Jewish people. The Christian Church identifies itself as the 'New Israel' and thus the inheritor of the promised privileges of God's Chosen People.

Jansenism The teachings associated with Cornelius JANSEN, that God's commandments can only be performed through his grace and that the operation of such grace is predetermined and irresistible.

Jesuits Members of the Society of Jesus founded by IGNATIUS LOYOLA in the sixteenth century.

Judaism The religion of the Jewish people.

Justification The act by which, through the grace of God, a human being becomes just and passes from a state of sin to righteousness.

Kenotic Christology The theory that during the earthly life of JESUS CHRIST, the Second Person of the Trinity 'emptied himself' and temporarily abandoned his divine attributes of omnipotence, omniscience and sovereignty.

Kingdom of God The established rule of God on earth. Christians are enjoined to pray for its coming.

Kirk   The Scottish equivalent of Church.

Knights Hospitallers   Also known as the Knights of Rhodes and the Knights of Malta, a religious order originally founded to provide hospitality for pilgrims and crusaders in the Holy Land.

Knights Templar   Order originally founded in the twelfth century to protect pilgrims from bandits in the Holy Land.

Koran   Sacred book of Islam.

Kulturkampf   The movement in Germany in the 1870s against the Roman Catholic Church.

Kyrie Eleison   'Lord have mercy!' A prayer for divine mercy.

Lambeth Conference   Assemblies of Anglican Bishops held every ten years.

Lateran Councils   Councils held in the Lateran Palace in Rome. Some Lateran Councils were Ecumenical Councils.

Laxism   A system of ethics which relaxed many of the traditional obligations set out in other moral systems.

Lay   Not belonging to the clergy.

Lay-Brothers/Sisters   Members of religious orders who are occupied with the manual work of the community and who are not bound to the regular recitation of the divine office.

Lay Investiture   The investiture of an Abbot or Bishop by the Emperor or Prince. See Investiture Controversy.

Lector   Reader/one of the minor orders of ministry.

Legate   A person entrusted with a specific office or authority by the Pope.

Lent   A forty-day period of abstinence in which JESUS's sojourn in the wilderness is remembered.

Liberalism   The willingness to accept new ideas and suggestions for reform. It is frequently juxtaposed with dogmatism.

Liberation Theology   A system of theology which initially arose in South America: it makes use of Marxist categories and stresses justice and God's bias to the poor.

Limbo   The abode of souls excluded from Heaven, but not condemned to punishment.

Liturgy   The prescribed services of the Church.

Logos   God's Word, the Second Person of the Trinity through which the world was created and which was incarnate in JESUS CHRIST.

Lollardy   The teachings of John WYCLIFFE.

Lutheranism   The theological system propounded by Martin LUTHER and his followers.

Manichaeism   The Gnostic beliefs associated with the followers of MANI.

Martyrs Those who die for their Christian beliefs.

Mass The central service of the Christian Church. See Eucharist.

Menaion The liturgical book which contains the particular monthly services of the Eastern Church.

Mendicants Members of religious orders which are forbidden to own property and work or beg for their livings.

Mennonism The beliefs associated with the followers of MENNO SIMONS.

Messiah Christ. The long-awaited anointed one of God who was expected by the Jewish people to right all wrongs and establish the Kingdom of God on earth.

Metaphysics The study of that which is beyond empirical experience.

Methodism The beliefs and organisation of the Churches founded by John WESLEY and his followers.

Metropolitan Bishops who exercise provincial rather than diocesan powers.

Millenarianism The expectation of the thousand-year period of blessedness as promised in the Book of Revelation.

Min-Jung Theology A theology which arose in Korea and which shares many of the characteristics of Latin American Liberation Theology.

Missionaries Those who dedicate their lives to spreading the good news of JESUS CHRIST.

Monks Men who are members of religious communities who live under vows of poverty, chastity and obedience.

Monophysitism The belief that in the person of JESUS CHRIST there was but one divine nature and that he was not fully human.

Monothelitism A modified form of Monophysitism; the belief that in JESUS CHRIST there was but one divine will.

Montanism A late second-century apocalyptic movement associated with MONTANUS.

Moravianism The Protestant Church which grew out of the Bohemian Brethren and was renewed under Count N.L. von ZINZENDORF.

Mormons The members of the Church of Latter Day Saints which was founded by Joseph SMITH and Brigham YOUNG.

Mosaic Cosmogeny The history of the creation of the world as set out in the early chapters of the Book of Genesis.

Muslims Members of the religion of Islam.

Mysticism The knowledge of God gained in this life through intense personal religious experience.

Natural Law The laws which human beings can discover by means of their own unaided reason.

Natural Theology The knowledge of God which can be derived from human reason alone without recourse to revelation.

Neo-Platonism   The philosophical system which derived many of its essential ideas from the thought of Plato and which sought to overcome the gap between thought and reality through the abstract knowledge of ultimate being.

Nestorianism   The beliefs associated with the teachings of NESTORIUS, that there were two separate persons in JESUS CHRIST, the divine and the human.

New Testament   The canonical Scriptures accepted by the Christian Church which are not recognised by the Jewish synagogue.

Nicene   The christology which was accepted by the Christian Church at the Council of Nicaea in 325 which was summoned to combat the teachings of ARIUS.

Nominalism   The theory of knowledge which denies reality to universal concepts.

Non-Conformity   The refusal to conform to the doctrines or discipline of any Established Church.

Non-Jurors   Members of the Church of England who refused to take the Oath of Allegiance to King William and Queen Mary after the revolution against King JAMES II in 1688.

Numinous   Word coined by Rudolf OTTO to describe the feelings of awe when undergoing religious experience.

Nuncio   A diplomatic representative of the Pope.

Nuns   Women who are members of religious communities living under vows of poverty, chastity and obedience.

Observantines   Members of the Franciscan Order who claimed to observe the original rule.

Octoechos   A liturgical book of the Eastern Church containing the variable parts of the service.

Office   The daily public liturgy of the Church.

Oecumenical   Universal; see Ecumenical.

Old Believers   The section of the Russian Orthodox Church which refused to accept the reforms of Patriarch NIKON.

Old Catholics   A group of small national Churches which at various times and for various reasons have separated themselves from the Church of Rome since 1724.

Old Testament   The Hebrew Scriptures.

Ontological Argument   Argument for the existence of God first formulated by St ANSELM and based on the idea of God's necessary existence.

Oratorio   The musical setting of a religious story involving orchestra soloists and chorus, but without scenery and costume.

Oratory   A chapel which is not a parish church.

Ordination   The service in which Bishops, priests and deacons are commissioned for their work. It is traditionally believed that ordination is an indelible Sacrament.

Original Sin   The state of sin which is inherent in all humanity since the time of the first man Adam. See Fall.

Orthodoxy   Correct (i.e. non heretical) belief; the Eastern Church.

Oxford Movement   The nineteenth-century movement within the Church of England which aimed to restore to that Church its High Church ideals.

Pacifism   The belief that participation in war is morally indefensible.

Paganism   The belief in many semi-anthropomorphic gods and goddesses.

Pallium   The garment which symbolises the authority of Popes and Archbishops.

Pantheism   The belief that God and the universe are identical.

Papal Infallibility   The belief that the Pope cannot err in his official teaching.

Parable   A comparison which is used to convey a spiritual meaning.

Parish   An area under the spiritual care of a resident clergyman.

Passion   The sufferings and death of JESUS CHRIST.

Passover   The Jewish festival which celebrates the liberation of the Israelites from slavery in Egypt.

Pastor   Shepherd. Spiritual leader in certain Protestant Churches.

Patriarch   The title of the holder of the important bishoprics of Rome, Alexandria, Antioch, Constantinople and Jerusalem. Later it was the title given to the heads of the various national Eastern Orthodox Churches.

Patristics   The study of the works of the early Church Fathers.

Paulists   Members of the Missionary Society of St PAUL founded by Isaac Thomas HECKER in the United States of America.

Pelagianism   The teachings associated with the heretic PELAGIUS.

Penal Substitution   The doctrine that JESUS CHRIST by his suffering and death took on the punishment which was due to all sinful human beings and thus enabled them to enter a state of grace.

Penance   The ritual punishment for sin.

Pentateuch   The first five books of the Hebrew Scriptures, traditionally believed to have been written by Moses.

Pentecostalism   The twentieth-century movement which stresses the reception of the more spectacular gifts of the Holy Spirit such as prophecy and speaking in tongues.

Pharisee   A member of a Jewish religious party which existed in the time of JESUS CHRIST. Pharisees stressed the oral interpretation of the written law of Moses.

Piarists   Members of an educational order founded by St JOSEPH CALASANCTIUS.

Pietism   The seventeenth-century movement associated with Philipp Jakob SPENER.

Pilgrimage   A journey to a holy place undertaken as an act of devotion.

Platonism   The ideas associated with the Greek philosopher Plato, in particular the conviction that underlying the changing phenomena of the physical world is the world of unchanging and eternal forms or ideas.

Pluralism The belief that the world consists of a plurality of ultimately distinct things or states; in modern times the belief that there are many possible paths to God.

Plymouth Brethren The group founded in England by John Nelson DARBY.

Pneumatomachi Heretics of the fourth century who denied the full godhead of the Holy Spirit.

Pontificate Period of office of a Pope.

Poor Clares Members of the order founded by St FRANCIS OF ASSISI and St CLARE in the early thirteenth century.

Pope The Bishop of Rome, the head of the Roman Catholic Church.

Prayer of Consecration Central prayer of the Eucharist over the bread and wine.

Preaching The deliverance of sermons or religious addresses.

Prebendary The holder of a cathedral benefice.

Predestination The divine decree by which some human beings are infallibily guided to salvation and others to destruction.

Premonstratensian Canons Members of the order founded by St NORBERT in the twelfth century.

Presbyterianism The system of Church government by presbyters.

Presbyters Elders; overseers of Churches.

Priests Members of the second rank of Christian ministry, below Bishops but above deacons.

Primate The title of the Bishop of the first national see.

Process Theology A modern school of theology which maintains that even God is in a process of development through his interaction with the evolving world.

Prophecy The speaking of God's word through the agency of the Holy Spirit.

Protestantism The system of belief and practice which arose as a result of the work of sixteenth-century Reformers such as Martin LUTHER, John CALVIN and Ulrich ZWINGLI.

Provincial One who exercises authority over a religious order or over a particular area.

Psalm One of the 150 Hebrew songs collected in the Old Testament Book of Psalms.

Ptolemaic System The astronomical system associated with Ptolemy in which the stars circle round the earth which remains stationary.

Pulpit An elevated stand used for preaching.

Purgatory A temporary state of punishment where the faithful expiate their sins before entering Heaven.

Puritanism Extreme English Protestantism current in the sixteenth and seventeenth centuries.

Quakers Members of the Society of Friends founded by George FOX in the seventeenth century.

Quietism   The movement associated with Miguel de MOLINOS, Mme GUYON and Archbishop FÉNELON, which stressed the importance of the passive contemplation of the divine. It was condemned by the Papacy as quasi-Protestant.

Realism   Philosophical doctrine that abstract concepts have objective existence.

Real Presence   The doctrine that the Body and Blood of JESUS CHRIST are actually present in the bread and wine of the Eucharist.

Recapitulation   The doctrine associated with St IRENAEUS that fallen humanity is restored to Communion with God through the obedience of JESUS CHRIST and that the incarnation is the summing up of all previous revelations of God to humanity.

Recollects   Members of either a Franciscan Observantine Order founded in the sixteenth century or an Augustinian Order of hermits founded in Spain, also in the sixteenth century.

Redemption   The deliverance from sin and the restoration of humanity's Communion with God through the saving death of JESUS CHRIST.

Reformation   The movement within Western Christendom which took place between the fourteenth and seventeenth centuries. Adherents initially demanded the reform of abuses within the Roman Catholic Church and finally established their own Protestant or Reformed Churches.

Relic   Remains of a saint which are venerated after his or her death.

Religious Orders   Congregations who live together in a community bound by vows.

Repentance   The turning away from and rejection of one's own sins.

Requiem Mass   A Eucharist offered for the dead.

Reservation   The practice of keeping consecrated bread and wine from the Eucharist service for the purpose of veneration.

Resurrection   The belief that JESUS CHRIST rose from the dead on the third day after his crucifixion.

Resurrection of the Dead   The belief that at the Second Coming of JESUS CHRIST all the dead will be raised before the Day of Judgement.

Retreat   A short period of retirement from the world to concentrate on spiritual matters.

Revelation   The truths about himself which God discloses to humanity and the process by which such knowledge comes to humanity.

Revivalism   Outbursts of religious fervour provoked by intensive preaching and prayer meetings.

Ritual   The prescribed form of the liturgy.

Ritualism   The emphasis on traditional Church ritual.

Rogation Days   Prescribed days of prayer dedicated to intercession for the harvest.

Roman Catholicism   The faith and practice of that portion of Western Christendom which accepts the authority of the Pope.

Rule   The regulations for conduct laid down for members of a religious order.

Sabbatarianism   Particular strictness in the observation of the Sabbath.

Sabbath   The day of rest. Jews observe the seventh day as the Sabbath (Saturday) while Christians observe Sunday, the day of the resurrection of JESUS CHRIST.

Sacrament   An outward and visible sign (such as water or bread and wine) of a spiritual grace (spiritual regeneration, the real presence of JESUS CHRIST). The seven Sacraments accepted by the Eastern and the Roman Catholic Churches are Baptism, Confirmation, the Eucharist, Penance, Marriage, Ordination and Extreme Unction.

Sacramentary   The liturgical book used for the celebration of the Eucharist in the Middle Ages.

Sacred Heart   The heart of JESUS CHRIST as an object of devotion in the Roman Catholic Church.

Sacrifice   The offering of a gift to God which is often associated with the making or renewing of covenants.

Sacrilege   The violation of a sacred person, place or object.

Saint   Holy or canonised person who is a subject of veneration in the Church.

Salvation   Act of saving or being saved from sin and its consequences.

Schism   Separation from the unity of the Church.

Scholasticism   The ideas associated with the teachings and educational traditions of the mediaeval schools of theology.

Schoolmen   The teachers of theology and philosophy at the mediaeval universities.

Second Coming   The return of JESUS CHRIST in glory to judge the world and end the present world order.

Sect   A religious denomination.

Secularism   The belief that morality or education should not be founded on religious teaching.

See   The area under the authority of a Bishop.

Semi-Arian   The teachings associated with the fourth-century group which taught a doctrine of the Sonship of JESUS CHRIST mid-way between that of the orthodox and that of ARIUS.

Seminary   A training college for ministers.

Sentences   Short expositions of the fundamental truths of Christianity, the best known of which was composed by PETER LOMBARD.

Separatists   Title first given to the followers of Robert BROWNE, but later used of any group which separated itself from the Church of England.

Septuagint   The early Greek translation of the Hebrew Scriptures.

Sermon   Spoken or written discourse on a religious subject often delivered from a pulpit during the course of a service.

Servites   Members of an order founded in Florence in the thirteenth century.

Simony   The purchase or sale of ecclesiastical positions.

Sin   Disobedience to the will of God. According to Christian theology death came into the world as a result of sin.

Sobernost   A term used in the Russian Church to signify both Catholicity and Conciliarity.

Society of Friends   See Quakers.

Socinianism   The teachings associated with Lelio Francesco Sozini and Fausto Paolo SOZZINI.

Soteriology   Theology which deals with the saving work of JESUS CHRIST.

Sophia   Divine wisdom.

Soul   The immortal, spiritual part of a human being.

Spiritual Franciscans   Those who wished to retain St FRANCIS OF ASSISI's original ideals of poverty in the Franciscan movement.

Stigmata   The marks of the wounds of JESUS's crucifixion.

Stylite   A solitary who lived on the top of a pillar, the most famous being St SIMEON STYLITES.

Subordinationism   Teaching about the Godhead which does not give full equality to the three persons of the Trinity.

Suffragan Bishop   An assistant Bishop appointed to help a diocesan Bishop.

Summa   A mediaeval compendium of theology, the most famous being that of St THOMAS AQUINAS.

Sunday School   An organisation in which religious instruction is given to children on Sundays.

Superior   The head of a religious congregation or order.

Synagogue   A meeting house used as a place of worship and instruction by the Jews.

Teleological Argument   Argument for God's existence based on the appearance of design in the world.

Tertiary   Member of an order of lay-people attached to an established religious order. They observe a rule and recite a liturgical office, but live their lives out in the world.

Theocracy   Government by God.

Theodicy   The part of theology concerned with explaining how the existence of evil in the world is compatible with the goodness and omnipotence of God.

Theology   The systematic study of divine revelation.

Theosophy   The esoteric teachings associated with Mme BLAVATSKY and Annie BESANT.

Theotokion   A verse of a liturgical hymn addressed to the Virgin MARY.

Theotokos 'God-bearer'; a title of the Virgin MARY.

Thomism The theological ideas associated with St THOMAS AQUINAS.

Tithe A tax exacted for the support of the clergy.

Tongues A traditional gift of the Holy Spirit; the ability to speak a strange heavenly language; it is a common feature of religious revivals.

Tonsure The shaving of part of the head which was a distinctive feature of clerics and monks in the Roman Catholic Church.

Tractarianism see Oxford Movement.

Transcendent Existing above and apart from the limitations of the material world.

Transubstantiation The belief that during the course of the Eucharist, the bread and wine changes in substance to the Body and Blood of JESUS CHRIST.

Trappists Members of a strict branch of the Cistercian Order founded by A.J. le B. DE RANCÉ in the seventeenth century.

Tridentine Mass The order of the Eucharist laid down in the sixteenth century at the Council of Trent.

Trinity The belief that the One God exists in Three Persons (Father, Son and Holy Spirit), but is of one substance.

Ultramontanism The tendency in the Roman Catholic Church to centralise authority in the Papacy and to discourage national or diocesan autonomy.

Unction The anointing with oil. This can take place at Baptism, Confirmation, at the coronation of a monarch and when visiting the terminally ill. Extreme unction is regarded as one of the seven Sacraments.

Unitarianism The belief in One God, but the rejection of the doctrine of the Trinity and the divinity of JESUS CHRIST. Various groups in the history of the Church have espoused unitarian beliefs.

Ursulines Members of the order founded in the sixteenth century by St ANGELA MERICI.

Usury The lending of money upon interest.

Vestments The special dress worn by clergy during liturgical services.

Victorines Members of the order founded by WILLIAM OF CHAMPEAUX in the early twelfth century.

Vulgate The Latin translation of the Bible which was mainly the work of St JEROME in the fourth century.

Waldensians Members of the community originally founded in the twelfth century by Peter VALDES.

Wesleyans see Methodists.

Western Church The Church of Western Europe; before the Reformation, the Roman Catholic Church.

Whitsunday   Pentecost: the day on which Christians celebrate the first coming of the Holy Spirit.

World Council of Churches   Organisation set up in 1948 to further ecumenical relations between the Churches.

Categories

- Popes
- Apostles and the First Generation
- Artists
- Composers
- Denomination/Sect Founders
- Devotional Writers
- Economists
- Ecumenists
- Educators
- Heretics and Early Excommunicates
- Historians
- Missionaries
- Monarchs
- Mystics
- Order Founders
- Philanthropists/Social Reformers
- Poets/Novelists
- Polemicists/Rebels
- Politicians/Statesmen
- Saints
- Scientists
- Theologians/Philosophers

Popes

(A) indicates Antipope; **bold** indicates entry.

Peter d. *c.* 64 AD
Linus *c.* 66–78
Anacletus *c.* 79–91
Clement I *c.* 91–101
Evaristus *c.* 100–109
Alexander I *c.* 109–116
Sixtus I *c.* 116–125
Telesphorus *c.* 125–*c.* 136
Hyginus *c.* 136–140
Pius I *c.* 140–154
Anicetus *c.* 154–166
Soter *c.* 166–175
Eleutherius 175–189
Victor I 189–198

Zephyrinus 198–217
Callistus I 217–222
(A) **Hippolytus** 217–*c.* 235
Urban I 222–230
Pontian 230–235
Anterus 235–236
Fabian 236–250
Cornelius 251–253
(A) **Novatian** 251–258
Lucius I 253–254
Stephen I 254–257
Sixtus II 257–258
Dionysius 260–268

Felix I 269–274
Eutychian 275–283
Caius 283–296
Marcellinus 296–304
Eusebius 310
Miltiades 311–314
Sylvester I 314–335
Mark 336
Julius I 337–352
Liberius 352–366
(A) Felix II 355–365
(A) Ursinus 366–367
Damasus I 366–384
Siricius 384–399

Anastasius I 399–400
Innocent I 402–417
Zosimus 417–418
(A) Eulalius 418–419
Boniface I 418–422
Celestine I 422–432
Sixtus III 432–440
Leo I 440–461
Hilarus 461–468
Simplicius 468–483
Felix II 483–492
Gelasius 492–496
Anastasius II 496–498
Symmachus 498–514
Hornisdas 514–523
John I 523–526
Felix IV 526–530
(A) Diascorus 530
Boniface II 530–532
John II 533–535
Agapetus I 535–536
Silverius 536–537
Virgilius 537–555
Pelagius I 556–561
John III 561–574
Benedict I 575–579
Pelagius II 579–590
Gregory I 590–604
Sabianus 604–606
Boniface III 607
Boniface IV 608–615
Adeodatus I 615–618
Boniface V 619–625
Honorius I 625–638
Severinus 640
John IV 640–642
Theodore I 642–649
Martin I 649–655
Eugenius I 654–667
Vitalian 657–672
Adeodatus II 672–676
Donus 676–678
Agatho 678–681
Leo II 682–683
Benedict II 684–685
John V 685–686
Conon 686–687
Sergius I 687–701
John VI 701–705
John VII 705–707

Sisinnius 708
Constantine 708–715
Gregory II 715–731
Gregory III 731–741
Zacharias 741–752
Stephen II 752
Stephen II 752–757
Paul I 757–767
Stephen III 768–772
Hadrian I 772–795
Leo III 795–816
Stephen IV 816–817
Paschal I 817–824
Eugenius II 824–827
Valentine 827
Gregory IV 827–844
Sergius II 844–847
Leo IV 847–855
(A) Anastasius 855
Benedict III 855–858
Nicholas I 858–867
Hadrian II 867–872
John VIII 872–882
Marinus I 882–884
Hadrian III 884–885
Stephen V 885–891
Formosus 891–896
Boniface VI 896
Stephen VI 896–897
Romanus 897
Theodore II 897
John IX 898–900
Benedict IV 900–903
Leo V 903
Sergius III 904–911
Anastasius III 911–913
Lando 913–914
John X 914–928
Leo VI 928
Stephen VII 928–931
John XI 931–935
Leo VII 936–939
Stephen VIII 939–942
Marinus II 942–946
Agapetus II 946–955
John XII 955–964
Leo VIII 963–965
Benedict V 964–966
John XIII 965–972
Benedict VI 973–974

(A) Boniface VII 974, 984–985
Benedict VII 974–983
John XIV 983–984
John XV 985–996
Gregory V 996–999
(A) John XVI 997–998
Sylvester II 999–1003
John XVII 1003
John XVIII 1003–1009
Sergius IV 1009–1012
(A) Gregory 1012
Benedict VIII 1012–1024
John XIX 1024–1032
Benedict IX 1032–1044
Sylvester III 1045
Gregory VI 1045–1046
Clement II 1046–1047
Benedict IX 1047–1048
Damasus II 1048
Leo IX 1048–1054
Victor II 1055–1057
Stephen IX 1057–1058
(A) Benedict X 1058–1059
Nicholas II 1059–1061
Alexander II 1061–1073
(A) Honorius II 1061–1072
Gregory VII 1073–1085
(A) Clement III 1080, 1084–1100
Victor III 1086–1087
Urban II 1088–1099
Paschal II 1099–1118
(A) Theodoric 1100–1102
Gelasius II 1118–1119
(A) Gregory VIII 1118–1121
Callistus II 1119–1124
(A) Celestine II 1124–1125
Honorius II 1124–1130
(A) Anacletus II 1130–1138
Innocent II 1130–1143
Celestine II 1143–1144
Lucius II 1144–1145
Eugenius III 1145–1153
Anastasius IV 1153–1154
Hadrian IV 1154–1159

(A) Victor IV 1159–1164
Alexander III 1159–1181
(A) Paschal III 1164–1168
(A) Callistus III 1168–1178
(A) Innocent III 1179–1180
Lucius III 1181–1185
Urban III 1185–1187
Gregory VIII 1187
Clement III 1187–1191
Celestine III 1191–1198
Innocent III 1198–1216
Honorius III 1216–1227
Gregory IX 1227–1241
Celestine IV 1241
Innocent IV 1243–1254
Alexander IV 1254–1261
Urban IV 1261–1264
Clement IV 1265–1268
Gregory X 1271–1276
Innocent V 1276
Hadrian V 1276
John XXI 1276–1277
Nicholas III 1277–1280
Martin IV 1281–1285
Honorius IV 1285–1287
Nicholas IV 1288–1292
Celestine V 1294
Boniface VIII 1294–1303
Benedict XI 1303–1304
Clement V 1305–1314
John XXII 1316–1334
Benedict XII 1334–1342
Clement VI 1342–1352
Innocent VI 1352–1362
Urban V 1362–1370

Gregory XI 1370–1378
Urban VI 1378–1389
(A) Clement VII 1378–1394
Boniface IX 1389–1404
(A) Benedict XIII 1394–1423
Innocent VII 1404–1406
Gregory XII 1406–1415
(A) Alexander V 1409–1410
(A) John XXIII 1410–1415
Martin V 1417–1431
(A) Clement VIII 1423–1429
(A) Benedict XIV 1425
Eugenius IV 1431–1447
(A) Felix V 1439–1449
Nicholas V 1447–1455
Callistus III 1455–1458
Pius II 1458–1464
Paul II 1464–1471
Sixtus IV 1471–1484
Innocent VIII 1484–1492
Alexander VI 1492–1503
Pius III 1503
Julius II 1503–1513
Leo X 1513–1521
Hadrian VI 1522–1523
Clement VII 1523–1534
Paul III 1534–1549
Julius III 1550–1555
Marcellus II 1555
Paul IV 1555–1559
Pius IV 1559–1565
Pius V 1566–1572
Gregory XIII 1572–1585
Sixtus V 1585–1590

Urban VII 1590
Gregory XIV 1590–1591
Innocent IX 1591
Clement VIII 1592–1605
Leo XI 1605
Paul V 1605–1621
Gregory XV 1621–1623
Urban VIII 1623–1644
Innocent X 1644–1655
Alexander VII 1655–1667
Clement IX 1667–1669
Clement X 1670–1676
Innocent XI 1676–1689
Alexander VIII 1689–1691
Innocent XII 1691–1700
Clement XI 1700–1721
Innocent XIII 1721–1724
Benedict XIII 1724–1730
Clement XII 1730–1740
Benedict XIV 1740–1758
Clement XIII 1758–1769
Clement XIV 1769–1774
Pius VI 1775–1799
Pius VII 1800–1823
Leo XII 1823–1829
Pius VIII 1829–1830
Gregory XVI 1831–1846
Pius IX 1846–1878
Leo XIII 1878–1903
Pius X 1903–1914
Benedict XV 1914–1922
Pius XI 1922–1939
Pius XII 1939–1958
John XXIII 1958–1963
Paul VI 1963–1978
John-Paul I 1978
John-Paul II 1978–

Apostles and the First Generation

Andrew
Barnabas
Bartholomew
Hermas
James the Greater
James the Less
James, the Lord's Brother
John the Apostle
John the Baptist

John the Elder
John the Evangelist
Joseph of Arimathaea
Joseph of Nazareth
Judas Iscariot
Jude
Lazarus
Levi
Longinus

Luke
Mark
Martha
Mary Magdalene
Mary of Bethany
Mary the Virgin
Matthew
Matthias
Nathaniel
Nicodemus
Onesimus
Paul
Peter
Philemon
Philip the Apostle
Philip the Deacon
Pilate

Priscilla
Silas
Simeon
Simon Magus
Simon of Cyrene
Simon the Apostle
Stephen
Thaddaeus
Thecla
Theophilus
Thomas
Timothy
Titus
Trophimus
Veronica
Zacchaeus

Artists

Angelico, Fra
Blake, William
Dürer, Albrecht
El Greco
Gill, Eric
Giotto
Grunewald, Matthis
Leonardo da Vinci

Michelangelo Buonarroti
Pugin, A.W.N.
Raphael
Rembrandt
Scott, George Gilbert
Titian
Wren, Chistopher

Composers

Bach, Johann Sebastian
Byrd, William
Gibbons, Orlando
Handel, George Friedrich
Monteverdi, Claudio

Mozart, Wolfgang Amadeus
Palestrina, Giovanni Pierluigi da
Purcell, Henry
Tallis, Thomas
Vaughan Williams, Ralph

Denomination Sect Founders

Albright, Jacob (Evangelical
  Association)
Allen, Richard (African Methodists)
Barclay, John (Bereans)
Besant, Annie (Theosophical Society)
Blavatsky, Helena (Theosophical
  Society)
Boehm, Martin (United Brethren)
Bourignon, Antoinette (Extreme
  Quietists)

Bourne, Hugh (Primitive Methodists)
Buchman, Frank (Moral Rearmament)
Bunting, Jabez (Methodism)
Campbell, Alexander (Disciples of
  Christ)
Channing, William Ellery (American
  Unitarians)
Chelcicky, Peter (Chelcic Brethren)
Clowes, William (Primitive Methodists)
Coke, Thomas (Methodism)

Darby, John Nelson (Plymouth Brethren)
Döllinger, Johann (Old Catholics)
Eddy, Mary Baker (Christian Science)
Emerson, Ralph Waldo
   (Transcendentalism)
Erskine, Ebenezer (Scottish Secession
   Church)
Fox, George (Society of Friends)
Frank, Jacob (Frankists)
Gichtel, Johann Georg (Angelic
   Brethren)
Gillespie, Thomas (the Relief)
Glas, John (Glasites, Sandemanians)
Grebel, Conrad (Anabaptists)
Gurney, Joseph John (Society of Friends)
Harris, Howel (Welsh Calvinist
   Methodists)
Helwys, Thomas (General Baptists)
Hicks, Elias (Hicksite Quakers)
Hutter, Jacob (Hutterite Anabaptists)
Irving, Edward (Catholic Apostolic
   Church)
Kelly, William (Kellyite Plymouth
   Brethren)
Kilham, Alexander (Methodist New
   Connexion)
Kim, Chi-Ha (Kitokyo Presbyterians)
Lee, Ann (Shakers)
Lefebvre, Marcel (Latin Tridentines)
Lenshina, Alice (Lumpa Church)
Mack, Alexander (New Baptists)
McPherson, Aimee Semple (Four-Square
   Gospel Church)
Melville, Andrew (Scottish
   Presbyterians)

Menno, Simons (Mennonites)
Miller, William (Seventh Day Adventists)
Moon, Sun-Myung (Unification Church)
Morison, James (Evangelical Union)
Muggleton, Ludowicke (Muggletonians)
Nayler, James (Ranters)
Nicholas, Henry (Family of Love)
Nicolas (Nicolaitans)
Ortleib of Strasbourg (Ortlibarii)
Otterbein, Philip William (United
   Brethren)
Ras Tafari (Rastafarians)
Reinkens, Joseph Hubert (Old
   Catholics)
Rosenkreutz, Christian (Rosicrucians)
Russell, Charles Taze (Jehovah's
   Witnesses)
Sancroft, William (Non-Jurors)
Sandeman, Robert (Sandemanians)
Schwenckfeld, Kaspar (Schwenkfelders)
Shembe, Isaiah (Ama-Nazaretha)
Smith, Joseph (Mormons)
Smyth, John (General Baptists)
Sozzini, Fausto (Socinianism)
Steiner, Rudolf (Anthroposophy)
Swedenborg, Emanuel
   (Swedenborgianism)
Valdes, Peter (Waldensians)
Voysey, Charles (Theistic Church)
Wesley, John (Methodism)
White, Ellen Gould (American Protest-
   ant Episcopalians)
Young, Brigham (Mormons)
Zizka, John (Taborites)

Devotional Writers

Adamnan
Andrewes, Launcelot
Avancini, Nikola
Baxter, Richard
Bayly, Lewis
Bunyan, John
Butler, Alban
Cassian, John
Catherine of Genoa
Catherine of Siena
Challoner, Richard

Chateaubriand, François
   René de
Chesterton, G.K.
Cyril of Jerusalem
Elias, John
Ephraem Syrus
Euthalius
Evagrius Ponticus
Faber, Federick William
Farrar, Frederic William
Fénelon, François

Fox, George
Francis of Sales
Froude, Richard Hurrell
Gerhard, Johann
Gerson, Jean le Charlier
   de
Gertrude the Great
Grignion de Montford,
   Louis-Marie
Guyon, Jeanne Marie
Henry, Matthew

Henry Suso
Herbert, George
Hildegard of Bingen
Hilton, Wilton
Hugh of St Victor
Ildefonsus
Inge, William Ralph
Isaac of Nineveh
John of Avila
John of the Cross
John of Damascus
Johnson, Samuel
Julian of Norwich
Kawaga, Toyohiko
Keble, John
Ken, Thomas
Kettlewell, John
King, Edward
Knox, Ronald
Law, William
Lawrence, Brother
Lewis, Clive Staples

Lingard, John
Ludolf of Saxony
Luis of Granada
Merton, Thomas
Molinos, Miguel de
More, Thomas
Moschius, John
Nicodemus of the Holy
　Mountain
Odo
Olier, Jean-Jacques
Pacian
Péguy, Charles Pierre
Penn, William
Peter the Venerable
Petrarch
Rabanus Maurus
Richard of St Victor
Rolle, Richard
Rossetti, Christina
Ruysbroeck, Jan van
Saint-Cyran, Abbé de

Sayers, Dorothy Leigh
Sheppard, Dick
Simeon, the New
　Theologian
Smith, Hanna Whitall
Southcott, Joanna
Spener, Philip Jakob
Spurgeon, Charles
　Haddon
Stillingfleet, Edward
Studdert Kennedy,
　Geoffrey Anketell
Surin, Jean-Joseph
Tatian
Tauler, Johann
Taylor, James Hudson
Teresa of Avila
Teresa of Lisieux
Thomas Tikhon
Underhill, Evelyn
Weatherhead, Leslie
　Dixon

Economists

Antoninus
Ball, John

Biel, Gabriel
Eck, Johann

Weber, Max

Ecumenists

Athenagoras
Aulen, Gustaf
Azariah, Vednayakam
　Samuel
Bell, George
Brent, Charles Henry
Bulgakov, Sergius
Dibelius, Martin
Döllinger, Johann

Eugenius IV
Florovsky, George
John XXIII
Küng, Hans
Leibniz, Gottfried
　Wilhelm
Mbiti, John S.
Mott, John
　Raleigh

Oldham, Joseph
　Houldsworld
Pannikar, Raimundo
Peake, Arthur Samuel
Soloviev, Vladimir
　Sergeevich
von Hügel, Friedrich
Zinzendorf, Nikolaus
　Ludwig

Educators

Alcuin
Alexander, Cecil Francis
Anselm
Aquaviva, Claudius

Arnold, Thomas
Barnardo, Thomas
Besant, Annie
Bosco, Giovanni Melchior

Bray, Thomas
Columbanus
Comenius, Johannes
　Amos

Coverdale, Miles
Cruden, Alexander
Fell, John
Fénelon, François
Francis Borgia
Fulbert
Huxley, T.H.
Illich, Ivan
Isidore of Seville

John Baptist de la Salle
Jones, Bob
Laubach, Frank Charles
Lucian of Antioch
Ludlow, John Malcolm
    Forbes
Margaret, Lady
Maurice, Frederick
    Denison

Moody, Dwight L.
Raikes, Robert
Ramabai, Pandita
Scopes, John Thomas
Trimmer, Sarah
Vaughan, Charles John
William of Wykeham
Woodard, Nathaniel
Yonge, Charlotte Mary

Heretics and Early Excommunicates

Apollinarius
Arius
Arnold of Brescia
Auxentius
Bardesanes
Barsumas of Nisibis
Basilides
Bonosus
Celestius
Cerinthus
Donatus

Eunomius
Eusebius of Nicomedia
Eutyches
Facundus
Hus, John
Jacob Bardaeus
Mani
Marcion
Marcus
Melitius
Montanus

Nestorius
Novatian
Paul of Samosata
Pelagius
Peter de Bruys
Priscillian
Tatian
Tyndal, William
Valentinus
Wycliffe, John

Historians

Bale, John
Bede
Belloc, Joseph Hilaire
    Pierre
Bloxam, John Rouse
Burchard, John
Butler, Alban
Carlyle, Thomas
Cranmer, Thomas
Dearmer, Percy
Dionysius, Exiguus
Döllinger, Johann
Eadmer
Eusebius of Caesarea
Evelyn, John
Foxe, John
Froissart, Jean
Geoffrey of Monmouth
Germanus of
    Constantinople
Gibbon, Edward
Goscelin

Gratian
Gregory of Tours
Grindal, Edmund
Hermann of Reichnau
Heylyn, Peter
Hume, David
Ildefonsus
Jacob of Voragine
Jerome
Joachim of Fiore
John the Evangelist
Julius Africanus
Lactantius
Lambert of Hersfeld
Leo IV
Liddon, Henry Parry
Lightfoot, Joseph Barber
Lingard, John
Luke
Mamertus
Mark
Matthew

Matthew Paris
Mesrob
Meyendorff, John
Moffatt, James
Möhler, Johann Adam
Muratori, Lodovico
    Antonio
Nicephoras
Nikon
Orosius Paulus
Ozanam, Frédéric
Palladius
Parker, Matthew
Philip Sidetes
Seeley, John Robert
Stanley, Arthur Penrhyn
Stillingfleet, Edward
Thomas of Celano
Ussher, James
Vico, Giovanni Battista
Weber, Max

Missionaries

Aidan (Northumbria)
Anskar (Scandinavia)
Asbury, Francis (America)
Augustine of Canterbury (Kent)
Aylward, Gladys (China)
Azariah, Vednyakam Samuel (India)
Beuno (North Wales)
Boniface (Frisia)
Brainerd, David (American Indians)
Bray, Thomas (Society for the Propagation of the Christian Gospel)
Campion, Edmund (England)
Carey, William (India)
Carroll, John (Maryland)
Chalmers, James (Polynesia)
Claver, Peter (Columbia)
Coke, Thomas (America)
Columba (Ireland, Holland)
Crowther, Samuel Ajayi (Niger)
Cuthbert (Northumbria)
Cyril (Moravia)
Damien, Father (Hawaii)
De Foucauld, Charles Eugène (North Africa)
De Nobili, Robert (India)
Elmo (Spain and Galicia)
Francis Borgia (Switzerland)
Francis Xavier (East Indies, Japan)
Frumentius (Ethiopia)
Giovanni, Capistrano (Bohemia)
Gossner, Johannes Evangelista (East India)
Graham, Billy (worldwide)
Gregory the Illuminator (Armenia)
Gregory Thaumaturgus (Pontus)
Guyard, Marie (Quebec)
Harris, Howel (Wales)
John of Aula (Spain)
Jones, Bob (USA)
Jones, Griffiths (Wales)
Judson, Adoniram (Burma)
Kentigern (Scotland)
Kilian (Franconia)

Knibb, William (Jamaica)
Las Casas, Bartolomé de (West Indies)
Laubach, Frank Charles ('Method')
Liddell, Eric (China)
Livingstone, David (East Africa)
Lull, Ramon (North Africa)
McPherson, Aimee Semple (USA, Britain)
Marsden, Samuel (Australia)
Martyn, Henry (India)
Methodius (Moravia)
Moffatt, Robert (Africa)
Moody, Dwight L. (USA, Britain)
Morrison, Robert (China)
Mott, John Raleigh (IMC)
Occom, Samson (American Indians)
Oldham, Joseph Houldsworld (IMC)
Otto (Pomerania)
Patrick (Ireland)
Patteson, John Coleridge (Melanesia)
Paulinus of York (Britain)
Ramabai, Pandita (India)
Raymond Nonnatus (Jews, Muslims)
Ricci, Matteo (China)
Roberts, Evan John (Wales)
Sankey, Ira David (USA, Britain)
Schweitzer, Albert (Africa)
Selwyn, George Augustus (New Zealand)
Simeon, Charles (CMS Jews)
Slessor, Mary (West Africa)
Stanley, Henry Morton (East Africa)
Studd, Charles Thomas (China, India, Africa)
Taylor, James Hudson (China)
Teresa, Mother (India)
Trotter, Isabella Lilias (North Africa)
Ulphilas (Gothia)
Weston, Frank (Zanzibar)
Whitefield, George (Britain, USA)
Williams, John (Polynesia)
Willibrord (Frisia)

Monarchs

Bertha (Kent)
Catherine (Sweden)

Charlemagne (Holy Roman Empire)
Charles I (England)

Charles V (HRE)
Clovis (Franconia)
Edward VI (England)
Elizabeth I (England)
Ethelbert (Kent)
Ferdinand V (Aragon)
Frederick I (HRE)
Frederick II (HRE)
Frederick III (Saxony)
Frederick III (Palatine)
Henry II (England)
Henry II (HRE)
Henry IV (HRE)
Henry IV (France)
Henry VI (England)
Henry VIII (England)
Heraclius (Eastern Empire)
Isabella (Spain)
James I (England)
James II (England)
Joseph II (HRE)
Julian (Roman Empire)
Justinian (Eastern Empire)
Khama III (Ngwato)
Ladislaus (Hungary)

Leo III (Eastern Empire)
Lewis I (HRE)
Louis XI (France)
Louis XIV (France)
Lucius (Britain)
Margaret (Scotland)
Mary I (England)
Offa (Britain)
Olave (Norway)
Oswald (Northumbria)
Otto I (HRE)
Pepin III (Franconia)
Peter (Russia)
Philip II (Spain)
Philip IV (France)
Prester John (Asia)
Pulcheria (Eastern Empire)
Stephen I (Hungary)
Theodora (Eastern Empire)
Theodosius I (Roman Empire)
Theodosius II (Eastern Empire)
Vladimir (Kiev)
Wenceslas (Bohemia)
Zeno (Eastern Empire)

Mystics

Alacoque, Marguérite
  Marie
Angela Merici
Antony of Egypt
Bernadette
Bernardino
Boehme, Jakob
Bonaventura
Bourignon, Antoinette
Bridget
Catherine of Genoa
Catherine of Siena
Cavasilas, Nikolas
Dionysius, Pseudo-
Eckhart, Meister
Elizabeth of the Trinity
Emmerick, Anna
  Katharina
Ficino, Marsilio
Frances of Rome
Francis of Assisi

Galgani, Gemma
Gerson, Jean le Charlier
  de
Gertrude the Great
Gichtel, Johann George
Gregory of Palamas
Griffiths, Ann
Groote, Geert de
Guyard, Marie
Guyon, Jeanne Marie
Hildegard of Bingen
Hilton, Walter
Hugh of St Victor
Jacopone da Todi
John of Avila
John of the Cross
Jones, Rufus Matthew
Joseph of Copertino
Julian of Norwich
Juliana of Liège
Kempe, Margery

La Badie, Jean de
Lawrence, Brother
Luis of Granada
Lull, Ramon
Macarius of Egypt
Maximus the Confessor
Mechthilde
Merton, Thomas
Molinos, Miguel de
Neumann, Thérèse
Nicholas, Henry
Paracelsus
Péguy, Charles Pierre
Richard of St Victor
Rolle, Richard
Ruysbroeck, Jan van
Santos, Lucia
Sergius of Radonezh
Simeon the New
  Theologian
Southcott, Joanna

Sundar Singh
Surin, Jean-Joseph
Swedenborg, Emanuel

Tauler, Johann
Teresa of Avila
Teresa of Lisieux

Underhill, Evelyn
Vaughan, Henry
William of St Thierry

Order Founders

Acarie, Barbe Jeanne (French Carmelites)
Angela Merici (Ursulines)
Athanasius (Mt Athos)
Benedict (Benedictines)
Bernard of Clairvaux (Cistercians)
Booth, William (Salvation Army)
Bosco, Giovanni Melchior (Salesians)
Bridget (Brigittines)
Bruno (Carthusians)
Cabrini, Frances-Xavier (Sisters of the Sacred Heart)
Cajetan (Theatines)
Camillus (Ministers of the Sick)
Carlile, Wilson (Church Army)
Celestine V (Celestines)
Clare (Poor Clares)
De Foucauld, Charles Eugène (Little Brothers and Sisters)
De Rancé, Armand-Jean le Bouthillier (Trappists)
Ferrar, Nicholas (Little Gidding)
Fey, Clara (Sisters of the Poor Child Jesus)
Fliedner, Theodor (Kaiserswerth Sisters)
Frances of Rome (Oblates of Tor de Specchi)
Francis of Assisi (Franciscans)
Francis of Paola (Minims)
Francis of Sales (Visitandines)
Gilbert of Sempringham (Gilbertines)
Gore, Charles (Community of the Resurrection)
Groote, Geerte de (Brothers of the Common Life)
Hecker, Isaac Thomas (Paulists)
Hilarion (Anchorites)
Hilda (Whitby)
Ignatius Loyola (Jesuits)
Ignatius, Father (Anglican Benedictines)
Jane Frances de Chantel (Visitation)
Jerome Emiliani (Somaschi)
John Baptist de la Salle (Brothers of the Christian Schools)

John Columbini (Gesuati)
John of the Cross (Discalced Carmelites)
John of God (Brothers Hospitallers)
John Gualbert (Vallumbrosians)
John of Malta (Trinitarians)
Joseph Calasanctius (Piarists)
Joseph of Volokolamsk (Volokolamsk)
La Badie, Jean de (Labadists)
Li, Florence (Anglican Women Priests)
Martin of Tours (Liguge)
Mechitar (Mechtarists)
Neale, John Mason (Sisters of St Margaret)
Norbert (Premonstratensians)
Odilia (Odilienberg)
Odo (CIuny)
Olier, Jean-Jacques (St Sulpice)
Ozanam, Frédéric (Society of St Vincent de Paul)
Pachomius (Community Monasticism)
Pallotti, Vincent (Pallottini Fathers)
Paul IV (Theatines)
Paul of the Cross (Passionists)
Peter of Alcantara (Alcantarines)
Peter Nolasco (Mercedarines)
Philip Neri (Oratorians)
Raymond of Peñafort (Mercedarians)
Robert of Arbrissel (Fontevrault)
Robert of Molesne (Cistercians)
Romauld (Camaldolesians)
Rosmini-Serbati, Antonio (Fathers of Charity)
Scholastica (Female Benedictines)
Schutz, Roger (Taizé)
Sellon, Priscilla Lydia (Society of the Most Holy Trinity)
Stephen Harding (Cistercians)
Teresa of Avila (Discalced Carmelites)
Teresa, Mother (Missionaries of Charity)
Tilak, Narayan Vaman (Baptised and Unbaptised Disciples)

Vincent de Paul (Lazarites, Sisters of Charity)
Ward, Mary (Institute of English Ladies)
William of Champeaux (Victorines)
Zinzendorf, Nikolaus Ludwig (Herrnhuter)

Philanthropists/Social Reformers

Barnardo, Thomas
Booth, William
Butler, Josephine
Cabrini, Frances-Xavier
Carlile, Wilson
Claver, Peter
Damien, Father
Fry, Elizabeth
Gossner, Johannes Evangelista
Gurney, Joseph John
Guthrie, Thomas
Headlam, Stewart
Howard, John
Howe, Julia Ward

Jerome Emiliani
John of God
Jones, Bob
Judson, Adoniram
Kagawa, Toyohiko
King, Edward
Kingsley, Charles
Ludlow, John Malcolm
Manning, Henry Edward
Mather, Cotton
Maurice, Frederic Denison
More, Thomas
Newton, John
Nightingale, Florence

Ozanam, Frédéric
Raikes, Robert
Rowntree, Joseph
Shaftesbury, Earl of
Stanton, Elizabeth Cady
Stowe, Harriet Beecher
Teresa, Mother
Tolstoy, Leo
Trimmer, Sarah
Wichern, Johann Heinrich
Wilberforce, William
Williams, George

Poets/Novelists

Alexander, Cecil Francis
Arnold, Matthew
Baker, Sir Henry Williams
Baxter, Richard
Belloc, Hilaire
Blake, William
Brooks, Phillips
Bunyan, John
Chesterton, G.K.
Coleridge, Samuel Taylor
Cosmas Melodus
Cowper, William
Dante
Dearmer, Percy
Donne, John
Dostoievsky, Fyodor
Eliot, T.S.
Ephraem Syrus
Francis of Assisi
Fulbert
Gerhardt, Paul
Gheon, Henri
Gottschalk of Orbais

Griffiths, Ann
Havergal, Frances Ridley
Hawthorne, Nathaniel
Heber, Reginald
Herbert, George
Hermann of Reichenau
Hilary of Poitiers
Hildegard of Bingen
Hopkins, Gerard Manley
Howe, Julia Ward
Hrosvit
Isaac the Great
Jacob of Sarug
Jacopone da Todi
John of the Cross
John of Damascus
Joseph the Hymnographer
Keble, John
Ken, Thomas
Kingsley, Charles
Lewis, C.S.
Macdonald, George
Mauriac, François

Milton, John
Neale, John Mason
Neander, Joachim
Newton, John
Paulinus of Nola
Petrarch
Pym, Barbara
Romanos
Rossetti, Christina
Sankey, Ira David
Sayers, Dorothy Leigh
Sergius of Radonezh
Sternhold, Thomas
Theodulf
Thompson, Francis
Tilak, Narayan Vaman
Tolstoy, Leo
Vaughan, Henry
Watts, Isaac
Wesley, Charles
Williams, Charles

Polemicists/Rebels

Aske, Robert
Bale, John
Ball, John
Barabbas
Barton, Elizabeth
Bell, George Kennedy
  Allen
Berggrav, Eivind
Bernard of Cluny
Boesak, Allan
Brewster, William
Brown, John
Cartwright, Thomas
Fawkes, Guy
Field, John
Gordon, Lord George
Helwys, Thomas

Henderson, Alexander
Heylyn, Peter
Hosius, Stanislaus
Hübmaier, Balthasar
Hung, Hsiu-Ch'uan
Hutten, Ulrich von
Joan of Arc
John of Leyden
Jurieu, Pierre
Kensit, John
Kim, Chi-Ha
King, Martin Luther
Knox, John
Las Casas, Bartolomé de
Law, William
Lilburne, John
Marprelate, Martin

Münzer, Thomas
Nayler, James
Nicephoras
Niemöller, Martin
O'Connell, Daniel
Oldcastle, Sir John
Peter the Hermit
Prynne, William
Robinson, John
Savonarola
Sickingen, Franz von
Stowe, Harriet Beecher
Swift, Jonathan
Tutu, Desmond
Warburton, William
William of Ockham

Politicians/Statesmen

Aberhart, William
Bacon, Francis
Boethius (St Severinus)
Coligny, Gaspard de
Cromwell, Oliver
Cromwell, Thomas
De Maistre, Joseph Marie
Du Plessis-Mornay,
  Philippe

Foliot, Gilbert
Gardiner, Stephen
Jefferson, Thomas
Kuyper, Abraham
Lamennais, Félicité
  Robert de
Laud, William
Lou, Tseng-Tsiang
Mazarin, Jules

More, Thomas
O'Connell, Daniel
Pilate, Pontius
Richelieu, Cardinal
Wolsey, Thomas
Ximénez de Cisneros,
  Francisco

Saints (see also Apostles)

Legendary

Agatha
Agnes
Anastasia
Barbara
Barlaam
Blasius
Catherine of Alexandria
Cecilia
Christopher
Dorothea

Eustace
Faith
George
Januarius
Joasaph
Leonard
Lucy
Magnus
Margaret of Antioch
Nicholas

Pancras
Pantaleon
Philomena
Sebastian
Tarsicius
Ursula
Valentine
Vitus

150–600

Alban
Ambrose

Antony of Egypt
Athanasius

Augustine of Canterbury
Augustine of Hippo

Basil the Great
Benedict
Bride
Chrysostom
Clement of Alexandria
Columba
Columbanus
Cyprian
Cyril of Alexandria
Cyril of Jerusalem
David
Demetrius
Denys
Dorotheus
Ephraem Syrus
Epiphanius
Ethelbert
Finnian
Frumentius
Gelasius I
Geneviève
Germanus of Paris
Gregory I
Gregory the Illuminator
Gregory of Nazianzus
Gregory of Nyssa
Helena

Hilarion
Hilary of Poitiers
Hippolytus
Ignatius
Irenaeus
Isaac
Isidore
Jacob of Nisibis
Jerome
Justin Martyr
Kentigern
Kevin
Laurence
Leo I
Leodegar
Liudhart
Lucian
Macarius of Egypt
Macarius of Jerusalem
Macrina
Mamertus
Martin
Mary of Egypt
Maurus
Maximus the Confessor
Melitius
Menas

Mesrob
Monica
Nerses
Pachomius
Pacian
Patrick
Paul of Thebes
Paulinus
Pelagia
Pius I
Polycarp
Proclus
Pulcherion
Remigius
Romanos
Scholastica
Simeon Stylites
Sixtus II
Spyridon
Stephen I
Sylvester I
Symmachus
Victor I
Victor of Capua
Vincent

600–1100

Adamnan
Alphege
Anselm
Anskar
Bede
Bernard
Beuno
Boniface
Bruno
Chad
Cosmas Melodus
Cuthbert
Cyril
Dominic
Dunstan
Francis of Assisi
Fulbert
Germanus of
  Constantinople

Gertrude
Gilbert of Sempringham
Giles
Gregory VII
Hilda
Hildegard
Hubert
Hugh of Cluny
Ildefonsus
Ivo
John of Damascus
John Gualbert
Joseph the Hymnographer
Kilian
Ladislaus
Leo III
Leo IV
Leo IX
Malachy

Margaret of Scotland
Martin I
Methodius
Nicephoras
Nicholas I
Norbert
Odilia
Odilio
Odo
Olave
Osmund
Oswald
Otto
Paschasius Radbertus
Paulinus
Peter Damian
Robert of Molesne
Romauld
Stanislaus

Stephen of Hungary
Swithin
Tarasius
Theodore of Studios
Theodore of Tarsus

Ulrich
Vladimir
Walburga
Wenceslas
Wilfrid

Willibrord
Winifred
Wulfstan

1100–1600

Albertus Magnus
Angela Merici
Antony of Padua
Becket, Thomas
Bellarmine
Bonaventura
Borromeo, Charles
Bridget of Sweden
Cajetan
Camillus
Campion, Thomas
Catherine of Genoa
Catherine of Siena
Celestine V
Clare
Clitherow, Margaret
Elizabeth of Hungary
Elmo
Fisher, John

Frances of Rome
Francis of Paola
Francis of Sales
Francis Xavier
Gertrude the Great
Giovanni Capistrano
Gregory Palamas
Hugh of Lincoln
Ignatius Loyola
Jane Frances de Chantel
Jerome Emiliani
Joan of Arc
John of Avila
John of the Cross
John of God
John of Malta
John of Nepomuk
Joseph Calasanctius
Juliana

Louis IX
Mary Magdalene de'Pazzi
Mechthilde
More, Thomas
Peter of Alcantara
Philip Neri
Pius V
Raymond Nonnatus
Raymond of Peñafort
Richard of Chichester
Roch
Rose of Lima
Sava
Teresa of Avila
Thomas Aquinas
Vincent de Paul
Vincent Ferrer
Zita

1600–Present

Alacoque, Marguérite
   Marie
Alphonsus Liguori
Bernadette
Bosco, Giovanni Melchior

Cabrini, Francis-Xavier
Galgani, Gemma
John Baptist de la Salle
Joseph of Cupertino
Paul of the Cross

Pius X
Plunket, Oliver
Teresa of Lisieux
Vianney, Jean-Baptiste
   Marie

Non-Catholic Saints

Avvakum (Old Catholic
   Church)
Cassian, John (Eastern
   Church)
Cranmer, Thomas (Prot-
   estant Martyr)
Hamilton, Patrick (Prot-
   estant Martyr)
Hooper, John (Protestant
   Martyr)
Hus, John (Reformer)

Hutter, Jacob (Anabaptist
   Martyr)
Joseph of Prague (Hussite
   Martyr)
Joseph of Volokolamsh
   (Eastern Church)
Latimer, Hugh (Protestant
   Martyr)
Nestorius (Assyrian
   Christian Church)
Nicodemus of the Holy

Mountain (Eastern
   Church)
Novatian (Novatian
   Church)
Photius (Eastern Church)
Ridley, Nicholas (Protest-
   ant Martyr)
Rogers, John (Protestant
   Martyr)
Seraphim of Sarov (East-
   ern Church)

Sergius of Radonezh
    (Eastern Orthodox
    Church)

Tikhon of Zadonsk
    (Eastern Orthodox
    Church)

Tyndale, William (Mar-
    tyred Reformer)

Scientists

Bacon, Roger
Browne, Sir Thomas
Darwin, Charles
Durkheim, Emile
Faraday, Michael
Frazer, James
Freud, Sigmund

Galileo
Gutenberg, Johann
Heisenberg, Werner
Huxley, T.H.
Jung, Carl Gustav
Kepler, Johann
Leonardo da Vinci

Lyell, Charles
Newton, Sir Isaac
Paracelsus
Pascal, Blaise
Scopes, John Thomas
Teilhard de Chardin, Pierre
Wren, Christopher

Theologians/Philosophers (see also **Heretics** and **Denomination Founders**)

100–600

Aphraates
Athanasius
Augustine of Hippo
Boethius
Cassian, John
Clement of Alexandria
Columbanus
Cyril of Alexandria
Dionysius, Pseudo-
Dorotheus of Gaza
Elkesai
Epiphanius
Gregory the Great
Gregory of Nazianzus
Gregory of Nyssa

Hilary of Poitiers
Hippolytus
Ibas
Ignatius of Antioch
Irenaeus
Jacob of Nisibis
Jerome
Justin Martyr
Lactantius
Leontius of Byzantium
Lucifer of Cagliari
Marcellus
Maximus the Confessor
Novatian
Optatus

Origen
Peter the Fuller
Philoxenus
Plotinus
Porphyry
Sabellius
Tertullian
Theodore of Mopsuestia
Theodoret
Theophilus
Ulphilas
Valentinus
Vincent of Lérins

600–1200

Abelard
Aelfric
Anselm of Canterbury
Anselm of Laon
Berengar
Bernard of Chartres
Bernard of Clairvaux
Erigena
Euthymius Zigabenus
Gaunilo
Gilbert de la Porrée
Gottschalk of Orbais

Honorius of Autun
Hugh of St Victor
Jacob of Edessa
John of Damascus
John of Salisbury
Lanfranc
Langton, Stephen
Paschasius Radbertus
Peter Damian
Peter Lombard
Photius
Rabanus Maurus

Roscellinus
Sergius of Radonezh
Theodulf
Thierry of Chartres
Valdes, Peter
Walter of St Victor
William of Champeaux
William of Conches
William of Paris
William of St Thierry
Wulfstan

1200–1600

Agricola, Johann
Albertus Magnus
Ames, William
Antoninus
Bacon, Francis
Bacon, Roger
Baius, Michel
Bancroft, Richard
Becon, Thomas
Bellarmine, Robert
Bernardino
Beza, Theodore
Biel, Gabriel
Blemmydes, Nicephorus
Bonaventura
Bradwardine, Thomas
Browne, Robert
Bucer, Martin
Bullinger, Johann
   Heinrich
Cajetan
Calvin, John
Cartwright, Thomas
Cavasilas, Nikolaus
Colet, John
Cox, Richard
Duns Scotus, Johannes
Durandus

Eck, Johann
Erasmus, Desiderius
Erastus, Thomas
Ficino, Marsilo
Fisher, John
Flacius, Matthias Illyricus
Gerhard, Johann
Gerson, Jean le Charlier de
Giles of Rome
Gregory Palamas
Gregory of Rimini
Grotius, Hugo
Herbert, George
Hobbes, Thomas
Hooker, Richard
Hosius, Stanislaus
Hus, John
Jansen, Cornelius
Jewel, John
John of Ragusa
Karlstadt, Andreas Bod-
   enstein von
Knox, John
Lucar, Cyril
Lull, Ramon
Luther, Martin
Major, Georg
Marsiglio of Padua

Melanchthon, Philip
Melville, Alexander
Menno Simon
Molina, Luis de
Montaigne, Michel de
More, Thomas
Nicholas of Cusa
Olivi, Petrus Johannis
Perkins, William
Peter Martyr
Pithou, Pierre
Saint-Cyran, Abbé de
Salesbury, William
Schwenkfeld, Kaspar
Servetus, Michael
Sozzini, Fausto
Suarez, Francisco de
Thomas Aquinas
Tremellius, John
   Immanuel
Tyndale, William
Vitoria, Francisco de
Vorstius, Conradus
William of Ockham
Wycliffe, John
Zwingli, Ulrich

1600–Present

Arnauld, Antoine
Aulen, Gustaf
Barclay, Robert
Barnes, Ernest William
Barth, Karl
Bauer, Walter
Baur, Ferdinand Christian
Bengel, Johannes Albrecht
Berdyaev, Nicolas
Bergson, Henri
Berkeley, George
Bérulle, Pierre de
Blondel, Maurice
Boesak, Allan
Boff, Leonardo
Bonhoeffer, Dietrich
Bonino, José Miguez

Bossuet, Jacques Bénigne
Browne, Sir Thomas
Brunner, Heinrich Emil
Bulgakov, Sergius
Bultmann, Rudolf
Bushnell, Horace
Butler, Joseph
Carlyle, Thomas
Channing, William Ellery
Chao, Tzu-Chen
Colenso, John William
Coleridge, Samuel Taylor
Cone, James Hal
Conzelmann, Hans
Cupitt, Don
Daly, Mary
Danjo, Ebina

De Maistre, Joseph
   Marie
Descartes, René
Dibelius, Martin
Dodd, Charles Harold
Durkheim, Emile
Edwards, Jonathan
Ellul, Jacques
Emerson, Ralph Waldo
Erskine, Ebenezer
Evelyn, John
Feuerbach, Ludwig
   Andreas
Fichte, Johann Gottlieb
Fiorenza, Elizabeth
   Schussler
Fletcher, Joseph

Flew, Antony Garrard
  Newton
Florovsky, George
Forsyth, Peter Taylor
Freud, Sigmund
Fuller, Andrew
Gibbon, James
Gore, Charles
Gorham, George
  Cornelius
Görres, Johann Joseph
  von
Graf, Karl Heinrich
Green, Thomas
Gutierrez, Gustavo
Hamann, Johann Georg
Hampden, Renn Dickson
Hampson, Daphne
Harnack, Adolf von
Hartshorne, Charles
Hegel, Friedrich
Heidegger, Martin
Hick, John Harwood
Hodge, Charles
Hofmann, Johann Christian Konrad von
Holland, Henry Scott
Hontheim, Johann
  Nikolaus von
Hort, Fenton John
  Anthony
Hoskyns, Sir Edwyn
  Clement
Howson, John Saul
Hume, David
Inge, William Ralph
James, William
Jaspers, Karl
Jefferson, Thomas
Jeremias, Joachim
Jones, Rufus Matthew
Jowett, Benjamin
Jung, Carl Gustav
Jurieu, Pierre
Kähler, Martin
Kant, Immanuel
Käsemann, Ernst
Keble, John
Khomyakoff, Alekssai
  Stepanovich

Kierkegaard, Søren
Kim, Chi-Ha
Kim, Jai-Jun
Koyama, Kosuke
Küng, Hans
Kuyper, Abraham
Lamennais, Félicité Robert de
Leibniz, Gottfried
  Wilhelm
Lessing, Gotthold
  Ephraim
Liddon, Henry Parry
Lightfoot, Joseph Barber
Linzey, Andrew
Lipsius, Richard Adelbert
Locke, John
Loisy, Alfred Firmin
Mackintosh, Hugh Ross
Macquarrie, John
Maritain, Jacques
Martensen, Hans Lassen
Marx, Karl
Mather, Cotton
Maurice, Frederick
  Denison
Mbiti, John S.
Meyendorff, John
Mogila, Peter
Möhler, Johann Adam
Moltmann, Jürgen
More, Thomas
Mowinckel, Sigmund
  Olaf Plytt
Muratori, Lodovico
  Antonio
Newman, John Henry
Nicole, Pierre
Niebuhr, Reinhold
Nietzsche, Friedrich
  Wilhelm
Noth, Martin
Otto, Rudolf
Paine, Thomas
Paley, William
Pannenberg, Wolfhart
Pannikar, Raimundo
Pascal, Blaise
Peake, Arthur Samuel
Philaret Drozdov

Pusey, Edward Bouverie
Rad, Gerhard von
Rahner, Karl
Ramsey, Michael
Rashdall, Hastings
Reimarus, Hermann
  Samuel
Renan, Joseph Ernest
Ritschl, Albrecht
Robinson, John Arthur
  Thomas
Rosmini-Serbati, Antonio
Rousseau, Jean-Jacques
Ruether, Rosemary
  Radford
Saint-Simon, Claude
  Henri de Rouvroi
Sartre, Jean-Paul
Schelling, Friedrich
  Wilhelm Joseph von
Schillebeeckx, Edward
  Cornelis Florentius
  Alfons
Schleiermacher, Friedrich
  Daniel Ernst
Schopenhauer, Arthur
Schweitzer, Albert
Segundo, Juan Luis
Sobrino, Jon
Sölle, Dorothee
Soloviev, Vladimir
  Sergeevich
Song, Choan-Seng
Spencer, John
Stanton, Elizabeth Cady
Stein, Edith
Strauss, David Friedrich
Streeter, Burnett Hillman
Suh, Nam-Dong
Swedenborg, Emanuel
Teilhard de Chardin,
  Pierre
Temple, William
Thielicke, Helmut
Tillich, Paul Johannes
Tindal, Matthew
Toland, John
Troeltsch, Ernst
Tyrrell, George
Unamuno, Miguel de

Vico, Giovanni Battista
Voltaire
Von Balthasar, Hans Urs
Von Hügel, Friedrich
Warfield, Benjamin
  Breckinridge

Weil, Simone
Weiss, Johannes
Wellhausen, Julius
Westcott, Brooke
  Foss
Whitehead, Alfred North

Williams, Charles Walter
  Stansby
Wittgenstein, Ludwig
Wrede, William

Encyclopaedias and reference works

D.J. Atkinson and D.H. Field (eds), *The New Dictionary of Christian Ethics and Pastoral Theology* (1995)

J. Bowden, *Who's Who in Theology* (1990)

R. Brownrigg, *Who's Who in the New Testament* (1986)

A. Bullock and R.B. Woodings (eds), *The Fontana Biographical Companion to Modern Thought* (1983)

The Catholic University of America, *The New Catholic Encyclopaedia* (1967)

R. Coggins, *Who's Who in the Bible* (1981)

F.L. Cross and E.A. Livingstone (eds), *The Oxford Dictionary of the Christian Church*, 2nd edn (1974)

J.D. Douglas (ed.), *The New International Dictionary of the Christian Church*, revised edition (1978)

P. Edwards (ed.), *The Encyclopaedia of Philosophy* (1967)

D.H. Farmer (ed.), *The Oxford Dictionary of Saints*, 3rd edn (1992)

J.N.D. Kelly (ed.) *The Oxford Dictionary of Popes* (1986)

E.A. Livingstone (ed.), *The Oxford Dictionary of the Christian Church*, revised edition (1997)

N. Lossky et al. (eds), *Dictionary of the Ecumenical Movement* (1991)

A.E. McGrath (ed.), *The Blackwell Encyclopaedia of Modern Christian Thought* (1993)

B.M. Metzger and M.D. Coogan (eds), *The Oxford Companion to the Bible* (1993)

A. Richardson and J. Bowden (eds), *A New Dictionary of Christian Theology* (1983)

L. Stephen (ed.), *Dictionary of National Biography* (1885 and supplements)

G.S. Wakefield (ed.), *A Dictionary of Christian Spirituality* (1983)